CW00972153

EU Data Protection Law

For Denis and Sabina

EU Data Protection Law

DENIS KELLEHER

BCL (UCC), H.Dip. Econ. Sc. (UCD), Barrister-at-Law (King's Inns), LL.D (UCD)

Head of Privacy (EMEA), LinkedIn

KAREN MURRAY

BA (NUIG), LL.B (NUIG), LL.M (QUB), Barrister-at-Law (King's Inns)

Lecturer in Law, National College of Ireland

Bloomsbury Professional

Bloomsbury Professional

An imprint of Bloomsbury Publishing Plc

Bloomsbury Professional Ltd	Bloomsbury Professional Ltd
The Fitzwilliam Business Centre	41–43 Boltro Road
26 Upper Pembroke Street	Haywards Heath
Dublin 2	RH16 1BJ
Ireland	UK

Bloomsbury Publishing Plc
50 Bedford Square
London
WC1B 3DP
UK

www.bloomsbury.com

BLOOMSBURY and the Diana logo are trademarks of

Bloomsbury Publishing Plc

First published 2018

© Bloomsbury Professional Ltd 2018

The authors has asserted their right under the Copyright, Designs and Patents Act 1988
to be identified as Author of this work.

All rights reserved. No part of this publication may be reproduced or transmitted in any form or by any means, electronic or mechanical, including photocopying, recording, or any information storage or retrieval system, without prior permission in writing from the publishers.

While every care has been taken to ensure the accuracy of this work, no responsibility for loss or damage occasioned to any person acting or refraining from action as a result of any statement in it can be accepted by the authors, editors or publishers.

British Library Cataloguing-in-Publication Data
A catalogue record for this book is available from the British Library.

ISBN:	HB:	978-1-7845-155-39
	ePDF:	978-1-7845-155-46
	ePub:	978-1-7845-155-60

Typeset by Pica Publishing Services

Printed and bound Great Britain by
CPI Group (UK) Ltd, Croydon, CR0 4YY

To find out more about our authors and books visit www.bloomsburyprofessional.com.
Here you will find extracts, author information, details of forthcoming events and the option to sign up for our newsletters

PREFACE

EU data protection law consists of provisions of the EU Treaties and Charter of Fundamental Rights, enactments of the EU legislature and judgments of the Court of Justice of the European Union. The purpose of this work is to provide a cohesive analysis of these constituents. Extraneous material, such as judgments of the courts of Member States is generally excluded, the one exception being the chapter devoted to judgments of the European Court of Human Rights. This focus is deliberate. EU data protection law now represents a distinctly EU discipline of law. As such it deserves its own distinct analysis, which is that which this work seeks to provide.

Providing such analysis is not without its challenges. EU data protection is technologically neutral by design. The flexibility of such an approach is undoubtedly appropriate to an environment that evolves as rapidly as that of data processing. But that flexibility sits uneasily with the contradiction that lies at the heart of EU data protection law. The EU's legislature lay down rules that ensure both '… the protection of individuals with regard to the processing of personal data …' and the '… the free movement of such data'. Until recently much attention has focused on the first of these tasks, as the General Data Protection Regulation wended its way through the EU legislature. In future greater attention may focus on the second. Recent judgments of the CJEU have made clear that right to data protection is of undoubted importance, but even a right such as this cannot exist in isolation. The EU Charter requires that the right to data protection be balanced with the other rights and freedoms that it and the EU Treaties provide. The only EU institution that can provide such balance is the EU's Court of Justice ('CJEU'). Technological neutrality means that Court must answer even the most basic questions, such as what is personal data? As a result, EU data protection law may become increasingly opaque to those who lack the skills to read CJEU judgments alongside legislative texts. That opacity may lead to frustration and confusion: EU data protection law often seems to mean quite different things to different people. However, there is ultimately only one opinion that matters: that of the CJEU. The function of this work is to examine how that Court has interpreted the various EU Treaty provisions, Charter protections and legislation to create what is now EU data protection law.

That function is complicated by the reality that whist the EU enacted new data protection laws in 2016, those laws will not apply until May 2018. It is these laws, particularly the GDPR, that are inevitably the focus of this work. Whilst the Data Protection Directive will remain part of EU data protection law for some months post-publication, its provisions are discussed only to the extent that they are of assistance in the interpretation of the GDPR's provisions. This approach reflects the reality of how privacy practitioners are approaching data protection throughout the EU. Otherwise we have made every endeavour to state the law as it is on 1 January 2018.

Writing this work would not have been possible without the assistance of our colleagues in Bloomsbury Professional: Amy Hayes, Marie Armah-Kwantreng and Sarah Sheehy. Denis would like to thank his former colleagues in the Central Bank of Ireland for all their help and support, in particular: Eadaoin Rock, Paschal Finn, Andrew Whitty, Louise Colgan, Feargal Byrne, Margaret Deveney, Simon Nolan, John Connolly and Deirdre Walsh. He would also like to thank his new colleagues in LinkedIn: Sara Harrington, Kalinda Raina, Sue Duke and Ciara Burke. Karen would like to thank her colleagues in the National College of Ireland and in particular Professor Jimmy Hill, Dr Colette Darcy, Dr Danielle McCartan-Quinn, Michele Kehoe, Mary Buckley, Tim Lawless and Maeve Byrne.

This book is written in our personal capacities and views expressed herein are our own and do not represent the views, opinions or interpretations of any other person.

Denis Kelleher, Dun Laoghaire, Co Dublin.
Karen Murray, National College of Ireland, Mayor Street, IFSC, Dublin 1.

http://www.ictlaw.com

12 January 2018

Contents

Part 7 Remedies, Liabilities and Penalties

Part 8 Criminal Justice

Part 9 Processing by Community Institutions

Part 10 ePrivacy Directive

TABLE OF CASES

C

D

E

F

G

H

I

P

R

S

W

X

Y

Z

TABLE OF STATUTES

TABLE OF EUROPEAN LEGISLATION

TABLE OF CONVENTIONS, PROTOCOLS AND TREATIES

TABLE OF LEGISLATION OF OTHER JURISDICTIONS

PART 1
THE EU RIGHT TO DATA PROTECTION

Chapter 1

THE EU RIGHT TO DATA PROTECTION

INTRODUCTION

[1.01] The purpose of EU data protection law is '… to ensure a consistent and high level of protection of natural persons and to remove the obstacles to flows of personal data within the (European) Union …'.[1] EU data protection law ensures that diverse national data protection rules States do not hinder the free flow of personal data between EU Member States. This is required by article 16 of the Treaty on the Functioning of the European Union (TFEU) which obliges the EU legislature to lay down both … the rules relating to the protection of individuals with regard to the processing of personal data … and the rules relating to the free movement of such data'.[2] It is a purpose that has been clear since the EU first enacted Directive 95/46,[3] the Recitals[4] to which explained:

> … the difference in levels of protection of the rights and freedoms of individuals, notably the right to privacy, with regard to the processing of personal data afforded in the Member States may prevent the transmission of such data from the territory of one Member State to that of another Member State; whereas this difference may therefore constitute an obstacle to the pursuit of a number of economic activities at Community level, distort competition and impede authorities in the discharge of their responsibilities under Community law; … this difference in levels of

---

1. GDPR, Recital 10.
2. TFEU, article 16(2); see similarly Article 39 of the Treaty on European Union (TEU), article 39.
3. Directive 95/46/EC of 24 October 1995 on the protection of individuals with regard to the processing of personal data and on the free movement of such data, OJ L 281, 23.11.1995, p 31–50.
4. Recitals form part of the Preamble to EU measures such as the GDPR. As such they may assist in its interpretation: 'Whilst a recital in the preamble to a regulation may cast light on the interpretation to be given to a legal rule, it cannot in itself constitute such a rule' (*Casa Fleischhandels* (Case R–215/88) (13 July 1989) para 31). However, recitals 'have … no binding legal force and cannot be relied on as a ground for derogating from the actual provisions of the act in question', *Nilsson* (Case C–162/97) (19 November 1998), para 54. Recitals may support interpretations of the actual provisions (*C* (Case C–435/06) (27 November 2007), para 53) expanding and clarifying them but without amending their meaning. (*Moskof* (Case C–244/95) (20 November 1997) para 45). As the CJEU held in *Manfredi* (Case C–308/97) (25 November 1998), para 30) : '… recital cannot be relied upon to interpret (an) Article … of (a) Regulation … in a manner clearly contrary to its wording'. See generally: Baratta, *Complexity of EU law in the domestic implementing process*, EU Commission, 19th Quality Of Legislation Seminar, Brussels 3rd July 2014: http://ec.europa.eu/dgs/legal_service/seminars/20140703_baratta_speech.pdf.

protection is due to the existence of a wide variety of national laws, regulations and administrative provisions.[5]

The objective of Directive 95/46 was '… to remove the obstacles to flows of personal data …', an objective which was:

> … vital to the internal market … especially in view of the scale of the divergences which currently exist between the relevant laws in the Member States and the need to coordinate the laws of the Member States so as to ensure that the cross-border flow of personal data is regulated in a consistent manner that is in keeping with the objective of the internal market.[6]

[1.02] Directive 95/46 itself was an internal market measure.[7] Its purpose was not to protect privacy or provide data protection rules; rather it was to ensure the harmonisation of those rules so as to avoid any interference with the internal market. Directive 95/46 itself made this clear, that its objective was to ensure that Member States:

> …protect the fundamental rights and freedoms of natural persons, and in particular their right to privacy with respect to the processing of personal data.

Before going onto provide that:

> Member States shall neither restrict nor prohibit the free flow of personal data between Member States for reasons connected with the protection afforded …[8] (above).

This anomaly, that EU data protection law is not a right in itself but rather as a mechanism to ensure the free flow of data within the EU's internal market, persisted until the entry into force of the Lisbon Treaty in December 2009. This had two significant effects. Firstly, the entry into force of that Treaty brought the Charter of Fundamental Rights of the European Union[9] ('the Charter') into effect. Article 8 of the Charter sets out the fundamentals of the EU right to data protection:

1. Everyone has the right to the protection of personal data concerning him or her.[10]

---

5. Directive 95/46, Recital 7.
6. Directive 95/46, Recital 8.
7. Directive 95/46 had its legal basis in TEC, article 100a.
8. Directive 95/46, article 1.
9. Charter of Fundamental Rights of the European Union, OJ C 326, 26.10.2012, p 391–407. The EU Charter of Fundamental Rights (the Charter, originally proclaimed on 1 December 2000, OJ 2000 C 364, p 1.) was originally part of the ill-fated Constitutional Treaty, which failed to be ratified in 2005 (Laursen, *The Rise and Fall of the EU's Constitutional Treaty* (Nijhoff, 2008).) The Charter was then excised from the Lisbon Treaty, thus appearing to slim down the text. However, this excision was more apparent than real, as the TEU now provides: 'The Union recognises the rights, freedoms and principles set out in the Charter of Fundamental Rights of the European Union of 7 December 2000, as adapted at Strasbourg, on 12 December 2007, which shall have the same legal value as the Treaties.' TEU, article 6(1). The Charter has applied to the EU since the entry of the Lisbon Treaty into force on 1 December 2009.
10. In *Avis 1/15* [2017] EUECJ (26 July 2017) (contd …/)

2.   Such data must be processed fairly for specified purposes and on the basis of the consent of the person concerned or some other legitimate basis laid down by law. Everyone has the right of access to data which has been collected concerning him or her, and the right to have it rectified.

3.   Compliance with these rules shall be subject to control by an independent authority.

[1.03] Secondly, article 16 of the Treaty on the Functioning of the European Union (TFEU)[11] now imposes a specific obligation upon the EU legislature to make data protection rules, providing that:

> The European Parliament and the Council, acting in accordance with the ordinary legislative procedure, shall lay down the rules relating to the protection of individuals with regard to the processing of personal data by Union institutions, bodies, offices and agencies, and by the Member States when carrying out activities which fall within the scope of Union law, and the rules relating to the free movement of such data.[12]

The EU Commission began the process of meeting this obligation in January 2012 when it proposed two new measures, which would become law in 2016:

- Regulation 679/2016/EU on the protection of natural persons with regard to the processing of personal data and on the free movement of such data, and repealing Directive 95/46/EC[13] (the General Data Protection Regulation, more commonly known by the anagram 'GDPR'); and

- Directive 2016/680/EU on the protection of natural persons with regard to the processing of personal data by competent authorities for the purposes of the prevention, investigation, detection or prosecution of criminal offences or the execution of criminal penalties, and on the free movement of such data (the 'PJCD').[14]

---

10.   (contd) the CJEU considered this to be identical in effect to TFEU, article 16(1), but although '... both of those provisions state that everyone has the right to the protection of personal data concerning him or her, only article 8 of the Charter lays down in a more specific manner, in para 2 thereof, the conditions under which such data may be processed' at para 120.

11.   Treaty on the Functioning of the European Union, OJ C 326, 26.10.2012, p 47–390.

12.   TFEU, article 16(2).

13.   Regulation 2016/679/EU on the protection of natural persons with regard to the processing of personal data and on the free movement of such data, and repealing Directive 95/46/EC, OJ L 119, 4.5.2016, p 1–88.

14.   Directive 2016/680/EU on the protection of natural persons with regard to the processing of personal data by competent authorities for the purposes of the prevention, investigation, detection or prosecution of criminal offences or the execution of criminal penalties, and on the free movement of such data, OJ L 119, 4.5.2016, p 89–131.

In addition, the EU has enacted a variety of other measures ranging from the Second Payment Services Directive (PSD2)[15] to the PNR Directive,[16] which enable the processing of personal data and also provide safeguards to ensure that processing complies with EU data protection rules. However, the CJEU has not waited for the EU legislature to act before taking account of the right to data protection set out in the charter.[17] This may be illustrated by contrasting the CJEU's analysis of Directive 2006/24 prior to the charter coming into effect, in *Ireland v Parliament and Council*,[18] with its analysis afterwards, in *Digital Rights Ireland*.[19] The objective of Directive 2006/24, more commonly known as the Data Retention Directive, was:

> ... to harmonise Member States' provisions concerning the retention, by providers of publicly available electronic communications services or of public communications networks, of certain data which are generated or processed by them, in order to ensure that the data are available for the purpose of the prevention, investigation, detection and prosecution of serious crime, such as organised crime and terrorism ...[20]

Directive 2006/24 was first considered by the CJEU in *Ireland v Parliament & Council*,[21] in a judgment delivered in February 2009, some ten months before the Charter came into effect. The CJEU did not consider the issue of fundamental rights at all, noting that: '... the action brought by Ireland relates solely to the choice of legal basis and not to any possible infringement of fundamental rights arising from interference with the exercise of the right to privacy'[22] and went on to uphold the validity of Directive 2006/24.

[1.04] The CJEU would return to consider Directive 2006/24 in *Digital Rights Ireland*. This judgment was delivered four years or so after the Charter came into effect. Reversing its earlier decision the CJEU found Directive 2006/24 to be invalid, on the basis that it entailed '... a wide-ranging and particularly serious interference ...' with the fundamental rights of privacy and data protection set out in the Charter. The view

---

15. Directive 2015/2366/EU of the European Parliament and of the Council of 25 November 2015 on payment services in the internal market, OJ L 337, 23.12.2015, p 35–127.
16. Directive 2016/681/EU of 27 April 2016 on the use of passenger name record (PNR) data for the prevention, detection, investigation and prosecution of terrorist offences and serious crime, OJ L 119, 4.5.2016, p 132–149.
17. Technically the Charter did not create any new rights, only reaffirmed pre-existing rights resulting '...from the constitutional traditions and international obligations common to the Member States, the European Convention for the Protection of Human Rights and Fundamental Freedoms, the Social Charters adopted by the Union and by the Council of Europe and the case law of the Court of Justice of the European Union and of the European Court of Human Rights' Preamble, Charter.
18. *Ireland v Parliament and Council* (Case C–301/06) (10 February 2009).
19. *Digital Rights Ireland* (Case C–293/12) (8 April 2014).
20. *Digital Rights Ireland* (Case C–293/12) (8 April 2014), para 24.
21. *Ireland v Parliament & Council* (Case C–301/06) (10 February 2009).
22. *Ireland v Parliament & Council* (Case C–301/06) (10 February 2009), para 57.

could be taken that this decision reflected the questions asked of the CJEU, as opposed to any change in the law. In recent years the CJEU has shown a fresh willingness provide 'full'[23] answers to data protection questions. This led it to find *EU Commission Decision 2000/520* (Safe Harbor) invalid in *Schrems*[24] even though it had not been formally asked to consider the validity of that Decision.[25]

[1.05] Contrasting *Lindqvist*[26] from 2003 with *Google Spain*[27] from 2014 gives a further illustration of how the CJEU's thinking about data protection has changed in recent years. In *Lindqvist* the CJEU concluded that the EU's legislature had failed to anticipate the global internet when enacting Directive 95/46.[28] In *Google Spain* the CJEU effectively disregarded its earlier decision and held that Directive 95/46 could be applied to the following activity:

> Google Search indexes websites throughout the world ... The information indexed by its 'web crawlers' or robots, that is to say, computer programs used to locate and sweep up the content of web pages methodically and automatically, is stored temporarily on servers whose State of location is unknown, that being kept secret for reasons of competition.[29]

---

23. '... in order to give the referring court a full answer, it should be examined whether that decision complies with the requirements stemming from Directive 95/46 read in the light of the Charter': *Schrems* (Case C–362/14) (6 October 2015), para 67.

24. *Schrems* (Case C–362/14) (6 October 2015).

25. The CJEU had been asked questions about the role of a supervisory authority and their conduct of investigations. Firstly whether '... in the course of determining a complaint which has been made to an independent office holder who has been vested by statute with the functions of administering and enforcing data protection legislation that personal data is being transferred to another third country (in this case, the United States of America) the laws and practices of which, it is claimed, do not contain adequate protections for the data subject, that office holder is absolutely bound by the Community finding to the contrary ...'. And secondly whether that supervisory authority must '... conduct his or her own investigation of the matter in the light of factual developments in the meantime since that Commission decision was first published': *Schrems* (Case C–362/14) (6 October 2015), para 36.

26. *Lindqvist* (Case C–101/01) (6 November 2003).

27. *Gonzalez v Google Spain and Google* (Case C–131/12) (13 May 2014).

28. In *Lindqvist v Sweden* (Case C–101/01) (6 November 2003) the CJEU considered the 'state of development of the internet at the time Directive 95/46 was drawn up' (para 68) and that the transborder data flows provisions of Directive 95/46 failed to 'lay down criteria for deciding whether operations carried out by hosting providers should be deemed to occur in the place of establishment of the service or at its business address or in the place where the computer or computers constituting the service's infrastructure are located' (para 67) The CJEU concluded that it could not be presumed that: 'Community legislature intended the expression transfer [of data] to a third country to cover the loading, by an individual in Mrs Lindqvist's position, of data onto an internet page, even if those data are thereby made accessible to persons in third countries with the technical means to access them'(para 68).

29. *Gonzalez v Google Spain and Google* (Case C–131/12) (13 May 2014), para 43.

Contrasting the CJEU judgments in *Lindqvist* and *Google Spain* illustrates that the changes in the approach of the CJEU reflect more than the EU's recognition of the Charter. Technology is changing, so too are the ways in which we use technology. As the Recitals to the GDPR explain:

> Rapid technological developments and globalisation have brought new challenges for the protection of personal data. The scale of the collection and sharing of personal data has increased significantly. Technology allows both private companies and public authorities to make use of personal data on an unprecedented scale in order to pursue their activities. Natural persons increasingly make personal information available publicly and globally. Technology has transformed both the economy and social life, and should further facilitate the free flow of personal data within the Union and the transfer to third countries and international organisations ...[30]

WHAT IS THE RIGHT TO DATA PROTECTION?

[1.06] In *Schecke*[31] that Court set out the EU right to data protection in the following terms:

> ... Article 8(1) of the Charter states that '[e]veryone has the right to the protection of personal data concerning him or her'. That fundamental right is closely connected with the right to respect of private life expressed in Article 7 of the Charter.[32]

The right to privacy is set out in Article 7 of the Charter, which is entitled 'Respect for private and family life' and provides:

> Everyone has the right to respect for his or her private and family life, home and communications.

However the right to privacy and the right to data protection are not the same. Information that has ceased to be private will remain subject to data protection rules. As the CJEU explained in *Satakunnan*:[33]

> ... a general derogation from the application of the directive in respect of published information would largely deprive the directive of its effect. It would be sufficient for the Member States to publish data in order for those data to cease to enjoy the protection afforded by the directive.[34]

A succinct analysis of the relationship between the right to privacy and the right to data protection was provided by the CJEU in *Google Spain:*

> Article 7 of the Charter guarantees the right to respect for private life, whilst Article 8 of the Charter expressly proclaims the right to the protection of personal data. Article 8(2) and (3) specify that such data must be processed fairly for

---

30. GDPR, Recital 6.
31. *Volker und Markus Schecke* (Case C–92/09) (9 November 2010).
32. *Volker und Markus Schecke* (Case C–92/09) (9 November 2010), para 47.
33. *Satakunnan Markkinaporssi* (Case C–73/07) (16 December 2008).
34. *Satakunnan Markkinaporssi* (Case C–73/07) (16 December 2008), para 48.

specified purposes and on the basis of the consent of the person concerned or some other legitimate basis laid down by law, that everyone has the right of access to data which have been collected concerning him or her and the right to have the data rectified, and that compliance with these rules is to be subject to control by an independent authority.[35]

These fundamental rights must always be taken into account when considering EU data protection laws, even those such as the GDPR that are intended to provide data protection rules. As the CJEU explained in *Schrems:*

… the provisions of Directive 95/46, inasmuch as they govern the processing of personal data liable to infringe fundamental freedoms, in particular the right to respect for private life, must necessarily be interpreted in the light of the fundamental rights guaranteed by the Charter.[36]

[1.07] Data protection is an important right, as the Court went onto explain:

The importance of both the fundamental right to respect for private life, guaranteed by Article 7 of the Charter, and the fundamental right to the protection of personal data, guaranteed by Article 8 thereof, is, moreover, emphasised in the case law of the Court …[37]

In *Google Spain* the CJEU considered that Directive 95/46 could not be interpreted restrictively in the light of its objective:

…of ensuring effective and complete protection of the fundamental rights and freedoms of natural persons, and in particular their right to privacy, with respect to the processing of personal data …[38]

The CJEU went on to explain that Directive 95/46 sought '… to ensure a high level of protection of the fundamental rights and freedoms of natural persons, in particular their right to privacy, with respect to the processing of personal data'.[39] The new rules that have been enacted by the EU legislature, the GDPR and the LED, should ensure even higher levels of data protection.

INTERFERENCE WITH THE RIGHT TO DATA PROTECTION

[1.08] It would seem that even quite limited processing of personal data may interference with a subjects rights of privacy an data protection. As the CJEU stated in *Schwarz:*[40]

… everyone has the right to respect for his or her private life … everyone has the right to the protection of personal data concerning him or her …

---

35. *Gonzalez v Google Spain and Google* (Case C–131/12) (13 May 2014), para 69.
36. *Schrems* (Case C–362/14) (6 October 2015), para 38.
37. *Schrems* (Case C–362/14) (6 October 2015), para 39.
38. *Google Spain* (Case C–131/12) (13 May 2014), para 53.
39. *Google Spain* (Case C–131/12) (13 May 2014), para 66.
40. *Schwarz v Stadt Bochum* (Case C–291/12) (17 October 2013).

It follows from a joint reading of those articles that, as a general rule, any processing of personal data by a third party may constitute a threat to those rights.[41]

Such rights may be interfered with by: '... the publication of data by name relating to ... beneficiaries ... and the precise amounts received by them ...';[42] the transfer of Passenger Name Records from the EU to Canada;[43] or by the '... general and indiscriminate retention of all traffic and location data of all subscribers and registered users relating to all means of electronic communication ...'.[44] To establish the existence of an interference in the right to data protection:

> ... it does not matter whether the information communicated is of a sensitive character or whether the persons concerned have been inconvenienced in any way... It suffices ... that data ... have been communicated to a third party.[45]

If the EU right to data protection existed in isolation then it would not be possible to process another's personal data without their agreement or consent. But as the CJEU explained in *Google Spain*:

> ... the provisions of Directive 95/46, in so far as they govern the processing of personal data liable to infringe fundamental freedoms, in particular the right to privacy, must necessarily be interpreted in the light of fundamental rights, which, according to settled case law, form an integral part of the general principles of law whose observance the Court ensures and which are now set out in the Charter.[46]

Data protection may be an integral principle of the EU law, but it is not an absolute right, as the CJEU stated in *Schecke*:[47]

> The right to the protection of personal data is not ... an absolute right, but must be considered in relation to its function in society.

And that Court went on to explain:

> Article 8(2) of the Charter thus authorises the processing of personal data if certain conditions are satisfied. It provides that personal data 'must be processed fairly for specified purposes and on the basis of the consent of the person concerned or some other legitimate basis laid down by law'.

---

41. *Schwarz v Stadt Bochum* (Case C–291/12) (17 October 2013), para 24-25.
42. *Volker und Markus Schecke (Approximation of laws)* (Case C–92/09) (9 November 2010), para 64.
43. *Transfer of Passenger Name Record data from the European Union to Canada* (Opinions of the Court) [2017] EUECJ Avis-1/15_OC (26 July 2017), para 36.
44. *Tele2 Sverige (Judgment)* (Case C–203/15) (21 December 2016), para 97.
45. *Österreichischer Rundfunk & Ors* (Approximation of laws) (Case C–465/00) (20 May 2003), para 75. Subsequently cited by the CJEU in *Digital Rights Ireland* (Case C–293/12) (8 April 2014), para 33; *Schrems* (Case C–362/14) (06 October 2015), para 87; and *Transfer of Passenger Name Record data from the European Union to Canada* [2017] EUECJ Avis-1/15_OC (26 July 2017) para 124.
46. *Google Spain and Google* (Case C–131/12) (13 May 2014), para 68.
47. *Volker und Markus Schecke* (Case C–92/09) (9 November 2010).

Article 52(1) of the Charter accepts that limitations may be imposed on the exercise of rights such as those set forth in Articles 7 and 8 of the Charter, as long as the limitations are provided for by law, respect the essence of those rights and freedoms and, subject to the principle of proportionality, are necessary and genuinely meet objectives of general interest recognised by the European Union or the need to protect the rights and freedoms of others.[48]

The manner in which such limitations may be imposed was considered by the CJEU in *Digital Rights Ireland*,[49] in which the validity of the EU's Data Retention Directive 2006/24[50] was challenged. Directive 2006/24 required the retention of certain telecommunications data by Telcos and enabled that data to be accessed by national authorities.[51] The CJEU considered that 'the obligation … to retain … data relating to a person's private life and to his communications … constitutes in itself an interference' with the rights of privacy and data protection and the court went on to restate the view of its Advocate General that in this case the interference was 'wide-ranging, and … particularly serious'.[52] The court then went on to consider whether interference with these rights could be justified in accordance with Article 52 of the Charter. It first found that the Directive satisfied 'an objective of general interest' given its use in the fight against terrorism and organised crime.[53] The court then considered whether Directive 2006/24 met the principle of proportionality, which:

requires that acts of the EU institutions be appropriate for attaining the legitimate objectives pursued by the legislation at issue and do not exceed the limits of what is appropriate and necessary in order to achieve those objectives.[54]

[**1.09**] It held that given the importance of data protection for the right to privacy and the seriousness of the interference caused by Directive 2006/24 for that right:

the EU legislature's discretion is reduced, with the result that review of that discretion should be strict.[55]

The court accepted that mobile phone data was 'a valuable tool for criminal investigations' and so retention of that data might be appropriate. However, data retention's value as a tool for combating terrorism and organised crime did not 'in itself' justify Directive 2006/24. It was the settled view of the court that: 'derogations and

---

48. *Volker und Markus Schecke* (Case C–92/09) (9 November 2010), paras 48–50.
49. *Digital Rights Ireland* (Case C–293/12) (8 April 2014).
50. Directive 2006/24/EC of the European Parliament and of the Council of 15 March 2006 on the retention of data generated or processed in connection with the provision of publicly available electronic communications services or of public communications networks and amending Directive 2002/58/EC ([2006] OJ L 105/54).
51. Directive 2006/24 was implemented in Ireland by the Communications (Retention of Data) Act 2011.
52. *Digital Rights Ireland* (Case C–293/12) (8 April 2014), paras 34–37.
53. *Digital Rights Ireland* (Case C–293/12) (8 April 2014), paras 41–44.
54. *Digital Rights Ireland* (Case C–293/12) (8 April 2014), para 46.
55. *Digital Rights Ireland* (Case C–293/12) (8 April 2014), para 48.

limitations in relation to the protection of personal data must apply only in so far as is strictly necessary'.[56]

This meant that the legislation had to 'lay down clear and precise rules' about the processing operation in question and impose 'minimum safeguards so that the persons whose data have been retained have sufficient guarantees to effectively protect their personal data against the risk of abuse and against any unlawful access and use of that data'. This was especially so where data was automatically processed and it was particularly vulnerable to unauthorised access.[57] The court found that Directive 2006/24 did not limit itself to what was 'strictly necessary' as it led to the retention of everyone's data, including those 'whose communications are subject … to the obligation of professional secrecy'[58] and did not 'require any relationship between the data whose retention is provided for and a threat to public security'. It failed to lay down objective criteria and substantial procedures to control access by national authorities to the data. There was no 'prior review … by a court or by an independent administrative body'.[59] Furthermore, Directive 2006/24 provided that the data might be retained for between six and 24 months, but did not provide any objective by which the appropriate retention period might be determined.[60] Finally, the Directive failed to 'require the data in question to be retained within the European Union'.[61]

[1.10] In *Digital Rights Ireland* the CJEU did find that objectives of combating organised crime and terrorism could justify the limitation of data protection rights. Such limitations might be imposed where strictly necessary and with appropriate controls, but not indiscriminately as was the case with Directive 2006/24. This finding against mass surveillance is highly significant, but the judgment's detailed analysis of how limitations upon rights of privacy and data protection must be imposed is of general application outside the criminal justice sphere.[62]

WHAT MUST THE RIGHT TO DATA PROTECTION BE BALANCED AGAINST?

[1.11] The Charter sets out the rights and freedoms of EU citizens across six chapters: Dignity, Freedoms, Equality, Solidarity, Citizens' Rights and Justice. The interaction

---

56.   *Digital Rights Ireland* (Case C–293/12) (8 April 2014), para 52.
57.   *Digital Rights Ireland* (Case C–293/12) (8 April 2014), paras 54–55.
58.   *Digital Rights Ireland* (Case C–293/12) (8 April 2014), para 58.
59.   *Digital Rights Ireland* (Case C–293/12) (8 April 2014), para 62.
60.   *Digital Rights Ireland* (Case C–293/12) (8 April 2014), para 64.
61.   *Digital Rights Ireland* (Case C–293/12) (8 April 2014), para 68.
62.   See also *ASNEF-EQUIFAX* (Case C–238/05) (23 November 2006) in which the CJEU held that when giving balance to rights under articles 7 and 8 of the Charter it was 'possible to take into consideration the fact that the seriousness of the infringement of the data subject's fundamental rights resulting from that processing can vary depending on whether or not the data in question already appear in public sources' (para 44). See also the analysis set out by the CJEU in *Transfer of Passenger Name Record data from the European Union to Canada* [2017] EUECJ Avis-1/15_OC (26 July 2017).

between those rights and freedoms that seem most likely to interact with rights of privacy and data protection are discussed below.

Free movement and the single market

[1.12] Data protection is a fundamental right, but as the CJEU has explained:

> ... it is settled case law that fundamental rights do not constitute unfettered prerogatives and may be restricted, provided that the restrictions in fact correspond to objectives of general interest pursued by the measure in question and that they do not involve, in the light of the objectives pursued, a disproportionate and intolerable interference which impairs the very substance of the rights guaranteed.[63]

TFEU, article 16 obliges the EU to legislate for data protection and provide 'rules relating to the free movement of such data'. In *Breyer*[64] the CJEU referred to the objective pursued by Directive 95/46: '...of maintaining a balance between the free movement of personal data and the protection of private life.'[65] As the CJEU explained in *Schrems:*

> ... the national supervisory authorities must, in particular, ensure a fair balance between, on the one hand, observance of the fundamental right to privacy and, on the other hand, the interests requiring free movement of personal data.[66]

Reconciling these twin objectives maybe a challenge as they are not necessarily compatible; a challenge that the CJEU acknowledged in *Commission v Germany:*[67]

> ...the free movement of personal data is liable to interfere with the right to private life as recognised ...[68] in ... the general principles of European Community law.[69]

When the EU Commission came forward with its GDPR Proposal in January 2012 it promised that enactment would:

> do away with the current fragmentation and costly administrative burdens, leading to savings for businesses of around €2.3 billion a year ... reinforce consumer confidence ... providing a much needed boost to growth, jobs and innovation in Europe.[70]

---

63. *Texdata Software* (Case C–418/11) (26 September 2013) para 84, citing *Dokter* (Case C–28/05), para 75, and *Alassini* (Joined Cases C–317/08 to C–320/08), para 63.
64. *Breyer* (Case C–582/14) (19 October 2016).
65. *Breyer* (Case C–582/14) (19 October 2016), para 58.
66. *Schrems* (Case C–362/14) (6 October 2015), para 42.
67. *Commission v Germany* (Case C–518/07) (9 March 2010).
68. Citing the following judgments of the ECtHR: *Amann v Switzerland* (16 February 2000) ECtHR, paras 69 and 80, and *Rotaru v Romania*, 4 May 2000, ECHR 2000-V.
69. *Commission v Germany* (Case C–518/07) (9 March 2010), para 21.
70. EU Commission, 'Commission proposes a comprehensive reform of data protection rules to increase users' control of their data and to cut costs for businesses' Press Release, 25 January 2012.

The free movement of data seems consistent with a number of freedoms set out in the TFEU: the internal market,[71] the free movement of goods;[72] and the free movement of persons, services and capital.[73] The relationship between privacy and such fundamental freedoms was considered by the CJEU in *Sayn-Wittgenstein*[74] in which the applicant was an Austrian who, as an adult, had been adopted in Germany. The purpose of the adoption was to enable her to use the surname 'Fürstin von Sayn-Wittgenstein', which sounded aristocratic (she was involved in the business of selling stately homes). However, the respondent insisted upon registering her name as 'Sayn-Wittgenstein' as Austrian law prohibits titles of nobility (hence the elimination of the aristocratic 'von'). Article 21(1) TFEU provides that 'Every citizen of the Union shall have the right to move and reside freely within the territory of the Member States'. The CJEU ruled that this article did not preclude the Austrian authorities from refusing to recognise the aristocratic title in question provided that this refusal was justified on public policy grounds.[75] The court noted that:

> the concept of public policy as justification for a derogation from a fundamental freedom must be interpreted strictly, so that its scope cannot be determined unilaterally by each Member State without any control by the European Union institutions[76] ... Thus, public policy may be relied on only if there is a genuine and sufficiently serious threat to a fundamental interest of society.[77]

The EU Commission is coming forward with further initiatives to build an EU Digital Single Market on the basis that:

> The completion of the EU Single Digital Market also needs a clear and stable legal environment to stimulate innovation, tackle market fragmentation and allow all

---

71. TFEU, Pt 3, Title I.
72. TFEU, Pt 3, Title II.
73. TFEU, Pt 3, Title IV.
74. *Sayn-Wittgenstein* (Case C–208/09) (22 December 2010).
75. *Sayn-Wittgenstein* (Case C–208/09) (22 December 2010), para 96. This decision was followed in *Runevič-Vardyn and Wardyn v Vilniaus miesto savivaldybės administracija* (Case C–391/09) 12 May 2011, in which the applicants were a Lithuanian from the Polish minority in Lithuania and her Polish husband. The respondents were Lithuanian municipal authorities. The facts of the case were that those authorities had registered the wife's name in its Lithuanian form but her husband's name in its Polish form, the significance of which was that Lithuanian does not use the letter 'W'. Hence husband and wife were required to spell their names differently. The CJEU considered that 'the objective pursued by national rules such as those at issue in the main proceedings, designed to protect the official national language by imposing the rules which govern the spelling of that language, constitutes, in principle, a legitimate objective capable of justifying restrictions on the rights of freedom of movement and residence provided for in Article 21 TFEU' (para 87).
76. Citing *Omega* (Case C–36/02), [2004] ECR I-9609, para 30; and *Jipa* (Case C–33/07), [2008] ECR I-5157, para 23.
77. *Sayn-Wittgenstein* (Case C–208/09) (22 December 2010), para 86. The CJEU considered that public policy did not justify a refusal to register a child's name in *Grunkin-Pau* (Case C–353/06), 14 October 2008. (contd .../)

players to tap into the new market dynamics under fair and balanced conditions. This will provide the bedrock of trust that is essential for business and consumer confidence.[78]

In particular the EU Commission has proposed a Regulation on a framework for the free flow of non-personal data in the European Union[79] which would:

> … ensure the free movement of data other than personal data within the Union by laying down rules relating to data localisation requirements, the availability of data to competent authorities and data porting for professional users.[80]

It would do so by providing that:

> Location of data for storage or other processing within the Union shall not be restricted to the territory of a specific Member State, and storage or other processing in any other Member State shall not be prohibited or restricted, unless it is justified on grounds of public security.[81]

Competition law

[1.13] The TFEU provides common rules on competition[82] banning agreements, decisions and concerted practices that distort competition[83] and abuses of dominant

---

77.   (contd)The child's parents were a German couple living in Denmark. They had been married, but 'did not use a common married name and refused to determine the surname of their child'. Under Danish law the child had therefore been given a double-barrelled name, composed of the surnames of both parents. This was a name that the German authorities refused to recognise, which was a problem as the child had German nationality but lived in Denmark. What this meant in practice, was that he had one name under Danish law which was not the same as the name that appeared in his passport and so 'every time the child concerned has to prove his identity in Denmark, the Member State in which he was born and has been resident since birth, he risks having to dispel doubts concerning his identity and suspicions of misrepresentation caused by the difference between the surname he has always used on a day-to-day basis, which appears in the registers of the Danish authorities and on all official documents issued in his regard in Denmark, such as, inter alia, his birth certificate, and the name in his German passport' (para 26). The court therefore ruled that the decision of the German authorities was an infringement of TFEU, article 21 (para 40).

78.   EU Commission, *Communication on the Mid-Term Review on the implementation of the Digital Single Market Strategy A Connected Digital Single Market for All*, Brussels, 10 May 2017, COM(2017) 228 final, para 1, p 2.

79.   EU Commission, *Proposal for a Regulation on a framework for the free flow of non-personal data in the European Union*, Brussels, 13 September 2017, COM(2017) 495 final.

80.   EU Commission, *Proposal for a Regulation on a framework for the free flow of non-personal data in the European Union*, Brussels, 13 September 2017, COM(2017) 495 final, article 1.

81.   EU Commission, *Proposal for a Regulation on a framework for the free flow of non-personal data in the European Union*, Brussels, 13 September 2017, COM(2017) 495 final, article 4(1).

82.   TFEU, Title VII, Ch 1.

83.   TFEU, article 101.

position.[84] This is a particular danger where data processing systems are concerned, as one former EU Competition Commissioner explained to the EU Parliament:

> The challenges of enforcing EU competition law in digital markets are mostly linked to their rapid evolution and to the fact that dominant companies can quickly rise to prominence and become gatekeepers for other market players. This is often the result of innovation and smart business models, which we have to support. Market dominance through internal growth, innovation and success is not a competition problem. However, the abuse of a dominant position is indeed a serious competition problem.[85]

Peter Thiel, founder of Paypal, is quite explicit on what he sees as the benefits of monopoly, benefits which he points out the State already recognises through its intellectual property laws:

> The dynamism of new monopolies ... explains why old monopolies don't strangle innovation ... Monopolies drive progress because the promise of years or even decades of monopoly profits provides a powerful incentive to innovate. Then monopolies can keep innovating[86] ... Creative monopoly means new products that benefit everybody ... Competition means ... a struggle for survival.[87]

Data processors that are in a dominant position are in a very good position to enter into contracts with their customers which provide a legitimate basis for personal data processing. Smaller competitors that lack such contracts may find themselves excluded from certain markets by their inability to comply with data protection law.[88] The CJEU has previously forced the licensing of intellectual property in order to prevent abuse of a dominant position. *IMS Health*[89] concerned a refusal to license a data format, which formed the structure of a database of pharmaceutical products. The CJEU held that a refusal to license intellectual property that is indispensable for carrying on a particular business will amount to an abuse of a dominant position where that refusal is: preventing the emergence of a new product for which there is a potential consumer demand; unjustified; and excluding competition on a secondary market.[90] This judgment was subsequently applied by the CJEU in *Microsoft*[91] in which it was held that the applicant's refusal to give access to information that would enable others to 'interoperate' with its Windows program and to refuse to authorise the use of that

---

84.   TFEU, article 102.

85.   Joaquin Almunia, Vice President of the European Commission responsible for Competition policy, *Presenting the Annual Competition Report,* EU Parliament, 23 September 2014.

86.   Thiel and Masters, *Zero to One* (Virgin Book, 2014), p 33.

87.   Thiel and Masters, *Zero to One* (Virgin Book, 2014), p 35.

88.   Spam is another illustration of the interaction between data protection and competition law. As the difficulties that smaller operators face in handling vast volumes of spam has driven consolidation in the e-mail market see: Rao and Reiley, *The Economics of Spam*, Journal of Economic Perspectives, Vol 26 (3), Summer 2012, p 87–110, at 91.

89.   *IMS Health* (Case C–418/01) (29 April 2004).

90.   *IMS Health* (Case C–418/01) (29 April 2004), para 38.

91.   *Microsoft* (Case T–167/08) (27 June 2012).

'interoperability information' was an abuse of its dominant position in the market for PC operating systems.[92] In *Deutsch Telekom*[93] the CJEU considered it appropriate for a German competition regulator to direct that the dominant German provider of directory services provide a copy of its database to competitors, notwithstanding that such a transfer had not been anticipated by some customers whose data was entered in the database. So, a subject's consent to have their data processed by one controller could be transferred to another, so long as the processing operations had the same purpose. The general application of this judgment may be limited, as the granting of access to a controller other than Deutsche Telekom was mandated by German domestic law.[94] However, *Deutsch Telekom* made clear that EU law may facilitate transfers of personal data in order to facilitate competition.[95]

Intellectual property

[1.14] Article 17 of the Charter provides:

> Everyone has the right to own, use, dispose of and bequeath his or her lawfully acquired possessions. No one may be deprived of his or her possessions, except in the public interest and in the cases and under the conditions provided for by law, subject to fair compensation being paid in good time for their loss. The use of property may be regulated by law in so far as is necessary for the general interest.[96]

As with any other Charter right, limitations may only be placed upon this right in accordance with article 52. In *Trabelsi v European Commission*[97] the applicant's assets had been subject to restrictions pursuant to an EU Decision.[98] He argued that these restrictions were a breach under his article 17 rights; the CJEU considered that claim in the context of article 52, which meant that the 'limitation on the exercise of the right to property must ... satisfy three conditions':[99]

1. the limitation must be 'provided for by law'[100] ... In other words, the measure in question must have a legal basis;

---

92. *Microsoft* (Case T–167/08) (27 June 2012), para 139.
93. *Deutsche Telekom* (Case C–543/09) (5 May 2011).
94. 'under Paragraphs 47(1), 104 and 105 of the [Telekommunikationsgesetz] ... any undertaking which assigns telephone numbers to end users is under an obligation to pass on to providers of publicly available directory enquiry services and directories who so request not only data relating to its own subscribers, but also data in its possession relating to subscribers of third-party service providers...': *Deutsche Telekom* (Case C–543/09) (5 May 2011), para 18.
95. See similarly *Tele2 (Netherlands)* (Case C–536/15) (15 March 2017).
96. Charter, article 17(1).
97. *Trabelsi v European Commission* (Case T–187/11) (28 May 2013).
98. Decision 2011/72/CFSP concerning restrictive measures directed against certain persons and entities in view of the situation in Tunisia ([2011] OJ L 28/62).
99. *Trabelsi v European Commission* (Case T–187/11) (28 May 2013), para 78.
100. Citing *Knauf Gips v Commission* (Case C–407/08 P) [2010] ECR I-6375, para 91.

2.   the limitation must refer to an objective of public interest, recognised as such by the European Union; and

3.   the limitation may not be excessive. First, it must be necessary and proportional to the aim sought[101] ... Second, the 'essential content', that is, the substance, of the right or freedom at issue must not be impaired.[102]

The CJEU went on to hold that the Decision should not apply to the applicant, as it lacked a legal base.[103] The interaction between rights to property and data protection has been considered in a number of cases and the Charter goes on to provide that: 'Intellectual property shall be protected.'[104]

[1.15] The interaction between rights of data protection and intellectual property was considered in *Promusicae*,[105] in which the applicant represented a number of music companies. It applied to the Spanish courts for an order requiring that the respondent 'disclose the identities and physical addresses of certain persons whom it provided with internet access services, whose IP address and date and time of connection were known',[106] and alleged that these persons were using the peer-to-peer service known as KaZaA to illegally share its members' intellectual property. The case made its way to the CJEU, which considered that:

> Directive 2002/58 ... authorises the Member States to adopt legislative measures to restrict the obligation of confidentiality of personal data where that restriction is necessary inter alia for the protection of the rights and freedoms of others ... Directive 2002/58 must be interpreted as expressing the Community legislature's intention not to exclude from their scope the protection of the right to property or situations in which authors seek to obtain that protection in civil proceedings.

[1.16] The CJEU was of the view that Member States could lay 'down an obligation to disclose personal data in the context of civil proceedings', but that Directive did not compel Member States to impose such an obligation.[107] It then went on to consider

---

101. Citing *Bosphorus* (Case C–84/95) [1996] ECR I-3953, point 26; *Kadi and Al Barakaat International Foundation v Council and Commission* (Case C–415/05) [2008] ECR I-6351, paras 355 and 360.
102. Citing *Nold v Commission* (Case 4/73) [1974] ECR 491, para 14; and *Kadi and Al Barakaat International Foundation v Council and Commission* (Case C–415/05) [2008] ECR I-6351, para 355.
103. *Trabelsi v European Commission* (Case T–187/11) (28 May 2013), paras 79–81 and 117.
104. Charter, article 17(2).
105. *Promusicae v Telefónica de España* (Case C–275/06), 29 January 2008. Applied in *LSG-Gesellschaft zur Wahrnehmung von Leistungsschutzrechten v Tele2* (Case C–557/07) ECJ, 19 February 2009.
106. *Promusicae* (Case C–275/06), paras 29–30.
107. *Promusicae* (Case C–275/06), paras 53–55.

articles 17 (the right to property) and 47 (the right to an effective remedy) of the Charter. The question asked of the CJEU was whether:

> an interpretation of those directives to the effect that the Member States are not obliged to lay down, in order to ensure the effective protection of copyright, an obligation to communicate personal data in the context of civil proceedings leads to an infringement of the fundamental right to property and the fundamental right to effective judicial protection.[108]

However, the CJEU explained that these two rights had to be balanced with the right to the protection of personal data. The CJEU concluded that when transposing the Directives cited to it, Member States would have to:

> take care to rely on an interpretation of them which allows a fair balance to be struck between the various fundamental rights protected by the Community legal order. Further, when implementing the measures transposing those directives, the authorities and courts of the Member States must not only interpret their national law in a manner consistent with those directives but also make sure that they do not rely on an interpretation of them which would be in conflict with those fundamental rights or with the other general principles of Community law, such as the principle of proportionality.[109]

The CJEU subsequently applied *Promusicae* in *Coty Germany*.[110] The applicant was a company which held an exclusive licence for the Community trade mark 'Davidoff Hot Water'. The applicant '…purchased a bottle of perfume bearing the trade mark Davidoff Hot Water on an Internet auction platform'.[111] It paid for this purchase by paying a sum into a bank account operated by a German bank. The bottle of perfume was then delivered to the applicant, which identified it as a counterfeit product. The applicant then:

> … asked that auction platform to provide it with the real name of the holder of the account of that platform from which the perfume had been sold to it (the sale having been made under an alias). The person named admitted to being the holder of that account, but denied being the seller of the product concerned and, relying on her right not to give evidence, refused to provide further information.[112]

The applicant then contacted the German Bank which operated the bank account into which it had paid the purchase price and asked it '… for the name and address of the holder …' of that bank account. However, that Bank invoked banking secrecy and refused. In response the applicant invoked article 8 of Directive 2004/48 on the enforcement of intellectual property rights.[113] This requires that Member States:

> … ensure that, in the context of proceedings concerning an infringement of an intellectual property right and in response to a justified and proportionate request

---

108. *Promusicae* (Case C–275/06), para 61.
109. *Promusicae* (Case C–275/06), para 70.
110. *Coty Germany* (Case C–580/13) (16 July 2015).
111. *Coty Germany* (Case C–580/13) (16 July 2015), paras 9–10.
112. *Coty Germany* (Case C–580/13) (16 July 2015), paras 9–10.
113. Directive 2004/48 of 29 April 2004 on the enforcement of intellectual property rights, OJ L 157, 30.4.2004, p 45–86.

of the claimant, ... competent judicial authorities may order that information on the origin and distribution networks of the goods or services which infringe an intellectual property right be provided by any person who was found to be providing on a commercial scale services used in the infringing activities.[114]

The CJEU held that this was intended '...to apply and implement the fundamental right to an effective remedy guaranteed in article 47 of the Charter, and thereby to ensure the effective exercise of the fundamental right to property ...'.[115] However, the CJEU went on to hold that '... the protection of intellectual property is not to hamper, inter alia, the protection of personal data ...'.[116] And so the case before the CJEU raised:

> ... the question of the need to reconcile the requirements of the protection of different fundamental rights, namely the right to an effective remedy and the right to intellectual property, on the one hand, and the right to protection of personal data, on the other ...[117]

[1.17] The CJEU suggested that it was for the German court to determine whether the German law implementing Directive 2006/48 allowed '... an unlimited refusal ...' to requests for information under article 8 without '... any condition or qualification ...' Such a law '... taken in isolation, is such as to seriously infringe the fundamental right to an effective remedy and, ultimately, the fundamental right to intellectual property, enjoyed by the holders of those rights, and that it does not, therefore, comply with the requirement to ensure a fair balance between, on the one hand, the various fundamental rights ...'.[118] The CJEU then concluded that Directive 2006/48:

> ... must be interpreted as precluding a national provision, such as that at issue in the main proceedings, which allows, in an unlimited and unconditional manner, a banking institution to invoke banking secrecy in order to refuse to provide ... information concerning the name and address of an account holder.[119]

[1.18] In *Bonnier Audio AB v Perfect Communication Sweden AB*[120] the applicants were again music publishers,[121] which had applied to the Swedish courts for an order disclosing the persons associated with certain IP addresses'.[122] The CJEU noted that the Swedish law which permitted the making of such orders:

> requires ... that, for an order for disclosure of the data in question to be made, there be clear evidence of an infringement of an intellectual property right, that the information can be regarded as facilitating the investigation into an infringement

---

114. *Coty Germany* (Case C–580/13) (16 July 2015), para 23.
115. *Coty Germany* (Case C–580/13) (16 July 2015), para 29.
116. *Coty Germany* (Case C–580/13) (16 July 2015), para 32.
117. *Coty Germany* (Case C–580/13) (16 July 2015), para 33.
118. *Coty Germany* (Case C–580/13) (16 July 2015), para 41.
119. *Coty Germany* (Case C–580/13) (16 July 2015), para 44.
120. *Bonnier Audio AB v Perfect Communication Sweden AB* (Case C–461/10), 19 April 2012.
121. *Bonnier Audio AB v Perfect Communication Sweden AB* (Case C–461/10), paras 25–26.
122. *Bonnier Audio AB v Perfect Communication Sweden AB* (Case C–461/10), para 28.

of copyright or impairment of such a right and that the reasons for the measure outweigh the nuisance or other harm which the measure may entail for the person affected by it or for some other conflicting interest.

As a result that legislation enabled the Swedish court to 'weigh the conflicting interests involved, on the basis of the facts of each case and taking due account of the requirements of the principle of proportionality' and 'to ensure a fair balance between the protection of intellectual property rights enjoyed by copyright holders and the protection of personal data enjoyed by internet subscribers or users'.[123] The CJEU therefore concluded that EU law did not preclude the Swedish court from making the order sought.[124]

Finally, *McFadden*[125] was an action brought by a German who provided:

> ... an anonymous access to a wireless local area network free of charge in the vicinity of his business ... Access to that network was intentionally not protected in order to draw the attention of customers of near-by shops, of passers-by and of neighbours to his company... [B]y means of the wireless local area network operated by Mr McFadden, a musical work was made available on the internet free of charge to the general public without the consent of the rightholders.[126]

The applicant asserted '... that he did not commit the infringement alleged' but he did '... not rule out the possibility that it was committed by one of the users of his network'.[127] This led to a dispute between Mr McFadden and Sony, which owned copyright in the musical work in question. That dispute came before the German courts, which referred a number of questions to the CJEU including whether EU law:

> ... must be interpreted as precluding the grant of an injunction ... which requires ... a provider of access to a communication network ... to prevent third parties from making a particular copyright-protected work ... available to the general public from an online (peer-to-peer) exchange platform ... where ... it has already been established that the only measures which the provider may in practice adopt consist in terminating or password-protecting the internet connection or in examining all communications passing through it.[128]

The CJEU held that it was for the referring court to ascertain whether '... a measure consisting in password-protecting an internet connection may dissuade the users of that connection from infringing copyright or related rights, provided that those users are required to reveal their identity in order to obtain the required password and may not

---

123. *Bonnier Audio AB v Perfect Communication Sweden AB* (Case C–461/10), paras 58–60.
124. *Bonnier Audio AB v Perfect Communication Sweden AB* (Case C–461/10), para 62.
125. *McFadden* (Case C–484/14) (15 September 2016).
126. *McFadden* (Case C–484/14) (15 September 2016), para 23.
127. *McFadden* (Case C–484/14) (15 September 2016), para 25.
128. *McFadden* (Case C–484/14) (15 September 2016), para 80.

therefore act anonymously ...'.[129] However, as there were no other lawful measures available to dissuade users from infringing copyright then:

> ... to consider that a communication network access provider need not secure its internet connection would thus be to deprive the fundamental right to intellectual property of any protection, which would be contrary to the idea of a fair balance.[130]

[1.19] In *McFadden* the CJEU made reference to its earlier decisions in *Promusicae, Scarlet Extended, UPC Telekabel Wien* and *Coty Germany*. What distinguishes this case from those is that the CJEU did not directly discuss data protection rights at all. This was notwithstanding that the applicant clearly thought those rights were at issue, as he had changed the name of his network '... to 'freiheitstattangst.de' in reference to a demonstration in favour of the protection of personal data and against excessive State surveillance'.[131]

Freedom to conduct a business

[1.20] Article 16 of the Charter sets out the 'freedom to conduct a business in accordance with Community law and national laws and practices'. In *SABAM*[132] the CJEU considered an injunction issued by a Belgian court which required that an ISP 'actively monitor all the data of each of its ... users in order to prevent any future infringement of intellectual-property rights'.[133] The CJEU held that the Belgian court was precluded from issuing such an injunction as *inter alia* it failed to respect 'the requirement that a fair balance be struck between ... the protection of the intellectual-property right enjoyed by copyright holders, and ... that of the freedom to conduct business enjoyed by operators such as hosting service providers'.[134] This freedom will similarly have to be balanced with other rights, such as data protection. Most significantly, this freedom may be a legitimate interest and so provide a legitimate criterion for the processing of personal data.

However, the imposition of costs may not, of itself, infringe upon this freedom. In *UPC Telekabel Wien*[135] the CJEU held that this freedom included 'the right for any business to be able to freely use, within the limits of its liability for its own acts, the economic, technical and financial resources available to it'. The applicant had been ordered to block its customers' access to certain websites on which the intellectual property of third parties was available. The court accepted that the injunctions 'represent a significant cost ... have a considerable impact on the organisation ... or require

---

129. *McFadden* (Case C–484/14) (15 September 2016), para 85.
130. *McFadden* (Case C–484/14) (15 September 2016), para 98.
131. *McFadden* (Case C–484/14) (15 September 2016), para 24.
132. *SABAM* (Information Society) (Case C–360/10) (16 February 2012).
133. *SABAM* (Information Society) (Case C–360/10) (16 February 2012), para 35.
134. *SABAM* (Information Society) (Case C–360/10) (16 February 2012), para 49.
135. *UPC Telekabel Wien* (Case C–314/12) (27 March 2014).

difficult and complex technical solutions' but this was not enough to 'infringe the very substance ... to conduct a business'.[136] Compliance with rules such as those of data protection will often impose costs on business, but these costs will not, of themselves, amount to an interference with this right.

Freedom of expression

[1.21] The Charter provides for a right to Freedom of expression and information:

> Everyone has the right to freedom of expression. This right shall include freedom to hold opinions and to receive and impart information and ideas without interference by public authority and regardless of frontiers.[137]

The balance between this right and that of data protection has been considered by the CJEU on many occasions. *Lindqvist*[138] concerned a Swedish catechist who '...followed a data processing course on which she had inter alia to set up a home page on the internet'.[139]

> The pages in question contained information about Mrs Lindqvist and 18 colleagues in the parish, sometimes including their full names and in other cases only their first names. Mrs Lindqvist also described, in a mildly humorous manner, the jobs held by her colleagues and their hobbies. In many cases family circumstances and telephone numbers and other matters were mentioned. She also stated that one colleague had injured her foot and was on half-time on medical grounds.[140]

Mrs Lindqvist was prosecuted for breaching Swedish data protection law. On foot of that prosecution the CJEU was asked to consider whether this action would '... bring about a restriction which conflicts with the general principles of freedom of expression ...'[141]. The CJEU held that the applicant's '... freedom of expression ... (has) to be weighed against the protection of the private life of ... individuals ...'.[142] In *Google Spain*[143] the applicant was a lawyer who objected to the fact that anyone who googled his name:

> would obtain links to two pages of La Vanguardia's newspaper ... on which ... Mr Costeja González's name appeared ... connected with attachment ... for the recovery of social security debts.[144]

---

136. *UPC Telekabel Wien* (Case C–314/12) (27 March 2014), paras 49–51.
137. Charter, article 11(1).
138. *Lindqvist* (Case C–101/01) (6 November 2003).
139. *Lindqvist* (Case C–101/01) (6 November 2003), para 12.
140. *Lindqvist* (Case C–101/01) (6 November 2003), para 13.
141. *Lindqvist* (Case C–101/01) (6 November 2003), para 72.
142. *Lindqvist* (Case C–101/01) (6 November 2003), para 86.
143. *Google Spain and Google* (Judgment of the Court) (Case C–131/12) (13 May 2014).
144. *Google Spain and Google* (Judgment of the Court) (Case C–131/12) (13 May 2014), para 14.

Mr González sought to enforce his right of objection, provided by Directive 95/46.[145] The Court held that this right meant that:

> the operator of a search engine is obliged to remove from the list of results displayed following a search made on the basis of a person's name links to web pages, published by third parties and containing information relating to that person ... even, as the case may be, when its publication in itself on those pages is lawful.

The CJEU went on to hold that the subject did not have to establish that he was being prejudiced by the making available of this information and the court went on to find that the subject's rights to privacy and data protection would typically override 'not only the economic interest of the operator of the search engine but also the interest of the general public in having access to that information upon a search relating to the data subject's name'. The only exception to this envisioned by the court was that the interference with the subject's fundamental rights was 'justified by the preponderant interest of the general public in having, on account of its inclusion in the list of results, access to the information in question'.[146]

[1.22] Directive 95/46 enabled Member States to reconcile rights of data protection with rights to freedom of expression and information.[147] GDPR, article 85(1) now provides:

> Member States shall by law reconcile the right to the protection of personal data pursuant to this Regulation with the right to freedom of expression and information, including processing for journalistic purposes and the purposes of academic, artistic or literary expression.[148]

[1.23] Member States shall therefore provide for exemptions or derogations if 'necessary to reconcile the right to the protection of personal data with the freedom of expression and information'. These exemptions or derogations will be from:

- Chapter II (principles),

- Chapter IV (controller and processor),

- Chapter V (transfer of personal data to third countries or international organisations),

- Chapter VI (independent supervisory authorities),

---

145. Directive 95/46, articles 12(b) and 14(a).

146. *Google Spain and Google* (Judgment of the Court) (Case C–131/12) (13 May 2014), para 100.

147. Directive 95/46, article 9, which provided 'Member States shall provide for exemptions or derogations from the provisions of this Chapter, Chapter IV and Chapter VI for the processing of personal data carried out solely for journalistic purposes or the purpose of artistic or literary expression only if they are necessary to reconcile the right to privacy with the rules governing freedom of expression'.

148. GDPR, article 85(1).

- Chapter VII (cooperation and consistency), and

- Chapter IX (specific data processing situations).[149]

[1.24] In *Satakunnan*[150] the CJEU considered the journalistic exemption provided by Directive 95/46. The CJEU held that the purpose of this exemption was to 'reconcile two fundamental rights: the protection of privacy and freedom of expression'. The court held that 'the exemptions and derogations provided for in article 9 of the Directive apply not only to media undertakings but also to every person engaged in journalism'. Secondly, the fact that publication is done for profit does not preclude it from being undertaken 'solely for journalistic purposes', and that the medium is irrelevant,[151] leading the court to conclude:

> activities ... may be classified as 'journalistic activities' if their object is the disclosure to the public of information, opinions or ideas, irrespective of the medium which is used to transmit them. They are not limited to media undertakings and may be undertaken for profit-making purposes.[152]

The exemption provided by article 9 seems to be quite specific in its application. Data published on a website may benefit from the journalistic exemption; data processed by a search engine will not. In *Google Spain* the CJEU held that:

> ... the processing by ... a web page ... in ... publication of information relating to an individual may, in some circumstances, be carried out 'solely for journalistic purposes' and thus benefit ... [from] ... Article 9 of Directive 95/46 ... whereas that does not appear to be so in the case of the processing carried out by the operator of a search engine.[153]

Right to communicate information

[1.25] Freedom of expression will count for nothing if that expression cannot be communicated. Data that cannot be found on a search engine is 'like a tree falling in the forest. There may be links out there, but if you can't find them through a search engine they might as well not exist'.[154] The first substantive decision of the CJEU on data protection was *Osterreichischer Rundfunk*,[155] which concerned a dispute between the Austrian State radio station and the Austrian Court of Auditors. Austrian law required

---

149. GDPR, article 85(2).
150. *Satakunnan* (Case C–73/07) (16 December 2008). See also *Anttila v Finland* (Case 16248/ 10) (Communicated Case) [2012] ECHR 1275 (3 July 2012).
151. '... the medium which is used to transmit the processed data, whether it be classic in nature, such as paper or radio waves, or electronic, such as the internet, is not determinative as to whether an activity is undertaken "solely for journalistic purposes"': *Satakunnan* (Case C– 73/07) (16 December 2008), para 60.
152. *Satakunnan* (Case C–73/07) (16 December 2008), para 61.
153. *Google Spain and Google* (Judgment of the Court) (Case C–131/12) (13 May 2014), para 85.
154. Toobin, 'The Solace of Oblivion' (2014) *New Yorker*, 29 September.
155. *Osterreichischer Rundfunk* (Case C–138/01) (20 May 2003).

that the former communicate to the latter '... the salaries and pensions exceeding a certain level paid by them to their employees and pensioners together with the names of the recipients, for the purpose of drawing up an annual report ...'.[156] This information was then made available to the Austrian parliament and public.[157] The CJEU concluded that the resulting interference with the right to privacy of those employees might be justified if it were concluded that:

> ... the wide disclosure not merely of the amounts of the annual income above a certain threshold of persons employed by the bodies ... but also of the names of the recipients of that income is both necessary for and appropriate to the aim of keeping salaries within reasonable limits ...[158]

[1.26] Article 8 of the Charter provides a right of privacy but it also provides that:

> Everyone has the right to respect for his or her ... communications.

The Charter recognises that freedom of expression is a right:

> ... to receive and impart information and ideas without interference by public authority and regardless of frontiers.[159]

That right goes on to provide that:

> The freedom and pluralism of the media shall be respected.[160]

[1.27] In *Degussa*[161] the EU Commission had found that the applicant had breached EU competition law. The applicant challenged this decision before the general court, the judgment of that court was appealed to the Grand Chamber of the CJEU, which held:

> ... that the right to protection of private life guaranteed in Article 8 of the ECHR and Article 7 of the Charter cannot prevent the disclosure of information which, like that whose publication is envisaged in the present case, concerns an undertaking's participation in an infringement of EU law relating to cartels ... since a person cannot ... complain of a loss of reputation which is the foreseeable consequence of his own actions ....[162]

Transparency and freedom of information

[1.28] Article 42 provides:

> Any citizen of the Union, and any natural or legal person residing or having its registered office in a Member State, has a right of access to documents of the institutions, bodies, offices and agencies of the Union, whatever their medium.

---

156. *Osterreichischer Rundfunk* (Case C–138/01) (20 May 2003), para 2.
157. *Osterreichischer Rundfunk* (Case C–138/01) (20 May 2003), para 87.
158. *Osterreichischer Rundfunk* (Case C–138/01) (20 May 2003), para 90.
159. Charter, article 11(1).
160. Charter, article 11(2).
161. *Degussa* (Case C–162/15) (14 March 2017).
162. *Degussa* (Case C–162/15) (14 March 2017), para 117.

[1.29] The CJEU has explained the balance struck by the EU's Transparency Regulation 1049/2001 between the right of access to public documents and the right to data protection in the following terms:

> Article 4(1)(b) of Regulation ... 1049/2001 ... provides that '[t]he institutions shall refuse access to a document where disclosure would undermine the protection of ... privacy and the integrity of the individual, in particular in accordance with [EU] legislation regarding the protection of personal data'. As is apparent from the case law, it is an indivisible provision and requires that any undermining of privacy and the integrity of the individual must always be examined and assessed in conformity with the EU legislation concerning the protection of personal data, and in particular with Regulation No 45/2001. Article 4(1)(b) of Regulation No 1049/2001 thus establishes a specific and reinforced system of protection of a person whose personal data could, in certain cases, be communicated to the public ...[163]

This balance has been considered by the CJEU on other occasions.[164] In *Dennekamp*[165] the applicant was a journalist who made a request pursuant to the Regulation.[166] In this request he sought '... all documents' relating to the additional pension scheme for Members of the European Parliament'.[167] The CJEU upheld a refusal of the EU Parliament to permit access to information as

> ... the risk of MEPs' legitimate interests, and thus their privacy, being undermined lies in the fact that, falling as they do into the private sphere of MEPs, the personal data at issue constitute a legitimate interest to be protected on the ground that they concern the personal financial situation of MEPs, pension contributions and resulting pension rights being private matters.[168]

A public document may relate to a living individual, and so might amount to their personal data and be subject to the right of access by that data subject. However, that will not make the document accessible to the public at large:

> the documents in question contain personal data concerning the applicant for access, the right of the latter to obtain their disclosure on the basis of the right of access to documents of the institutions cannot have the consequence of opening a right of access of the public in general to the said documents.

---

163. *McCullough* (Case T–496/13) (11 June 2015), para 43. See similarly *Internationaler Hilfsfonds* (Case T–300/10) (22 May 2012).
164. See *Strack* (Case C–127/13) (2 October 2014), *Mayer* (Case T–493/14) (17 February 2017)
165. *Dennekamp* (Case T–115/13) (15 July 2015).
166. Regulation 1049/2001 of 30 May 2001 regarding public access to European Parliament, Council and Commission documents, OJ 2001 L 145, p 43.
167. *Dennekamp* (Case T–115/13) (15 July 2015), para 2.
168. *Dennekamp* (Case T–115/13) (15 July 2015), para 139.

Chapter 2

EU RIGHT TO DATA PROTECTION AND THE ECHR

INTRODUCTION

[2.01] The EU '… is founded on the values of … respect for human rights …'[1] and has long recognised that respect for human rights formed part of the 'unwritten law' of the EU.[2] That respect is now reflected in the text of the Treaty on European Union (TEU), which states:

> Fundamental rights, as guaranteed by the European Convention for the Protection of Human Rights and Fundamental Freedoms and as they result from the constitutional traditions common to the Member States, shall constitute general principles of the Union's law.[3]

The European Convention for the Protection of Human Rights and Fundamental Freedoms, better known as the European Convention on Human Rights (ECHR) was opened for signature in November 1950 following 'difficult'[4] negotiations. All EU Member States have acceded to the ECHR; the EU, however, has not. This follows a negative opinion of the CJEU on the proposed accession of the EU to the ECHR pursuant to TEU, article 6(2).[5] The ECHR and the Charter may be similar, but they are not the same. As its Preamble explains, the Charter reaffirms fundamental rights:

> … with due regard for the powers and tasks of the Community and the Union.

As the CJEU explained in *Digital Rights Ireland*:

> So far as concerns the right to respect for private life, the protection of that fundamental right requires, according to the Court's settled case law, in any event, that derogations and limitations in relation to the protection of personal data must apply only in so far as is strictly necessary.[6]

---

1. TEU, article 2.
2. *Stauder v City of Ulm Sozialamt* (Case C–29/69), also *Nold v Commission* (Case C–4/73).
3. TEU, article 6(3).
4. Clayton and Tomlinson, *The Law of Human Rights* (OUP, 2000).
5. Is the draft EU agreement re: accession of the European Union to the Convention for the Protection of Human Rights and Fundamental Freedoms compatible with the Treaties? (Opinions of the Court) [2014] EUECJ Avis-2/13 (18 December 2014).
6. *Digital Rights Ireland* (Judgment of the Court) (Case C–293/12) (8 April 2014), para 52 citing *Institut Professionnel des Agents Immobiliers (IPI) v Englebert* (Case C–473/12) (7 November 2013), para 39 which cited S*atakunnan Markkinapörssi and Satamedia* (Case C–73/07) [2008] ECR I-9831 para 56, and *Volker und Markus Schecke and Eifert* (Joined Cases C–92/09 and C–93/09), [2010] ECR I-11063, paras 77 and 86 in turn.

The ECHR contains no equivalent to the EU Treaties' obligation to give 'due regard' to tasks such as the building of the single market. Hence what may be necessary under the EU's Charter and Treaties may not be necessary under the ECHR. In its negative opinion on the proposed accession of the EU to the ECHR, the CJEU expressed a concern that accession to the ECHR was '... liable to upset the underlying balance of the EU and undermine the autonomy of EU law'.[7] It remains to be seen whether this will lead to a significant divergence between the European Court of Human Rights (ECtHR) in Strasbourg and the CJEU in Luxembourg. Should significant differences emerge between the CJEU and the ECtHR then it may prove significant that judgments of the CJEU are directly enforceable against Member States, whilst judgments of the ECtHR are not.[8] Of course the critical difference between the EU right to data protection and the ECHR right to privacy is that, pursuant to TFEU, article 16 and the GDPR, the former right may be enforced against individuals whereas the ECHR may only be invoked against States that have ratified the ECHR.

ARTICLE 8, ECHR

[2.02] Article 8 ECHR is entitled 'Right to respect for private and family life' and provides:

> Everyone has the right to respect for his private and family life, his home and his correspondence.[9]

Article 8 ECHR is about much more than a right to privacy, as the ECtHR explained in *A, B and C v Ireland*:[10]

> the notion of 'private life' within the meaning of Article 8 of the Convention is a broad concept which encompasses, *inter alia*, the right to personal autonomy and personal development[11] ... It concerns subjects such as gender identification, sexual orientation and sexual life[12] ... a person's physical and psychological

---

7. *Is the draft EU agreement re: accession of the European Union to the Convention for the Protection of Human Rights and Fundamental Freedoms compatible with the Treaties? (Opinions of the Court)* [2014] EUECJ Avis-2/13 (18 December 2014), para 194.
8. Compare TFEU, article 260(2) 'If the Commission considers that the Member State concerned has not taken the necessary measures to comply with the judgment of the Court, it may bring the case before the Court ... It shall specify the amount of the lump sum or penalty payment to be paid by the Member State concerned...' with ECHR, article 46(4)–(5): 'If the Committee of Ministers considers that a High Contracting Party refuses to abide by a final judgment in a case to which it is a party, it may ... refer to the Court the question whether that Party has failed to fulfil its obligation ... If the Court finds a violation ... it shall refer the case to the Committee of Ministers'.
9. ECHR, article 8(1).
10. *A, B and C v Ireland* No 25579/05 [2010] ECHR 2032 (16 December 2010).
11. Citing *Pretty v United Kingdom* (29 April 2002) ECtHR, para 61.
12. Citing *Dudgeon v United Kingdom* (22 October 1981) ECtHR, pp 18–19, para 41; and *Laskey, Jaggard and Brown v United Kingdom* (19 February 1997) ECtHR, p 131, para 36.

integrity[13] ... as well as decisions both to have and not to have a child or to become genetic parents.[14]

Article 8 ECHR does not just protect 'privacy'; it protects one's 'private life'. So article 8 impacts on a broad range of issues, as the ECtHR stated in *Niemetz v Germany*:[15]

> The Court does not consider it possible or necessary to attempt an exhaustive definition of the notion of 'private life'. However, it would be too restrictive to limit the notion to an 'inner circle' in which the individual may live his own personal life as he chooses and to exclude therefrom entirely the outside world not encompassed within that circle. Respect for private life must also comprise to a certain degree the right to establish and develop relationships with other human beings.
>
> There appears, furthermore, to be no reason of principle why this understanding of the notion of 'private life' should be taken to exclude activities of a professional or business nature since it is, after all, in the course of their working lives that the majority of people have a significant, if not the greatest, opportunity of developing relationships with the outside world. This view is supported by the fact that ... it is not always possible to distinguish clearly which of an individual's activities form part of his professional or business life and which do not. Thus, especially in the case of a person exercising a liberal profession, his work in that context may form part and parcel of his life to such a degree that it becomes impossible to know in what capacity he is acting at a given moment of time.[16]

In *Niemetz* the plaintiff was a German lawyer who objected to the collection of church tithes by the German state and was active in anti-clerical circles. He was suspected of involvement in the sending of a fax to the office in a court involved in the prosecution of an employer who refused to deduct tithes from his employee's wages. A prosecution was initiated and his offices were searched. He objected to that search and made his way to the ECtHR, where he argued that 'the search of his law office had given rise to a breach of Article 8 of the Convention'.[17] The court found in his favour, holding that the right to respect for one's private life extended to 'certain professional or business activities or premises'.[18]

---

13.   Citing *Tysiąc v Poland* (7 February 2006) ECtHR.
14.   Citing *Evans v United Kingdom* [GC], No 6339/05, ECHR 2007 IV. *A, B and C v Ireland*, No 25579/05 [2010] ECHR 2032 (16 December 2010), para 212. Not everything will be a breach of privacy, however. The ECtHR refused to admit a claim that a hunting ban was a breach of article 8 in *Friend v the United Kingdom*, No 16072/06 [2009] ECHR 2068 (24 November 2009).
15.   *Niemetz v Germany* [1993] 16 EHRR 97 (16 December 1992).
16.   *Niemetz v Germany* [1993] 16 EHRR 97 (16 December 1992), para 29.
17.   *Niemetz v Germany* [1993] 16 EHRR 97 (16 December 1992), para 26.
18.   *Niemetz v Germany* [1993] 16 EHRR 97 (16 December 1992), para 31. The ECtHR reapplied *Niemietz v Germany* in *Turan v Hungary*, No 33068/05 [2010] ECHR 1058 (6 July 2010). The applicant was a Hungarian lawyer whose offices were searched by the police, without her being present, which was contrary to Hungarian law. (contd .../)

In *Pretty v United Kingdom*[19] the ECtHR took a broad interpretation of the meaning of 'private life' and reiterated previous remarks that:

> the concept of 'private life' is a broad term not susceptible to exhaustive definition. It covers the physical and psychological integrity of a person ... It can sometimes embrace aspects of an individual's physical and social identity ... Elements such as, for example, gender identification, name and sexual orientation and sexual life fall within the personal sphere protected by Article 8 ... Article 8 also protects a right to personal development, and the right to establish and develop relationships with other human beings and the outside world ... Although no previous case has established as such any right to self-determination as being contained in Article 8 of the Convention, the Court considers that the notion of personal autonomy is an important principle underlying the interpretation of its guarantees.

In *Von Hannover v Germany*[20] the ECtHR extended the remit of article 8 to public spaces, holding that:

> the public does not have a legitimate interest in knowing where the applicant is and how she behaves generally in her private life even if she appears in places that cannot always be described as secluded and despite the fact that she is well known to the public.[21]

The applicant in question was a member of the royal family of Monaco.[22] A number of German magazines had published photographs of her in restaurants, on horseback, shopping, playing tennis, riding a bike and canoeing with her children. The applicant claimed that these photographs interfered with her rights under article 8. The ECtHR agreed. It held that:

> private life, in the Court's view, includes a person's physical and psychological integrity; the guarantee afforded by Article 8 of the Convention is primarily intended to ensure the development, without outside interference, of the personality of each individual in his relations with other human beings ... [t]here is ... a zone of interaction of a person with others, even in a public context, which may fall within the scope of private life ...[23]

---

18.   (contd) The ECtHR therefore held that there had been a breach of article 8. See also *Kilic v Turkey*, No 70845/01 [2006] ECHR 894 (24 October 2006).

19.   *Pretty v United Kingdom* (29 April 2002) ECtHR, para 61.

20.   *Von Hannover v Germany* (24 June 2004) ECtHR.

21.   *Von Hannover v Germany* (24 June 2004) ECtHR, para 75.

22.   The political impotence of the applicant's position was significant. The ECtHR made 'a fundamental distinction ... between reporting facts – even controversial ones – capable of contributing to a debate in a democratic society relating to politicians in the exercise of their functions, for example, and reporting details of the private life of an individual who, moreover, as in this case, does not exercise official functions'. *Von Hannover v Germany* (24 June 2004) ECtHR, para 63. The private lives of politicians may, thus, be more vulnerable than those of princesses. See *Karhuvaara v Finland* (16 November 2004) ECtHR.

23.   *Von Hannover v Germany* (24 June 2004) ECtHR, para 50.

Whilst the applicant was a public person, the court accepted that this did not mean that she was not entitled to a private life:

> although the public has a right to be informed, which is an essential right in a democratic society that, in certain special circumstances, can even extend to aspects of the private life of public figures, particularly where politicians are concerned ... this is not the case here. The situation here does not come within the sphere of any political or public debate because the published photos and accompanying commentaries relate exclusively to details of the applicant's private life ...[24]

[2.03] The ECtHR has adopted a flexible interpretation of the meaning of 'home'. In *Gillow v United Kingdom*[25] it held that a property which the plaintiffs had not lived in for 19 years, although they had retained ownership in it, rented it out and intended to return to it upon their retirements was a home. In *Buckley v United Kingdom*[26] a caravan site where the plaintiff lived with her family in breach of planning permission was held to be a home. Evictions may fall within the scope of article 8 as will investigations by child welfare services,[27] prosecutions[28] and flights to and from airports in the middle of the night.[29] The article 8 rights of a mother were found to have been breached where:

> ... the continuing harassment of ... her disabled son for whom she has been taking care, and the incidents of harassment which also concerned her personally ... had an adverse effect on her private and family life. Indeed, the moral integrity of an individual is covered by the concept of private life. The concept of private life extends also to the sphere of the relations of individuals between themselves.[30]

A failure to properly investigate an allegation of rape may be 'a violation of the procedural aspect of ... Article 8'.[31] The German court's failure to even consider a

---

24. *Von Hannover v Germany* (24 June 2004) ECtHR, para 64.
25. *Gillow v United Kingdom* (1986) 11 EHRR 335.
26. *Buckley v United Kingdom* (1996) 23 EHRR 101. See also *Chichester District Council v First Secretary of State and Ors* [2004] EWCA Civ 1248.
27. In *KT v Norway*, No 26664/03 [2008] ECHR 890 (25 September 2008) the ECtHR held that investigations carried out by child welfare services were not a breach of article 8 ECHR. But contrast this to *Moser v Austria*, No 12643/02 [2006] ECHR 799 (21 September 2006).
28. In *SXH v Crown Prosecution Service* [2014] EWCA Civ 90 (6 February 2014) the applicant claimed that the decision to prosecute him breached his rights under ECHR, article 8. The English Court of Appeal rejected that claim whilst accepting that '... there may be circumstances in which a decision to prosecute engages article 8 ECHR, even when the offence with which the defendant is charged does not itself constitute interference with private life' (para 79).
29. *Hatton v UK* [2002] EHRR 1. But see *Hamalainen v Finland*, No 37359/09 [2014] ECHR 787 (16 July 2014) in which the ECtHR held that refusal to change ID number of trans-gender individual was not a breach of article 8 and *SAS v France* [2014] ECHR 695 (1 July 2014) in which the ECtHR held that a '...ban on wearing clothing designed to conceal one's face in public places...' was not a breach (para 30).
30. *Dordevic v Croatia*, No 41526/10, HEJUD [2012] ECHR 1640 (24 July 2012), para 97.
31. *DJ v Croatia*, No 42418/10, HEJUD [2012] ECHR 1642 (24 July 2012), para 104.

complaint about the state's refusal 'to grant [the applicant]'s late wife authorisation to acquire a lethal dose of drugs allowing her to end her life'[32] was a breach of the applicant's rights under article 8. In *X v Finland*[33] the ECtHR found that the 'forced administration of medication ... without proper legal safeguards'[34] was in violation of article 8. Dismissals from work have been held to be a breach of a person's article 8 rights. The ECtHR held that an unlawful dismissal from work could amount to a breach of article 8 in *Kyriakides v Cyprus*.[35] The applicant 'was accused ... of negligence in respect of the involvement of other officers under his command in the torture of suspects'. This accusation was made by a commission of enquiry which 'received considerable publicity and led to the applicant's dismissal from the police force'.[36] The ECtHR held that the failure of the Cypriot courts to award damages for the unlawful administrative act of dismissal was a breach of article 8.[37]

The ECHR, article 8 right can apply to non-living persons such as companies. In *Bernh Larsen v Norway*[38] the ECtHR held that an order requiring that a company provide a copy of its servers was an interference with its right to respect for 'home' and 'correspondence' under article 8 ECHR.

The relevance of Article 8, ECHR to EU data protection law

[2.04] The relationship between article 8, ECHR and EU data protection law was first substantially considered by the CJEU in *Osterreichischer Rundfunk*.[39] The CJEU began its analysis by noting:

> ... that Article 8 of the Convention while stating in paragraph 1 the principle that the public authorities must not interfere with the right to respect for private life, accepts in paragraph 2 that such an interference is possible where it is in accordance with the law and is necessary in a democratic society in the interests of national security, public safety or the economic well-being of the country, for the prevention of disorder or crime, for the protection of health or morals, or for the protection of the rights and freedoms of others.[40]

The CJEU went on to find that:

> ... while the mere recording by an employer of data by name relating to the remuneration paid to his employees cannot as such constitute an interference with

---

32. *Koch v Germany*, No 497/09 [2012] ECHR 1621 (19 July 2012), para 3.
33. *X v Finland*, No 34806/04 [2012] ECHR 1371 (3 July 2012).
34. *X v Finland*, No 34806/04 [2012] ECHR 1371 (3 July 2012), paras 221–222.
35. *Kyriakides v Cyprus*, No 39058/05 [2008] ECHR 1087.
36. *Kyriakides v Cyprus*, No 39058/05 [2008] ECHR 1087 (16 October 2008), para 47.
37. See also *Taliadorou and Stylianou v Cyprus*, No 39627/05 [2008] ECHR 1088 (16 October 2008).
38. *Bernh Larsen v Norway* [2013] ECHR 220 (14 March 2013).
39. *Osterreichischer Rundfunk* (Case C–138/01) (20 May 2003).
40. *Osterreichischer Rundfunk* (Case C–138/01) (20 May 2003) para 71.

private life, the communication of that data to third parties … infringes the right of the persons concerned to respect for private life, whatever the subsequent use of the information thus communicated, and constitutes an interference within the meaning of Article 8 of the Convention.[41]

The CJEU then held that it was for the Austrian courts to decide whether:

… the wide disclosure not merely of the amounts of the annual income … but also of the names of the recipients of that income is both necessary for and appropriate to the aim of keeping salaries within reasonable limits …[42]

Finally it was the judgment of the CJEU that if the Austrian courts were to:

… conclude that the national legislation at issue is incompatible with Article 8 of the [ECHR] that legislation is also incapable of satisfying the requirement of proportionality in … Directive 95/46.[43]

The relationship between the ECHR and the EU right to data protection is now subject to article 52(3) of the Charter itself, which provides:

In so far as this Charter contains rights which correspond to rights guaranteed by the Convention for the Protection of Human Rights and Fundamental Freedoms, the meaning and scope of those rights shall be the same as those laid down by the said Convention. This provision shall not prevent Union law providing more extensive protection.[44]

The CJEU explained the relationship between the EU Charter rights to privacy and data protection with the ECHR right to privacy as follows in *Schecke*:[45]

… according to Article 52(3) of the Charter, in so far as it contains rights which correspond to rights guaranteed by the Convention, the meaning and scope of those rights are to be the same as those laid down by the Convention. Article 53 of the Charter further states that nothing in the Charter is to be interpreted as restricting or adversely affecting the rights recognised inter alia by the Convention … In those circumstances, it must be considered that the right to respect for private life with regard to the processing of personal data, recognised by Articles 7 and 8 of the Charter, concerns any information relating to an identified or identifiable individual[46] … and the limitations which may lawfully be imposed on the right to the protection of personal data correspond to those tolerated in relation to Article 8 of the [ECHR].[47]

---

41. *Osterreichischer Rundfunk* (Case C–138/01) (20 May 2003), para 74.
42. *Osterreichischer Rundfunk* (Case C–138/01) (20 May 2003), para 90.
43. *Osterreichischer Rundfunk* (Case C–138/01) (20 May 2003), para 91.
44. Charter, article 52(3).
45. *Volker und Markus Schecke* (Case C–92/09) (9 November 2010).
46. Citing *Amann v Switzerland, Rotaru v Romania*.
47. *Volker und Markus Schecke* (Case C–92/09) (9 November 2010), paras 51 & 52.

[2.05] In *Tele2 Sverige*[48] the CJEU was asked to consider questions about national data retention laws following its finding in *Digital Rights Ireland* that the EU's Data Retention Directive was invalid. The CJEU was asked to consider:

> … whether, in the Digital Rights judgment, the Court interpreted Articles 7 and/or 8 of the Charter in such a way as to expand the scope conferred on Article 8 ECHR by the European Court of Human Rights.[49]

The CJEU began its consideration by recalling that:

> … whilst, as Article 6(3) TEU confirms, fundamental rights recognised by the ECHR constitute general principles of EU law, the ECHR does not constitute, as long as the European Union has not acceded to it, a legal instrument which has been formally incorporated into EU law …[50]

And that:

> … the interpretation of Directive 2002/58, which is at issue in this case, must be undertaken solely in the light of the fundamental rights guaranteed by the Charter …[51]

The CJEU bore in mind that article 52(3) of the Charter:

> … is intended to ensure the necessary consistency between the Charter and the ECHR, 'without thereby adversely affecting the autonomy of Union law and … that of the Court of Justice of the European Union'.[52] In particular … the first sentence of Article 52(3) does not preclude Union law from providing protection that is more extensive than the ECHR. It should be added, finally, that Article 8 of the Charter concerns a fundamental right which is distinct from that enshrined in Article 7 of the Charter and which has no equivalent in the ECHR.[53]

However, the CJEU went on to rule that the specific question asked was inadmissible.[54] However in *Orsi*[55] the CJEU stated:

> … as Article 6(3) TEU confirms, fundamental rights recognised by the ECHR constitute general principles of the European Union's law and whilst Article 52(3) of the Charter provides that the rights contained in the Charter which correspond to rights guaranteed by the ECHR are to have the same meaning and scope as those laid down by that convention, the latter does not constitute, as long as the European Union has not acceded to it, a legal instrument which has been formally incorporated into EU law… Therefore, the examination of the question referred

---

48. *Tele2 Sverige* (Case C–203/15) (21 December 2016).
49. *Tele2 Sverige* (Case C–203/15) (21 December 2016), para 126.
50. *Tele2 Sverige* (Case C–203/15) (21 December 2016), para 127.
51. *Tele2 Sverige* (Case C–203/15) (21 December 2016), para 128.
52. Citing *JN v Staatssecretaris van Veiligheid en Justitie* (Case C–601/15) (15 February 2016), para 47
53. *Tele2 Sverige* (Case C–203/15) (21 December 2016), para 129.
54. *Tele2 Sverige* (Case C–203/15) (21 December 2016), para 133.
55. *Orsi* (Case C–217/15) (5 April 2017).

must be undertaken solely in the light of the fundamental rights guaranteed by the Charter...[56]

This strongly suggests that article 8 ECHR and its discussion by the ECtHR are of limited, if any, relevance to EU data protection law at the present time. However there are a number of reasons for continuing to consider article 8 ECHR in the context of EU data protection law: one is that the ECHR still constitutes a general principle of EU law; another is that it remains open to the EU to accede to the ECHR in future; and finally the wide variety of privacy issues considered by the ECtHR mean that the judgments of that Court remain relevant to discussions of EU data protection law.

So while the above may suggest that article 8 ECHR and its discussion by the ECtHR are of limited relevance to EU data protection law, this is not the final judgment of the CJEU. And there are a number of reasons for continuing to consider article 8, ECHR in the context of EU data protection law: one is that the ECHR still constitutes a general principle of EU law; another is that it remains open to the EU to accede to the ECHR in future; and finally the wide variety of privacy issues considered by the ECtHR mean that the judgments of that Court remain relevant to discussions of EU data protection law.

[2.06] The CJEU has cited judgments of the ECtHR when considering EU data protection law on a number of occasions (though not since its judgment in *Tele2 Sverige*). In *Digital Rights Ireland* the CJEU cited judgments of the ECtHR in *Leander v Sweden*,[57] *Rotaru v Romania*[58] and *Weber v Germany*[59] in support of its finding that '... the access of the competent national authorities to the data constitutes a further interference with that fundamental right ... (to privacy)'.[60] The CJEU went on to cite the judgment of the ECtHR in *S and Marper v the United Kingdom*[61] in support of its view that the EU's legislature's discretion was limited '... where interferences with fundamental rights are at issue ...'[62] and that:

> EU legislation ... must lay down clear and precise rules governing the scope and application of the (data retention) measure ... and imposing minimum safeguards so that the persons whose data have been retained have sufficient guarantees to effectively protect their personal data against the risk of abuse and against any unlawful access and use of that data ...[63]

---

56. *Orsi* (Case C–217/15) (5 April 2017), para 15.
57. *Leander v Sweden* (1987) 9 EHRR 433.
58. *Rotaru v Romania* [GC], No 28341/95, para 46, ECHR 2000-V.
59. *Weber v Germany* No 54934/00, § 79, ECHR 2006-XI.
60. *Digital Rights Ireland* (Case C–293/12) (8 April 2014), para 35; see similarly *Digital Rights Ireland* (Judgment of the Court) (Case C–293/12) (8 April 2014).
61. *S and Marper v the United Kingdom* [GC], Nos 30562/04 and 30566/04, para 102, 2008-V.
62. *Digital Rights Ireland* (Case C–293/12) (8 April 2014), para 47.
63. The CJEU also cited the ECtHR judgments in *Liberty and Ors v the United Kingdom* (1 July 2008) ECtHR, paras 62 and 63; *Rotaru v Romania*, paras 57 to 59, *Digital Rights Ireland* (Case C–293/12) (8 April 2014), para 54.

In *Schwarz*[64] the CJEU again cited *S and Marper v the United Kingdom* in support of its finding that fingerprints constitute personal data.

Application of Article 8 ECHR to personal data

[2.07] In *Von Hannover v Germany* the ECtHR suggested that:

> increased vigilance in protecting private life is necessary to contend with new communication technologies which make it possible to store and reproduce personal data.[65]

In *S and Marper v The United Kingdom*[66] the CJEU described what might be described as the ECHR right to data protection in the following terms:

> The protection of personal data is of fundamental importance to a person's enjoyment of his or her right to respect for private and family life, as guaranteed by Article 8 of the Convention. The domestic law must afford appropriate safeguards to prevent any such use of personal data as may be inconsistent with the guarantees of this Article ...[67] The need for such safeguards is all the greater where the protection of personal data undergoing automatic processing is concerned, not least when such data are used for police purposes. The domestic law should notably ensure that such data are relevant and not excessive in relation to the purposes for which they are stored; and preserved in a form which permits identification of the data subjects for no longer than is required for the purpose for which those data are stored[68] ... The domestic law must also afford adequate guarantees that retained personal data was efficiently protected from misuse and abuse[69] .... The above considerations are especially valid as regards the protection of special categories of more sensitive data[70] ... and more particularly of DNA information, which contains the person's genetic make-up of great importance to both the person concerned and his or her family.[71]

Where personal data is contained in correspondence or stored in a person's home, then its privacy is explicitly protected by article 8 ECHR. However, the ECtHR has been

---

64. *Schwarz v Stadt Bochum* (Case C–291/12) (17 October 2013).
65. *Von Hannover v Germany* (24 June 2004) ECtHR, para 70.
66. *S and Marper v The United Kingdom* (4 December 2008) ECtHR.
67. Citing *mutatis mutandis, Z v Finland*, (25 February 1997), § 71, Reports of Judgments and Decisions 1997 I, 25 EHRR 371, para 95.
68. Citing the Strasbourg Convention 108, article 5 and the preamble thereto and Principle 7 of Recommendation R(87)15 of the Committee of Ministers regulating the use of personal data in the police sector.
69. Citing Data Protection Convention, article 7.
70. Citing Data Protection Convention, article 6. See also *LH v Latvia* No 52019/07, 29 April 2014 in which the collection of the applicant's medical data was held to have violated ECHR, article 8.
71. Citing Recommendation No R(92)1 of the Committee of Ministers on the use of analysis of DNA within the framework of the criminal justice system. *S and Marper v The United Kingdom* (4 December 2008) ECtHR, para 103.

willing to extend article 8 ECHR to encompass personal data stored by others outside the home and to photographs taken by third parties. The ECtHR has held that a failure to keep accurate data may amount to a breach of article 8 ECHR. In *Babylonova v Slovakia*[72] the applicant and her husband bought a house. The vendors undertook to deregister themselves as residents of the house, but one of them failed to do so as he was unable to establish a permanent residence elsewhere. The ECtHR agreed that the fact that this person remained registered as a resident of the applicant's home amounted to a breach of her rights under article 8. In *Nikolova v Bulgaria*[73] the ECtHR reiterated that '… the gathering, storing and release of information relating to an individual's "private life" come within the scope of article 8' (ECHR).[74] The ECtHR has repeatedly held that the entry of a person's personal information on a register or database may amount to a breach of their rights under article 8 ECHR.[75]

[2.08] The application of the ECHR to data processing operations is not unlimited, as is clear from *Smith v United Kingdom*.[76] The applicant was the former director of a firm that had been refused funding by a bank, and had been declared bankrupt as a result. The applicant had sought access to the bank's notes of a meeting with himself under the UK's Data Protection Act 1998, but was refused. He applied to the ECtHR, arguing that 'he had been denied access to documents held by a bank in breach of Article 8 (ECHR)'. This application was rejected by the court, which began by noting 'that it is not its role to assess whether the domestic courts have correctly interpreted domestic or European legislation on data protection'. The court also noted that 'the information allegedly in the files concerned a business transaction' and this appeared to the court to be 'an oblique application for discovery of documentary evidence'. The court distinguished this case from:

> a case where the applicant seeks access to files holding information about his identity or personal history, whether with a view to correcting any errors in those records or preventing misuse of personal information[77] … or to uncovering information with formative implications for his or her personality[78] … Nor was the information in the documents obtained through any measure invasive of the applicant's privacy or held on a data base which is in current use or involves the possibility of release of personal information to others.

---

72. *Babylonova v Slovakia*, No 69146/01 [2006] ECHR 630 (20 June 2006).
73. *Nikolova v Bulgaria*, No 20688/04, Chamber Judgment [2013] ECHR 1291 (17 December 2013).
74. *Nikolova v Bulgaria*, No 20688/04, Chamber Judgment [2013] ECHR 1291 (17 December 2013), para 105 citing *Leander v Sweden* (1987) 9 EHRR 433, and *Antunes Rocha v Portugal* (31 May 2005) ECtHR.
75. See: *Brunet v France* [2014] ECHR 970 (18 September 2014); *MK v France*, 19522/09, 18 April 2013, *Khelili v Switzerland*, 18 October 2011, *Shimovolos v Russia* (21 June 2012) ECtHR, *Dimitrov-Kazakov v Bulgaria*, 10 February 2011.
76. *Smith v United Kingdom*, No 39658/05 [2007] ECHR 85 (4 January 2007).
77. Citing eg *Rotaru v Romania* [GC], No 28341/95, ECHR 2000 V.
78. Citing eg *Gaskin v United Kingdom* (1989) 12 EHRR 3; *Mikulić v Croatia*, No 53176/99, para 54, ECHR 2002 I.

Recording of personal data undoubtedly occurred in *Rotaru v Romania*.[79] The applicant in question was a lawyer who had published a couple of articles in 1946; he was arrested, convicted and sentenced to a term of one year's imprisonment. After the fall of Communism the plaintiff sought to have his prison term used in the calculation of his pension. When he brought his case before the courts a letter was produced from Romanian intelligence services alleging that the plaintiff was a member of an extreme right-wing organisation.[80] The plaintiff brought his case to the ECtHR, where the Romanian government:

> denied that Article 8 was applicable, arguing that the information in the ... letter ... related not to the applicant's private life but to his public life. By deciding to engage in political activities and have pamphlets published, the applicant had impliedly waived his right to the 'anonymity' inherent in private life. As to his questioning by the police and his criminal record, they were public information.[81]

The court rejected this claim, reiterating that 'the storing of information relating to an individual's private life in a secret register and the release of such information comes within the scope of Article 8(1) (ECHR)'.[82] In *Cemalettin Canli v Turkey*[83] the applicant had been acquitted on charges of membership of an illegal organisation in 1990. He was subsequently charged with entirely separate offences in 2003. At his trial, the police submitted records to the court that the applicant had been a member of an illegal organisation in 1990. The applicant complained to the ECtHR that 'the preparation of and submission to ... court ... of the police report had been arbitrary and unlawful'[84] and that this was a breach of his article 8 ECHR rights. The ECtHR agreed, dismissing the respondent's argument that this was public, not private, information.

[2.09] Depending upon context, the issue of whether or not data is recorded may determine whether or not an interference with article 8 ECHR has occurred. In *PG and JH v United Kingdom*[85] the ECtHR considered that:

> [a] person who walks down the street will, inevitably, be visible to any member of the public who is also present. Monitoring by technological means of the same public scene (for example, a security guard viewing through closed-circuit television) is of a similar character. Private-life considerations may arise, however, once any systematic or permanent record comes into existence of such material from the public domain.[86]

---

79.   *Rotaru v Romania* (4 May 2000) ECtHR.
80.   Where membership of such an organisation would have disqualified the plaintiff's pension claim.
81.   *Rotaru v Romania* (4 May 2000) ECtHR, para 42.
82.   *Rotaru v Romania* (4 May 2000) ECtHR, para 43.
83.   *Cemalettin Canli v Turkey*, No 22427/04 [2008] ECHR 14588 (18 November 2008).
84.   *Cemalettin Canli v Turkey*, No 22427/04 [2008] ECHR 14588 (18 November 2008), para 31.
85.   *PG and JH v United Kingdom* (25 September 2001) ECtHR. See similarly *Vetter v France* (31 May 2005) ECtHR in which listening devices were installed in the applicant's flat.
86.   *PG and JH v United Kingdom* (25 September 2001) ECtHR, para 57.

Justification under Article 8(2) ECHR

[2.10] The rights provided by article 8(1) ECHR may be interfered with in accordance with article 8(2) ECHR, which provides:

> There shall be no interference by a public authority with the exercise of this right except such as is in accordance with the law and is necessary in a democratic society in the interests of national security, public safety or the economic well-being of the country, for the prevention of disorder or crime, for the protection of health or morals, or for the protection of the rights and freedoms of others.

It may seem obvious, but a plaintiff must establish that his right has been interfered with by the State. In *Halford v United Kingdom* the plaintiff submitted that 'she should not be required to establish that there was a "reasonable likelihood" that calls made on her home telephone were intercepted'.[87] However, the court rejected this submission and held that it did 'not find it established that there was an interference with Ms Halford's rights to respect for her private life and correspondence in relation to her home telephone'.[88] In *Amann v Switzerland*[89] it was 'not disputed that the Public Prosecutor's Office intercepted and recorded a telephone call received by the applicant ... from a person at the former Soviet embassy in Berne'.[90] The court held that this interception and recording of calls was an interference by a public authority. In *Rotaru v Romania* the court pointed out that:

> both the storing by a public authority of information relating to an individual's private life and the use of it and the refusal to allow an opportunity for it to be refuted amount to interference with the right to respect for private life secured in Article 8(1) of the Convention.

The fact that a law exists, even if it is not enforced, may be sufficient to amount to interference. In *Norris v Ireland:*

> the Government relied on the fact that the applicant had been able to maintain an active public life side by side with a private life free from any interference on the part of the State or its agents.[91]

This argument was rejected by the court, which cited its own decision in *Dudgeon v United Kingdom*:[92]

> the maintenance in force of the impugned legislation constitutes a continuing interference with the applicant's right to respect for his private life ... the very existence of this legislation continuously and directly affects his private life.[93]

---

87. *Halford v United Kingdom* (25 June 1997) ECtHR, para 53.
88. *Halford v United Kingdom* (25 June 1997) ECtHR, para 60.
89. *Amann v Switzerland* (2000) 30 EHRR 843.
90. *Amann v Switzerland* (2000) 30 EHRR 843, para 45.
91. *Amann v Switzerland* (2000) 30 EHRR 843, para 37.
92. *Dudgeon v United Kingdom* (1981) 4 EHRR 149.
93. *Dudgeon v United Kingdom* (1981) 4 EHRR 149, para 38.

Such an interference must be justified in accordance with the law. This means that the action must have a basis in domestic law and it must be accessible and foreseeable.[94] This requirement is illustrated by the case of *Malone v United Kingdom*.[95] The plaintiff was charged with handling stolen goods, and at trial it emerged that phone calls to his home had been intercepted. He sought redress from the ECtHR which reiterated that the expression 'in accordance with the law' must be interpreted in the light of the following principles: first, the word law means written and unwritten law; second, the interference must have some basis in domestic law. The court reiterated that 'the phrase 'in accordance with the law' does not merely refer back to domestic law but also relates to the quality of the law, requiring it to be compatible with the rule of law ... The phrase thus implies ... that there must be a measure of legal protection in domestic law against arbitrary interferences by public authorities with ...' the right to privacy. The court went on to hold that:

> the law must be sufficiently clear in its terms to give citizens an adequate indication as to the circumstances in which and the conditions on which public authorities are empowered to resort to this secret and potentially dangerous interference with the right to respect for private life and correspondence.[96]

It concluded that: 'in view of the attendant uncertainty and obscurity in this essential aspect[97] ... the interferences with the applicant's right ... to respect for his private life and correspondence ... were not 'in accordance with the law'.'[98] In *Rotaru v Romania* the court concluded that:

> the holding and use ... of information on the applicant's private life was not 'in accordance with the law', a fact that suffices to constitute a violation of Article 8. In the instant case that fact prevents the court from reviewing the legitimacy of the aim pursued by the measures ordered and determining whether they were— assuming the aim to have been legitimate—'necessary in a democratic society'.[99]

However, it is clear from the judgments of the court in *Klass v Germany* and *Malone v United Kingdom* that these exceptions must be interpreted narrowly. Justification on the grounds of national security was held to exist in *Klass v Germany* where the court commented that:

> The first [justification] consists of the technical advances made in the means of espionage and, correspondingly, of surveillance; the second is the development of terrorism in Europe in recent years. Democratic societies nowadays find

---

94. See *Turek v Slovakia*, Application No 57986/00, 14 February 2006, which concerned a former Czechoslovak Communist Security Agency file which identified the applicant as one of his agents. The file was retained on the basis of rules to which the applicant had no access, which the CJEU held was a breach of article 8. See also *Soro v Estonia* (3 September 2015) ECtHR.

95. *Malone v United Kingdom* (1984) 7 EHRR 14.

96. *Malone v United Kingdom* (1984) 7 EHRR 14, para 67.

97. *Malone v United Kingdom* (1984) 7 EHRR 14, para 79.

98. *Malone v United Kingdom* (1984) 7 EHRR 14, para 80.

99. *Rotaru v Romania* (4 May 2000) ECtHR, para 62.

themselves threatened by highly sophisticated forms of espionage and by terrorism, with the result that the State must be able, in order effectively to counter such threats, to undertake the secret surveillance of subversive elements operating within its jurisdiction.[100]

[2.11] In *Leander v Sweden*[101] the plaintiff was a temporary museum employee who applied for a permanent post. He was then reviewed by the Swedish security services and it was:

> uncontested that the secret police-register contained information relating to Mr Leander's private life. Both the storing and the release of such information, which were coupled with a refusal to allow Mr Leander an opportunity to refute it, amounted to an interference with his right to respect for private life.[102]

The court noted that the aim of this register, the protection of national security, was undoubtedly legitimate[103] and in accordance with the law.[104] As regards it being necessary in a democratic society, the court held that:

> [t]here can be no doubt as to the necessity, for the purpose of protecting national security, for the Contracting States to have laws granting the competent domestic authorities power, first, to collect and store in registers not accessible to the public information on persons and, secondly, to use this information when assessing the suitability of candidates for employment in posts of importance for national security.[105]

[2.12] In *Antunes Rocha v Portugal*[106] the applicant got a job with the Portuguese National Council for Emergency Civil Planning. As part of her job, she was subject to a security vetting, this being a requirement of NATO, of which Portugal was a member. However, she resigned when she discovered that as part of this vetting her home had been placed under surveillance and close acquaintances had been questioned. The applicant complained to the ECtHR alleging that her right to privacy had been breached. The ECtHR held that gathering information about the applicant in this way did indeed amount to an interference with her private life. The ECtHR then examined whether this interference was in accordance with the law. The ECtHR noted that the investigation was undertaken pursuant to Portuguese law and that the aim of this legislation was clear; that is, to establish whether the applicant was totally honest and loyal and whether her reputation, habits, social life, discretion and common sense were such as to permit her to be given access to confidential files. However, the ECtHR went on to find that the legislation was defective in a number of other aspects. Firstly, it was too vague.

---

100. *Klass v Germany* (1979–80) 2 EHRR 214, para 48.
101. *Leander v Sweden* (1987) 9 EHRR 433.
102. *Leander v Sweden* (1987) 9 EHRR 433, para 48.
103. *Leander v Sweden* (1987) 9 EHRR 433, para 49.
104. *Leander v Sweden* (1987) 9 EHRR 433, para 57.
105. *Leander v Sweden* (1987) 9 EHRR 433, para 59.
106. *Antunes Rocha v Portugal* [2005] ECHR 335.

Secondly, it did not alert those concerned to the fact that they might be subject to measures such as surveillance of their home. Finally, the legislation did not contain any control mechanisms or provide any safeguards for individuals. In consequence, the ECtHR ruled that the legislation did not indicate with sufficient clarity the scope of security investigations or the manner in which they were to be carried out. Therefore, the ECtHR ruled that Portugal was in breach of the ECHR.

[2.13] The economic well-being of the country is quite broadly defined. In *MS v Sweden*[107] the plaintiff suffered an injury in the course of her employment and made a claim for compensation under the Swedish Industrial Injury Insurance Act whereupon she discovered that her confidential medical records had been reviewed by the authorities. The court held this interference was justified as necessary for the determination of her claim for compensation and it was necessary for the economic well-being of Sweden that public funds were only dispensed to deserving applicants.

[2.14] The prevention of disorder or crime was held to justify the entry into and search of the home of Mrs Murray, whom the UK authorities suspected was a terrorist, in *Murray v United Kingdom*.[108] In *Campbell v United Kingdom*[109] it was held to justify the interception of the correspondence of prisoners[110] and in *Ludi v Switzerland*[111] it was held to justify police surveillance.[112] In *Z v Finland*[113] the court accepted that:

> the interests of a patient and the community as a whole in protecting the confidentiality of medical data may be outweighed by the interest in investigation and prosecution of crime and in the publicity of court proceedings ... where such interests are shown to be of even greater importance.[114]

Interference on the grounds of health and morals has justified the taking of children into care,[115] the placing of restrictions on gypsy caravans[116] and a ban on assisted suicide.[117] Interference for the protection of the rights and freedoms of others was invoked in *TV v*

---

107. *MS v Sweden* (27 August 1997) [1997] ECHR 49, No 20837/92.

108. *Murray v United Kingdom* (1994) 19 EHRR 193.

109. *Campbell v United Kingdom* (1992) 15 EHRR 137.

110. See also *De Wilde v Belgium* (1971) 1 EHRR 373; *Schonenberger v Switzerland* (1988) 11 EHRR 202.

111. *Ludi v Switzerland* (1992) 15 EHRR 173.

112. See also *Klass v Germany* (1979–80) 2 EHRR 214; *Greuter v Netherlands* (19 March 2002) ECtHR.

113. *Z v Finland* (1997) 25 EHRR 371.

114. *Z v Finland* (1997) 25 EHRR 371, para 97.

115. See *W v United Kingdom* (1987) 10 EHRR 29; *B v United Kingdom* (1987) 10 EHRR 87; *R v United Kingdom* (1987) 10 EHRR 74.

116. *Chapman v United Kingdom* [2001] ECHR 43, *Coster v United Kingdom* (18 January 2001) ECtHR, *Beard v United Kingdom* (18 January 2001) ECtHR, *Lee v United Kingdom* (18 September 2012) ECtHR and *Smith v United Kingdom* (2001) EHRR 18.

117. *Pretty v United Kingdom* (2002) 12 BHRC 149.

Finland.[118] This was a decision of the European Commission on Human Rights, in which it was held that disclosing the HIV status of a prisoner to prison officers was justified in 'the interests of others'. In *Bouchacourt v France*[119] the applicant had been convicted of rape; the ECtHR held that the inclusion of his data on a national database of sex offenders struck a fair balance between his interests and those of the public.

Does Article 8 ECHR provide a right to data protection?

[2.15] Some 47 European states have given legal undertakings to comply with the ECHR and have agreed to supervision of their compliance by the ECtHR. Perhaps as a result of the broader range of States from which cases may be taken to the ECtHR, the jurisprudence of that court is now quite broad. Of course, this jurisprudence of the ECtHR cannot be compared to the complexity and detail of EU data protection law. But these judgments do allow the parameters of what might be termed the ECHR right to data protection to be sketched out. Judgments of the ECtHR have discussed the following issues:

- surveillance;

- data retention;

- privacy at work;

- information;

- access;

- security; and

- dissemination and disclosure of personal information.

Surveillance

[2.16] Correspondence has been held to mean letters sent through the postal service, particularly to and from prisoners.[120] Telephone calls are also correspondence.[121] In *Klass v Germany*[122] the court held that telephone conversations fell within the ambit of article 8.[123] In *Halford v UK*[124] the court held that 'the conversations held by … [the

---

118. *TV v Finland* (1994) 76A DR 140.

119. *Bouchacourt v France*, No 5335/06 [2009] ECHR 2276 (17 December 2009).

120. Eg *Campbell v United Kingdom* (1992) 15 EHRR 165.

121. See *Malone v United Kingdom* (1984) 7 EHRR 14.

122. *Klass v Germany* (1979–80) 2 EHRR 214.

123. 'Although telephone conversations are not expressly mentioned in para 1 of article 8, the Court considers, as did the Commission, that such conversations are covered by the notions of 'private life' and 'correspondence' referred to by this provision': (1979–80) 2 EHRR 214, para 41.

124. *Halford v UK* [1997] ECHR 32.

plaintiff] ... on her office telephones fell within the scope of the notions of "private life" and "correspondence"'.[125] Similarly, in *Kruslin v France*[126] the applicant was a man of no fixed abode, who made phone calls in relation to a murder from a phone box. These calls were recorded by the French police. On appeal to the ECtHR it was held that this amounted to an interference with the applicant's 'private life' and his 'correspondence' and so was an interference with article 8(1) ECHR.[127]

[2.17] In *Uzun v Germany*[128] the applicant was 'suspected of participation in offences committed by the so-called Anti-Imperialist Cell ... an organisation which was pursuing the armed combat abandoned since 1992 by the Red Army Faction'[129] and so the German authorities subjected the applicant to intense surveillance. Initially they installed transmitters in the applicant's car, but he 'detected and destroyed the transmitters'.[130] Instead the German authorities built a GPS receiver into a car owned by an accomplice of the applicant. The data from this device was downloaded every couple of days, and used along with other data to build up an account of his movements, which was subsequently used in his trial. The applicant argued that this amounted to a breach of his rights under article 8 ECHR. The court noted that 'GPS surveillance is by its very nature to be distinguished from other methods of visual or acoustical surveillance which are, as a rule, more susceptible of interfering with a person's right to respect for private life, because they disclose more information on a person's conduct, opinions or feelings'. To some extent the ECtHR seemed to be expressing a preference for GPS surveillance, but the court then went on to say that in this case the use of GPS, the processing of data derived from that GPS and the use of that data in court amounted to an interference with the applicant's rights under article 8.[131] The court went on to find that this surveillance was in accordance with the relevant German law and that it was necessary and proportionate given that the applicant was being investigated in relation to 'several counts of attempted murder for which a terrorist movement had claimed responsibility and to prevent further bomb attacks'.[132] The court therefore held that there had been no breach of article 8 ECHR.

[2.18] In *RE v United Kingdom*[133] the applicant was arrested and detained by Northern Irish police. The ECtHR held that covert surveillance of consultations with his solicitor breached the ECHR, but covert surveillance of his meetings with 'appropriate adults' did not.[134] In *Zakharov v Russia*[135] the applicant was the editor-in-chief of a publishing

---

125. *Halford v UK* [1997] ECHR 32, para 46. See also *Kopp v Switzerland* [1998] ECHR 18.
126. *Kruslin v France and Huvig v France* (24 April 1990) ECtHR.
127. *Kruslin v France and Huvig v France* (28 September 1995), para 26.
128. *Uzun v Germany* (2 September 2010) ECtHR.
129. *Uzun v Germany* (2 September 2010) ECtHR, para 6.
130. *Uzun v Germany* (2 September 2010) ECtHR, para 11.
131. *Uzun v Germany* (2 September 2010) ECtHR, para 52.
132. *Uzun v Germany* Application (2 September 2010) ECtHR, para 77.
133. *RE v United Kingdom* [2013] ECHR 387 (11 April 2013).
134. Compare to *Wisse v France* (2005) ECHR 71611/01.
135. *Zakharov v Russia*, No 47143/06 [2015] ECHR 1065 (4 December 2015).

company and of a magazine, he was also prominently involved in a NGO which monitored the freedom of Russian media. He brought '... judicial proceedings against three mobile network operators, claiming that there had been an interference with his right to the privacy of his telephone communications ...' as they '... had installed equipment which permitted the Federal Security Service ('the FSB') to intercept all telephone communications without prior judicial authorisation'.[136] The applicant was unable to prove that his communications had actually been intercepted, however the ECtHR held that there was a '... need to ensure that the secrecy of surveillance measures does not result in the measures being effectively unchallengeable and outside the supervision of ... the Court ...'. The ECtHR therefore accepted that '... an applicant can claim to be the victim of a violation occasioned by the mere existence of secret surveillance measures, or legislation permitting secret surveillance measures ...'. However, such an applicant would have to satisfy the following conditions: firstly they would have to show that they fell within the scope of the measures either because they belonged to a group that was targeted by those measures or else '... because the legislation directly affects all users of communication services ...';[137] and, secondly they would have to show that they lacked an effective remedy at national level. The ECtHR went on to conclude that:

> Russian legal provisions governing interceptions of communications do not provide for adequate and effective guarantees against arbitrariness and the risk of abuse which is inherent in any system of secret surveillance ... the circumstances in which public authorities are empowered to resort to secret surveillance measures are not defined with sufficient clarity. Provisions on discontinuation of secret surveillance measures do not provide sufficient guarantees against arbitrary interference. The domestic law permits automatic storage of clearly irrelevant data and is not sufficiently clear as to the circumstances in which the intercept material will be stored and destroyed after the end of a trial. The authorisation procedures are not capable of ensuring that secret surveillance measures are ordered only when 'necessary in a democratic society.[138]

The ECtHR went on to find that Russia lacked an independent, effective and competent supervisory mechanism; it also lacked effective remedies. *Szabo & Vissy v Hungary*[139] concerned a Hungarian law which allowed the authorities '... to search and keep under surveillance the applicants' homes secretly, to check their postal mail and parcels, to monitor their electronic communications and computer data transmissions and to make recordings of any data acquired through these methods ...'.[140] The ECtHR held that: 'In the mere existence of the legislation itself there is involved ... a menace of surveillance

---

136. *Zakharov v Russia*, No 47143/06 [2015] ECHR 1065 (4 December 2015), para 10.

137. *Zakharov v Russia*, No 47143/06 [2015] ECHR 1065 (4 December 2015), para 171.

138. *Zakharov v Russia*, No 47143/06 [2015] ECHR 1065 (4 December 2015), para 302.

139. *Szabo & Vissy v Hungary*, No 37138/14 [2016] ECHR 579 (12 January 2016). See also: *Dragojevic v Croatia*, No 68955/11, [2015] ECHR 28 (15 January 2015); *Mustafa Sezgin Tanrikulu v Turkey*, No 27473/06 [2017] ECHR 669 (18 July 2017).

140. *Szabo & Vissy v Hungary*, No 37138/14 [2016] ECHR 579 (12 January 2016), para 52.

...'.[141] The ECtHR went on to hold that: 'In view of the risk that a system of secret surveillance set up to protect national security may undermine or even destroy democracy under the cloak of defending it, the Court must be satisfied that there are adequate and effective guarantees against abuse'.[142] The ECtHR noted that '... it is a natural consequence of the forms taken by present-day terrorism that governments resort to cutting-edge technologies in pre-empting such attacks ... The techniques applied ... have ... reached a level of sophistication which is hardly conceivable for the average citizen ...'. And the ECtHR explained that it had to '... scrutinise the question as to whether the development of surveillance methods resulting in masses of data collected has been accompanied by a simultaneous development of legal safeguards ...'. The ECtHR warned that:

> ... it would defy the purpose of government efforts to keep terrorism at bay ... if the terrorist threat were paradoxically substituted for by a perceived threat of unfettered executive power intruding into citizens' private spheres by virtue of uncontrolled yet far-reaching surveillance techniques and prerogatives.[143]

The ECtHR interpreted the requirement that such surveillance be 'necessary in a democratic society' as meaning 'strict necessity' where 'cutting edge surveillance technologies' would be used: '... only if ... strictly necessary ... for the safeguarding the democratic institutions and ... for the obtaining of vital intelligence in an individual operation'.[144] The ECtHR went on to hold that '... supervision by a politically responsible member of the executive, such as the Minister of Justice, does not provide the necessary guarantees ... (that surveillance would only be authorised where strictly necessary)'.[145]

[2.19] Surveillance for civil purposes can also breach article 8, ECHR. In *Vukota-Bojic v Switzerland*:[146]

> ... the applicant was systematically and intentionally watched and filmed by professionals acting on the instructions of her insurance company on four different dates over a period of twenty-three days. The material obtained was stored and selected and the captured images were used as a basis for an expert opinion and, ultimately, for a reassessment of her insurance benefits.[147]

The CJEU observed that Swiss law did not indicate: '... any procedures to follow for the authorisation or supervision of the implementation of secret surveillance measures in the specific context of insurance disputes' and failed to provide '... any details as

---

141. *Szabo & Vissy v Hungary*, No 37138/14 [2016] ECHR 579 (12 January 2016), para 53.
142. *Szabo & Vissy v Hungary*, No 37138/14 [2016] ECHR 579 (12 January 2016), para 57.
143. *Szabo & Vissy v Hungary*, No 37138/14 [2016] ECHR 579 (12 January 2016), para 68.
144. *Szabo & Vissy v Hungary*, No 37138/14 [2016] ECHR 579 (12 January 2016), para 73.
145. *Szabo & Vissy v Hungary*, No 37138/14 [2016] ECHR 579 (12 January 2016), para 77.
146. *Vukota-Bojic v Switzerland*, No 61838/10 [2016] ECHR 899 (18 October 2016).
147. *Vukota-Bojic v Switzerland*, No 61838/10 [2016] ECHR 899 (18 October 2016), para 58.

regards the maximum duration of the surveillance measures or the possibility of their judicial challenge'. In addition, Swiss law:

> ... equally remained silent on the procedures to be followed for storing, accessing, examining, using, communicating or destroying the data collected through secret measures of surveillance. It thus remained unclear where and how long the report containing the impugned footage and photographs of the applicant would remain stored, which persons would have access to it and whether she had any legal means of contesting the handling of the said report. The foregoing necessarily increased the risk of unauthorised access to, or disclosure of, the surveillance materials.[148]

The Swiss government argued that '... the interference with the applicant's right to privacy by way of secret surveillance was relatively small ...'. And the ECtHR agreed that this surveillance '... must be considered to interfere less with a person's private life than, for instance, telephone tapping ...'.[149] However, it went on to decide that '... notwithstanding the arguably minor interference ...' there had been a breach of the applicant's rights under article 8 ECHR particularly as the Swiss law failed to 'set out sufficient safeguards against abuse'.[150]

Data retention

[2.20] The use of DNA was considered by the ECtHR in *S and Marper v United Kingdom*[151] where the first applicant had been arrested 'at the age of eleven and charged with attempted robbery'. His fingerprints and DNA samples were taken, but he was subsequently acquitted. The second applicant had been 'charged with harassment of his partner'. Again, his fingerprints and DNA samples were taken. He then reconciled with his partner and charges were dropped. Both applicants then 'asked for their fingerprints and DNA samples to be destroyed, but in both cases the police refused'.[152] They sought judicial review of this decision, but without success and so complained to the ECtHR that 'the retention of their fingerprints, cellular samples and DNA profiles'[153] was a breach of article 8 ECHR:

> The mere storing of data relating to the private life of an individual amounts to an interference within the meaning of Article 8[154] ... The subsequent use of the stored information has no bearing on that finding[155] ... However, in determining whether

---

148. *Vukota-Bojic v Switzerland*, No 61838/10 [2016] ECHR 899 (18 October 2016), paras 74-75.

149. *Vukota-Bojic v Switzerland*, No 61838/10 [2016] ECHR 899 (18 October 2016), paras 76.

150. *Vukota-Bojic v Switzerland*, No 61838/10 [2016] ECHR 899 (18 October 2016), para 77.

151. *S and Marper v United Kingdom* (4 December 2008) ECtHR. See also *W v the Netherlands*, No 20689/08 [2009] ECHR 277 (20 January 2009) and *Avcaquer v France*, 22 June 2016.

152. *S and Marper v United Kingdom* (4 December 2008) ECtHR, paras 10–12.

153. *S and Marper v United Kingdom* (4 December 2008) ECtHR, para 58.

154. Citing *Leander v Sweden* (1987) 9 EHRR 433.

155. Citing *Amann v Switzerland* [GC], No 27798/95, § 69, ECHR 2000-II, 30 EHRR 843.

the personal information retained by the authorities involves any of the private-life aspects mentioned above, the Court will have due regard to the specific context in which the information at issue has been recorded and retained, the nature of the records, the way in which these records are used and processed and the results that may be obtained.[156][157]

In *MM v The United Kingdom*[158] a Northern Irish grandmother had taken her grandson overnight against the wishes of his mother, who wished to bring the boy to Australia with her. The child was returned unharmed and a caution was administered. The grandmother then sought employment as a 'Health Care Family Support Worker' but a job offer was withdrawn when the caution was disclosed by the vetting process. The ECtHR held that both the retention and the disclosure of this data was a breach of article 8 ECHR. In addition, the court was:

> ... not satisfied that there were, and are, sufficient safeguards in the system for retention and disclosure of criminal record data to ensure that data relating to the applicant's private life have not been, and will not be, disclosed in violation of her right to respect for her private life. The retention and disclosure of the applicant's caution data accordingly cannot be regarded as being in accordance with the law. There has therefore been a violation of Article 8 of the Convention in the present case ...[159]

In *Brunet v France*[160] the ECtHR held that there had been a violation of the applicant's article 8 ECHR rights where his information had been added to a police database following the discontinuance of criminal proceedings against him. In *MK v France*[161] the ECtHR found that the retention of the applicant's finger prints on a database following his acquittal on criminal charges was a breach of article 8, ECHR.

Privacy at work

[2.21] The right to privacy at work was first recognised by the ECtHR in *Niemetz v Germany* (discussed above). In *Peev v Bulgaria*[162] the applicant was a criminologist and a friend of a prosecutor who had made serious allegations against the Chief Prosecutor and then committed suicide. The applicant contemplated resignation and drafted two resignation letters, which he kept in his desk. His office was searched, the draft letters removed and he was then informed that his resignation had been accepted. He

---

156. Citing *mutatis mutandis*, *Friedl v Austria* (31 January 1995) ECtHR, 21 EHRR 83 and *Peck v the United Kingdom*, cited above).
157. *S and Marper v The United Kingdom* (4 December 2008) ECtHR, para 67.
158. *MM v The United Kingdom*, No 24029/07, HEJUD [2012] ECHR 1906 (13 November 2012).
159. *MM v The United Kingdom*, No 24029/07, HEJUD [2012] ECHR 1906 (13 November 2012), para 207; see also *Leander v Sweden* (1987) 9 EHRR 433 and *Rocha v Portugal* [2005] ECHR 335.
160. *Brunet v France* [2014] ECHR 970 (18 September 2014).
161. *MK v France*, No 19522/09, 18 April 2013.
162. *Peev v Bulgaria,* No 64209/01 [2007] ECHR 655 (26 July 2007).

complained that this was a breach of article 8 ECHR. The ECtHR agreed holding that the applicant did have a reasonable expectation of privacy, 'if not in respect of the entirety of his office, at least in respect of his desk and his filing cabinets'. The court considered that this expectation was demonstrated by 'the great number of personal belongings that he kept there', but furthermore:

> such an arrangement is implicit in habitual employer–employee relations and there is nothing in the particular circumstances of the case – such as a regulation or stated policy of the applicant's employer discouraging employees from storing personal papers and effects in their desks or filing cabinets – to suggest that the applicant's expectation was unwarranted or unreasonable. The fact that he was employed by a public authority and that his office was located on government premises does not of itself alter this conclusion ... Therefore, a search which extended to the applicant's desk and filing cabinets must be regarded as an interference with his private life.[163]

In *Halford v United Kingdom*[164] the ECtHR concluded that the applicant's expectation of privacy would extend to the phone she used at work. She was a senior policewoman who had been refused a further promotion and had then initiated proceedings before the UK's Industrial Tribunal. She alleged that 'calls made from her home and her office telephones were intercepted for the purposes of obtaining information to use against her in the discrimination proceedings'.[165] The respondent argued this was not a breach of article 8 ECHR as she could have had no reasonable expectation of privacy in relation to calls made from her office, arguing that an employer should in principle and without the prior knowledge of the employee be able to monitor calls made by the latter on telephones provided by the employer.[166] The ECtHR disagreed:

> it is clear from its case law that telephone calls made from business premises as well as from the home may be covered by the notions of 'private life' and 'correspondence' within the meaning of Article 8[167] ... There is no evidence of any warning having been given to Ms Halford ... that calls ... would be liable to interception. She would, the Court considers, have had a reasonable expectation of privacy for such calls[168] ... Article 8 ... is therefore applicable.

In *Copland v United Kingdom*[169] an employee's telephone, email and internet usage were subjected to monitoring by her employer.[170] The ECtHR held that it logically followed

---

163. *Peev v Bulgaria*, No 64209/01 [2007] ECHR 655 (26 July 2007), para 39.
164. *Halford v United Kingdom* (25 June 1997) ECtHR.
165. *Halford v United Kingdom* (25 June 1997) ECtHR, para 17.
166. *Halford v United Kingdom* (25 June 1997) ECtHR, para 43.
167. *Halford v United Kingdom* (25 June 1997) ECtHR, para 44.
168. *Halford v United Kingdom* (25 June 1997) ECtHR, para 45.
169. *Copland v United Kingdom* [2007] ECHR 253 (3 April 2007).
170. '... people to whom she had made calls were in turn telephoned ... to identify the callers and the purpose of the call ... her personal movements, both at work and when on annual or sick leave, were the subject of surveillance' *Copland v United Kingdom* [2007] ECHR 253 (3 April 2007), paras 10, 16.

from its decision in *Halford* that: 'e-mails sent from work should be similarly protected ... as should information derived from the monitoring of personal internet usage'.[171]

Kopke v Germany[172] concerned a complaint to the ECtHR that an employee's right to privacy had been breached by her employer's covert surveillance of her. The court deemed the complaint inadmissible, noting that the surveillance had not commenced until after an 'arguable suspicion' that cash was being stolen had been raised. The surveillance was 'limited in time – it was carried out for two weeks' and 'was restricted in respect of the area it covered in that it did not extend to the applicant's workplace in the supermarket ... but covered only the area behind and including the cash desk, the cashier and the area immediately surrounding the cash desk'. The CCTV footage was only viewed by a limited number of persons and only processed for the purposes of the complainant's dismissal. As regards the balance to be struck between the rights of the employee and those of the employer, the ECtHR held as follows:

> It must be considered essential for its employment relationship with ... a person to whom it had entrusted the handling of a till, that it could rely on her not to steal money contained in that till. The Court ... agrees ... that the employer's interest in the protection of its property rights could only be effectively safeguarded if it could collect evidence in order to prove the applicant's criminal conduct ... This ... served the public interest in the proper administration of justice ... to establish the truth as far as possible ... Furthermore, the covert video surveillance of the applicant served to clear from suspicion other employees who were not guilty of any offence.

In addition, the court observed that 'there had not been any other equally effective means to protect the employer's property rights which would have interfered to a lesser extent with the applicant's right to respect for her private life'. Hence the ECtHR deemed the complaint inadmissible.[173]

---

171. *Copland v United Kingdom* [2007] ECHR 253 (3 April 2007), para 41. Compare this to the decision of the EAT in *Felix Adeagbo v Mitie Facilities Management* UD692/2013, 14 September 2014. The appellant was a security guard who 'was looking at U Tube and various websites on the respondent's computer and this was forbidden' when the complex he was supposed to be guarding was broken into.

172. *Kopke v Germany*, No 420/07 [2010] ECHR 1725 (5 October 2010).

173. See similarly the EAT decision of *Roche v BRC McMahon Reinforcements* [2009] 12 JIEC 1402 in which an employer had received complaints that some employees were smoking in the staff canteen. Smoking in the workplace is an offence (see Public Health (Tobacco) Act 2002, ss 46 and 47 as amended by Public Health (Tobacco) (Amendment) Act 2004, ss 15 and 16) and '... a no smoking policy was a condition of the respondent's insurance cover'. The employer knew that smoking was going on, but not who the smokers were. So, the employer installed CCTV: 'The covert surveillance was in place in the canteen for three days ... and it clearly showed the three employees, including the claimant, smoking'. The claimant was then dismissed and brought an unfair dismissal claim to the EAT. At hearing the claimant argued 'that the covert CCTV surveillance in the canteen was a breach of the claimant's rights under the Data Protection Acts'. This argument was rejected by the EAT as the employer had ascertained that the covert surveillance was necessary: it had evidence that a criminal offence was being committed and had no other means of identifying the culprit. (contd .../)

[2.22] In *Barbulescu*[174] the applicant was a Romanian who '... created an instant messaging account for his employer'. The applicant was informed of his employer's internet usage policy, which included the following provision: 'Any disturbance of order and discipline on company premises shall be strictly forbidden, in particular: ... personal use of computers, photocopiers, telephones or telex or fax machines'.[175] The applicant was subsequently asked by his employer to explain his internet usage and provided with a 45-page '... transcript of the messages which the applicant had exchanged with his brother and his fiancée during the period when he had been monitored; the messages related to personal matters and some were of an intimate nature'.[176] His employment was then terminated. The applicant challenged his dismissal and on foot of that challenge an application was made to the ECtHR which observed that:

> ... the kind of internet instant messaging service at issue is just one of the forms of communication enabling individuals to lead a private social life. At the same time, the sending and receiving of communications is covered by the notion of 'correspondence', even if they are sent from an employer's computer.[177]

The ECtHR noted that the applicant had been instructed '... to refrain from any personal activities in the workplace'[178] but went on to observe that:

> ... an employer's instructions cannot reduce private social life in the workplace to zero. Respect for private life and for the privacy of correspondence continues to exist, even if these may be restricted in so far as necessary.[179]

[2.23] The Court considered that '... proportionality and procedural guarantees against arbitrariness are essential' and went on to suggest that the following criteria were relevant:

(i)   whether the employee has been notified of the possibility of monitoring by the employer;

(ii) the extent of the monitoring by the employer and the degree of intrusion into the employee's privacy;

(iii) whether the employer has provided legitimate reasons to justify monitoring the communications and accessing their actual content. Since monitoring of the content of communications is by nature a distinctly more invasive method, it requires weightier justification;

---

173. (contd) The use of covert CCTV would also seem proportionate, as it was only installed for three days.
174. *Barbulescu v Romania* [2017] ECHR 754 (5 September 2017).
175. *Barbulescu v Romania* [2017] ECHR 754 (5 September 2017), para 12.
176. *Barbulescu v Romania* [2017] ECHR 754 (5 September 2017), para 21.
177. *Barbulescu v Romania* [2017] ECHR 754 (5 September 2017), para 74.
178. *Barbulescu v Romania* [2017] ECHR 754 (5 September 2017), para 74.
179. *Barbulescu v Romania* [2017] ECHR 754 (5 September 2017), para 80.

(iv) whether it would have been possible to establish a monitoring system based on less intrusive methods and measures than directly accessing the content of the employee's communications;

(v) the consequences of the monitoring for the employee subjected to it; and,

(vi) whether the employee had been provided with adequate safeguards.[180]

The ECtHR went on to conclude that the Romanian authorities had violated the applicant's article 8 ECHR rights as they had:

> ... failed to determine ... whether the applicant had received prior notice from his employer of the possibility that his communications ... might be monitored; nor did they have regard either to the fact that he had not been informed of the nature or the extent of the monitoring, or to the degree of intrusion into his private life and correspondence. In addition, they failed to determine, firstly, the specific reasons justifying the introduction of the monitoring measures; secondly, whether the employer could have used measures entailing less intrusion into the applicant's private life and correspondence; and thirdly, whether the communications might have been accessed without his knowledge ...[181]

[2.24] *Antović* was brought by two professors at the University of Montenegro, which had decided to install CCTV in their classrooms. The ECtHR rejected the Montenegran government's claim that no privacy issue was at stake as the area under surveillance had been a public, working area.[182]

Access

[2.25] In *Gaskin v United Kingdom*[183] the applicant was taken into care by the state while he was less than a year old. He spent virtually all of his childhood in different forms of care until he attained the age of majority. He then sought access to confidential records held in a file. The UK argued before the Commission that 'the file as such, being information compiled for and by the local authority, did not form a part of the applicant's private life. Accordingly, ... neither its compilation nor the question of access thereto fall within the scope of Article 8 (ECHR)'.[184] However, it was the opinion

---

180. *Barbulescu v Romania* [2017] ECHR 754 (5 September 2017), para 121.
181. *Barbulescu v Romania* [2017] ECHR 754 (5 September 2017), para 140.
182. *Antović & Anor v Montenegro*, Application No 70838/13.
183. *Gaskin v United Kingdom* (1989) 12 EHRR 36. Contrast with *Odièvre v France* Application No 42326/98, 13 February 2003.
184. *Gaskin v United Kingdom* (1989) 12 EHRR 36, para 35. See also *Szulc v Poland* [2012] ECHR 1908 (13 November 2012) in which the ECtHR held that the applicant should have access 'to all relevant information that would allow her to contest her classification by the security services as their secret informant' (para 94). Also *Segerstedt-Wiberg v Sweden* [2006] ECHR 597 (6 June 2006); *MG v the United Kingdom* [2002] ECHR 632 (24 September 2002); *Odièvre v France* [2003] ECHR 86 (13 February 2003); and *Guerra v Italy* [1998] ECHR 7 (19 February 1998).

of the Commission that 'the file provided a substitute record for the memories and experience of the parents of the child who is not in care'. It no doubt contained information concerning highly personal aspects of the applicant's childhood, development and history and thus could constitute his principal source of information about his past and formative years. Consequently, lack of access thereto did raise issues under article 8 (ECHR).[185] The court agreed with the Commission, holding that '[t]he records contained in the file undoubtedly do relate to Mr. Gaskin's "private and family life" in such a way that the question of his access thereto falls within the ambit of Article 8 (ECHR)'.[186]

[2.26] In *McGinley and Egan v The United Kingdom*,[187] the plaintiffs were former soldiers who had been lined up facing away from a nuclear bomb and had been ordered to shut their eyes when it exploded. The plaintiffs were 'denied access to the records compiled in relation to radiation levels and the medical treatment they had received following the explosions'.[188] The court considered that 'the issue of access to information which could either have allayed the applicants' fears ... or enabled them to assess the danger to which they had been exposed, was sufficiently closely linked to their private and family lives within the meaning of Article 8 (ECHR) as to raise an issue under that provision'.[189] In *KH v Slovakia*[190] the applicants were a group of Roma women who suspected that 'a sterilisation procedure was performed on them by medical personnel'[191] in various hospitals. They sought access to their medical records, but the Slovak courts ruled that they could only view their records and take notes, they could not photocopy them. The women brought a case to the ECtHR. They argued that:

> the mere possibility of consulting the files and making handwritten excerpts thereof did not provide them with effective access to the relevant documents concerning their health. In particular, medical records contained charts, graphs, drawings and other data which could not be properly reproduced through

---

185. *Gaskin v United Kingdom* (1989) 12 EHRR 36, para 36.
186. *Gaskin v United Kingdom* (1989) 12 EHRR 36, para 37. Although the court did comment that: 'This finding is reached without expressing any opinion on whether general rights of access to personal data and information may be derived from Article 8(1) of the Convention. The court is not called upon to decide *in abstracto* on questions of general principle in this field but rather has to deal with the concrete case of Mr Gaskin's application.' It should be noted that Walsh J dissented, stating that: 'In my opinion Article 8 of the Convention is not applicable in the present case. The information sought by the applicant was for the purpose of furthering his legal action for damages against the Liverpool City Council. It was not sought in defence of or to further his right to respect for his private and family life.' (1989) 12 EHRR 36, para 1 of the dissent of Walsh J.
187. *McGinley and Egan v The United Kingdom* (1998) 27 EHRR 1. Compare to *Roche v the United Kingdom*, Application No 32555/96, (19 October 2005).
188. *McGinley and Egan v The United Kingdom* (1998) 27 EHRR 1, para 64.
189. *McGinley and Egan v The United Kingdom* (1998) 27 EHRR 1, para 97.
190. *KH v Slovakia*, No 32881/04 [2009] ECHR 709 (28 April 2009).
191. *KH v Slovakia*, No 32881/04 [2009] ECHR 709 (28 April 2009), para 7.

handwritten notes. They were voluminous as a rule and their transcript by hand was not only insufficient but also time consuming and burdensome.[192]

Security

[2.27] A failure to secure a person's personal data may be a breach of article 8 ECHR. In *I v Finland*[193] the applicant was a nurse who had been diagnosed as HIV positive. Her medical records were held in the hospital in which she worked, where 'hospital staff had free access to the patient register which contained information on patients' diagnoses and treating doctors'.[194] She suspected that her colleagues knew her HIV status; she then lost her job and sought to find out who had accessed her records. However, the hospital was unable to tell her as it had no system for monitoring access to those records. The applicant sued in the Finnish courts, lost and then complained to the ECtHR. She then alleged that the hospital 'had failed in its duties to establish a register from which her confidential patient information could not be disclosed'.[195] The court upheld her complaint, noting that the applicant had 'lost her civil action because she was unable to prove on the facts a causal connection between the deficiencies in the access security rules and the dissemination of information about her medical condition'. The ECtHR disagreed with this decision, considering that 'to place such a burden of proof on the applicant is to overlook the acknowledged deficiencies in the hospital's record keeping at the material time'.[196] A failure to destroy data may also result in a breach of the ECHR. In *Reklos and Davourlis v Greece*[197] the applicants were the parents of a boy who had been photographed shortly after birth by the staff of a Greek hospital. The purpose of doing so was apparently to sell the photograph to the parents, who instead objected and sought the destruction of the image. The ECtHR held that the taking of the photograph was a breach of the child's right under article 8 ECHR as the parents' permission for the taking of the photograph had not been sought first.[198]

Dissemination and disclosure of personal information

[2.28] In *Von Hannover v Germany* the ECtHR suggested that increased vigilance should apply to 'the systematic taking of specific photos and their dissemination to a broad section of the public'.[199] The ECtHR held that:

> there is no doubt that the publication by various German magazines of photos of the applicant in her daily life either on her own or with other people falls within the scope of her private life.[200]

192. *KH v Slovakia*, No 32881/04 [2009] ECHR 709 (28 April 2009), para 38.
193. *I v Finland*, No 20511/03 [2008] ECHR 623 (17 July 2008).
194. *I v Finland*, No 20511/03 [2008] ECHR 623 (17 July 2008), para 7.
195. *I v Finland*, No 20511/03 [2008] ECHR 623 (17 July 2008), para 26.
196. *I v Finland*, No 20511/03 [2008] ECHR 623 (17 July 2008), para 44.
197. *Reklos and Davourlis v Greece*, No 1234/05 [2009] ECHR 200 (15 January 2009).
198. *Reklos and Davourlis v Greece*, No 1234/05 [2009] ECHR 200 (15 January 2009), para 43.
199. *Von Hannover v Germany* (24 June 2004) ECtHR, para 70.
200. *Von Hannover v Germany* (24 June 2004) ECtHR, para 53.

In *Peck v United Kingdom*[201] the applicant 'argued that … the disclosure of that record of his movements to the public in a manner in which he could never have foreseen … gave rise to … an interference'[202] with his article 8 ECHR right. The applicant was recorded on CCTV attempting to kill himself. The council which operated the CCTV released the recording to various media outlets. The applicant claimed that this was an interference in his private life. The ECtHR concurred, concluding that:

> the disclosures by the Council of the CCTV material in the CCTV News and to the Yellow Advertiser, Anglia Television and the BBC were not accompanied by sufficient safeguards to prevent disclosure inconsistent with the guarantees of respect for the applicant' private life contained in Article 8. As such, the disclosure constituted a disproportionate and therefore unjustified interference with his private life and a violation of Article 8 of the Convention.[203]

In *LL v France*[204] the ECtHR held that use of the applicant's medical records in divorce proceedings without his consent was a breach of his rights under article 8 ECHR.

---

201. *Peck v United Kingdom* [2003] ECHR 44.

202. *Peck v United Kingdom* [2003] ECHR 44, para 60.

203. *Peck v United Kingdom* [2003] ECHR 44, para 87. See also the decision of the English House of Lords in *Ashworth Hospital Authority v MGN* [2002] UKHL 29, (2002) 12 BHRC 443. This case is interesting as the House ordered the disclosure of one individual's personal data in order to preserve the privacy of others. The House ordered that a newspaper disclose to the hospital which of its employees was the source for leaking the medical records of the 'Moors Murderer' Ian Brady to the newspaper. The justification for ordering the disclosure of the identity of the source was that '[t]he source's disclosure was wholly inconsistent with the security of the records and the disclosure was made worse because it was purchased by a cash payment' per Woolf J at para 66. See also *Draksas v Lithuania*, No 36662/04, HEJUD [2012] ECHR 1660 (31 July 2012) in which phone conversations between a political associate of the state president, his business partners and the state president himself were recorded. These recordings were subsequently played during impeachment proceedings of the president. The ECHR ruled that this was not a breach of article 8; however, the separate release of such recordings was.

204. *LL v France*, No 7508/02, 10 October 2016 see similarly *Panteleyenko v Ukraine* (29 June 2006) ECtHR.

PART 2
THE GENERAL DATA PROTECTION
REGULATION (GDPR)

Chapter 3

SCOPE AND THE APPLICATION OF THE GDPR

APPLICATION

[3.01] One of the distinctive features of the GDPR is its broad application to activities, territories and technology. The breath of this application is highly unusual, possibly unprecedented. The GDPR applies to pretty much all processing of personal data outside the home, criminal justice and state security. This broad application of the GDPR mimics the all-pervasive nature of personal data processing technologies, which are generally to process personal data by default. This default is already built-into data processing technologies of all kinds, from CCTV, to smartphones and the Internet-of-Things. Such technologies will process personal data by default unless they are specifically designed or instructed not to. The GDPR will similarly apply by default unless specific steps are taken to switch it off, such as by anonymising data or switching data processing devices off. How these defaults will align in practice remains to be seen, but if the GDPR is successful then it will fundamentally alter how personal data is processed. The GDPR:

> … applies to the processing of personal data wholly or partly by automated means
> and to the processing other than by automated means of personal data which form
> part of a filing system or are intended to form part of a filing system.[1]

It is this application to the automated processing of personal data that makes the GDPR significant. At present this processing takes place almost entirely on conventional computers, once it would have taken place on punched-cards,[2] soon it may take place on quantum systems.[3] However, personal data processing can also be undertaken on paper files,[4] to which the protections of the GDPR extend. The GDPR justifies this extension as an anti-avoidance measure:

> In order to prevent creating a serious risk of circumvention, the protection of
> natural persons should be technologically neutral and should not depend on the
> techniques used. The protection of natural persons should apply to the processing
> of personal data by automated means, as well as to manual processing, if the
> personal data are contained or are intended to be contained in a filing system.[5]

---

1. GDPR, article 2(1).
2. Campbell-Kelly & Garcia-Swartz, *From Mainframes to Smartphones* (Harvard University Press, 2015).
3. 'Quantum Devices, here, there and everywhere', (2017) *The Economist*, 11 March.
4. Most notoriously this was undertaken by the Stasi, the secret police of the former East Germany. See http://www.bstu.bund.de/DE/Home/home_node.html (Federal Commissioner for the Records of the State Security Service of the former German Democratic Republic).
5. GDPR, Recital 15.

[3.02] Filing systems are defined as '...any structured set of personal data which are accessible according to specific criteria, whether centralised, decentralised or dispersed on a functional or geographical basis'.[6] The Recitals provide some further definition providing that 'Files or sets of files, as well as their cover pages, which are not structured according to specific criteria should not fall within the scope of this Regulation'.[7] A structured file means one that is structured in accordance with criteria, such as alphabetically in order of the subject's surname. An interesting feature of the GDPR is that its definition of manual filing system is much broader than that which appeared in Directive 95/46. The old definition required that a filing system be structured in such a way that it allowed '... easy access to the personal data'.[8] This language no longer appears in the GDPR, so it must be assumed that the GDPR will apply to any filing system that is structured in such a way as to allow access to personal data, whether easily or otherwise. Broadening the scope of the definition of manual data in this way is consistent with the approach taken elsewhere in the GDPR.

EXCLUSIONS FROM THE APPLICATION OF THE GDPR

[3.03] The GDPR provides a number of exclusions from its application.[9] These exclusions are narrow however and it seems likely that they will be narrowly interpreted by the CJEU following judgments such as *Tele2 Sverige*[10] where the CJEU held that EU data protection law still applied to national measures introduced under a derogation from the ePrivacy Directive, and *Rynes*,[11] in which the CJEU significantly circumscribed the exemption for domestic data processing. These exclusions are considered below.

(a) ... in the course of an activity which falls outside the scope of Union law

[3.04] The GDPR will not apply to the processing of personal data '... in the course of an activity which falls outside the scope of Union law'.[12] The competencies of the EU are set out in the EU Treaties, primarily in TFEU, Title 1, Pt 1. TFEU, article 3.1 provides that the EU has exclusive competence[13] in the following areas:

    (a)   customs union;

---

6.   GDPR, article 2(6).
7.   GDPR, Recital 15.
8.   GDPR, Recital 27, Directive 95/46.
9.   GDPR, article 2(2).
10.   *Tele2 Sverige* (Case C–203/15) (21 December 2016).
11.   *Rynes* (Case C–212/13) (11 December 2014).
12.   A quite comprehensive analysis was undertaken by the UK government in advance of the UK's Brexit referendum in June 2016. See: https://www.gov.uk/guidance/review-of-the-balance-of-competences.
13.   TFEU, article 2(1) explains that where the EU Treaties '...confer on the Union exclusive competence in a specific area, (contd .../)

(b) the establishing of the competition rules necessary for the functioning of the internal market;

(c) monetary policy for the Member States whose currency is the euro;

(d) the conservation of marine biological resources under the common fisheries policy;

(e) common commercial policy.[14]

[3.05] In addition, article 2(3) provides that '... Member States shall coordinate their economic and employment policies within arrangements as determined by this Treaty, which the Union shall have competence to provide'. And article 2(4) provides that the EU '... shall have competence, in accordance with the provisions of the Treaty on European Union, to define and implement a common foreign and security policy, including the progressive framing of a common defence policy'. TFEU, article 4(1) then goes on to provide that the EU will share competence[15] with the Member States in the following areas:

(a) internal market;

(b) social policy, for the aspects defined in this Treaty;

(c) economic, social and territorial cohesion;

(d) agriculture and fisheries, excluding the conservation of marine biological resources;

(e) environment;

(f) consumer protection;

(g) transport;

(h) trans-European networks;

(i) energy;

---

13. (contd) only the Union may legislate and adopt legally binding acts, the Member States being able to do so themselves only if so empowered by the Union or for the implementation of Union act'.

14. In addition, TFEU, article 3(2) provides that the EU '... shall also have exclusive competence for the conclusion of an international agreement when its conclusion is provided for in a legislative act of the Union or is necessary to enable the Union to exercise its internal competence, or in so far as its conclusion may affect common rules or alter their scope'.

15. TFEU, article 2(2) explains that 'When the Treaties confer on the Union a competence shared with the Member States in a specific area, the Union and the Member States may legislate and adopt legally binding acts in that area. The Member States shall exercise their competence to the extent that the Union has not exercised its competence. The Member States shall again exercise their competence to the extent that the Union has decided to cease exercising its competence'.

(j)   area of freedom, security and justice;

(k)   common safety concerns in public health matters, for the aspects defined in this Treaty.[16]

[3.06] Article 5 provides that '... Member States shall coordinate their economic policies within the Union' and that the EU Council shall provide '... broad guidelines for these policies'. That article goes on to provide that the EU '... shall take measures to ensure coordination of the employment policies of the Member States...' and by defining guidelines for those policies in particular. Article 5 concludes by providing that the EU '... may take initiatives to ensure coordination of Member States' social policies'.

[3.07] Finally, article 6 provides that the EU will have '... competence to carry out actions to support, coordinate or supplement the actions of the Member States'. At a European level these areas of competence are:

(a)   protection and improvement of human health;

(b)   industry;

(c)   culture;

(d)   tourism;

(e)   education, vocational training, youth and sport;

(f)   civil protection;

(g)   administrative cooperation.

It is evident from the above that the EU Treaties were drafted to carefully split competencies between the EU and its Member States. Some competencies are exclusive to the EU, others are shared with Member States. However, the GDPR dispenses with this differentiated approach and simply states that it will apply to every activity that does not fall outside the scope of EU law. This broad application of GDPR reflects the status of data protection as an EU fundamental right. It is the settled case law of the CJEU that '... the fundamental rights guaranteed in the legal order of the European Union are applicable in all situations governed by European Union law...'.[17]

---

16.   TFEU, article 3(3) and (4) provides that the EU shall have competence in '... areas of research, technological development and space ...' and '... areas of development cooperation and humanitarian aid ...' but such competencies '... shall not result in Member States being prevented from exercising theirs'.

17.   *Aklagaren v Akerberg Fransson* (Case C–617/10) (26 February 2013), para 19. See also *Siragusa v Sicilia ...* (Judgment of the Court) (Case C–206/13) (6 March 2014).

(b) … by the Member States when carrying out activities which fall within the scope of Chapter 2 of Title V of the TEU …

[3.08] Title V, Chapter 2, TFEU sets out provisions on the EU's Common Foreign and Security policy. The exclusion of these provisions from the scope of the GDPR does not mean that data protection rules do not apply to them. But as TFEU, article 16(2) acknowledges, the data protection rules that apply to such processing must be made pursuant to TEU, article 38, which provides:

> … the Council shall adopt a decision laying down the rules relating to the protection of individuals with regard to the processing of personal data by the Member States when carrying out activities which fall within the scope of this Chapter …[18]

Activities that fall within the scope of Title V, Chapter 2, TFEU include tasks such as '… peace-keeping, conflict prevention and strengthening international security …' and '… the progressive framing of a common Union defence policy …'.[19]

(c) … by a natural person in the course of a purely personal or household activity …

[3.09] The meaning of the equivalent exclusion from the scope of Directive 95/46 was considered by the CJEU in *Rynes*.[20] The respondent and his family '… had for several years been subjected to attacks by persons unknown whom it had not been possible to identify[21] 'and so he '… installed and used a camera system located under the eaves of his family home. The camera was installed in a fixed position and could not turn; it recorded the entrance to his home, the public footpath and the entrance to the house opposite.' The functioning of this system was limited, it:

> '… allowed only a visual recording, which was stored on recording equipment in the form of a continuous loop, that is to say, on a hard disk drive. As soon as it reached full capacity, the device would record over the existing recording, erasing the old material. No monitor was installed on the recording equipment, so the images could not be studied in real time. Only the respondent had direct access to the system and the data.[22]

Following the installation of this system one of the respondent's windows was broken '… by a shot from a catapult'.[23] Footage from the respondent's video surveillance system was analysed and this analysis enabled the identification of two suspects. This

---

18. Such an EU Council Decision has yet to be proposed as of 1 December 2017.
19. TEU, article 42(1) and (2).
20. *Rynes* (Case C–212/13) (11 December 2014).
21. *Rynes* (Case C–212/13) (11 December 2014), para 14.
22. *Rynes* (Case C–212/13) (11 December 2014), para 13.
23. *Rynes* (Case C–212/13) (11 December 2014), para 15.

footage was handed over to the police and used to prosecute the suspects, one of whom then complained to the Czech Data Protection Authority, which found that the respondent had breached Czech data protection by using '… a camera system to collect, without their consent, the personal data of persons moving along the street or entering the house opposite'; and not informing '… those persons of the processing of that personal data, the extent and purpose of that processing, by whom and by what means the personal data would be processed, or who would have access to the personal data'.[24] This decision was challenged by the respondent and the challenge made its way to the CJEU by way of a request for a preliminary ruling. The question referred being:

> Can the operation of a camera system installed on a family home for the purposes of the protection of the property, health and life of the owners of the home be classified as the processing of personal data 'by a natural person in the course of a purely personal or household activity' …, even though such a system also monitors a public space?[25]

The answer of the CJEU was that it could not. The CJEU took the view that this exception would apply '…only where it is carried out in the purely personal or household setting of the person processing the data'[26] and that:

> … to the extent that video surveillance such as that at issue in the main proceedings covers, even partially, a public space and is accordingly directed outwards from the private setting of the person processing the data in that manner, it cannot be regarded as an activity which is a purely 'personal or household' activity …[27]

This led the CJEU to conclude that the relevant provision of Directive 95/46 had to be:

> … interpreted as meaning that the operation of a camera system…installed by an individual on his family home for the purposes of protecting the property, health and life of the home owners, but which also monitors a public space, does not amount to the processing of data in the course of a purely personal or household activity …[28]

The Court went on to explain that '… so far as natural persons are concerned, correspondence and the keeping of address books constitute … a "purely personal or household activity" even if they incidentally concern or may concern the private life of other persons'.[29]

---

24. *Rynes* (Case C–212/13) (11 December 2014), para 16. In addition, the Czech SA found that the respondent had '…not fulfilled the obligation to report that processing to the Office'. Directive 95/46's obligation to register has been dropped from the GDPR.

25. *Rynes* (Case C–212/13) (11 December 2014), para 18.

26. *Rynes* (Case C–212/13) (11 December 2014), para 31.

27. *Rynes* (Case C–212/13) (11 December 2014), para 33.

28. Paragraph 36.

29. *Rynes* (Case C–212/13) (11 December 2014), para 33.

[3.10] *Rynes* considered Directive 95/46, Recital 12, which provided a domestic exemption relatively broader than that to be found in the GDPR, stating that:

> ... there should be excluded the processing of data carried out by a natural person in the exercise of activities which are exclusively personal or domestic, such as correspondence and the holding of records of addresses.[30]

The equivalent provision in the GDPR is Recital 18 which provides that it:

> ...does not apply to the processing of personal data by a natural person in the course of a purely personal or household activity and thus with no connection to a professional or commercial activity. Personal or household activities could include correspondence and the holding of addresses, or social networking and online activity undertaken within the context of such activities.[31]

The GDPR makes clear that its personal or household exemption only applies to processing that has '...no connection to a professional or commercial activity.' The reference to 'domestic' in Directive 95/46 is dropped and replaced with 'household', which might be read as suggesting a tie to a physical location, such as a house. The GDPR does go on to explicitly provide that this exemption will apply to a '... social networking and online activity undertaken within the context of such activities'. So, setting up one's own personal Facebook page would still benefit from this exemption, so long as that page was not used to share or process the personal data of other data subjects.[32] And a family Facebook group could similarly argue that they were outside the scope of the GDPR, as they were a 'domestic' activity. But if non-family members were to join the group then the domestic exemption might fail to apply. Of course, concepts of family are more fluid now than they once were, even so, the decision in *Rynes* suggests that the CJEU will take a narrow view of what amounts to '... a purely personal or household activity'.

Finally, the GDPR makes clear that it '... applies to controllers or processors which provide the means for processing personal data for such personal or household activities'.[33] So while the application of the GDPR to the hypothetical family Facebook group may be discussed, there is no question that the GDPR applies to Facebook itself.

(d) ... by competent authorities for the purposes of the prevention, investigation, detection or prosecution of criminal offences or the execution of criminal penalties, including the safeguarding against and the prevention of threats to public security

[3.11] The enactment of the new Data Protection Directive 2016/680 means that this exclusion has less significance than its predecessor provision in Directive 95/46. The

---

30. Pararaph 3(12).
31. GDPR, Recital 18.
32. Though the GDPR would apply to a third party, who was not a family member, if they were to link to or, like or copy that page.
33. GDPR, Recital 18.

fact that data is being processed for criminal justice purposes no longer means that EU data protection rules no longer apply.[34] This is clear from the judgment of the CJEU in *Digital Rights Ireland*,[35] a successful challenge to the EU's Data Retention Directive 2006/24.[36] Directive 2006/24 had required the retention of certain telecommunications data by telecommunications operators and enabled that data to be accessed by national authorities such as the police. The CJEU considered that 'the obligation ... to retain ... data relating to a person's private life and to his communications ... constitutes in itself an interference' with the rights of privacy and data protection and the court went on to restate the view of its Advocate General that in this case the interference was 'wide-ranging, and ... particularly serious'.[37] The court then went on to consider whether interference with these rights could be justified in accordance with Article 52 of the Charter. It first found that the Directive satisfied 'an objective of general interest' given its use in the fight against terrorism and organised crime.[38] The court considered whether Directive 2006/24 met the principle of proportionality, which:

> requires that acts of the EU institutions be appropriate for attaining the legitimate objectives pursued by the legislation at issue and do not exceed the limits of what is appropriate and necessary in order to achieve those objectives.[39]

This judgment was reaffirmed by the CJEU in *Tele2 Sverige*[40] which concerned a national data retention law, which held that the Charter precluded: '...national

---

34. Until 2009 EU law was divided into pillars: European Communities (EC); Common Foreign and Security Policy (CFSP) Police and Judicial Co-operation in Criminal Matters, more commonly known as Justice and Home Affairs (JHA). As the Data Protection Directive was an EC measure it fell under the EC pillar and as such had no application to JHA. See: *Parliament v Council* (Transport) (Case C–317/04) (30 May 2006) in which the CJEU agreed with the EU Parliament that 'the transfer of PNR data ... constitutes processing operations concerning public security and the activities of the State in areas of criminal law' (para 56) and so Council Decision 2004/496/EC of 17 May 2004 on the conclusion of an Agreement between the European Community and the United States of America on the processing and transfer of PNR data by Air Carriers to the United States Department of Homeland Security, Bureau of Customs and Border Protection (OJ 2004 L 183, p 83, and corrigendum at OJ 2005 L 255, p. 168), did not '... not fall within the scope of ... Directive [95/46]' (para 59).

35. *Digital Rights Ireland* (Case C–293/12) (8 April 2014).

36. Directive 2006/24/EC of the European Parliament and of the Council of 15 March 2006 on the retention of data generated or processed in connection with the provision of publicly available electronic communications services or of public communications networks and amending Directive 2002/58/EC ([2006] OJ L 105/54).

37. *Digital Rights Ireland* (Case C–293/12) (8 April 2014), paras 34–37.

38. *Digital Rights Ireland* (Case C–293/12) (8 April 2014), paras 41–44.

39. *Digital Rights Ireland* (Case C–293/12) (8 April 2014), para 46, citing the settled case law of: *Afton Chemical* (Case C–343/09), para 45; *Volker und Markus Schecke and Eifert* (Cases C–92/09 and C–93/09), para 74; and *Nelson and Ors* (Cases C–629/10 and C–581/10), para 71; *Sky Österreich* (Case C–283/11) EU:C:2013:28, para 50; and *Schaible* (Case C–101/12) EU:C:2013:661, para 29.

40. *Tele2 Sverige* (Case C–203/15) (21 December 2016).

legislation which, for the purpose of fighting crime, provides for general and indiscriminate retention of all traffic and location data of all subscribers and registered users relating to all means of electronic communication'. The EU rules on the processing of personal data by law enforcement authorities are discussed at **Chapter 21** below.

EU institutions, bodies, offices and agencies

[3.12] EU institutions, bodies, offices and agencies are subject to a specific data protection regime: Regulation 45/2001. The GDPR[41] provides that Regulation 45/2001 will continue to apply although '… adapted to the principles and rules of this Regulation in accordance with Article 98'.[42]

The eCommerce Directive

[3.13] The GDPR is stated to be without prejudice to the application of the eCommerce Directive,[43] in particular of the liability rules of intermediary service providers that are set out in Articles 12 to 15 of that Directive.

Chapter IX, specific applications of the GDPR

[3.14] GDPR, Ch IX provides for its application to certain specific situations. Some of these reflect the practicalities of data protection, such as its application in the context of employment. Others reflect more fundamental conflicts, such as its reconciliation with freedom of expression. Each of these is considered below.

Processing and freedom of expression and information

[3.15] Freedom of expression is an EU fundamental right,[44] however the GDPR leaves it to the Member States to set a precise balance between rights of data protection and freedom of expression. GDPR, article 85 provides that:

> Member States shall by law reconcile the right to the protection of personal data pursuant to this Regulation with the right to freedom of expression and information, including processing for journalistic purposes and the purposes of academic, artistic or literary expression.[45]

---

41. GDPR, article 2(3).
42. GDPR, article 98 provides that the EU Commission may '… submit legislative proposals with a view to amending other Union legal acts on the protection of personal data, in order to ensure uniform and consistent protection of natural persons with regard to processing. This shall in particular concern the rules relating to the protection of natural persons with regard to processing by Union institutions, bodies, offices and agencies and on the free movement of such data'.
43. Directive 2000/31/EC on certain legal aspects of information society services, in particular electronic commerce, in the Internal Market, OJ L 178, 17.7.2000, pp 1–16.
44. The reconciliation of these rights of data protection with that of freedom of expression under the Charter is dealt with more fully in **Chapter 1**.
45. GDPR, article 85(1).

Article 85 then goes on to list out the chapters of the GDPR that Member States must provide derogations from for '… journalistic purposes and the purposes of academic, artistic or literary expression'. The requirement to provide exemptions is not absolute. Exemptions need only be provided where '… they are necessary to reconcile the right to the protection of personal data with the freedom of expression and information'. The chapters from which such exemptions may be provided are:

- Chapter II (principles);
- Chapter III (rights of the data subject);
- Chapter IV (controller and processor);
- Chapter V (transfer of personal data to third countries or international organisations);
- Chapter VI (independent supervisory authorities);
- Chapter VII (cooperation and consistency); and
- Chapter IX (specific data processing situations).

In other words, exemptions may be provided from all operationally significant provisions of the GDPR other than VIII, (remedies, liability and penalties). The other Chs I, X and XI that are not listed in GDPR, article 85(2) relate to the scope, enactment and general administration of the GDPR itself.

[3.16] Member States have to notify the Commission of any law that they adopt pursuant to GDPR, article 85 and any amendment to that law.[46] However they do not need to consult with the Commission prior to enactment (though they may need to consult with their SA).[47]

Processing and public access to official documents

[3.17] Transparency is another EU fundamental right.[48] Again, the GDPR provides that it is for Member States to set the balance between transparency and data protection, stating that:

> Personal data in official documents held by a public authority or a public body or a private body for the performance of a task carried out in the public interest may be disclosed by the authority or body in accordance with Union or Member State law to which the public authority or body is subject in order to reconcile public access to official documents with the right to the protection of personal data pursuant to this Regulation.[49]

---

46.   GDPR, article 85.3.
47.   GDPR, article 57(1)(c).
48.   The reconciliation of these rights of data protection with that of transparency under the Charter is dealt with more fully above.
49.   GDPR, article 86.

The Recitals explain that the purpose of this provision is to allow '… the principle of public access to official documents to be taken into account when applying this Regulation …'.

The reason for this is that 'Public access to official documents may be considered to be in the public interest'. The Recitals go on to assert that EU or Member State laws on public access to documents:

> … should reconcile public access to official documents and the reuse of public sector information with the right to the protection of personal data and may therefore provide for the necessary reconciliation with the right to the protection of personal data …[50]

The reference to the reuse of public sector information in the above is worthy of note. It is a good example of how the Recitals can subtly extend the meaning of provisions within the main text. Reuse of public sector information may be read as a reference to the Directive on the Re-Use of Public Sector Information.[51] This Directive notes that:

> Public sector information is an important primary material for digital content products and services and will become an even more important content resource with the development of wireless content services.[52]

And so, it provides that 'Member States shall ensure that documents to which this Directive applies … shall be re-usable for commercial or non-commercial purposes …'.[53] Where document is defined as meaning '… any content whatever its medium (written on paper or stored in electronic form or as a sound, visual or audiovisual recording) …'.[54]

Processing of the national identification number

[3.18] In *Rigas*[55] the CJEU found that it was 'common ground' that an 'identity document number' constituted '… information concerning an identified or identifiable natural person and, therefore, "personal data"…'.[56] Such numbers would fall within the category of identification numbers that are specified by the GDPR as a type of personal data.[57] Given that national identification numbers are processed by the State and public bodies, then such processing will almost invariably have to take place on the lawful basis

---

50.   GDPR, Recital 154.

51.   Directive 2003/98/EC on the re-use of public sector information OJ L 345, 31.12.2003, p 90 as amended by Directive 2013/37/EU on the re-use of public sector information OJ L 175, 27.6.2013, p 1–8.

52.   GDPR, Recital 5, Directive 2003/98/EC on the re-use of public sector information.

53.   GDPR, article 3(1), Directive 2003/98/EC on the re-use of public sector information.

54.   GDPR, article 2(3)(a), Directive 2003/98/EC on the re-use of public sector information.

55.   *Rigas satiksme* (Case C–13/16) (4 May 2017),

56.   *Rigas satiksme* (Case C–13/16) (4 May 2017), para 24.

57.   GDPR, article 4(1).

of an EU or Member State law, which will have to comply with GDPR, article 6(3). In addition, GDPR, article 88 provides:

> Member States may further determine the specific conditions for the processing of a national identification number or any other identifier of general application. In that case the national identification number or any other identifier of general application shall be used only under appropriate safeguards for the rights and freedoms of the data subject pursuant to this Regulation.[58]

Processing in the context of employment

[3.19] As the Article 29 WP has pointed out '… many activities performed routinely in the employment context entail the processing of personal data of workers, sometimes of very sensitive information'.[59] GDPR, article 88 provides that Member States may:

> …by law or by collective agreements, provide for more specific rules to ensure the protection of the rights and freedoms in respect of the processing of employees' personal data in the employment context…

The Recitals suggest that the purpose of this derogation is to allow for collective agreements or 'works agreements' that: '… provide for specific rules on the processing of employees' personal data in the employment context, in particular for the conditions under which personal data in the employment context may be processed on the basis of the consent of the employee …'.[60] This does raise the question of whether an employee can be deemed to have given his consent through a collective bargaining process. In *Pfeiffer*[61] the applicant's contract of employment referenced a collective bargaining agreement. The CJEU considered that this was insufficient to imply the subject's consent to an extension of working time where that consent had to be given individually, expressly and freely. However, this decision did not directly consider data protection law.

Article 88 GDPR goes on to state that Member States may provide for more specific rules to ensure the protection of such rights:

> … in particular for the purposes of the recruitment, the performance of the contract of employment, including discharge of obligations laid down by law or by collective agreements, management, planning and organisation of work, equality and diversity in the workplace, health and safety at work, protection of employer's or customer's property and for the purposes of the exercise and enjoyment, on an individual or collective basis, of rights and benefits related to employment, and for the purpose of the termination of the employment relationship.[62]

It should be noted that this derogation does not extend to the EU, only the Member States. Of course, this does not necessarily mean that the EU will not be legislating for

---

58. GDPR, article 87.
59. Article 29 WP *Opinion 8/2001 on the processing of personal data in the employment context*, WP 48, Brussels, 13 September 2001, p 2.
60. GDPR, Recital 155.
61. *Pfeiffer* (Case C–397/01) (5 October 2004).
62. GDPR, article 88(1).

the processing of personal data in an employment context. The EU is required to '...
take measures to ensure coordination of the employment policies of the Member States,
in particular, by defining guidelines for these policies'[63] and it is quite possible that this
will result in the EU legislating for the processing of personal data in an employment
context. For example, in *Worten*[64] an employer was accused by the Portuguese Authority
for Working Conditions of failing to immediately produce a record of its workers'
working time to ensure compliance with the Portuguese implementation of the Directive
on Working Time.[65] The employer argued that it was excessive for the authority to be
able to immediately consult records of working time as this was an interference in
workers' private lives. The employer argued that the purpose of this processing was to
'... provide workers with a means of proving the hours they have actually worked ...'
and '... monitoring, inter alia, working hours exemptions ...'. For these purposes '... the
immediate availability of those records does not ... provide any added value'.[66] The EU
Commission argued that '... the employer's obligation to allow immediate consultation
of the record of working time ensures that data is not altered during the interval between
the inspection visit ... and the actual verification of those data ...'.[67] The CJEU
concluded that it was for the national court to consider '... whether the employer's
obligation to provide the competent national authority access to the record of working
time so as to allow its immediate consultation can be considered necessary for the
purposes of the performance by that authority of its monitoring task ...'.[68]

[3.20] Rules introduced on foot of article 88 GDPR must:

> ...include suitable and specific measures to safeguard the data subject's human
> dignity, legitimate interests and fundamental rights, with particular regard to the
> transparency of processing, the transfer of personal data within a group of
> undertakings, or a group of enterprises engaged in a joint economic activity and
> monitoring systems at the work place.

Member States may notify to the Commission any laws that are adopted on foot of
article 88(1) GDPR. Again, there is no obligation that they consult with the Commission
prior to enactment (though they may need to consult with their SA.[69]

Safeguards and derogations

[3.21] That we live in a knowledge economy is one of the enduring clichés of modern
life, but it is a cliché that reflects reality. Modern methods of statistical research, now

---

63.   TFEU, article 5(2).
64.   *Worten* (Case C–342/12) (30 May 2013).
65.   Directive 2003/88/EC concerning certain aspects of the organisation of working time (OJ
      2003 L 299, p 9).
66.   *Worten* (Case C–342/12) (30 May 2013), para 42.
67.   *Worten* (Case C–342/12) (30 May 2013), para 41.
68.   *Worten* (Case C–342/12) (30 May 2013), para 43.
69.   GDPR, article 57(1)(c).

commonly referred to under the modern rubric of 'big data', are creating new forms of knowledge and insight. As a report for the US government explained:

> Big data technologies can derive value from large datasets in ways that were previously impossible—indeed, big data can generate insights that researchers didn't even think to seek.[70]

[3.22] The power of big data means that researchers can no longer rely upon the anonymization of personal data to avoid the GDPR's controls; modern analytics lessen the challenge of reversing anonymization processes. To enable research to continue, article 89 GDPR provides a specific regime for the processing of personal data '… for archiving purposes in the public interest, scientific or historical research purposes or statistical purposes'. It provides that:

> Processing for archiving purposes in the public interest, scientific or historical research purposes or statistical purposes, shall be subject to appropriate safeguards, in accordance with this Regulation, for the rights and freedoms of the data subject. Those safeguards shall ensure that technical and organisational measures are in place in particular in order to ensure respect for the principle of data minimisation. Those measures may include pseudonymisation provided that those purposes can be fulfilled in that manner. Where those purposes can be fulfilled by further processing which does not permit or no longer permits the identification of data subjects, those purposes shall be fulfilled in that manner.

Article 89(1) GDPR suggests pseudonymisation or anonymization as a mechanism by which researchers may continue to work in accordance with the GDPR. Article 89(1) seems to suggest safeguards to '…ensure that technical and organisational measures are in place…' to ensure that pseudonymisation or anonymization, which are what article 89(1) means by data minimisation, cannot be reversed. Recital 156 GDRP then go on to provide for an overarching set of derogations for processing for the purposes of '… archiving … in the public interest, scientific or historical research purposes or statistical purposes'. It provides that Member States:

> …should be authorised to provide, under specific conditions and subject to appropriate safeguards for data subjects, specifications and derogations with regard to the information requirements and rights to rectification (Article 16), to erasure, to be forgotten (Article 17), to restriction of processing (Article 18), to data portability (Article 20), and to object (Article 21) when processing personal data…

Recital 156 GDPR suggests that the conditions and safeguards referred to above:

> … may entail specific procedures for data subjects to exercise those rights if this is appropriate in the light of the purposes sought by the specific processing along with technical and organisational measures aimed at minimising the processing of personal data in pursuance of the proportionality and necessity principles.

---

70.   Executive Office of the President, President's Council of Advisors on Science and Technology, *Big Data and Privacy: a Technological Perspective*, May 2014, p 5.

The Recital concludes by noting that the '… processing of personal data for scientific purposes should also comply with other relevant legislation such as on clinical trials'.[71]

[3.23] Article 89(2) and (3) GDPR then go on to set out two separate sets of derogations: one for scientific, historic or statistical research; the other for archiving in the public interest. Where processing of personal data for either set of derogations '… serves at the same time another purpose' then article 89(4) GDPR provides that these derogations shall apply only to processing for the purposes referred to in article 89(2) and (3).

As regards processing for scientific, historic or statistical research, Article 89(2) GDPR provides that where personal data is:

> …processed for scientific or historical research purposes or statistical purposes, Union or Member State law may provide for derogations from the rights referred to in Articles 15 (access), 16 (rectification), 18 (restriction) and 21 (objection) … in so far as such rights are likely to render impossible or seriously impair the achievement of the specific purposes, and such derogations are necessary for the fulfilment of those purposes.

Omitted from this list is the right to portability, which the recitals[72] suggest might be provided where personal data is processed for 'scientific or historical research purposes or statistical purposes' is not listed here. The recitals then go on to reference the importance of registries[73] and scientific research.[74] The recitals do not make any detailed

---

71. GDPR, Recital 156.
72. GDPR, Recital 156.
73. 'By coupling information from registries, researchers can obtain new knowledge of great value with regard to widespread medical conditions such as cardiovascular disease, cancer and depression. On the basis of registries, research results can be enhanced, as they draw on a larger population. Within social science, research on the basis of registries enables researchers to obtain essential knowledge about the long-term correlation of a number of social conditions such as unemployment and education with other life conditions. Research results obtained through registries provide solid, high-quality knowledge which can provide the basis for the formulation and implementation of knowledge-based policy, improve the quality of life for a number of people and improve the efficiency of social services. In order to facilitate scientific research, personal data can be processed for scientific research purposes, subject to appropriate conditions and safeguards set out in Union or Member State law' GDPR, Recital 157.
74. 'Where personal data are processed for scientific research purposes, this Regulation should also apply to that processing. For the purposes of this Regulation, the processing of personal data for scientific research purposes should be interpreted in a broad manner including for example technological development and demonstration, fundamental research, applied research and privately funded research. In addition, it should take into account the Union's objective under Article 179(1) TFEU of achieving a European Research Area. Scientific research purposes should also include studies conducted in the public interest in the area of public health. (contd …/)

provision for historical research[75] but they do provide for statistical processing, stating that the GDPR applies to the processing of personal data for statistical purposes. The Recitals define statistical purposes as:

> …any operation of collection and the processing of personal data necessary for statistical surveys or for the production of statistical results.[76]

The Recitals suggest that the processing of personal data for statistical purposes: '… implies that the result of processing … is not personal data, but aggregate data, and that this result or the personal data are not used in support of measures or decisions regarding any particular natural person'.[77] EU or Member State law may '… determine statistical content, control of access, specifications for the processing of personal data for statistical purposes and appropriate measures to safeguard the rights and freedoms of the data subject and for ensuring statistical confidentiality'. And the Recitals provide that '… statistical results may further be used for different purposes, including a scientific research purpose'. Article 90 GDPR[78] provides for obligations of secrecy, the Recitals explain that the '… confidential information which the Union and national statistical authorities collect for the production of official European and official national statistics should be protected'.[79]

---

74. (contd) To meet the specificities of processing personal data for scientific research purposes, specific conditions should apply in particular as regards the publication or otherwise disclosure of personal data in the context of scientific research purposes. If the result of scientific research in particular in the health context gives reason for further measures in the interest of the data subject, the general rules of this Regulation should apply in view of those measures', GDPR, Recital 159.

75. 'Where personal data are processed for historical research purposes, this Regulation should also apply to that processing. This should also include historical research and research for genealogical purposes, bearing in mind that this Regulation should not apply to deceased persons', GDPR, Recital 160.

76. GDPR, Recital 162.

77. GDPR, Recital 162.

78. This allows Member State legislatures to integrate the supervisory authorities under the GDPR with other regulatory agencies, which will operate under specific secrecy regimes. Article 53 of Directive 2013/36/EU of the European Parliament and of the Council of 26 June 2013 on access to the activity of credit institutions and the prudential supervision of credit institutions and investment firms, OJ L 176, 27.6.2013, pp 338–436, provides that competent authorities, such as Central Banks or financial regulators in the financial services sector are subject to obligations of professional secrecy. Article 90 of the GDPR allows the legislatures of Member States to enable such competent authorities to exchange information with supervisory authorities under the GDPR.

79. The Recital goes on to say that 'European statistics should be developed, produced and disseminated in accordance with the statistical principles as set out in Article 338(2) TFEU, while national statistics should also comply with Member State law. Regulation (EC) No 223/2009 of the European Parliament and of the Council (Regulation (EC) No 223/2009 of the European Parliament and of the Council of 11 March 2009 on European statistics and repealing Regulation (EC, Euratom) No 1101/2008 of the European Parliament (contd .../)

[3.24] As regards archiving in the public interest, article 89(3) provides where 'personal data are processed for archiving purposes in the public interest' then EU or Member State law:

> ...may provide for derogations from the rights referred to in Articles 15 (access), 16 (rectification), 18 (restriction), 19 (notification of restriction), 20 (data portability) and 21 (right to object) subject to the conditions and safeguards referred to (above) in so far as such rights are likely to render impossible or seriously impair the achievement of the specific purposes, and such derogations are necessary for the fulfilment of those purposes.

The Recitals narrowly defined the archives to which these derogations should apply. These are 'Public authorities or public or private bodies that hold records of public interest ...' which provide services pursuant to obligations imposed by EU or Member State law. Such archives must be legally obliged to:

> ...acquire, preserve, appraise, arrange, describe, communicate, promote, disseminate and provide access to records of enduring value for general public interest.

The Recitals go on to provide that 'Member States should also be authorised to provide for the further processing of personal data for archiving purposes'. The Recitals suggest that such archiving might be undertaken:

> ...with a view to providing specific information related to the political behaviour under former totalitarian state regimes, genocide, crimes against humanity, in particular the Holocaust, or war crimes.[80]

Existing data protection rules of churches and religious associations

[3.25] As its Recitals explain, the GDPR '...respects and does not prejudice the status under existing constitutional law of churches and religious associations or communities in the Member States, as recognised in Article 17 TFEU'.[81] Article 17 TFEU provides that the EU '... respects and does not prejudice the status under national law of churches and religious associations or communities in the Member States'.[82]

The TFEU also provides that the EU '... equally respects the status under national law of philosophical and non-confessional organisations'[83] and concludes with a recognition of these churches and organisations '... identity and ... specific

---

79. (contd) and of the Council on the transmission of data subject to statistical confidentiality to the Statistical Office of the European Communities,Council Regulation (EC) No 322/97 on Community Statistics, and Council Decision 89/382/EEC, Euratom establishing a Committee on the Statistical Programmes of the European Communities (OJ L 87, 31.3.2009, p. 164).) provides further specifications on statistical confidentiality for European statistics'. GDPR, Recital 163.

80. GDPR, Recital 158.

81. GDPR, Recital 165.

82. TFEU, article 17(1).

83. TFEU, article 17(2).

contribution' which requires that the EU: 'maintain an open, transparent and regular dialogue with these churches and organisations'.[84] Notwithstanding this promise of equality the GDPR provides for its application to churches, religious associations or communities only, providing that:

> Where in a Member State, churches and religious associations or communities apply, at the time of entry into force of this Regulation, comprehensive rules relating to the protection of natural persons with regard to processing, such rules may continue to apply, provided that they are brought into line with this Regulation.[85]

The GDPR goes on to provide:

> Churches and religious associations which apply comprehensive rules... shall be subject to the supervision of an independent supervisory authority, which may be specific, provided that it fulfils the conditions laid down in Chapter VI of this Regulation.[86]

Data relating to religious beliefs is a special category of data,[87] the Recitals also provide that:

> ... the processing of personal data by official authorities for the purpose of achieving the aims, laid down by constitutional law or by international public law, of officially recognised religious associations, is carried out on grounds of public interest.[88]

---

84.   TFEU, article 17(3).
85.   GDPR, article 91(1).
86.   GDPR, article 91(2).
87.   GDPR, article 9(1).
88.   GDPR, Recital 55.

Chapter 4

DEFINITIONS

INTRODUCTION

[4.01] The GDPR is 'technologically neutral'[1] as its Recitals make clear:

> In order to prevent creating a serious risk of circumvention, the protection of natural persons should be technologically neutral and should not depend on the techniques used.[2]

Technological neutrality means that the GDPR's definitions are phrased generally, they are not specific to a particular technology. This technological neutrality has meant adaptability: it allowed the old Directive 95/46 to retain relevance a quarter-century after it was first conceived and may allow the new GDPR to aspire towards similar longevity. Such adaptability is not without risk. What might seem technologically neutral to some might seem unacceptably vague to others. As the CJEU warned in *Schrems*:

> … EU legislation involving interference with the fundamental rights guaranteed by Articles 7 and 8 of the Charter must, according to the Court's settled case law, lay down clear and precise rules governing the scope and application of a measure and imposing minimum safeguards, so that the persons whose personal data is concerned have sufficient guarantees enabling their data to be effectively protected against the risk of abuse and against any unlawful access and use of that data …[3]

However, the CJEU has repeatedly held that provisions of Directive 95/46 were 'sufficiently precise to be relied on by individuals and applied by the national courts'.[4]

---

1. The Rand Corporation cited the following features of Directive 95/46 as justifying its description as technologically neutral in research undertaken for the UK's ICO: no reference to specific technologies; security measures not specified; and, concept of personal data broad enough to be technologically neutral. Rand Europe, *Review of the European Data Protection Directive; technical report,* ICO, 2009, p 4.

2. GDPR, Recital 14. See also Rand Europe, *Review of the European Data Protection Directive; technical report,* ICO, 2009, p 4.

3. *Schrems* (Judgment) (Case C–362/14) (6 October 2015), para 91; see also *Digital Rights Ireland* (Case C–293/12) (8 April 2014), para 54.

4. *Osterreichischer Rundfunk* (Case C–139/01) (20 May 2003), para 100; *Asociacion Nacional de Establecimientos Financieros de Credito* (Case C–468/10) (24 November 2011), para 52. See also *Huber* (Case C–524/06) (16 December 2008), para 52; and *Transfer of Passenger Name Record data from the European Union to Canada* [2017] EUECJ Avis-1/15_OC (26 July 2017), para 54.

THE DATA SUBJECT AND THEIR PERSONAL DATA

[4.02] As did Directive 95/46, the GDPR merges its definition of data subject into that of personal data. Personal data is defined as meaning:

> ... any information relating to an identified or identifiable natural person ('data subject'); an identifiable natural person is one who can be identified, directly or indirectly, in particular by reference to an identifier such as a name, an identification number, location data, an online identifier or to one or more factors specific to the physical, physiological, genetic, mental, economic, cultural or social identity of that natural person.[5]

The new definition is basically the same as the old, albeit with slight differences, to that which was to be found in Directive 95/46. One interesting change is the repetition of the requirement that the data in question relate to a 'natural person'. Directive 95/46 mentioned this requirement once; the new definition repeats it three times. Such repetition suggests a determination to prevent the extension of data protection rights to non-living persons such as companies or artificial intelligence.[6] The GDPR also suggests the following as identifiers:

- *names* are now specified as an identifier, though the omission of these was probably an oversight in Directive 95/46;

- *location data*, such as that generated by mobile phone networks;

- *online identifiers*, such identifiers might include cookies or Internet Protocol (IP) addresses;[7] and

- *genetic* factors, the obvious example of this is information derived from DNA and RNA.[8] However, the definition of genetic data is broader than this capturing all '... personal data relating to the inherited or acquired genetic characteristics

---

5.   GDPR, article 4(1).
6.   Such an extension has already occurred under the ECHR, at least in the case of companies (see *Bernh Larsen v Norway* [2013] ECHR 220 (14 March 2013). The possibility that artificial intelligence entities might someday benefit from data protection rights is far beyond the scope of this book. Artificial intelligence is a rapidly advancing technological field, but truly autonomous systems remain a far distant prospect (for an analysis of the regulatory challenge posed by super-intelligent AI see Bostrom, *Superintelligence,* OUP, 2014). But if, as *Brenh Larsen* suggests companies can have privacy rights then why not machines?
7.   Natural persons may be associated with online identifiers provided by their devices, applications, tools and protocols, such as internet protocol addresses, cookie identifiers or other identifiers such as radio frequency identification tags. This may leave traces which, in particular when combined with unique identifiers and other information received by the servers, may be used to create profiles of the natural persons and identify them,' GDPR, Recital 30.
8.   This is clear from GDPR, Recital 34, which provides that '... Genetic data should be defined as personal data relating to the inherited or acquired genetic characteristics of a natural person which result from the analysis of a biological sample from the natural person in question, (contd .../)

of a natural person which give unique information about the physiology or the health of that natural person ...'. The GDPR goes on to specify that this will include data that results '... in particular, from an analysis of a biological sample from the natural person in question'.[9] However, it seems clear that the definition of genetic data is broader than that of data derived from the analysis of DNA or RNA alone.

The CJEU has repeatedly considered the issue of what is personal data. At its most basic level it is clear that a person's name is their personal data. In *McCullough*[10] the applicant sought access to the minutes of a meeting held by the European Centre for the Development of Vocational Training (Cedefop).[11] Cedefop considered that the names of the members of its Governing Board and its Bureau, which were contained in those minutes, constituted personal data.[12] The CJEU agreed, holding that:

> ... surnames are personal data and are therefore protected ... The fact that the members of Cedefop's decision-making bodies participated in the meetings of those bodies in connection with the exercise of their public duties and not in the private sphere, or indeed the fact that the surnames of the members of the Governing Board and the Bureau were published in the *Official Journal of the European Union* or on the Internet, does not affect the characterisation of their surnames as personal data.[13]

[4.03] In *Internationaler Hilfsfonds* the CJEU held that:

> ... the act of referring, on a communication support, to various persons and identifying them by name or by other means, for instance by giving their telephone number or information regarding their working conditions and hobbies, constitutes a 'processing of data' ...[14]

The test of what is, or is not, personal data is an objective one. The context within which information is processed is irrelevant to the questions of whether that information is personal data. So just because information about a person is published into the public domain does not mean that ceases to be personal data. As the CJEU explained in *Satakunnan*:[15]

> ... a general derogation from the application of the directive in respect of published information would largely deprive the directive of its effect. It would be

---

8.   (contd) in particular chromosomal, deoxyribonucleic acid (DNA) or ribonucleic acid (RNA) analysis, or from the analysis of another element enabling equivalent information to be obtained'.

9.   GDPR, article 4(13).

10. *McCullough* [2015] (Case T–496/13) (11 June 2015).

11. Regulation 1049/2001/EC of the European Parliament and of the Council of 30 May 2001 regarding public access to European Parliament, Council and Commission documents.

12. *McCullough* [2015] (Case T–496/13) (11 June 2015), para 8.

13. *McCullough* [2015] (Case T–496/13) (11 June 2015), para 8.

14. *Internationaler Hilfsfonds* (Case T–300/10) (22 May 2012), para 116, citing *Lindqvist*, para 27.

15. *Satakunnan Markkinaporssi* (Case C–73/07) (16 December 2008).

sufficient for the Member States to publish data in order for those data to cease to enjoy the protection afforded by the directive.[16]

Similarly, the fact that information about a person is processed in an employment or professional context is irrelevant to the question of whether that information is personal data. In *ClientEarth*[17] the applicant had sought the names of external experts who had assisted the European Food Safety Authority under the EU's transparency rules. The applicant argued that: '... the fact that an expert issues, in a professional capacity, a scientific opinion is not covered by the concept of privacy'.[18] However, the CJEU held that '... the fact that information is provided as part of a professional activity does not mean that it cannot be characterised as a set of personal data'.[19]

At its core the definition of personal data is short, succinct and incredibly broad. The GDPR defines personal data as '... any information relating to an identified or identifiable natural person ...'.

The Recitals provide further detail on what the GDPR means by 'identifiable':

> To determine whether a natural person is identifiable, account should be taken of all the means reasonably likely to be used, such as singling out, either by the controller or by another person to identify the natural person directly or indirectly. To ascertain whether means are reasonably likely to be used to identify the natural person, account should be taken of all objective factors, such as the costs of and the amount of time required for identification, taking into consideration the available technology at the time of the processing and technological developments.[20]

[4.04] The CJEU has repeatedly considered what personal data is and found the following to be so:

- '... data ... which relate both to the monies paid by certain bodies and the recipients ...'.[21]

- '... the name of a person in conjunction with his telephone coordinates or information about his working conditions or hobbies'.[22]

- A subject's 'name, given name, date and place of birth, nationality, marital status, sex; a record of his entries into and exits from Germany, and his residence status; particulars of passports issued to him; a record of his previous statements as to domicile; and reference numbers ... particulars of the authorities which supplied the data and the reference numbers used by those authorities'.[23]

---

16. *Satakunnan Markkinaporssi* (Case C–73/07) (16 December 2008), para 48.
17. *ClientEarth* (Case C–615/13 P) (16 July 2015).
18. *ClientEarth* (Case C–615/13 P) (16 July 2015), para 25.
19. *ClientEarth* (Case C–615/13 P) (16 July 2015), para 30.
20. GDPR, Recital 26.
21. *Osterreichischer Rundfunk* (Case C–138/01) (20 May 2003), para 64.
22. *Lindqvist* (Case C–101/01) (6 November 2003), para 23.
23. *Huber* (Case C–524/06) (16 December 2008), paras 31, 42 and 43.

- '... the surname and given name of certain natural persons whose income exceeds certain thresholds as well as the amount, to the nearest EUR 100, of their earned and unearned income ...'.[24]

- A person's '... name and address ...'.[25]

- '... surnames and forenames ...'.[26]

- 'Fingerprints ... as they objectively contain unique information about individuals which allows those individuals to be identified with precision ...'.[27]

- Data '... collected by ... private detectives ... relat(ing) to persons acting as estate agents and concern(ing) identified or identifiable natural persons'.[28]

- '... data necessary to trace and identify the source of a communication and its destination, to identify the date, time, duration and type of a communication, to identify users' communication equipment, and to identify the location of mobile communication equipment, data which consist, inter alia, of the name and address of the subscriber or registered user, the calling telephone number, the number called and an IP address for Internet services'.[29]

- '... data found, indexed and stored by search engines ...'.[30]

- 'a record of working time ... which includes an indication, for each worker, hours of beginning and end of work as well as interruptions or corresponding breaks ...'.[31]

- '... the image of a person recorded by a camera ... inasmuch as it makes it possible to identify the person concerned.'[32]

- '... tax data relating to ... income'.[33]

- '... the identity document number and the address of (a) passenger ...'.[34]

- '... the name(s) of the air passenger(s), information necessary to the reservation, such as the dates of intended travel and the travel itinerary, information relating to tickets, groups of persons checked-in under the same

---

24. *Satakunnan Markkinaporssi and Satamedia* (Approximation of laws) (Case C–73/07) (16 December 2008), para 35.

25. *Rijkeboer* (Approximation of laws) (Case C–553/07) (7 May 2009), para 42. See also *Puskar* (Case C–73/16) (27 September 2017), para 33.

26. *Commission v Bavarian Lager* (Case C–28/08) (29 June 2010), para 68.

27. *Schwarz v Stadt Bochum* (Case C–291/12) (17 October 2013), para 27.

28. *IPI* (Case C–473/12) (7 November 2013), para 26.

29. *Digital Rights Ireland* (Judgment of the Court) [2014] (Case C–293/12) (8 April 2014), para 26.

30. *Costeja Gonzalez v Google Spain and Google* (Judgment of the Court) (Case C–131/12) (13 May 2014), para 27.

31. *Pharmacontinente* (Case C–683/13_CO) (19 June 2014), para 13.

32. *Rynes* (Judgment) (Case C–212/13) (11 December 2014), para 22.

33. *Bara* (Case C–201/14) (1 October 2015), para 15.

34. *Rigas satiksme* (Case C–13/16) (4 May 2017), para 24.

reservation number, passenger contact information, information relating to the means of payment or billing, information concerning baggage and general remarks regarding the passenger'.[35]

- '... an identification number...' of '...a candidate at a professional examination... placed either on the examination script itself or on its cover sheet'.[36]

[4.05] The breadth of this definition was considered by the CJEU in a series of cases that considered the processing of IP addresses. IP addresses were described by the CJEU in *Breyer*:[37]

... most of those websites store information on all access operations in logfiles. The information retained in the logfiles after those sites have been accessed include ... the IP address of the computer from which access was sought.[38]

The CJEU explained that such addresses were a:

'... series of digits assigned to networked computers to facilitate their communication over the internet ... internet service providers allocate to the computers of internet users either a 'static' IP address or a 'dynamic' IP address, that is to say an IP address which changes each time there is a new connection to the internet. Unlike static IP addresses, dynamic IP addresses do not enable a link to be established, through files accessible to the public, between a given computer and the physical connection to the network used by the internet service provider.[39]

[4.06] The first of these decisions, *Promusicae*,[40] was brought by a Spanish organisation of '... producers and publishers of musical and audiovisual recording' which asked that Telefonica, a Spanish electronic communications network, '... disclose the identities and physical addresses of certain persons whom it provided with internet access services, whose IP address and date and time of connection were known'.[41] However, it was not disputed that the '... communication sought by Promusicae of the names and addresses of certain users ... involves the making available of personal data ...'.[42] Similarly in the second of these decisions, *Bonnier Audio*,[43] an owner of copyright sought from an internet service provider '...the communication of the name and address of an internet subscriber or user using the IP address from which it is presumed that an unlawful exchange of files containing protected works took place, in order to identify

---

35.   *Transfer of Passenger Name Record data from the European Union to Canada* (Opinions of the Court) [2017] EUECJ Avis-1/15_OC (26 July 2017), para 121.

36.   *Nowak* (Case C–434/16) (20 December 2017), para 29.

37.   *Breyer* (Case C–582/14) (19 October 2016).

38.   *Breyer* (Case C–582/14) (19 October 2016), para 14.

39.   *Breyer* (Case C–582/14) (19 October 2016), paras 15–16.

40.   *Promusicae* (Case C–275/06) (29 January 2008).

41.   *Promusicae* (Case C–275/06) (29 January 2008), paras 29–30.

42.   *Promusicae* (Case C–275/06) (29 January 2008), para 45.

43.   *Bonnier Audio* (Case C–461/10) (19 April 2012).

that person'.[44] Hence both *Promusicae* and *Bonnier Audio* were actions taken against internet service providers who were in a position to identify data subjects from personal data that they were already processing.

[4.07] *Breyer,* the most recent of these decisions, suggests a significant broadening of the definition of personal data. The applicant was a German who had '... accessed several websites operated by German Federal institutions'.[45] The applicant then objected to the retention of his IP address by those websites.[46] At issue was the storage of 'dynamic' as opposed to 'static' IP addresses. A static address will typically be assigned to a significant internet user, such as that of a university, government department or e-commerce firm. Because the address is permanent the string of numbers that make it up serve as a straightforward identifier of the website. But few individual users of the internet will be assigned a static IP address. Instead their ISP will assign them a temporary or 'dynamic' IP address when they go on-line, which they will lose when they go off-line, whereupon the dynamic IP address will be reassigned to another user.[47] These dynamic IP addresses did not enable the identification of data subjects on their own.[48]

[4.08] The question before the CJEU was whether a dynamic IP address could amount to data about an 'identifiable natural person'. The CJEU held that it could as: '... in the event of cyber attacks legal channels exist so that the online media services provider is able to contact the competent authority, so that the latter can take the steps necessary to obtain that information from the internet service provider and to bring criminal proceedings'.[49] And so the CJEU concluded that the website operator:

> ... has the means which may likely reasonably be used in order to identify the data subject, with the assistance of other persons, namely the competent authority and the internet service provider, on the basis of the IP addresses stored.

---

44. *Bonnier Audio* (Case C–461/10) (19 April 2012), para 51.
45. *Breyer* (Case C–582/14) (19 October 2016), para 14.
46. *Breyer* (Case C–582/14) (19 October 2016), paras 15–16.
47. As the CJEU explained: '... internet service providers allocate to the computers of internet users either a 'static' IP address or a 'dynamic' IP address, that is to say an IP address which changes each time there is a new connection to the internet. Unlike static IP addresses, dynamic IP addresses do not enable a link to be established, through files accessible to the public, between a given computer and the physical connection to the network used by the internet service provider'. *Breyer* (Case C–582/14) (19 October 2016), para 16. See also the discussion by Charleton J in *EMI Records v Eircom* [2010] IEHC 108 (16 April 2010), para 14.
48. '... a dynamic IP address does not constitute information relating to an 'identified natural person', since such an address does not directly reveal the identity of the natural person who owns the computer from which a website was accessed, or that of another person who might use that computer' *Breyer* (Case C–582/14) (19 October 2016), para 38.
49. *Breyer* (Case C–582/14) (19 October 2016), para 47.

This sets what appears to be a low threshold for data to be considered identifiable. A number of parties would have to interact before the data subjects in question could be identified: the website operator themselves, the police or other 'competent authorities' and the subject's own internet service provider. As the CJEU itself pointed out this interaction would have to take place through 'legal channels'. And as the CJEU held in *Digital Rights Ireland* this cannot be a simple matter of the German police writing to an ISP and asking that they send over a list of names and addresses. The CJEU expects that such 'legal channels' should be '... dependent on a prior review carried out by a court or by an independent administrative body whose decision seeks to limit access to the data and their use to what is strictly necessary for the purpose of attaining the objective pursued and which intervenes following a reasoned request of those authorities submitted within the framework of procedures of prevention, detection or criminal prosecutions'.[50] Furthermore, it is far from clear that the website operator would itself be able to identify the subjects in question, unless those subjects were actually prosecuted. In *Digital Rights Ireland* the CJEU made clear that it expected that such legal channels would impose rules by which: '... the number of persons authorised to access and subsequently use the data retained is limited to what is strictly necessary in the light of the objective pursued'.[51]

[4.09] In *Breyer* the CJEU considered that a subject was 'identifiable' from data even though a legal process would have to be engaged before they could be identified and even then their identity might not be revealed to the controller. The only limits that are set on what is meant by 'identifiable' are set out in Recital 26; a controller need only consider 'all the means reasonably likely to be used' by them or someone else to identify a subject. So it is not necessary to consider every possible process by which a person might be identified, only those reasonably likely to be used. But that still leaves us with a definition of personal data that is very broad.

The definition of personal data applied by the CJEU in *Breyer* was very broad; it was however objective. In *Nowak*[52] the CJEU then expanded this definition to include subjective elements such as the effect that the processing would have on the subject. This case was brought by a trainee accountant who had failed an open book examination and then sought a copy of his examination script by way of an access request. His request was refused and his challenge to that refusal resulted in the Irish Supreme Court referring questions to the CJEU, which that Court summarised as whether:

> ... the written answers submitted by a candidate at a professional examination and
> any examiner's comments with respect to those answers constitute personal data
> ...[53]

The CJEU began its consideration of this question by reciting that there was: 'no requirement that all the information enabling the identification of the data subject must

---

50. *Digital Rights Ireland* (Case C–293/12) (8 April 2014), para 62.
51. *Digital Rights Ireland* (Judgment of the Court) (Case C–293/12) (8 April 2014), para 62.
52. *Nowak* (Case C–434/16) (20 December 2017).
53. *Nowak* (Case C–434/16) (20 December 2017), para 27.

be in the hands of one person'. The CJEU went onto note that '... the scope of Directive 95/46 is very wide and the personal data covered by that directive is varied'[54] explaining that:

> The use of the expression 'any information' in the definition of the concept of 'personal data'..., reflects the aim of the EU legislature to assign a wide scope to that concept, which is not restricted to information that is sensitive or private, but potentially encompasses all kinds of information, not only objective but also subjective, in the form of opinions and assessments, provided that it 'relates' to the data subject.[55]

The CJEU went onto identify the ways in which the applicant's written answers were linked to him. Firstly, '... the content of those answers reflects the extent of the candidate's knowledge and competence in a given field and, in some cases, his intellect, thought processes, and judgment. In the case of a handwritten script, the answers contain, in addition, information as to his handwriting'. Secondly, '... the purpose of collecting those answers is to evaluate the candidate's professional abilities and his suitability to practice the profession concerned'. Finally, the use of the written answers was liable to have an effect on the applicant's rights and interests. Such an effect might be '... the candidate's success or failure at the examination concerned ...' which would '... determine or influence ... the chance of entering the profession aspired to or of obtaining the post.'[56] What makes *Nowak* particularly interesting is that subject matter of the examination in question was Strategic Finance and Management Accounting and the examination was open book.[57] Hence it might be anticipated that such an examination might give the subject a limited capacity to express his personal opinions. However, the CJEU held that:

> ... equally true that the written answers submitted by a candidate at a professional examination constitute information that relates to that candidate by reason of its content, purpose or effect, where the examination is, as in this case, an open book examination.[58]

The CJEU went onto repeat the view of its Advocate General that:

> the aim of any examination is to determine and establish the individual performance of a specific person, namely the candidate, and not, unlike, for example, a representative survey, to obtain information that is independent of that person.[59]

The CJEU went onto explain that the definition of personal data can encompass information which relates to a number of subjects. It noted that comments made by the

---

54. *Nowak* (Case C–434/16) (20 December 2017), para 33.
55. *Nowak* (Case C–434/16) (20 December 2017), para 34.
56. *Nowak* (Case C–434/16) (20 December 2017), para 39.
57. *Nowak* (Case C–434/16) (20 December 2017), para 18.
58. *Nowak* (Case C–434/16) (20 December 2017), para 40.
59. *Nowak* (Case C–434/16) (20 December 2017), para 41.

examiner '... reflects the opinion or the assessment of the examiner of the individual performance of the candidate in the examination, particularly of his or her knowledge and competences in the field concerned. The purpose of those comments is, moreover, precisely to record the evaluation by the examiner of the candidate's performance, and those comments are liable to have effects for the candidate ...'.[60] The CJEU went onto explain that the:

> ... same information may relate to a number of individuals and may constitute for each of them, provided that those persons are identified or identifiable, personal data ...[61]

[4.10] The definition of personal data may be broad, but it only encompasses information that 'relates' to an identified or identifiable data subject. Just because information is of interest or relevance to such a subject does not mean that it will relate to them. This is clear from the CJEU decision in *YS*.[62] The applicant had sought a residence permit from the respondent, the Dutch Minister for Immigration. This application contained personal information which was then reviewed by that Minister, whose civil servants undertook a legal analysis. The CJEU was in 'no doubt that the data relating to the applicant for a residence permit and contained in a minute, such as the applicant's name, date of birth, nationality, gender, ethnicity, religion and language, are ... "personal data"'. However, the Court went on to hold that whilst 'data in the legal analysis contained in the minute are 'personal data'... by contrast, that analysis cannot in itself be so classified'.[63]

The CJEU is due to again consider the definition of personal data in *Nowak*,[64] in which the CJEU is being asked whether 'information recorded in/as answers given by a candidate during a professional examination (is) capable of being personal data'.[65]

Data subject

[4.11] The definition of personal data may be broad, but the definition of data subject is not. There is only one type of data subject recognised by the GDPR: a living natural

---

60.   *Nowak* (Case C–434/16) (20 December 2017), para 43.

61.   *Nowak* (Case C–434/16) (20 December 2017), para 45.

62.   *YS* (Case C–141/12) (17 July 2014).

63.   *YS* (Case C–141/12) (17 July 2014), para 48. This judgment may be particular to the right of access as '... extending the right of access ... to that legal analysis would not in fact serve the directive's purpose of guaranteeing the protection of the applicant's right to privacy with regard to the processing of data relating to him, but would serve the purpose of guaranteeing him a right of access to administrative documents ...' *YS* (Case C–141/12) (17 July 2014), para 46 ...'.

64.   *Nowak* (Case C–434/16), Application: OJ C 364 from 03.10.2016, p 11.

65.   The opinion of Advocate General Bot issued on 20 July 2017.

person. Dead people cannot be data subjects[66] as is made clear by the recitals to the GDPR:

> This Regulation does not apply to the personal data of deceased persons. Member States may provide for rules regarding the processing of personal data of deceased persons.[67]

However, as the article 29 WP has explained, 'the data of the deceased may still indirectly receive some protection in certain cases'.[68] One such case is where the controller is not in a position to ascertain whether a subject is still alive. Another would be where data that relates to a dead person, may also relate to someone who is still alive. So information that a dead person had suffered from a genetic disease might also amount to the personal data of their living descendants who might have inherited the disease in question.

[4.12] Legal persons cannot be data subjects as they are not natural persons. In the second *Digital Rights Ireland*[69] decision, the applicant was a legal person which sought to challenge the EU Commission's Privacy Shield decision, which enabled the transfer of personal data to the USA. However, the applicant was a legal person. And as the CJEU explained:

> ... in so far as the protection of personal data guaranteed by Article 8 of the Charter of Fundamental Rights of the European Union concerns any information relating to an identified or identifiable individual, legal persons can claim the protection of that provision only in so far as the official title of the legal person identifies one or more natural persons ...[70]

This mean that: '... annulment of the contested decision ... is not capable of having ... legal consequences for the applicant or of procuring for it an advantage in that regard'.[71] The CJEU went onto hold that the applicant did 'not have an interest in bringing proceedings'[72] and deemed its application inadmissible.[73]

The recitals to the GDPR state:

> This Regulation does not cover the processing of personal data which concerns legal persons and in particular undertakings established as legal persons, including the name and the form of the legal person and the contact details of the legal person.[74]

---

66. 'The dead have no rights and can suffer no wrongs.' *R v Ensor* (1887) 3 TLR 366.
67. GDPR, Recital 27.
68. Article 29 Working Party, *Opinion 4/2007 on the concept of personal data,* 01248/07/EN WP 136, 20 June 2009, 22.
69. *Digital Rights Ireland* (Case T–670/16) (27 November 2017).
70. *Digital Rights Ireland* (Case T–670/16) (27 November 2017), para 25.
71. *Digital Rights Ireland* (Case T–670/16) (27 November 2017), para 28.
72. *Digital Rights Ireland* (Case T–670/16) (27 November 2017), para 43.
73. *Digital Rights Ireland* (Case T–670/16) (27 November 2017), para 60.
74. GDPR, Recital 14.

This might seem to overturn the judgment of the CJEU in *Schecke*[75] in which the CJEU considered an EU Regulation[76] which provided for the publication of beneficiaries from certain EU agricultural funds. This publication was challenged by two German farmers, on the basis that it amounted to a breach of rights to privacy and data protection under the Charter of Fundamental Rights of the EU. One of the farmers was a legal person, not a living individual. The court held that: 'legal persons can claim the protection of Article … 8 of the Charter in relation to such identification only in so far as the official title of the legal person identifies one or more natural persons'.[77]

But caution should be exercised before assuming that all legal persons fall outside the definition of personal data. Data relating to a large company which happens to be named after its founder will not amount to the personal data of that living individual, as data relating to the company will not necessarily relate to the founder. However, many independent service providers will operate through companies. To the extent that data relating to such a company may be related to an identifiable living person, then it may be argued that it is that subject's personal data. In the same way data that relates to an object may be personal data if the latter may be related to an individual data subject. So in *Pharmacontinente,*[78] the CJEU held that time cards which indicated the hours when individual workers had begun and ended work, as well as interruptions or breaks, would fall within the concept of 'personal data'.[79] The EU's Fundamental Rights Agency cites the ECtHR decision in *Uzun v Germany*[80] in support of its view that:

> where there is a close link between an object or an event – eg a mobile phone, a
> car, an accident – on the one hand, and a person – eg as its owner, user, victim – on

---

75. *Volker und Markus Schecke and Eifert* (Joined Cases C–92/09 & C–93/09) (9 November 2010).

76. Commission Regulation 259/2008/EC of 18 March 2008 laying down detailed rules for the application of Regulation No 1290/2005 as regards the publication of information on the beneficiaries of funds deriving from the European Agricultural Guarantee Fund (EAGF) and the European Agricultural Fund for Rural Development (EAFRD) [2008] OJ L 76/28. The court also reviewed Council Regulation 1290/2005/EC of 21 June 2005 on the financing of the common agricultural policy [2005] OJ L 209/1, as amended by Council Regulation 1437/2007/EC of 26 November 2007 [2007] OJ L 322/1 ('Regulation No 1290/ 2005'), and Directive 2006/24/EC of the European Parliament and of the Council of 15 March 2006 on the retention of data generated or processed in connection with the provision of publicly available electronic communications services or of public communications networks and amending Directive 2002/58/EC [2006] OJ L 105/54.

77. *Volker und Markus Schecke and Eifert* (Joined Cases C–92/09 & C–93/09) (9 November 2010), para 53. See also European Data Protection Supervisor, *Executive Summary of the Opinion of the European Data Protection Supervisor on the Commission Proposal for a Directive of the European Parliament and of the Council on single-member private limited liability companies*, OJ 2014 C 390/02, (5 November 2014).

78. *Pharmacontinente* (Case C–683/13) (19 June 2014). See similarly *Worten v Autoridade para as Condicoes de Trabalho (ACT)* (Case C–342/12) (30 May 2013).

79. *Pharmacontinente* (Case C–683/13) (19 June 2014), para 13.

80. *Uzun v Germany* No 35623/05 (2 September 2010), which concerned a GPS tracking device hidden in an individual's car.

the other, information about an object or about an event ought also to be considered personal data.[81]

In *Worten*[82] the CJEU was asked to consider whether '… a record of working time … containing the indication, in relation to each worker, of the times when working hours begin and end, as well as the corresponding breaks and intervals, constitutes "personal data" …'[83] The CJEU concluded that it was. In *Osterreichischer Rundfunk*[84] the CJEU noted that data relating to what certain employees were paid was personal data.[85] Other examples are names and other personal details in an identification database.[86]

Anonymisation and pseudonymisation

[4.13] The breadth of the definition of personal data means that the definition of anonymous data must be correspondingly narrow. Given the quantities of data that are in existence and sophistication of the algorithms that are used by so-called 'big-data'[87] systems, successful anonymisation of personal data is increasingly difficult, if not impossible.[88] This may have significant implications. Suppose a medical researcher is conducting research into a medical condition. This research is conducted on the basis of anonymous data provided by hospitals and medical practitioners. It is reasonably possible that their research may identify a sub-group of patients who might benefit from

81. EU Fundamental Rights Agency, *Handbook on European Data Protection Law* (2014), 42.
82. *Worten* (Case C–342/12) (30 May 2013).
83. *Worten* (Case C–342/12) (30 May 2013), para 18.
84. *Osterreichischer Rundfunk* (Case C–138/01) (20 May 2003).
85. *Osterreichischer Rundfunk* (Case C–138/01) (20 May 2003), para 64.
86. *Huber* (Case C–524/06) (16 December 2008), para 43 and *Rijkeboer* (Case C–553/07) (7 May 2009), para 42.
87. 'Big data is big in two different senses. It is big in the quantity and variety of data that are available to be processed. And, it is big in the scale of analysis (termed 'analytics') that can be applied to those data, ultimately to make inferences and draw conclusions. By data mining and other kinds of analytics, nonobvious and sometimes private information can be derived from data that, at the time of their collection, seemed to raise no, or only manageable, privacy issues.' Executive Office of the President, President's Council of Advisors on Science and Technology, *Big Data and Privacy: a Technological Perspective,* May 2014, p ix.
88. In 2006 Netflix, the online movie rental service, launched the 'Netflix prize', a $1 million reward for whoever could best improve their movie recommendations. As part of this competition Netflix made an anonymised database of the movie rentals of almost 500,000 subscribers available. Researchers were able to 'de-anonymise' this database by combining it with the publically expressed preferences of users on another site, the Internet Movie Database (IMDb). Narayanan, Shmatikov, 'How To Break Anonymity of the Netflix Prize Dataset', Cornell University Library, Computer Science > Cryptography and Security, 18 Oct 2006. These results have since been replicated, see Su, Shukla, Goel, *Narayanan De-anonymizing Web Browsing Data with Social Networks,* Proceedings of the 26th International Conference on World Wide Web, April 2017, pp 1261–126.

a particular course of treatment.[89] Identifying these patients might reasonably mean deanonymising the data upon which the research is based. This might mean reversing the anonymisation process, but this might well prove possible by matching the research data to the original personal data. So is the research data not always personal data? The judgment in *Breyer* suggests that it may be, so long as means exist that might reasonably be used to identify the subjects. This does not mean that this data cannot be processed for research, but that research must be undertaken in accordance with the GDPR.

[4.14] 'Big-data' systems are a significant challenge for EU data protection law, since often the most effective route to compliance may be for a controller to use anonymisation techniques to ensure that they are not processing personal data. The GDPR recognises data minimisation as a principle of data protection law[90] and requires the use of techniques such as anonymisation and pseudonymisation.[91] As the Recitals explain:

> Personal data which have undergone pseudonymisation,[92] which could be attributed to a natural person by the use of additional information should be considered to be information on an identifiable natural person. To determine whether a natural person is identifiable, account should be taken of all the means reasonably likely to be used, such as singling out, either by the controller or by another person to identify the natural person directly or indirectly. To ascertain whether means are reasonably likely to be used to identify the natural person, account should be taken of all objective factors, such as the costs of and the

---

89. This occurred in France in the early 1990s, where research was carried out into instances of hereditary glaucoma in Boulogne-sur-Mer, which had an unusually high incidence of this disease. The research traced the family trees of three families who were known to be suffering from glaucoma back fifteen generations to a blind couple who had lived in the sixteenth century. It was then relatively straightforward to trace all the descendants of that couple and identify those who were at an increased risk of suffering from glaucoma. If glaucoma is caught early enough it can be halted by the application of eye drops; however, the only treatment for late-disease glaucoma is surgery, or blindness may result. Prior to contacting the descendants the researchers consulted the French data protection agency but were told that under French data protection law they could not, under any circumstances, inform the descendants of what they had discovered. See Laurie, *Genetic Privacy* (CUP, 2002), p 117.

90. See GDPR, article 5.

91. See GDPR, article 25. Notwithstanding the reliance that the GDPR places upon anonymisation and pseudononymisation techniques, it would seem that EU data protection law does not itself provide an absolute right to anonymity. This seems clear from the judgment of the CJEU in *McFadden* (Case C–484/14) (15 September 2016).

92. The GDPR defines 'pseudonymisation' as meaning:
   '… the processing of personal data in such a manner that the personal data can no longer be attributed to a specific data subject without the use of additional information, provided that such additional information is kept separately and is subject to technical and organisational measures to ensure that the personal data are not attributed to an identified or identifiable natural person', GDPR, article 4(5).

amount of time required for identification, taking into consideration the available technology at the time of the processing and technological developments. The principles of data protection should therefore not apply to anonymous information, namely information which does not relate to an identified or identifiable natural person or to personal data rendered anonymous in such a manner that the data subject is not or no longer identifiable. This Regulation does not therefore concern the processing of such anonymous information ...

The GDPR defines pseudonymisation as:

... the processing of personal data in such a manner that the personal data can no longer be attributed to a specific data subject without the use of additional information, provided that such additional information is kept separately and is subject to technical and organisational measures to ensure that the personal data are not attributed to an identified or identifiable natural person.[93]

[4.15] The GDPR's Recitals suggest that pseudonymisation can: '...reduce the risks to the data subjects concerned and help controllers and processors to meet their data-protection obligations'.[94] However, as the Recitals go on to explain, pseudonymised data remains personal data:

The principles of data protection should apply to any information concerning an identified or identifiable natural person. Personal data which have undergone pseudonymisation, which could be attributed to a natural person by the use of additional information, should be considered to be information on an identifiable natural person.[95]

It is further recited that the 'explicit introduction of 'pseudonymisation' in this Regulation is not intended to preclude any other measures of data protection'.[96] Since the GDPR explicitly accepts that pseudonymised data is personal data,[97] it is not clear that this concept has any real meaning. Nevertheless, the Recitals suggest that pseudonymisation should be incentivised and in order to create such incentives:

... measures of pseudonymisation should, whilst allowing general analysis, be possible within the same controller when that controller has taken technical and

---

93. GDPR, article 4(5).
94. GDPR, Recital 28.
95. GDPR, Recital 26.
96. GDPR, Recital 28.
97. See also the judgment of the CJEU in *Nowak* (Case C–434/16) (20 December 2017), para 30, in which the CJEU held that '... it is of no relevance ... whether the examiner can or cannot identify the candidate at the time when he/she is correcting and marking the examination script' (para 30) noting that '... in the event that the examiner does not know the identity of the candidate when he/she is marking the answers submitted by that candidate in an examination, the body that set the examination ... does, however, have available to it the information needed to enable it easily and infallibly to identify that candidate through his identification number, placed on the examination script or its cover sheet, and thereby to ascribe the answers to that candidate' (para 31).

organisational measures necessary to ensure, for the processing concerned, that this Regulation is implemented, and that additional information for attributing the personal data to a specific data subject is kept separately. The controller processing the personal data should indicate the authorised persons within the same controller.[98]

[4.16] The GDPR imposes some restrictions upon the extent to which a controller may be required to de-anonymise data. GDPR, article 11 provides that:

If the purposes for which a controller processes personal data do not or do no longer require the identification of a data subject by the controller, the controller shall not be obliged to maintain, acquire or process additional information in order to identify the data subject for the sole purpose of complying with this Regulation.[99]

In such cases where '… the controller is able to demonstrate that it is not in a position to identify the data subject, the controller shall inform the data subject accordingly, if possible.' The rights set out in GDPR, articles 15 to 20, will not apply in respect of such personal data unless the data subject '… provides additional information enabling his or her identification'.[100] However, the Recitals go on to provide that '… the controller should not refuse to take additional information provided by the data subject in order to support the exercise of his or her rights. Identification should include the digital identification of a data subject, for example through authentication mechanisms such as the same credentials, used by the data subject to log-in to the on-line service offered by the data controller'.[101]

Processing

[4.17] As with its definitions of data subject and personal data the GDPR adopts a definition of processing that is very broad. The GDPR defines processing as:

… any operation or set of operations which is performed on personal data or on sets of personal data, whether or not by automated means, such as collection, recording, organisation, structuring, storage, adaptation or alteration, retrieval, consultation, use, disclosure by transmission, dissemination or otherwise making available, alignment or combination, restriction, erasure or destruction.[102]

This definition is broad enough to encompass anything that can be done with personal data. As such it is largely unaltered from the definition to be found in Directive 95/46[103] albeit with some subtle differences: processing applies to operations performed on both data and sets of personal data; it may include structuring; and a reference to the

---

98.   GDPR, Recital 29.
99.   GDPR, article 11(1).
100. GDPR, article 11(2).
101. GDPR, Recital 57.
102. GDPR, article 4(2).
103. Directive 95/46, article 2(b).

'blocking' of personal data is removed and replaced with restriction. However, the two definitions are essentially the same, which is useful as the CJEU considered Directive 95/46's definition on a number of occasions. In *Bodil Lindqvist*[104] the CJEU concluded that:

> ... the act of referring, on an internet page, to various persons and identifying them by name or by other means, for instance by giving their telephone number or information regarding their working conditions and hobbies, constitutes the processing of personal data wholly or partly by automatic means.[105]

This definition was considered by the CJEU[106] in *Google Spain* in which Google argued that:

> ... the activity of search engines cannot be regarded as processing of the data which appear on third parties' web pages displayed in the list of search results, given that search engines process all the information available on the internet without effecting a selection between personal data and other information. Furthermore, even if that activity must be classified as 'data processing', the operator of a search engine cannot be regarded as a 'controller' in respect of that processing since it has no knowledge of those data and does not exercise control over the data.[107]

However, the court held that:

> in exploring the internet automatically, constantly and systematically in search of the information which is published there, the operator of a search engine 'collects' such data which it subsequently 'retrieves', 'records' and 'organises' within the framework of its indexing programmes, 'stores' on its servers and, as the case may be, 'discloses' and 'makes available' to its users in the form of lists of search results. As those operations are referred to expressly and unconditionally in Article 2(b) of Directive 95/46, they must be classified as 'processing' within the meaning of that provision, regardless of the fact that the operator of the search engine also carries out the same operations in respect of other types of information and does not distinguish between the latter and the personal data.[108]

This finding was not affected by 'the fact that those data have already been published on the internet and are not altered by the search engine'.[109] The court pointed out that this was consistent with its approach in *Satakunnan*, in which it held that:

> an activity in which data on the earned and unearned income and the assets of natural persons are: ...collected from documents in the public domain held by the

---

104. *Bodil Lindqvist* (Case C–101/01) (6 November 2003).
105. *Bodil Lindqvist* (Case C–101/01) (6 November 2003), para 27.
106. The CJEU also considered that disclosing personal data in response to an FOI request will amount to the processing of that data (*Commission v Bavarian Lager* (Case C–28/08) (29 June 2010), para 69).
107. *Google Spain* (Case C–131/12) (13 May 2014), para 22.
108. *Google Spain* (Case C–131/12) (13 May 2014), para 28.
109. *Google Spain* (Case C–131/12) (13 May 2014), para 29.

tax authorities and processed for publication, published alphabetically in printed form by income bracket and municipality in the form of comprehensive lists, transferred onward on CD-ROM to be used for commercial purposes, and processed for the purposes of a text-messaging service whereby mobile telephone users can, by sending a text message containing details of an individual's name and municipality of residence to a given number, receive in reply information concerning the earned and unearned income and assets of that person, must be considered as the 'processing of personal data.[110]

[4.18] In *Schrems* the CJEU held that the act of sending personal data outside the EU was a form of processing within the Member State from which it was sent.[111] In *Osterreichischer Rundfunk*[112] it was held that '... the collection, recording, organisation, storage, consultation, and use of such data by an employer, as well as their transmission by that employer to the national authorities responsible for monitoring working conditions ... represent the 'processing of personal data'.[113] In *Huber*[114] it was held that the collection, storage and transmission of personal data on a register amounted to the processing of that data.

[4.19] The CJEU has held that the following amount to the processing of personal data:

- The '... recording and use ... and their transmission ... and inclusion ... in a report intended to be communicated to various political institutions and widely diffused ...'.[115]

- '... the act of referring, on an internet page, to various persons and identifying them by name or by other means, for instance by giving their telephone number or information regarding their working conditions and hobbies ...'.[116]

- '... the operation of loading personal data on an internet page ...'.[117]

- '... collection, storage and transmission (of personal data) by the body responsible for the management of (a) register ...'.[118]

- The collection of '...public data from the Finnish tax authorities for the purposes of publishing extracts from those data in ... editions of...(a) newspaper ...'.[119]

---

110. *Satakunnan* (Case C–73/07) (16 December 2008), para 37.
111. '... the operation consisting in having personal data transferred from a Member State to a third country constitutes, in itself, processing of personal data ...carried out in a Member State' *Schrems* (Case C–362/14) (6 October 2015), para 45.
112. *Osterreichischer Rundfunk* (Case C–138/01) (20 May 2003).
113. *Osterreichischer Rundfunk* (Case C–138/01) (20 May 2003), para 20.
114. *Huber* (Case C–524/06) (16 December 2008), para 43.
115. *Osterreichischer Rundfunk* (Case C–138/01) (20 May 2003), para 64.
116. *Lindqvist* (Case C–101/01) (6 November 2003), para 27.
117. *Costeja Gonzalez v Google Spain and Google* (Case C–131/12), para 26, citing *Lindqvist*, para 25. See also *Weltimmo* (Judgment) (Case C–230/14) (1 October 2015), para 37.
118. *Huber* (Case C–524/06) (16 December 2008), para 43.
119. *Satakunnan Markkinaporssi and Satamedia* (Approximation of laws) (Case C–73/07) (16 December 2008), para 25.

- '... to take a person's fingerprints and [keep] ... those fingerprints ... in the storage medium in that person's passport'.[120]

- 'retention of data for the purpose of possible access to them by the competent national authorities'.[121]

- 'exploring the internet automatically, constantly and systematically in search of the information which is published there, the operator of a search engine 'collects' such data which it subsequently 'retrieves', 'records' and 'organises' within the framework of its indexing programmes, 'stores' on its servers and, as the case may be, 'discloses' and 'makes available' to its users in the form of lists of search results'.[122]

- 'Surveillance in the form of a video recording of persons ... which is stored on a continuous recording device — the hard disk drive — constitutes ... the automatic processing of personal data'.[123]

- '... the communication, by ... a banking institution, of the name and address of one of its customers ...'.[124]

- '... both the transfer of PNR data from the European Union to the Canadian Competent Authority and the framework negotiated by the European Union with Canada of the conditions concerning the retention of that data, its use and its subsequent transfer to other Canadian authorities, Europol, Eurojust, judicial or police authorities of the Member States or indeed to authorities of third countries ...'.[125]

- '... collection and ... use by the various tax authorities ...'.[126]

[4.20] As with its predecessor, Directive 95/46, the GDPR applies to processing by automated means and also:

> to the processing other than by automated means of personal data which form part of a filing system or are intended to form part of a filing system.

This is an anti-avoidance measure. The Strasbourg Convention 108, the original European data protection convention, applied to electronic data processing systems only. This gave rise to data controllers utilising old-fashioned filing systems to avoid national

---

120. *Schwarz v Stadt Bochum* [2013] (Case C–291/12) (17 October 2013), para 29.
121. *Digital Rights Ireland* (Judgment of the Court) (Case C–293/12) (8 April 2014), para 29.
122. *Costeja Gonzalez v Google Spain and Google* (Case C–131/12), para 28.
123. *Rynes* (Judgment) (Case C–212/13) (11 December 2014), para 25.
124. *Coty Germany GmbH v Stadtsparkasse Magdeburg* (Case C–580/13) (16 July 2015), para 26.
125. *Transfer of Passenger Name Record data from the European Union to Canada (Opinions of the Court)* [2017] EUECJ Avis-1/15_OC (26 July 2017), para 125.
126. *Puskar (Charter of Fundamental Rights of the European Union - Processing of personal data* (Judgment) (Case C–73/16) (27 September 2017), para 34.

provisions introduced on foot of Convention 108. As the Recitals to the GDPR explain, it was therefore necessary to extend EU data protection law to such systems:

> In order to prevent creating a serious risk of circumvention, the protection of natural persons should be technologically neutral and should not depend on the techniques used. The protection of natural persons should apply to the processing of personal data by automated means, as well as to manual processing, if the personal data are contained or are intended to be contained in a filing system. Files or sets of files, as well as their cover pages, which are not structured according to specific criteria should not fall within the scope of this Regulation.[127]

The GDPR defines 'filing system' as meaning:

> ... any structured set of personal data which are accessible according to specific criteria, whether centralised, decentralised or dispersed on a functional or geographical basis.[128]

This would encompass files held in a filing cabinet, which are filed in order of subject's surname, address, identification or in some similar structure.

Controller

[4.21] The GDPR defines 'controller' as meaning:

> ... the natural or legal person, public authority, agency or other body[129] which, alone or jointly with others, determines the purposes and means of the processing of personal data; where the purposes and means of such processing are determined by Union or Member State law, the controller or the specific criteria for its nomination may be provided for by Union or Member State law.[130]

This definition is essentially the same as that which appeared in Directive 95/46. That definition was considered by the CJEU on a number of occasions. In *Google Spain* the respondent's search engine (Google) explored:

> ... the internet automatically, constantly and systematically in search of the information which is published there, the operator of a search engine 'collects' such data which it subsequently 'retrieves', 'records' and 'organises' within the framework of its indexing programmes, 'stores' on its servers and, as the case may be, 'discloses' and 'makes available' to its users in the form of lists of search results.[131]

---

127. GDPR, Recital 15.
128. GDPR, article 4(6). The definition is unchanged from Directive 95/46, the only change being that the American spelling of centralised and decentralised has been dropped.
129. The only significant change between this and the original definition to be found in Directive 95/46 is the elimination of the work 'any' from the reference to other body. This may have the effect of making the definition somewhat more focused.
130. GDPR, article 4(7).
131. *Costeja Gonzalez v Google Spain and Google* (Case C–131/12), para 28.

The key question was 'who was the controller of the data processed by that search engine?'. The CJEU held that it was:

> ... the search engine operator which determines the purposes and means of that activity and thus of the processing of personal data that it itself carries out within the framework of that activity and which must, consequently, be regarded as the 'controller' in respect of that processing.[132]

[4.22] In *Manni* the CJEU held that a public body which maintained a register was the controller of personal data where it was responsible for '...transcribing and keeping that information in the register and communicating it, where appropriate, on request to third parties ...'.[133] In *Worten* the CJEU held that an employer was the controller of its employees' data.[134] The definition of controller was considered by the Article 29 WP, which considered that it contained 'three main building blocks':

- 'the natural or legal person, public authority, agency or any other body';
- 'which alone or jointly with others';
- 'determines the purposes and means of the processing of personal data'.[135]

The Article 29 WP considered that the concept of controller was a factual one 'in the sense that it is intended to allocate responsibilities where the factual influence is' and the Working Party thought that the power to determine 'the purposes and means of the processing of personal data' was key to deciding who was or was not a data controller. It went on to conclude that 'a body which has neither legal nor factual influence to determine how personal data are processed cannot be considered as a controller.' Such influence might have a variety of bases, including:

> an explicit legal competence, when the law appoints the controller or confers a task or duty to collect and process certain data; common legal provisions or existing traditional roles that normally imply a certain responsibility within certain organisations (for example, the employer in relation to data of its employees); [or] factual circumstances and other elements (such as contractual relations, actual control by a party, visibility towards data subjects, etc).

[4.23] The GDPR anticipates that data may be jointly controlled, providing that:

> Where two or more controllers jointly determine the purposes and means of processing, they shall be joint controllers.

Such joint controllers must '... in a transparent manner determine their respective responsibilities for compliance with the obligations under ...' the GDPR. This must be

---

132. *Costeja Gonzalez v Google Spain and Google* (Case C–131/12) (13 May 2014), para 33.
133. *Manni* (Approximation of laws Approximation of laws Data protection Freedom of establishment (Judgment) (Case C–398/15) (9 March 2017), para 35.
134. *Worten* (Case C–342/12) (30 May 2013), para 23.
135. Article 29 Working Party, *Opinion 1/2010 on the concepts of 'controller' and 'processor'*, 00264/10/EN WP 169, Brussels, (16 February 2010), p 7.

done '... by means of an arrangement between them ...'[136] which must '... duly reflect the respective roles and relationships of the joint controllers *vis-à-vis* the data subjects'[137] and be made available to data subjects.[138] The controller cannot use this arrangement to purport to limit the rights of those subjects as the GDPR goes on to provide that subjects may exercise their rights '... in respect of and against each of the controllers'.[139] By requiring that they define their relationship in this way the GDPR effectively forces controllers to define their own relationship. Thus the GDPR does not have to anticipate the great variety of relationships that may exist between different types of joint controllers. That definition is something that those joint controllers must themselves provide, whilst respecting the rights of data subjects.

Processor

[4.24] The term 'processor' is defined by the GDPR as meaning:

> ... a natural or legal person, public authority, agency or other body[140] which processes personal data on behalf of the controller.[141]

The Article 29 WP has suggested that there are 'two basic conditions for qualifying as processor', namely:

- 'being a separate legal entity with respect to the controller'; and
- 'processing personal data on his behalf'.

The Working Party was anxious to emphasize that the distinction between controller and processor was not hard-and-fast: 'the same entity may act at the same time as a controller for certain processing operations and as a processor for others'. The Working Party saw processors as performing functions delegated to them by the controller: 'a processor is called to implement the instructions given by the controller at least with regard to the purpose of the processing and the essential elements of the means'. The Working Party thought that a controller might retain a 'certain degree of discretion about how to best serve the controller's interests'.[142] However, if a processor went substantially beyond its instructions then it would become a joint-controller.

[4.25] In *Probst v mr nexnet*[143] the applicant had challenged the imposition of charges imposed by an internet access provider (ISP). The provider had then sold the debt to a

136. GDPR, article 26(1).
137. GDPR, article 26(2).
138. GDPR, article 26(3).
139. GDPR, article 26(3).
140. As with the definition of controller the reference to 'any' other body is eliminated here.
141. GDPR, article 4(8).
142. Article 29 Working Party, *Opinion 1/2010 on the concepts of 'controller' and 'processor'*, 00264/10/EN WP 169, Brussels, 16 February 2010, p 25.
143. *Probst v mr.nexnet* (Case C–119/12) (22 November 2012).

factoring company,[144] mr nexnet. The applicant argued that the ISP should not have transferred his personal data in this way. The provider argued that this was permitted by Directive 2002/58 as the transfer was under its authority. The CJEU considered this transfer in the context of the obligations of confidentiality and security applied to processors by articles 16 and 17 of Directive 95/46. The CJEU held that these:

> … set out the level of control that the controller must exercise over the processor which it appoints, that that processor acts only on the controller's instructions and that the controller ensures compliance with the measures agreed in order to protect personal data against any form of unlawful processing.[145]

The CJEU went on to conclude that the transfer of this data would be permitted where:

> … first, that it acts under the authority of the service provider as regards the processing of those data and, second, that that assignee confines itself to processing the traffic data necessary for the purposes of recovering the claims assigned.[146]

This suggests that in order to distinguish between a controller, joint controller or a processor it is necessary to have regard to the agreement between them. The obligations of confidentiality that controllers were required to impose upon processors by article 17 of Directive 95/46 have been expanded upon by GDPR, article 28. If there is a contract or other legal act in place, which contains provisions that fulfil the requirements of GDPR, article 28 then the relationship between two parties may be that of controller and processor. If the contract or other legal act does not fulfil those requirements, then this may be an 'arrangement' for the purposes of GDPR, article 26 and the parties will be joint controllers. If however no such contract, legal act or arrangement is in place then the parties will each be a controller in their own right.

[4.26] The GDPR does not attempt to define or describe the great variety of relationships that can exist between controller and processor. As with joint controllers the GDPR requires that such definition be provided by controllers and processors themselves. GDPR, article 28 requires that 'Processing by a processor shall be governed by a contract or other legal act …'.

This document must set out '…the subject-matter and duration of the processing, the nature and purpose of the processing, the type of personal data and categories of data subjects and the obligations and rights of the controller'.[147] In particular it must '… stipulate ... that the processor … processes the personal data only on documented instructions from the controller …'.[148]

---

144. 'Under the factoring contract nexnet bears the risk of debtor default' *Probst v mr.nexnet* (Case C–119/12) (22 November 2012), para 11.
145. *Probst v mr.nexnet* (Case C–119/12) (22 November 2012), para 25.
146. *Probst v mr.nexnet* (Case C–119/12) (22 November 2012), para 29.
147. GDPR, article 28(3).
148. GDPR, article 28(3)(a).

This would seem to be the key distinction between controllers and processors; the former must issue instructions to the latter. A processor that processes personal data without such instructions runs the risk of either becoming a controller or else breaching the GDPR. This distinction may become significant if subjects should seek compensation pursuant to GDPR, article 82, which provides that 'A processor shall be liable for the damage caused by processing ... where it has acted outside or contrary to lawful instructions of the controller'.[149]

Recipient

[4.27] 'Recipient' is defined as a meaning:

> ... natural or legal person, public authority, agency or another body, to which the personal data are disclosed, whether a third party or not.[150]

The GDPR identifies one exception to this definition: public authorities that receive personal data in the framework of a particular inquiry in accordance with Union or Member State law. The GDPR goes on to provide that: '... the processing of those data by those public authorities shall be in compliance with the applicable data protection rules according to the purposes of the processing'.[151] The Recitals expand upon the bodies that benefit from this:

> Public authorities to which personal data are disclosed in accordance with a legal obligation for the exercise of their official mission, such as tax and customs authorities, financial investigation units, independent administrative authorities, or financial market authorities responsible for the regulation and supervision of securities markets should not be regarded as recipients if they receive personal data which are necessary to carry out a particular inquiry in the general interest, in accordance with Union or Member State law.

They go on to describe how those bodies may benefit from this exclusion:

> The requests for disclosure sent by the public authorities should always be in writing, reasoned and occasional and should not concern the entirety of a filing system or lead to the interconnection of filing systems. The processing of personal data by those public authorities should comply with the applicable data-protection rules according to the purposes of the processing.[152]

Consent

[4.28] The GDPR defines 'consent of the data subject' as meaning:

> ... any freely given, specific, informed and unambiguous indication of the data subject's wishes by which he or she, by a statement or by a clear affirmative

---

149. GDPR, article 82(2).
150. GDPR, article 4(9).
151. GDPR, article 4(9).
152. GDPR, Recital 31.

action, signifies agreement to the processing of personal data relating to him or her.[153]

Restriction of processing

[4.29] The restriction of processing is defined as meaning: '… the marking of stored personal data with the aim of limiting their processing in the future'.[154] The Recitals go on to provide that:

> In automated filing systems, the restriction of processing should in principle be ensured by technical means in such a manner that the personal data are not subject to further processing operations and cannot be changed.[155]

Profiling

[4.30] One of the GDPR's most interesting innovations is the explicit restrictions it places upon the profiling of subjects.[156] 'Profiling' is defined as:

> … any form of automated processing of personal data consisting of the use of personal data to evaluate certain personal aspects relating to a natural person, in particular to analyse or predict aspects concerning that natural person's performance at work, economic situation, health, personal preferences, interests, reliability, behaviour, location or movements.

Third party

[4.31] The GDPR defines 'third party' as meaning:

> … a natural or legal person, public authority, agency or body other than the data subject, controller, processor and persons who, under the direct authority of the controller or processor, are authorised to process personal data.[157]

Personal data breach

[4.32] The GDPR defines 'personal data breach' as meaning:

> …a breach of security leading to the accidental or unlawful destruction, loss, alteration, unauthorised disclosure of, or access to, personal data transmitted, stored or otherwise processed.[158]

---

153. GDPR, article 4(11).
154. GDPR, article 4(3).
155. GDPR, Recital 67.
156. GDPR, article 21.
157. GDPR, article 4(10).
158. GDPR, article 4(12).

Genetic data

[4.33] The GDPR defines 'genetic data' as meaning:

> ... personal data relating to the inherited or acquired genetic characteristics of a natural person which give unique information about the physiology or the health of that natural person and which result, in particular, from an analysis of a biological sample from the natural person in question.[159]

Biometric data

[4.34] The GDPR defines 'biometric data' as meaning:

> ... personal data resulting from specific technical processing relating to the physical, physiological or behavioural characteristics of a natural person, which allow or confirm the unique identification of that natural person, such as facial images or dactyloscopic data.[160]

Data concerning health

[4.35] The GDPR defines 'data concerning health' as meaning:

> ... personal data related to the physical or mental health of a natural person, including the provision of health care services, which reveal information about his or her health status.[161]

Main establishment

[4.36] The GDPR defines 'main establishment' as meaning:

(a) 'as regards a controller with establishments in more than one Member State, the place of its central administration in the Union, unless the decisions on the purposes and means of the processing of personal data are taken in another establishment of the controller in the Union and the latter establishment has the power to have such decisions implemented, in which case the establishment having taken such decisions is to be considered to be the main establishment';

(b) 'as regards a processor with establishments in more than one Member State, the place of its central administration in the Union, or, if the processor has no central administration in the Union, the establishment of the processor in the Union where the main processing activities in the context of the activities of an establishment of the processor take place to the extent that the processor is subject to specific obligations under this Regulation.'[162]

---

159. GDPR, article 4(13).
160. GDPR, article 4(14).
161. GDPR, article 4(15).
162. GDPR, article 4(16).

Representative

[4.37] The GDPR defines 'representative' as meaning:

> ... a natural or legal person established in the Union who, designated by the controller or processor in writing pursuant to Article 27, represents the controller or processor with regard to their respective obligations under this Regulation.[163]

Enterprise

[4.38] The GDPR defines 'enterprise' as meaning:

> a natural or legal person engaged in an economic activity, irrespective of its legal form, including partnerships or associations regularly engaged in an economic activity.[164]

Group of undertakings

[4.39] The GDPR defines a 'group of undertakings' as meaning 'a controlling undertaking and its controlled undertakings'.[165]

Binding corporate rules

[4.40] The GDPR defines 'binding corporate rules' as meaning:

> personal data protection policies which are adhered to by a controller or processor established on the territory of a Member State for transfers or a set of transfers of personal data to a controller or processor in one or more third countries within a group of undertakings, or group of enterprises engaged in a joint economic activity.[166]

Supervisory authority

[4.41] The GDPR defines 'supervisory authority' as meaning 'an independent public authority which is established by a Member State pursuant to Article 51'.[167]

---

163. GDPR, article 4(17).
164. GDPR, article 4(18).
165. GDPR, article 4(19).
166. GDPR, article 4(20).
167. GDPR, article 4(21).

Supervisory authority concerned

[4.42] The GDPR defines 'supervisory authority concerned' as meaning:

'a supervisory authority which is concerned by the processing of personal data because:

(a) 'the controller or processor is established on the territory of the Member State of that supervisory authority;

(b) 'data subjects residing in the Member State of that supervisory authority are substantially affected or likely to be substantially affected by the processing; or

(c) 'a complaint has been lodged with that supervisory authority'.[168]

Cross-border processing

[4.43] The GDPR defines 'cross-border processing' as meaning either:

(a) 'processing of personal data which takes place in the context of the activities of establishments in more than one Member State of a controller or processor in the Union where the controller or processor is established in more than one Member State; or

(b) 'processing of personal data which takes place in the context of the activities of a single establishment of a controller or processor in the Union but which substantially affects or is likely to substantially affect data subjects in more than one Member State.'[169]

Relevant and reasoned objection

[4.44] The GDPR defines 'relevant and reasoned objection' as meaning:

an objection to a draft decision as to whether there is an infringement of this Regulation, or whether envisaged action in relation to the controller or processor complies with this Regulation, which clearly demonstrates the significance of the risks posed by the draft decision as regards the fundamental rights and freedoms of data subjects and, where applicable, the free flow of personal data within the Union.[170]

---

168. GDPR, article 4(22).
169. GDPR, article 4(23).
170. GDPR, article 4(24).

Information society service

[4.45] The GDPR[171] effectively defines 'information society service' as 'any service normally provided for remuneration, at a distance,[172] by electronic means[173] and at the individual request of a recipient of service'.[174] This would not cover services such as 'consultation of an electronic catalogue in a shop with the customer on site'; 'automatic cash or ticket dispensing machines' for banknotes or rail tickets; or radio and television broadcasts.[175]

International organisation

[4.46] The GDPR defines 'international organisation' as meaning:

> an organisation and its subordinate bodies governed by public international law, or any other body which is set up by, or on the basis of, an agreement between two or more countries.[176]

---

171. GDPR, article 4(25) cross references to point (b) of article 1(1) of Directive 2015/1535/EU of 9 September 2015 laying down a procedure for the provision of information in the field of technical regulations and rules relating to information society services, OJ L 241, 17 September 2015.

172. Point (b)(i) of article 1(1) of Directive 2015/1535/EU defines 'at a distance' as meaning '… that the service is provided without the parties being simultaneously present'.

173. Point (b)(ii) of article 1(1) of Directive 2015/1535/EU defines 'by electronic means' as meaning that 'the service is sent initially and received at its destination by means of electronic equipment for the processing (including digital compression) and storage of data, and entirely transmitted, conveyed and received by wire, by radio, by optical means or by other electromagnetic means'.

174. Point (b)(iii) of art1(1) of Directive 2015/1535/EU defines 'at the individual request of a recipient of services' as meaning that the service is provided through the transmission of data on individual request.

175. Directive 2015/1535/EU, Sch 1.

176. GDPR, article 4(26).

Chapter 5

TERRITORIAL SCOPE OF THE GDPR AND TRANSFERS OUTSIDE THE EU

INTRODUCTION

[5.01] Privacy and data protection laws exist outside the EU that have objectives not dissimilar to those of the EU. A good example of this being the Council of Europe's Strasbourg Convention 108,[1] which has now been ratified or acceded to by some 50 countries including those of the EEA[2] (at one point it was even mooted that the USA might join).[3] The US legal system actively protects the privacy rights of its citizens,[4] on occasion awarding extraordinary sums of damages to some who have suffered intrusions upon their privacy.[5] However, these protections cannot really be compared to those provided by EU law. The Strasbourg Convention 108 may have provided the foundation upon which EU data protection laws have been built, but its protections have long been surpassed by those provided by the EU. American law may provide some with rigorous privacy protections, but often only to those willing or able to finance the expensive court-room battle that may be required to vindicate those rights.[6] And these protections may only be available to US citizens, non-US citizens may not benefit.[7]

Accordingly, whilst many non-EEA countries may have data privacy laws, few can really be compared to those provided by the EU. We know this to be so because the EU Commission actively examines the data privacy regimes of non-EEA jurisdictions to assess whether they are adequate by EU standards. To date it has only found 11 such 'third countries' have adequate protections together with its controversial Privacy Shield arrangements with the USA. Obtaining such a decision requires that the third country in question convince the EU Commission that its data privacy laws, supervisory structures and international obligations are essentially equivalent to those of the EU. Even then not

---

1. Council of Europe, Convention for the Protection of Individuals with regard to Automatic Processing of Personal Data, ETS No108, Strasbourg, 28 January 1981.
2. https://www.coe.int/en/web/conventions/full-list/-/conventions/treaty/108/signatures?p_auth=Le39t5fc.
3. https://epic.org/privacy/intl/coeconvention/.
4. For example, the US Privacy Act of 1974 'governs the protection of personally identifiable information ('PII'). It regulates how Executive Branch agencies and departments collect, store, use, and give out PII ...' https://www.consumerfinance.gov/privacy/privacy-policy-non-us-citizens/.
5. Madigan, Somaiya, 'Hulk Hogan Awarded $115 Million in Privacy Suit Against Gawker', (2016) *New York Times*, 18 March.
6. Mac, Drange, 'This Silicon Valley Billionaire Has Been Secretly Funding Hulk Hogan's Lawsuits Against Gawker', (2016) *Forbes*, 24 May.
7. 'The [US] Privacy Act does not apply to non-U.S. citizens who are not Legal Permanent Residents ...' https://www.consumerfinance.gov/privacy/privacy-policy-non-us-citizens/.

everyone may be convinced by such an assessment. In November 2017 the Article 29 WP issued a statement on Privacy Shield, which indicated that it had:

> ... identified a number of significant concerns that need to be addressed by both the Commission and the U.S. authorities. Therefore the WP29 calls upon the Commission and the U.S. competent authorities to restart discussions. An action plan has to be set up immediately in order to demonstrate that all these concerns will be addressed. In particular the appointment of an independent Ombudsperson should be prioritized and the rules of procedure be further explained including by declassification ... Those prioritized concerns need to be resolved by 25 May 2018.[8]

Not every third country will want to alter its domestic and international arrangements to meet the demands of the EU Commission, but there is a significant incentive for those that do. Once a country has an adequacy ruling then data may be transferred to it freely, without '... any specific authorisation'. Even if a third country is willing to amend its data protection laws to ensure that they are adequate from an EU perspective this will not necessarily guarantee entirely free flows of personal data from the EU. The CJEU has repeatedly held that transfers of sensitive personal data outside the EU are prohibited.[9] *Tele2 Sverige* was a challenge to a Swedish data retention law; the CJEU held that:

> Given the quantity of retained data, the sensitivity of that data and the risk of unlawful access to it... national legislation must make provision for the data to be retained within the European Union.[10]

Although the EU cannot commit to allow data freely flow outside its borders it does want to enhance global privacy and data protection laws. The GDPR asks that the Commission and Supervisory Authorities enhance data privacy laws globally. For as its Recitals warn, once:

> ... personal data moves across borders outside the Union it may put at increased risk the ability of natural persons to exercise data protection rights ... supervisory authorities may find that they are unable to pursue complaints or conduct investigations ...

And so, article 50 GDPR requires that the EU Commission and EU Data Protection Supervisory Authorities take 'appropriate steps' to ensure co-operation with other countries and:

> (a) develop international cooperation mechanisms to facilitate the effective enforcement of legislation for the protection of personal data;
>
> (b) provide international mutual assistance in the enforcement of legislation for the protection of personal data, including through notification, complaint

---

8. Article 29 WP, *First annual Joint Review of the Privacy Shield*, Press Release, November 2017.

9. In *Opinion 1/15* it held that: '... Articles 7, 8 and 21 and Article 52(1) of the Charter preclude ... the transfer of sensitive data to Canada ...' (para 167)

10. *Tele2 Sverige* (Case C–203/15) (21 December 2016), para 122.

referral, investigative assistance and information exchange, subject to
appropriate safeguards for the protection of personal data and other
fundamental rights and freedoms;

(c) engage relevant stakeholders in discussion and activities aimed at furthering
international cooperation in the enforcement of legislation for the protection
of personal data;

(d) promote the exchange and documentation of personal data protection
legislation and practice, including on jurisdictional conflicts with third
countries.

[5.02] As the Recitals explain, this is to enable the EU Commission and the DPSAs to
'... exchange information and cooperate ... with competent authorities in third
countries, based on reciprocity and in accordance with this Regulation'. As the EU
Commission has said:

> Greater compatibility between different data protection systems would facilitate
> international flows of personal data, whether for commercial purposes or
> cooperation between public authorities (eg law enforcement). The EU should seize
> this opportunity to promote its data protection values and facilitate data flows by
> encouraging convergence of legal systems.[11]

The EU Commission promises to '... strive to seek greater upward convergence of data
protection principles internationally ...'.[12] There are big advantages for the EU if it can
establish its data protection rules in general and the GDPR in particular as the global
standard for data privacy. The EU witnessed such advantages in the past, such as the
adoption of GSM as a global standard for mobile phones.[13] The EU sees its role as
making globalisation a 'convergence to the top' rather than a 'race to the bottom' for
data privacy.[14]

However, the EU is not alone in seeking the global application of its laws.[15] In the

---

11. EU Commission, *Exchanging and Protecting Personal Data in a Globalised World*,
Brussels, 10 January 2017, COM(2017) 7 final, p 2.

12. EU Commission, *Exchanging and Protecting Personal Data in a Globalised World,*
Brussels, 10 January 2017, COM(2017) 7 final, p 16.

13. Commission Staff Working Document, *The External Dimension Of The Single Market
Review,* Brussels, SEC(2007) 1519, 20 November, 2007.

14. Commission Staff Working Document, *The External Dimension Of The Single Market
Review,* Brussels, SEC(2007) 1519, 20 November, 2007, p 7.

15. See in particular, the US Foreign Account Tax Compliance Act (FATCA) (HR 3933), which
now comprises Chapter 4 of the US Internal Revenue Code. FATCA has led to the creation
of a regime for the international sharing of tax information. Initially FATCA required that
financial institutions outside the USA report information about financial accounts held by
their institutions by US taxpayers or by foreign entities in which US taxpayers hold a
substantial ownership interest. But once the FATCA model was established, others began to
follow suit. France, Germany, Italy, Spain and the UK announced their intention to
exchange FATCA-type information amongst themselves; other countries quickly joined this
initiative. (contd .../)

US case of *Microsoft v US Department of Justice*[16] the American authorities sought to direct that the applicant provide it with copies of e-mails that were stored on a server within the EU.[17] In an effort to protect personal data within the EU from orders such as this the GDPR provides that:

> Any judgment of a court or tribunal and any decision of an administrative authority of a third country requiring a controller or processor to transfer or disclose personal data may only be recognised or enforceable in any manner if based on an international agreement, such as a mutual legal assistance treaty, in force between the requesting third country and the Union or a Member State ...[18]

JURISDICTION OF THE GDPR

[5.03] The GDPR takes a bifurcated approach to jurisdiction. On the one hand, Article 3 GDPR asserts a global jurisdiction for EU data protection law. On the other, Chapter V GDPR sets out a variety of mechanisms to control the transfer of data outside the EU. The former article's assertion of a global jurisdiction should, in theory, be all that is required; from a theoretical perspective one might say that the latter just adds a layer of pointless complexity. But in practice the assertion of a a global jurisdiction for EU data protection may prove problematic. And so the EU has no option but to retain the latter mechanisms, cumbersome as they may be.

---

15.   (contd) Now there is a global standard (the OECD in its Automatic Exchange of Financial Account Information, Background Information Brief, 29 October 2014) and amendments are being made to the EU's Savings Tax Directive (Council Directive 2014/48/EU of 24 March 2014 amending Directive 2003/48/EC on taxation of savings income in the form of interest payments, [2014] OJ L 111/50–78) and the Administrative Cooperation Directive (Implementing Regulation (1156/2012) of 6 December 2012 laying down detailed rules for implementing certain provisions of Council Directive 2011/16/EU on administrative cooperation in the field of taxation [2012] OJ L 335/42.) The Article 29 WP issued a 'Statement on automatic inter-state exchanges of personal data for tax purposes' in which it stated the following principles: The automatic exchange of personal data for tax purposes should meet data protection requirements, namely the principles of purpose limitation and necessity; Member States that roll out the model of automatic massive storage and then forward this data for tax purposes, should be aware that they may incur increased (security) risks and liability under EU data protection laws; and, confirmed its approach on providing additional guidance to increase data protection safeguards in this area, 4 February 2015, WP230.

16.   *Microsoft Corp v United States*, No 14-2985 (2d Cir 2017).

17.   This direction was issued in the USA under US law, but was successfully challenged by the applicant before the US courts: *US court refuses to reconsider decision in Microsoft email case*, Irish Times, 25 January 2017. That refusal is now under appeal to the US Supreme Court: Edwards, 'US Supreme Court to hear appeal in Microsoft warrant case', (2017) *Irish Times*, 16 October.

18.   GDPR, article 48.

Article 3: Territorial Scope

[5.04] Article 3 GDPR asserts a global role for the GDPR, stating that it:

> ... applies to the processing of personal data in the context of the activities of an establishment of a controller or a processor in the Union, regardless of whether the processing takes place in the Union or not.[19]

This approach is consistent with that previously adopted by the CJEU in *Google Spain*,[20] which was a challenge brought by a Spaniard to the processing of his personal data by Google's search engine. Google Spain was engaged only in the 'promotion and sale of advertising space', the actual processing of personal data was undertaken by Google Search in the USA. However, the fact that Google Spain was established in the EU was sufficient to ensure that EU data protection law applied to it. The GDPR explanation for what is meant by 'establishment' is as follows:

> Establishment implies the effective and real exercise of activity through stable arrangements. The legal form of such arrangements, whether through a branch or a subsidiary with a legal personality, is not the determining factor in that respect.[21]

[5.05] The question of whether or not a controller or processor is established within the EU at all must be distinguished from that of which precise Member State that controller or processor may have its main establishment in. *Google Spain* suggests that the threshold for being established in the EU is very low. Google Spain has a 'separate legal personality'[22] from Google Inc, on behalf of which it sold advertising space. The CJEU held that this was sufficient to establish Google in the EU as:

> ... the activities of the operator of the search engine and those of its establishment situated in the Member State concerned are inextricably linked since the activities relating to the advertising space constitute the means of rendering the search engine at issue economically profitable and that engine is, at the same time, the means enabling those activities to be performed.[23]

The CJEU did not enquire into the nature of Google Spain's establishment within the EU, whether or not it had a bank account, a postal address or engaged in litigation. Any

---

19.   GDPR, article 3.1. This remedies a key defect in Directive 95/46, identified in *Lindqvist v Sweden* (Case C–101/01) (6 November 2003) in which the CJEU concluded that it could not be presumed that 'Community legislature intended the expression transfer [of data] to a third country to cover the loading, by an individual in Mrs Lindqvist's position, of data onto an internet page, even if those data are thereby made accessible to persons in third countries with the technical means to access them' at para 68.

20.   *Costeja Gonzalez v Google Spain and Google* (Judgment of the Court) (Case C–131/12) (13 May 2014).

21.   GDPR, Recital 22.

22.   *Costeja Gonzalez v Google Spain and Google* (Judgment of the Court) (Case C–131/12) (13 May 2014), para 49.

23.   *Costeja Gonzalez v Google Spain and Google* (Judgment of the Court) (Case C–131/12) (13 May 2014), para 56.

activity seems to have been sufficient to establish Google within the EU and so subject it to EU data protection laws. In contrast in *Weltimmo*[24] the CJEU considered that a wide variety of factors had to be taken into account when deciding in which precise Member State of the EU a controller's main establishment would be.

[5.06] The GDPR may also apply '... to the processing of personal data of data subjects who are in the Union by a controller or processor not established in the Union'. This will occur where the processing in question is related to:

(a) the offering of goods or services, irrespective of whether a payment of the data subject is required, to such data subjects in the Union; or

(b) the monitoring of their behaviour as far as their behaviour takes place within the Union.

So even if Google were to dispense with the services of Google Spain it would still be subject to the GDPR as it is '... offering ... goods or services, irrespective of whether a payment of the data subject is required, to ... data subjects in the Union ...'. There is no requirement that such goods or services be sold to the subjects in question, only that they be 'offered' to subjects within the EU. Similarly, it is sufficient that a controller or processor outside the EU monitor the behaviour of subjects within the Union, regardless of whether the controller or processor in question interacts with any data subjects within the EU.[25]

[5.07] Article 27 GDPR provides that where it applies: '... the controller or the processor shall designate in writing a representative[26] in the Union'.

---

24. *Weltimmo* (Case C–230/14) (1 October 2015).

25. Article 3(4) GDPR provides that it applies '... to the processing of personal data by a controller not established in the Union, but in a place where Member State law applies by virtue of public international law'. This is similar in effect to article 4(1)(g) of Directive 95/46 which was considered by the article 29 WP in its Opinion 8/2010 on applicable law, 0836-02/10/EN WP 179, 16 December 2010. The article 29 WP's opinion was that this meant that 'External criteria stemming from international public law will determine in specific situations the extension of the application of a national data protection law beyond the national boundaries, as for example in the case of embassies or ships' (p 30). However, the article 29 WP thought it important to '... highlight that national data protection law may not apply to foreign missions or international organisations on EU territory to the extent in which they have a special status under international law, either in general or via a headquarter agreement ...'. So an '... EU Member State's embassy in Canada is subject to the national data protection law of that Member State, and not to the Canadian data protection law ...'. In contrast 'Any country's embassy in the Netherlands is not subject to the Dutch data protection law as any embassy has a special status under international law' (p 18).

26. The term 'representative' is defined as meaning '... a natural or legal person established in the Union who, designated by the controller or processor in writing pursuant to Article 27, represents the controller or processor with regard to their respective obligations under this Regulation' GDPR, article 4(17).

This obligation does not apply to '... processing which is occasional, does not include, on a large scale, processing of special categories of data ... or processing of personal data relating to criminal convictions and offences ... and is unlikely to result in a risk to the rights and freedoms of natural persons, taking into account the nature, context, scope and purposes of the processing'. Nor does it apply to 'a public authority or body'.[27]

[5.08] A controller or processor that is subject to Article 27 GDPR cannot establish their representative in any Member State of the EU but must establish that representative '... in one of the Member States where the data subjects, whose personal data are processed in relation to the offering of goods or services to them, or whose behaviour is monitored, are'.[28] That representative must be:

> ... mandated by the controller or processor to be addressed in addition to or instead of the controller or the processor by, in particular, supervisory authorities and data subjects, on all issues related to processing, for the purposes of ensuring compliance with this Regulation.[29]

Given that such representatives may be established by controllers or processors that have no substantive operations within the EU it may well be that those controllers or processors will have no substantive assets that an EU Court or SA could easily attach. Hence there is a risk that any action taken against such a controller or processor in a jurisdiction where they may have assets will be met with the argument that this is a claim that must be addressed to the controller or processor's representative within the EU. The GDPR addresses this risk by providing that:

> The designation of a representative by the controller or processor shall be without prejudice to legal actions which could be initiated against the controller or the processor themselves.[30]

Subjects have a right to be informed of the identity of the controller or processor's representative.[31] The representative must also '... maintain a record of processing activities under its responsibility'.[32] This presumably does not mean records of the processing activities undertaken by the controller or processor outside the EEA, since the representative is not responsible for these (if it were then it would be a controller or processor itself). They must also '... maintain a record of all categories of processing activities carried out on behalf of a controller ...'.[33] They must make these records

---

27. GDPR, article 27(2). Such an exclusion may seem at odds with the serious concerns expressed by the CJEU about the processing of EU personal data by the US authorities, but it would be contrary to public international law for the GDPR to require non-EU States to establish representation within the EU.
28. GDPR, article 27(3).
29. GDPR, article 27(4).
30. GDPR, article 27(5).
31. GDPR, articles 13(1)(a), 14(1)(a).
32. GDPR, article 30(1).
33. GDPR, article 30(2).

available to the relevant SA upon request[34] and must '... cooperate, on request, with the supervisory authority in the performance of its tasks'.[35] Finally, the SA will have the power to: '... order ... the controller's or the processor's representative to provide any information it requires for the performance of its tasks'.[36]

However, the GDPR does not provide any other powers that may be used to enforce its provisions against controllers or processors outside the EEA. Although the GDPR asserts a global jurisdiction it does not specify an effective mechanism by which such powers may be enforced. Of course, this does not preclude the possibility that the EU Commission or SAs will identify such mechanism, which might perhaps be provided through co-operation and reciprocity with supervisory authorities outside the EEA. But for now, the EU has been unable to dispense with the broad prohibition upon transfers of personal data outside the EEA which is set out in GDPR, Ch V.

Chapter V, Transfers of personal data to third countries or international organisations

[5.09] The GDPR Recitals express a positive view of transfers of personal data outside the EEA:

> Flows of personal data to and from countries outside the Union and international organisations[37] are necessary for the expansion of international trade and international cooperation.[38]

Similarly, the EU Commission has expressed its view that '... the EU should proactively engage with third countries on this matter'. As:

> A strong data protection system facilitates data flows by building consumer confidence in those companies that care about the way they handle their customers' personal data. High data protection standards thus become an advantage in the global digital economy.[39]

However, the EU's support for international flows of personal data is far from unambiguous. As the GDPR's Recitals explain:

> The increase in such flows has raised new challenges and concerns with regard to the protection of personal data ... when personal data are transferred from the Union to controllers, processors or other recipients in third countries or to

---

34. GDPR, article 30(4).
35. GDPR, article 31.
36. GDPR, article 58(1)(a).
37. International organisations are defined by GDPR, article 4(26) as '... an organisation and its subordinate bodies governed by public international law, or any other body which is set up by, or on the basis of, an agreement between two or more countries'.
38. GDPR, Recital 101.
39. EU Commission, *Exchanging and Protecting Personal Data in a Globalised World*, Brussels, 10 January 2017, COM(2017) 7 final, p 16.

international organisations, the level of protection of natural persons ensured in the Union by this Regulation should not be undermined ...[40]

And so, GDPR, article 44 provides:

Any transfer of personal data which are undergoing processing or are intended for processing after transfer to a third country or to an international organisation shall take place only if, subject to the other provisions of this Regulation, the conditions laid down in this Chapter are complied with by the controller and processor, including for onward transfers... All provisions in this Chapter shall be applied in order to ensure that the level of protection of natural persons guaranteed by this Regulation is not undermined.

[5.10] This is a rather convoluted way of saying that it is not permissible to transfer personal data outside the EEA unless one of the conditions for transfer set out in GDPR, Ch V are complied with. A variety of such conditions are provided by the GDPR, these are considered in detail below, but they may be grouped as transfers that are subject to:

1.   adequacy decisions;

2.   appropriate safeguards; or

3.   specific derogations.

Chapter V suggests that this is not a list but rather a hierarchy with adequacy decisions at the top and derogations at the bottom. Article 46 specifies that its appropriate safeguards may be relied upon in the absence of an adequacy decision, whilst GDPR, article 49 specifies that its derogations may be relied upon in the absence of an adequacy decision or appropriate safeguards. However, the Recitals suggest that controllers and processors may have some discretion as it suggests that if the Commission has not issued an adequacy decision then:

... the controller or processor should make use of solutions that provide data subjects with enforceable and effective rights as regards the processing of their data in the Union once those data have been transferred so that that they will continue to benefit from fundamental rights and safeguards.[41]

Article 49 seems to suggest that if a controller or processor cannot bring itself within one of the mechanisms set out in Ch V then the transfer may not take place. But there are a couple of other bases upon which data may be transferred outside the EU. One is that the GDPR has 'EEA relevance', which suggest that the GDPR may apply to countries within the European Economic Area (EEA) under the EEA agreement. This agreement created a single market consisting of the EU together with Iceland, Liechtenstein and Norway. Hence the GDPR should apply seamlessly to transfers between the 31 Member States of the EEA.[42] And the GDPR will not necessarily

---

40.   GDPR, Recital 101.
41.   GDPR, Recital 114.
42.   As of 1 November 2017 the GDPR was under scrutiny by EFTA with a view to it being incorporated into the EEA agreement and entered into force within the EEA. See: http://www.efta.int/eea-lex/32016R0679.

prejudice international agreements between the Union and third countries regulating the transfer of personal data, provided such agreements include appropriate safeguards for the data subjects. Member States may conclude international agreements which involve the transfer of personal data to third countries or international organisations, as far as such agreements do not affect this Regulation or any other provisions of Union law and include an appropriate level of protection for the fundamental rights of the data subjects.[43]

Adequacy decisions

[5.11] GDPR, article 45 provides for transfers of personal data outside the EEA in the following circumstances:

> A transfer of personal data to a third country or an international organisation may take place where the Commission has decided that the third country, a territory or one or more specified sectors within that third country, or the international organisation in question ensures an adequate level of protection. Such a transfer shall not require any specific authorisation.[44]

This confers a broad discretion upon the EU Commission to recognise the adequacy of different countries, sectors or international organisations. This discretion was considered by the CJEU in *Schrems,*[45] a successful challenge to the adequacy of the EU/ US Safe Harbour Agreement.[46] A complaint had been made to the Irish Supervisory Authority requesting that it prohibit '... Facebook Ireland from transferring his personal data to the United States'.[47] The Irish SA refused to entertain this complaint as '... the Commission had found ... that the United States ensured an adequate level of protection'.[48] The CJEU held that the Irish SA was correct in this regard as:

> ... until such time as the Commission decision is declared invalid by the Court, the Member States and their organs, which include their independent supervisory authorities ... cannot adopt measures contrary to that decision ... Measures of the EU institutions are in principle presumed to be lawful and accordingly produce legal effects until such time as they are withdrawn, annulled in an action for annulment or declared invalid following a reference for a preliminary ruling or a plea of illegality ...[49]

However, the issue of an EU Commission Adequacy Decision could neither prevent a complaint being lodged nor the investigation of that complaint by that SA, which

---

43.   GDPR, Recital 102.
44.   GDPR, article 45(1).
45.   *Schrems* (Case C–362/14) (6 October 2015).
46.   Commission Decision 2000/520/EC pursuant to Directive 95/46 on the adequacy of the protection provided by the safe harbour privacy principles and related frequently asked questions issued by the US Department of Commerce. OJ 2000 L 215, p 7.
47.   *Schrems* (Case C–362/14) (6 October 2015), para 28.
48.   *Schrems* (Case C–362/14) (6 October 2015), para 29.
49.   *Schrems* (Case C–362/14) (6 October 2015), para 52.

remained responsible for the oversight of transfers of personal data to third countries such as the USA. The CJEU held that a SA '… must be able to examine, with complete independence, whether the transfer of that data complies with the requirements laid down by the directive'.[50] The DPSA could just investigate the complaint;[51] but only the CJEU had the power to actually invalidate an EU Commission Adequacy Decision:

> … the Court alone has jurisdiction to declare … an EU act … invalid, the exclusivity of that jurisdiction having the purpose of guaranteeing legal certainty by ensuring that EU law is applied uniformly …[52]

The reference to the 'court' must be read as a reference to the CJEU itself; national courts do not have the power to invalidate an EU law nor do SAs themselves.[53] So if the SA should conclude that the claim made was unfounded the data subject must '… have access to judicial remedies enabling him to challenge such a decision adversely affecting him before the national courts' which would then consider whether to '… stay proceedings and make a reference to the Court for a preliminary ruling on validity …'. If the SA concluded that the complaint was well-founded then it might seek a reference to the CJEU itself.[54]

[5.12] The EU Commission might be assumed to have quite considerable discretion when deciding whether a third country's data protections are adequate. Such a decision is one that only the CJEU can find invalid; that can only happen once considerable time, money and effort have been expended getting a review of that decision before that Court. The procedure by which national courts interact with the CJEU will further limit that review, which will not be a full re-examination of the Commission decision but rather takes the form of responses to questions asked by the national court.[55] However the CJEU was clear in *Schrems* that the EU Commission has a quite limited discretion

---

50. 'If that were not so, persons whose personal data has been or could be transferred to the third country concerned would be denied the right, guaranteed by article 8(1) and (3) of the Charter, to lodge with the national supervisory authorities a claim for the purpose of protecting their fundamental rights…'. *Schrems* (Case C–362/14) (6 October 2015), paras 57–58, citing *Digital Rights Ireland* (Case C–293/12) (8 April 2014).

51. Though it was '… incumbent upon the national supervisory authority to examine the claim with all due diligence', *Schrems* (Case C–362/14) (6 October 2015), para 63.

52. *Schrems* (Case C–362/14) (6 October 2015), para 61, citing *Melki and Abdeli* (Cases C–188/10 and C–189/10), para 54, and *CIVAD* (Case C–533/10), para 4.

53. *Schrems* (Case C–362/14) (6 October 2015), para 62, citing *Foto-Frost* (Case 314/85), paras 15 to 20, and *IATA and ELFAA* (Case C–344/04), para 27.

54. *Schrems* (Case C–362/14) (6 October 2015), paras 64–65.

55. Such a challenge will typically come before the CJEU by way of a preliminary ruling (TFEU, article 267) though a challenge to the Privacy Shield Adequacy Decision (Commission Implementing Decision (EU) 2016/1250 pursuant to Directive 95/46/EC of the European Parliament and of the Council on the adequacy of the protection provided by the EU-US Privacy Shield, OJ L 207, 1.8.2016, p 1–112, has been taken pursuant to TFEU, article 263, see *Digital Rights Ireland v Commission* (Case T-670/16) OJ C 410 from 07.11.2016, p 26.

when making an adequacy decision. Under the GDPR these limitations are imposed by GDPR, article 45(2), which sets out three elements that the EU Commission must 'in particular' take into account when assessing the adequacy of a third state's data protections. In *Schrems* the CJEU held that the equivalent provisions in Directive 95/46 had to be strictly applied and that the EU Commission's discretion in making an Adequacy Decision was 'reduced'. It further stated that:

> ... the term 'adequate level of protection' must be understood as requiring the third country in fact to ensure, by reason of its domestic law or its international commitments, a level of protection of fundamental rights and freedoms that is essentially equivalent to that guaranteed within the European Union by virtue of Directive 95/46 read in the light of the Charter.[56]

This suggests that the list set out in GDPR, article 45(2) is no more than an outline; the adequacy of a third country or an international organisation's data protection must be assessed against the entire corpus of EU data protection law including, but not limited to, the GDPR. Indeed, the Recitals suggest that adequacy may be assessed against criteria that are not quite the same as those set out in GDPR, article 45(2):

> The third country should offer guarantees ensuring an adequate level of protection essentially equivalent to that ensured within the Union, in particular where personal data are processed in one or several specific sectors ... and the data subjects should be provided with effective and enforceable rights and effective administrative and judicial redress.[57]

The CJEU did not object to such an approach in *Avis 1/15* in which the Court held that although:

> '... the means intended to ensure such a level of protection may differ from those employed within the European Union in order to ensure that the requirements stemming from EU law are complied with, those means must nevertheless prove, in practice, effective in order to ensure protection essentially equivalent to that guaranteed within the European Union'.[58]

[5.13] The elements set out in GDPR, article 45(2) are as follows:

   (a)   the rule of law, respect for human rights and relevant legislation;

   (b)   the existence and effective functioning of independent supervisory authorities; and

   (c)   international commitments the third country or international organisation concerned has entered into.

As regards the first of the above the EU Commission must consider 'relevant legislation, both general and sectoral'. It must examine legislation 'concerning public security,

---

56.   *Schrems* (Case C–362/14) (6 October 2015), para 78.
57.   GDPR, Recital 104.
58.   *Transfer of Passenger Name Record data from the European Union to Canada* [2017] EUECJ Avis-1/15_OC (26 July 2017), para 134.

defence, national security and criminal law and the access of public authorities to personal data, as well as the implementation of such legislation'. This examination will presumably enable the EU Commission to assess how EU personal data may be processed by the third country concerned. Then it must consider the protections for personal data that the legislation of that country may provide.[59] This seems to amount to something of a balancing exercise; the powers provided by the former being balanced with the protections provided by the latter. In *Schrems* the CJEU held that the Safe Harbour Adequacy Decision[60] failed to set an appropriate balance. On the one hand that Decision permitted US authorities to interfere with EU personal data[61] but on the other hand it failed to provide any adequate data protection controls.[62] The CJEU went on to explain that for the laws of a third country to be adequate they would have to:

> ... lay down clear and precise rules governing the scope and application of a measure and imposing minimum safeguards, so that the persons whose personal data is concerned have sufficient guarantees enabling their data to be effectively protected against the risk of abuse and against any unlawful access and use of that data. The need for such safeguards is all the greater where personal data is subjected to automatic processing and where there is a significant risk of unlawful access to that data.[63]

In addition, EU data protection law required that '... derogations and limitations in relation to the protection of personal data ... apply only in so far as is strictly necessary'.[64]

---

59. '... data protection rules, professional rules and security measures, including rules for the onward transfer of personal data to another third country or international organisation which are complied with in that country or international organisation, case law, as well as effective and enforceable data subject rights and effective administrative and judicial redress for the data subjects whose personal data are being transferred ...' GDPR, article 45(2)(a).
60. Decision 2000/520/EC.
61. The Safe Harbour Adequacy Decision enabled: '... interference, founded on national security and public interest requirements or on domestic legislation of the United States, with the fundamental rights of the persons whose personal data is or could be transferred from the European Union to the United States' *Schrems* (Case C–362/14) (6 October 2015), para 87.
62. 'the Commission found that the United States authorities were able to access the personal data transferred ... and process it in a way incompatible, in particular, with the purposes for which it was transferred, beyond what was strictly necessary and proportionate to the protection of national security ... data subjects had no administrative or judicial means of redress enabling... the data relating to them to be accessed and, as the case may be, rectified or erased', *Schrems* (Case C–362/14) (6 October 2015), para 90.
63. Para 91 (Judgment in *Digital Rights Ireland* and Ord (Case C–293/12) and (Case C–594/12).
64. *Schrems* (Case C–362/14) (6 October 2015), paras 91–92. The CJEU went on to hold that 'Legislation is not limited to what is strictly necessary where it authorises, on a generalised basis, storage of all the personal data of all the persons whose data has been transferred from the European Union to the United States without any differentiation, (contd .../)

The case *Avis 1/15*[65] concerned an '... envisaged agreement between Canada and the European Union on the transfer and processing of Passenger Name Record data'.[66] The CJEU began its consideration by holding that the transfer of personal data to Canada and the onward transfer of that data to other authorities constituted interferences with the rights guaranteed by Articles 7 and 8 of the Charter.[67] The CJEU went onto hold that the right to data protection:

> ... requires ... that the high level of protection of fundamental rights and freedoms conferred by EU law continues where personal data is transferred from the European Union to a non-member country.

The CJEU went on to conclude that the agreement between Canada and the EU on the transfer of PNR data would have to fulfil the following criteria:

(a) The agreement would have to be clear and precise;

(b) The processing enabled by the agreement would have to be 'specific, reliable, non-discriminatory and limited';

(c) Any subsequent processing or disclosures of data after passengers arrived in Canada would have to be '... subject to substantive and procedural conditions based on objective criteria; make that use and that disclosure, except in cases of validly established urgency, subject to a prior review carried out either by a court or by an independent administrative body'.

(d) Data would only be retained in relation to passengers who had left Canada where there was '... objective evidence from which it may be inferred that they may present a risk in terms of the fight against terrorism and serious transnational crime'.

(e) Disclosures by the Canadian authorities to the authorities of other countries would be '... subject to the condition that there be either an equivalent agreement between the EU and that third country or else an adequacy decision of the European Commission'.

---

64. (contd) limitation or exception being made in the light of the objective pursued and without an objective criterion being laid down by which to determine the limits of the access of the public authorities to the data, and of its subsequent use, for purposes which are specific, strictly restricted and capable of justifying the interference which both access to that data and its use entail... legislation permitting the public authorities to have access on a generalised basis to the content of electronic communications must be regarded as compromising the essence of the fundamental right to respect for private life...' *Schrems* (Case C–362/14) (6 October 2015), para 93–94.

65. *Transfer of Passenger Name Record data from the European Union to Canada* [2017] EUECJ Avis-1/15_OC (26 July 2017).

66. *Transfer of Passenger Name Record data from the European Union to Canada* [2017] EUECJ Avis-1/15_OC (26 July 2017), para 1.

67. *Transfer of Passenger Name Record data from the European Union to Canada* [2017] EUECJ Avis-1/15_OC (26 July 2017), paras 125-126.

(f)   It mist provide for the notification of individuals if their data should be used or disclosed pursuant to the agreement.

(g)   It must guarantee that the oversight of the agreement be carried out by an independent supervisory authority.[68]

[5.14] One of the bases upon which the CJEU found the Safe Harbour Adequacy Decision invalid in *Schrems* was that it purported to limit the power of EU SAs.[69] The second element set out in GDPR, article 45(2) is the effectiveness of the supervisory authority in the third country or international organisation to which the EU personal data is to be sent. It is insufficient that such an authority exists; it also has to be 'effective'. In particular, it must have:

> … responsibility for ensuring and enforcing compliance with the data protection rules, including adequate enforcement powers, for assisting and advising the data subjects in exercising their rights and for cooperation with the supervisory authorities of the Member States …[70]

The third element is the international commitments which the third country or international organisation concerned has entered into. Such commitments or obligations may arise '… from legally binding conventions or instruments as well as from its participation in multilateral or regional systems, in particular in relation to the protection of personal data'.[71] One such convention would of course be the Council of Europe's Strasbourg Convention, 108.[72]

[5.15] The EU Commission must first assess the adequacy of data protection having regard to the above elements. It may then issue an Adequacy Decision, which may be issued in respect of '… a territory or one or more specified sectors within a third country, or an international organisation …'. This may be done by way of an implementing act, which must contain the following provisions:

- it must provide for its periodic review, at least every four years; [73]
- specify the Decisions '… territorial and sectoral application…'; and,
- '… identify the supervisory authority or authorities …' established by the third country or international organisation to which the data is being sent.[74]

---

68.   *Transfer of Passenger Name Record data from the European Union to Canada* [2017] EUECJ Avis-1/15_OC (26 July 2017), para 232.
69.   *Schrems* (Case C–362/14) (6 October 2015), paras 99–106.
70.   GDPR, article 45(2)(b).
71.   GDPR, article 45(2)(c).
72.   'In particular, the third country's accession to the Council of Europe Convention of 28 January 1981 for the Protection of Individuals with regard to the Automatic Processing of Personal Data and its Additional Protocol should be taken into account' GDPR, Recital 105.
73.   Such a review '… shall take into account all relevant developments in the third country or international organisation'.
74.   GDPR, article 45(3). The Adequacy Decision must be adopted by means of an implementing act in accordance with the procedure referred to at GDPR, article 93(2).

Once an Adequacy Decision is made the EU Commission must keep the third country or international organisation in respect of which it has been issued under review.[75] It must '… on an ongoing basis, monitor developments …'.[76] that could affect the functioning of the Adequacy Decisions it has made and those previously made pursuant to Directive 95/46, article 25(6). The EU Commission issued Adequacy Decisions under Directive 95/46 in respect of: Andorra,[77] Argentina,[78] Canada,[79] Faroe Islands,[80] Jersey,[81] Guernsey,[82] the Isle of Man,[83] Israel,[84] New Zealand,[85]

---

75.   GDPR, Recital 106 provides some further detail about this process 'For the purposes of monitoring and of carrying out the periodic reviews, the Commission should take into consideration the views and findings of the European Parliament and of the Council as well as of other relevant bodies and sources. The Commission should evaluate, within a reasonable time, the functioning of the latter decisions and report any relevant findings to the Committee … to the European Parliament and to the Council'.

76.   GDPR, article 45(4).

77.   Commission Decision of 19 October 2010 pursuant to Directive 95/46/EC of the European Parliament and of the Council on the adequate protection of personal data in Andorra [2010] OJ L 277/27–29.

78.   Commission Decision of 30 June 2003 pursuant to Directive 95/46/EC of the European Parliament and of the Council on the adequate protection of personal data in Argentina [2003] OJ L 168/19–22.

79.   Commission Decision of 20 December 2001 pursuant to Directive 95/46/EC of the European Parliament and of the Council on the adequate protection of personal data provided by the Canadian Personal Information Protection and Electronic Documents Act [2002] OJ L 2/13; see also EU Commission Staff Working Document: The application of Commission Decision 2002/2/EC of 20 December 2001 pursuant to Directive 95/46/EC of the European Parliament and of the Council on the adequate protection of personal data provided by the Canadian Personal Information Protection and Electronic Documentation Act.

80.   Commission Decision of 5 March 2010 pursuant to Directive 95/46/EC of the European Parliament and of the Council on the adequate protection provided by the Faeroese Act on processing of personal data [2001] OJ L 58/17–19.

81.   Commission Decision of 8 May 2008 pursuant to Directive 95/46/EC of the European Parliament and of the Council on the adequate protection of personal data in Jersey [2008] OJ L 138/21–23.

82.   Commission Decision of 21 November 2003 on the adequate protection of personal data in Guernsey [2003] OJ L 308/27.

83.   Commission Decision of 28 April 2004 on the adequate protection of personal data in the Isle of Man [2004] OJ L 151/48–51.

84.   Commission Decision of 31 January 2011 pursuant to Directive 95/46/EC of the European Parliament and of the Council on the adequate protection of personal data by the State of Israel with regard to automated processing of personal data [2011] OJ L 27/ 39–42.

85.   Commission Implementing Decision of 19 December 2012 pursuant to Directive 95/46/EC of the European Parliament and of the Council on the adequate protection of personal data by New Zealand [2013] OJ L 28/12–14.

Switzerland[86] and Uruguay.[87] These Adequacy Decisions remain in place after 25 May 2018.[88] Although given the very significant differences between Directive 95/46 and the GDPR they may well be subject to some form of review in early course.

[5.16] Article 46 GDPR goes on to provide for the revocation of Adequacy Decisions. Where '… available information reveals …' that a third country or international organisation '… no longer ensures an adequate level of protection …' then it shall '… to the extent necessary, repeal, amend or suspend the decision referred …'.[89] This revocation will not have retrospective (retro-active) effect.[90] If such a revocation decision is issued then the EU Commission shall enter into discussions with the third country or international organisation concerned with a view to remedying the situation that led to the revocation decision being made.[91] And if such a revocation decision is made this will be without prejudice to other transfer mechanisms such as consent or binding corporate rules.[92] Finally the EU Commission is required to publish lists of all those third countries, territories and specified sectors within a third country and international organisations in respect of which it has issued adequacy or revocation decisions.[93]

---

86. Commission Decision of 26 July 2000 pursuant to Directive 95/46/EC of the European Parliament and of the Council on the adequate protection of personal data provided in Switzerland [2000] OJ L 215/1; see also Commission Staff Working Document: The application of Commission Decision 2000/518/EC of 26 July 2000 pursuant to Directive 95/46/EC of the European Parliament and of the Council on the adequate protection of personal data provided in Switzerland.

87. Commission Implementing Decision of 21 August 2012 pursuant to Directive 95/46/EC of the European Parliament and of the Council on the adequate protection of personal data by the Eastern Republic of Uruguay with regard to automated processing of personal data [2012] OJ L 227/11–14.

88. 'Decisions adopted by the Commission on the basis of Article 25(6) of Directive 95/46/EC shall remain in force until amended, replaced or repealed by a Commission Decision adopted in accordance with para 3 or 5 of this Article.' GDPR, article 45(9) and Recital 171.

89. 'The Commission may also decide, having given notice and a full statement setting out the reasons to the third country or international organisation, to revoke such a decision' GDPR, Recital 103.

90. GDPR, article 45(4). Such a revocation shall be adopted on the basis of the examination procedure set out in article 93(2) but where there are '… duly justified imperative grounds of urgency …' then the Commission shall '… adopt immediately applicable implementing acts in accordance with the procedure referred to in Article 93(3)'.

91. GDPR, article 45.6. Recital 107 provides some further detail about what should happen: 'The Commission should, in a timely manner, inform the third country or international organisation of the reasons and enter into consultations with it in order to remedy the situation'.

92. GDPR, article 45.7.

93. GDPR, article 45.8.

Transfers subject to appropriate safeguards

[5.17] The transfer mechanism preferred by the GDPR is that of an adequacy decision, however such decisions are relatively uncommon. In the absence of such a decision other mechanisms may be considered. These must provide:

- 'appropriate safeguards';

- 'enforceable data subject rights'; and,

- 'effective legal remedies for data subjects'.[94]

[5.18] Article 45 GDPR then proceeds to outline a number of mechanisms which may provide appropriate safeguards.[95] These are divided into two sets, the first is those that do not require a specific authorisation from a SA. These are:

(a) a legally binding and enforceable instrument between public authorities or bodies;

(b) binding corporate rules;

(c) & (d) standard data protection clauses adopted either by the Commission or a SA;

(e) an approved code of conduct; or

(f) an approved certification mechanism.

Each of these is considered in further detail below.

[5.19] The Recitals suggest that this may be an agreement between public authorities 'with corresponding duties or functions'. The GDPR does not anticipate that international treaties would be required. Rather it may be sufficient for such public authorities to insert '… provisions … into administrative arrangements, such as a memorandum of understanding, providing for enforceable and effective rights for data subjects'.[96] International agreements entered into under Directive 95/46 remain in force under the GDPR '… until amended, replaced or revoked'.[97]

[5.20] Binding corporate rules (BCRs) are an innovation developed by the WP, Article 29 Working Party itself, which explained that: '… some multinational

---

94. GDPR, article 45.1.
95. GDPR, article 49.5 provides that 'In the absence of an adequacy decision, Union or Member State law may, for important reasons of public interest, expressly set limits to the transfer of specific categories of personal data to a third country or an international organisation. Member States shall notify such provisions to the Commission'. This derogation does not appear to be specific to transfers under article 49 itself, although it does not specify that may apply to transfers under article 46.
96. GDPR, Recital 108.
97. GDPR, article 96.

companies due to their complex architectural structures worldwide would like to benefit from the possibility to adopt "codes of conduct for international transfers"… dealing with the international transfer of personal data within the same corporate group at a multinational level subject to the authorisation of the relevant data protection authorities …'.[98] BCRs are defined as:

> … personal data protection policies which are adhered to by a controller or processor established on the territory of a Member State for transfers or a set of transfers of personal data to a controller or processor in one or more third countries within a group of undertakings, or group of enterprises engaged in a joint economic activity.[99]

The Recitals explain that:

> A group of undertakings,[100] or a group of enterprises[101] engaged in a joint economic activity, should be able to make use of approved binding corporate rules for its international transfers from the Union to organisations within the same group of undertakings, or group of enterprises engaged in a joint economic activity, provided that such corporate rules include all essential principles and enforceable rights to ensure appropriate safeguards for transfers or categories of transfers of personal data.[102]

[5.21] GDPR, article 47 provides that competent SAs may adopt such BCRs.[103] The Commission may specify the format and procedures for the exchange of information between controllers, processors and supervisory authorities for binding corporate rules.[104] But otherwise BCRs are a matter for the SAs, which may approve BCRs that:

(a) are legally binding and apply to and are enforced by every member concerned of the group of undertakings, or group of enterprises engaged in a joint economic activity, including their employees;

(b) expressly confer enforceable rights on data subjects with regard to the processing of their personal data; and

(c) fulfil the requirements set out in GDPR, article 47(2).

---

98. Article 29 WP, *Working Document: Transfers of personal data to third countries: Applying Article 26 (2) of the EU Data Protection Directive to Binding Corporate Rules for International Data Transfers,* 11639/02/EN, WP 74, 3 June 2003, p 5.
99. GDPR, article 4(19).
100. A 'group of undertakings' is defined as meaning '…a controlling undertaking and its controlled undertakings' GDPR, article 4(19).
101. An 'enterprise' is defined as meaning '…natural or legal person engaged in an economic activity, irrespective of its legal form, including partnerships or associations regularly engaged in an economic activity' GDPR, Recital 4(18).
102. GDPR, Recital 110.
103. '… in accordance with the consistency mechanism set out in 63 …'.
104. GDPR, article 47(3). Such specifications are to be set out in implementing acts adopted in accordance with the examination procedure set out in article 93(2).

The requirements set out in article 47(2) are that BCRs must contain the following:

(a) the structure and contact details of the group of undertakings, or group of enterprises engaged in a joint economic activity and of each of its members;

(b) the data transfers or set of transfers, including the categories of personal data, the type of processing and its purposes, the type of data subjects affected and the identification of the third country or countries in question;

(c) their legally binding nature, both internally and externally;

(d) the application of the general data protection principles, in particular, purpose limitation, data minimisation, limited storage periods, data quality, data protection by design and by default, legal basis for processing, processing of special categories of personal data, measures to ensure data security, and the requirements in respect of onward transfers to bodies not bound by the BCRs;

(e) the rights of data subjects in regard to processing and the means to exercise those rights, including the right not to be subject to decisions based solely on automated processing, including profiling, the right to lodge a complaint with the competent supervisory authority and before the competent courts of the Member States, and to obtain redress and, where appropriate, compensation for a breach of the BCRs;

(f) the acceptance by the controller or processor established on the territory of a Member State of liability for any breaches of the BCRs by any member concerned not established in the Union; the controller or the processor shall be exempt from that liability, in whole or in part, only if it proves that that member is not responsible for the event giving rise to the damage;

(g) how the information on the BCRs is to be provided to data subjects;

(h) the tasks of any DPO or other person or entity in charge of monitoring compliance with the BCRs within the group of undertakings, or group of enterprises engaged in a joint economic activity, as well as monitoring training and complaint-handling;

(i) complaint procedures;

(j) mechanisms within the group of undertakings[105] for ensuring the verification of compliance with the BCRs;[106]

(k) the mechanisms for reporting and recording changes to the rules and reporting those changes to the supervisory authority;

---

105. '... or ... group of enterprises engaged in a joint economic activity ...'.

106. 'Such mechanisms shall include data protection audits and methods for ensuring corrective actions to protect the rights of the data subject. Results of such verification should be communicated to the DPO or other persons and to the board of the controlling undertaking of a group of undertakings and should be available upon request to the competent supervisory authority'.

(l)   the cooperation mechanism with the SA in particular by making available to the SA the results of verifications referred to in point (j) above;

(m) the mechanisms for reporting to the competent supervisory authority any legal requirements to which a member of the group of undertakings[107] is subject in a third country which are likely to have a substantial adverse effect on the guarantees provided by the BCRs; and

(n) the appropriate data protection training to personnel having permanent or regular access to personal data.[108]

The Article 29 WP has issued a Working Document setting up a table with the elements and principles to be found in Binding Corporate Rules[109] which serves to:

> … to facilitate the use of Binding Corporate Rules for Controllers (BCR-C) by a corporate group or a group of enterprises engaged in a joint economic activity for international transfers from organisations established in the EU to organisations within the same group established outside the EU …[110]

[5.22] These clauses are intended to set minimum standards for data protection. As the Recitals explain, the approval of these will not '… prevent controllers or processors from adding other clauses or additional safeguards .... Controllers and processors should be encouraged to provide additional safeguards via contractual commitments that supplement standard protection clauses'.[111] Three sets of such contractual clauses were approved by the EU Commission under Directive 95/46:

(1)   Commission Decision 2001/497/EC on standard contractual clauses for the transfer of personal data to third countries;[112]

(2)   Commission Decision 2004/915/EC alternative set of standard contractual clauses for the transfer of personal data to third countries,[113] and

(3)   Commission Decision 2010/87/: of 5 February 2010 on standard contractual clauses for the transfer of personal data to processors established in third countries.[114]

---

107. '… or group of enterprises engaged in a joint economic activity …'.

108. GDPR, article 47(2).

109. Article 29 WP, *Working Document setting up a table with the elements and principles to be found in Binding Corporate Rules*, 17/EN WP 256, 29 November 2017.

110. Article 29 WP, *Working Document setting up a table with the elements and principles to be found in Binding Corporate Rules,* 17/EN WP 256, 29 November 2017, p 2.

111. GDPR, Recital 109.

112. Commission Decision 2001/497/EC on standard contractual clauses for the transfer of personal data to third countries; OJ L 181, 4.7.2001, p 19–31.

113. Commission Decision 2004/915/EC alternative set of standard contractual clauses for the transfer of personal data to third countries, OJ L 385, 29.12.2004, p 74–84.

114. Commission Decision 2010/87/ on standard contractual clauses for the transfer of personal data to processors established in third countries, OJ L 39, 12.2.2010, p 5–18.

Such clauses may not seem particularly robust, as the contractual requirements imposed by the GDPR are so different to those imposed by Directive 95/46. But they remain valid and will remain so until such time as they are 'amended, replaced or repealed'.[115] Controllers or processors are entitled to rely upon them until then; it is clear from *Google Spain* that only the CJEU can find these clauses invalid in the absence of such a decision. However, the Irish courts have referred the validity of such clauses to the CJEU.[116]

[5.23] Codes of conduct allowing for transfers may be approved pursuant to article 40, such a code will be in addition to '... binding and enforceable commitments of the controller or processor in the third country to apply the appropriate safeguards, including as regards data subjects' rights'.

[5.24] Certification mechanisms may be approved pursuant to article 42, again such mechanism will be in addition to '... binding and enforceable commitments of the controller or processor in the third country to apply the appropriate safeguards, including as regards data subjects' rights'.

A second set of safeguards are those that are specifically authorised by a SA. The GDPR is silent as to the process by which a controller or processor may obtain such authorisations, merely that they may be obtained. The GDPR goes on to provide that '... the consistency mechanism referred to in Article 63 ...' must be applied to such authorisations. However, it is the SA to which an application for such an authorisation is made that must apply this mechanism, not the applicant. Presumably SAs will themselves set out the procedures to be followed by such applicants, but the GDPR does not provide for such procedures to be set out in national law. Such safeguards may be provided for by:

(a) contractual clauses between the controller or processor and the controller, processor or the recipient of the personal data in the third country or international organisation; or

(b) provisions to be inserted into administrative arrangements between public authorities or bodies which include enforceable and effective data subject rights.

Such authorisations issued on the basis of Directive 95/46[117] will '... remain valid until amended, replaced or repealed ...' by the SA that issued them.[118]

---

115. GDPR, article 46(5).

116. See *Data Protection Commissioner v Facebook Ireland Ltd* [2017] IEHC 545 (3 October 2017) in which the Irish High Court concurred with the Irish supervisory authority '... that there are well founded grounds for believing that the [clause] decisions are invalid and furthermore that it is extremely important that there be uniformity in the application of the Directive throughout the Union on this vitally important issue' (at para 338). Accordingly the Irish High Court decided to refer these decisions '... to the CJEU for a preliminary ruling' (para 340).

117. Directive 95/46/EC, article 26(2) specifically.

118. GDPR, article 46(5).

Specific derogations

[5.25] At the bottom of the GDPR's apparent hierarchy of transfer mechanisms lie 'Derogations for specific situations'. GDPR, article 49 provides that in the absence of an adequacy decision pursuant to article 45 or appropriate safeguards pursuant to article 46 then a transfer of personal data outside the EU shall take place only on one of the following conditions:

(a) the data subject has explicitly consented to the proposed transfer, after having been informed of the possible risks of such transfers for the data subject due to the absence of an adequacy decision and appropriate safeguards, this condition cannot be relied upon by a public authority exercising its public powers;

(b) the transfer is necessary for the performance of a contract between the data subject and the controller or the implementation of pre-contractual measures taken at the data subject's request, again this condition cannot be relied upon by a public authority exercising its public powers;

(c) the transfer is necessary for the conclusion or performance of a contract concluded in the interest of the data subject between the controller and another natural or legal person, and again this condition cannot be relied upon by a public authority exercising its public powers;[119]

(d) the transfer is necessary for important reasons of public interest, which must be recognised by EU law or the law of the Member State to which the controller is subject;[120] the recitals suggest that this derogation would apply in cases of international data exchange between competition authorities, tax or customs administrations, between financial supervisory authorities, between services competent for social security matters, or for public health, for example in the case of contact tracing for contagious diseases or in order to reduce and/or eliminate doping in sport.[121]

(e) the transfer is necessary for the establishment, exercise or defence of legal claims;[122]

(f) the transfer is necessary in order to protect the vital interests of the data subject or of other persons, where the data subject is physically or legally incapable of giving consent. The recitals suggest that the subject's 'physical integrity or life' would amount to such a vital interest; the Recitals go on to suggest that a '... transfer to an international humanitarian organisation of personal data of a data subject who is physically or legally incapable of giving consent, with a view to

---

119. GDPR, article 46(3).
120. GDPR, article 49(4).
121. GDPR, Recital 112.
122. The Recitals provide that this condition applies not just to judicial procedures but also '... an administrative or any out-of-court procedure, including procedures before regulatory bodies' GDPR, Recital 111.

accomplishing a task incumbent under the Geneva Conventions or to complying with international humanitarian law applicable in armed conflicts, could be considered to be necessary for an important reason of public interest or because it is in the vital interest of the data subject';[123]

(g)   the transfer is made from a register which, according to Union or Member State law, is intended to provide information to the public and which is open to consultation either by the public in general or by any person who can demonstrate a legitimate interest, but only to the extent that the conditions laid down by Union or Member State law for consultation are fulfilled in the particular case. Such transfers shall not involve the entirety of the personal data or entire categories of the personal data contained in the register. Where the register is intended for consultation by persons having a legitimate interest, the transfer shall be made only at the request of those persons or if they are to be the recipients.[124] The decision to transfer shall take '… into full account the interests and fundamental rights of the data subject'.[125]

Where neither GDPR, articles 45, 46 nor one of the above conditions can be relied upon, then the second paragraph of GDPR, article 49(1) provides that a transfer to a third country or international organisation may take place only if:

* the transfer is not repetitive;

* concerns only a limited number of data subjects;

* is necessary for the purposes of compelling legitimate interests pursued by the controller which are not overridden by the interests or rights and freedoms of the data subject; and

* the controller has assessed all the circumstances surrounding the data transfer and has on the basis of that assessment provided suitable safeguards with regard to the protection of personal data. In making this decision the Recitals suggest that the controller should give particular consideration to the nature of the personal data, the purpose and duration of the proposed processing operation or operations, as well as the situation in the country of origin, the third country and the country of final destination. This assessment and the safeguards provided must be documented in accordance with GDPR, article 30.[126]

The Recitals suggest that this basis should only be relied upon '… in residual cases where none of the other grounds for transfer are applicable'. The Recitals then go on to suggest that such transfers might take place for '… scientific or historical research purposes or statistical purposes' where the legitimate expectations of society for an

123. GDPR, Recital 112.
124. GDPR, article 49(2).
125. GDPR, Recital 111.
126. GDPR, article 49(6).

increase of knowledge should be taken into consideration'.[127] In addition, the controller must inform the SA of the transfer.[128] It must also inform the subject, this obligation being in addition to those imposed by GDPR, articles 13 and 14. The subject must be informed of the compelling legitimate interests pursued.[129]

---

127. GDPR, Recital 113.
128. GDPR, article 49(1), Recital 113.
129. GDPR, article 49(1).

PART 3
RULES OF DATA PROCESSING

Chapter 6

THE PRINCIPLES RELATING TO PROCESSING OF PERSONAL DATA

INTRODUCTION

[6.01] The principles relating to the processing of personal data set out the basic rules that apply to the processing of personal data; they provide the foundations for European data protection law. They first appeared in the Strasbourg Convention, though the principles that appear in the GDPR are not quite the same as those that first appeared in 1981: they have been renamed and rearranged; they have been joined by an additional principle, that of accountability; and, most significantly they must be read in conjunction with a variety of new rules such as lawful basis, introduced by Directive 95/46 and procedural rules for controllers and processors set out in GDPR, Ch IV.

[6.02] The principles of data protection are:

(a) lawfulness, fairness and transparency;

(b) purpose limitation;

(c) data minimisation;

(d) accuracy;

(e) storage limitation;

(f) integrity and confidentiality; and

(g) accountability.

The principles cannot be considered in isolation as the GDPR's rules on processing are interlinked with one another. So the principle that data processing be transparent imposed by GDPR, article 5(1)(a), requires that subjects be informed of the purpose of the processing under GDPR, articles 13 and 14, that information will allow subjects to determine whether the processing goes beyond what is necessary and so contrary to GDPR, article 5(1)(c). Each of these principles is discussed in further detail below.

LAWFULNESS, FAIRNESS AND TRANSPARENCY

[6.03] GDPR, article 5(1)(a) sets out that personal data must be '… processed lawfully, fairly and in a transparent manner in relation to the data subject'. As its title suggests this principle may be broken down into three elements: lawfulness; fairness; and transparency. Lawfulness must mean that the data processing operation in question complies with the law in general, not just the EU law on data protection. There are a great variety of such laws at an EU and Member State level. This principle makes clear that data processing must be compliant not just with the GDPR itself, but also with the broader legal environment. What makes this interesting is that the GDPR provides subjects with remedies which may not be available under other laws. Suppose personal data is extracted from a database in breach of the database right[1] provided by the Database Directive.[2] The Database Directive will not provide the subject of that data with a remedy for the breach of the database right, but since the processing is unlawful it may breach the GDPR, which does.

[6.04] Fairness is a more nebulous concept. It might be read as importing the concept of data ethics into the GDPR.[3] But it may be more appropriate to read it as a reference to the concept of proportionality, as provided for in article 52(1) of the Charter. As the CJEU explained in *Volker und Markus Schecke*:[4]

> It is settled case law that the principle of proportionality which is one of the general principles of European Union law, requires that measures implemented by acts of the European Union are appropriate for attaining the objective pursued and do not go beyond what is necessary to achieve it.[5]

In other words, it is insufficient that processing be on the basis of a law, that law must itself be appropriate and proportionate. The CJEU went on to further explain in *Digital Rights Ireland*,[6] a challenge to the validity of the Data Retention Directive:[7]

> ... the principle of proportionality requires that acts of the EU institutions be appropriate for attaining the legitimate objectives pursued by the legislation at issue and do not exceed the limits of what is appropriate and necessary in order to achieve those objectives.

[6.05] The CJEU noted that:

> ... where interferences with fundamental rights are at issue, the extent of the EU legislature's discretion may prove to be limited, depending on a number of factors,

1. Directive 96/9/EC, Ch III on the legal protection of databases.
2. Directive 96/9/EC on the legal protection of databases, OJ L 77, 27.3.1996, p 20–28.
3. 'Data ethics is the concept that '... the idea that something is right or wrong, is more universal than the typically western notions of privacy and data protection', Buttarelli, European Data Protection Supervisor, Ethics at the Root of Privacy and as the Future of Data Protection, Berkman Center for Internet and Society, Harvard University, 19 April 2016. The EDPS has established an Ethics Advisory Group to 'analyse ethical dimensions of data protection ... submit recommendations to the EDPS' and 'produce at least two public reports' article 2(1), European Data Protection Supervisor decision establishing an external advisory group on the ethical dimensions of data protection ('the Ethics Advisory Group'), OJ C 33, 28 January 2016.
4. *Volker und Markus Schecke* (Case C–92/09) (9 November 2010).
5. *Volker und Markus Schecke* (Case C–92/09) (9 November 2010), para 74, citing *Vodafone and Ors* (Case C–58/08) [2010] ECR I-0000, para 51.
6. *Digital Rights Ireland* (Case C–293/12) (8 April 2014).
7. Directive 2006/24/EC of the European Parliament and of the Council of 15 March 2006 on the retention of data generated or processed in connection with the provision of publicly available electronic communications services or of public communications networks.

including, in particular, the area concerned, the nature of the rights at issue guaranteed by the Charter, the nature and seriousness of the interference and the object pursued by the interference.

And concluded:

… in view of the important role played by the protection of personal data in the light of the fundamental rights to respect for private life and the extent and seriousness of the interference with that right caused by [the Data Retention Directive] … the EU legislature's discretion is reduced, with the result that review of that discretion should be strict.[8]

The GDPR sets out an indicative list of what such a law may contain at para 6(2), but such a law must '… meet an objective of public interest and be proportionate to the legitimate aim pursued'.

Transparency must be read in conjunction with the specific obligations set out in GDPR, articles 12, 13 and 14. The Recitals explain that:

The principle of transparency requires that any information and communication relating to the processing of those personal data be easily accessible and easy to understand, and that clear and plain language be used. That principle concerns, in particular, information to the data subjects on the identity of the controller and the purposes of the processing and further information to ensure fair and transparent processing in respect of the natural persons concerned and their right to obtain confirmation and communication of personal data concerning them which are being processed. Natural persons should be made aware of risks, rules, safeguards and rights in relation to the processing of personal data and how to exercise their rights in relation to such processing.[9]

PURPOSE LIMITATION

[6.06] Article 5(1)(b) provides that data must be:

collected for specified, explicit and legitimate purposes and not further processed in a manner that is incompatible with those purposes.[10]

Again, the requirement that purposes be specified and explicit must be read in conjunction with obligations of transparency set out elsewhere in the GDPR.[11] Article 13(1)(c) specifies that where personal data is collected directly from the subject then they must be informed of 'the purposes of the processing for which the personal data are intended'.[12] It is clear from both wording of article 5(1)(b) and the judgment of the

---

8.   *Digital Rights Ireland* (Case C–293/12), paras 46-48.
9.   GDPR, Recital 39.
10.   It goes on to provide that 'further processing for archiving purposes in the public interest, scientific or historical research purposes or statistical purposes shall, in accordance with Article 89(1), not be considered to be incompatible with the initial purposes'.
11.   GDPR, articles 5(1)(b), 12, 13 and 14.
12.   GDPR, article 14(1)(c) similarly provides where data are not obtained from the subject.

CJEU in *Bara*[13] that the requirement that information given to subjects be specific. This precludes controllers providing subjects with generic or general descriptions of how they intend to process their data. Nor is this an issue that may be deferred, the recitals provide:

> In particular, the specific purposes for which personal data are processed should be explicit and legitimate and determined at the time of the collection of the personal data.[14]

So, the purpose limitation principle imposes a significant limitation on the data processing even where processing in question is legitimate and lawful as controllers will inevitably lack the prescience to anticipate and specify how they intend to process data.

[6.07] In *Avis 1/15* the CJEU considered a proposed agreement for the transfer of Passenger Name Records from the EU to Canada. The CJEU pointed out that this entailed a change of purpose:

> ... the processing of PNR data under the envisaged agreement pursues a different objective from that for which that data is collected by air carriers ... Consequently, the processing cannot be regarded as being based on the consent of the air passengers to the collection of that data by the air carriers for reservation purposes, and it therefore itself requires either the air passengers' own consent or some other legitimate basis laid down by law.[15]

In *Deutsche Telekom*[16] the CJEU made clear that the purpose limitation is about how data is processed, not who is doing the processing. Deutsche Telekom amalgamated telephone numbers that are assigned by itself and other telecoms providers into a database of phone numbers, which it used to publish directories and operate a directory enquiry service. The German telecommunications regulator had directed Deutsche Telekom to grant a third party access to this database. The CJEU distinguished between a change of controller and a change of purpose '... if it is guaranteed that the data in question will not be used for purposes other than those for which the data were collected with a view to their first publication'.[17]

[6.08] GDPR, article 6(4) goes on to set out a test to enable controllers to decide whether data may be processed for a purpose other than that for which it was originally collected. The GDPR makes clear that this test will not apply where '... the data

---

13. *Bara and Ors v Preşedintele Casei Naţionale de Asigurări de Sănătate, Casa Naţională de Asigurări de Sănătate and Agenţia Naţională de Administrare Fiscală (ANAF)* (Case C–201/14).

14. GDPR, Recital 39.

15. *Transfer of Passenger Name Record data from the European Union to* Canada [2017] EUECJ Avis-1/15_OC (26 July 2017) paras 142–143.

16. *Deutsche Telekom* (Case C–543/09) (5 May 2011) applied in *Tele2 (Netherlands)* (Case C–536/15) (15 March 2017).

17. *Deutsche Telekom* (Case C–543/09) (5 May 2011), para 65.

subject's consent or on a Union or Member State law …'.[18] (in those cases the controller will either have to get a new consent or else seek a change to the law). In order to '… ascertain whether processing for another purpose is compatible with the purpose for which the personal data are initially collected …' the controller must take the following factors into account, inter alia:

(i)   any link between the purposes for which the personal data have been collected and the purposes of the intended further processing;

(ii)   the context in which the personal data have been collected, in particular regarding the relationship between data subjects and the controller;

(iii) the nature of the personal data, in particular whether special categories of personal data are processed, pursuant to article 9, or whether personal data related to criminal convictions and offences are processed, pursuant to article 10;

(iv)   the possible consequences of the intended further processing for data subjects; and,

(v)   the existence of appropriate safeguards, which may include encryption or pseudonymisation.[19]

DATA MINIMISATION

[6.09] Data minimisation means that data must be '… adequate, relevant and limited to what is necessary in relation to the purposes for which they are processed'.[20] In *Osterreichischer Rundfunk*[21] the CJEU held that the equivalent provision[22] in Directive 95/46 was an 'unconditional obligation' that was 'sufficiently precise to be relied on by individuals and applied by the national court'.[23] That provision was again considered by the CJEU in *Google Spain* which concerned a complaint that when someone entered the complainant's name in the Google search engine they would obtain links to pages of a newspaper from some sixteen years before '… on which an announcement mentioning Mr Costeja González's name appeared for a real-estate auction connected with attachment proceedings for the recovery of social security debt'.[24] The CJEU noted that:

> … even initially lawful processing of accurate data may, in the course of time, become incompatible with the directive where those data are no longer necessary

18.   GDPR, article 6(4) goes on to specify that this must be a law '… which constitutes a necessary and proportionate measure in a democratic society to safeguard the objectives referred to in Article 23(1) …'.

19.   See also GDPR, Recital 50.

20.   GDPR, article 5(1)(c).

21.   *Osterreichischer Rundfunk* (Case C–139/01) (20 May 2003).

22.   Member States shall provide that personal data must be … adequate, relevant and not excessive in relation to the purposes for which they are collected and/or further processed,' Directive 95/46, article 6(1)(c).

23.   *Osterreichischer Rundfunk* (Case C–139/01) (20 May 2003), para 100.

24.   *Costeja Gonzalez v Google Spain and Google* (Case C–131/12) (13 May 2014), para 14.

in the light of the purposes for which they were collected or processed. That is so in particular where they appear to be inadequate, irrelevant or no longer relevant, or excessive in relation to those purposes and in the light of the time that has elapsed.[25]

The CJEU went on to find that if:

> ... the inclusion in the list of results displayed following a search ... is, at this point in time, incompatible with ... the directive because that information appears, having regard to all the circumstances of the case, to be inadequate, irrelevant or no longer relevant, or excessive in relation to the purposes of the processing at issue carried out by the operator of the search engine, the information and links concerned in the list of results must be erased.[26]

The equivalent provision in Directive 95/46 required that data be processed in a manner that was 'not excessive,' a phrase now replaced with 'what is necessary'. The meaning of 'excessive' was considered by the CJEU in a different context in *X*,[27] which considered the fee that a controller might charge for complying with an access request. Directive 95/46 stipulated that this should be 'not excessive', which the CJEU considered meant that '... the level of those fees must not exceed the cost of communicating such data'.[28] The CJEU did not suggest that the controller needed to seek out the lowest cost mechanism for communicating that data. Minimisation, the term now used in the GDPR, suggests that the controller should. 'Not excessive' suggest that controllers should not process more data than they need, data minimisation however suggests that controllers go beyond this and actively seek to limit or minimise the amount of data that they process. As the Recitals explain:

> Personal data should be processed only if the purpose of the processing could not reasonably be fulfilled by other means.[29]

The principle of data minimisation set out in article 5(1)(c) must be read in conjunction with the obligations of data protection by design and default set out in article 25. These require that controllers actively pursue the minimisation of personal data; article 30 requires that they record how they have done so.

ACCURACY

[6.10] As regards GDPR, article 5(1)(d) provides that:

> ... accurate and, where necessary, kept up to date; every reasonable step must be taken to ensure that personal data that are inaccurate, having regard to the purposes for which they are processed, are erased or rectified without delay.[30]

---

25.   *Costeja Gonzalez v Google Spain and Google* (Case C–131/12) (13 May 2014), para 93.
26.   *Costeja Gonzalez v Google Spain and Google* (Case C–131/12) (13 May 2014), para 94.
27.   *X* (Case C–486/12) (12 December 2013), see also *Rijkeboer* (Case C–553/07) (7 May 2009).
28.   *X* (Case C–486/12) (12 December 2013), para 31.
29.   GDPR, Recital 39.
30.   GDPR, article 5(1)(d).

Accuracy is an important principle. It underlay the right of access in Directive 95/46, the Recitals to which explained that subjects had a right of access '… in order to verify in particular the accuracy of the data …'.[31] One of the arguments successfully made against granting a subject access to a legal opinion in *YS*[32] was that the legal opinion '… is not in itself liable to be the subject of a check of its accuracy by that applicant …'.[33] However the Recitals to the GDPR no longer suggest that the right of access is to be used, or perhaps limited, to this purpose. And just because data is accurate does not mean, of itself, that it can be processed.[34]

The principle of accuracy should be read in conjunction with the Right of Rectification, which grants subjects the right '… to obtain from the controller without undue delay the rectification of inaccurate personal data concerning him or her'.[35]

[6.11] In *Nowak* the CJEU explained what the right to accurate data meant in the context of examination answers:

> … the assessment of whether personal data is accurate and complete must be made in the light of the purpose for which that data was collected. That purpose consists, as far as the answers submitted by an examination candidate are concerned, in being able to evaluate the level of knowledge and competence of that candidate at the time of the examination. That level is revealed precisely by any errors in those answers. Consequently, such errors do not represent inaccuracy …, which would give rise to a right of rectification …[36]
>
> On the other hand, it is possible that there might be situations where the answers of an examination candidate and the examiner's comments with respect to those answers prove to be inaccurate… for example due to the fact that, by mistake, the examination scripts were mixed up in such a way that the answers of another candidate were ascribed to the candidate concerned, or that some of the cover sheets containing the answers of that candidate are lost, so that those answers are incomplete, or that any comments made by an examiner do not accurately record the examiner's evaluation of the answers of the candidate concerned.[37]

STORAGE LIMITATION

[6.12] Data should be kept no longer than is necessary. GDPR, article 5(1)(e) provides that it should be:

> … kept in a form which permits identification of data subjects for no longer than is necessary for the purposes for which the personal data are processed.[38]

---

31. Directive 95/46, Recital 41.
32. *YS* (Case C–141/12) (17 July 2014).
33. *YS* (Case C–141/12) (17 July 2014), para 45.
34. *Costeja Gonzalez v Google Spain and Google* (Case C–131/12) (13 May 2014), para 93.
35. GDPR, article 16.
36. *Nowak* (Case C–434/16) (20 December 2017), para 53.
37. *Nowak* (Case C–434/16) (20 December 2017), para 54.
38. Going onto provide that 'personal data may be stored for longer periods in so far as the personal data will be processed solely for archiving purposes (contd .../)

As the CJEU explained in *Avis 1/15* there must be '... a connection between the personal data to be retained and the objective pursued (by the retention)'.[39] The Recitals suggest that this means '... ensuring that the period for which the personal data are stored is limited to a strict minimum ... In order to ensure that the personal data are not kept longer than necessary, time limits should be established by the controller for erasure or for a periodic review'.[40] The CJEU held invalid two laws that provided for the retention of personal data in *Digital Rights Ireland*[41] and *Tele2 Sverige*,[42] though in both cases the grounds for invalidity went far beyond the length of time for which data was being retained. One of the grounds upon which the CJEU held the Data Retention Directive invalid in *Digital Rights Ireland* was that it required that 'data be retained for a period of at least six months, without any distinction being made between the categories of data ... the basis of their possible usefulness for the purposes of the objective pursued or according to the persons concerned'. That Directive set the maximum retention period at 24 months '... but it is not stated that the determination of the period of retention must be based on objective criteria in order to ensure that it is limited to what is strictly necessary'.[43] *Tele2 Sverige* concerned a Swedish national measure, which similarly provided for the retention of data but at a national level. The CJEU held that the Charter:

> ... must be interpreted as precluding national legislation which, for the purpose of fighting crime, provides for the general and indiscriminate retention of all ... data of all subscribers ...[44]

What the above suggest is that EU data protection law expects that specific retention periods will be set for specific categories of personal data. In *Tele2 Sverige* the CJEU made it clear that national laws could provide for the retention of quite broad categories of personal data relating to quite broad categories of person:

> ... national legislation must be based on objective evidence which makes it possible to identify a public whose data is likely to reveal a link, at least an indirect one, with serious criminal offences, and to contribute in one way or another to fighting serious crime or to preventing a serious risk to public security. Such limits may be set by using a geographical criterion where the competent national authorities consider, on the basis of objective evidence, that there exists, in one or more geographical areas, a high risk of preparation for or commission of such offences.[45]

---

38.   (contd) in the public interest, scientific or historical research purposes or statistical purposes in accordance with Article 89(1) subject to implementation of the appropriate technical and organisational measures required by this Regulation in order to safeguard the rights and freedoms of the data subject'.

39.   *Transfer of Passenger Name Record data from the European Union to Canada (Opinions of the Court)* [2017] EUECJ Avis-1/15_OC (26 July 2017), para 191.

40.   GDPR, Recital 39.

41.   *Digital Rights Ireland* (Case C–293/12) (8 April 2014).

42.   *Tele2 Sverige* (Case C–203/15) (21 December 2016).

43.   *Digital Rights Ireland* (Case C–293/12) (8 April 2014), paras 63-64.

44.   *Tele2 Sverige* (Case C–203/15) (21 December 2016), para 112.

45.   *Tele2 Sverige* (Case C–203/15) (21 December 2016), para 111.

The CJEU was not saying that it was not possible to have national data retention laws; only that such laws could not be 'general and indiscriminate'. What the GDPR does require is that controllers should assess how long they need to retain data for, build procedures that ensure those retention periods are complied with and periodically review their retention policies and the data that they retain to see if that retention is still necessary.

[6.13] The principle of storage limitation must be considered in conjunction with the right to erasure or the right to be forgotten, which is set out in GDPR, article 17. This right was given effect in *Google Spain,* which considered the display of links to certain pages on a newspaper's website on the search engine's result page. *Google Spain* explicitly did not consider the deletion of the pages themselves, which the CJEU accepted might well be lawful.[46] The CJEU considered how long it may be lawful to retain data for in two cases: *Manni*[47] and *Rijkeboer.*[48] *Manni* was brought by an Italian who was director of a company that had been unable to sell apartments in a tourist complex. Mr Manni believed this was because a company register disclosed that he had been director of a company '… which had been declared insolvent in 1992 and struck off the companies register, following liquidation proceedings, on 7 July 2005'.[49] Mr Manni challenged the availability of this personal data in the company register before the Italian courts, which referred the question of whether he was entitled to seek limitations upon access to his data to the CJEU. That Court noted the view of its Advocate General that it was '… common ground that even after the dissolution of a company, rights and legal relations relating to it continue to exist' and that data such as that retained on the Italian company register '… may be necessary in order, inter alia, to assess the legality of an act carried out on behalf of that company during the period of its activity …'. The CJEU noted that '… questions requiring such data may arise for many years after a company has ceased to exist.' And so, it was:

> impossible, at present, to identify a single time limit, as from the dissolution of a company, at the end of which the inclusion of such data in the register and their disclosure would no longer be necessary.[50]

The CJEU did note that there might be:

> … specific situations in which the overriding and legitimate reasons relating to the specific case of the person concerned justify exceptionally that access to personal data entered in the register is limited, upon expiry of a sufficiently long period after the dissolution of the company in question, to third parties who can demonstrate a specific interest in their consultation.

---

46. *Costeja Gonzalez v Google Spain and Google* (Case C–131/12) (13 May 2014), para 94.
47. *Manni* (Case C–398/15) (9 March 2017).
48. *Rijkeboer* (Case C–553/07) (7 May 2009).
49. Paragraph 24.
50. *Manni* (Case C–398/15) (9 March 2017), paras 53-55.

But that '… the need to protect the interests of third parties in relation to joint-stock companies and limited liability companies and to ensure legal certainty, fair trading and thus the proper functioning of the internal market'[51] would take precedence. It is particularly worth noting that in *Manni* the CJEU was not considering whether data might be deleted from the register, only whether limitations should be placed upon access to that data. The CJEU held that it was a matter for national legislatures to decide whether such limitations on access should be placed. If the Italian legislature were to decide that it was appropriate then it would be a matter for the Italian courts to decide:

> … having regard to all the relevant circumstances and taking into account the time elapsed since the dissolution of the company concerned, the possible existence of legitimate and overriding reasons which, as the case may be, exceptionally justify limiting third parties' access to the data concerning Mr Manni in the company register …

However, the CJEU did point out that:

> … the mere fact that, allegedly, the properties of a tourist complex … do not sell because of the fact that potential purchasers of those properties have access to that data in the company register, cannot be regarded as constituting such a reason, in particular in view of the legitimate interest of those purchasers in having that information.[52]

[6.14] *Manni* is a significant judgment for a number of reasons. Firstly, the CJEU held that the failure of EU law to stipulate a retention period for this personal data did not:

> … result in disproportionate interference with the fundamental rights of the persons concerned and particularly their right to respect for private life and their right to protection of personal data as guaranteed by Articles 7 and 8 of the Charter.[53]

Secondly, the CJEU clearly considered that limiting access to data could offer an appropriate alternative to deletion. Finally, the CJEU was clearly of the view that subjects who knowingly engage in particular activities must then accept that their data will be processed in particular ways:

> … it appears justified that natural persons who choose to participate in trade through … a company are required to disclose the data relating to their identity and functions within that company, especially since they are aware of that requirement when they decide to engage in such activity.[54]

[6.15] The selective deletion of certain categories of personal data was considered by the CJEU in *Rijkeboer*. A Dutch authority retained the subject's name and address for a very long time,[55] but deleted data relating to the persons to which that data was disclosed

---

51. *Manni* (Case C–398/15) (9 March 2017), para 60.
52. *Manni* (Case C–398/15) (9 March 2017), para 63.
53. *Manni* (Case C–398/15) (9 March 2017), para 57.
54. *Manni* (Case C–398/15) (9 March 2017), para 59.
55. *Rijkeboer* (Case C–553/07) (7 May 2009), para 42.

after a year.[56] The subject wanted to find out who his data had been disclosed to over the two years prior to his access request, but was unable to do so as it had been deleted after one. The CJEU held that:

> The setting of a time-limit with regard to the right to access to information on the recipients or categories of recipient of personal data and on the content of the data disclosed must allow the data subject to exercise the different rights laid down in the Directive ...[57]

The CJEU went on to hold that it was:

> ... for the Member States to fix a time-limit for storage of information ... which constitutes a fair balance between, on the one hand, the interest of the data subject in protecting his privacy, in particular by way of his rights to rectification, erasure and blocking of the data ... and rights to object and to bring legal proceedings and, on the other, the burden which the obligation to store that information represents for the controller.[58]

And that:

> ... rules limiting the storage of information on the recipients or categories of recipient of personal data and on the content of the data disclosed to a period of one year and correspondingly limiting access to that information, while basic data is stored for a much longer period, do not constitute a fair balance of the interest and obligation at issue, unless it can be shown that longer storage of that information would constitute an excessive burden on the controller.[59]

Whether it could be shown that information storage is excessively burdensome is an open question. The straight-forward storage of data has become relatively cheap. What is burdensome is managing that data and, in particular, complying with data protection obligations such as request for access and rectification. A better argument for the selective deletion of personal data is that doing so would be in the interests of the subject, as it is no longer necessary for the controller to process the data in question.

The CJEU considered how long it might be necessary to retain examination answers and examiners comments in *Nowak:*

> Taking into consideration the purpose of the answers submitted by an examination candidate and of the examiner's comments with respect to those answers, their retention in a form permitting the identification of the candidate is, a priori, no longer necessary as soon as the examination procedure is finally closed and can no longer be challenged, so that those answers and comments have lost any probative value.[60]

---

56. *Rijkeboer* (Case C–553/07) (7 May 2009), para 43.
57. *Rijkeboer* (Case C–553/07) (7 May 2009), para 57.
58. *Rijkeboer* (Case C–553/07) (7 May 2009), para 64.
59. *Rijkeboer* (Case C–553/07) (7 May 2009), para 71.
60. *Nowak* (Case C–434/16) (20 December 2017), para 55.

[6.16] What is clear from the judgments of the CJEU is that each controller has to itself consider its retention periods for data. A retention period that may be lawful and appropriate for one controller will not be for another. This is clear from the judgment of the CJEU in *Google Spain.* Google argued that:

> ... the operator of a search engine is obliged to remove from the list of results displayed following a search made on the basis of a person's name links to web pages ... when its publication in itself on those pages is lawful.[61]

The CJEU did not agree and held that if the subject requested the removal of his data from the search engine's result page then the controller of that results page had to consider whether:

> the inclusion in the list of results displayed following a search made on the basis of his name of the links to web pages published lawfully by third parties and containing true information relating to him personally is, at this point in time, incompatible with [the principles] because that information appears, having regard to all the circumstances of the case, to be inadequate, irrelevant or no longer relevant, or excessive in relation to the purposes of the processing at issue carried out by the operator of the search engine, the information and links concerned in the list of results must be erased.[62]

The fact that the newspaper was able to process the subject's data in its archive or on its website did not mean that Google was able to process that data in its search engine or on its results page.

INTEGRITY AND CONFIDENTIALITY

[6.17] The principle of integrity and confidentiality should mean something more than simple security. The obligation to secure data is specifically set out in article 32, which requires that controllers '... implement appropriate technical and organisational measures to ensure a level of security appropriate to the risk ...'[63] to personal data. However, the text of GDPR, article 5(1)(f) requires only that personal data be:

> ... processed in a manner that ensures appropriate security of the personal data, including protection against unauthorised or unlawful processing and against accidental loss, destruction or damage, using appropriate technical or organisational measures ...

But to argue that the principle of integrity and confidentiality is an irrelevant repetition of what is in article 32 would be to confuse the means with the result. An appropriate standard of security for personal data is that which results in its integrity and confidentiality. Both articles 5(1)(f) and 32 replicate equivalent provisions in Directive

---

61.   *Google Spain* (Case C–131/12) (13 May 2014), para 62.
62.   *Google Spain* (Case C–131/12) (13 May 2014), para 94.
63.   GDPR, article 32(1).

95/46.[64] The CJEU clearly considers security important, one which may require the processing of personal data in certain circumstances.

[6.18] In *Breyer*[65] websites operated on behalf of the German government stored the IP addresses of visitors. Germany argued that this was:

> ... necessary to guarantee the security and continued proper functioning of the online media services that it makes accessible to the public, in particular, enabling cyber attacks known as "denial-of-service" attacks, which aim to paralyse the functioning of the sites by the targeted and coordinated saturation of certain web servers with huge numbers of requests, to be identified and combated.[66]

And the CJEU did accept that '... the objective aiming to ensure the general operability of those services may justify the use of those data after a consultation period of those websites'.[67] In *McFadden*[68] the applicant was operating an open WiFi network which was allegedly being used to permit the illegal downloading of the respondent's music. The CJEU held that the applicant could be required to secure his network to prevent this happening. In particular the CJEU did not preclude: '... the grant of an injunction ... which requires... a provider of access to a communication network ... prevent third parties from making a particular copyright-protected work ... available to the general public from an online (peer-to-peer) exchange platform'. The CJEU said it was for the applicant to choose the means to comply with such an injunction, which might issue:

> ... even if such a choice is limited to a single measure consisting in password-protecting the internet connection, provided that those users are required to reveal their identity in order to obtain the required password and may not therefore act anonymously ...[69]

Finally, in *Tele2 Sverige*[70] the CJEU held that access to retained telecommunications data might be necessary '... where ... vital national security, defence or public security interests are threatened by terrorist activities, access to the data of other persons might ... be granted where there is objective evidence from which it can be deduced that that data might, in a specific case, make an effective contribution to combating such activities'.[71]

[6.19] The importance that the CJEU attaches to security in general is reflected in the importance that it attaches to personal data security in particular. One of the concerns that the CJEU had in *Tele2 Sverige* was that retained communications data would have

---

64. Articles and Directive 95/46 respectively.
65. *Breyer* (Case C–582/14) (19 October 2016).
66. *Breyer* (Case C–582/14) (19 October 2016), para 27.
67. *Breyer* (Case C–582/14) (19 October 2016), para 65.
68. *McFadden* (Case C–484/14) (15 September 2016).
69. *McFadden* (Case C–484/14) (15 September 2016), para 102.
70. *Tele2 Sverige* (Judgment) (Case C–203/15) (21 December 2016).
71. *Tele2 Sverige* (Judgment) (Case C–203/15) (21 December 2016), para 119.

to be kept securely. This was a challenge to Swedish and UK data retention laws. The CJEU emphasised that to be valid such laws would have to 'ensure the full integrity and confidentiality of that data' that they retained. And that those laws should in particular '... make provision for the data to be retained within the European Union and for the irreversible destruction of the data at the end of the data retention period data'.[72] In *Digital Rights Ireland*[73] the CJEU held that the Data Retention Directive should have provided:

> ... minimum safeguards so that the persons whose data have been retained have sufficient guarantees to effectively protect their personal data against the risk of abuse and against any unlawful access and use of that data.[74]

The CJEU went on to find that the Directive should have laid down: '... rules which are specific and adapted to (i) the vast quantity of data whose retention is required by that directive, (ii) the sensitive nature of that data and (iii) the risk of unlawful access to that data, rules which would serve, in particular, to govern the protection and security of the data in question in a clear and strict manner in order to ensure their full integrity and confidentiality.' It should also have imposed '... minimum safeguards so that the persons whose data have been retained have sufficient guarantees to effectively protect their personal data against the risk of abuse and against any unlawful access and use of that data' And should have ensured: '... the irreversible destruction of the data at the end of the data retention period'.[75]

[6.20] Finally, in *Schrems*[76] the CJEU reiterated that subjects must:

> ... have sufficient guarantees enabling their data to be effectively protected against the risk of abuse and against any unlawful access and use of that data. The need for such safeguards is all the greater where personal data is subjected to automatic processing and where there is a significant risk of unlawful access to that data.[77]

The CJEU went on to hold that laws which permitted public authorities:

> ... to have access on a generalised basis to the content of electronic communications must be regarded as compromising the essence of the fundamental right to respect for private life ...[78]

[6.21] The judgments in *Tele2 Sverige, Digital Rights Ireland* and *Schrems* were all challenges to EU and national legislation, which may make their discussion of legislative principles seem somewhat remote from day-to-day issues of security. What they do make clear is the very great importance that the CJEU attaches to data security.

---

72.   *Tele2 Sverige* (Judgment) (Case C–203/15) (21 December 2016), para 122.
73.   *Digital Rights Ireland* (Case C–293/12) (8 April 2014).
74.   *Digital Rights Ireland* (Case C–293/12) (8 April 2014), para 54.
75.   *Digital Rights Ireland* (Case C–293/12) (8 April 2014), paras 66-67.
76.   *Schrems* (Case C–362/14) (6 October 2015).
77.   *Schrems* (Case C–362/14) (6 October 2015), para 91.
78.   *Schrems* (Case C–362/14) (6 October 2015), para 94.

As the CJEU judgments in *Breyer* and *McFadden* demonstrate, the CJEU has no difficulty becoming embroiled in the details of cyber security.

ACCOUNTABILITY

[6.22] Accountability is a new addition to the principles; it is set apart from the others in GDPR, article 5(2), which provides:

> The controller shall be responsible for, and be able to demonstrate compliance with [the other principles].

Setting the principle of accountability apart makes clear that it is an overarching principle which applies jointly and equally to the six principles set out in GDPR, article 5(1). This is also clear from the text of GDPR, article 5(1) itself, which makes clear that the controller is responsible for demonstrating compliance with the principles set out in GDPR, article 5(1). Accountability is a significant addition to the principles of data protection as it ensures that subjects may seek remedies against controllers who fail to discharge their compliance obligations under GDPR, Ch IV. Those obligations, such as those of record keeping pursuant to GDPR, article 30 and communication pursuant to GDPR, article 34 will facilitate subjects in this regard.

Chapter 7

LAWFULNESS OF PROCESSING

INTRODUCTION

[7.01] Article 8(2) of the Charter provides that personal data must be:

> … processed … on the basis of the consent of the person concerned or some other legitimate basis laid down by law.

These legitimate bases are set out in GDPR, article 6, which provides that processing will be lawful if, and only if at least one of the following applies:

(a) consent;

(b) contract;

(c) compliance with a legal obligation;

(d) protection of the vital interests of the subject or another natural person;

(e) necessity in the public interest; and,

(f) legitimate interests of the controller or a third party.

Processing can have more than one legal basis as is clear from the text of article 6(1) itself. This stipulates that processing must have at least one lawful basis, suggesting that it may have more than one. An example of a processing operation with more than one lawful basis is given by the CJEU decision in *Deutsch Telekom*.[1] Customers of the applicant had consented to the publication of their data in a phone directory, the German telecommunications regulator then ordered that this data be provided to the controller of another, identical phone directory.[2] The CJEU held that a further consent was not required to give effect to this order, provided that subjects were informed of the resulting data transfer.[3] Hence the processing in this case had dual lawful bases: consent and a legal obligation.

[7.02] The list of bases is egalitarian; it is not a hierarchy. Although consent is the only one of the above lawful bases to be explicitly mentioned in the Charter and appears at the beginning of the list it is not in any real way 'superior' to the others. The CJEU considered the argument that subjects were entitled to withhold their consent notwithstanding that their data could be lawfully processed on another legal basis in *Schwarz*.[4] At issue was EU Council Regulation 2252/2004/EU on standards for security

---

1. *Deutsche Telekom* (Case C–543/09) (5 May 2011).
2. *Deutsche Telekom* (Case C–543/09) (5 May 2011), para 21.
3. *Deutsche Telekom* (Case C–543/09) (5 May 2011), para 67.
4. *Schwarz v Stadt Bochum* (Case C–291/12) (17 October 2013).

features and biometrics in passports and travel documents issued by Member States[5] which provided that:

> ... biometric identifiers should be integrated in the passport or travel document in order to establish a reliable link between the genuine holder and the document.[6]

Regulation 2252/2004/EU went on to require that 'Passports and travel documents shall ... include two fingerprints taken flat in interoperable formats'.[7] The applicant was a German who had '... applied ... for a passport, but refused at that time to have his fingerprints taken'.[8] The CJEU held that:

> ... concerning the condition requiring the consent of persons applying for passports before their fingerprints can be taken, it should be noted that, as a general rule, it is essential for citizens of the Union to own a passport in order, for example, to travel to non-member countries and that that document must contain fingerprints pursuant to ... Regulation ... 2252/2004. Therefore, citizens of the Union wishing to make such journeys are not free to object to the processing of their fingerprints. In those circumstances, persons applying for passports cannot be deemed to have consented to that processing.[9]

The CJEU went on to find that the applicant had revealed nothing capable of invalidating Regulation 2252/2004's requirement that he submit his fingerprints when applying for a passport. That Court in effect found that Regulation 2252/2014 provided a valid lawful basis for the processing of the applicant's personal data notwithstanding that the applicant wished to withhold his consent to the processing of it. In other words, a law could provide a legal basis of equal validity to that of the subject's consent.

[7.03] Although the list of legal bases is not a hierarchy it may be useful to structure that list in order of the level of discretion granted to the subject about how their data is processed. Such a structure looks like this:

1.   consent;
2.   legitimate interests of controller;
3.   necessity in the public interest;
4.   contract;
5.   lawful obligation; and
6.   vital interests of subject or another natural person.

---

5.   Council Regulation 2252/2004/EC of 13 December 2004 on standards for security features and biometrics in passports and travel documents issued by Member States (OJ 2004 L 385, p 1), as amended by Regulation 444/2009/EC of the European Parliament and of the Council of 6 May 2009 (OJ 2009 L 142, p 1; corrigendum: OJ 2009 L 188, p 127) ('Regulation No 2252/2004').
6.   Regulation 2252/2004, Recital 2.
7.   Regulation 2252/2004, article 1(2).
8.   Regulation 2252/2004, para 11.
9.   *Schwarz v Stadt Bochum* (Case C–291/12) (17 October 2013), para 32.

Obviously, this list is not intended to be definitive in any real sense. Consent is at the top since the subject may withdraw it at any time; the vital interests of the subject or someone else are at the bottom since these may override even lawful obligations. The legitimate interests of controller and necessity in the public interest follow consent as the subject may object to processing on these bases. Contract is next as although the subject has a discretion as to whether he enters into a contract, once that contract is made the controller has the legal right to continue processing the subject's personal data for as long as is necessary for the purposes of discharging that contract. Then there is a lawful obligation such as an obligation imposed by legislation. But none of these lawful bases is 'better' than any of the others; each may or may not apply depending upon the circumstances in which processing is undertaken.

Each of these lawful bases is considered in further detail below.

The data subject has given consent

[7.04] The concept of consent under the GDPR is not simple; obtaining consent in accordance with the GDPR will never be straightforward. Consent can provide a valid basis for the processing of personal data,[10] but relying on consent will not be easy. What distinguishes consent from other lawful bases for processing is that it may be withdrawn by the subject at any time and without penalty. Controllers must therefore have systems in place to ensure that such withdrawals of consent are given effect. Given these procedural safeguards and the application of other safeguards such as Directive 93/13 on unfair terms in consumer contracts, consent under the GDPR may be more easily understood as a revocable contract. One reason not to do so may be that a contract requires consideration to pass between controller and subject. But it is unsurprising that many controllers prefer to structure their relationships with their clients on the basis of formal, irrevocable, contracts, not consent.[11]

GDPR, article 4 defines 'consent' as meaning:

> … any freely given, specific, informed and unambiguous indication of the data subject's wishes by which he or she, by a statement or by a clear affirmative action, signifies agreement to the processing of personal data relating to him or her.[12]

---

10. 'Consent is sometimes a weak basis for justifying the processing of personal data and it loses its value when it is stretched or curtailed to make it fit to situations that it was never intended to be used in. The use of consent "in the right context" is crucial'. WP29 Opinion 15/2011 on the definition of consent (01197/11/EN WP187). Adopted 13/7/2011.

11. See, eg, https://www.facebook.com/terms: 'By using or accessing Facebook Services, you agree that we can collect and use such content and information in accordance with the Data Policy as amended from time to time' or https://twitter.com/tos?lang=en: 'In consideration for Twitter granting you access to and use of the Services, you agree that Twitter and its third-party providers and partners may place advertising on the Services …'.

12. GDPR, article 4(11).

[7.05] Article 7 then goes on to set out the conditions that must be complied with before a consent can be said to have been issued. First of all, it provides that where processing is based on consent then:

> ... the controller shall be able to demonstrate that the data subject has consented to processing of his or her personal data.[13]

This places the burden of proving that a valid consent was obtained squarely on the shoulders of the controller. Of course, this obligation should not be read in isolation. Regard must also be had to other obligations including the principle of accountability set out in GDPR, article 5, the responsibilities imposed by article 24 and the record keeping obligations provided by article 30. There is no explicit obligation that a consent be recorded in writing,[14] indeed the Recitals acknowledge that a consent may be given by means of '... an oral statement'.[15] But the obligation that controllers record that consent has been obtained may often amount to the same thing in practice. And the GDPR does anticipate that consent may be given by way of a '... written declaration ...'. Where consent is given by way of a written declaration which also concerns other matters, then:

> ... the request for consent shall be presented in a manner which is clearly distinguishable from the other matters, in an intelligible and easily accessible form, using clear and plain language.

The Recitals expand on what the controller needs to do in order to demonstrate that the data subject has given consent to the processing operation. In particular, if the subject has given '... a written declaration on another matter' then '... safeguards should ensure that the data subject is aware of the fact that and the extent to which consent is given'.

[7.06] As regards the requirement that consent be 'freely given' the GDPR makes clear that subjects should not feel pressurised into giving consent. In particular, consent will not be freely given where '... the controller is a public authority and it is therefore unlikely that consent was freely given in all the circumstances of that specific situation'.[16] Article 7 goes on to explain that:

> When assessing whether consent is freely given, utmost account shall be taken of whether, *inter alia*, the performance of a contract, including the provision of a service, is conditional on consent to the processing of personal data that is not necessary for the performance of that contract.[17]

If the controller should formulate and present its own declaration of consent[18] then that declaration should not contain unfair terms that would be contrary to Directive 93/13 on

---

13.   GDPR, article 7(1).
14.   Although the Recitals do provide that consent may be given by '... a written statement, including by electronic means.' GDPR, Recital 32.
15.   GDPR, Recital 32.
16.   GDPR, Recital 43.
17.   GDPR, article 7(4).
18.   It would seem logical to apply the guidance provided by Directive 93/13 when deciding whether a term has been formulated and provided by the controller. Directive 93/13, (contd .../)

unfair terms in consumer contracts.[19] Directive 93/13 provides that a contract shall be regarded as unfair:

> ... if, contrary to the requirement of good faith, it causes a significant imbalance in the parties' rights and obligations arising under the contract, to the detriment of the consumer.[20]

The Recitals expand upon the above, providing that:

> ... consent should not provide a valid legal ground for the processing of personal data in a specific case where there is a clear imbalance between the data subject and the controller ... Consent is presumed not to be freely given if it does not allow separate consent to be given to different personal data processing operations despite it being appropriate in the individual case, or if the performance of a contract, including the provision of a service, is dependent on the consent despite such consent not being necessary for such performance.[21]

This prevents consents being bundled with one another. Where it is intended to process personal data in a variety of different ways then consent should cover all processing activities carried out for the same purpose or purposes. When the processing has multiple purposes, consent should be given for all of them.[22]

[7.07] For consent to be informed, the data subject should be aware at least of the identity of the controller and the purposes of the processing for which the personal data are intended, this is simply a partial replication of the obligations of providing information imposed by GDPR, articles 12 and 13. In addition article 7(3) requires that subjects be informed that they have the right to withdraw their consent at any time and

---

18. (contd) article 3(2) provides that a '... term shall always be regarded as not individually negotiated where it has been drafted in advance and the consumer has therefore not been able to influence the substance of the term, particularly in the context of a pre-formulated standard contract'. Directive 93/13 goes on to provide that just because one aspect of a term may have been individually negotiated does not means that the rest of the term is not pre-formulated standard contract. Finally, the burden of proof of proving that a term was not pre-formulated will be borne by the supplier who asserts that such is so.

19. GDPR, Recital 42 cites that such a declaration should accord with Directive 93/13/EEC on unfair terms in consumer contracts (OJ L 95, 21.4.1993, p. 29).

20. Directive 93/13/EEC, article 3(1). Many subjects may give consent to the processing of their personal data when acting as consumers, but many will also do so when acting in the course of their professional lives. As the CJEU held in *ClientEarth* (Case C–615/13 P), 16 July 2015, '... the fact that information is provided as part of a professional activity does not mean that it cannot be characterised as a set of personal data' (para 30). Hence GDPR, Recital 42 may extend Directive 93/13 to consent agreements for the processing of personal data in a professional capacity; as such this may mark a significant extension of that Directive.

21. GDPR, Recital 43.

22. GDPR, Recital 32.

that this withdrawal will not operate retrospectively. The Recitals expand upon what subjects should be informed providing that:

> ... a declaration of consent pre-formulated by the controller should be provided in an intelligible and easily accessible form, using clear and plain language and it should not contain unfair terms. For consent to be informed, the data subject should be aware at least of the identity of the controller and the purposes of the processing for which the personal data are intended. Consent should not be regarded as freely given if the data subject has no genuine or free choice or is unable to refuse or withdraw consent without detriment.[23]

Consent cannot be implied; silence cannot be deemed to be consent. The definition of consent is that it is an '... unambiguous indication of the data subject's wishes ... by a statement or by a clear affirmative action'.[24] This statement or action must signify the subject's agreement to the processing of their personal data. As the Recitals further explain the giving of consent:

> ... could include ticking a box when visiting an internet website, choosing technical settings for information society services or another statement or conduct which clearly indicates in this context the data subject's acceptance of the proposed processing of his or her personal data. Silence, pre-ticked boxes or inactivity should not therefore constitute consent.[25]

The Recitals specify that this means that '... safeguards should ensure that the data subject is aware of the fact that and the extent to which consent is given'.[26] This may avoid consent for the processing of personal data being buried deep within a set of notifications. The failure of subjects to read such notifications and consider what they are consenting to is a persistent challenge to consent as a lawful basis for processing. Requiring that controllers make such a consent 'clearly distinguishable' may help, but only if subjects read the relevant terms and conditions. The Recitals provide that:

> If the data subject's consent is to be given following a request by electronic means, the request must be clear, concise and not unnecessarily disruptive to the use of the service for which it is provided.[27]

However, the reality remains that many subjects may not consider what they are consenting to at all.[28] A controller who proffers a declaration that breaches this, or any other provision of the GDPR such as article 13, will find that the consent will not be binding.[29]

---

23.   GDPR, Recital 42.
24.   GDPR, article 4(11).
25.   GDPR, Recital 32.
26.   GDPR, Recital 42.
27.   GDPR, Recital 32.
28.   'Nobody reads terms and conditions: it's official', Out-Law.com, 19 April 2010.
29.   GDPR, article 7(2).

[7.08] A distinctive feature of consent is that it can be withdrawn. The subject has:

> ... the right to withdraw his or her consent at any time ... It shall be as easy to withdraw as to give consent.[30]

The subject must be informed about their right of withdrawal prior to consent being given. Consent must be 'informed', which means the subject must have been informed of their right of withdrawal for consent to be valid. Or, to be more precise, the controller must be able to demonstrate that it has informed the subject of this right. The requirement that consent should be informed would seem to go beyond this, however. In addition, the controller must provide the subject with the information set out in article 13: identity of controller, purpose of processing, recipients and so forth.

Hence controllers that wish to rely upon consent as a lawful basis will need systems in place to record that subjects have been given the requisite information, to record the giving of the consent itself and to ensure that the cessation of processing if that consent should be withdrawn. A withdrawal of consent will not be retrospective. The GDPR provides that:

> The withdrawal of consent shall not affect the lawfulness of processing based on consent before its withdrawal.[31]

The GDPR imposes specific safeguards in relation to the consent of children; the implementation of which may prove controversial in practice. The Recitals explain that:

> Children merit specific protection with regard to their personal data, as they may be less aware of the risks, consequences and safeguards concerned and their rights in relation to the processing of personal data.[32]

[7.09] GDPR, article 8 then provides specific 'Conditions applicable to child's consent in relation to information society services'[33] providing that where the consent of a child is sought:

> ... in relation to the offer of information society services directly to a child, the processing of the personal data of a child shall be lawful where the child is at least

---

30. GDPR, article 7(3).
31. GDPR 6(3).
32. GDPR, Recital 38.
33. GDPR, article 4(25) defines 'information society service' as '... a service as defined in point (b) of Article 1(1) of Directive 2015/1535 laying down a procedure for the provision of information in the field of technical regulations and of rules on Information Society services (OJ L 241, 17.9.2015, p. 1)' para (b) of which defines such a service as '... any service normally provided for remuneration, at a distance, by electronic means and at the individual request of a recipient of services' Where 'at a distance' means that the service is provided without the parties being simultaneously present;
   'by electronic means' means that the service is sent initially and received at its destination by means of electronic equipment for the processing (including digital compression) and storage of data, and entirely transmitted, conveyed and received by wire, by radio, by optical means or by other electromagnetic means; and 'at the individual request of a recipient of services' means that the service is provided through the transmission of data on individual request. An indicative list of services that are not covered by this definition is set out in Directive 2015/1535, Annex I.

16 years old.[34] Where the child is below the age of 16 years, such processing shall be lawful only if and to the extent that consent is given or authorised by the holder of parental responsibility over the child.

Article 8(2) goes on to provide that it is for the controller to identify who is, or is not, a child:

> The controller shall make reasonable efforts to verify in such cases that consent is given or authorised by the holder of parental responsibility over the child, taking into consideration available technology.

The identification and protection of children online has been a challenge since the earliest days of internet regulation.[35] The days are long gone where one cartoon canine could turn to another and say 'On the Internet nobody knows you're a dog'.[36] Instead identification verification is becoming a service that both companies and countries are endeavouring to provide. Facebook requires: 'people to provide the name they use in real life; that way, you always know who you're connecting with'.[37] Estonia is issuing 'ID cards to non-resident "satellite Estonians", thereby creating a global, government-standard digital identity'.[38] The EU anticipates the market for such identity services with its Regulation 910/2014 on electronic identification and trust services for electronic

---

34.   GDPR, article 8(1) goes on to provide that: 'Member States may provide by law for a lower age for those purposes provided that such lower age is not below 13 years'.

35.   *Reno v American Civil Liberties Union*, 521 US 844.

36.   The cartoon was by Peter Steiner and was published in the *New Yorker* magazine Vol 69, 5 July 1993, p 61. It's hard to believe the subterfuge described in the first edition of this work succeeding today: 'One early case concerned a male, middle aged, psychiatrist from New York. He developed a much racier online persona as 'Talkin' Lady' whose fiancé had been killed in the car accident which had left her paralysed in a wheelchair. In this persona he, or she, became an important and supportive member of his, or her, online community, until the subterfuge was discovered to the chagrin of many' (para 21.01). But it does. In one example, a 68-year old theoretical particle physicist met a dark haired Czech bikini model on a dating website. She wanted to talk marriage, children, but asked that he pick up a 'special' package in Buenos Aires first. When searched by Argentinian customs officers the package turned out to contain two kilos of cocaine. (Swann, 'The Professor, the Bikini Model and the Suitcase full of Trouble', (2013) *New York Times*, 8 March). More bizarre was the American footballer from Notre Dame who met and became engaged to a girl whom he had never met but who had apparently graduated from Stanford University and died of leukaemia before being revealed as a man who was very much alive. ('Hoaxer Denies Te'o Involved', (2013) *New York Times*, 31 January).

37.   https://www.facebook.com/help/112146705538576 (30 December 2014). Some suggest that Google persists with the 'ghost town' of Google+ because: 'once you sign up for Plus, it becomes your account for all Google products, from Gmail to YouTube to maps, so Google sees who you are and what you do across its services': Cain-Miller, 'The Plus in Google Plus? It's Mostly for Google' (2014) New York Times, 14 February. 'Facebook, Google and Twitter are all trying to make their accounts a form of ID. But these are issued without verification, so pseudonyms are rife and impersonation easy': 'Digital Identity Cards: Estonia takes the plunge' (2014) *The Economist*, 28 January.

38.   'Digital Identity Cards: Estonia takes the plunge' (2014) *The Economist*, 28 January.

transactions in the internal market,[39] which 'lays down the conditions under which Member States recognise electronic identification means of natural … persons'.[40]

[7.10] The Recitals go on to provide that the specific protections of article 7 should:

> … in particular, apply to the use of personal data of children for the purposes of marketing or creating personality or user profiles and the collection of personal data with regard to children when using services offered directly to a child.

The Recitals also place some limitations on the application of article 7, stating that:

> The consent of the holder of parental responsibility should not be necessary in the context of preventive or counselling services offered directly to a child.[41]

Further protections for children are provided elsewhere in the GDPR. Information and communications must be provided '… subject in a concise, transparent, intelligible and easily accessible form, using clear and plain language, in particular for any information addressed specifically to a child.[42] The GDPR goes on to suggest that Codes of Conduct be prepared that provide for: 'the information provided to, and the protection of, children, and the manner in which the consent of the holders of parental responsibility over children is to be obtained'.[43] Children also have a specific right to obtain the erasure of personal data that has been processed in accordance with article 8.[44] The limitations placed upon obtaining the consent of children are significant as children typically lack the capacity to enter into contracts under the laws of the Member States. Article 7 specifies that it does not:

> … affect the general contract law of Member States such as the rules on the validity, formation or effect of a contract in relation to a child.[45]

Processing is necessary for the performance of a contract at the request of the data subject prior to entering into a contract

[7.11] The CJEU has considered personal data that was processed on the basis of a contract without commenting on the legal basis on a number of occasions. The contract concluded between the parties provided the lawful basis for the processing of the applicant's personal data in *Schrems*,[46] questions raised by a challenge to transfers from

---

39. Regulation 910/2014 on electronic identification and trust services for electronic transactions in the internal market, OJ L 257, 28.8.2014, p 73–114.
40. Regulation 910/2014, article 1(1)(a).
41. GDPR, Recital 38.
42. GDPR, article 12(1).
43. GDPR, article 40(2)(g).
44. GDPR, article 17(1)(f).
45. GDPR, article 7(3).
46. *Schrems* (Case C–362/14) (6 October 2015), para 27. In *Deutsche Telekom* (Case C–543/09) (5 May 2011) the applicant had 'concluded contracts for the acquisition of subscriber data with approximately 100 undertakings' (para 19). See also *Verein fur Konsumenteninformation* (Case C–191/15) (28 July 2016).

the EU to the USA on the basis of such contractual provisions has been referred to the CJEU by the Irish courts. The lawfulness of data processing on the basis of a contract was considered by the CJEU in *Probst v mr.nexnet*[47] in which the applicant was '... the owner of a telephone line ... through which his computer is connected to the internet'. He was charged for this access by his phone company, the amounts appearing on his bill as 'amounts due to other providers'.[48] He failed to pay and '... nexnet, as assignee of that debt pursuant to a factoring contract concluded between the legal predecessors to Verizon and to nexnet, claimed payment of the amounts billed together with various charges'. Billing the applicant meant providing the respondent, mr nexnet, with the traffic data about his internet usage. At issue was whether the processing of this data on the basis of a contract between the applicant's telecommunications provider and mr nexnet provided a lawful basis for the processing of personal data. The CJEU held that it did. And it is worthy of note that the applicant was not a party to the contract which provided this legal basis, which was between the applicant's telecommunications provider and the respondent to whom the debt was assigned. The CJEU did impose limitations on processing on such a basis:

> ... the contract concluded between the service provider which assigns its claims for payment and the party to which those claims are assigned must contain provisions of such a kind as to ensure the lawful processing of traffic data by the latter and must allow the service provider to ensure at all times that those provisions are being complied with by the assignee.[49]

The CJEU suggest that the contract in this case complied with the above conditions as it:

> ... allows the processing of traffic data by the assignee of claims for payment only in so far as such processing is necessary for the collection of those debts and imposes on that assignee the obligation immediately and irreversibly to erase or return those data as soon as knowledge thereof is no longer necessary for the recovery of the claims concerned. Furthermore, it allows the service provider to check whether there is compliance with the rules on security and data protection on the part of the assignee, which may, on simple request, be obliged to erase or to return the traffic data.[50]

The CJEU did not consider the contact between the applicant and his telecommunications provider; nor did it consider the extent to which the applicant should have been informed that his data had been or was to be transferred in this way. The CJEU's subsequent decision in *Bara*,[51] where data was transferred on the basis of a lawful obligation, suggests that the applicant should be informed.[52]

---

47. *Probst v mr.nexnet* (Case C–119/12) (22 November 2012).
48. *Probst v mr.nexnet* (Case C–119/12) (22 November 2012), para 11.
49. *Probst v mr.nexnet* (Case C–119/12) (22 November 2012), para 27.
50. *Probst v mr.nexnet* (Case C–119/12) (22 November 2012), para 28.
51. *Bara* (Case C–201/14) (1 October 2015).
52. The provision of information to the subject seems unlikely to be an issue in the case of debt recovery services, which tend to take a very proactive approach to contacting debtors.

This lawful basis applies to both data processing on the basis of a contract as well as data processing '… in order to take steps at the request of the data subject prior to entering into a contract'. This might seem like consent, but it is not. Data may be processed prior to entering into a contract for the purposes of drawing up the contract itself: conduct or credit reference checks and so forth. The difference between this and consent is that this legal basis is an explicitly temporary one. If the subject decides to enter into the contract then it is that contract that will provide a legal basis for the continued processing of his personal data. If the subject or the controller decides not to enter into the contract then this legal basis will fall away. Of course, other legal bases may exist, for example a controller may need to retain some personal data as evidence that it has complied with equality legislation. The temporary nature of this legal basis may explain why, unlike consent, the GDPR does not specify the detail of what subjects must be informed of before entering a contract (though such information must be provided pursuant to article 13). The GDPR does set out in some considerable detail what must be contained in a contract between a controller and processor.[53] The relative paucity of guidance on what must be contained in contracts between subjects and controllers may ultimately be resolved by the EU's ongoing project for the standardisation of EU contract terms. This had led to a proposal for a Common EU Sales law,[54] but this proposal was withdrawn.[55]

Processing is necessary for compliance with a legal obligation

[7.12] This lawful basis must be considered in conjunction with that of GDPR, article 7(1)(e):

> … processing is necessary for the performance of a task carried out in the public interest or in the exercise of official authority vested in the controller.

Hence three different lawful bases are rolled into one: compliance with a legal basis, performance of a task in the public interest and the exercise of an official authority. As the Recitals explain:

> A law as a basis for several processing operations based on a legal obligation to which the controller is subject or where processing is necessary for the performance of a task carried out in the public interest or in the exercise of an official authority may be sufficient.[56]

Often it will be problematic, and probably pointless, to draw a line between these two legal bases. So, a Supervisory Authority (SA) that seeks access to personal data held by

---

53. GDPR, article 28(3).

54. Proposal for a Regulation on a Common European Sales Law, COM/2011/0635 final - 2011/0284 (COD).

55. 'Common European Sales Law proposals to be replaced as new consultation is opened on online sales barriers', out-law.com, (17 Jun 2015).

56. GDPR, Recital 45.

a controller may do so under the powers provided by GDPR, article 58(1)(e). This then will be an exercise of that SA's official authority, and so would seem to have a legal basis in GDPR, article 7(1)(e). However in seeking that information the SA will be discharging their tasks under GDPR, article 57(1), particularly the monitoring and enforcement of its provisions. In doing so will the SA be complying with a legal obligation or exercising their official authority? An argument can be made for either legal basis, but it is probably correct to say that seeking access in this way would have both legal bases. However, there need be no discussion about the legal basis upon which the controller from which access is sought will process that data. This will clearly be article 7(1)(c) a legal obligation to which that controller is subject.

[7.13] Tasks carried out in the public interest and exercises of official authority will often be imposed by way of legislation, which will then impose legal obligations upon the bodies or authorities required to undertake those tasks. Sometimes those bodies or authorities will be public in nature; other times they will not. So, the Fourth AML Directive[57] imposes a variety of legal obligations upon obliged entities such as credit and financial institutions.[58] Is such an institution that undertakes customer due diligence pursuant to Chapter II of that directive doing so in compliance with a legal obligation, performing a task in the public interest or exercising an official authority? A good argument can be made that any or all of these provide a lawful basis for the processing.

A further lawful basis may be found in the legitimate interests of the controller or a third party. A good example of how these various legal bases can interact is given by the CJEU decision in *Satakunnan*[59] in which the respondent '… collected public data from the Finnish tax authorities for the purposes of publishing extracts from those data in … the *Veropörssi* newspaper'. This was done pursuant to a Finnish law which provided that 'Information relating to tax matters shall be in the public domain in accordance with the detailed rules laid down in this law'.[60] This enabled the applicant to publish the personal data of some 1.2 million Finnish data subjects who were tax payers. The data in question included their '… surname and given name … the amount … of their earned and unearned income and details relating to wealth tax …'.[61] The applicant argued that its processing of personal data '… must be considered as activities involving the processing of personal data carried out solely for journalistic purposes'.[62]

The CJEU concluded that it was for the Finnish Courts to strike a balance between the data protection rights of tax payers and freedom of expression '… relating to data from documents which are in the public domain under national legislation'. The CJEU

---

57. Directive 2015/849 on the prevention of the use of the financial system for the purposes of money laundering or terrorist financing, OJ L 141, 5.6.2015, p 73–117.

58. Directive 2015/849 on the prevention of the use of the financial system for the purposes of money laundering or terrorist financing, OJ L 141, 5.6.2015, p 73–117, article 2(1).

59. *Satakunnan Markkinapörssi* (Case C–73/07) (16 December 2008).

60. *Satakunnan Markkinapörssi* (Case C–73/07) (16 December 2008), para 22.

61. *Satakunnan Markkinapörssi* (Case C–73/07) (16 December 2008), paras 25-26.

62. *Satakunnan Markkinapörssi* (Case C–73/07) (16 December 2008), para 50.

did not consider the legal basis for this processing, but a good argument could be made that the obtaining and publication of this personal data was processing necessary for the performance of a task carried out in the public interest. Alternatively, or in addition, it could be argued that the publication of this personal data was 'necessary for the purposes of the legitimate interests pursued by the controller'.

[7.14] The decision of the CJEU in *Satakunnan*[63] follows from the earlier decision of the CJEU in *Österreichischer Rundfunk*,[64] which concerned an obligation imposed by Austrian law on '... public bodies ... to communicate ... the salaries and pensions exceeding a certain level paid by them to their employees ... for the purpose of drawing up an annual report to be ... made available to the general public ...'.[65] The CJEU concluded that EU data protection law did '... not preclude national legislation such as that at issue in the main proceedings, provided that it is shown that the wide disclosure ... is necessary for and appropriate to the objective of proper management of public funds pursued by the legislature ...'.[66]

A wide variety of legal acts providing for the processing of personal data have been considered by the CJEU over the years. In *Huber*[67] the CJEU set out the requirements that would have to be met by a German law establishing a central register of foreign nationals.[68] In *Deutsch Telekom*[69] it held that the ePrivacy Directive did not preclude national laws that required one telecommunications provider to provide personal data relating to its own subscribers and those of third parties to the providers of director enquiry services. As noted above the CJEU upheld the processing of personal data on the basis of Regulation 2252/2014 in *Schwarz*.

---

63. *Satakunnan Markkinapörssi* (Case C–73/07) (16 December 2008).

64. *Österreichischer Rundfunk* (Cases C–465/00, C–138/01 and C–139/01) (20 May 2003).

65. *Österreichischer Rundfunk* (Cases C–465/00, C–138/01 and C–139/01) (20 May 2003), para 2.

66. *Österreichischer Rundfunk* (Cases C–465/00, C–138/01 and C–139/01) (20 May 2003), para 102.

67. *Huber* (Case C–524/06) (16 December 2008).

68. Those standards being that the German register could contain only the necessary data and its '... centralised nature enables the legislation relating to the right of residence to be more effectively applied as regards Union citizens who are not nationals of that Member State' *Huber* (Case C–524/06) (16 December 2008), para 82.

69. *Deutsche Telekom* (Case C–543/09) (5 May 2011) a decision applied by the CJEU in *Tele2 (Netherlands)* (Case C–536/15) (15 March 2017). See also *KPN Telecom* (Case C–109/03) (25 November 2004) in which the CJEU held (at para 32) that: '... the protection of personal data and privacy is a factor of the first importance to be taken into account in determining the data that an operator is required to make available to a third-party competitor. In fact a broad approach requiring the indiscriminate provision of all the data at an operator's disposal, with the exception, however, of those concerning subscribers who in no way wish to appear on a published list, is not reconcilable either with the protection of those data or with the privacy of the persons concerned'.

[7.15] In *Manni*[70] the CJEU considered the processing of personal data on a company register. The CJEU noted that this processing appeared to have twin lawful bases:

> ... the activity of a public authority consisting in the storing, in a database, of data which undertakings are obliged to report on the basis of statutory obligations, permitting interested persons to search for that data and providing them with print-outs thereof, falls within the exercise of public powers[71] ... Moreover, such an activity also constitutes a task carried out in the public interest within the meaning of that provision.[72]

It is clear from these judgments that the CJEU recognises that EU or national laws can provide a lawful basis for the processing of personal data.[73] But it is also clear that the CJEU considers that such laws must respect EU data protection rules. So in *Digital Rights Ireland*[74] the CJEU held that the EU's Data Retention Directive was invalid as it failed to '... lay down clear and precise rules governing the scope and application of the measure in question and imposing minimum safeguards so that the persons whose data have been retained have sufficient guarantees to effectively protect their personal data against the risk of abuse and against any unlawful access and use of that data'.[75] And in *Tele2* it agreed that the *ePrivacy Directive* allowed Sweden introduce a data retention law of its own, which limited the privacy and data protection rights of subjects but '... any limitation on the exercise of the rights and freedoms recognised by the Charter must be provided for by law and must respect the essence of those rights and freedoms ... limitations may be imposed on the exercise of those rights and freedoms only if they are necessary and if they genuinely meet objectives of general interest recognised by the European Union or the need to protect the rights and freedoms of others ...'.[76] Such a law had to have due regard to the principle of proportionality, which meant '... that derogations from and limitations on the protection of personal data should apply only in so far as is strictly necessary'.[77]

[7.16] The Recitals make clear that the GDPR does not:

> ... require a specific law for each individual processing. A law as a basis for several processing operations based on a legal obligation to which the controller is subject or where processing is necessary for the performance of a task carried out in the public interest or in the exercise of an official authority may be sufficient.[78]

---

70. *Manni* (Case C–398/15) (9 March 2017).
71. Citing *Compass-Datenbank* (Case C–138/11) (12 July 2012), paras 40 and 41.
72. *Manni* (Case C–398/15) (9 March 2017), para 43.
73. See also *Willems* (Case C–446/12) (16 April 2015) and *TR & P Fisher* (Case C–369/98) (14 September 2000).
74. *Digital Rights Ireland* (Case C–293/12) (8 April 2014).
75. *Digital Rights Ireland* (Case C–293/12) (8 April 2014), para 54.
76. *Tele2 Sverige (Judgment)* (Case C–203/15) (21 December 2016), para 94.
77. *Tele2 Sverige (Judgment)* (Case C–203/15) (21 December 2016), para 96.
78. GDPR, Recital 45.

The use of a generally phrased law to provide a legal basis for a specific processing operation was considered by the CJEU in *Bara*,[79] which concerned the transfer of personal data from the Romanian tax authorities to health insurance funds. The legal bases of these transfers was a Romanian law which expressly provided that:

> the data necessary to certify that the person concerned qualifies as an insured person are to be communicated free of charge to the health insurance funds by the authorities, public institutions or other institutions in accordance with a protocol.[80]

The CJEU did not dispute the validity of this legal base, but held that the law in question could not '... constitute ... prior information enabling the data controller to dispense with his obligation to inform the persons from whom data relating to their income are collected as to the recipients of those data'.[81] The CJEU went on to hold the transfer invalid in the absence of that information.[82] It is open to question whether a law such as this could provide a valid lawful basis for the processing of information under the GDPR. However, the Recitals do provide that a reference to a legal basis or a legislative measure in the GDPR:

> ... does not necessarily require a legislative act adopted by a parliament, without prejudice to requirements pursuant to the constitutional order of the Member State concerned. However, such a legal basis or legislative measure should be clear and precise and its application should be foreseeable to persons subject to it, in accordance with the case law of the Court of Justice of the European Union ('Court of Justice') and the European Court of Human Rights.[83]

Hence a processing operation may have a legal basis in a judgment of court, a constitutional provision or even an administrative scheme, if such can provide a legal basis under the constitutional order of the Member State in question. Whatever the legal basis in question it must be sufficiently precise and provide subjects with information as to how it will apply to them. Whether a court judgment in particular can provide such a legal basis will depend upon the facts of the case in question, but judgments can tend to be quite specific to the facts set before the Court in question. Lawyers may be equipped with the skills to apply those judgments to other sets of facts, but many subjects will not have those skills. Hence courts judgments may only provide a legal basis that is limited to particular circumstances.

[7.17] GDPR, article 6(2) provides that:

> Member States may maintain or introduce more specific provisions to adapt the application of the rules of this Regulation with regard to processing for compliance with points (c) and (e) of para 1 by determining more precisely specific requirements for the processing and other measures to ensure lawful and

---

79. *Bara* (Case C–201/14) (1 October 2015).
80. *Bara* (Case C–201/14) (1 October 2015), para 37.
81. *Bara* (Case C–201/14) (1 October 2015), para 38.
82. *Bara* (Case C–201/14) (1 October 2015), para 47.
83. GDPR, Recital 41.

fair processing including for other specific processing situations as provided for in Chapter IX.

Member States will have to adapt their laws in the public sector to take account of the GDPR. Article 6(2) allows for this process to take effect, some Member States may wish to do so by undertaking an omnibus provision, others may do so by amending individual laws. These laws may be those that deal with the situations to which GDPR, Ch IX applies: journalists, artists, academics and authors; freedom of information and transparency; national identification numbers; employment; archiving, scientific, historic or statistical research; secrecy; and, churches. However the scope of article 6(2) is not limited to those situations that are set out in Ch IX but suggests that Member States may wish to introduce more general provisions.

[7.18] GDPR, article 6(3) provides that where a law provides a legal basis for processing then it must meet an objective of public interest and be proportionate to the legitimate aim pursued. This is consistent with the approach of the CJEU. Any law which provides for the processing of personal data must necessarily limit the exercise of subjects data protection rights. In *Avis I-15* the CJEU explained that:

> any limitation on the exercise of the rights and freedoms recognised by the Charter must be provided for by law and respect the essence of those rights and freedoms. Under the second sentence of Article 52(1) of the Charter, subject to the principle of proportionality, limitations may be made to those rights and freedoms only if they are necessary and genuinely meet objectives of general interest recognised by the Union or the need to protect the rights and freedoms of others.[84]

Similarly in *Tele2 Sverige* the CJEU considered how a national data retention law might be limited to what was necessary:

> ... if it is to be ensured that data retention is limited to what is strictly necessary... conditions may vary according to the nature of the measures taken... the retention of data must continue nonetheless to meet objective criteria, that establish a connection between the data to be retained and the objective pursued. In particular, such conditions must be shown to be such as actually to circumscribe,
> in practice, the extent of that measure and, thus, the public affected.[85]

However it would not be sufficient to limit the processing of personal data to a particular objective. In addition national law would have to '... lay down substantive and procedural conditions governing the access of national authorities to the retained data'.[86] In *Schrems* the CJEU held that:

> Legislation is not limited to what is strictly necessary where it authorises, on a generalised basis, storage of all the personal data of all the persons whose data has been transferred from the European Union to the United States without any

---

84. *Transfer of Passenger Name Record data from the European Union to Canada* [2017] EUECJ Avis-1/15_OC (26 July 2017), para 138.
85. *Tele2 Sverige* (Case C–203/15) (21 December 2016), para 110.
86. *Tele2 Sverige* (Case C–203/15) (21 December 2016), para 118.

differentiation, limitation or exception being made in the light of the objective pursued and without an objective criterion being laid down by which to determine the limits of the access of the public authorities to the data, and of its subsequent use, for purposes which are specific, strictly restricted and capable of justifying the interference which both access to that data and its use entail …[87]

Such a limitation would have to be proportionate, in order to observe this principle the CJEU held that such a law would have to '… apply only in so far as is strictly necessary'.[88] In *Tele2 Sverige* the CJEU suggested that in order to ensure proportionality:

the national legislation must be based on objective evidence which makes it possible to identify a public whose data is likely to reveal a link, at least an indirect one, with serious criminal offences, and to contribute in one way or another to fighting serious crime or to preventing a serious risk to public security. Such limits may be set by using a geographical criterion where the competent national authorities consider, on the basis of objective evidence, that there exists, in one or more geographical areas, a high risk of preparation for or commission of such offences.[89]

Any law would have to be clearly defined. As the CJEU went onto state:

… any limitation on the exercise of fundamental rights must be provided for by law implies that the legal basis which permits the interference with those rights must itself define the scope of the limitation on the exercise of the right concerned.[90]

And such legislation would have to:

… lay down clear and precise rules governing the scope and application of the measure in question and imposing minimum safeguards, so that the persons whose data has been transferred have sufficient guarantees to protect effectively their personal data against the risk of abuse. It must, in particular, indicate in what circumstances and under which conditions a measure providing for the processing of such data may be adopted, thereby ensuring that the interference is limited to what is strictly necessary. The need for such safeguards is all the greater where personal data is subject to automated processing. Those considerations apply particularly where the protection of the particular category of personal data that is sensitive data is at stake …[91]

Hence it is clear that the simple existence of a law which may provide for the processing of personal data may not, of itself, but sufficient to provide a lawful basis for that

---

87. *Schrems* (Case C–362/14) (06 October 2015), para 93.
88. *Transfer of Passenger Name Record data from the European Union to Canada* [2017] EUECJ Avis-1/15_OC (26 July 2017), para 140.
89. *Tele2 Sverige* (Case C–203/15) (21 December 2016), para 111.
90. *Transfer of Passenger Name Record data from the European Union to Canada* [2017] EUECJ Avis-1/15_OC (26 July 2017), para 139.
91. *Transfer of Passenger Name Record data from the European Union to Canada* [2017] EUECJ Avis-1/15_OC (26 July 2017), para 141.

processing. As the CJEU has outlined about, there are certain elements that such a law must contain in order to provide a lawful basis. And consistent with the approach of the CJEU, Article 6(2) GDPR goes onto provide that such a law may contain certain specific provisions:

(a) general conditions governing the lawfulness of processing by the controller;

(b) types of data which are subject to the processing;

(c) data subjects concerned;

(e) purpose limitation;

(f) storage periods;

(g) processing operations and processing procedures, including measures to ensure lawful and fair processing such as those for other specific processing situations such as Freedom of Information, national identification numbers, employment, archiving, research, statistics and churches.[92]

Both the CJEU and the GDPR have set out specific criteria as to what a law must contain. However the CJEU has taken a broad view as to what may amount to a law. In *Avis 1/15* the EU Parliament argued that an agreement between the US and Canada did not '... fall within the notion of "law", within the meaning of Article 8(2) of the Charter and, therefore, of Article 52(1) thereof inasmuch as it does not constitute a "legislative act". The CJEU rejected this argument on two grounds. One ground was that it had not been argued '... the envisaged agreement may not meet the requirements as to accessibility and predictability required ...' by the Court. This is not inconsistent with the approach of the Court in *Bara*, in which it was held that a Romanian law could not provide for a transfer of data as it did not '... constitute ... prior information enabling the data controller to dispense with his obligation to inform the persons from whom data relating to their income are collected as to the recipients of those data'.[93] The other ground was that although the agreement in question was not an internal law '... such an agreement may be regarded as being the equivalent, externally, of that which is a legislative act internally'. The CJEU therefore found that it to follow that this transfer of data was:

> ...based on 'some other basis' that is 'laid down by law', within the meaning of Article 8(2) of the Charter.[94]

This may suggest that it is not absolutely necessary for legislation to contain all the elements set out in Article 6(3) GDPR so long as the existing framework met the CJEU's requirements as to accessibility and predictability. It is possible that the CJEU would find that a combination of legislation that provides a general power to process personal

---

92. These are the various types of processing operations provided for in Chapter IX, GDPR, article 6.3.

93. *Bara & Ors* (Judgment) (Case C–201/14) (1 October 2015), para 38.

94. *Transfer of Passenger Name Record data from the European Union to Canada* [2017] EUECJ Avis-1/15_OC (26 July 2017), paras 146–147.

data together with a legally binding memorandum which provided the detail required by Article 6(3) GDPR could amount to 'some other basis' that is 'laid down by law'.

[7.19] Where a law is proposed which provides for the processing of personal data then SAs may be consulted in relation to its content. GDPR, article 58(3)(b) provides that SAs have the power to:

> ... issue, on its own initiative or on request, opinions to the national parliament, the Member State government or, in accordance with Member State law, to other institutions and bodies as well as to the public on any issue related to the protection of personal data.

This creates a gateway for the governments and legislatures of Member States to consult with SAs prior to the enactment of laws that provide for the processing of personal data. However, it does not require that such consultation take place. Once such a law is enacted then the SA will be bound by it, though this does not mean that neither a SA nor a subject can challenge its provisions. This is clear from the judgment of the CJEU in *Schrems*.[95] At issue was a decision of the EU Commission that the Safe Harbor Agreement between the EU and USA provided an adequate level of data protection. The CJEU held that:

> ... until such time as the Commission decision is declared invalid by the Court, the Member States and their organs, which include their independent supervisory authorities ... cannot adopt measures contrary to that decision ... Measures of the EU institutions are in principle presumed to be lawful and accordingly produce legal effects until such time as they are withdrawn, annulled in an action for annulment or declared invalid following a reference for a preliminary ruling or a plea of illegality ...[96]

The CJEU went on to explain that this did not mean that such a law was beyond challenge. Such an EU Commission decision could neither prevent a subject making a complaint to a SA[97] nor prevent that SA investigating such a complaint.[98] However, only the CJEU:

> ... has jurisdiction to declare that an EU act ... is invalid, the exclusivity of that jurisdiction having the purpose of guaranteeing legal certainty by ensuring that EU law is applied uniformly ...[99]

And so, while '... national courts are ... entitled to consider the validity of an EU act ... they are not ... endowed with the power to declare such an act invalid themselves.' And so, when national SAs '... examine a claim ... they are not entitled to declare that decision invalid themselves'.[100] Instead either SAs or subjects should apply to their

---

95. *Schrems* (Case C–362/14) (6 October 2015).
96. *Schrems* (Case C–362/14) (6 October 2015), para 52.
97. *Schrems* (Case C–362/14) (6 October 2015), para 53.
98. *Schrems* (Case C–362/14) (6 October 2015), para 56.
99. *Schrems* (Case C–362/14) (6 October 2015), para 61.
100. *Schrems* (Case C–362/14) (6 October 2015), para 62.

national courts with a view to referring the validity of the EU act in question to the CJEU.[101] A similar approach would presumably be taken in relation to national legislation, the validity of which might be referred to a national court, which might then refer any questions arising in relation to the interpretation of the GDPR to the CJEU. GDPR, article 79 suggests that an impatient data subject may refer the validity of such a law to the courts without first making a complaint to their SA, providing that:

> Without prejudice to any available administrative or non-judicial remedy ... each data subject shall have the right to an effective judicial remedy where he or she considers that his or her rights under this Regulation have been infringed as a result of the processing of his or her personal data in non-compliance with this Regulation.[102]

How many subjects will be willing to take this route remains to be seen. Going to court can be costly, whilst a complaint to a SA can be made for free.

[7.20] The Article 29 WP adopted *Guidelines on Consent under Regulation 2016/679*[103] in November 2017, which were undergoing public consultation at the time of this work's publication. These provide some useful guidance as to how consent may be applied in practice. The Article 29 WP notes that the GDPR requires 'explicit consent' in relation to the processing of sensitive personal data,[104] transborder data flows[105] and profiling,[106] Article 29 WP explains that while a 'clear affirmative act' is a prerequisite for 'regular' consent, explicit consent requires 'that the data subject must give an express statement of consent. An obvious way to make sure consent is explicit would be to expressly confirm consent in a written statement'.[107] As regards retention periods, the guidelines note that: 'There is no specific time limit in the GDPR for how long consent will last. How long consent lasts will depend on the context, the scope of the original consent and the expectations of the data subject. If the processing operations change or evolve considerably then the original consent is no longer valid.'[108] Finally, the Article 29 WP explain that controllers do not need to renew consents simply due to the GDPR's application:

> Controllers that currently process data on the basis of consent in compliance with national data protection law are not automatically required to completely refresh all existing consent relations with data subjects in preparation for the GDPR.

---

101. *Schrems* (Case C–362/14) (6 October 2015), paras 64–65.

102. GDPR, article 79(1).

103. A29 WP *Guidelines on Consent under Regulation 2016/679,* 17/EN WP259, 28 November 2017.

104. GDPR, article 9.

105. GDPR, article 49.

106. GDPR, article 22.

107. A29 WP *Guidelines on Consent under Regulation 2016/679,* 17/EN WP259, 28 November 2017, p 18.

108. A29 WP *Guidelines on Consent under Regulation 2016/679,* 17/EN WP259, 28 November 2017, p 20.

Consent which has been obtained to date continues to be valid in so far as it is in line with the conditions laid down in the GDPR.[109]

Processing is necessary in order to protect vital interests

[7.21] This lawful basis is directed at issues such as those that arose in France in the early 1990s, where research was carried out into instances of hereditary glaucoma in Boulogne-sur-Mer, which had an unusually high incidence of this disease. The research traced the family trees of three families who were known to be suffering from glaucoma back fifteen generations to a blind couple who had lived in the sixteenth century. It was then relatively straightforward to trace all the descendants of that couple and identify those who were at an increased risk of suffering from glaucoma. If glaucoma is caught early enough it can be halted by the application of eye drops; however, the only treatment for late-disease glaucoma is surgery, or blindness may result. Prior to contacting the descendants, the researchers consulted the French data protection agency but were told that under French data protection law they could not, under any circumstances, inform the descendants of what they had discovered.[110] As the Recitals explain:

> Processing of personal data based on the vital interest of another natural person should in principle take place only where the processing cannot be manifestly based on another legal basis. Some types of processing may serve both important grounds of public interest and the vital interests of the data subject as for instance when processing is necessary for humanitarian purposes, including for monitoring epidemics and their spread or in situations of humanitarian emergencies, in particular in situations of natural and man-made disasters.[111]

There has been little consideration of this as a lawful basis for the processing of personal data by the CJEU. In *Tele2 Sverige*[112] the CJEU did suggest that access to retained telecommunications data might be permitted:

> ... in particular situations, where for example vital national security, defence or public security interests are threatened by terrorist activities, access to the data of other persons might also be granted where there is objective evidence from which it can be deduced that that data might, in a specific case, make an effective contribution to combating such activities.[113]

This suggests that if personal data is to be processed on the basis that it is in the vital interests of the subject or another person then there must be objective evidence to support the view that this processing would in fact make an effective contribution to the

---

109. A29 WP *Guidelines on Consent under Regulation 2016/679,* 17/EN WP259, 28 November 2017, p 29.
110. Laurie, *Genetic Privacy* (CUP, 2002), p 117.
111. GDPR, Recital 46.
112. *Tele2 Sverige* (Case C–203/15) (21 December 2016).
113. *Tele2 Sverige* (Case C–203/15) (21 December 2016), para 119.

vital interest of the subject or other persons. In *Manni*[114] the CJEU considered that the interest that purchasers of apartments might have in knowing that the vendor had previously been the sole director of a company which had been declared insolvent and liquidated could justify the continuing processing of the applicants' personal data on a company register many years afterward.

Processing is necessary for the performance of a task carried out in the public interest or in the exercise of official authority vested in the controller

[7.22] In *Puskar*[115] the subject's name appeared on '… a list of persons considered by the Finance Directorate to be "front-men" …'.[116] He challenged his appearance on that list and the Czech courts asked the CJEU to consider:

> … whether Directive 95/46 and Articles 7 and 8 of the Charter are to be interpreted as precluding the processing of personal data by the authorities of a Member State for the purpose of collecting tax and combating tax fraud such as that effected by drawing up the contested list in the main proceedings without the consent of the data subjects.[117]

The CJEU noted the equivalent provision to Article 6(1)(e) GDPR in Directive 95/46 and suggested that '… establishment of the contested list appears likely to fall within that provision.[118] It appeared to the Court:

> … that the collection of the tax and combating tax fraud, for the purposes of which the contested list is established, must be regarded as tasks carried out in the public interest within the meaning of that provision.[119]

However the CJEU considered it important … to ensure that the principle of proportionality is respected. The protection of the fundamental right to respect for private life at the European Union level requires that derogations from the protection of personal data and its limitations be carried out within the limits of what is strictly necessary'.[120] The CJEU therefore concluded that the Directive 95/46 equivalent of Article 6(1)(e) could provide a lawful basis for the processing of the list in question by the Czech authorities:

> … provided that, first, those authorities were invested by the national legislation with tasks carried out in the public interest within the meaning of that article, that the drawing-up of that list and the inclusion on it of the names of the data subjects in fact be appropriate and necessary for the purpose of attaining the objectives

---

114. *Manni* (Case C–398/15) (9 March 2017), para 63.
115. *Puskar* (Case C–73/16) (27 September 2017).
116. *Puskar* (Case C–73/16) (27 September 2017), para 2.
117. *Puskar* (Case C–73/16) (27 September 2017), para 99.
118. *Puskar* (Case C–73/16) (27 September 2017), para 107.
119. *Puskar* (Case C–73/16) (27 September 2017), para 108.
120. *Puskar* (Case C–73/16) (27 September 2017), para 112.

pursued and that there be sufficient indications to assume that the data subjects are rightly included in that list and, second, that all of the conditions for the lawfulness of that processing of personal data imposed by Directive 95/46 be satisfied.[121]

Processing is necessary for the purposes of the legitimate interests pursued by the controller or by a third party

[7.23] Reliance upon this lawful basis requires that the legitimate interests of the controller be balanced with the interests or fundamental rights and freedoms, not just the data protection rights, of the data subject.[122] This requires that an analysis be undertaken and that the outcome of that analysis be recorded.[123] The GDPR does not stipulate that this analysis be undertaken by means of a Data Protection Impact Assessment (DPIA), but the use of a DPIA seems appropriate. A DPIA must contain 'a systematic description of the envisaged processing operations and the purposes of the processing, including, where applicable, the legitimate interest pursued by the controller'[124] and 'an assessment of the risks to the rights and freedoms of data subjects'.[125] This analysis will enable the controller '... to demonstrate compliance with this Regulation taking into account the rights and legitimate interests of data subjects and other persons concerned'.[126] Controllers are accountable[127] and so prudent controllers that wish to process data on the basis of article 6(1)(f) may wish to undertake a DPIA before doing so in order to demonstrate that compliance.

[7.24] The assessment of what may amount to a legitimate interest of a controller was considered by the CJEU in *Rynes*.[128] The applicant was a householder who had been the victim of vandalism. The CJEU held that the CCTV system he had erected to monitor such activity was subject to Directive 95/46, however it suggested that '... the

---

121. *Puskar* (Case C–73/16) (27 September 2017), para 117.
122. See also WP29 Party Opinion 06/2014 on the notion of legitimate interests of the data controller under Directive 95/46/EC, article 7. 844/14/EN WP 217.
123. GDPR, article 30.
124. GDPR, article 35(7)(a).
125. GDPR, article 35(7)(c).
126. GDPR, article 35(7)(d).
127. GDPR, article 5(2).
128. *Rynes* (Case C–212/13) (11 December 2014). In *Dennekamp v Parliament* (Case T–115/13) (15 July 2015) access to information about the pensions of MEPs was sought pursuant to EU transparency rules (Regulation (EC) No 1049/2001 of the European Parliament and of the Council of 30 May 2001 regarding public access to European Parliament, Council and Commission documents (OJ 2001 L 145, p. 43). The CJEU upheld the refusal of the EU Parliament to permit access to this information as '... the risk of MEPs' legitimate interests, and thus their privacy, being undermined lies in the fact that, falling as they do into the private sphere of MEPs, the personal data at issue constitute a legitimate interest to be protected on the ground that they concern the personal financial situation of MEPs, pension contributions and resulting pension rights being private matters' (para 139).

application of Directive 95/46 makes it possible, where appropriate, to take into account ... legitimate interests pursued by the controller, such as the protection of the property, health and life of his family and himself ...'.[129] The Recitals do offer some guidance as to what may amount to a legitimate interest of a controller:

> Such legitimate interest could exist for example where there is a relevant and appropriate relationship between the data subject and the controller in situations such as where the data subject is a client or in the service of the controller. At any rate the existence of a legitimate interest would need careful assessment including whether a data subject can reasonably expect at the time and in the context of the collection of the personal data that processing for that purpose may take place.[130]

This initial guidance is rather vague, but the Recitals go on to specify that:

> Controllers that are part of a group of undertakings or institutions affiliated to a central body may have a legitimate interest in transmitting personal data within the group of undertakings for internal administrative purposes, including the processing of clients' or employees' personal data.[131]

The Recitals also suggest that information security may be a legitimate interest. In *Breyer* the applicant had '... accessed several websites operated by German Federal institutions'.[132] He discovered that: 'With the aim of preventing attacks and making it possible to prosecute "pirates", most of those websites store information on all access operations in logfiles'.[133] The CJEU accepted that '... the objective aiming to ensure the general operability of those services may justify the use of those data after consultation of those websites'.[134] This is consistent with the Recitals of the GDPR, which suggest that the following will constitute a legitimate interest of the data controller:

> The processing of personal data to the extent strictly necessary and proportionate for the purposes of ensuring network and information security, i.e. the ability of a network or an information system to resist, at a given level of confidence, accidental events or unlawful or malicious actions that compromise the availability, authenticity, integrity and confidentiality of stored or transmitted personal data, and the security of the related services offered by, or accessible via, those networks and systems, by public authorities, by computer emergency response teams (CERTs), computer security incident response teams (CSIRTs), by providers of electronic communications networks and services and by providers of security technologies and services ... This could, for example, include preventing unauthorised access to electronic communications networks and malicious code distribution and stopping 'denial of service' attacks and damage to computer and electronic communication systems.[135]

---

129. *Rynes* (Case C–212/13) (11 December 2014), para 34.
130. GDPR, Recital 47.
131. GDPR, Recital 48.
132. *Breyer* (Case C–582/14) (19 October 2016), para 13.
133. *Breyer* (Case C–582/14) (19 October 2016), para 14.
134. *Breyer* (Case C–582/14) (19 October 2016), para 64.
135. GDPR, Recital 49.

In addition, the Recitals provide that:

> Where the data subject has given consent or the processing is based on Union or Member State law which constitutes a necessary and proportionate measure in a democratic society to safeguard, in particular, important objectives of general public interest, the controller should be allowed to further process the personal data irrespective of the compatibility of the purposes. In any case, the application of the principles set out in this Regulation and in particular the information of the data subject on those other purposes and on his or her rights including the right to object, should be ensured. Indicating possible criminal acts or threats to public security by the controller and transmitting the relevant personal data in individual cases or in several cases relating to the same criminal act or threats to public security to a competent authority should be regarded as being in the legitimate interest pursued by the controller. However, such transmission in the legitimate interest of the controller or further processing of personal data should be prohibited if the processing is not compatible with a legal, professional or other binding obligation of secrecy.[136]

Finally, the Recitals suggest that the '... processing of personal data strictly necessary for the purposes of preventing fraud also constitutes a legitimate interest of the data controller concerned' and that the '... processing of personal data for direct marketing purposes may be regarded as carried out for a legitimate interest'.[137]

[7.25] These legitimate interests of the controller or third parties have to be balanced with the interests, rights and freedoms of the data subject. The GDPR explains that:

> The interests and fundamental rights of the data subject could in particular override the interest of the data controller where personal data are processed in circumstances where data subjects do not reasonably expect further processing.[138]

The impact that the processing of personal data by an internet search engine might have upon the interests of the subject was considered by the CJEU in *Google Spain*[139] albeit in the context of the right to object.[140] The CJEU held that the:

> processing of personal data ... carried out by the operator of a search engine is liable to affect significantly the fundamental rights to privacy and to the protection of personal data when the search by means of that engine is carried out on the basis of an individual's name, since that processing enables any internet user to obtain through the list of results a structured overview of the information relating to that individual that can be found on the internet — information which potentially concerns a vast number of aspects of his private life and which, without the search engine, could not have been interconnected or could have been only with great difficulty — and thereby to establish a more or less detailed profile of him. Furthermore, the effect of the interference with those rights of the data

---

136. GDPR, Recital 51.
137. GDPR, Recital 47.
138. GDPR, Recital 47.
139. *Google Spain* (Case C–131/12) (13 May 2014).
140. Now GDPR, article 17.

subject is heightened on account of the important role played by the internet and search engines in modern society, which render the information contained in such a list of results ubiquitous ...[141]

As regards balancing the interests, rights and freedoms of the subject with the legitimate interests of the controller the CJEU held:

> In the light of the potential seriousness of that interference, it is clear that it cannot be justified by merely the economic interest which the operator of such an engine has in that processing.

However, the CJEU did allow that third parties might have a legitimate interest in the processing of this personal data. The Court accepted '... that the data subject's rights ... override, as a general rule, that interest of internet users, that balance may however depend, in specific cases, on the nature of the information in question and its sensitivity for the data subject's private life and on the interest of the public in having that information, an interest which may vary, in particular, according to the role played by the data subject in public life'.[142]

[7.26] The GDPR makes clear that public authorities cannot rely upon their legitimate interests to provide a lawful basis for the processing of personal data in the performance of their tasks.[143] The Recitals explain that this is because:

> ... it is for the legislator to provide by law for the legal basis for public authorities to process personal data.[144]

Finally, GDPR, article 6(2) provides that:

> ... Member States may maintain or introduce more specific provisions to adapt the application of the rules of this Regulation with regard to processing for compliance with points (c) and (e) of para 1 by determining more precisely specific requirements for the processing and other measures to ensure lawful and fair processing including for other specific processing situations as provided for in Chapter IX.

Such a national provision was considered by the CJEU in *ASNEF*.[145] At issue was a Spanish law which added '... to the condition relating to the legitimate interest in data processing without the data subject's consent, a condition, which does not exist in Directive 95/46, to the effect that the data should appear in public sources'.[146] The CJEU considered that:

> A distinction ... must be made between national measures that provide for additional requirements amending the scope of a principle ... on the one hand, and national measures which provide for a mere clarification of one of those

---

141. *Google Spain* (Case C–131/12) (13 May 2014), para 80.
142. *Google Spain* (Case C–131/12) (13 May 2014), para 81.
143. GDPR, article 6(1) concludes with a statement that 'point (f) ... . Shall not apply to processing carried out by public authorities in the performance of their tasks'.
144. GDPR, Recital 47.
145. *ASNEF* (Case C–468/10) (24 November 2011).
146. *ASNEF* (Case C–468/10) (24 November 2011), para 17.

principles, on the other hand. The first type of national measure is precluded. It is only in the context of the second type of national measure that Member States have ... a margin of discretion.

The CJEU noted that Directive 95/46, article 7(f), the equivalent of GDPR, article 6(1)(f):

... sets out two cumulative conditions that must be fulfilled in order for the processing of personal data to be lawful: firstly, the processing of the personal data must be necessary for the purposes of the legitimate interests pursued by the controller or by the third party or parties to whom the data are disclosed; and, secondly, such interests must not be overridden by the fundamental rights and freedoms of the data subject.[147]

This led the CJEU to conclude that 'article 7(f) of Directive 95/46 precludes any national rules which, in the absence of the data subject's consent, impose requirements that are additional to the two cumulative conditions set out in the preceding paragraph'.[148] Given that Directive 95/46, article 7(f) is essentially the same as GDPR, article 6(1)(f) the judgment of the CJEU in ASNEF would seem to apply, meaning that national legislatures have a quite limited discretion if they should introduce measures in accordance with GDPR, article 6(2).

---

147. *ASNEF* (Case C–468/10) (24 November 2011), para 38.
148. *ASNEF* (Case C–468/10) (24 November 2011), para 39.

Chapter 8

SPECIAL CATEGORIES OF DATA

INTRODUCTION

[8.01] The GDPR repeals and replaces its predecessor, Directive 95/46, but retains its supervisory structures. This continuity has many advantages but it also means that some provisions have been retained that may no longer be useful or effective. One such may be GDPR, article 10, which prohibits the processing of certain 'special categories' of personal data. The recitals explain that this is because:

> Personal data which are, by their nature, particularly sensitive in relation to fundamental rights and freedoms merit specific protection as the context of their processing could create significant risks to the fundamental rights and freedoms.[1]

There are two difficulties with categorising certain types of data as 'special'. One is that the categories themselves seem rather arbitrary. Trade union membership may have been sensitive data in 1980s Poland, but is it really sensitive now? Many people feel 'sensitive' about their financial records and bank details, however this is not one of the categories of data listed as 'sensitive' in GDPR, article 10. Mobile phone location data is another example of data that some might consider worthy of special protection, but which is not listed in GDPR, article 10. What is interesting about mobile phone location data is that it is the CJEU that is making the case for it to be treated as 'sensitive'. In *Tele2*[2] the CJEU referred to such data as being:

> … information that is no less sensitive, having regard to the right to privacy, than the actual content of communications.[3]

As the CJEU would be well aware the content of communications are not defined as 'sensitive' by either Directive 95/46 or the GDPR.

[8.02] The other difficulty is that the advent of 'big data' means that it is no longer necessary to process categories of data explicitly labelled race or sexuality to process data about a person's racial origin or sexual orientation. The implications of big data for privacy have been the subject of reports by both President Obama's White House[4] and

---

1. GDPR, Recital 51.
2. *Tele2 Sverige* (Case C–203/15) (21 December 2016).
3. *Tele2 Sverige* (Case C–203/15) (21 December 2016), para 99. The CJEU went on to refer to the '… the sensitivity …' of retained communications data at para 122.
4. Executive Office of the President, President's Council of Advisors on Science and Technology, *Big Data and Privacy: a Technological Perspective*, May 2014.

the European Data Protection Supervisor[5] (EDPS). As the Obama Whitehouse report explains:

> Big data is big in two different senses. It is big in the quantity and variety of data that are available to be processed. And, it is big in the scale of analysis (termed 'analytics') that can be applied to those data, ultimately to make inferences and draw conclusions. By data mining and other kinds of analytics, non-obvious and sometimes private information can be derived from data that, at the time of their collection, seemed to raise no, or only manageable, privacy issues.[6]

Such analytics allow the identities discussed above to be combined; as the American survey explains:

> Analytics, comprising a number of different computational technologies, is what fuels the big data revolution. Analytics is what creates the new value in big datasets, vastly more than the sum of the values of the parts.[7]

Big data analytics may operate discretely, subjects may never be aware of options that some big data analysis has decided should not be made.[8] Such techniques are very sophisticated and so incomprehensible to anyone other than experts, whose expertise may be rare and expensive. Even then it is very difficult to understand what exactly is happening within a computer program, especially for an outsider. Algorithms may be designed which attach weightings to be attached to certain key items of data,[9] instead of being asked intimate questions a subject might just have to 'like' or not a number of disparate images.[10] It is one thing to ask someone whether or not they are gay; it is quite another to ask them whether they like 'Wicked the Musical'.[11]

[8.03] Analysis of the GDPR's rules on the processing of 'sensitive' or 'special' categories of personal data are complicated by the CJEU's expansions of these rules.

---

5.   European Data Protection Supervisor, Preliminary Opinion, Privacy and competitiveness in the age of big data: The interplay between data protection, competition law and consumer protection in the Digital Economy, March 2014.

6.   Executive Office of the President, President's Council of Advisors on Science and Technology, *Big Data and Privacy: a Technological Perspective,* May 2014, p ix.

7.   Executive Office of the President, President's Council of Advisors on Science and Technology, *Big Data and Privacy: a Technological Perspective*, May 2014, para 3.2, p 24.

8.   This is discussed further at **Chapter 22** below.

9.   'Armed with vast data sets produced by tech firms, microeconomists can produce startlingly good forecasts of human behaviour. Silicon Valley firms have grown to love them: by bringing a cutting-edge economist in house, they are able to predict what customers or employees are likely to do next' *A long way from dismal*, The Economist, 10 January 2015.

10.   'Users on the site gave the scientists access to their Facebook 'likes' and completed a personality questionnaire created by psychologists'. The scientists used this data to build a model which '… was able to judge personality more accurately than a work colleague though analysing just 10 Facebook likes, a friend with 70 likes, a family member through 150 likes, and a wife or husband using 300 likes. On average, a Facebook user has 227 likes on their social network profile', Ahmed, 'Facebook understands you better than your spouse', (2015) *Financial Times*, 12 January.

11.   Halliday, 'Facebook users unwittingly revealing intimate secrets, study finds', (2013) *The Guardian*, 11 March.

One notable expansion is that the CJEU has repeatedly held that such data may not be transferred outside the EU. In *Avis 1/15* the CJEU held that an agreement for the transfer of Passenger Name Record data was:

> incompatible with Articles 7, 8 and 21 and Article 52(1) of the Charter in so far as it does not preclude the transfer of sensitive data from the European Union to Canada and the use and retention of that data.[12]

And in *Tele2 Sverige* the CJEU noted that retained telecommunications data:

> ... taken as a whole, is liable to allow very precise conclusions to be drawn concerning the private lives of the persons whose data has been retained, such as everyday habits, permanent or temporary places of residence, daily or other movements, the activities carried out, the social relationships of those persons and the social environments frequented by them.

The CJEU went onto describe that data as '... no less sensitive, having regard to the right to privacy, than the actual content of communications'.[13] It was the 'sensitivity' of this data that, in part, led the CJEU to impose a requirement that such data '... be retained within the European Union and for the irreversible destruction of the data at the end of the data retention period'.[14] Hence the categories of sensitive data may be expanding before the application of the GDPR. A further impetus to this expansion may be given by PSD2's provisions on the processing of 'sensitive payment data' which it defines as:

> ... data, including personalised security credentials which can be used to carry out fraud. For the activities of payment initiation service providers and account information service providers, the name of the account owner and the account number do not constitute sensitive payment data.[15]

Article 9 GDPR defines the following categories of data as being 'special':

(a) The processing of personal data revealing:

   (i)   racial or ethnic origin,[16]

   (ii) political opinions,

   (iii) religious or philosophical beliefs, or

---

12. *Transfer of Passenger Name Record data from the European Union to Canada (Opinions of the Court)* [2017] EUECJ Avis-1/15_OC (26 July 2017), para 232. See also: *Digital Rights Ireland* (Case C–293/12) (8 April 2014) para 68; *Tele2 Sverige* (Case C–203/15) (21 December 2016), para 122.

13. *Tele2 Sverige* (Case C–203/15) (21 December 2016), para 99.

14. *Tele2 Sverige* (Case C–203/15)15 (21 December 2016), para 122.

15. Directive 2015/2366 on payment services in the internal market, OJ L 337, 23rd December 2015, p 35–127, article 4(32).

16. The Recitals reassure that the GDPR's '... use of the term 'racial origin' in this Regulation does not imply an acceptance by the Union of theories which attempt to determine the existence of separate human races' GDPR, Recital 51.

(iv) trade union membership;

(b) the processing of:

    (i)   genetic data,

    (ii)   biometric data for the purpose of uniquely identifying a natural person,

    (iii) data concerning health, or

    (iv) data concerning a natural person's sex life or sexual orientation.

[8.04] These special categories of data contain two new categories of sensitive personal data that were not to be found in GDPR, article 10's predecessor provision, article 8 of Directive 95/46. These are genetic and biometric data. Genetic data is defined as meaning:

> ... personal data relating to the inherited or acquired genetic characteristics of a natural person which give unique information about the physiology or the health of that natural person and which result, in particular, from an analysis of a biological sample from the natural person in question.[17]

Biometric data is defined as meaning:

> ... personal data resulting from specific technical processing relating to the physical, physiological or behavioural characteristics of a natural person, which allow or confirm the unique identification of that natural person, such as facial images or dactyloscopic data.[18]

[8.05] The Recitals go on to explain that 'The processing of photographs should not systematically be considered to be processing of special categories of personal data as they are covered by the definition of biometric data only when processed through a specific technical means allowing the unique identification or authentication of a natural person'.[19] This suggests that the use of a CCTV may not amount to the processing of special categories of data; it is only when that CCTV is connected to facial recognition technology that it will be subject to the article 9 prohibition.

[8.06] Data concerning health is defined as meaning:

> ... personal data related to the physical or mental health of a natural person, including the provision of health care services, which reveal information about his or her health status.[20]

---

17.   GDPR, article 4(13).
18.   GDPR, article 4(14).
19.   GDPR, Recital 51.
20.   GDPR, article 4(15).

[8.07] Article 9(2) sets out derogations to the general prohibition on the processing of biometric, genetic and health data. In addition, article 9(4) provides that Member States may also impose additional limitations on the processing of such data:

> Member States may maintain or introduce further conditions, including limitations, with regard to the processing of genetic data, biometric data or data concerning health.[21]

However, the Recitals suggest that such limitations should not hamper the free flow of personal data within the Union when those conditions apply to cross-border processing of such data.[22]

[8.08] GDPR, article 9(1) provides that the processing of personal data falling within the above categories shall be prohibited. Article 9(2) goes on to set out various exceptions to this prohibition. Member States will have some discretion in relation to these exceptions, the Recitals stating that:

> ... Member States law may lay down specific provisions on data protection in order to adapt the application of the rules of this Regulation for compliance with a legal obligation or for the performance of a task carried out in the public interest or in the exercise of official authority vested in the controller.[23]

It is important to understand that the prohibition on the processing of special categories of data is in addition to the rest of the GDPR. As the Recitals explain:

> In addition to the specific requirements for such processing, the general principles and other rules of this Regulation should apply, in particular as regards the conditions for lawful processing.[24]

[8.09] The derogations provided by GDPR, article 9(2) are only exceptions to the prohibition imposed by GDPR, article 9(1); they are not derogations from the GDPR in its entirety. A data processing operation that fits within one of the derogations set out in article 9(2) cannot be assumed to have a valid legal basis or to comply with the principles of data processing simply because it benefits from such a derogation. GDPR, article 9(2) provides the following derogations to the prohibition on the processing of sensitive personal data.

(a) the data subject has given explicit consent to the processing of those personal data for one or more specified purposes,

The GDPR provides that either EU or Member State law may provide that the prohibition on the processing of personal data '... may not be lifted by the data subject', thus allowing for this derogation to be itself restricted.[25]

---

21. GDPR, article 9(4).
22. GDPR, Recital 53.
23. GDPR, Recital 51.
24. GDPR, Recital 51.
25. For a full discussion on the area of consent see **Chapter 6**.

(b) processing is necessary for the purposes of carrying out the obligations and exercising specific rights of the controller or of the data subject in the field of employment and social security and social protection law in so far as it is authorised by Union or Member State law or a collective agreement pursuant to Member State law providing for appropriate safeguards for the fundamental rights and the interests of the data subject;

Special categories of data will have to be processed in the course of employment, details of trade union membership may be processed by employers which deduct employee wages for union dues for example. Health data, such as medical certificates, may also have to be processed by employers. Neither form of processing may benefit from this derogation, though they may instead take place on the basis of consent. This derogation will only apply to the processing of personal data that is authorised by law or a collective agreement. Those laws or agreements must provide what the main text refers to as appropriate and the recitals refer to as suitable safeguards. The Recitals also suggest that such a derogation should be '... in the public interest to do so'. The Recitals go on to suggest that such a derogation might be adopted:

... in particular processing personal data in the field of employment law, social protection law including pensions and for health security, monitoring and alert purposes ...[26]

(c) processing is necessary to protect the vital interests of the data subject or of another natural person where the data subject is physically or legally incapable of giving consent;

The need for this derogation is obvious; it may be necessary to take steps to preserve the life or the assets of a person who is unconscious or otherwise incapable of consenting to the processing of sensitive data such as their health records. This derogation essentially replicates the lawful basis set out in GDPR, article 6(1)(d), notwithstanding this the controller must still be able to separately demonstrate compliance with this and all the other requirements of the GDPR.

(d) processing is carried out in the course of its legitimate activities with appropriate safeguards by a foundation, association or any other not-for-profit body with a political, philosophical, religious or trade-union aim and on condition that the processing relates solely to the members or to former members of the body or to persons who have regular contact with it in connection with its purposes and that the personal data are not disclosed outside that body without the consent of the data subjects;

This derogation enables organisations such as churches, political parties and trade unions to process special categories of data relating to their members, former members and associates. But it does not permit the processing of special categories of data relating to passive or potential supporters. This may limit the

---

26. GDPR, Recital 52.

ability of political parties within the EU to adopt the sophisticated (though sometimes ineffective[27]) software used in US elections.[28] The limitations placed by the GDPR upon the processing of personal data relating to political opinions would seem to preclude the use of data which claims to be able to identify voters who may be receptive to particular viewpoints. The furthest that the GDPR will allow political parties to go is to process the data of persons who have 'regular contact' with them. This would seem to preclude parties identifying and reaching out to existing and potential supporters, who do not have 'regular' contact with them. The language of this derogation suggests that it is the supporters who must have 'regular contact' with the party, not *vice-versa*. Any well-established political party will have long-standing supporters whose interaction is limited to voting at election times. Such contact may be neither frequent nor regular, indeed the voter may never directly contact 'their' party at all. And if no such direct contact is made then this derogation will not apply. The Recitals carry over one of the Recitals for Directive 95/46 and provide that:

Where in the course of electoral activities, the operation of the democratic system in a Member State requires that political parties compile personal data on people's political opinions, the processing of such data may be permitted for reasons of public interest, provided that appropriate safeguards are established.[29]

Similar issues may arise in relation to religious organisations such as churches. Some churches may have large numbers of nominal members with whom they have minimal contact, other than participating in ceremonies for significant life events such as births, marriages and deaths. An argument may be made that such interaction is sufficient to amount to regular contact for the purposes of the GDPR. But it is not at all inconceivable that someone could be a churchgoer for many years, indeed their entire life, without leaving any sort of data trail after they reach adulthood. Somewhat ironically the GDPR may impel political parties and churches to become active compilers of membership lists so that they can remain in regular contact with their loosely affiliated supporters.

The Recitals suggest that a further derogation should be provided: '… where the data subject gives his or her explicit consent or in respect of specific needs in particular where the processing is carried out in the course of legitimate activities by certain associations or foundations the purpose of which is to permit the exercise of fundamental freedoms'.[30] This would allow a Non-Governmental-Organisation (NGO) that campaigns for groups on the basis of their racial origin or sexual orientation to process the data of subjects who consent to the NGO doing so. This derogation might alternatively apply where the subject has

27. Alllen & Parnes, Shattered: *Inside Hillary Clinton's Doomed Campaign* (Crown Publishing, 2017).

28. Confessore & Hakim, 'Data Firm Says 'Secret Sauce' Aided Trump; Many Scoff', (2017) *New York Times*, 6 March.

29. GDPR, Recital 56. This previously appeared as Directive 95/46, Recital 36.

30. GDPR, Recital 51.

specific needs. The GDPR does not specify what such needs may be but they must presumably be related to the exercise of the subject's fundamental freedoms. Again these may be any of the subject's fundamental freedoms such as freedom of expression[31] or to conduct a business.[32]

(e) processing relates to personal data which are manifestly made public by the data subject;

A subject who reveals details of their personal life to the public will no longer be able to rely upon the prohibition provided by GDPR, article 9 in relation to data such as that relating to their health, sex life or sexual orientation. However, they will still be able to rely on all the other protections provided by the GDPR. Just because personal data is in the public domain does not mean that EU data protection law no longer applies to it. As the CJEU stated in *Satakunnan*:[33]

... a general derogation from the application of the directive in respect of published information would largely deprive the directive of its effect. It would be sufficient for the Member States to publish data in order for those data to cease to enjoy the protection afforded by the directive.[34]

(f) processing is necessary for the establishment, exercise or defence of legal claims or whenever courts are acting in their judicial capacity;

The Courts will be in a position to provide the safeguards and controls required by EU data protection law for the processing of these special categories of data. The Recitals suggest that this derogation may be extended to administrative or out-of-court procedures. Any such derogation would still have to ensure the same safeguards and controls.

(g) processing is necessary for reasons of substantial public interest, on the basis of Union or Member State law which shall be proportionate to the aim pursued, respect the essence of the right to data protection and provide for suitable and specific measures to safeguard the fundamental rights and the interests of the data subject;

This very broad derogation allows the EU or Member States to introduce such derogations as may be required by '*reasons of substantial public interest*'. The Recitals do suggest that one such public interest ground may be '... the processing of personal data by official authorities for the purpose of achieving the aims, laid down in constitutional law or international public law, of officially recognised religious associations ...'.[35]

---

31. Charter, article 11.
32. Charter, article 16.
33. *Satakunnan Markkinaporssi* (Case C–73/07) (16 December 2008).
34. *Satakunnan Markkinaporssi* (Case C–73/07) (16 December 2008), para 48.
35. GDPR, Recital 55.

(h)   processing is necessary for the purposes of preventive or occupational medicine, for the assessment of the working capacity of the employee, medical diagnosis, the provision of health or social care or treatment or the management of health or social care systems and services on the basis of Union or Member State law or pursuant to contract with a health professional and subject to the conditions and safeguards referred to in para 3;

This is the first of two derogations that specifically allow for the processing of health data. In addition, the Recitals suggest that Member States are allowed to impose limitations on the processing of health data such as:

... further conditions, including limitations, with regard to the processing of genetic data, biometric data or data concerning health. However, this should not hamper the free flow of personal data within the Union when those conditions apply to cross-border processing of such data.[36]

The GDPR anticipates that health data will be processed in three situations: firstly, for the purposes of treating the individual subject themselves; secondly, for the purposes of managing the health system; and finally for the purposes of managing the overall health of workplaces and society as a whole, preventative medicine, disease monitoring and so forth. As the Recitals explain:

Special categories of personal data which merit higher protection should be processed for health-related purposes only where necessary to achieve those purposes for the benefit of natural persons and society as a whole ...[37]

As regards the first situation, treating the individual subject, GDPR, article 9(2)(h) does not just provide a derogation for treatment or processes that are sought by the subject. It extends to an 'assessment of the working capacity of the employee', which the subject may not necessarily control. This derogation also applies to 'medical diagnosis' and 'pursuant to contract with a health professional and subject to the conditions and safeguards referred to in paragraph 3'. The conditions and safeguards referred to are that the data in question must be:

... processed by or under the responsibility of a professional subject to the obligation of professional secrecy under Union or Member State law or rules established by national competent bodies or by another person also subject to an obligation of secrecy under Union or Member State law or rules established by national competent bodies.[38]

As regards the second situation, management of the health system, GDPR, article 9(2)(h) provides that health data may be processed for '... the provision of health or social care or treatment or the management of health or social care systems and services on the basis of Union or Member State law ...'. In addition,

36.   GDPR, Recital 53.
37.   GDPR, Recital 53.
38.   GDPR, article 9(3).

the Recitals provide that '... a derogation may be made for health purposes, including public health and the management of health-care services, especially in order to ensure the quality and cost-effectiveness of the procedures used for settling claims for benefits and services in the health insurance system'.[39] The Recitals go on to provide that a derogation may be provided:

> ... in particular in the context of the management of health or social care services and systems, including processing by the management and central national health authorities of such data for the purpose of quality control, management information and the general national and local supervision of the health or social care system, and ensuring continuity of health or social care and cross-border healthcare or health security, monitoring and alert purposes, or for archiving purposes in the public interest, scientific or historical research purposes or statistical purposes, based on Union or Member State law which has to meet an objective of public interest, as well as for studies conducted in the public interest in the area of public health.[40]

The third situation, that of managing society's overall health and that of particular parts of society such as workplaces, GDPR, article 9(2)(h) provides a derogation for:

> processing ... necessary for the purposes of preventive or occupational medicine
> ...

The Recitals suggest that a derogation should be provided for '... the prevention or control of communicable diseases and other serious threats to health'.[41] GDPR, article 9(2)(i) then goes on to provide for a derogation where:

(i) processing is necessary for reasons of public interest in the area of public health, such as protecting against serious cross-border threats to health or ensuring high standards of quality and safety of health care and of medicinal products or medical devices, on the basis of Union or Member State law which provides for suitable and specific measures to safeguard the rights and freedoms of the data subject, in particular professional secrecy;

The Recitals explain that:

> 'public health' should be interpreted as defined in Regulation 1338/2008 [on Community statistics on public health and health and safety at work],[42] namely all elements related to health, namely health status, including morbidity and disability, the determinants having an effect on that health status, health care needs, resources allocated to health care, the provision of, and universal access to,

---

39. GDPR, Recital 52.
40. GDPR, Recital 53.
41. GDPR, Recital 52.
42. Regulation 1338/2008/EC of the European Parliament and of the Council of 16 December 2008 on Community statistics on public health and health and safety at work (OJ L 354, 31.12.2008, p 70).

health care as well as health care expenditure and financing, and the causes of mortality.[43]

Then Recitals make clear that this '... should not result in personal data being processed for other purposes by third parties such as employers or insurance and banking companies'.[44]

(j)   processing is necessary for archiving purposes in the public interest, scientific or historical research purposes or statistical purposes in accordance with article 89(1) based on Union or Member State law which shall be proportionate to the aim pursued, respect the essence of the right to data protection and provide for suitable and specific measures to safeguard the fundamental rights and the interests of the data subject.

This is consistent with the approach taken elsewhere in the GDPR, particularly in Ch IX, article 89 but also in article 5 of enabling the processing of data for scientific, historical research or statistical purposes.

CRIMINAL RECORDS

[8.10] GDPR, article 10 imposes strict controls on the processing of criminal record data, providing that:

> Processing of personal data relating to criminal convictions and offences or related security measures based on Article 6(1) shall be carried out only under the control of official authority or when the processing is authorised by Union or Member State law providing for appropriate safeguards for the rights and freedoms of data subjects. Any comprehensive register of criminal convictions shall be kept only under the control of official authority.

This essentially provides that criminal record data may only be processed where that processing is either pursuant to an official authority or authorised by the law. Any such law must provide appropriate safeguards for the rights and freedoms of the subject concerned, not just their data protection rights. So if criminal record checks are being undertaken then safeguards will have to be in place to ensure that there are adequate safeguards for the subject's 'Freedom to choose an occupation and right to engage in work'.[45]

DATA PROTECTION IMPACT ASSESSMENT (DPIA)

[8.11] In order to assist controllers in complying with the GDPR and demonstrate compliance with its provisions data controllers may be required to carry out a DPIA. The GDPR does not require a DPIA to be carried out for all processing operations but

---

43.   GDPR, Recital 54.
44.   GDPR, Recital 54.
45.   Charter, article 15.

rather is required where processing is 'likely to result in a high risk to the rights and freedoms of natural persons'. The assessment in that case will be required in order to assess the impact of the envisaged processing operations on the protection of personal data.[46] In particular such an assessment will be required in the case of 'processing on a large scale of special categories of personal data' (as set out in article 9(1)) or personal data relating to criminal convictions and offences (as set out in article 10).[47] The recitals explain that the processing of personal data would not be considered to be on a 'large scale' where a doctor processes his patient's data or a lawyer processes his clients and so a DPIA would not be mandatory.[48] The failure to carry out a DPIA can result in the imposition of administrative fines in circumstances where the controller is obliged to carry out the assessment but fails to do so.[49]

---

46.   GDPR, article 35(1).
47.   GDPR, article 35(3).
48.   GDPR, Recital 91.
49.   GDPR, article 83(4)(a).

PART 4
RIGHTS OF THE DATA SUBJECT

Chapter 9

RIGHTS OF THE DATA SUBJECT

INTRODUCTION

[9.01] Data protection's supervisory model is quite unlike that for medical devices or financial services. Nobody expects a patient to check the reliability of a pacemaker before it is inserted into their heart[1] or stress test a bank before they open a current account.[2] And so the law does not provide patients and bank customers with tools that they would need to undertake such checks. Data protection is different: it expects that data subjects will do their own research and make their own decisions. The GDPR provides subjects with the tools to undertake those tasks. Subjects have the right to access their data, object to its processing, seek rectifications and corrections. These rights are not new. Similar rights were to be found in the GDPR's predecessors, the Strasbourg Convention and Directive 95/46. The difference is that the GDPR provides real supervisory and enforcement mechanisms to ensure that these rights can be successfully invoked. These mechanisms may be invoked by the supervisors established by the GDPR, but also by the subjects themselves. This supervisory structure makes the GDPR an experiment in supervision by subjects themselves; if the GDPR succeeds then its supervisory model will have implications for other regulated industries and activities.

The rights of data subjects have their basis in the Charter, which confers two specific rights upon subjects. It states:

> Everyone has the right of access to data which has been collected concerning him or her, and the right to have it rectified.[3]

[9.02] In *Nowak* the CJEU made clear that subjects cannot be deprived of their rights simply because the operation of those rights may have consequences for data controllers that are inconvenient. The CJEU began by recalling that where information is classified as personal data then:

> … a number of principles and safeguards … are attached to that classification and follow from that classification …[4]'

---

1. Regulation 745/2017/EU of the European Parliament and of the Council of 5 April 2017 on medical devices, OJ L 117, 5 May 2017, p 1.
2. A task conferred on the ECB by article 4 of Council Regulation 1024/2013/EU of 15 October 2013 conferring specific tasks on the European Central Bank concerning policies relating to the prudential supervision of credit institutions OJ L 287, 29.10.2013, p. 63–89.
3. Charter, article 8(2).
4. *Nowak* (Case C–434/16) (20 December 2017), para 47.

The CJEU disagreed with the proposition that the adverse consequences for rights and duties could taken into account when deciding whether information was personal data. As the CJEU explained, if the applicant's answers and his examiner's written comments were not his personal data then:

> that would have the effect of entirely excluding that information from the obligation to comply not only with the principles and safeguards that must be observed in the area of personal data protection, and, in particular, the principles relating to the quality of such data and the criteria for making data processing legitimate ... but also with the rights of access, rectification and objection of the data subject... and with the supervision exercised by the supervisory authority ...[5]

[9.03] The GDPR then expands this out into a list of some ten subject rights:

1. rights to information about how data is being processed;

2. a right to access their own data;

3. a right to rectification;

4. a right to erasure known as 'The Right to Be Forgotten';

5. a right to restriction;

6. a right to ensure the notification of third parties of the rectification or erasure of personal data;

7. a right to data portability;

8. a right to object generally to the processing of personal data;

9. a right to object specifically to the processing of personal data for the purpose of direct marketing;

10. a right not to be subject to automated individual decision making; a right not to be subject to profiling.

Each of these rights is considered in succession below. In addition, the GDPR sets out the modalities by which such rights must be exercised and provides for the restriction of these rights in certain circumstances. These rights are discussed in the Chapter.

RIGHTS TO INFORMATION

[9.04] Effective exercise of subject rights such as the right of access is dependent on subjects being aware that their data is being processed. The CJEU notedin *Avis 1/15*, which concerned the transfer of PNR data from the EU to Canada, that it had previously held that the purpose of subject rights was to enable them to: 'be certain that his personal data are processed in a correct and lawful manner'.[6] The CJEU then went onto

---

5.   *Nowak* (Case C–434/16) (20 December 2017), para 49.

6.   *Avis 1/15* [2017] EUECJ Avis-1/15_OC (26 July 2017), para 219.

hold that subjects could only be certain that these rights were being complied with if they were:

> ... notified of the transfer of their ... data ... and of its use ... That information is, in fact, necessary to enable the air passengers to exercise their rights to request access to ... data concerning them and ... rectification of that data, and ... to an effective remedy before a tribunal.[7]

In *Bara*[8] the CJEU considered transfers from one Romanian State body to another, the CJEU did not dispute the legal basis upon which the transfers were being made but held that the right to information precluded:

> ... national measures ... which allow a public administrative body of a Member State to transfer personal data to another public administrative body and their subsequent processing, without the data subjects having been informed of that transfer or processing.[9]

Similarly, in *Deutsch Telekom*[10] the CJEU held that subscriber data could be transferred from one operator of a telephone directory to another provided that: '... subscribers have been informed, before the first inclusion of their data in a public directory, of the purpose of that directory and of the fact that those data could be communicated to another telephone service provider ...'.[11]

[9.05] The right of subjects to be informed about who is to process their data and how it is to be processed is set out in GDPR, articles 13 and 14. These two rights are similar, but they are not the same. Article 13 GDPR sets out the information to be provided to the data subject where personal data are collected from them directly. It provides that the controller must provide the subject with three sets of information. This must be done '... at the time when personal data are obtained ...'. Although the obligation will not apply '... where and insofar as the data subject already has the information ...'.[12] The first set of information to be provided are:

(a)   the identity and the contact details of the controller and, where applicable, of the controller's representative;

(b)   the contact details of the data protection officer, where applicable;

---

7.   *Avis 1/15* [2017] EUECJ Avis-1/15_OC (26 July 2017), para 220.

8.   *Bara* (Case C–201/14) (1 October 2015).

9.   *Bara* (Case C–201/14) (1 October 2015), para 47.

10.   *Deutsche Telekom* (Case C–543/09) (5 May 2011).

11.   *Deutsche Telekom* (Case C–543/09), (5 May 2011), para 68. This judgment was followed in *Tele2 (Netherlands)* (Case C–536/15) (15 March 2017) in which it was held the subscriber data could be transferred form one directory provider to another so long as subscribers had been '... informed, before the first inclusion of their data in a public directory, of the purpose of that directory and of the fact that those data may be communicated to another telephone service provider ...' (para 34).

12.   GDPR, article 13(4).

    (c)   the purposes of the processing for which the personal data are intended as well as the legal basis for the processing;

    (d)   the legitimate interests pursued by the controller or by a third party, where the lawful basis of the processing lies in those legitimate interests;

    (e)   the recipients or categories of recipients of the personal data, if any;

    (f)   If the controller intends to transfer personal data to a third country or international organisation whether on the basis or absence of an adequacy decision by the Commission, or may in the case of transfers subject to appropriate safeguards[13] or binding corporate rules,[14] or a contract.[15] If so, then the subject must be provided with reference to the appropriate or suitable safeguards and the means by which to obtain a copy of them or where they have been made available'.[16]

[9.06] The second set of information are in addition to the first. The GDPR explains the distinction between the two on the basis that the second set are '… necessary to ensure fair and transparent processing',[17] which links this obligation back to the principle of fairness and transparency set out in GDPR, article 5(1)(a). The second set of information is:

    (a)   the period for which the personal data will be stored, or if that is not possible, the criteria used to determine that period;

    (b)   the existence of the right to request from the controller access to and rectification or erasure of personal data or restriction of processing concerning the data subject or to object to processing as well as the right to data portability;

    (c)   where the processing is based on consent, the existence of the right to withdraw consent at any time, without affecting the lawfulness of processing based on consent before its withdrawal;

    (d)   the right to lodge a complaint with a supervisory authority;

    (e)   whether the provision of personal data is a statutory or contractual requirement, or a requirement necessary to enter into a contract, as well as whether the data subject is obliged to provide the personal data and of the possible consequences of failure to provide such data;

    (f)   the existence of automated decision-making, including profiling and meaningful information about the logic involved, as well as the significance and the envisaged consequences of such processing for the data subject.

---

13.   On the basis of GDPR, article 46.
14.   On the basis of GDPR, article 47.
15.   As set out in the second subpara of GDPR, article 49(1).
16.   GDPR, article 13(1).
17.   GDPR, article 13(2).

Both sets of information contain elements that may be quite generic in practice such as the contact details of the controller and the DPO in the first set and the right to lodge a complaint with a SA in the second. Both sets also contain elements that may vary from case to case, such as purpose in the first set and retention period in the second. One distinction between the two sets seems to be that the first set have to be provided when data is collected from the subject, whilst the second has to be provided when data is 'obtained' which suggests that it may be collected otherwise than from the data subject. This seems to envisage a process whereby the data controller may initially collect data from a subject, providing them with the information stipulated in GDPR, article 13(1). Then, if the controller subsequently 'obtains' data from elsewhere they have to provide the subject with the information set out in article 13(2). As the Recitals explain:

> The information in relation to the processing of personal data relating to the data subject should be given to him or her at the time of collection from the data subject, or, where the personal data are obtained from another source, within a reasonable period, depending on the circumstances of the case.[18]

The third set of information contains a single element which must be provided where '... the controller intends to further process the personal data for a purpose other than that for which the personal data were collected.' This must be provided 'prior to that further processing'. The information in question is:

> ... information on that other purpose.[19]

[9.07] In addition, the controller must provide the subject with the relevant further information required by GDPR, article 13(2). Two additional clarifications are provided by the Recitals:

1. Where personal data can be legitimately disclosed to another recipient, the data subject should be informed when the personal data are first disclosed to the recipient.

2. Where the origin of the personal data cannot be provided to the data subject because various sources have been used, general information should be provided.[20]

The controller will still have to provide subjects with information where data are not obtained from the subject. Where personal data have not been obtained from the data subject, the controller must provide the data subject with up to three sets of information. This information must be provided:

> within a reasonable period after obtaining the personal data, but at the latest within one month, having regard to the specific circumstances in which the personal data are processed.

---

18. GDPR, Recital 61.
19. GDPR, article 13(3).
20. GDPR, Recital 61.

However, one month is the longest period that can be allowed to pass before information is provided. Shorter periods will apply in two scenarios. If personal data is to be used to communicate with a data subject, then they must be informed '… at the latest at the time of the first communication to that data subject …'. If communication to someone other than the data subject is envisaged, then that subject must be informed '… at the latest when the personal data are first disclosed'.[21]

[9.08] GDPR, article 14 sets out the information that must be provided to subjects where data is ·not obtained from the data subject. A controller will have to provide this information unless it can be shown that the subject already has the information. This creates an incentive for controllers that acquire data from others to ensure that their suppliers inform subjects of the disclosure. If it cannot be demonstrated that the old controller provided the requisite information under GDPR, article 13 then the new controller will have to do so under GDPR, article 14.

Two such sets of information have to be provided to the subject, both at the same time. One distinction between the two sets is that the first simply has to be provided by the controller to the subject, whilst the second has to be provided '… to ensure fair and transparent processing in respect of the data subject'. This creates an explicit link back to the principle of fairness and transparency set out in GDPR, article 5(1). However, the provision of information pursuant to article 14(1) would seem to also ensure fairness and transparency.

[9.09] Article 14(1) states that the first set of information to be provided by the controller to the subject is:

(a) the identity and the contact details of the controller and, if any, of the controller's representative;

(b) the contact details of the data protection officer, where applicable;

(c) the purposes of the processing for which the personal data are intended as well as the legal basis for the processing;

(d) the categories of personal data concerned;

(e) the recipients or categories of recipients of the personal data, where applicable;

(f) if the controller intends to transfer personal data to a third country or international organisation whether on the basis or absence of an adequacy decision by the Commission, or may in the case of transfers subject to appropriate safeguards[22] or binding corporate rules,[23] or a contract.[24] If so, then the subject must be provided with reference to the appropriate or suitable

---

21.   GDPR, article 14(3).
22.   On the basis of GDPR, article 46.
23.   On the basis of GDPR, article 47.
24.   As set out in the second subpara of GDPR, article 49(1).

safeguards and the means by which to obtain a copy of them or where they have been made available'.[25]

[9.10] Article 14(2) states the second set of information that must be provided to the subject in addition to the first:

(a) the period for which the personal data will be stored, or if that is not possible, the criteria used to determine that period;

(b) the legitimate interests pursued by the controller or by a third party, where the processing relies upon legitimate interest to provide a lawful basis,

(c) the existence of the right to request from the controller access to and rectification or erasure of personal data or restriction of processing concerning the data subject and to object to processing as well as the right to data portability;

(d) where processing is based on consent the existence of the right to withdraw consent at any time, without affecting the lawfulness of processing based on consent before its withdrawal;

(e) the right to lodge a complaint with a supervisory authority; from which source the personal data originate, and if applicable, whether it came from publicly accessible sources;

(f) the existence of automated decision-making, including profiling and meaningful information about the logic involved, as well as the significance and the envisaged consequences of such processing for the data subject.

A third set of information must be provided where '... the controller intends to further process the personal data for a purpose other than that for which the personal data were obtained'. In that case the controller must provide the subject with information on that other purpose and with any relevant further information set out in the second set above. This must be done prior to the commencement of that further processing.

[9.11] The Article 29 WP adopted *Guidelines on transparency under Regulation 2016/ 679*,[26] which are undergoing public consultation at the time of publication. These Guidelines explain that:

> Transparency is an overarching obligation under the GDPR applying to three central areas: (1) the provision of information to data subjects related to fair processing; (2) how data controllers communicate with data subjects in relation to their rights under the GDPR; and (3) how data controllers facilitate the exercise by data subjects of their rights.[27]

These guidelines recommend '... that layered privacy statements/notices should be used to link to the various categories of information which must be provided to the data

---

25. GDPR, article 14(1).
26. A29 WP, *Guidelines on transparency under Regulation 2016/679,* 17/EN WP260.
27. A29 WP, *Guidelines on transparency under Regulation 2016/679,* 17/EN WP260, p 5.

subject, rather than displaying all such information in a single notice on the screen, in order to avoid information fatigue'.[28]

[9.12] The obligation to provide information to the data subject will not apply in the circumstances set out below:

(a) the data subject already has the information. This creates a substantive incentive for controllers who receive data from other controllers to insist that the controller who originally obtained the data informs subjects of the transfer. It also means that such a recipients cannot avoid responsibility for ensuring that subjects right to information is upheld;

(b) the provision of such information proves impossible or would involve a disproportionate effort. The GDPR suggests that this may occur 'in particular' in relation to processing for archiving purposes in the public interest, scientific or historical research purposes or statistical purposes. Such processing must be subject to the conditions and safeguards stipulated by GDPR, article 89(1). The first set of information, set out in article 14(1), need not be provided if doing so would be likely to render impossible or seriously impair the achievement of these public interest, scientific, historical research or statistical purposes. The Recitals suggest that when deciding whether providing the information would prove impossible or involve disproportionate effort the following factors should be taken into consideration: 'the number of data subjects, the age of the data and any appropriate safeguards adopted'.[29] Presumably none of the information required by article 14 needs to be provided, once it is ascertained that provision of the information set out in article 14(1) would cause a serious impairment. If this exception is availed of then the controller must take appropriate measures to protect the data subject's rights and freedoms and legitimate interests, including making the information publicly available.

(c) The obtaining or disclosure of data is expressly laid down by Union or Member State law to which the controller is subject and which provides appropriate measures to protect the data subject's legitimate interests; or

(d) Where the personal data must remain confidential subject to an obligation of professional secrecy regulated by Union or Member State law, including a statutory obligation of secrecy.

Recital 31 effectively limits the application of Articles 13 and 14 GDPR to requests for information made by public authorities, providing that:

> Public authorities to which personal data are disclosed in accordance with a legal obligation for the exercise of their official mission, such as tax and customs authorities, financial investigation units, independent administrative authorities, or financial market authorities responsible for the regulation and

---

28.   A29 WP, *Guidelines on transparency under Regulation 2016/679,* 17/EN WP260, p 17.
29.   GDPR, Recital 62.

supervision of securities markets should not be regarded as recipients if they receive personal data which are necessary to carry out a particular inquiry in the general interest, in accordance with Union or Member State law.

This adjustment of the definition of recipients means that if, say, the tax authorities of a member state seek the personal data relating to an individual customer of a bank, then neither the bank nor the tax authority will be obliged to inform the subject that the tax authority is now a 'recipient' of their data. This adjustment is limited in its effect. It only applies to particular inquiries and Recital 31 goes onto provide that:

> The requests for disclosure sent by the public authorities should always be in writing, reasoned and occasional and should not concern the entirety of a filing system or lead to the interconnection of filing systems. The processing of personal data by those public authorities should comply with the applicable data-protection rules according to the purposes of the processing.

RIGHT OF ACCESS

[9.13] The right of a subject to access their personal data forms a fundamental part of the right to data protection, being explicitly referenced in article 8 of the EU Charter of Fundamental Rights. As the CJEU explained in *Avis 1/15*:

> ... the fundamental right to respect for private life... means that the person concerned may be certain that his personal data are processed in a correct and lawful manner. In order to carry out the necessary checks, that person must have a right of access to the data relating to him which is being processed.[30]

The Recitals suggest that this right is provided so that subjects may:

> ... be aware of, and verify, the lawfulness of the processing.

The Recitals go on to provide that subjects should be able 'to exercise that right easily and at reasonable intervals'.[31]

The right of access provided by the GDPR goes far beyond a simple right to access personal data.[32] Article 15 provides data subjects with the right to obtain from the controller confirmation as to whether or not personal data concerning him or her are

---

30. *Transfer of Passenger Name Record data from the European Union to Canada* [2017] EUECJ Avis-1/15_OC (26 July 2017), para 219.

31. GDPR, Recital 63.

32. As was pointed out by the referring court in *X* (Case C–486/12) (12 December 2013): '... access to a display screen does not constitute a communication for the purposes of Article 12(a) of [Directive 95/46] ... Article 8 of the Charter of Fundamental Rights of the European Union ... protects only the right to access data. Access to data via a display screen has the additional disadvantage that, unlike a certified transcript, it cannot be accepted as authentic and accurate by the public authorities ... and cannot provide an historical overview of the data registered' (para 14).

being processed. Where their data is being processed subjects have firstly the right to access the personal data in question and then the right to be provided with:

> ... a copy of the personal data undergoing processing.[33]

These rights, of access and to be provided with a copy of the data in question, appear to be separate. This suggests that a subject which wishes to view the data within the subject's systems may have to be facilitated in doing so. If this is so then the right of access may include a right of inspection, a right to view their data as it is being processed by the controller's systems. Such an analysis is supported by the separation of the right to access data in article 15(1) from the right to receive a copy in article 15(3). The Recitals confirm that subjects have to be given a right to inspect their data on the controller's system where 'possible'. This direct access may be provided by means of 'remote access to a secure system'.[34]

[9.14] A subject is entitled to receive a copy of their personal data, not just '... a full summary of those data in an intelligible form'.[35] This is clear from the decision of the CJEU in *YS*[36] which considered the subject's right to access their personal data contained in a minute created by the Dutch Interior Ministry. The applicant argued that he had a 'right to obtain a copy of the minute'.[37] The EU Commission and others argued that there were '... other possible ways of disclosing, in an intelligible form, the personal data contained in such a document, inter alia by providing him with a full and comprehensible summary of those data'.[38] However, the CJEU held that for the right to data protection to be complied with:

> ... it is sufficient for the applicant to be provided with a full summary of those data in an intelligible form, that is, a form which allows him to become aware of those data and to check that they are accurate and processed in compliance with that directive, so that he may, where relevant, exercise the rights conferred on him by that directive.[39]

---

33. The subject may seek further copies of their data but GDPR, article 15(2) goes on to provide that 'For any further copies requested by the data subject, the controller may charge a reasonable fee based on administrative costs. Where the data subject makes the request by electronic means, and unless otherwise requested by the data subject, the information shall be provided in a commonly used electronic form'. In *X* (Case C–486/12) (12 December 2013) the CJEU held that '... in order to ensure that fees levied when the right to access personal data is exercised are not excessive for the purposes of that provision, the level of those fees must not exceed the cost of communicating such data' (para 31).
34. GDPR, Recital 63.
35. *YS* (Case C–141/12) (17 July 2014), para 50.
36. *YS* (Case C–141/12) (17 July 2014).
37. *YS* (Case C–141/12) (17 July 2014), para 52.
38. *YS* (Case C–141/12) (17 July 2014), para 53.
39. *YS* (Case C–141/12) (17 July 2014), para 60. Someone who wanted their data in its original form might utilise their right of data portability under GDPR, article 20.

A subject's right to access their personal data should not be confused with their rights to obtain information under other transparency or freedom of information rules. In *Bavarian Lager* the CJEU was considering the transparency and data protection regulations that apply to EU institutions. The CJEU explained that:

> … it must be borne in mind that those regulations have different objectives. The first is designed to ensure the greatest possible transparency of the decision-making process of the public authorities and the information on which they base their decisions. It is thus designed to facilitate as far as possible the exercise of the right of access to documents, and to promote good administrative practices. The second is designed to ensure the protection of the freedoms and fundamental rights of individuals, particularly their private life, in the handling of personal data.[40]

This was applied by the CJEU in *YS* in which the CJEU held that extending the subject's right to access his personal data to encompass a legal opinion:

> … would not in fact serve the directive's purpose of guaranteeing the protection of the applicant's right to privacy with regard to the processing of data relating to him, but would serve the purpose of guaranteeing him a right of access to administrative documents, which is not however covered by Directive 95/46.[41]

In addition to these twin rights, to access the data and receive a copy of it, article 15(1) sets out a variety of information that the subject must also receive:

(a)   the purposes of the processing;

(b)   the categories of personal data concerned;

(c)   the recipients or categories of recipient to whom the personal data have been or will be disclosed, in particular recipients in third countries or international organisations;

(d)   where possible, the envisaged period for which the personal data will be stored, or, if not possible, the criteria used to determine that period;

(e)   the existence of the right to request from the controller rectification or erasure of personal data or restriction of processing of personal data concerning the data subject or to object to such processing;

(f)   the right to lodge a complaint with a supervisory authority;

(g)   where the personal data are not collected from the data subject, any available information as to their source;

(h)   the existence of automated decision-making, including profiling[42] and meaningful information about the logic involved, as well as the significance and the envisaged consequences of such processing for the data subject. This

---

40.   *Bavarian Lager* (Case C–28/08) (29 June 2010), para 49.
41.   *YS* (Case C–141/12) (17 July 2014), para 46.
42.   As referred to in GDPR, article 22(1) and (4).

information must be provided 'at least' where automated decision-making or profiling is being undertaken. Controllers who are processing personal data in other ways may therefore provide this information if they wish, but are not under any obligation to do so.[43]

In addition to the above the subject also has the right to be informed of the appropriate safeguards provided pursuant to GDPR, article 46 where personal data are transferred to a third country or to an international organisation.[44] In addition, the Recitals specify that this right:

> ... includes the right for data subjects to have access to data concerning their health, for example the data in their medical records containing information such as diagnoses, examination results, assessments by treating physicians and any treatment or interventions provided.[45]

[9.15] As regards the provision of copies the GDPR essentially provides that the subject has the right of selecting the format he or she wants to receive these. Article 15(3) provides that where the data subject makes their request by electronic means then the information shall be provided in a commonly used electronic form 'unless otherwise requested by the data subject'.

On the other hand, article 15(4) provides that the provision of a copy under article 15(3) 'shall not adversely affect the rights and freedoms of others'. One obvious way in which the GDPR could infringe the rights and freedoms of others is if the data of one subject becomes intermingled with that of another. The Recitals suggest that this provision is aimed at preserving '... trade secrets or intellectual property and in particular the copyright protecting the software.' The Recitals go on to provide that 'the result of those considerations should not be a refusal to provide all information to the data subject'.[46]

Finally, the Recitals do address some practical issues that may arise when controllers are responding to access requests. One is that controllers:

> ... should use all reasonable measures to verify the identity of a data subject who requests access, in particular in the context of online services and online identifiers.[47]

[9.16] In addition, the Recitals suggest that:

> Where the controller processes a large quantity of information concerning the data subject, the controller should be able to request that, before the information is delivered, the data subject specify the information or processing activities to which the request relates.[48]

---

43.   GDPR, article 15(1).
44.   GDPR, article 15(2).
45.   GDPR, Recital 63.
46.   GDPR, Recital 63.
47.   GDPR, Recital 64.
48.   GDPR, Recital 63.

Finally, it is recited that a controller 'should not retain personal data for the sole purpose of being able to react to potential requests'.[49] This recital may be aimed at the judgment of the CJEU in *Rijkeboer*,[50] which arose from an access request made to the 'Board of Aldermen of Rotterdam'. The subject had sought access to a list of those persons to whom his data had been disclosed in the preceding two years. However, the respondent only retained that data for the preceding year. The CJEU held that:

> rules limiting the storage of information on the recipients or categories of recipient of personal data and on the content of the data disclosed to a period of one year and correspondingly limiting access to that information, while basic data is stored for a much longer period, do not constitute a fair balance ... unless it can be shown that longer storage of that information would constitute an excessive burden on the controller.[51]

The ability of a controller to limit the uses to which personal data obtained through an access request may be put was considered by the CJEU in *Puskar*.[52] The subject had discovered that his name appeared on '... a list of persons considered by the Finance Directorate to be "front-men"...'.[53] This list was deemed inadmissible by the Czech courts as it been obtained "... without the consent, legally required, of the person responsible for processing that data'.[54] The CJEU accepted that '... the objective of avoiding the unauthorised use of internal documents in judicial proceedings is capable of constituting a legitimate general interest objective' and that '... where a list, such as the contested list, is intended to remain confidential and also contains personal data of other natural persons, there is a need to protect the rights of those persons'.[55] However the CJEU went onto suggest that '... if the person whose personal data is on the list enjoys a right of access to those data, such rejection appears disproportionate to those very objectives'.[56]

RIGHT TO RECTIFICATION

[9.17] As with access the right to rectification has the distinction of being specified by the Charter, which provides:

> Everyone has the right of access to data which has been collected concerning him or her, and the right to have it rectified.[57]

---

49.   GDPR, Recital 64.
50.   *Rijkeboer* (Case C–553/07) (7 May 2009).
51.   *Rijkeboer* (Case C–553/07) (7 May 2009, para 66.
52.   *Puskar* (Case C–73/16) (27 September 2017).
53.   *Puskar* (Case C–73/16) (27 September 2017), para 2.
54.   *Puskar* (Case C–73/16) (27 September 2017), para 77.
55.   *Puskar* (Case C–73/16) (27 September 2017), para 92.
56.   *Puskar* (Case C–73/16) (27 September 2017), para 94.
57.   GDPR, article 8(2).

[9.18] In *Google Spain*[58] the CJEU noted that compliance with the principles of data protection, which are now set out in GDPR, article 5 meant that: '… the controller must take every reasonable step to ensure that data which do not meet the requirements of that provision are erased or rectified'.[59] One of the defects identified by the CJEU in *Schrems*,[60] was that 'the data subjects had no administrative or judicial means of redress enabling, in particular, the data relating to them to be accessed and, as the case may be, rectified or erased'.[61]

[9.19] GDPR, article 16 provides some further detail about this right:

> The data subject shall have the right to obtain from the controller without undue delay the rectification of inaccurate personal data concerning him or her. Taking into account the purposes of the processing, the data subject shall have the right to have incomplete personal data completed, including by means of providing a supplementary statement.

Essentially this right splits into two parts. First, there is the straightforward right to have inaccurate data rectified or corrected. The fact that the subject has a right to correct their data does not mean that the controller can avoid their duty to ensure the accuracy of that data under GDPR, article 5(1)(d). As the CJEU noted in *Huber*,[62] an authority entrusted with the management of a database '… is responsible for the accuracy of the data registered in it'.[63] Secondly, there is the right to have information completed. It is possible that subjects who feel that their data is incomplete or reflects poorly upon them will use this right to insist upon inserting statements into their data.

RIGHT TO ERASURE OR 'RIGHT TO BE FORGOTTEN'

[9.20] The right to erasure, otherwise known as the right to be forgotten, is the most ambiguous of the rights conferred by the GDPR. Whether any item of data can ever be fully or properly erased is very much open to question.[64] The right to be forgotten is the name given to the right articulated by the CJEU in *Google Spain,* but all that was required in that case was the deletion of certain references to the subject in the respondent's search results. The data to which those results were linking was allowed to remain on-line and available. And in *Manni,* the CJEU decision that followed *Google*

---

58. *Costeja González v Google Spain and Google* (Case C–131/12) (13 May 2014).

59. *Costeja González v Google Spain and Google* (Case C–131/12) (13 May 2014), para 72.

60. *Schrems* (Case C–362/14) (6 October 2015).

61. *Schrems* (Case C–362/14) (6 October 2015), para 90.

62. *Huber* (Case C–524/06) (16 December 2008).

63. *Huber* (Case C–524/06) (16 December 2008), para 21.

64. For example the personal data of users of Ashley-Madison were released by hackers in 2015, including the data of subjects who had paid $15 to have their data deleted from the site. Adee, 'The traces we leave online can return to haunt us', *New Scientist*, Vol. 227, Issue 3032, 1 August 2015.

Spain, the CJEU was unwilling to mandate a time period beyond which personal data could no longer be retained.

[9.21] In *Google Spain*[65] the applicant, Costeja González, was a Spanish lawyer who had been the subject of liquidation proceedings some years before. His complaint was that when an internet user entered his name:

> ... in the search engine of the Google group ('Google Search'), he would obtain links to two pages of La Vanguardia's newspaper, of 19 January and 9 March 1998 respectively, on which an announcement mentioning Mr Costeja González's name appeared for a real-estate auction connected with attachment proceedings for the recovery of social security debts.[66]

Initially the applicant requested that the newspaper 'be required either to remove or alter those pages so that the personal data relating to him no longer appeared or to use certain tools made available by search engines in order to protect the data.' The Spanish court took the view 'that the publication ... of the information in question was legally justified as it took place upon order of the Ministry of Labour and Social Affairs and was intended to give maximum publicity to the auction in order to secure as many bidders as possible'.[67] One might question whether it was necessary to make this particular item of personal data publicly available through an archive some 16 years after the sale in question. However, no question about this finding was asked of the CJEU. And that Court was careful not to pass any judgment on the display of personal data on the archive in question referring to it in the following terms '... even, as the case may be, when its publication in itself on those pages is lawful'.[68]

[9.22] There are a number of bases upon which the publication of the newspaper advertisements in question might be lawful. One might be 'the performance of a task carried out in the public interest', in this case the publication of an official advertisement; another might be the legitimate interests of the controller as the publisher of a newspaper. In addition, publication of a newspaper archive is arguably '... processing for journalistic purposes', which forms part of the right to freedom of expression, which must be balanced with the right to data protection.[69] The CJEU suggested that this might provide a lawful basis for the continuing processing of this personal data in the newspaper archive:

> the processing by the publisher of a web page consisting in the publication of information relating to an individual may, in some circumstances, be carried out 'solely for journalistic purposes' and thus benefit ... from derogations from the requirements laid down by the directive, whereas that does not appear to be so in the case of the processing carried out by the operator of a search engine.

---

65. *Google Spain* (Case C–131/12) (13 May 2014).
66. *Google Spain* (Case C–131/12) (13 May 2014), para 14.
67. *Google Spain* (Case C–131/12) (13 May 2014), para 16.
68. *Google Spain* (Case C–131/12) (13 May 2014), para 100.
69. GDPR, article 85.

The CJEU then refused to rule out that 'in certain circumstances' the right to object might be exercisable against the operator of a search engine but not the publisher of a webpage.[70] The CJEU was again asked about the right of erasure in *Manni*.[71] The applicant was the sole director of' '... a building company which was awarded a contract for the construction of a tourist complex'.[72] He claimed that '... the properties in that complex were not selling because it was apparent from the companies register that he had been the sole director and liquidator of ... Immobiliare Salentina ... which had been declared insolvent in 1992 and struck off the companies' register, following liquidation proceedings, on 7 July 2005'.[73] He sought an order requiring that this company register 'erase, anonymise or block the data linking him to the liquidation of Immobiliare Salentina'.[74] The applicant was initially successful, but the Italian Court of Appeal decided to refer certain questions arising to the CJEU.[75]

[9.23] The CJEU considered the relevant companies' legislation and concluded that it was '... impossible, at present, to identify a single time limit, as from the dissolution of a company, at the end of which the inclusion of such data in the register and their disclosure would no longer be necessary'.[76] And so the CJEU concluded that the applicant did not:

> have the right to obtain, as a matter of principle, after a certain period of time from the dissolution of the company concerned, the erasure of personal data concerning them, which have been entered in the register pursuant to the latter provision, or the blocking of that data from the public.[77]

That court considered that refusing to order the deletion of the applicant's data was not disproportionate for two reasons. Firstly, the law in question only required the disclosure of certain data, 'namely those relating to the identity and the respective functions'.[78] Secondly it noted that:

> the only safeguards that joint-stock companies and limited liability companies offer to third parties are their assets, which constitutes an increased economic risk for the latter. In view of this, it appears justified that natural persons who choose to participate in trade through such a company are required to disclose the data

---

70. *Google Spain* (Case C–131/12) (13 May 2014), para 85. The CJEU was not asked to consider the validity of Commission Decision 2000/520 in *Schrems* [2015] (Case C–362/14) (6 October 2015), but that did not prevent the Court making a finding of invalidity in its judgment.
71. *Manni* (Case C–398/15) (9 March 2017).
72. Paragraph 23.
73. Paragraph 24.
74. Paragraph 26.
75. Paragraph 29.
76. Paragraph 55.
77. Paragraph 56.
78. Paragraph 58.

relating to their identity and functions within that company, especially since they are aware of that requirement when they decide to engage in such activity.[79]

The CJEU then went on to point out that 'in the weighting to be carried ... the need to protect the interests of third parties in relation to joint-stock companies and limited liability companies and to ensure legal certainty, fair trading and thus the proper functioning of the internal market take precedence'. The CJEU did not exclude that there might be 'specific situations in which the overriding and legitimate reasons relating to the specific case of the person concerned justify exceptionally that access to personal data entered in the register is limited, upon expiry of a sufficiently long period after the dissolution of the company in question, to third parties who can demonstrate a specific interest in their consultation'.[80] However the CJEU did not seem to envisage that such situations would frequently arise, it merely did not exclude the possibility that they might, on occasion, arise.

Hence the right to be forgotten described by the CJEU in *Google Spain* may not apply as broadly as may sometimes be assumed. In *Google Spain* the subject invoked his right 'to object at any time on compelling legitimate grounds relating to his particular situation to the processing of data relating to him' pursuant to article 14 Directive 95/46. The CJEU considered that:

> processing of personal data ... carried out by the operator of a search engine is liable to affect significantly the fundamental rights to privacy and to the protection of personal data when the search by means of that engine is carried out on the basis of an individual's name, since that processing enables any internet user to obtain through the list of results a structured overview of the information relating to that individual that can be found on the internet — information which potentially concerns a vast number of aspects of his private life and which, without the search engine, could not have been interconnected or could have been only with great difficulty — and thereby to establish a more or less detailed profile of him.[81]

The CJEU considered that the resulting interference with the subject's data protection rights was of such severity that 'it cannot be justified by merely the economic interest which the operator of such an engine has in that processing'. However, the CJEU acknowledged that 'the removal of links from the list of results could, depending on the information at issue, have effects upon the legitimate interest of internet users potentially interested in having access to that information'. And so 'a fair balance' had to be sought between these diverse interests. The CJEU considered that the subject's right to privacy and data protection under articles 7 and 8 of the Charter would:

> override, as a general rule, that interest of internet users, that balance may however depend, in specific cases, on the nature of the information in question and its sensitivity for the data subject's private life and on the interest of the public in

---

79. Paragraph 59.
80. Paragraph 60.
81. Paragraph 80.

having that information, an interest which may vary, in particular, according to the role played by the data subject in public life.[82]

[9.24] In *Google Spain* the CJEU was considering article 14 of Directive 95/46; that right to object has now been greatly expanded by GDPR, article 17. This new right broadens out the circumstances where the right to erasure will apply, sets out how that right may apply and sets out a number of situations where it will not. Article 17 GDPR begins by setting out what the right to object is:

> The data subject shall have the right to obtain from the controller the erasure of personal data concerning him or her without undue delay and the controller shall have the obligation to erase personal data without undue delay ...

[9.25] The Recitals go on suggest methods by which such erasure can take effect, including: 'temporarily moving the selected data to another processing system, making the selected personal data unavailable to users, or temporarily removing published data from a website'.[83] GDPR, article 17(1) then goes on to set out the circumstances where this right will apply:

(a)   the personal data is no longer necessary in relation to the purposes for which they were collected or otherwise processed;

(b)   the data subject has withdrawn their consent and there is no other legal ground for the processing;

(c)   the data subject objects to the processing pursuant to GDPR, article 21;

(d)   the personal data has been unlawfully processed;

(e)   the personal data has to be erased for compliance with a legal obligation in Union or Member State law to which the controller is subject;

(f)   the personal data has been collected in relation to the offer of information society services to a child.[84]

As regards the last of the above circumstances, the Recitals note that the right to erasure is particularly relevant: 'where the data subject has given his or her consent as a child and is not fully aware of the risks involved by the processing, and later wants to remove such personal data, especially on the internet. The data subject should be able to exercise that right notwithstanding the fact that he or she is no longer a child'.[85]

---

82.   Paragraph 81.
83.   GDPR, Recital 67 which goes on to provide that 'In automated filing systems, the restriction of processing should in principle be ensured by technical means in such a manner that the personal data are not subject to further processing operations and cannot be changed. The fact that the processing of personal data is restricted should be clearly indicated in the system'.
84.   As referred to in article 8(1).
85.   GDPR, Recital 65.

[9.26] GDPR, article 17(3) then sets out grounds upon which the right to object may be refused. This dis-application is not absolute; article 17(3) will only allow such a refusal: '... to the extent that processing is necessary' for the following reasons:

(a) exercising the right of freedom of expression and information;

(b) compliance with a legal obligation which requires processing by Union or Member State law to which the controller is subject or for the performance of a task carried out in the public interest or in the exercise of official authority vested in the controller;

(c) reasons of public interest in the area of public health;[86]

(d) archiving purposes in the public interest, scientific or historical research purposes or statistical purposes in so far as the right to erasure is likely to render impossible or seriously impair the achievement of the objectives of that processing; or

(e) the establishment, exercise or defence of legal claims.

So the right to erasure might be invoked by a subject on the basis that the processing of that data was no longer necessary. However, that invocation of the right might not be successful if the controller could demonstrate that the subject was a public figure and the processing of the data in question was necessary for the exercise of freedom of expression and information.[87]

[9.27] The right to erasure may require that the controller delete certain data about a subject. Article 17(2) may impose an additional burden upon that controller providing that:

> Where the controller has made the personal data public and is obliged ... to erase the personal data, the controller, taking account of available technology and the cost of implementation, shall take reasonable steps, including technical measures, to inform controllers which are processing the personal data that the data subject

---

86. These must be 'in accordance with points (h) and (i) of Article 9(2) as well as Article 9(3)'.

87. This is what happened to Mario Costeja González. Following his success before the CJEU he sought the erasure of his data on Google, however the Spanish SA held that there was '... a preponderant interest of the public in the comments about the famous case that gave rise to the CJEU judgment of May 13, 2014'. And so his '... right-to-be-forgotten case appears to have ended up in a big Streisand effect'. Peguera, *No More Right-To-BeForgotten For Mr Costeja, Says Spanish Data Protection Authority*, 3 October 2015. http://cyberlaw.stanford.edu/blog/2015/10/no-more-right-be-forgotten-mr-costeja-says-spanishdata-protection-authority. The 'Streisand effect' referred to above is a reference to the possibility that efforts to protect a subject's privacy have the counter-effect of attracting more attention. The effect takes its name from US film star 'Barbra Streisand's failed effort to suppress in court an aerial photograph of her home for privacy reasons, which only seemed to stoke interest. The photograph now illustrates Wikipedia's Streisand Effect article', Cohen, 'On Wikipedia, Echoes of 9/11 'Edit Wars' (2011) *New York Times*, 11 September.

has requested the erasure by such controllers of any links to, or copy or replication of, those personal data.

This may impose a very significant burden upon controllers, who have to undertake 'reasonable steps' to ensure that data which they have erased will also be erased by third parties that have a copy. Controllers may invoke the grounds for refusal set out in GDPR, article 17(3), but neither provision explicitly suggests that a controller can refuse to contact such third parties on the basis that doing so would impose an excessive burden or be impossible. 'Reasonable steps' may amount to the same thing, but article 17(2) does not explicitly state this to be so. What the Recitals do say is that deciding what are 'reasonable steps' may take '… into account available technology and the means available to the controller, including technical measures, to inform the controllers which are processing the personal data of the data subject's request'.[88]

[9.28] The Recitals make clear that this obligation is imposed in order to '… strengthen the right to be forgotten in the online environment …'. It is intended as an extension of the right to erase '… in such a way that a controller who has made the personal data public should be obliged to inform the controllers which are processing such personal data to erase any links to, or copies or replications of those personal data'.[89] It seems that this amounts only to an obligation to inform other controllers that such links should be erased, the GDPR does not provide that controllers have to require such erasure and does not provide a specific mechanism by which controllers could require such erasure.

RIGHT TO RESTRICTION

[9.29] One of the new rights conferred by the GDPR is the right of restriction of processing. GDPR, article 8 confers upon subjects the right to seek the restriction of the processing of their data where one of the following applies:

(a) the accuracy of the personal data is contested by the data subject. In this case the processing of the data would only be restricted for the period enabling the controller to verify the accuracy of the personal data;

(b) the processing is unlawful and the data subject opposes the erasure of the personal data and requests the restriction of their use instead;

(c) the controller no longer needs the personal data for the purposes of the processing, but they are required by the data subject for the establishment, exercise or defence of legal claims;

(d) the data subject has objected to processing pursuant to GDPR, article 21(1) and verification of whether the legitimate grounds of the controller override those of the data subject is awaited.

---

88. GDPR, Recital 66.
89. GDPR, Recital 66.

[9.30] The GDPR defines 'restriction of processing' as:

> ... the marking of stored personal data with the aim of limiting their processing in the future.[90]

[9.31] Article 18(2) goes on to provide that where data has been restricted then, with the exception of storage:

> ... such personal data shall ... only be processed with the data subject's consent or for the establishment, exercise or defence of legal claims or for the protection of the rights of another natural or legal person or for reasons of important public interest of the Union or of a Member State.

[9.32] The Recitals go on to provide some further guidance on what is meant by restriction of data in practice:

> Methods by which to restrict the processing of personal data could include, inter alia, temporarily moving the selected data to another processing system, making the selected personal data unavailable to users, or temporarily removing published data from a website.

The Recitals also suggest that in automated filing systems:

> ... the restriction of processing should in principle be ensured by technical means in such a manner that the personal data are not subject to further processing operations and cannot be changed. The fact that the processing of personal data is restricted should be clearly indicated in the system.[91]

Finally, GDPR, article 18(3) provides:

> A data subject who has obtained restriction of processing ... shall be informed by the controller before the restriction of processing is lifted.

There is a danger that the ability of subjects to restrict the processing of their data may give rise to abuse. For example, a subject with a poor credit history might challenge the accuracy of the data processed by credit bureaux and seek a restriction on that basis. Many subjects will do so quite appropriately, but some may seek such a restriction with a view to hiding their poor credit history when they apply for further loans. In that situation the credit bureaux might still process the data on the basis that it was necessary for '... the protection of the rights of another natural or legal person ...' Of course it is relatively easy to anticipate how restricting the processing of a subject's poor credit history will cause a risk to the rights of other persons who might then advance that subject a loan. There may be other situations where such an assessment cannot be so easily made. Article 19 provides what may amount to a safeguard for such situations.

---

90. GDPR, article 4(3).
91. GDPR, Recital 67.

NOTIFICATION OF RECTIFICATION, ERASURE OR RESTRICTION

[9.33] GDPR, article 19 obliges controllers to let third parties to which they have disclosed personal data know of any rectification, erasure or restriction of that personal data. The only exception to this obligation is where such a communication '... proves impossible or involves disproportionate effort.' In *Rijkeboer*[92] the CJEU considered the extent to which controllers were obliged to retain records of persons to whom data were disclosed suggested that where:

> ... relevant recipients are numerous ... the obligation to keep the information on the recipients or categories of recipient of personal data ... could represent an excessive burden on the controller.[93]

It might similarly be argued that notifying numerous recipients might impose an excessive or disproportionate effort, but the success of such an argument would depend upon the facts of any particular case. In addition, the controller is obliged to inform the data subject about those recipients if the data subject requests it.

DATA PORTABILITY

[9.34] The EU grew out of the European Economic Community. This growth means that the EU is no longer just about Europe's internal market, the aim of the EU is now '... to promote peace, its values and the well-being of its peoples'.[94] However, the internal market remains an integral part of the EU. The EU is required to '... establish an internal market' which shall be based upon '... a highly competitive social market economy'.[95] The form that this market is to take is set out in Pt 3, Title 1 of the TFEU. One of the peculiarities of Directive 95/46 was that it was an internal market measure. This was a peculiarity with real consequences: any conflict between the privacy rights of individuals would have to be resolved in favour of the internal market. This peculiarity was addressed by the Lisbon Treaty, which requires that a more balanced approach be taken. Article 16(2) TFEU provides that the EU's legislature:

> ... lay down the rules relating to the protection of individuals with regard to the processing of personal data ... and the rules relating to the free movement of such data ...

[9.35] The free movement of data within the EU faces a variety of challenges, one of which is anti-competitive behaviour. By their nature information technologies have

---

92.   *Rijkeboer* (Case C–553/07) (7 May 2009).
93.   *Rijkeboer* (Case C–553/07) (7 May 2009), para 59.
94.   TEU, article 3(1).
95.   TEU, article 3(3).

tended towards monopolies, which have been the subject of repeated EU Commission investigations and prosecutions over the years.[96]

[9.36] The GDPR contains a single provision that seems designed with a view to ensuring greater competition in the market-place. This is the right to portability which enables subjects to extract their data from one controller and transmit it to another. Article 20 GDPR provides:

> The data subject shall have the right to receive the personal data concerning him or her, which he or she has provided to a controller, in a structured, commonly used and machine-readable format and have the right to transmit those data to another controller without hindrance from the controller to which the personal data have been provided …[97]

[9.37] This right may be invoked in the following circumstances:

(a) 'the processing is based on consent[98] … or on a contract[99] …; and

(b) 'the processing is carried out by automated means'.

This limits the application of the right to portability to situations where the subject had previously agreed to the processing of their data, whether by giving consent or entering into a contract. Hence it will not apply to the situation where a subject's data is processed by the State on the basis of a legal obligation[100] or by a search engine on the

---

96.   The most prominent of these cases may be those taken by the EU Commission against Microsoft (see *Microsoft v Commission* (Case T–201/04) (17 September 2007), EU Commission, Antitrust: Commission fines Microsoft for non-compliance with browser choice commitments, Press Release, 6 March 2013) and Intel (*Intel v Commission* (Case T–286/09) (12 June 2014)).

97.   GDPR, article 20(1). The Article 29 WP has published, *Guidelines on the right to data portability, which were revised and adopted on 5 April 2017*, (16/EN, WP 242 rev 01). These suggest that as good practice: '… data controllers should start developing the means that will contribute to answer data portability requests, such as download tools and Application Programming Interfaces. They should guarantee that personal data are transmitted in a structured, commonly used and machine-readable format, and they should be encouraged to ensure the interoperability of the data format provided in the exercise of a data portability request' and 'recommends that industry stakeholders and trade associations work together on a common set of interoperable standards and formats to deliver the requirements of the right to data portability' (p 3).

98.   '… pursuant to point (a) of Article 6(1) or point (a) of Article 9(2 …' GDPR, article 20(1).

99.   '… pursuant to point (b) of Article 6(1)', GDPR, article 20(1).

100. GDPR, article 20(3) provides: 'That right shall not apply to processing necessary for the performance of a task carried out in the public interest or in the exercise of official authority vested in the controller'. The Recitals explain that: 'By its very nature, that right should not be exercised against controllers processing personal data in the exercise of their public duties. It should therefore not apply where the processing of the personal data is necessary for compliance with a legal obligation to which the controller is subject or for the performance of a task carried out in the public interest or in the exercise of an official authority vested in the controller', GDPR, Recital 68.

basis of its legitimate interest. Although the right to portability will apply where data is being processed on the basis of a contract the Recitals make clear that this right cannot '... imply the erasure of personal data concerning the data subject which have been provided by him or her for the performance of a contract to the extent that and for as long as the personal data are necessary for the performance of that contract'.[101]

[9.38] Where the right to data portability is invoked:

> ... the data subject shall have the right to have the personal data transmitted directly from one controller to another, where technically feasible.[102]

The Recitals explain this means that '... the data subject should also be allowed to receive personal data concerning him or her which he or she has provided to a controller in a structured, commonly used, machine-readable and interoperable format ...' In order to ensure the effectiveness of this right the Recitals go on to provide that data controllers:

> ... should be encouraged to develop interoperable formats that enable data portability.

However, the Recitals make clear that this will not '... create an obligation for the controllers to adopt or maintain processing systems which are technically compatible'.[103] The right to portability is stated to be without prejudice to the right to be forgotten, set out in article 17 of the GDPR. This means that a subject can request both the transfer of their data under article 20 of the GDPR and its erasure under article 17. The portability of data has been considered by the CJEU on two occasions: *Deutsche Telekom*[104] and *Tele2 (Netherlands)*.[105] In neither case was the transfer of data being sought by the subjects themselves. Rather companies that wished to provide directory enquiry services were seeking to have data transferred from telecommunications companies to themselves. That said the CJEU did not see any difficulty with directions being given that required such transfers of data.

[9.39] If remains to be seen how widely this power will be used. One difficulty with data portability is that whilst it may enable an individual subject to transfer their own data, it will not enable subjects to bring data relating to their social networks with them.[106] The GDPR is very clear about this, providing that the right of data portability:

> ... shall not adversely affect the rights and freedoms of others.[107]

---

101. GDPR, Recital 68.
102. GDPR, article 20(2).
103. GDPR, Recital 68.
104. *Deutsche Telekom* (Case C–543/09) (5 May 2011).
105. *Tele2 (Netherlands)* (Case C–536/15) (15 March 2017).
106. The recitals make clear that it is precisely this situation that GDPR, article 20(4) is concerned with providing that: '... in a certain set of personal data, more than one data subject is concerned, the right to receive the personal data should be without prejudice to the rights and freedoms of other data subjects in accordance with this Regulation' GDPR, Recital 68.
107. GDPR, article 20(4).

[9.40] Transferring the personal data of a third party would clearly interfere with their rights, at the very least it would involve the processing of their personal data but it might also interfere with their rights to privacy,[108] freedom of expression[109] or property.[110] The balance that must be struck between such rights and the right to portability may limit the effectiveness of the latter right.

RIGHT TO OBJECT

[9.41] The GDPR provides subjects with the right to object to the processing of their personal data. It is a right that has been invoked on a couple of occasions,[111] most significantly it was one of the bases upon which the CJEU held in *Google Spain* that:

> … the operator of a search engine is obliged to remove from the list of results displayed following a search made on the basis of a person's name links to web pages, published by third parties and containing information relating to that person.[112]

[9.42] The decision in *Google Spain* was grounded in both the right to object and the right to erasure. A trend may therefore emerge of these two rights being invoked simultaneously, but it remains to be seen if this actually occurs. These rights are not the same. In particular, the right to object may be applied much more narrowly than the right to be forgotten. The right to object can only be invoked where data is being processed on the basis that the processing in question is necessary:

(a) for the performance of a task carried out in the public interest or in the exercise of an official authority;[113] or

(b) for the purposes of the legitimate interests pursued by the controller or by a third party.[114]

[9.43] GDPR, article 21(1) explicitly extends the right to object to profiling that relies on these legal bases. As well as objecting, subjects may also withdraw consent, but this will only be effective where data is being processed on the basis of that consent. But subjects do not have the right prevent the processing of personal data on the basis of a contract or a legal obligation.[115] Of course they may challenge the validity of either instrument, but this may well entail going to court.[116]

---

108. Charter, article 7.
109. Charter, article 11.
110. Charter, article 17.
111. *Costeja González v Google Spain and Google* (Case C–131/12) (13 May 2014), *Commission v Bavarian Lager* (Case C–28/08) (29 June 2010).
112. *Costeja González v Google Spain and Google* (Case C–131/12) (13 May 2014), para 100(3).
113. GDPR, article 6(1)(e).
114. GDPR, article 6(1)(f).
115. *Schwarz* (Case C–291/12) (17 October 2013).
116. *Schrems* (Case C–362/14) (6 October 2015), paras 60–64.

[9.44] Where the subject invokes their right to object they may do so '... on grounds relating to his or her particular situation' and 'at any time'. If such an objection is made, then:

> The controller shall no longer process the personal data unless the controller demonstrates compelling legitimate grounds for the processing which override the interests, rights and freedoms of the data subject or for the establishment, exercise or defence of legal claims.

The Recitals make clear that the burden of demonstrating that this right cannot be invoked rests on the controller, not the subject. In other words, processing of personal data must cease, unless the controller can:

> ... demonstrate that its compelling legitimate interest overrides the interests or the fundamental rights and freedoms of the data subject.[117]

[9.45] The manner in which such a balance would be struck was considered by the CJEU in *Google Spain*, which held that:

> ... when appraising the conditions for the application of those provisions, it should inter alia be examined whether the data subject has a right that the information in question relating to him personally should ... no longer be linked to his name by a list of results displayed following a search made on the basis of his name ... As the data subject may ..., request that the information in question no longer be made available to the general public on account of its inclusion in such a list of results, those rights override, as a rule, not only the economic interest of the operator of the search engine but also the interest of the general public in having access to that information upon a search relating to the data subject's name.

It seems clear from the above passage that the subject's right to object will normally overrule the controller's economic interest in processing the data in question. However, the rights of the subject may have to be balanced with other rights. The CJEU went on to explain that the right to object might not be successfully invoked:

> ... if it appeared ... such as the role played by the data subject in public life, that the interference with his fundamental rights is justified by the preponderant interest of the general public in having, on account of its inclusion in the list of results, access to the information in question.[118]

[9.46] In *Manni* the applicant objected to the inclusion of his personal data in a company register. The CJEU held that:

> ... in the weighting to be carried out ...in principle, the need to protect the interests of third parties in relation to joint-stock companies and limited liability companies and to ensure legal certainty, fair trading and thus the proper functioning of the internal market take precedence, it cannot be excluded, however, that there may be specific situations in which the overriding and

117. GDPR, Recital 69.
118. *Schrems* (Case C–362/14) (6 October 2015), para 130.

legitimate reasons relating to the specific case of the person concerned justify exceptionally that access to personal data entered in the register is limited, upon expiry of a sufficiently long period after the dissolution of the company in question, to third parties who can demonstrate a specific interest in their consultation.[119]

[9.47] GDPR, article 21 goes on to specify how the right to object will apply in three circumstances: in the context of the use of information society services; direct marketing; and processing for scientific, historic research or statistical purposes.

If the right to object should be invoked in the context of the use of information society services, then notwithstanding the ePrivacy Directive, the subject may:

> exercise his or her right to object by automated means using technical specifications.

What is presumably anticipated here is that information systems, such as web-browsers, may be set to automatically object to the processing of personal data, such as by refusing to accept cookies. How this will work out in practice remains to be seen as rejection of cookies may limit the ability of many websites to target advertising at their users.[120] However, the right to object to profiling is not limited to a specific technology such as cookies; subjects have the right to object to their being profiled, the GDPR does not specify what technologies are to be used to undertake such profiling.

[9.48] The GPR provides that where data is processed for direct marketing purposes then:

> ... the data subject shall have the right to object at any time to processing of personal data concerning him or her for such marketing, which includes profiling to the extent that it is related to such direct marketing.[121]

The GDPR goes on to provide that once a data subject objects to the processing of their personal data 'for direct marketing purposes, the personal data shall no longer be processed for such purposes'.[122] Subjects have to be notified of this right in the first communication made to the subject at the latest. This notification must be:

> ... explicitly brought to the attention of the data subject and shall be presented clearly and separately from any other information.[123]

---

119. *Manni* (Case C–398/15) (9 March 2017), para 60.
120. Reilly, *The cookie is dead. Here's how Facebook, Google, and Apple are tracking you now*, Venturebeat, 6 October 2014. Whether the move away from cookies will ensure better privacy is an open question: Edwards, *Think Cookies Hurt Your Privacy? You'll Beg For Their Return Once You See What Google And Facebook Are Planning*, Business Insider, 1 February 2014.
121. GDPR, article 21(2).
122. GDPR, article 21(3).
123. GDPR, article 21(4).

Finally, where personal data is being processed for scientific, historical research purposes or statistical purposes[124] then the data subject will have the right to object to that processing, 'on grounds relating to his or her particular situation'. The exception to this being where 'processing is necessary for the performance of a task carried out for reasons of public interest'. So a patient could not, necessarily, object to the processing of their personal data for the purposes of medical research.

AUTOMATED INDIVIDUAL DECISION-MAKING, INCLUDING PROFILING

[9.49] The inclusion of a right not to be subject to automated decision making in Directive 95/46 may have reflected the optimism about the future of artificial intelligence a quarter century ago.[125] But, progress has proven slower than was then thought and this right is only beginning to seem really relevant now. There are two reasons for this. One is very real progress in artificial intelligence systems, which now have the potential to take over jobs ranging from truck drivers[126] to lawyers.[127] The other is that the right itself has been expanded; it is no longer a right to object to decisions that are made without human input. Now it is also a right to object to the profiling of individuals. This broadening of the right ensures its relevance even before artificial intelligence becoming a reality.[128] GDPR, article 22(1) provides:

> The data subject shall have the right not to be subject to a decision based solely on automated processing,[129] including profiling, which produces legal effects concerning him or her or similarly significantly affects him or her.

---

124. Pursuant to GDPR, article 89(1).
125. 'Throughout the 1980s … AI was enjoying increased popularity and commercial successes and then suffering funding cuts and a wintry season …' Nilsson, *The Quest for Artificial Intelligence*, (2009) Cambridge University Press, p 433 https://ai.stanford.edu/~nilsson/QAI/qai.pdf.
126. Vanian, (2017) 'In 10 Years, Artificial Intelligence Will Transform Trucking, Says Otto Exec', *Fortune*, 27 March.
127. Lohr, (2017) 'A.I. Is Doing Legal Work. But It Won't Replace Lawyers, Yet', (2017) *New York Times*, 19 March.
128. 'We're in an awkward phase of the tech industry, one marked by incremental improvements to technologies that we think of as boring — and lots of exciting promises about far-off tech that isn't quite ready for prime time' Manjoo, 'Google, Not the Government, Is Building the Future', (2017) *New York Times*, 17 May.
129. Knowing that their application or case will be considered by a human may be comforting to some, though such human intervention may have no impact on the decision made. Humans can be required to follow procedures in much the same way as computers can be required to follow programs. Indeed 'computer' is a term originally used to describe humans (often women) who undertook calculations by hand; see Grier, *Computers Were Human* (Princeton University Press, 2007).
    This could be read as a partial imposition of the Charter's Right of Good Administration upon data controllers who use automated decision-making systems. (contd .../)

The GDPR does not offer any guidance as to what a 'legal effect concerning an individual' may amount to. WP29 has suggested that legal effects might include:

> ... automated decisions that mean someone is:
>
> - entitled to or denied a particular social benefit granted by law, such as child or housing benefit;
>
> - refused entry at the border;
>
> - subjected to increased security measures or surveillance by the competent authorities; or
>
> - automatically disconnected from their mobile phone service for breach of contract because they forgot to pay their bill before going on holiday.[130]

The meaning of the phrase 'legal effect' was considered by the CJEU in *Reynolds Tobacco v Commission*,[131] an appeal from a decision of the Court of First Instance that a decision by the EU Commission to commence a civil action against certain tobacco companies could not be judicially reviewed. What is now Article 230 of the EC Treaty provided that:

> The Court of Justice shall review the legality of acts adopted jointly by the European Parliament and the Council, of acts of the Council, of the Commission and of the ECB, other than recommendations and opinions, and of acts of the European Parliament intended to produce legal effects vis-à-vis third parties.

The Court of First Instance had held that:

> ... the contested decisions may have had the effect of informing the applicants that they were running a real risk of having penalties imposed on them by the United States court, this is a mere consequence of fact and not a legal effect which the contested decisions are intended to produce.[132]

The CJEU went on to dismiss the appeal as:

> ... it is not only preparatory acts which fall outside the scope of the judicial review provided for in Article 230 EC but any act not producing legal effects which are binding on and capable of affecting the interests of the individual, such as

---

129. (contd) GDPR, article 20(2) may be compared to Charter, article 41(2) which provides for: 'the right of every person to be heard, before any individual measure which would affect him or her adversely is taken' A previous attempt to use the UK Data Protection Act 1998 to extend administrative law controls to private decision making failed in *Johnson v Medical Defence Union* [2007] EWCA Civ 262 (28 March 2007). Article 20 could be read as a reverse of this view, at least in relation to automated decision-making. How this right will impact upon the development of Automated Decision Making systems within the EU remains to be seen.

130. WP29, *Guidelines on Automated individual decision-making and Profiling for the purposes of Regulation 2016/679*, 17/EN, WP 251, 3 October 2017, p 10.

131. *Reynolds Tobacco v Commission* (Case C–131/03) (12 September 2006)

132. Para 118 of *Philip Morris International v Commission* (Case T–377/00) (15 January 2003)

> confirmatory measures and implementing measures ... mere recommendations
> and opinions ... in principle, internal instructions.[133]

In *Alro v Commission*[134] the CJEU held that: '... commercial uncertainty and the perceptions of ... other(s)' did not amount to a legal effect. And so, the CJEU found that a decision to initiate an investigation of the subject could not be the subject of a judicial review as it did not produce any 'legal effects'. Such uncertainties and perceptions were:

> ... mere consequences of fact and not legal effects that the decision to initiate the
> formal investigation procedure is intended to have ...[135]

In *Hungary v Commission*[136] the applicant sought to annul an entry in the list of quality wines produced pursuant to Regulation No 1493/1999. This list then became the basis for the e-Bacchus database. Again, the General Court was asked to consider whether this entry had legal effects. The Court began its consideration by noting that:

> binding legal effects of a measure must be assessed in accordance with objective
> criteria ...[137]'

The CJEU went on to find that the database entry simply rellected the underlying facs and had no 'legal effect'.[138]

The right not to be subject to automated decision making is quite different from other rights set out in Ch III of the GDPR, such as access, restriction and objection, which are rights that a subject must invoke for them to be effective. In contrast, controllers have to respect the right not to be subject to decisions based on automated processing without any steps being taken by the subject. GDPR, article 22(1) does not just apply to decisions that produce legal effects; it also applies to decisions that may significantly affect a subject. What the GDPR means by 'significantly affect' a subject is unclear. The argument could be made that this might be something that affects a subject's Charter rights, such as the right to privacy,[139] freedom of expression[140] or conduct a business[141] or else one of their Freedoms under the EU Treaty such as freedom from discrimination on grounds of nationality[142] or freedom to supply goods[143] or services.[144] Hence it could be argued that even where the automated processing does not directly result in a decision being taken, it does create inputs into that decision-making

---

133. *Reynolds Tobacco v Commission* (Case C–131/03), para 55.
134. *Alro v Commission* (Case T–517/12) (16 October 2014).
135. *Alro v Commission* (Case T–517/12) (16 October 2014), para 63.
136. *Hungary v Commission* (Case C–31/13) (13 February 2014).
137. *Hungary v Commission* (Case C–31/13) (13 February 2014), para 55.
138. *Hungary v Commission* (Case C–31/13) (13 February 2014), para 63.
139. Charter, article 9.
140. Charter, article 11.
141. Charter, article 16.
142. TEU, article 18.
143. TFEU, Pt 3, Title II.
144. TFEU, Pt 3, Title IV, Ch 3.

process that will 'significantly affect' the subject in question. WP29 has suggested that processing that significantly affects an individual:

> For data processing to significantly affect someone the effects of the processing must be more than trivial and must be sufficiently great or important to be worthy of attention … The decision must have the potential to significantly influence the circumstances, behaviour or choices of the individuals concerned. At its most extreme,the decision may lead to the exclusion or discrimination of individuals.[145]

[9.50] Article 22(2) disapplies this right where the subject has either agreed to the processing or else it has been authorised by EU or Member State law.[146] The Recitals go on to provide that:

> … automated decision-making based on such processing, including profiling, should be allowed where expressly authorised by Union or Member State law to which the controller is subject, including for fraud and tax-evasion monitoring and prevention purposes conducted in accordance with the regulations, standards and recommendations of Union institutions or national oversight bodies and to ensure the security and reliability of a service provided by the controller …[147]

Article 22(3) goes on to provide that where automated decisions are taken or profiling used on the basis of the subjects' agreement then:

> … the data controller shall implement suitable measures to safeguard the data subject's rights and freedoms and legitimate interests, at least the right to obtain human intervention on the part of the controller, to express his or her point of view and to contest the decision.

The Recitals provide that automated decisions, which may include a measure '… should not concern a child'.[148] This latter safeguard may effectively limit the use of such measures to situations in which the controller can verify the identity and age of the subject, since it requires that controllers know that they are not profiling. Even where decisions have a legal basis in the agreement of the subject or a lawful obligation then article 22(4) provides that such decisions cannot be based on special categories of personal data. There are exceptions to this: where the subject has given their explicit consent[149] or else where processing is necessary for grounds of substantial public

---

145. WP29, *Guidelines on Automated individual decision-making and Profiling for the purposes of Regulation 2016/679*, 17/EN, WP 251, 3 October 2017, p 11.

146. GDPR, article 22(2) provides that the right does not apply if the decision in question '… is necessary for entering into, or performance of, a contract between the data subject and a data controller; … is authorised by Union or Member State law to which the controller is subject and which also lays down suitable measures to safeguard the data subject's rights and freedoms and legitimate interests; or … is based on the data subject's explicit consent'.

147. GDPR, Recital 71.

148. GDPR, Recital 71.

149. In accordance with GDPR, article 9(2)(a).

interest.[150] In addition, '… suitable measures to safeguard the data subject's rights and freedoms and legitimate interests …' have to be put in place.

[9.51] Article 22 is not just a right not to be subject to automated decision making, it is also a right not to be subject to profiling,[151] which is defined by GDPR, article 4(4) as meaning:

> … any form of automated processing of personal data consisting of the use of personal data to evaluate certain personal aspects relating to a natural person, in particular to analyse or predict aspects concerning that natural person's performance at work, economic situation, health, personal preferences, interests, reliability, behaviour, location or movements.

Profiling is integral to the business models of search engines such as Google and social media providers such as Facebook.[152] Article 22 may particularly impact upon companies such as Google which may process personal data on the basis of their legitimate interest. In *Google Spain* the CJEU considered the lawful basis upon which such searches were being undertaken was that '… it is necessary for the purposes of the legitimate interests pursued by the controller or by the third party or parties to whom the data are disclosed …'[153] Google's search engine is fully automated; it is a computer that decides what responses to return in response to a term being entered into the search engine. To that extent Google Search will fall within the scope of article 22, but those search results will not, of themselves, give rise to legal effects about a subject. Someone who views such results may make a decision on foot of doing so. Someone might decide not to hire a lawyer because Google Search displays results indicating that he was subject to debt recovery proceedings many years before (the display of such results was the subject of *Google Spain*). However that will be the decision of the person looking for a lawyer, that decision will not be solely based on automated processing.

GDPR, article 22(1) is the most prominent of a suite of rights that the GDPR provides in relation to profiling. Additional rights are provided in relation to rights of

---

150. In accordance with GDPR, article 9(2)(g).
151. GDPR, Recital 72 provides that 'Profiling is subject to the rules of this Regulation governing the processing of personal data, such as the legal grounds for processing or data protection principles. The European Data Protection Board established by this Regulation (the 'Board') should be able to issue guidance in that context'.
152. Sometimes the results generated by such profiling can be amusing, such as a US broker which profiled visitors to its website, only to learn that staff of the US Securities and Exchange Commission (SEC) were the most frequent visitors. Shortly afterwards the SEC closed them down. Murphy, 'Calling out white males, aged 45–54, working in the Washington DC area …', (2015) *Financial Times*, 2 June. However, such profiling can give rise to significant concerns such as the racial profiling of Facebook users (Hern, 'Facebook's "ethnic affinity" advertising sparks concerns of racial profiling', (2016) *The Guardian*, 22 March). Facebook has since placed some limitations upon the ways to which such 'ethnic affinity' advertising can be used (Hern, 'Facebook stops advertisers illegally discriminating by race', (2017) *The Guardian*, 9 February).
153. *Costeja González v Google Spain and Google* (Case C–131/12), para 74.

information,[154] access[155] and objection[156] in relation to such profiling. Of perhaps greatest significance is that Data Protection Impact Assessments must be undertaken before such profiling begins:

> A data protection impact assessment … shall in particular be required in the case of … a systematic and extensive evaluation of personal aspects relating to natural persons which is based on automated processing, including profiling, and on which decisions are based that produce legal effects concerning the natural person or similarly significantly affect the natural person.[157]

[9.52] GDPR, articles 13(1)(f), 14(2)(g) and 15(1)(h) provide for subjects to be given information about 'the existence of automated decision-making, including profiling'. How useful this information will be remains to be seen. It can be very difficult to explain the sophisticated algorithms that underlie big data programs, even to experts. In addition, it may be even harder to verify the accuracy of such explanations when given. The Recitals outline measures that controllers may use to '… ensure fair and transparent processing in respect of the data subject, taking into account the specific circumstances and context in which the personal data are processed'. These measures include the use of '… appropriate mathematical or statistical procedures for the profiling …' And the implementation of '… technical and organisational measures …'. These should be appropriate:

(a) To ensure '… that factors which result in inaccuracies in personal data are corrected and the risk of errors is minimised …';

(b) To '… secure personal data in a manner that takes account of the potential risks involved for the interests and rights of the data subject …';

(c) To prevent '… discriminatory effects on natural persons on the basis of racial or ethnic origin, political opinion, religion or beliefs, trade union membership, genetic or health status or sexual orientation, or that result in measures having such an effect'.

[9.53] Subjects have the right to object to being profiled pursuant to GDPR, article 21. It remains to be seen if controllers that engage in profiling argue that articles 21 and 22 must be read together and that they only have to cease profiling under article 22 where the subject has objected under article 21.

---

154. GDPR, articles 13(2)(f) and 14(2)(g).
155. GDPR, article 15(1)(h).
156. GDPR, article 21(1).
157. GDPR, article 35(3)(a).

Chapter 10

MODALITIES AND RESTRICTIONS

[10.01] The GDPR sets out the rights of the data subject between article 12, which explains the 'modalities' by which those rights are to be exercised, and article 23, which explains how those rights may be restricted. These standardise the operation of the various rights of subjects that are set out between these two provisions. Hence the GDPR makes no particular distinction between any of these rights: it is intended that each and any right may be exercised in the same way as each or any of the others.

MODALITIES

[10.02] These modalities primarily apply to the exercise of rights pursuant to GDPR, articles 13 to 22. However, they can have application to some other provisions of GDPR, such as article 34, which provides for the communication of data breaches to the subject. The first of these modalities is that any information or communications given by the controller to the subject[1] must be provided:

> in a concise, transparent, intelligible and easily accessible form, using clear and plain language.

The Recitals add that this information should:

> ... be concise ... easy to understand ... and, additionally, where appropriate, visualisation be used.

This is particularly so where information is being provided to a child. The Recitals add:

> Given that children merit specific protection, any information and communication, where processing is addressed to a child, should be in such a clear and plain language that the child can easily understand.

That information must be provided in writing and may be by electronic means, where appropriate. As the Recitals explain:

> Such information could be provided in electronic form, for example, when addressed to the public, through a website. This is of particular relevance in situations where the proliferation of actors and the technological complexity of practice make it difficult for the data subject to know and understand whether, by whom and for what purpose personal data relating to him or her are being collected, such as in the case of online advertising.[2]

---

1. That provision of information may take place pursuant to articles 13 and 14 and any communication under GPRR, articles 15 to 22 and 34.
2. GDPR, Recital 58.

[10.03] The electronic provision of such information might not necessarily mean the provision of information by e-mail or on a web-page. It could also mean setting up a website to interact with browsers in a particular way. Alternatively, the information may be provided orally, provided that this is requested by the subject, whose identity must be proven by other means.[3] This is an off-hand reference to one of the most significant obligations imposed on data controllers, that of verifying that those who assert subject rights are who they say they are. GDPR, article 12(6) goes on to provide:

> Without prejudice to Article 11, where the controller has reasonable doubts concerning the identity of the natural person making the request referred to in Articles 15 to 21, the controller may request the provision of additional information necessary to confirm the identity of the data subject.

This obligation to verify the identity of data subjects has to be read in the context of the principle of integrity and confidentiality imposed by GDPR, article 5(1)(d). This means more than ensuring that data is kept secure; allowing another to invoke the rights of rectification, erasure, restriction or objection might also cause this principle to be breached.

This need to ensure the correct identification of data subjects should not be allowed to interfere with the ability of those subjects to exercise their rights. Controllers are obliged to '... facilitate the exercise of data subject rights under Articles 15 to 22 ...'.[4] Hence the controller cannot act in a manner which might suggest that he was seeking to frustrate the subject, such as insisting upon overly complex identity checks.

[10.04] The time limits imposed by the GDPR are short and strict. GDPR, article 12(3) provides that the controller must:

> ... provide information on action taken on a request under Articles 15 to 22 to the data subject without undue delay and in any event within one month of receipt of the request ...

So controllers must respond to requests as soon as possible, although they may take as long as a month to respond.[5] They must decide whether or not they intend to respond to

---

3.   GDPR, article 12(1).
4.   Specific provision is made for facilitating the exercise of rights under article 11(2).
5.   Regulation 1182/71/EU determining the rules applicable to periods, dates and time limits, (OJ L 124, 8.6.1971, p. 1–2) begins by noting that '... numerous (EU) acts ... employ the terms "working days" or "public holidays" and that "...it is necessary to establish uniform general rules on the subject". Although it goes onto note that "...no authority to establish such rules is provided for in the Treaties.'. Regulation 1182/71 goes onto provide that: 'Where a period, expressed in ... months ... is to be calculated from the moment at which an event occurs or an action takes place, the day during which that event occurs or that action takes place shall not be considered as falling within the period in question' (Article 3(1)). It goes onto provide that '... a period expressed in ... months ... shall start at the beginning of the first hour of the first day of the period, and shall end with the expiry of the last hour of whichever day in the last ... month ... is the same day of the week, or falls on the same date, as the day from which the period runs. (contd .../)

the request within the first month.[6] It is only where an extension of time is necessary to comply with a request that controllers can extend for a further two months. In deciding how long is 'necessary' the controller may take into account '... the complexity and number of the requests'. If the controller decides that it needs such an extension then it must inform the subject '... within one month of receipt of the request, together with the reasons for the delay'. Where the data subject makes the request by electronic means, the information must be provided by electronic means where possible, unless otherwise requested by the data subject.[7]

This obligation to facilitate the subject is reflected in the elimination of fees. Rights can be exercised and communications must be provided free of charge.[8] The only exception to this is where requests '... are manifestly unfounded or excessive, in particular because of their repetitive character ...' In such circumstances the controller may either:

(a) charge a reasonable fee taking into account the administrative costs of providing the information or communication or taking the action requested; or

(b) refuse to act on the request.

[10.05] Demonstrating that a request is 'manifestly unfounded or excessive' may prove a challenge. Modern data processing systems make it easy for data to be amended or changed. Hence a subject may be justified in repeatedly exercising their rights in relation to such data, even in a short period of time. This is particularly so if the data is of type, such as credit history, which might have a significant impact upon the subject. If a controller suspects that a subject may be making 'manifestly unfounded or excessive' requests, then that controller will '... bear the burden of demonstrating the manifestly unfounded or excessive character of the request'.[9] This would mean having some process in place to demonstrate that the request is 'manifestly unfounded or excessive'. It would be insufficient to demonstrate that the request is 'merely' unfounded or excessive; the request must be 'manifestly' so. Manifestly is derived from the adjective manifest, defined by the OED as: 'Clear or obvious to the eye or mind'.[10] If a controller comes to the conclusion that the requests are in fact 'manifestly unfounded or excessive' then it has two options: charge the subject a 'reasonable fee'; or refuse to process the

---

5. (contd) If, in a period expressed in months ... the day on which it should expire does not occur in the last month, the period shall end with the expiry of the last hour of the last day of that month" (Article 3(2)(c)). Regulation 1182/71 continues that the '... periods concerned shall include public holidays, Sundays and Saturdays ... (Article 3(3)) and that 'Where the last day of a period expressed otherwise than in hours is a public holiday, Sunday or Saturday, the period shall end with the expiry of the last hour of the following working day' (Article 3(4)).

6. GDPR, article 12(4).

7. GDPR, article 12(3).

8. This includes all information and communications provided pursuant to articles 13 to 22 and 34.

9. GDPR, article 12(5).

10. *Concise Oxford English Dictionary* (10th edn, Oxford University Press, revised 1999).

request. The controller must facilitate the subject in the exercise of their rights, which suggests that it may be for the subject to decide whether they want to avail of either of these two options. The controller has to provide the subject with the reasons why their request is being refused. It may be difficult for a controller to maintain such a refusal if the subject responds that they would prefer to pay a 'reasonable fee'.

[10.06] The issue of what level a fee might be set at was considered by the CJEU in *X*,[11] which concerned a subject who had been charged €12.80 for being provided with a certified copy of her personal data.[12] The CJEU held that fees had to be fixed:

> ... at a level which constitutes a fair balance between, on the one hand, the interest of the data subject in protecting his privacy, in particular through his right to have the data communicated to him ... so that he is able ... to exercise his rights to rectification, erasure and blocking of the data ... and, on the other, the burden which the obligation to communicate such data represents for the controller.

The CJEU went on to hold that such a fee '... may not be fixed at a level likely to constitute an obstacle to the exercise of the right of access ...'.[13] What this meant was that:

> ... the level of those fees must not exceed the cost of communicating such data ...[14]

Whilst the cost of communicating personal data by registered post may be quite high, the cost of communicating it through electronic means may be very low. This is particularly so as the GDPR encourages controllers to facilitate subjects by using electronic means to provide information to the subject[15] and by providing remote and direct access to it.[16] A controller who facilitates subjects in such ways may find it difficult to justify charging subjects anything for upholding their rights; it is hard to see why the GDPR would advantage those who do not facilitate subjects by using more costly means to communicate such as registered post. Hence it may be difficult for controllers to charge subjects anything at all as a 'reasonable fee' for exercising their subject rights.

If a controller decides to refuse a request, then they must:

> ... inform the data subject without delay and at the latest within one month of receipt of the request of the reasons for not taking action and on the possibility of lodging a complaint with a supervisory authority and seeking a judicial remedy.

---

11. *X* (Case C–486/12) (12 December 2013).
12. The data in question was her addresses. A fine had been imposed on X for traffic offences, her defence was that '... she had never received the notices requesting payment of that fine, as they had been sent to the wrong address' (para 7).
13. *X* (Case C–486/12) (12 December 2013), paras 28–29.
14. *X* (Case C–486/12) (12 December 2013), para 31.
15. GDPR, article 12(1).
16. GDPR, Recital 63.

[10.07] Article 12 anticipates that information may be provided to subjects by more and less sophisticated means. Less sophisticated means would be:

> standardised icons … to give in an easily visible, intelligible and clearly legible manner a meaningful overview of the intended processing.[17]

What these icons might look like is a matter for the EU Commission which is '… empowered to adopt delegated acts[18] for the purpose of determining the information to be presented by the icons and the procedures for providing standardised icons'.[19] More sophisticated means would be ensuring that these icons are machine readable when they are provided electronically. This might facilitate subjects who wished to set their systems to reject requests from controllers which indicated that the data given might be subject to disclosure or retained for a long period of time, for example.

RESTRICTIONS

[10.08] GDPR, Ch III begins by setting out how controllers may facilitate subjects in the exercise of their rights; it concludes by setting out how those rights may be restricted. GDPR, Section 5 of Ch III contains the single article 23, which sets out the restrictions that may be imposed upon the processing of personal data. These restrictions will be limited; the GDPR sets out an exhaustive set of requirements that must be fulfilled before a restriction can be imposed.

(1) the restriction must be set in EU law or the law of a Member State;

(2) that law must take the form of a legislative measure;

(3) the restriction must respect '… the essence of the fundamental rights and freedoms';

(4) be a 'necessary and proportionate measure in a democratic society';

(5) safeguard one of the interests set out in GDPR, article 23(1); and

(6) contain at least the specific provisions set out in GDPR, article 23(2).

These requirements should mean that the rights of subjects cannot be easily restricted. In particular, it requires that EU or Member State legislatures take a conscious decision to restrict those rights. Article 23 requires that such a legislative measure be relatively complex, such complexity will increase the frictional costs of legislating for the restriction of subject rights. The provisions required by article 23(2) may increase the political costs of such restrictions by requiring that such legislation make clear the nature of the restrictions being imposed.

Article 23(1) begins by providing that EU law or that of a Member State may impose restrictions upon the rights of subjects. These restrictions must take the form of a

---

17.   GDPR, article 12(7).

18.   '…in accordance with Article 92 …' GDPR.

19.   GDPR, article 12(8).

'legislative measure', thus precluding that they might be set out in a judgment of a court. However, it is very clear that the courts may restrict data protection rights so that they may be balanced with the rights and freedoms of others. Data protection is just one set of rights that are recognised by the Charter, article 52 of which provides:

> Any limitation on the exercise of the rights and freedoms recognised by this Charter must be provided for by law ... Subject to the principle of proportionality, limitations may be made only if they are necessary and genuinely meet objectives of general interest recognised by the Union or the need to protect the rights and freedoms of others.[20]

This allows that limitations may be provided for by law, it does not require that such limitations be set out in legislation. And the courts may well impose limitations on the rights of subjects. In *Google Spain*[21] the CJEU held that the data protection rights of the subject meant that '... the operator of a search engine is obliged to remove from the list of results displayed following a search made on the basis of a person's name links to web pages ...'. However, this right was not unlimited. The CJEU held that 'that would not be the case if it appeared ... that the interference with his fundamental rights is justified by the preponderant interest of the general public in having ... access to the information in question'.[22] Of course this interference could be regarded as having a legislative basis in GDPR, article 85, which requires that the laws of Member States reconcile rights of data protection with those of expression and information. However, the GDPR does not accord any such legislative status to the right of property or to conduct a business. In *McFadden*[23] the CJEU held that these rights were being interfered with by the actions of the applicant and held that:

> Where several fundamental rights protected under EU law are at stake, it is for the national authorities or courts concerned to ensure that a fair balance is struck between those rights.[24]

[10.09] The Court went on to find that the rights of the respondent had to be balanced with the data protection rights of the applicant's customers (at least one of whom had used his wi-fi network to download material in breach of copyright). This means that the respondent might have to start '... password-protecting an internet connection' in order to '... dissuade the users of that connection from infringing copyright or relating rights'.[25] This would force the applicant to start processing his customer's personal data and prevent them accessing the internet anonymously.

[10.10] To the extent that EU or national legislatures can place restrictions on rights such as access or rectification, then the judgment of the CJEU in *Nowak* suggests that

---

20. Charter, article 52(1).
21. *Gonzalez v Google Spain* (Case C–131/12) (13 May 2014).
22. *Gonzalez v Google Spain* (Case C–131/12) (13 May 2014), para 100.
23. *McFadden* (Case C–484/14) (15 September 2016).
24. *McFadden* (Case C–484/14) (15 September 2016), para 83.
25. *McFadden* (Case C–484/14) (15 September 2016), para 96.

such restrictions must be specific implementations of article 23 GDPR. In *Nowak* the CJEU was considering the possibility that restrictions might be placed on the ability of examination candidates to access their answers and comments of examiners. The CJEU began by holding that:

> ... to give a candidate a right of access to those answers and to those comments... serves the purpose ... of guaranteeing the protection of that candidate's right to privacy with regard to the processing of data relating to him ... irrespective of whether that candidate does or does not also have such a right of access under the national legislation applicable to the examination procedure.[26]

This seems to suggest that the right of access exists independently or 'irrespective' of existing national regimes. The CJEU considers that the right of access will apply regardless of what existing national rules may say. The CJEU goes onto note that both '... Directive 95/46 and Regulation 2016/679 which replaces the directive both provide for certain restrictions on those rights'.[27] The CJEU went onto note that:

> ... Article 23(1)(e) of Regulation 2016/679 extends the list of grounds justifying restrictions ... to 'other important objectives of general public interest of the Union or of a Member State'. Further, Article 15(4) of Regulation 2016/679, that article relating to the data subject's right of access, provides that the right to obtain a copy of personal data must not adversely affect the rights and freedoms of others.[28]

The relationship between the rights of access and those of rectification and erasure was explained:

> ... the protection of the fundamental right to respect for private life means, inter alia, that any individual may be certain that the personal data relating to him is correct and that it is processed in a lawful manner ... it is in order to be in a position to carry out the necessary checks that the data subject has ... right of access to the data relating to him which is being processed. That right of access is necessary, inter alia, to enable the data subject to obtain, depending on the circumstances, the rectification, erasure or blocking of his data by the data controller and consequently to exercise the right (of rectification or erasure) ...[29]

[10.11] The GDPR has to be read as compatible with the Charter and the Recitals do provide '... restrictions should be in accordance with the requirements set out in the Charter and in the European Convention for the Protection of Human Rights and Fundamental Freedoms'. Article 23 might therefore be viewed as applying only to restrictions that are imposed by EU or Member States' legislatures. It does not apply to restrictions imposed by the Courts, which will have a separate legal basis in article 52 of the Charter. So a Court can restrict subject rights and its judgment will not have to include the provisions set out in article 23(2).

---

26. *Nowak* (Case C–434/16) (20 December 2017), para 56.
27. *Nowak* (Case C–434/16) (20 December 2017), para 59.
28. *Nowak* (Case C–434/16) (20 December 2017), para 61.
29. *Nowak* (Case C–434/16) (20 December 2017), para 57.

Any such restrictions must respect both 'the essence of the fundamental rights and freedoms' and be '... a necessary and proportionate measure in a democratic society'. This requirement is consistent with the text of the Charter. Similar requirements have been discussed by the CJEU on many occasions. In *Tele2 Sverige*[30] the CJEU held that:

> ... limitations may be imposed on the exercise of those rights and freedoms only if they are necessary and if they genuinely meet objectives of general interest recognised by the European Union or the need to protect the rights and freedoms of others ...[31]

[10.12] As regards proportionality the CJEU held that:

> ... the protection of the fundamental right to respect for private life at EU level requires that derogations from and limitations on the protection of personal data should apply only in so far as is strictly necessary ...[32]

At issue in *Tele2 Sverige* was EU Member State legislation providing for the retention of traffic data such as when (and where) a phone call was made. The CJEU held that EU law:

> ... must be interpreted as precluding national legislation which, for the purpose of fighting crime, provides for the general and indiscriminate retention of all traffic and location data of all subscribers and registered users relating to all means of electronic communication.[33]

However, the CJEU did not suggest that all such data retention laws were invalid; only those providing for 'general and indiscriminate retention'. Before this conclusion, the CJEU discussed what a valid data retention law would contain. By its nature such a law must restrict the rights of data subjects, hence this discussion is highly relevant to other laws that may similarly restrict the rights of data subjects. The CJEU begins its discussion by noting that the data[34] retained:

> ... taken as a whole, is liable to allow very precise conclusions to be drawn concerning the private lives of the persons whose data has been retained, such as everyday habits, permanent or temporary places of residence, daily or other

---

30.   *Tele2 Sverige* (Case C–203/15) (21 December 2016).
31.   *Tele2 Sverige* (Case C–203/15) (21 December 2016), para 94.
32.   *Tele2 Sverige* (Case C–203/15) (21 December 2016), para 96.
33.   *Tele2 Sverige* (Case C–203/15) (21 December 2016), para 112.
34.   The data retained '... makes it possible to trace and identify the source of a communication and its destination, to identify the date, time, duration and type of a communication, to identify users' communication equipment, and to establish the location of mobile communication equipment. That data includes, inter alia, the name and address of the subscriber or registered user, the telephone number of the caller, the number called and an IP address for internet services. That data makes it possible, in particular, to identify the person with whom a subscriber or registered user has communicated and by what means, and to identify the time of the communication as well as the place from which that communication took place. Further, that data makes it possible to know how often the subscriber or registered user communicated with certain persons in a given period': para 97.

movements, the activities carried out, the social relationships of those persons and the social environments frequented by them.[35]

[10.13] The CJEU analysis of the interference caused to the rights of subjects is careful and structured. Member States that wish to restrict subject rights under article 23 will have to undertake a similarly structured analysis. They may have to undertake a DPIA,[36] for example, and consult with their SA before and perhaps after they legislate.[37] The CJEU found that the interference with the rights of the subjects was '... very far-reaching and must be considered to be particularly serious'.[38] The CJEU therefore held that given the severity of this interference '... only the objective of fighting serious crime is capable of justifying such a measure'.[39] Whatever restrictions are imposed pursuant to article 23 will have to be similarly proportionate to the end pursued. What this will mean in practice is that restrictions will have to be focused on specific risks. A particularly broad restriction will have to be justified by a particularly significant risk. This was an issue that the CJEU had with the Swedish legislation which was:

> ... not restricted to retention in relation to (i) data pertaining to a particular time period and/or geographical area and/or a group of persons likely to be involved, in one way or another, in a serious crime, or (ii) persons who could, for other reasons, contribute, through their data being retained, to fighting crime ...

So it will not be enough for a restriction to safeguard one of the purposes set out in article 23(1); any restriction will have to be focused on a proportionate aspect of that purpose. So a restriction for the purpose of safeguarding 'national security' would have to ensure that such restrictions would only apply to times, places or persons who posed a particular risk. The CJEU went on to require that such data retention legislation would have to '... lay down clear and precise rules governing the scope and application of such a ... measure and imposing minimum safeguards'. Such requirements are set out in detail in GDPR, article 23(2). These rules and safeguards should ensure that those whose rights are restricted '... have sufficient guarantees of the effective protection of their personal data against the risk of misuse'.[40]

[10.14] In *Tele2 Sverige* the CJEU set out further elements that data retention legislation must contain, which are relevant to the restriction of subject rights. One is that the legislation '... must, in particular, indicate in what circumstances and under which conditions a data retention measure may ... be adopted, thereby ensuring that such a measure is limited to what is strictly necessary'.[41] So a measure cannot be adopted that sets out where restrictions are to apply in general terms; it must be specific. Another is

---

35. *Tele2 Sverige* (Case C–203/15) (21 December 2016), para 98.
36. GDPR, article 35.
37. GDPR, article 36.
38. *Tele2 Sverige* (Case C–203/15) (21 December 2016), para 100.
39. *Tele2 Sverige* (Case C–203/15) (21 December 2016), para 102.
40. *Tele2 Sverige* (Case C–203/15) (21 December 2016), para 109.
41. *Tele2 Sverige* (Case C–203/15) (21 December 2016), para 109.

that the operation of such a measure must '... continue nonetheless to meet objective criteria, that establish a connection between the data to be retained and the objective pursued. In particular, such conditions must be shown to be such as actually to circumscribe, in practice, the extent of that measure and, thus, the public affected.' In other words, it is not enough that legislation be adopted which appears to comply with article 23; that legislation must be operated in practice in a manner which complies with the data protection rules in general and the GDPR in particular. Finally, the operation of such restrictions must be 'based on objective evidence'. In the case of data retention this would mean that such retention '... makes it possible to identify a public whose data is likely to reveal a link, at least an indirect one, with serious criminal offences ...'. Similar objective evidence would be required before restrictions could be imposed upon the rights of subjects in an individual case.

Article 23 provides that Member States may legislate to safeguard one of the following:

(a) national security (the Recitals expand this to include 'the protection of human life especially in response to natural or manmade disasters');[42]

(b) defence;

(c) public security (the Recitals expand this out to '... including the safeguarding against and the prevention of threats to public security';

(d) the prevention, investigation, detection or prosecution of criminal offences or the execution of criminal penalties, including the safeguarding against and the prevention of threats to public security;

(e) other important objectives of general public interest of the Union or of a Member State, in particular an important economic or financial interest of the Union or of a Member State, including monetary, budgetary and taxation matters, public health and social security;

(f) the protection of judicial independence and judicial proceedings;

(g) the prevention, investigation, detection and prosecution of breaches of ethics for regulated professions;

(h) a monitoring, inspection or regulatory function connected, even occasionally, to the exercise of official authority in the cases referred to in points (a), (b), (c), (d), (e) and (g);

(i) the protection of the data subject or the rights and freedoms of others (the Recitals include in this 'social protection, public health and humanitarian purposes');[43]

(j) the enforcement of civil law claims.

42. GDPR, Recital 73.
43. GDPR, Recital 73.

[10.15] The Recitals add a couple of further elements to this list: '... the keeping of public registers kept for reasons of general public interest' and '... further processing of archived personal data to provide specific information related to the political behaviour under former totalitarian state regimes'.[44]

Article 23(2) then goes on to set specific provisions that must be included in any such legislative measure 'where relevant':

- (a) the purposes of the processing or categories of processing;
- (b) the categories of personal data;
- (c) the scope of the restrictions introduced;
- (d) the safeguards to prevent abuse or unlawful access or transfer;
- (e) the specification of the controller or categories of controllers;
- (f) the storage periods and the applicable safeguards taking into account the nature, scope and purposes of the processing or categories of processing;
- (g) the risks to the rights and freedoms of data subjects; and
- (h) the right of data subjects to be informed about the restriction, unless that may be prejudicial to the purpose of the restriction.

---

44. GDPR, Recital 73.

PART 5
CONTROLLER AND PROCESSORS

Chapter 11

CONTROLLER AND PROCESSOR

INTRODUCTION

[11.01] Of all the changes that the GDPR makes to EU data protection law, article 5(2) may arguably be the most significant. Article 5(2) adds an additional principle to those originally set out in Directive 95/46, which are repeated and renamed by the GDPR. This principle, that of 'accountability' is short and succinct:

> The controller shall be responsible for, and be able to demonstrate compliance with … (the principles relating to processing of personal data).

Chapter IV of the GDPR, then goes on to set out how controllers (and processors) may demonstrate compliance with these principles. This obligation is primarily imposed upon controllers. Article 24 provides:

> Taking into account the nature, scope, context and purposes of processing as well as the risks of varying likelihood and severity for the rights and freedoms of natural persons, the controller shall implement appropriate technical and organisational measures to ensure and to be able to demonstrate that processing is performed in accordance with this Regulation. Those measures shall be reviewed and updated where necessary.

This obligation is broader than the principle of accountability, as the controller is expected to be able to demonstrate compliance with the GDPR in its entirety. This obligation is not confined to a particular point in time, but rather is continuous, as the controller must review and update their measures. GDPR, article 24 goes on to specify 'the implementation of appropriate data protection policies by the controller' as measures that may be used by controllers to demonstrate compliance where 'proportionate'.[1] The CJEU considers the principle of proportionality to be settled by its case law, describing it as:

> … one of the general principles of European Union law, (which) requires that measures implemented by acts of the European Union are appropriate for attaining the objective pursued and do not go beyond what is necessary to achieve it.[2]

This suggests that the CJEU will expect that controllers will use, review and update such measures as necessary to demonstrate compliance. In addition, controllers may also adhere to codes of conduct or approved certification mechanism. Article 24(3) suggests that these may be used:

> … as an element by which to demonstrate compliance with the obligations of the controller.

---

1. GDPR, article 24(2).
2. *Volker und Schecke* (Case C–93/09) (9 November 2010), para 74.

[11.02] The structure of article 24 significantly broadens out the controller's obligation. Article 24 initially imposes upon controllers the straightforward duty that a controller be able to demonstrate compliance with the obligations imposed by the GDPR. It then extends out that obligation to data protection policies that the controller may implement and codes of conduct to which it may adhere. Of course controllers could implement or adhere to such policies and codes without any provision being made by article 24. Specifically mentioning such policies and codes makes implementation or adherence part of the obligation imposed by that article. What this may mean in practice is that a prudent controller who wishes to demonstrate compliance may adopt appropriate policies and follow relevant codes. That controller will then find that adherence to those policies and codes is part of his compliance burden. Therefore, it is not illogical to wonder why a controller would bother with the additional burden imposed by such adherence. However, controllers may have little choice but to do so. The obligations imposed by the GDPR are very high-level, policies and codes may therefore be needed to apply those obligations to the specific data processing systems of a controller and the risks that processing may pose for the rights and freedoms of data subjects.

[11.03] A variety of obligations are imposed by GDPR, Ch IV. These obligations are significant; they are also interlinked. It may be useful to divide these obligations into two sets: those that relate to governance and those that relate to risk management. The obligations that relate to governance are:

- the Data Protection Officer (DPO);

- the relationship between controllers, joint controllers and processors;

- record keeping & Cooperation with the Supervisory Authority (SA).

The obligations that relate to risk are:

- data protection by default and design;

- data protection impact assessment (including prior consultation);

- the assessment of appropriate security measures; and,

- the assessment of where a personal data breach is high risk.

These two sets of obligations are considered separately in the two chapters that follow.

Chapter 12

CONTROLLER AND PROCESSOR: GOVERNANCE

[12.01] The GDPR obliges controllers, and to a lesser extent, processors, to fundamentally alter their management structures. In doing so the GDPR takes no account of the relative size of different controllers, focusing instead upon the relative risks that a processing operation may pose to subjects. That is appropriate, one of the distinctive features of information technology is that it enables tiny firms to process data relating to hundreds of millions of people.[1] But the burden imposed on small firms may prove significant. The Recitals however suggest that these obligations may need to be moderated, but only make specific provision with regard to record-keeping. The Recitals state that:

> To take account of the specific situation of micro, small and medium-sized enterprises, this Regulation includes a derogation for organisations with fewer than 250 employees with regard to record-keeping. In addition, the Union institutions and bodies, and Member States and their supervisory authorities, are encouraged to take account of the specific needs of micro, small and medium-sized enterprises in the application of this Regulation ...[2]

Other than this specific exemption with regard to record keeping the GDPR will apply to all controllers equally. The compliance burden on small firms may prove significant, a firm that considers it necessary to appoint a DPO may find that it needs to also improve the compliance function that will interact with that DPO. Such functions may require skills and personnel that many micro, small and medium-sized firms simply will not have.

THE DATA PROTECTION OFFICER (DPO)

[12.02] The concept of the Data Protection Officer (DPO) originated in Germany.[3] It is perhaps the most distinctive feature of a supervisory structure and is quite different to that found in areas such as financial or communications services. In those latter areas firms that are subject to supervision pay their regulators costs by way of levies or fees. Under the GDPR data controllers appoint and pay for their own, internal, supervisor.

---

1. Instagram for example has less than 500 employees, but around 700 million users worldwide; Wagner, 'Inside Instagram's reinvention', (2017) *Recode*, 23 January.
2. GDPR, Recital 13 which goes on to say that 'The notion of micro, small and medium-sized enterprises should draw from Article 2 of the Annex to Commission Recommendation 2003/361/EC of 6 May 2003 concerning the definition of micro, small and medium-sized enterprises (C(2003) 1422) (OJ L 124, 20.5.2003, p 36).
3. Meyer, 'What will mandatory DPOs look like under the GDPR? Germany could tell you', The Privacy Advisor, IAPP, 6 June 2016.

This is the DPO, who will have a senior, independent function within a data controller's operation. Their role is a combination of advisor, educator and point of contact for both the supervisory authority (SA) and subjects.

A DPO must be designated in any one of three situations:

(a) where the processing is carried out by a public authority or body, except for courts acting in their judicial capacity;

(b) where the core activities of the controller or the processor consist of processing operations which, by virtue of their nature, their scope and/or their purposes, require regular and systematic monitoring of data subjects on a large scale; or

(c) where the core activities of the controller or the processor consist of processing on a large scale of special categories of data pursuant to Article 9 and personal data relating to criminal convictions and offences referred to in Article 10.

[12.03] All public bodies must appoint a DPO. This obligation may not prove as onerous as it seems as GDPR, article 35 goes on to provide that a single DPO may be designated for several such public authorities. The GDPR does not define what precisely is meant by 'a public authority or body' but the WP29 'considers that such a notion is to be determined under national law.' Whilst acknowledging that there may be no legal obligation to do so, the WP29 suggests that 'private organisations carrying out public tasks or exercising public authority' should also designate a DPO.[4] Courts do not have to appoint a DPO, but may instead have their own supervisory authority.

DPOs must also be appointed where the 'core activities' of the controller or the processor '... require regular and systematic monitoring of data subjects on a large scale'. The GDPR does not define what it means by 'core activities' but the Recitals suggest that:

> the core activities of a controller relate to its primary activities and do not relate to
> the processing of personal data as ancillary activities.[5]

So, a security firm that provides CCTV monitoring services might have to appoint a DPO because regular or systemic monitoring will be one of its primary activities.[6] An accountancy firm that installed a CCTV camera to monitor its car park might not however, as such monitoring would be ancillary to its primary activity of accountancy.[7]

---

4.   Article 29 WP, *Guidelines on Data Protection Officers* ('DPOs'), revised and adopted on 5 April 2017, 16/EN, WP 243 rev 01, p 6.

5.   GDPR, Recital 97.

6.   The W29 gives the example of a hospital whose core activity is to provide health care. This activity could not be performed safely and effectively without processing health data such as patient health records. Processing this data 'should be considered to be one of any hospital's core activities' and therefore requires the appointment of a DPO. WP29 *Guidelines on Data Protection Officers* ('DPOs') 16/EN WP243 adopted on 13 December 2016, p 7.

7.   Similarly, W29 suggests that provision of IT support or paying employees are support functions for an organisation's core activity: (contd .../)

It will be interesting to see where the line is drawn between primary and ancillary activities. A supermarket that installs CCTV in all its stores might argue that such monitoring is ancillary to its primary activity of selling groceries and other goods, but is that correct if CCTV cameras are in every store, monitoring every customer coming in and out?

In addition, the monitoring must also be 'regular[8] and systemic'[9] for this obligation to apply.[10] The OED[11] defines a system as a '... set of things working together as parts of a mechanism or an interconnecting network; a complex whole'. So if an accountancy firm installed a CCTV camera to monitor its car park this would not be systemic, but if a number of cameras were installed, monitoring every possible pedestrian or vehicular exit then it might be argued that this was 'systemic'. And, the installation of CCTV throughout a supermarket chain might as this would almost certainly be 'systemic'. Again it will be interesting to see where the line is drawn between isolated and systemic monitoring; this may well depend upon whether the monitoring is 'large scale'.

[12.04] The GDPR does not define what it means by 'large-scale'. In the context of whether or not a Data Protection Impact Assessment (DPIA) is required the Recitals provide that:

> The processing of personal data should not be considered to be on a large scale if the processing concerns personal data from patients or clients by an individual physician, other health care professional or lawyer.[12]

---

7.   (contd) 'Even though these activities are necessary or essential, they are usually considered ancillary functions rather than the core activity. WP29 *Guidelines on Data Protection Officers* ('DPOs') 16/EN, WP 243 rev 01 revised and adopted on 5 April 2017, p 7.

8.   The WP29 interprets regular as meaning one or more of the following: 'Ongoing or occurring at particular intervals for a particular period... Recurring or repeated at fixed times... Constantly or periodically taking place' Article 29 WP, *Guidelines on Data Protection Officers* ('DPOs'), revised and adopted on 5 April 2017, 16/EN, WP 243 rev 01, p 8–9.

9.   The WP29 has suggested that systemic means one or more of the following 'Occurring according to a system ... Pre-arranged, organised or methodical ... Taking place as part of a general plan for data collection ... Carried out as part of a strategy' Article 29 WP, Guidelines on Data Protection Officers ('DPOs'), revised and adopted on 5 April 2017, 16/EN, WP 243 rev 01, p 9.

10.   WP29 suggest the following examples of what may constitute regular and systemic monitoring of data subjects: 'operating a telecommunications network; providing telecommunications services; email retargeting; data-driven marketing activities; profiling and scoring for purposes of risk assessment (eg for purposes of credit scoring, establishment of insurance premiums, fraud prevention, detection of money-laundering); location tracking, for example, by mobile apps; loyalty programs; behavioural advertising; monitoring of wellness, fitness and health data via wearable devices; closed circuit television; connected devices eg smart meters, smart cars, home automation, etc.' Article 29 WP, Guidelines on Data Protection Officers ('DPOs'), revised and adopted on 5 April 2017, 16/EN, WP 243 rev 01, p 9

11.   *Concise Oxford English dictionary* (OUP, 10th edn, 1999).

12.   GDPR, Recital 91.

The use of the singular may be significant here; it suggests that whilst processing undertaken by an individual professional may not be 'large-scale', that undertaken by a partnership or practice may be. This does suggest that a data processing operation can become 'large-scale' quite swiftly. The WP29 recommends that the following factors be taken into account when considering whether or not a data processing operation is large-scale:

(a) the number of data subjects concerned – either as a specific number or as a proportion of the relevant population;

(b) the volume of data and/or the range of different data items being processed;

(c) the duration, or permanence, of the data processing activity;

(d) the geographical extent of the processing activity.

[12.05] The WP29 provide the following examples of large-scale processing:

(a) processing of patient data in the regular course of business by a hospital;

(b) processing of travel data of individuals using a city's public transport system (eg tracking via travel cards);

(c) processing of real time geo-location data of customers of an international fast food chain for statistical purposes by a processor specialised in providing these services;

(d) processing of customer data in the regular course of business by an insurance company or a bank;

(e) processing of personal data for behavioural advertising by a search engine;

(f) processing of data (content, traffic, location) by telephone or internet service providers.[13]

Finally, a controller or processor may have to appoint a DPO where the core activities include the processing of sensitive data and criminal conviction data. The WP29 suggests that this should not be read as meaning that a DPO need only be appointed where both categories of data are being processed as 'there is no policy reason for the two criteria having to be applied simultaneously. The text should therefore be read to say 'or'.[14] This seems correct. If it were not so, then a DPO might be seldom appointed under article 37(1)(c), since many of the obvious situations where both sensitive and criminal conviction data would be processed would be covered by Directive 2016/680.

---

13. Article 29 WP, *Guidelines on Data Protection Officers* ('DPOs'), revised and adopted on 5 April 2017, 16/EN, WP 243 rev 01, p 8.

14. Article 29 WP, *Guidelines on Data Protection Officers* ('DPOs'), revised and adopted on 5 April 2017, 16/EN, WP 243 rev 01, p 9.

[12.06] Controllers and processors must separately assess whether it is necessary for them to appoint a DPO. Therefore, situations may arise where a controller will appoint a DPO but its processor will not. In such situations the WP29 has suggested that it may nevertheless 'be good practice' for the processor to do so.[15] The WP29 recommends that unless it is clear that a controller or processor is not required to designate a DPO, then controllers and processors should:

> … document the internal analysis carried out to determine whether or not a DPO is to be appointed, in order to be able to demonstrate that the relevant factors have been taken into account properly.[16]

The WP29 notes that controllers or processors which do not employ a DPO may nevertheless employ staff or outside consultants with tasks relating to data protection. In such cases:

> It is important to ensure that there is no confusion regarding their title, status, position and tasks. Therefore, it should be made clear, in any communications within the company, as well as with data protection authorities, data subjects, and the public at large, that the title of this individual or consultant is not a 'DPO'.[17]

Qualifications

[12.07] Article 37(5) describes the criteria for being designated a DP in the following terms.

> The data protection officer shall be designated on the basis of professional qualities and, in particular, expert knowledge of data protection law and practices and the ability to fulfil the tasks referred to in Article 39.

A DPO needs a very broad skill set. The tasks set out in article 39(1) require that they act as a combination of advisor, educator, auditor and compliance officer and must have a knowledge of risk. Article 39(2) stipulates that they shall:

> … in the performance of his or her tasks have due regard to the risk associated with processing operations, taking into account the nature, scope, context and purposes of processing.

In particular, DPOs must advise upon DPIAs that may be undertaken by the controller or processor that employs or engages them.[18] Such DPIAs are risk analyses in large part. In addition, DPOs must also provide indications of:

> Guidance on the implementation of appropriate measures and on the demonstration of compliance by the controller or the processor, especially as regards the identification of the risk related to the processing, their assessment in

---

15. WP29 *Guidelines on Data Protection Officers* ('DPOs') revised and adopted on 5 April 2017, 16/EN, WP 243 rev 01, p 9.
16. WP29 *Guidelines on Data Protection Officers* ('DPOs') revised and adopted on 5 April 2017, 16/EN, WP 243 rev 01, p 5.
17. WP29 *Guidelines on Data Protection Officers* ('DPOs') revised and adopted on 5 April 2017, 16/EN, WP 243 rev 01, p 6.
18. GDPR, article 35(2).

terms of origin, nature, likelihood and severity, and the identification of best
practices to mitigate the risk ...[19]

[12.08] A DPO must be professional or at least be designated on the basis of their
professional qualities. The GDPR does not specify exactly which professional qualities
are needed, but the use of the term 'professional' may suggest that qualifications as a
DPO may be integrated with the existing EU structures for recognition of professional
qualifications.[20] There is no formal EU standard that professional DPOs can adhere to
but it is clear that DPOs do not have to be lawyers. However, the EU framework for
recognised legal qualifications does offer a model for what an EU DPO profession
might look like. Directive 98/5/EC[21] sets out the framework that enables lawyers
qualified in one Member State to work in another. Such a lawyer will be bound by rules
of professional conduct'[22] and may be subject to disciplinary proceedings.[23] A good
argument can be made that similar rules are required by DPOs, particularly given their
quasi-independent status. A controller who wishes to dismiss or penalise a DPO on
grounds of incompetence or misfeasance may be met with the allegation that the
controller is seeking to impinge upon the independence of the DPO. One of the
functions of regulated professions is to resolve such allegations and counter-allegations,
by regulating the conduct of their members. If DPOs are not established as a regulated
profession then such allegations would have to be litigated under the employment laws
of individual member states. Employment laws of some Member States may find the
idea of an employee operating in the independent manner required of a DPO quite alien.
Alternatively, supervisory authorities might operate a sort of fitness and probity regime
similar to that which already operates in the financial services sector,[24] but the GDPR
does not make any provision for this. As well as having such professional qualities,
DPOs must also have expert knowledge of 'data protection law and practices,' together
with the ability to fulfil the tasks of a DPO. But the GDPR does not specify any
qualification that such a DPO is required to have.

---

19.   GDPR, Recital 77.

20.   Directive 2005/36/EC of the European Parliament and of the Council of 7 September 2005
      on the recognition of professional qualification, OJ L 255, 30.9.2005, pp 22–14.

21.   Directive 98/5/EC of the European Parliament and of the Council of 16 February 1998 to
      facilitate practice of the profession of lawyer on a permanent basis in a Member State other
      than that in which the qualification was obtained. OJ L 77, 14.3.1998, pp 36–4.

22.   Directive 98/5/EC.

23.   Directive 98/5/EC.

24.   See, for example, the guidelines issued by the European Banking Authority pursuant to
      article 91(12) of Directive 2013/36/EU of the European Parliament and of the Council of
      26 June 2013 on access to the activity of credit institutions and the prudential supervision of
      credit institutions and investment firms, OJ L 176, 27.6.2013, pp 338–436.

Role

[12.09] The DPO will be defined by their seniority, reporting to someone who is at the highest management level of the controller or the processor. Such seniority should ensure that the DPO cannot be ignored. The DPO may be a member of staff of the employee of the controller or processor; alternatively, they may '... fulfil the tasks on the basis of a service contract'. Both arrangements come with advantages and disadvantages for the controller but the DPO must be independent. The Recitals provide that:

> Such data protection officers, whether or not they are an employee of the controller, should be in a position to perform their duties and tasks in an independent manner.[25]

This clear statement of independence must be read in conjunction with GDPR, article 38(3), which provides:

> The controller and processor shall ensure that the data protection officer does not receive any instructions regarding the exercise of those tasks.

[12.10] The WP29 suggest that DPOs 'must not be instructed to take a certain view of an issue related to data protection law, for example, a particular interpretation of the law.' So if the DPO is not a lawyer they may need independent legal advice; if they are a lawyer then they may need the advice of a risk consultant. Such advice may form part of the resources necessary for the DPO to carry out their tasks, which the controller or processor must provide pursuant to GDPR, article 38(2). WP29 suggest that '... the more complex and/or sensitive the processing operations, the more resources must be given to the DPO'. Other resources that the WP29 suggest that the DPO may require include:

- Active support of the DPO's function by senior management (such as at board level).
- Sufficient time for DPOs to fulfil their duties.
- Financial resources, infrastructure (premises, facilities, equipment) and staff where appropriate.
- Official communication of the designation of the DPO to all staff.
- Access to other services, such as Human Resources, legal, IT, security, etc.

Continuous training

[12.11] WP29 go onto suggest that depending upon the size and structure of an organisation, it may be necessary to set up a DPO team.[26]

---

25. GDPR, Recital 97.
26. WP29 *Guidelines on Data Protection Officers* ('DPOs') revised and adopted on 5 April 2017, 16/EN, WP 243 rev 01, p 14.

This is on foot of article 38(2) which provides that:

> The controller and processor shall support the data protection officer in performing the tasks referred to in Article 39 by providing resources necessary to carry out those tasks and access to personal data and processing operations, and to maintain his or her expert knowledge.

So in addition to resources along the lines of what is set out above, the DPO must also be able to access adequate training and other materials. The GDPR goes on to provide that the DPO:

> ... shall not be dismissed or penalised by the controller or the processor for performing his tasks.[27]

[12.12] The WP29 suggest that such penalties might include 'absence or delay of promotion; prevention from career advancement; denial from benefits that other employees receive. It is not necessary that these penalties be actually carried out, a mere threat is sufficient as long as they are used to penalise the DPO on grounds related to his/her DPO activities'. It goes on to suggest that a DPO could be dismissed legally in cases of 'theft, physical, psychological or sexual harassment or similar gross misconduct)'. The WP29 also notes that the GDPR does not specify how and when a DPO can be dismissed or replaced by another person.[28] This may make managing the role of the DPO a challenging one. Who will adjudicate between a controller, that wishes to discipline or dismiss a DPO on grounds of incompetence and a DPO who asserts that the controller's actions are motivated by a desire to punish the DPO for the diligence with which he or she has monitored compliance with the GDPR? Normal employment dispute resolution mechanisms may not be competent to adjudicate on such issue; the GDPR does not provide any mechanism by which such an issue could be appealed to the relevant supervisory authority. Article 77 provides subjects with a right to make a complaint to the supervisory authority, not DPOs. Similarly, GDPR, article 79 provides that subjects have a right to an effective judicial remedy, not DPOs.

Given such complications a controller or processor might prefer to appoint a DPO on the basis of a service contract as an alternative to employing a DPO directly. This arrangement however, comes with its own disadvantages. It may or may not be appropriate to refer to data as 'the new oil'[29] but the processing of personal data is clearly central to the operations of an increasing number of controllers and processors.[30] Prudent controllers or processors may think it unwise to grant a third party access to processes that are central to their operations.[31] Providing such services is not without risks. The tasks of a DPO include advising on and monitoring compliance with the GDPR. It would not be unreasonable for a controller or processors to rely upon a DPO to advise competently and monitor diligently. Such reasonable reliance implies liability. A

---

27.   GDPR, article 38(3).

28.   WP29 *Guidelines on Data Protection Officers* ('DPOs') revised and adopted on 5 April 2017, 16/EN, WP 243 rev 01.

29.   'The world's most valuable resource is no longer oil, but data' (2017) *The Economist*, 6 May.

controller or processor subject to a significant penalty or award of damages might seek to recover that award, in whole or in part, from a DPO who failed to properly advise upon or monitor its data processing operations. Such potential liabilities may mean that those firms that provide DPO services will need professional liability insurance. Given that these liabilities might potentially be significant, then such insurance may prove to be similarly expensive.

[12.13] GDPR, article 38(5) provides that the DPO:

> ... shall be bound by secrecy or confidentiality concerning the performance of his or her tasks, in accordance with Union or Member State law.[32]

Functions and tasks of the DPO may include acting as point of contact for data subjects and cooperating with supervisory authorities. Such functions and tasks mean that the DPO will be in receipt of confidential information, which they will have to keep secret, presumably from the controller or employer who has employed or engaged them. Whilst the DPO must co-operate with the SA, these roles are distinct from one another. So the DPO may come into possession of confidential information about the controller or processor. The obligation of confidence may similarly apply to such information; meaning that it would be inappropriate for the DPO to disclose it to the SA. What would be appropriate would be for the DPO to advise the controller to disclose this information to the SA.

[12.14] It would appear not to be the role of the DPO to disclose details of potential infringements to the SA. The GDPR does not provide any gateway which would allow the DPO to disclose such details. EU laws that impose confidentiality obligations equivalent to GDPR, article 38(5) generally provide 'gateway' provisions that enable such disclosures to be made. In the absence of such provisions no disclosures may be possible; DPOs should be cautious of breaching a statutory obligation of confidentiality, which may expose them to significant liabilities. The issue of confidentiality indicates the essence of what the DPO's role is. The DPO must provide assistance and co-ordination to a diverse set of stakeholders: the controller or processor who employs or engages them, data subjects and the SA. As the WP29 has said the role of the DPO is to:

> act as intermediaries between relevant stakeholders (eg supervisory authorities, data subjects and business units within an organisation).[33]

---

30. 'Data are to this century what oil was to the last one: a driver of growth and change. Flows of data have created new infrastructure, new businesses, new monopolies, new politics and—crucially—new economics. Digital information is unlike any previous resource; it is extracted, refined, valued, bought and sold in different ways. It changes the rules for markets and it demands new approaches from regulators. Many a battle will be fought over who should own, and benefit from, data' (2017) *The Economist*, 6 May.

31. 'Potential customers are also very cautious about control of the data that reveal the inner workings of their operations,' Crooks, 'The internet of things: industry's digital revolution', (2017) *Financial Times*, 27 June.

32. GDPR, article 38(5).

The DPO is not a 'mini-supervisor'; it is not their role to either inform on their employer to the SA or to manage interactions with subjects on their employer's behalf. If such were the role of the DPO then they would be given appropriate powers to exchange information or conduct investigations.

[12.15] Clear definition of the tasks of the DPO may be particularly significant where the individual who acts as DPO fulfils other tasks and duties. The GDPR allows for DPOs to undertake other tasks, but provides that:

> The controller or processor shall ensure that any such tasks and duties do not result in a conflict of interests.[34]

These additional tasks and duties will presumably take advantage of the same skill-set as led to the individual in question being appointed DPO. Hence it may not be immediately obvious which tasks are being fulfilled as DPO and which are not. The WP29 suggest that in order to avoid such conflicts it might be best practice to:

- identify the positions which would be incompatible with the function of DPO;

- draw up internal rules to avoid conflicts of interests;

- to include a more general explanation about conflicts of interests;

- to declare that their DPO has no conflict of interests as a way of raising awareness of this requirement;

include safeguards in the internal rules of the organisation and to ensure that the vacancy notice for the position of DPO or the service contract is sufficiently precise and detailed in order to avoid a conflict of interests.[35]

Tasks

[12.16] The tasks of the DPO have to be distinguished from the functions of the controller; the DPO is not accountable for how the controller processes personal data. The controller or processor must ensure that:

> … the data protection officer is involved, properly and in a timely manner, in all issues which relate to the protection of personal data.[36]

This general obligation makes clear that the tasks of the DPO are broader than the five tasks set out in GDPR, article 39(1). A notable omission from that list is the task of

---

33.   WP29 *Guidelines on Data Protection Officers* ('DPOs') revised and adopted on 5 April 2017, 16/EN, WP 243 rev 01, p 4.

34.   GDPR, article 38(6).

35.   WP29 *Guidelines on Data Protection Officers* ('DPOs') revised and adopted on 5 April 2017, 16/EN, WP 243 rev 01, p 16.

36.   GDPR, article 38(1).

acting as point of contact with data subjects. This is clearly a function of the DPO. GDPR, article 38(2) provides:

> Data subjects may contact the data protection officer with regard to all issues related to processing of their personal data and to the exercise of their rights under this Regulation.

This function is undoubtedly important. The GDPR requires that controllers and processors 'publish the contact details of the data protection officer',[37] record[38] and provide them to the SA.[39] Subjects must also be informed of the contact details of the DPO.[40] The function of assisting data subjects is not one of the tasks listed in GDPR, article 39. Whether this omission matters is open to question. The list of tasks set out in article 39 GDPR is clearly not intended to be exhaustive. But, the GDPR's protections for DPOs only apply where they are performing 'the tasks referred to in Article 39'. Article 38(2) provides that:

> The controller and processor shall support the data protection officer in performing the tasks referred to in Article 39 by providing resources necessary to carry out those tasks and access to personal data and processing operations, and to maintain his or her expert knowledge.

[12.17] GDPR, article 38(3) then provides that the controller or processor may not penalise or dismiss a DPO for performing 'those tasks'. Ultimately, it may be for the courts to decide what 'those tasks' are. There is a good argument to be made that facilitating subjects is not, in fact, a task of the DPO but rather the duty of the controller.[41] As the WP29 has explained:

> DPOs are not personally responsible in case of non-compliance with the GDPR. The GDPR makes it clear that it is the controller or the processor who is required to ensure and to be able to demonstrate that the processing is performed in accordance with its provisions ... Data protection compliance is a responsibility of the controller or the processor.[42]

[12.18] Anyone taking up the role of DPO would be well-advised to ensure that their contract of employment or engagement clearly sets out what their tasks are. If those tasks should be broader than those listed in GDPR, article 39 then that contract should specify whether or not they will be performed as DPO and set out the supports and

---

37. GDPR, article 37(7).
38. GDPR, article 30(1)(a).
39. GDPR, article 37(7).
40. GDPR, article 13(1)(b) and 14(1)(b).
41. GDPR, article 12(2).
42. Article 29 WP, *Guidelines on Data Protection Officers* ('DPOs'), revised and adopted on 5 April 2017, 16/EN, WP 243 rev 01, p 4.

protections the DPO will receive when doing them. Article 39(1) GDPR provides that the DPO shall have 'at least' the following tasks:

(a) to inform and advise the controller or the processor and the employees who carry out processing of their obligations pursuant to this Regulation and to other Union or Member State data protection provisions;

(b) to monitor compliance with this Regulation, with other Union or Member State data protection provisions and with the policies of the controller or processor in relation to the protection of personal data, including the assignment of responsibilities, awareness-raising and training of staff involved in processing operations, and the related audits;

(c) to provide advice where requested as regards the data protection impact assessment and monitor its performance pursuant to article 35;

(d) to cooperate with the supervisory authority; and,

(e) to act as the contact point for the supervisory authority on issues relating to processing, including the prior consultation referred to in article 36, and to consult, where appropriate, with regard to any other matter.

CONTROLLERS, JOINT CONTROLLERS AND PROCESSORS

[12.19] Directive 95/46 conceived controllers and processors as having clearly defined and separate roles. The reality of this separation may have been open to question even back in 1995, but changes in technologies and business models have broken this separation down.[43] GDPR, articles 26 to 29 seek to update the rules that apply to the relationships between controllers and processors. As the Recitals explain:

> The protection of the rights and freedoms of data subjects as well as the responsibility and liability of controllers and processors, also in relation to the monitoring by and measures of supervisory authorities, requires a clear allocation of the responsibilities under this Regulation, including where a controller determines the purposes and means of the processing jointly with other controllers or where a processing operation is carried out on behalf of a controler.[44]

---

43. As the WP29 recognised in 2010: 'the concrete application of the concepts of data controller and data processor is becoming increasingly complex. This is mostly due to the increasing complexity of the environment in which these concepts are used ...', WP29 *Opinion 1/2010 on the concepts of 'controller' and 'processor'*, 16 February 2010, p 2. The WP29 recognised that this complexity was causing particular problems in the case of cloud computing: 'there may be situations in which a provider of cloud services may be considered either as a joint controller or as a controller in their own right depending on concrete circumstances. For instance, this could be the case where the provider processes data for its own purposes ...'. WP29, *Opinion 05/2012 on Cloud Computing,* 1 July 2012, p 8.

44. GDPR, Recital 79.

However, the GDPR does not itself provide this clear allocation of responsibilities; the GDPR's definitions of controller and processor are little different to those that appeared in Directive 95/46. Instead, the GDPR requires that controllers and processors must themselves define their relationship. This approach is consistent with the technologically neutral approach that the GDPR adopts, but it means that the relationship between controller, joint controller and processor will be somewhat opaque. The GDPR requires that these parties reduce the essentials of their relationship to writing, but only someone with both the time and the skills necessary to understand the resulting agreement, arrangement or contract will be able to properly comprehend the relationship between the parties. Control may remain key to such comprehension; the distinction between controller and processor is that the former will issue instructions to the latter. If no instructions are issued, or if such instructions as are issued are vague and high level, it may be that the parties are in fact joint controllers as opposed to being controller and processor.

[12.20] Controllers, joint controllers and processors will want to be clear about their relationship because GDPR, article 82 provides for the allocation of their liabilities should an infringement of subject rights occur. Article 82(1) provides that subjects have a right to compensation where an infringement of the GDPR has occurred. The remainder of article 82 sets out how such liabilities are allocated: between controller and processor (article 82(2)) or joint controllers and joint processors (article 82(4)). Article 82 concludes by providing for the joint and several liability of controllers and processors. Hence sensible controllers, joint controllers and processors will want to ensure that any agreements, arrangements or contracts clearly set out where this liability will lie.

Relationship between joint controllers

[12.21] GDPR, article 26 begins by defining joint controllers as being two or more controllers who:

> ... jointly determine the purposes and means of processing ...

These joint controllers must '... in a transparent manner determine their respective responsibilities for compliance with the obligations ...'. They may do this by means '... of an arrangement between them ...'.[45] That arrangement must determine '... in a transparent manner ...' each of the joint controllers' '... respective responsibilities for compliance with the(ir) obligations ...' under the GDPR '... in particular as regards the exercising of the rights of the data subject and their respective duties to provide the information referred to in Articles 13 and 14 ...'. That arrangement may also '... designate a contact point for data subjects'.[46] This arrangement must '... duly reflect the

---

45. Although such an arrangement will not be necessary '...in so far as, the respective responsibilities of the controllers are determined by Union or Member State law to which the controllers are subject.' GDPR, article 26(1).

46. GDPR, article 26(1).

respective roles and relationships of the joint controllers regarding the data subjects.' Its 'essence', which presumably does not mean the actual text, must be made available to data subjects.[47] However, irrespective of what the arrangement says subjects may exercise their rights under the GDPR in '... respect of and against each of the controllers'.[48]

Relationship between controllers and processors

[12.22] Controllers may out-source the processing of the data that they control, but they cannot outsource their responsibilities. GDPR, article 28(1) makes this clear, providing that:

> ... the controller shall use only processors providing sufficient guarantees to implement appropriate technical and organisational measures in such a manner that processing will meet the requirements of this Regulation and ensure the protection of the rights of the data subject.

The controller must enter into a contract with the processor. When doing so the controller will have to take the principles of data protection by design and default into account. The Recitals specifically require that these principles be '... taken into consideration in the context of public tenders'.[49] However it is hard to see how this requirement can be confined to the public sector alone; there is nothing in the GDPR to suggest that a controller in the private sector does not have to similarly take data protection by design and default into account when tendering for suppliers of data processing services.

This contract (or other legal act) must be 'binding on the processor with regard to the controller' and must set out:

(a)   the subject-matter and duration of the processing;

(b)   the nature and purpose of the processing;

(c)   the type of personal data;

(d)   categories of data subjects; and

(e)   the obligations and rights of the controller.

In addition, that contract (or other legal act) must stipulate that the processor:

(a)   processes the personal data only on documented instructions from the controller, including with regard to transfers of personal data to a third country or an international organisation, unless required to do so by Union or Member State law to which the processor is subject; in such a case, the processor shall inform

---

47.   GDPR, article 26(2).
48.   GDPR, article 26(3).
49.   GDPR, Recital 78.

the controller of that legal requirement before processing, unless that law prohibits such information on important grounds of public interest;

(b) ensures that persons authorised to process the personal data have committed themselves to confidentiality or are under an appropriate statutory obligation of confidentiality;

(c) takes all measures required pursuant to article 32 (data security);

(d) respects the conditions referred to in paras 2 and 4 for engaging another processor;

(e) taking into account the nature of the processing, assists the controller by appropriate technical and organisational measures, insofar as this is possible, for the fulfilment of the controller's obligation to respond to requests for exercising the data subject's rights laid down in Ch III;

(f) assists the controller in ensuring compliance with the obligations pursuant to articles 32 to 36 (data security, notification of breaches, DPIA, prior consultation with DPC) taking into account the nature of processing and the information available to the processor;

(g) at the choice of the controller, deletes or returns all the personal data to the controller after the end of the provision of services relating to processing, and deletes existing copies unless Union or Member State law requires storage of the personal data;

(h) makes available to the controller all information necessary to demonstrate compliance with the obligations laid down in this Article and allow for and contribute to audits, including inspections, conducted by the controller or another auditor mandated by the controller.

If any of the above elements are missing from the contract then it may be argued that this is an arrangement between joint controllers, not a contract between controller and processor. Hence it will be in the processor's interests to ensure that all the above elements are included in the contract. What distinguishes a processor from a controller is that the former will process data on the instructions of the latter, doing so may ensure that processors have a defence to an action for damages if data should be processed in breach of the GDPR.[50] GDPR, article 29 makes explicitly clear that only the controller can direct the processing of personal data:

> The processor and any person acting under the authority of the controller or of the processor, who has access to personal data, shall not process those data except on instructions from the controller, unless required to do so by Union or Member State law.

---

50. GDPR, article 82(2).

[12.23] GDPR, article 28(6) provides that:

> ... if a processor infringes this Regulation by determining the purposes and means of processing, the processor shall be considered to be a controller in respect of that processing.[51]

This is stated to be without prejudice to articles 82 (compensation and liability), 83 (fines) and 84 (penalties). So, if a controller has engaged a processor then exceeds their instructions by determining how and why data is processed that processor will become controller in respect of that data processing operation. However, this does not mean that liabilities, fines or other penalties cannot be imposed on the original controller. Although the controller will retain primary responsibility for how data is processed, this will not allow the processor to abdicate all responsibility. GDPR, article 26(3)(h) above requires that processors assist controllers in demonstrating compliance with the GDPR, including assisting in audits. However, it goes on to provide that:

> ... the processor shall immediately inform the controller if, in its opinion, an instruction infringes this Regulation or other Union or Member State data protection provisions.[52]

[12.24] It will be interesting to see how the courts will assign liability between a controller who has instructed a processor to breach the GDPR and a processor who failed to inform the controller that this instruction was illegal. A processor who fails to inform a controller that an instruction breaches the GDPR may find that this will be taken into account by a SA when imposing an administrative penalty. Factors that the SA may take into account when imposing such a penalty include 'the intentional or negligent character of the infringement' and 'any action taken by the controller or processor to mitigate the damage suffered by data subjects'.[53]

[12.25] Controllers must assert their control over their entire out-sourcing chain; they cannot simply hire a single data processor and allow them to appoint sub-processors as they may see fit. The GDPR requires that controllers approve, in writing, sub-processors prior to their appointment. This approval may be specific or general. Where a general authorisation is given then:

> ... the processor shall inform the controller of any intended changes concerning the addition or replacement of other processors, thereby giving the controller the opportunity to object to such changes.[54]

Hence the controller is required to take responsibility for each processor that is engaged either directly by it or on its behalf. The GDPR allows the controller to outsource both data processing itself and the engagement of sub-processors to undertake that processing. Controllers can engage processors directly or indirectly without reviewing

---

51.   GDPR, article 28(10).
52.   GDPR, article 28(3).
53.   GDPR, article 83(2)(b) and (c).
54.   GDPR, article 28(2).

whether they are competent or trustworthy. What controllers cannot do is avoid accountability for the actions of their data processors; so while the GDPR does not explicitly require that controllers be cautious when engaging data processors it does strongly encourage such an approach.

Similarly, the processor cannot avoid its liability by engaging another processor. Article 28(4) provides:

> Where a processor engages another processor for carrying out specific processing activities on behalf of the controller, the same data protection obligations as set out in the contract or other legal act ... shall be imposed on that other processor by way of a contract or other legal act ...

This contract or other legal act must in particular provide '... guarantees to implement appropriate technical and organisational measures in such a manner that the processing will meet the requirements of (the GDPR)'. If the sub-processor should fail to fulfil its data protection obligations, the initial processor will remain fully liable to the controller for the performance of the sub-processor's obligations.

[12.26] Contracts (or other legal acts) between controllers, processors and sub-processors '...shall be in writing, including in electronic form'.[55] The GDPR provides for the standardisation of both contractual terms and contract management mechanisms. Such standardised contractual clauses are stated to be 'without prejudice' to the individual contract (or other legal act) between controller and processor.[56] Standard clauses for contracts between controllers and processors and processors and sub-processors may be laid down by the EU Commission[57] or adopted by a SA.[58]

One of the most significant changes that the GDPR makes to the relationship between controller and processor is that both will have to actively manage their relationship. Of course it may be assumed that they would have done so anyway, but the GDPR creates specific obligations that will have to be managed if the specific liabilities, fines and penalties that may be imposed pursuant to the GDPR are to be avoided. Such management processes may be recognised by certifications granted pursuant to GDPR, articles 42 and 43; alternatively, they may form part of an approved code of conduct as referred to in GDPR, article 40 or an approved certification mechanism as referred to in article 42 GDPR. Adherence to such codes of conduct or certification mechanisms may help demonstrate sufficient guarantees that appropriate technical and organisational measures will be implemented.[59] Finally the Recitals provide that:

> After the completion of the processing on behalf of the controller, the processor should, at the choice of the controller, return or delete the personal data, unless

---

55.   GDPR, article 28(9).
56.   GDPR, article 28(5).
57.   '... in accordance with the examination procedure referred to in Article 93(2)' GDPR, article 28(7).
58.   '... in accordance with the consistency mechanism referred to in Article 63' GDPR, article 28(8).
59.   GDPR, article 28(5).

there is a requirement to store the personal data under Union or Member State law to which the processor is subject.[60]

Record keeping and cooperation with the supervisory authorities

[12.27] Directive 95/46 had required that certain data controllers and processors had to notify their SA that they were processing personal data. This obligation might have been relevant in the 1970s, when Europe's first modern data protection laws were enacted and the Strasbourg Convention was conceived. But it was rendered obsolete by the invention of the personal computer, which made computers available to all. Even by then it was neither reasonable nor practical to expect data controllers to register with a central authority or for SAs to maintain such a register. Any pretence that this obligation retained some relevance would have dissolved once the iPhone came to market in 2007. However, it took until 2016 for the obligation to register to be formally repealed; a repeal that did not take effect for a further two years. That obligation has now been replaced with a duty to maintain records. Article 30 GDPR provides that:

> Each controller and, where applicable, the controller's representative, shall maintain a record of processing activities under its responsibility.

[12.28] The GDPR then sets out a list of what such records must contain:

(a) the name and contact details of the controller and, where applicable, the joint controller, the controller's representative and the data protection officer;

(b) the purposes of the processing;

(c) a description of the categories of data subjects and of the categories of personal data;

(d) the categories of recipients to whom the personal data have been or will be disclosed including recipients in third countries or international organisations;

(e) where applicable, transfers of personal data to a third country or an international organisation, including the identification of that third country or international organisation and, in the case of transfers referred to in the second subparagraph of article 49(1), the documentation of suitable safeguards;

(f) where possible, the envisaged time limits for erasure of the different categories of data;

(g) where possible, a general description of the technical and organisational security measures referred to in article 32(1).

This is almost identical to the contents of notification that were required under article 19 of Directive 95/46 (the one addition is the envisaged time limits). GDPR, article 30(2) provides that processors and their representatives must maintain a record of all

---

60. GDPR, Recital 81.

categories of processing activities carried out on behalf of a controller, containing the following:

(a) the name and contact details of the processor or processors and of each controller on behalf of which the processor is acting, and, where applicable, of the controller's or the processor's representative, and the data protection officer;

(b) the categories of processing carried out on behalf of each controller;

(c) where applicable, transfers of personal data to a third country or an international organisation, including the identification of that third country or international organisation and, in the case of transfers referred to in the second subparagraph of article 49(1), the documentation of suitable safeguards; and,

(d) where possible, a general description of the technical and organisational security measures referred to in article 32(1).

All of the above records must be retained in writing, which may include 'electronic form'. The Recitals explain that the purpose of maintaining records is in '... order to demonstrate compliance with this Regulation'.[61] However the records that are required to be retained pursuant to GDPR, article 30 must surely represent a minimum of what would be required to demonstrate compliance. Article 30 GDPR does not require the retention of DPIAs or contracts with processors, even though both may be required pursuant to the GDPR. Hence the lists set out in article 30(1) should not be considered as exhaustive indications of all the records that need to be retained in order to comply with the GDPR.

[12.29] Article 30 provides an exemption from the specific record keeping obligation that it imposes for SMEs.[62] This exemption may not be of any great value, the information required to be retained by article 30 is high level and should be obvious to any competently managed controller or processor. And it is an exemption specific to article 30; it does not exempt controllers or processors from the obligation to demonstrate compliance with the GDPR. Demonstrating compliance will in many cases require that controllers retain records far more detailed than those required by article GDPR, article 30.

The duty to retain records is linked to the duty to cooperate with the SA. GDPR, article 30(4) provides that:

> The controller or the processor and, where applicable, the controller's or the processor's representative, shall make the record available to the supervisory authority on request.

---

61. GDPR, Recital 82.

62. 'The obligations referred to in paras 1 and 2 shall not apply to an enterprise or an organisation employing fewer than 250 persons unless the processing it carries out is likely to result in a risk to the rights and freedoms of data subjects, the processing is not occasional, or the processing includes special categories of data as referred to in Article 9(1) or personal data relating to criminal convictions and offences referred to in Article 10' GDPR, article 30(6).

[12.30] The Recitals go on to provide that:

> Each controller and processor should be obliged to cooperate with the supervisory authority and make those records, on request, available to it, so that it might serve for monitoring those processing operations.[63]

[12.31] GDPR, article 31 provides that:

> The controller and the processor and, where applicable, their representatives, shall cooperate, on request, with the supervisory authority in the performance of its tasks.

Although cooperation may sound like a vague, high-level concept it comes with some real duties. Cooperation is a familiar concept in EU law. TEU, article 4(3) requires that Member States and the EU institutions assist one another 'in full mutual respect' and 'pursuant to the principle of sincere cooperation'. The duties that this duty of co-operation impose are real. So Member States cannot unilaterally undertake actions in international organisations that may ultimately contradict that of the EU, even where discussions of that EU position have been postponed.[64] This principle requires that EU Member States refrain from adopting measures that would compromise the result of an EU Directive during the period laid down for that Directive's implementation.[65]

[12.32] It may be assumed that the CJEU will interpret the duty to cooperate under the GDPR in the same manner as it interprets the duty to cooperate under the EU Treaties. If so, then this would then mean that controllers and processors cannot do anything that would contradict the position of their SA. So if the SA has issued guidance, the controller or processor would have to follow that guidance. If the SA has commenced an initial inquiry into a processing operation, then the controller or processor is prohibited from doing anything that might prejudice or compromise that inquiry. This makes the link drawn by the Recitals between record-keeping and cooperation with the SA significant. Since such a link may suggest that controllers and processors must retain the records required for their cooperation with the SA. This might limit the ability of controllers and processors to destroy or delete records that a SA required for an investigation, for example. The duty to cooperate is not general; it must be invoked 'on request' by the SA. But once invoked it may prove far-reaching.

63.　GDPR, Recital 82.

64.　*Commission v Sweden* (Case C–246/07), [2010] ECR I–3317.

65.　*Inter-Environnement Wallonie* (Case C–2129/96) (18 December 1997).

Chapter 13

CONTROLLER AND PROCESSOR: RISK

INTRODUCTION

[13.01] The GDPR embraces a risk-based approach to supervision. Some may find this ironic, given that the GDPR was proposed shortly after the EU had witnessed a crisis in which '... risk monitoring and management practices ... dramatically failed ...'.[1] But it would be a mistake to use such failures as a justification for ignoring risk; if anything they serve as a lesson of the importance of properly assessing and anticipating risks. Such assessments are never going to be perfect; risks by their nature are difficult to assess. And, in truth, EU data protection law has long recognised that certain types of data pose particular types of risk. Sensitive data, which relates to health, sexuality, religion and so forth, was granted special protections by Directive 95/46. The GDPR takes this approach further, one of the justifications for its enactment is:

> ... a widespread public perception that there are significant risks to the protection of natural persons.[2]

An awareness of the risks that modern data processing systems may pose to the privacy and data protection rights of subjects is a feature of the GDPR. The Recitals provide that:

> The risk to the rights and freedoms of natural persons, of varying likelihood and severity, may result from personal data processing which could lead to physical, material or non-material damage, in particular: where the processing may give rise to discrimination, identity theft or fraud, financial loss, damage to the reputation, loss of confidentiality of personal data protected by professional secrecy, unauthorised reversal of pseudonymisation, or any other significant economic or social disadvantage; where data subjects might be deprived of their rights and freedoms or prevented from exercising control over their personal data; where personal data are processed which reveal racial or ethnic origin, political opinions, religion or philosophical beliefs, trade union membership, and the processing of genetic data, data concerning health or data concerning sex life or criminal convictions and offences or related security measures; where personal aspects are evaluated, in particular analysing or predicting aspects concerning performance at work, economic situation, health, personal preferences or interests, reliability or behaviour, location or movements, in order to create or use personal profiles; where personal data of vulnerable natural persons, in particular of children, are

---

1.   The de Larosière Group, The High Level Group on Financial Supervision in the EU, Report, Brussels, 25 February 2015, Para 122, p32, http://ec.europa.eu/internal_market/finances/docs/de_larosiere_report_en.pdf.
2.   GDPR, Recital 9.

processed; or where processing involves a large amount of personal data and affects a large number of data subjects.[3]

This Recital could be read as a summation of the risks that the GDPR hopes may be managed. Such a list can not be exhaustive; it could never be given the pace at which data processing technology changes and its uses evolve. In practice the determination of what these risks are will fall to the controller. Article 24(1) is very clear about this, providing that:

> Taking into account the nature, scope, context and purposes of processing as well as the risks of varying likelihood and severity for the rights and freedoms of natural persons, the controller shall implement appropriate technical and organisational measures to ensure and to be able to demonstrate that processing is performed in accordance with this Regulation. Those measures shall be reviewed and updated where necessary.

Thus it is for the controller to determine '... the risks of varying likelihood and severity for the rights and freedoms of natural persons ...; When determining the 'likelihood and severity of the risk to the rights and freedoms of the data subject' the controller should have:

> reference to the nature, scope, context and purposes of the processing. Risk should be evaluated on the basis of an objective assessment, by which it is established whether data processing operations involve a risk or a high risk.[4]

[13.02] The GDPR does not anticipate that the controller will have to manage such risks in isolation. The Recitals suggest that 'approved codes of conduct, approved certifications, guidelines provided by the Board or indications provided by a data protection officer' may provide:

> Guidance on the implementation of appropriate measures and on the demonstration of compliance by the controller or the processor, especially as regards the identification of the risk related to the processing, their assessment in terms of origin, nature, likelihood and severity, and the identification of best practices to mitigate the risk ...

In addition, the EDPB '... may also issue guidelines on processing operations that are considered to be unlikely to result in a high risk to the rights and freedoms of natural persons and indicate what measures may be sufficient in such cases to address such risk'.[5] The concept of risk permeates the GDPR, which provides four main mechanisms for the management of risk:

1. data protection by design and default;
2. the data protection impact assessment;
3. the assessment of appropriate security measures; and,
4. the assessment of where a personal data breach is high risk.

Each of these risk assessment processes is discussed in turn below.

---

3.   GDPR, Recital 75.
4.   GDPR, Recital 76.
5.   GDPR, Recital 77.

DATA PROTECTION BY DESIGN AND DEFAULT

[13.03] Data minimisation underlies the concepts of data protection by design and default. Article 5(1)(c) provides that personal data must be:

> … adequate, relevant and limited to what is necessary in relation to the purposes for which they are processed …

[13.04] Article 25 seeks to put this principle into effect. This multi-faceted approach to data protection is much more sophisticated than that which was to be found in the GDPR's predecessor Directive 95/46.[6] The difficulty with enforcing a principle such as this is that it is very high level; it is difficult to say what exactly is adequate or relevant. Article 25 requires that data controllers put a process in place to make this decision. The decision as to what is adequate or relevant remains difficult and highly subjective; it is much easier to assess whether controllers have a process in place to make that decision and whether that process is adequate. As the Recitals explain:

> In order to be able to demonstrate compliance with this Regulation, the controller should adopt internal policies and implement measures which meet in particular the principles of data protection by design and data protection by default.[7]

Article 25(1) sets out what is meant by data protection by design.

> Taking into account the state of the article, the cost of implementation and the nature, scope, context and purposes of processing as well as the risks of varying likelihood and severity for rights and freedoms of natural persons posed by the processing, the controller shall, both at the time of the determination of the means for processing and at the time of the processing itself, implement appropriate technical and organisational measures, such as pseudonymisation, which are designed to implement data-protection principles, such as data minimisation, in an effective manner and to integrate the necessary safeguards into the processing in order to meet the requirements of this Regulation and protect the rights of data subjects.

Of course data protection by design is about complying with the requirements of the GDPR as a whole, not just data minimisation. But the most effective way of discharging the controller's burden of demonstrating compliance with the GDPR is to avoid processing personal data in the first place. Article 25(1) suggests one method by which this may be done, pseudnonymisation. Further suggestions are to be found in the Recitals:

> Such measures could consist, inter alia, of minimising the processing of personal data, pseudonymising personal data as soon as possible, transparency with regard to the functions and processing of personal data, enabling the data subject to monitor the data processing, enabling the controller to create and improve security features.[8]

---

6. Directive 95/46, article 6(1)(c) see also Strasbourg Convention, article 5(c).
7. GDPR, Recital 78.
8. GDPR, Recital 78.

But it leaves it to the controller to decide what the appropriate technical and organisational measures are to implement the data protection principles.

Article 25(2) sets out what is meant by data protection by default, providing that:

> The controller shall implement appropriate technical and organisational measures for ensuring that, by default, only personal data which are necessary for each specific purpose of the processing are processed. That obligation applies to the amount of personal data collected, the extent of their processing, the period of their storage and their accessibility.

[13.05] The Recitals explain that:

> When developing, designing, selecting and using applications, services and products that are based on the processing of personal data or process personal data to fulfil their task, producers of the products, services and applications should be encouraged to take into account the right to data protection when developing and designing such products, services and applications and, with due regard to the state of the article, to make sure that controllers and processors are able to fulfil their data protection obligations.

In other words, what this means is that data protection cannot be an afterthought. Controllers must take it into account at the design and development stage. And they must be able to demonstrate that they have complied with this obligation. Article 25(3) suggests one approach which might assist controllers in doing so providing that:

> An approved certification mechanism pursuant to Article 42 may be used as an element to demonstrate compliance ... (with the obligations of design and default).

[13.06] Although the obligations of design and default are set out in general terms in the GDPR it does identify two specific situations where such obligations must take effect. One is that technical and organisational measures implemented by the controller:

> ... shall ensure that by default personal data are not made accessible without the individual's intervention to an indefinite number of natural persons.[9]

The other is that:

> The principles of data protection by design and by default should also be taken into consideration in the context of public tenders.[10]

DATA PROTECTION IMPACT ASSESSMENT (DPIA)

[13.07] DPIAs are 'important tools for accountability'[11] which provide 'a process for building and demonstrating compliance'. A DPIA is not a requirement for every

---

9.   GDPR, article 25(2).
10. GDPR, Recital 78.
11. WP29 *Guidelines on Data Protection Impact Assessment (DPIA) and determining whether processing is 'likely to result in a high risk' for the purposes of Regulation 2016/679*, 17/EN WP 248. Adopted on 4 April 2017, p 4.

processing operation, only those that are 'high risk'. Of course deciding whether or not a processing operation is high risk requires an assessment of the risks posed by a particular processing operation. Even where a controller concludes that the operation in question is not high risk it will want to retain a record of that assessment, so that it can demonstrate compliance with its obligation to consider article 35. The process of undertaking a DPIA and answering this question may be divided into six steps:

1. description – is this processing 'likely to result in a high risk to the rights and freedoms of natural persons'?;

2. analysis: 'a systematic description of the … purposes of the processing …';

3. consultation;

4. conclusion:

    (a) necessity and proportionality;

    (b) risk rating;

    (c) do '… measures envisaged …address the risks … to ensure the protection of personal data and to demonstrate compliance … taking into account the rights and legitimate interests of data subjects and other persons concerned';

5. prior consultation; and

6. repetition.

As WP29 has said 'the GDPR sets out the basic requirements of an effective DPIA'.[12] These requirements have been used to generate the DPIA template set out at Sch 1.

A DPIA must be undertaken by the controller who must first consider who he will ask to actually do the work of carrying out the DPIA on his behalf. Given the amount of work and the variety of skills that may be required to undertake a successful DPIA, it may be difficult for a single person to undertake such a project. Hence it may well be that a team of persons will have to participate in the DPIA. One option would be for a controller to appoint external experts to do this work, which may be appropriate in some cases. There may be a number of disadvantages to such an approach, however. One is cost. Another is the time it may take a controller to explain its processes to external consultants. Finally, and perhaps most significantly someone who undertakes a DPIA must have a complete understanding of how the controller is processing personal data. Wise controllers will carefully consider the risks of the giving such an understanding to external consultants. Hence many controllers may want to use in-house resources to undertake such DPIAs. A DPIA should not be the DPO. The role of the DPO is to advise upon the DPIA, not to undertake it.

---

12. WP29 *Guidelines on Data Protection Impact Assessment (DPIA) and determining whether processing is 'likely to result in a high risk' for the purposes of Regulation 2016/679*, 17/EN WP 248 rev 01. Adopted on 4 October, p 19.

Description

[13.08] The first step in undertaking the DPIA will be drawing up an initial description of the data processing operation in question and making a decision as to whether it is necessary to undertake a DPIA. At first glance this step may seem redundant; why would a controller appoint someone to undertake a DPIA if he did not think one was needed? But the controller is obliged to be able to demonstrate that he is in compliance with the GDPR. In some cases, it may well be self-evident that no DPIA is required. But in marginal cases a prudent controller may wish to undertake an initial description of the data processing operation in question and document their conclusion whether or not to recommend that a DPIA be undertaken. That person may want to consult with the DPO before making a recommendation. The GDPR does not explicitly require that the DPO be consulted on this question, only once the DPIA is being carried out. However, DPOs are supposed to be '... involved, properly and in a timely manner, in all issues which relate to the protection of personal data'.[13] This suggests that the DPO should be consulted on the issue of whether a DPIA is necessary.

[13.09] Once an initial description of the data processing operation has been drawn up the controller will have to decide whether or not a DPIA is required. GDPR, article 35(1) provides that a DPIA will be required:

> Where a type of processing in particular using new technologies, and taking into account the nature, scope, context and purposes of the processing, is likely to result in *a high risk* to the rights and freedoms of natural persons, the controller shall, prior to the processing, carry out an assessment of the impact of the envisaged processing operations on the protection of personal data.[14]

It is clear that the GDPR requires a very broad analysis of the risks posed by a processing operation. There must be a consideration of all risks to 'rights and freedoms', not just data protection rights. The WP29 suggest that such consideration:

> primarily concerns the rights to data protection and privacy but may also involve other fundamental rights such as freedom of speech, freedom of thought, freedom of movement, prohibition of discrimination, right to liberty, conscience and religion.[15]

Article 16(2) of the TFEU provides a lawful basis for the GDPR; this requires that the EU legislate for both data protection and the free movement of personal data. This may suggest some context for assessing what may amount to a high risk. If, perchance, a controller was restricting the processing of personal data to the territory of a particular Member State then such a restriction might poses a high risk to the free movement of data, which would entail undertaking a DPIA. Another example is offered by the CJEU

---

13.   GDPR, article 38(1).
14.   GDPR, article 35(1).
15.   WP29 *Guidelines on Data Protection Impact Assessment (DPIA)* and determining whether processing is 'likely to result in a high risk' for the purposes of Regulation 2016/679, 17/EN WP 248, rev 01. Adopted on 4 October 2017, p 6.

judgment in *McFadden,* in which the applicant permitted anyone to anonymously use the internet for free. This posed a high risk to the intellectual property rights of authors and copyright owners, so a DPIA might have been required. Article 35(1) requires that risks to the rights and freedoms of 'natural persons' be considered. This is broader that data subjects, so a DPIA must assess the risks to all natural persons who will be affected by the processing not just those data subjects to whom the processing directly or indirectly relates.[16]

[13.10] It is not necessary to undertake an individual DPIA in respect of each individual data processing operation. The GDPR provides that:

> A single assessment may address a set of similar processing operations that present similar high risks.[17]

This should not be read as meaning that a controller can undertake a single DPIA in respect of all his data processing operations. A single DPIA can cover operations that present similar risks, but if different operations present different risks then separate DPIAs may need to be undertaken. The Recitals suggest that there may be:

> ... circumstances under which it may be reasonable and economical for the subject of a data protection impact assessment to be broader than a single project, for example where public authorities or bodies intend to establish a common application or processing platform or where several controllers plan to introduce a common application or processing environment across an industry sector or segment or for a widely used horizontal activity.[18]

[13.11] The WP29 suggest that a single DPIA could be used to assess multiple processing operations that are 'similar in terms of the risks presented, provided adequate consideration is given to the specific nature, scope, context and purposes of the processing. This might mean where similar technology is used to collect the same sort of data for the same purposes'.[19] It gives the example of a group of municipal authorities setting up similar CCTV systems. A single DPIA might cover all the processing.

When the processing involves joint controllers, the WP29 suggest that they each define their respective obligations precisely.[20] It also suggests that a fresh DPIA will not

---

16. As a result *McFadden* is not a perfect example of where a DPIA might have been required, as Sony records, which had taken the original German court action against the respondent is not a natural person. *McFadden* (Case C–484/14) (15 September 2016), para 26.
17. GDPR, article 35(1).
18. GDPR, Recital 92.
19. WP29 *Guidelines on Data Protection Impact Assessment (DPIA) and determining whether processing is 'likely to result in a high risk' for the purposes of Regulation 2016/679,* 17/EN WP 248. Adopted on 4 April 2017, p 6.
20. WP29 *Guidelines on Data Protection Impact Assessment (DPIA) and determining whether processing is 'likely to result in a high risk' for the purposes of Regulation 2016/679,* 17/EN WP 248 rev 01. Adopted on 4 October 2017, p 7.

be required 'when the nature, scope, context and purposes of the processing are very similar to the processing for which DPIA have been carried out'.[21]

[13.12] Article 35(1) make clear that it is for the controller to decide whether a proposed processing operation is so high risk that it merits a DPIA. To assist in that decision article 35(3) suggests a number of circumstances where DPIAs shall 'in particular' be required:

(a) a systematic and extensive evaluation of personal aspects relating to natural persons which is based on automated processing, including profiling, and on which decisions are based that produce legal effects concerning the natural person or similarly significantly affect the natural person;

(b) processing on a large scale of special categories of data referred to in Article 9(1), or of personal data relating to criminal convictions and offences referred to in Article 10; or

(c) a systematic monitoring of a publicly accessible area on a large scale. The Recitals go on to explain that a DPIA is required '... for monitoring publicly accessible areas on a large scale, especially when using optic-electronic devices or for any other operations where the competent supervisory authority considers that the processing is likely to result in a high risk to the rights and freedoms of data subjects, in particular because they prevent data subjects from exercising a right or using a service or a contract, or because they are carried out systematically on a large scale'.[22]

The above sets out three situations where a DPIA is required; profiling, the processing of sensitive data or criminal records or where surveillance systems such as CCTV are being installed. As WP29 have pointed out, the use of the words 'in particular' indicate that this is a non-exhaustive list: 'There may be "high risk" processing operations that are not captured by this list, but yet pose similarly high risks'.[23] These are just examples of where DPIAs must be undertaken. Another example is offered by the Recitals, which suggest that public bodies may be under a particular duty to undertake DPIAs:

> In the context of the adoption of the Member State law on which the performance of the tasks of the public authority or public body is based and which regulates the specific processing operation or set of operations in question, Member States may deem it necessary to carry out such assessment prior to the processing activities.[24]

21. WP29 *Guidelines on Data Protection Impact Assessment (DPIA) and determining whether processing is 'likely to result in a high risk' for the purposes of Regulation 2016/679*, 17/EN WP 248 rev 01. Adopted on 4 October 2017, p 10.

22. GDPR, Recital 91.

23. WP29 *Guidelines on Data Protection Impact Assessment (DPIA) and determining whether processing is 'likely to result in a high risk' for the purposes of Regulation 2016/679*, 17/EN WP 248, rev 01. Adopted on 4 October 2017, p 7.

24. GDPR, Recital 93.

However, article 35(10) provides that where processing has a lawful basis in EU law or that of a Member State and a DPIA was undertaken as part of the general impact assessment when that law was being enacted then it may not be necessary to undertake a further DPIA prior to the commencement of processing.[25]

[13.13] Controllers will have to undertake an assessment in each individual situation as to whether a DPIA is required. The Recitals provide further guidance that a DPIA may be needed for:

> ... large-scale processing operations which aim to process a considerable amount of personal data at regional, national or supranational level and which could affect a large number of data subjects and which are likely to result in a high risk, for example, on account of their sensitivity, where in accordance with the achieved state of technological knowledge a new technology is used on a large scale[26] as well as to other processing operations which result in a high risk to the rights and freedoms of data subjects, in particular where those operations render it more difficult for data subjects to exercise their rights.

This is much broader than the three specific situations set out in article 35. It also suggests that the scale of the data processing operations as regards both the amount of data processed, where it is from and the numbers of data subjects are relevant issues. Such an approach is consistent with that of the CJEU, which in cases such as *Tele2 Sverige*[27] has expressed particular concern about mass surveillance operations.[28] Other factors to be taken into account are the technologies involved are new and may make it more difficult for subjects to exercise their rights. The Recitals offer one example of where a DPIA may not be required or at least may not be 'mandatory':

> The processing of personal data should not be considered to be on a large scale if the processing concerns personal data from patients or clients by an individual physician, other health care professional or lawyer.[29]

---

25. 'Where processing pursuant to point (c) or (e) of Article 6(1) has a legal basis in Union law or in the law of the Member State to which the controller is subject, that law regulates the specific processing operation or set of operations in question, and a data protection impact assessment has already been carried out as part of a general impact assessment in the context of the adoption of that legal basis, paragraphs 1 to 7 shall not apply unless Member States deem it to be necessary to carry out such an assessment prior to processing activities'. GDPR, article 35(10).
26. The WP29 suggest that a DPIA can be useful for assessing the data protection impact of new technology, for example new software or hardware. WP29 *Guidelines on Data Protection Impact Assessment (DPIA) and determining whether processing is 'likely to result in a high risk' for the purposes of Regulation 2016/679*, 17/EN WP 248, 17/EN WP 248, rev 01. Adopted on 4 October 2017, p 8.
27. *Tele2 Sverige* (Case C–203/15) (21 December 2016).
28. *Tele2 Sverige* (Case C–203/15) (21 December 2016), paras 97–100.
29. GDPR, Recital 91.

[13.14] The WP29 offer the following list of criteria that should also be considered in making the decision of whether or not to carry out a DPIA:

1. Evaluation or scoring, including profiling such as a bank screening customers against a credit reference database or a biotechnology company offering genetic tests to consumers in order to predict disease or health risks.

2. Automated decision making with legal or similar significant effect such as processing that might discriminate against individuals.

3. Systematic monitoring of data subjects including data collected through a 'systematic monitoring of a publicly accessible area' for example where data is collected and data subjects are not aware of who is collecting their data and how it will be used or where they are unable to avoid being subjected to such processing.

4. Sensitive data which WP29 suggest includes data falling within articles 9 and 10 of the GDPR such as information about a person's political opinions or criminal records, health records, financial data, location data. In addition WP29 goes onto suggest that this may also include data that 'can be considered as increasing the possible risk to the rights and freedoms of individuals'. This might include data that is 'linked to household and private activities', data that impacts on the exercise of a fundamental right such as location data or data that may impact upon a subject's daily life, such as financial data that might be used for the purposes of a financial fraud. WP29 go onto suggest that 'whether the data has already been made publicly available by the data subject or by third parties may be relevant'.

5. Data processed on a large scale. WP29 suggest that this depends on the number of data subjects concerned, the volume of data, duration or permanence of the data processing activity and the geographical extent of the processing activity.

6. Datasets that have been matched or combined for example originating from two or more data processing operations performed for different purposes and/or by different controllers in a way that a data subject would not reasonably expect.

7. Data concerning vulnerable data subjects. A DPIA may be necessary given the imbalance of power between the data controller and data subjects meaning that the data subject is unable to give a real consent to the processing. The WP29 gives the examples of employees and new HR processing operations, or children, mentally ill persons, asylum seekers, the elderly and patients.

8. Innovative use or applying technological or organisational solutions such as combining the use of fingerprints and facial recognition data for improved physical entry onto a premises.

When the processing itself prevents the data subject from exercising a right or using a service or a contract such as where a bank carries out a reference check in deciding whether to offer a loan to a customer.[30]

WP29 suggest that 'a data controller can consider that a processing meeting two criteria would require a DPIA to be carried out' but goes onto warn that there may be cases where 'a processing meeting only one of these criteria requires a DPIAD'.[31]

In any event, Supervisory Authorities must establish and publicise lists of processing operations in respect to which DPIAs are[32] and are not[33] required. Such lists must be communicated to the EDPB, which may take steps to ensure that such lists are kept consistent within the EU.[34]

[13.15] Ultimately, the decision as to whether a DPIA should be undertaken is one that must be made by the controller alone but in making that decision the controller must keep in mind that he is accountable for demonstrating that his decision complied with the GDPR. If the controller does not undertake a DPIA in circumstances where the SA subsequently determines one should have been done then a fine of up to 10 million or up to 2 per cent of global turnover (whichever is the higher) may be imposed.[35] If a DPIA has not been done then the SA may order that one be done '... in a specified manner and within a specified period'[36] and it may limit or ban the controller from processing personal data in the meantime.[37] And subjects may seek compensation for material or non-material damage that they have suffered as a result of processing undertaken in the absence of a DPIA.[38]

---

30. This Opinion was first adopted in April 2017 then revised and readopted in October of that year. It is worth noting that the October Opinion dispensed with Data transfer across borders outside the EU as a category of risk WP29 *Guidelines on Data Protection Impact Assessment (DPIA) and determining whether processing is 'likely to result in a high risk' for the purposes of Regulation 2016/679,* 17/EN WP 248. Adopted on 4 April 2017, p 10.

31. WP29 *Guidelines on Data Protection Impact Assessment (DPIA) and determining whether processing is 'likely to result in a high risk' for the purposes of Regulation 2016/679,* 17/EN WP 248 Rev 1. Adopted on 4 October 2017, p 9-12.

32. GDPR, article 35(4).

33. GDPR, article 35(5).

34. 'Prior to the adoption of the lists referred to in paragraphs 4 and 5, the competent supervisory authority shall apply the consistency mechanism referred to in article 63 where such lists involve processing activities which are related to the offering of goods or services to data subjects or to the monitoring of their behaviour in several Member States, or may substantially affect the free movement of personal data within the Union' GDPR, article 35(6).

35. GDPR, article 83(4)(a).

36. GDPR, article 58(2)(d).

37. GDPR, article 58(2)(f).

38. GDPR, article 82.

Analysis

[13.16] Article 35(7)(a) provides that a DPIA must contain:

> a systematic description of the envisaged processing operations and the purposes of the processing, including, where applicable, the legitimate interest pursued by the controller.

Hence the DPIA will have to describe how personal data will be processed, together with a description of its lawful basis and purpose. This will probably mean explaining how the processing operation in question will comply with the principles of data protection set out in Article 5. This will take time. WP29 recommends that the DPIA be carried out 'as early as practical in the design of the processing operation even if some of the processing operations are still unknown'. It may also be necessary to repeat individual steps of the assessment as the development process continues and the WP29 make it clear that merely because the DPIA may need to be updated once processing has begun is not a valid reason for postponing or not carrying out the assessment. It is a 'continual process, not a one-time exercise'.[39]

The DPIA process requires that the controller take into account '… the nature, scope, context and purposes of the processing …' In order to do this the controller must fully describe the processing operation in question. The complexity of modern data processing operations means that such a process may not be easy. But the accuracy of this description is essential to the validity of the DPIA. If the description is inaccurate or insufficiently comprehensive it may have to be repeated.

Consultation

[13.17] The controller is obliged to carry out the DPIA but the GDPR specifies that consultations must be undertaken with two sets of persons. One is the DPO, who must provide advice on request in relation to the DPIA.[40] The GDPR does not specify when such advice must be sought, but the DPO must be involved '… properly and in a timely manner, in all issues which relate to the protection of personal data'.[41] This strongly suggests that the DPO should be involved throughout the DPIA process. The other set of persons are data subjects or their representatives, whose views may be sought 'where appropriate'. However, the seeking of these views will be '… without prejudice to the protection of commercial or public interests or the security of processing operations'.[42] If the views of the subjects or their representatives are to be sought, then that may not occur until quite late in the process, after a preliminary analysis has been undertaken. The WP29 consider that those views could be obtained through different means such as

---

39. WP29 *Guidelines on Data Protection Impact Assessment (DPIA) and determining whether processing is 'likely to result in a high risk' for the purposes of Regulation 2016/679,* 17/EN WP 248 rev 01. Adopted on 4 October 2017, p 14.
40. GDPR, article 39(1)(c).
41. GDPR, article 38(1).
42. GDPR, article 35(9).

a formal question to employees or trade unions, or a survey sent to customers. It suggests that where the views of the controller differ from that provided by these parties, the reasons should be documented and where the controller believes that it is 'not appropriate' to seek their views, the justification should also be documented.[43] Processors do not have a formal role in the DPIA process but the Recitals note that they'... should assist the controller, where necessary and upon request, in ensuring compliance with the obligations deriving from the carrying out of data protection impact assessments and from prior consultation of the supervisory authority'.[44]

Conclusion

[13.18] Article 35(7) stipulates that in addition to a systemic description of the processing a DPIA must contain 'at least' the following:

- an assessment of the necessity and proportionality of the processing operations in relation to the purposes;
- an assessment of the risks to the rights and freedoms of data subjects; and
- the measures envisaged to address the risks, including safeguards and mechanisms to ensure the protection of personal data and to demonstrate compliance with this Regulation taking into account the rights and legitimate interests of data subjects and other persons concerned.[45]

The conclusion of a DPIA may therefore be divided into three sub-parts. Firstly, is the processing operation in question 'necessary and proportionate'? Secondly, an assessment of the risks posed by the processing operation in question and the measures, safeguards and mechanisms envisaged to address those risks. Finally, the DPIA must conclude whether those measures, safeguards and mechanisms are sufficient '... to demonstrate compliance with this Regulation taking into account the rights and legitimate interests of data subjects and other persons concerned'. This assessment of what the risks of a processing operation are and how those risks may be addressed lies at the core of a DPIA. The risks in question are risks to all the rights and freedoms of the subjects, not just data protection rights. So the DPIA might have to consider whether the processing in question might affect data subject rights to freedom of expression,[46] ownership of property,[47] freedom of movement,[48] rights to liberty,[49] thought, conscience, religion[50] or their ability to carry on a business[51] for example. This assessment may also

---

43. WP29 *Guidelines on Data Protection Impact Assessment (DPIA) and determining whether processing is 'likely to result in a high risk' for the purposes of Regulation 2016/679,* 17/EN WP 248 Rev 1. Adopted on 4 October 2017, p 15.
44. GDPR, Recital 95.
45. GDPR, article 35(7).
46. Charter, article 11.
47. Charter, article 17.
48. TFEU, article 45.
49. Charter, article 6.
50. Charter, article 10.
51. Charter, article 16.

take into account compliance with approved codes of conduct by the controller and processor.[52]

[13.19] There is no legal obligation to publish the DPIA but WP29 suggests that data controllers should consider publishing their DPIA. 'The purpose of such a process would be to help foster trust in the controller's processing operations, and demonstrate accountability and transparency. It is particularly good practice to publish a DPIA where members of the public are affected by the processing operation. This could particularly be the case where a public authority carries out a DPIA'.[53]

Prior consultation – Supervisory Authority

[13.20] Not every EU supervisory regime requires that undertakings seek authorisation before commencing trading in a particular sector, but many do. Some supervisory regimes require that authorisations be obtained before opening a bank, providing insurance or telecommunications services. Others, such as EU competition law, require that authorisations be obtained before certain courses of action are embarked upon, such as acquiring a business rival or the provision of State Aid. The GDPR takes the latter approach, providing that only certain controllers have to obtain prior authorisation from their SA before commencing processing. As such the authorisation requirements imposed by the GDPR may not be as onerous as those imposed by CRD IV[54] or Solvency II,[55] but they are real and potentially onerous. Getting authorisation to open a bank or insurer in the EU may be a complex, expensive and lengthy process but the application of the rules that apply to that process are clear: if you want to provide banking or insurance services within the EU you will have to apply for authorisation. Deciding whether or not you need to seek authorisation to process personal data raises highly subjective questions which only the controller can answer. The difficulty for the controller is that if they answer those questions incorrectly and process personal data without undertaking a DPIA or obtaining prior authorisation from a SA in circumstances where they should have, then they will be unable to demonstrate compliance with the GDPR. The controller will then run the risk of being subject to fines or compensation claims, as well as the disruption that will be caused if they cannot

52.   GDPR, article 35(8).
53.   WP29 *Guidelines on Data Protection Impact Assessment (DPIA) and determining whether processing is 'likely to result in a high risk' for the purposes of Regulation 2016/679*, 17/EN WP 248 rev 01. Adopted on 4 October 2017, p 18.
54.   Directive 2013/36/EU of the European Parliament and of the Council of 26 June 2013 on access to the activity of credit institutions and the prudential supervision of credit institutions and investment firms, amending Directive 2002/87/EC and repealing Directives 2006/48/EC and 2006/49/EC. Text with EEA relevance.
55.   Directive 2009/138/EC of the European Parliament and of the Council of 25 November 2009 on the taking-up and pursuit of the business of Insurance and Reinsurance, OJ L 335, 17.12.2009, pp 1–155.

do ongoing business until the necessary DPIA or prior consultation processes are completed.

[13.21] If the controller concludes that its processing operation will give rise to a high risk, then it must consult with the SA. The obligation to consult is set out in article 36(1) which provides that:

> The controller shall consult the supervisory authority prior to processing where a data protection impact assessment under Article 35 indicates that the processing would result in a high risk in the absence of measures taken by the controller to mitigate the risk.[56]

This would appear to suggest that consultation should take place even if the controller concludes that they can employ measures that are adequate to mitigate the risk in question but that is contradicted by the Recitals which provide:

> Where a data protection impact assessment indicates that the processing would, in the absence of safeguards, security measures and mechanisms to mitigate the risk, result in a high risk to the rights and freedoms of natural persons and the controller is of the opinion that the risk cannot be mitigated by reasonable means in terms of available technologies and costs of implementation, the supervisory authority should be consulted prior to the start of processing activities.[57]

This clarifies that prior consultation need only take place if high risks[58] to the rights and freedoms of natural persons (not just data subjects) cannot be mitigated by measures taken by the controller. The WP29 agree and explain that:

> where a DPIA reveals high residual risks, the data controller will be required to seek prior consultation for the processing from the supervisory authority... As part of this, the DPIA must be fully provided... The supervisory authority may provide its advice, and will not compromise trade secrets or reveal security vulnerabilities, subject to the principles applicable in each Member State on public access to official documents.[59]

WP29 go onto suggest that:

> An example of an unacceptable high residual risk includes instances where the data subjects may encounter significant, or even irreversible, consequences, which

---

56. GDPR, Recital 89 further provides that the SA should only be consulted in relation to '... those types of processing operations which are likely to result in a high risk to the rights and freedoms of natural persons by virtue of their nature, scope, context and purposes ...'.

57. GDPR, Recital 44.

58. GDPR, Recital 94 explains that such high risks are '... likely to result from certain types of processing and the extent and frequency of processing, which may result also in a realisation of damage or interference with the rights and freedoms of the natural person'.

59. WP29 *Guidelines on Data Protection Impact Assessment (DPIA) and determining whether processing is 'likely to result in a high risk' for the purposes of Regulation 2016/679*, 17/EN WP 248 Rev 1. Adopted on 4 October 2017, p 18.

they may not overcome... and/or when it seems obvious that the risk will occur ...[60]

[13.22] Article 36(2) suggests that the purpose of such consultation is to enable the SA to assess whether the safeguards proposed by the controller are adequate. It provides that where the SA forms the opinion:

> that the intended processing ... would infringe this Regulation, in particular where the controller has insufficiently identified or mitigated the risk, the supervisory authority shall ... provide written advice to the controller and, where applicable to the processor ...

The SA must provide this written advice within eight weeks, a period which may be extended by a further six weeks 'taking into account the complexity of the intended processing'. The SA shall inform the controller of its intention to extend this period within one month of receiving the request for consultation, a communication which must include the reasons for the delay. This information may also be given to the processor. One potential difficulty for the controller is that these consultation periods '... may be suspended until the supervisory authority has obtained information it has requested for the purposes of the consultation'.[61] However if the SA does not respond this does not necessarily mean that the controller can commence processing. The Recitals provide:

> The supervisory authority should respond to the request for consultation within a specified period. However, the absence of a reaction of the supervisory authority within that period should be without prejudice to any intervention of the supervisory authority in accordance with its tasks and powers laid down in this Regulation, including the power to prohibit processing operations.[62]

So the fact that the controller is still waiting for the SA to respond to a prior consultation cannot be relied upon to challenge the ability of the SA to utilise its power under the GDPR.

[13.23] The GDPR specifies that Member States must consult with the SA: '... during the preparation of a proposal for a legislative measure to be adopted by a national parliament, or of a regulatory measure based on such a legislative measure, which relates to processing'.[63] In addition Member States '... may require controllers to consult with, and obtain prior authorisation from, the supervisory authority in relation to processing by a controller for the performance of a task carried out by the controller in the public interest, including processing in relation to social protection and public health'.[64]

---

60.   WP29 *Guidelines on Data Protection Impact Assessment (DPIA) and determining whether processing is 'likely to result in a high risk' for the purposes of Regulation 2016/679*, 17/EN WP 248 Rev 1. Adopted on 4 October 2017, p 19.
61.   GDPR, article 36(2).
62.   GDPR, Recital 94.
63.   GDPR, article 36(4).
64.   GDPR, article 36(5).

The controller must provide the SA with the following material when engaging in prior consultation:

(a) where applicable, the respective responsibilities of the controller, joint controllers and processors involved in the processing, in particular for processing within a group of undertakings;

(b) the purposes and means of the intended processing;

(c) the measures and safeguards provided to protect the rights and freedoms of data subjects pursuant to this Regulation;

(d) where applicable, the contact details of the data protection officer;

(e) the data protection impact assessment provided for in article 35; and

(f) any other information requested by the supervisory authority.[65]

The stated purpose of the prior consultation process is to enable the SA to advise the controller. However, the GDPR makes clear that the SA: '… may use any of its powers referred to in Article 58.' Such powers include:

(a) ordering '… the controller or processor to bring processing operations into compliance …'[66] with the GDPR;

(b) imposing '… a temporary or definitive limitation including a ban on processing';[67] and,

(c) ordering '… the rectification or erasure of personal data or restriction of processing …'.[68]

In essence article 35 is an authorisation regime. If the SA is unhappy with the information provided or unconvinced that the controller can process data in accordance with the GDPR then it can direct that such processing be either brought into compliance or else cease.

Repetition

[13.24] The DPO must monitor the performance of the DPIA[69] and the controller will have to review the DPIA where there has been a change to the risk. A controller must:

> … carry out a review to assess if processing is performed in accordance with the data protection impact assessment at least when there is a change of the risk represented by processing operations.[70]

---

65. GDPR, article 35(3).
66. GDPR, article 58(1)(d).
67. GDPR, article 58(1)(e).
68. GDPR, article 58(1)(f).
69. GDPR, article 39(1)(b) and (c).
70. GDPR, article 35(11).

WP29 suggests that 'a DPIA should be continuously reviewed and regularly re-assessed'.[71] It may therefore be prudent for the DPIA to set out what would trigger such a reassessment. That trigger might be the passage of a set period of time, such as a number of months or years. Alternatively that trigger might take the form of a specific event, such as the attainment of specific performance indicators.

Conclusion – will the DPIA and prior consultation processes work?

[13.25] The GDPR suggests that the justification for a DPIA is to provide an effective alternative to Directive 95/46's obligation to register certain data processing operations with the SA. The Recitals state that:

> Directive 95/46/EC provided for a general obligation to notify the processing of personal data to the supervisory authorities. While that obligation produces administrative and financial burdens, it did not in all cases contribute to improving the protection of personal data. Such indiscriminate general notification obligations should therefore be abolished, and replaced by effective procedures and mechanisms which focus instead on those types of processing operations which are likely to result in a high risk to the rights and freedoms of natural persons by virtue of their nature, scope, context and purposes.[72]

This makes clear that the output of a DPIA will be a decision whether or not to engage in a prior consultation process with the SA. The requirement that controllers undertake DPIAs justified the removal of the general obligation to notify the SA. The purpose of the DPIA process is to ensure that controllers only notify high risk data processing operations to the SA. It will be interesting to see if the DPIA process succeeds in this regard. The GDPR requires that the prior consultation process last from eight to fourteen weeks or even longer if the controller does not respond promptly to queries from the SA. However, a DPIA may take a lot longer. Given the complexity of compiling a DPIA it seems likely that any controller who completes a DPIA will conclude that they may as well consult with their SA. The disadvantage of doing so is that such a consultation may take eight weeks or more. However, the advantage is that the SA may save the controller from a costly mistake, if it should prevent or limit the processing. But if the SA accedes to the processing, however vague that accession may be, then the controller will have demonstrated their compliance with the GDPR in the clearest manner possible. Some controllers may consider such a *de facto* endorsement attractive. And other than time, the costs of consulting with a SA may fall primarily on the SA, not the controller. Had the EU legislature wanted to discourage controllers from prior consulting as a matter of course it might perhaps have allowed SAs to charge controllers who engage in such prior consultations an appropriate fee, but it does not.

---

71. WP29 *Guidelines on Data Protection Impact Assessment (DPIA) and determining whether processing is 'likely to result in a high risk' for the purposes of Regulation 2016/679*, 17/EN WP 248 rev 01. Adopted on 4 October 2017, p 14.

72. GDPR, Recital 89.

ASSESSMENT OF APPROPRIATE SECURITY MEASURES

[13.26] Integrity and confidentiality is one of the principles of data protection,[73] the controller must ensure:

> ... appropriate security of the personal data, including protection against unauthorised or unlawful processing and against accidental loss, destruction or damage, using appropriate technical or organisational measures.[74]

In *Digital Rights Ireland* the CJEU commented adversely upon a provision in the Data Retention Directive 2006/24. The CJEU held that Directive 2006/24 did not provided '... sufficient safeguards ... to ensure effective protection of the data retained against the risk of abuse and against any unlawful access and use of that data'. The made a two-fold criticism of that Directive. Firstly that it failed to:

> ... lay down rules which are specific and adapted to (i) the vast quantity of data whose retention is required by that directive, (ii) the sensitive nature of that data and (iii) the risk of unlawful access to that data, rules which would serve, in particular, to govern the protection and security of the data in question in a clear and strict manner in order to ensure their full integrity and confidentiality.

Secondly, Directive 2006/24 when read in conjunction with the security obligations imposed by Directive 95/46 failed to:

> ...ensure that a particularly high level of protection and security is applied by those providers by means of technical and organisational measures, but permits those providers... to have regard to economic considerations when determining the level of security which they apply, as regards the costs of implementing security measures.[75]

This criticism formed one of the bases upon which the CJEU held that Directive 2006/24 was invalid. The CJEU returned to this criticism in *Tele2 Sverige* in which it set out what safeguards it expected that a national data retention law would provide. One such safeguard related to data security. The CJEU held that '... the providers of electronic communications services must, in order to ensure the full integrity and confidentiality of that data, guarantee a particularly high level of protection and security by means of appropriate technical and organisational measures'.[76] However the CJEU did not repeat its earlier criticism of Directive 2006/24 that it failed to specify particular security measures.

Given the frequency and magnitude of malicious hacking events,[77] it is not illogical to focus on hacking as the main threat to the security of personal data. But this is just one of the threats that personal data has to be secured against. There are many others:

73.　GDPR, article 5(1)(f).
74.　GDPR, article 5(1)(f).
75.　*Digital Rights Ireland* (Case C–293/12) (8 April 2014) paras 66-67.
76.　*Tele2 Sverige* (Case C–203/15) (21 December 2016), para 122.
77.　Jones and Kuchler, 'The shadow arms bazaar that fuels global cyber crime', (2017) *Financial Times*, 19 May.

loss of equipment, fires and floods are also significant threats. Hard-drive failure may seem mundane, but it is a common cause of data loss.[78] Data breaches can occur when unencrypted DVDs are lost in the post[79] or unsecured smartphones are left behind in an airport.[80] The GDPR requires that data processing systems are designed to be secure by default, providing that technical and organisational measures implemented by the controller:

> … shall ensure that by default personal data are not made accessible without the individual's intervention to an indefinite number of natural persons.[81]

The Recitals suggest that:

> In order to maintain security and to prevent processing in infringement of the GDPR, the controller or processor should evaluate any processing risks and implement measures to mitigate those risks by using for example encryption.[82]

[13.27] This suggests that the controller undertake a risk assessment. That requirement is made explicit by article 32(1) which provides that taking into account the state of the article, the costs of implementation and the nature, scope, context and purposes of processing as well as the risk of varying likelihood and severity for the rights and freedoms of natural persons, the controller and the processor must implement appropriate technical and organisational measures to ensure a level of security appropriate to the risk, including inter alia as appropriate:

(a)   the pseudonymisation and encryption of personal data;

(b)   the ability to ensure the ongoing confidentiality, integrity, availability and resilience of processing systems and services;

(c)   the ability to restore the availability and access to personal data in a timely manner in the event of a physical or technical incident;

(d)   a process for regularly testing, assessing and evaluating the effectiveness of technical and organisational measures for ensuring the security of the processing.

---

78.   Nunic, *What's The #1 Data Loss Cause In The World In 2016?* Krollonline, 10 February 2017 https://www.krollontrack.co.uk/blog/the-world-of-data/whats-1-data-loss-cause-world.

79.   Pidd, 'Manchester police fined £150,000 over victim interviews lost in post', (2017) *The Guardian*, 4 May.

80.   In 2017 the US government fined a Texas Hospital some $3.2 million in respect of '… the loss of an unencrypted, non-password protected BlackBerry device at the Dallas/Fort Worth International Airport on November 19, 2009,' US Department of Health and Human Services, *Lack of timely action risks security and costs money*, 1 February 2017, https://www.hhs.gov/about/news/2017/02/01/lack-timely-action-risks-security-and-costs-money.html.

81.   GDPR, article 25(2).

82.   GDPR, Recital 83.

[13.28] In order to assess the appropriate level of security, the risks that are presented by processing, in particular from accidental or unlawful destruction, loss, alteration, unauthorised disclosure of, or access to personal data transmitted, stored or otherwise processed must be taken into account.[83] Whether the controller or processor has complied with an approved code of conduct or approved certification mechanism may be used as an element by which to demonstrate compliance with the requirements set out above.[84] The controller and processor must take steps to ensure that any natural person acting under the authority of the controller or the processor who has access to personal data does not process them except on instructions from the controller, unless he or she is required to do so by Union or Member State law.[85] The Recitals provide that the controller should be responsible for the carrying-out of a data protection impact assessment to evaluate, in particular, the origin, nature, particularity and severity of that risk. The outcome of the assessment should be taken into account when determining the appropriate measures to be used in order to demonstrate that the processing of personal data complies with the Regulation. Where a data-protection impact assessment indicates that processing operations involve a high risk which the controller cannot mitigate by appropriate measures in terms of available technology and costs of implementation, a consultation of the supervisory authority should take place prior to the processing.[86]

ASSESSMENT OF WHERE A PERSONAL DATA BREACH IS A RISK OR HIGH RISK

[13.29] The Recitals note that a general obligation to notify of data breaches existed under the Data Protection Directive (95/46/EC) but that it did not always improve the protection of personal data. The Recitals call for the abolition of 'such indiscriminate general notification obligations' and replacement by 'effective procedures and mechanisms which focus instead on those types of processing operations which are likely to result in a high risk to the rights and freedoms of natural persons by virtue of their nature, scope, context and purposes'.[87]

The justification for breach notification is that a personal data breach may, if not addressed in an appropriate and timely manner, result in physical, material or non-material damage such as loss of control over their personal data or limitation of their rights, discrimination, identity theft or fraud, financial loss, unauthorised reversal of pseudonymisation, damage to reputation, loss of confidentiality of personal data protected by professional secrecy or any other significant economic or social

---

83. GDPR, article 32(2).
84. GDPR, article 32(3).
85. GDPR, article 32(4).
86. GDPR, Recital 84.
87. GDPR, Recital 89.

disadvantage to the natural person concerned.[88] The GDPR defines a personal data breach as:

> ... a breach of security leading to the accidental or unlawful destruction, loss, alteration, unauthorised disclosure of, or access to, personal data transmitted, stored or otherwise processed.[89]

Where a personal data breach occurs the GDPR may require that the controller notify personal data breaches to the SA or the subject themselves. Such notifications may have significant repercussions for the controller, particularly if a notification is made to the subject themselves. Such a notification may effectively amount to an admission of liability, which may be used against the controller in any subsequent action for damages under article 82 GDPR.

[13.30] The Recitals provide that in setting rules concerning the format and procedures surrounding notifications for data breaches, consideration should be given to the circumstances of that breach such as whether or not personal data had been protected by appropriate technical protection measures which would effectively limit the likelihood of identity fraud or other forms of misuse. Any rules or procedures should take into account the legitimate interests of law-enforcement authorities where early disclosure could unnecessarily hamper the investigation of the circumstances of a personal data breach.[90]

Notification of a personal data breach to the Supervisory Authority

[13.31] Where there is a personal data breach, then article 33(1) requires that the controller without undue delay and, where feasible, not later than 72 hours after having become aware of it, notify the personal data breach to the SA. The controller will not have to provide such notification if it determines that:

> ... the personal data breach is unlikely to result in a risk to the rights and freedoms of natural persons.[91]

If the data breach is not notified within the 72-hour period, reasons for the delay must be provided. The controller's notification of a personal data breach must at least:

(a) describe the nature of the personal data breach including where possible, the categories and approximate number of data subjects concerned and the categories and approximate number of personal data records concerned;

(b) communicate the name and contact details of the data protection officer or other contact point where more information can be obtained;

---

88. GDPR, Recital 85.
89. GDPR, article 4(12).
90. GDPR, Recital 88.
91. In accordance with the accountability principle, GDPR, Recital 85.

(c) describe the likely consequences of the personal data breach;

(d) describe the measures taken or proposed to be taken by the controller to address the personal data breach, including, where appropriate, measures to mitigate its possible adverse effects. [92]

If it is not possible to provide this information at the same time, the information may be provided in phases without undue further delay.[93] The controller is obliged to document any personal data breaches, comprising the facts relating to the personal data breach, its effects and the remedial action taken. That documentation will enable the supervisory authority to verify compliance with the controller's notification obligations.[94] In the case of a processor, the processor must notify the controller without undue delay after becoming aware of a personal data breach.[95]

[13.32] The Recitals provide that the fact that the notification was made without undue delay should be established taking into account in particular the nature and gravity of the personal data breach and its consequences and adverse effects for the data subject. Such notification may result in an intervention of the supervisory authority.[96] WP29 has suggested that in certain circumstances controllers may be able to 'bundle' their notifications:

> Strictly speaking, each individual breach is a reportable incident. However, to avoid being overly burdensome, the controller may be able to submit a 'bundled' notification representing all these breaches, provided that they concern the same type of personal data breached in the same way, over a relatively short space of time.[97]

Communication of a personal data breach to the data subject

[13.33] Under article 34(1) when the personal data breach is likely to result in a high risk to the rights and freedoms of natural persons, the controller must communicate the personal data breach to the data subject 'without undue delay'. According to the Recitals this is to enable the data subject to take the necessary precautions. The Recitals further provide that the communication should be made to the data subject as soon as reasonably feasible and in close cooperation with the supervisory authority, respecting guidance provided by it or by other relevant authorities such as law enforcement authorities. It suggests that the need to mitigate an immediate risk of damage would call for a prompt communication with the data subject whereas the need to implement appropriate measures against continuing or similar personal data breaches may justify

---

92. GDPR, article 33(3).

93. GDPR, article 32(4).

94. GDPR, article 33(5).

95. GDPR, article 33(2).

96. GDPR, Recital 87.

97. WP29, *Guidelines on Personal data breach notification under Regulation 2016/679*, 17/EN, WP250, adopted on 3 October 2017, p 14.

more time.[98] The communication to the data subject must be in clear and plain language and set out the nature of the personal data breach and at least the following information: the name and contact details of the data protection officer or other contact point where more information can be obtained, a description of the likely consequences of the personal data breach and a description of the measures taken or proposed to be taken by the controller to address the breach including where appropriate, measures to mitigate its possible adverse effects.[99] There is no requirement to communicate this information to the data subject if any of the following conditions are met:

(a) the controller has implemented appropriate technical and organisational protection measures, and that those measures were applied to the personal data affected by the personal data breach, in particular those that render the personal data unintelligible to any person who is not authorised to access it, such as encryption;

(b) the controller has taken subsequent measures which ensure that the high risk to the rights and freedoms of data is no longer likely to materialise;

(c) it would involve disproportionate effort. In this case, a public communication or some other similar measure may be made so that subjects are informed in an equally effective manner.[100]

If the controller has not already communicated the personal data breach to the data subject, the supervisory authority, having considered the likelihood of the personal data breach resulting in a high risk, may require it to do so or may decide that any of the conditions in (a), (b) and (c) are met.[101]

How should the risk of a data breach be assessed?

[13.34] Article 33 requires that controllers notify their supervisory authority where a data breach is not '… unlikely to result in a risk to the rights and freedoms of natural persons'.[102] Article 34 requires that controllers notify subjects where a '… personal data breach is likely to result in a high risk to the rights and freedoms of natural persons'.[103] WP29 has issued guidelines which set out criteria which controllers may take into account when assessing such risks. These criteria are:

• the type of breach;

• the nature, sensitivity, and volume of personal data;

• ease of identification of individuals;

---

98.   GDPR, Recital 86.
99.   GDPR, article 34(2). This information is set out in GDPR, article 33(3)(b), (c) and (d).
100. GDPR, article 34(3).
101. GDPR, article 34(4).
102. GDPR, article 33(1).
103. GDPR, article 34(1).

- severity of consequences for individuals;

- special characteristics of the individual;

- the number of affected individuals;

- special characteristics of the data controller.

WP29 conclude with the following comment:

> ... when assessing the risk that is likely to result from a breach, the controller should consider a combination of the severity of the potential impact on the rights and freedoms of individuals and the likelihood of these occurring. Clearly, where the consequences of a breach are more severe, the risk is higher and similarly where the likelihood of these occurring is greater, the risk is also heightened. If in doubt, the controller should err on the side of caution and notify.[104]

---

104. WP29, *Guidelines on Personal data breach notification under Regulation 2016/679*, 17/EN, WP250, Adopted on 3 October 2017, p 22.

Chapter 14

CODES OF CONDUCT AND CERTIFICATION

INTRODUCTION

[14.01] Chapter IV, s 5 GDPR provides for codes of conduct and certification. The Recitals explain why codes of conduct are useful:

> Guidance on the implementation of appropriate measures and on the demonstration of compliance by the controller or the processor, especially as regards the identification of the risk related to the processing, their assessment in terms of origin, nature, likelihood and severity, and the identification of best practices to mitigate the risk, could be provided in particular by means of approved codes of conduct, approved certifications, guidelines provided by the Board or indications provided by a data protection officer. The Board may also issue guidelines on processing operations that are considered to be unlikely to result in a high risk to the rights and freedoms of natural persons and indicate what measures may be sufficient in such cases to address such risk.[1]

Codes of conduct for data protection are not a new development; Directive 95/46 encouraged '… the drawing up of codes of conduct…'.[2] A number of such codes exist at an EU level, one example being that for Cloud Service providers[3] another being that for Cloud Infrastructure Services Providers.[4]

The GDPR suggest that adherence to an approved code of conduct or approved certification mechanisms may be used by the controller to show compliance with his obligations[5] and compliance with data protection by design and default.[6] The Recitals add that such codes of conduct could calibrate the obligations of controllers and processing.[7] Compliance with approved codes of conduct by controllers and processors can be taken into account in assessing the impact of processing operations, in particular for the purposes of the DPIA.[8] Recital 77 provides that codes of conduct and

---

1. GDPR, Recital 77.
2. Directive 95/46, article 27(1).
3. Cloud Select Industry Group (C-SIG), *EU Data Protection Code of Conduct for Cloud Service Providers*, Version 1.7, May 2017, https://eucoc.cloud/en/home/#c2055 See Article 29 WP, Opinion 02/2015 on C-SIG Code of Conduct on Cloud Computing, 2588/15/EN WP 232, 22 September 2015.
4. Cloud Infrastructure Service Providers in Europe (CISPE), *Data Protection, Code of Conduct for Cloud Infrastructure Service Providers* January 2017 https://cispe.cloud/wp-content/uploads/2017/02/CISPE-CodeOfConduct-27012017.pdf.
5. GDPR, article 24(3).
6. GDPR, article 25(3).
7. GDPR, Recital 98.
8. GDPR, article 35(8).

certifications could provide guidance on the implementation of appropriate measures, particularly as regards risk.

CODES OF CONDUCT

[14.02] The GDPR encourages the creation of codes of conduct and provides in article 40(1) that:

> The Member States, the supervisory authorities, the Board and the Commission shall encourage the drawing up of codes of conduct intended to contribute to the proper application of this Regulation, taking account of the specific features of the various processing sectors and the specific needs of micro, small and medium-sized enterprises.[9]

In addition, associations and other bodies that represent categories of controllers or processors may prepare codes of conduct, or amend or extend such codes in order to specify the application of the GDPR:

> such as with regard to:
>
> (a) fair and transparent processing;
>
> (b) the legitimate interests pursued by controllers in specific contexts;
>
> (c) the collection of personal data;
>
> (d) the pseudonymisation of personal data;
>
> (e) the information provided to the public and to data subjects;
>
> (f) the exercise of the rights of data subjects;
>
> (g) the information provided to, and the protection of, children, and the manner in which the consent of the holders of parental responsibility over children is to be obtained;
>
> (h) the measures and procedures referred to in Articles 24 (responsibilities of the controller) and 25 (data protection by design and default) and the measures to ensure security of processing referred to in Article 32;
>
> (i) the notification of personal data breaches to supervisory authorities and the communication of such personal data breaches to data subjects;
>
> (j) the transfer of personal data to third countries or international organisations; or
>
> (k) out-of-court proceedings and other dispute resolution procedures for resolving disputes between controllers and data subjects with regard to processing, without prejudice to the rights of data subjects pursuant to Articles 77 and 79.[10]

---

9.   GDPR, article 40(1).
10.   GDPR, article 40(2).

Associations and other bodies intending to prepare a code of conduct, amend or extend an existing code of conduct must submit the draft code, amendment or extension to the competent SA which must provide an opinion on whether it complies with the GDPR. If it believes that there are sufficient safeguards, then the draft code, amendment or extension will be approved.[11] The Recitals explain that such associations and other bodies should consult relevant stakeholders, including data subjects when drawing up, amending or extending such codes, where feasible and have regard to their submissions and views.[12] The code must be registered and published by the SA unless it relates to processing activities in several member states. [13] A code of conduct drawn up by an association or body must contain mechanisms which enable an accredited body[14] to carry out the mandatory monitoring of compliance with its provisions by the controllers or processors which undertake to apply it. This is without prejudice to the tasks and powers of SAs.[15]

[14.03] Where a draft code of conduct relates to processing activities in several Member States, the competent supervisory authority must submit the code, amendment or extension to the European Data Protection Board (EDPB)[16] before approval. The EDPB will provide an opinion on whether it complies with the GDPR or, as the case may be, provides appropriate safeguards.[17] Where the EDPB's opinion confirms that this is the case, it will submit its opinion to the Commission.[18] The Commission may, by way of implementing acts, decide that it has general validity within the Union and those implementing acts must be adopted in accordance with the examination procedure.[19] Approved codes having such general validity must be appropriately publicised by the Commission.[20] The EDPB is tasked with collating all approved codes of conduct, amendments and extensions in a register and must make them publicly available by way of appropriate means.[21]

Codes of conduct must be adhered to by controllers and processors subject to the GDPR. But in addition, where codes of conduct have been approved by the SA and it has been decided that the code of conduct has general validity by the Commission, these may also be adhered to by controllers or processors that are not subject to the GDPR:

> in order to provide appropriate safeguards within the framework of personal data transfers to third countries or international organisations[22] ....Those controllers or processors must make binding and enforceable commitments, via contractual or

---

11. GDPR, article 40(5).
12. GDPR, Recital 99.
13. GDPR, article 40(6).
14. GDPR, article 41(1).
15. GDPR, article 40(4).
16. Following the procedure in GDPR, article 63.
17. GDPR, article 40(7).
18. GDPR, article 40(8).
19. The examination procedure as set out in GDPR, article 93. GDPR, article 40(9).
20. GDPR, article 40(10).
21. GDPR, article 40(11).
22. As described in GDPR, article 46(2)(e).

other legally binding instruments, to apply those appropriate safeguards including with regard to the rights of data subjects.[23]

Monitoring of approved codes of conduct

[14.04] Article 41 provides that the monitoring of approved codes of conduct may be carried out by a body which has an appropriate level of expertise in relation to the subject-matter of the code and is accredited for that purpose by the competent supervisory authority.[24] Such a body must have:

(a) demonstrated its independence and expertise in relation to the subject-matter of the code to the satisfaction of the competent SA;

(b) established procedures which allow it to assess the eligibility of controllers and processors concerned to apply the code, to monitor their compliance with its provisions and to periodically review its operation;

(c) established procedures and structures to handle complaints about infringements of the code or the manner in which the code has been, or is being, implemented by a controller or processor, and to make those procedures and structures transparent to data subjects and the public; and

(d) demonstrated to the satisfaction of the competent SA that its tasks and duties do not result in a conflict of interests.[25]

The competent SA must submit the draft criteria for accreditation of a body to the EDPB in accordance with the consistency mechanism.[26] That accredited body must, subject to appropriate safeguards, take appropriate action in cases where there has been an infringement of the code by a controller or processor. This might include suspending or excluding the controller or processor from the code. In that case, it must inform the competent SA of its actions and reasons for such action.[27]

The competent SA must revoke the accreditation of a body if the conditions for accreditation are not, or are no longer, met or where actions taken by the body infringe the GDPR.[28] Article 41 does not apply to processing carried out by public authorities and bodies.[29]

CERTIFICATION

[14.05] Article 42 provides that Member States, the supervisory authorities, the EDPB and the Commission must encourage, particularly at Union level:

> the establishment of data protection certification mechanisms and of data protection seals and marks, for the purpose of demonstrating compliance with this

---

23.   GDPR, article 40(3).
24.   GDPR, article 41(1).
25.   GDPR, article 41(2).
26.   GDPR, article 41(3).
27.   GDPR, article 41(4).
28.   GDPR, article 41(5).
29.   GDPR, article 41(6).

Regulation of processing operations by controllers and processors. The specific needs of micro, small and medium-sized enterprises shall be taken into account.

The setting up of certification mechanisms and data protection seals and marks is to 'enhance transparency and compliance' according to the recitals.[30] Such data protection certification mechanisms, seals or marks may be established for the purpose of demonstrating the existence of appropriate safeguards provided by controllers or processors that are not subject to this Regulation where there are personal data transfers to third countries or international organisations. Such controllers or processors must make binding and enforceable commitments, via contract or other legally binding instruments, to apply those appropriate safeguards, including with regard to the rights of data subjects.[31]

[14.06] The certification must be voluntary and available via a transparent process.[32] A certification pursuant to this Article does not reduce the responsibility of the controller or the processor for compliance with the GDPR and is without prejudice to the tasks and powers of the competent supervisory authorities.[33]

A certification must be issued by the certification bodies as set out in article 43 or by the competent SA, on the basis of criteria approved by that competent SA in accordance with its authorisation and advisory powers in article 58(3) or by the EDPB. Where the criteria are approved by the Board, this may result in a common certification, the European Data Protection Seal.[34]

A controller or processor submitting its processing to the certification mechanism must provide the certification body 'with all information and access to its processing activities which are necessary to conduct the certification procedure'.[35] Certification is issued for a maximum period of three years and is renewable under the same conditions, provided that the relevant requirements continue to be met. Where they are not or are no longer being met, Certification must be withdrawn, as applicable, by the certification bodies.[36] The EDPB must collate all certification mechanisms and data protection seals and marks in a register and make them publicly available by any appropriate means.[37]

Certification bodies

[14.07] Without prejudice to the tasks and powers of the competent SA, certification bodies which have an appropriate level of expertise in relation to data protection must,

---

30. GDPR, Recital 100.
31. GDPR, article 42(2).
32. GDPR, article 42(3).
33. GDPR, article 42(4).
34. GDPR, article 42(5).
35. GDPR, article 42(6).
36. GDPR, article 42(7).
37. GDPR, article 42(8).

after informing the SA in order to allow it to exercise its powers pursuant to point (h) of article 58(2) where necessary, issue and renew certification.

Member States must ensure that certification bodies are accredited by one or both of the following:

(a) the competent supervisory authority;[38]

(b) the national accreditation body named in accordance with Regulation 765/2008/ EC on setting out the requirements for accreditation and market surveillance relating to the marketing of products[39] in accordance with EN-ISO/IEC 17065/ 2012 and with the additional requirements established by the competent SA.[40]

Such certification bodies must be accredited 'only where they have':

(a) demonstrated their independence and expertise in relation to the subject-matter of the certification to the satisfaction of the competent SA;

(b) undertaken to respect approved criteria; (that is, criteria approved by the competent SA or EDPB. In the case of certification bodies accredited by the national accreditation body (in article 43(1)(b) above) those requirements must complement those envisaged in Regulation 765/2008/EC and the technical rules that describe the methods and procedures of the certification bodies.[41] These requirements and criteria must be made public by the SA in an easily accessible form and must be transmitted to the EDPB. The EDPB is tasked with collating all certification mechanisms and data protection seals in a register and must make them publicly available by any appropriate means.[42]

(c) established procedures for the issuing, periodic review and withdrawal of data protection certification, seals and marks;

(d) established procedures and structures to handle complaints about infringements of the certification or the manner in which the certification has been, or is being, implemented by the controller or processor, and to make those procedures and structures transparent to data subjects and the public; and

(e) demonstrated, to the satisfaction of the competent SA, that their tasks and duties do not result in a conflict of interests.[43]

The certification bodies are responsible for 'the proper assessment leading to the certification or the withdrawal of such certification without prejudice to the responsibility of the controller or processor for compliance' with the GDPR. The accreditation is issued for a maximum period of five years and may be renewed on the

---

38. As set out in GDPR, article 55 or 56.
39. Regulation 765/2008/EC of the European Parliament and of the Council.
40. GDPR, article 43(1).
41. GDPR, article 43(3).
42. GDPR, article 43(6).
43. GDPR, article 43(2).

same conditions provided that the certification body meets the requirements as set out above.[44] Certification bodies must provide the competent SA with the reasons for granting or withdrawing the requested certification.[45]

[14.08] Without prejudice to the remedies, liabilities and penalties set out in the GDPR, the competent SA or the national accreditation body can revoke an accreditation of a certification body where the conditions for the accreditation are not, or are no longer, met or where actions taken by a certification body infringe the GDPR.[46]

The Commission has the power to adopt delegated acts for the purpose of specifying the requirements to be taken into account for the data protection certification mechanisms[47] and may adopt implementing acts:

> laying down technical standards for certification mechanisms and data protection seals and marks, and mechanisms to promote and recognise those certification mechanisms, seals and marks.[48]

---

44. GDPR, article 43(4).
45. GDPR, article 43(5).
46. GDPR, article 43(7).
47. GDPR, article 43(8).
48. GDPR, article 43(9).

PART 6
SUPERVISORY AUTHORITIES

Chapter 15

SUPERVISORY AUTHORITIES

INTRODUCTION

[15.01] Data Protection Authorities[1] (Supervisory Authorities) have been a feature of European data protection law since its inception. First, the Strasbourg Convention provided for their designation:[2] Directive 95/46 required their establishment,[3] and finally the Lisbon Treaty made the obligation to establish Supervisory Authorities part of the EU's basic law when it entered into force in 2009. Now TFEU, article 16(2) requires that the EU legislature lay down data protection rules and provides that:

> Compliance with these rules shall be subject to the control of independent authorities.

The importance of such Supervisory Authorities was emphasised by the CJEU in *Schrems,* which held that:

> The establishment in Member States of independent supervisory authorities is ... an essential component of the protection of individuals with regard to the processing of personal data.[4]

This emphasis is repeated by the Recitals to the GDPR:

> The establishment of supervisory authorities in Member States, empowered to perform their tasks and exercise their powers with complete independence, is an essential component of the protection of natural persons with regard to the processing of their personal data.[5]

[15.02] GDPR, article 51(1) provides for the establishment of what it terms 'supervisory authorities' by Member States, providing that:

> Each Member State shall provide for one or more independent public authorities to be responsible for monitoring the application of this Regulation, in order to protect the fundamental rights and freedoms of natural persons in relation to processing and to facilitate the free flow of personal data within the Union.

---

1. Data Protection Authorities or Supervisory Authorities have been used interchangeably with the term supervisory authorities by the CJEU and the A29 WP. Either term is arguably correct, although the GDPR refers solely to supervisory authorities. The difficulty with using this term is that the various regulatory schemes now adopted by the EU have given rise to a great number of supervisory authorities. Hence the term Data Protection Authorities or Supervisory Authorities used here.
2. Strasbourg Convention 108, article 13.
3. Directive 95/46, article 28.
4. Paragraph 41.
5. GDPR, Recital 117.

[15.03] Member States can have more than one Supervisory Authority; as the GDPR provides:

> Member States should be able to establish more than one supervisory authority, to reflect their constitutional, organisational and administrative structure [6]

EU data protection law requires, in effect, that Member States have at least two Supervisory Authorities: one to supervise data protection in general, and one to supervise data protection in relation to data processing by courts. GDPR, article 55(3) provides that Supervisory Authorities will '… not be competent to supervise processing operations of courts acting in their judicial capacity'.[7] This does not mean data processing by the courts will go unsupervised; the Recitals suggest that:

> It should be possible to entrust supervision of such data processing operations to specific bodies within the judicial system of the Member State, which should, in particular ensure compliance with the rules of this Regulation, enhance awareness among members of the judiciary of their obligations under this Regulation and handle complaints in relation to such data processing operations.[8]

If, or rather when, a Member State has established '… more than one supervisory authority …' then:

> … that Member State shall designate the supervisory authority which is to represent those authorities in the Board and shall set out the mechanism to ensure compliance by the other authorities with the rules relating to the consistency mechanism referred to in Article 63.[9]

This effectively requires that each Member State designate a lead Supervisory Authority, which will attend the EDPB and take responsibility for ensuring that its other national Supervisory Authorities comply with the GDPR's consistency mechanism. The GDPR provides:

> Where a Member State establishes several supervisory authorities, it should establish by law mechanisms for ensuring the effective participation of those supervisory authorities in the consistency mechanism. That Member State should in particular designate the supervisory authority which functions as a single contact point for the effective participation of those authorities in the mechanism, to ensure swift and smooth cooperation with other supervisory authorities, the Board and the Commission.[10]

[15.04] At least one Supervisory Authority must be established prior to 25 May 2018. Member States must notify to the Commission the provisions of the law upon which their Supervisory Authority has been established before that date '… and, without delay, any subsequent amendment affecting them'.[11]

---

6.   GDPR, Recital 117.
7.   GDPR, article 55(3).
8.   GDPR, Recital 20.
9.   GDPR, article 51(3).
10.   GDPR, Recital 119.
11.   GDPR, article 51(4).

Each member of a Supervisory Authority must be appointed by means of a 'transparent procedure'. This appointment must be made by either the Member States parliament, government, head of State or an independent body entrusted with the appointment under Member State law.[12] Each member must have '… the qualifications, experience and skills, in particular in the area of the protection of personal data, required to perform its duties and exercise its powers'.[13] Article 52 states that each Member State shall provide for all of the following by law:

(a)   the establishment of each supervisory authority;

(b)   the qualifications and eligibility conditions required to be appointed as member of each supervisory authority;

(c)   the rules and procedures for the appointment of the member or members of each supervisory authority;

(d)   the duration of the term of the member or members of each supervisory authority of no less than four years;[14]

(e)   whether and, if so, for how many terms the member or members of each supervisory authority is eligible for reappointment;

(f)   the conditions governing the obligations of the member or members and staff of each supervisory authority, prohibitions on actions, occupations and benefits incompatible therewith during and after the term of office and rules governing the cessation of employment.[15]

[15.05] Members and staff of a Supervisory Authority will be subject to duties of professional secrecy:

> … with regard to any confidential information which has come to their knowledge in the course of the performance of their tasks or exercise of their powers.

This obligation shall apply '… both during and after their term of office …' however article 54 ends with a statement that:

> During their term of office, that duty of professional secrecy shall in particular apply to reporting by natural persons of infringements of this Regulation.[16]

[15.06] It is not made clear in the GDPR as to why the duty of professional secrecy makes this distinction between complaints received before or after a member's term of office, given that the obligation of professional secrecy continues to apply.

---

12.   GDPR, article 53(1).
13.   GDPR, article 53(2).
14.   The GDPR allows an exception to this '… for the first appointment after 24 May 2016, part of which may take place for a shorter period where that is necessary to protect the independence of the supervisory authority by means of a staggered appointment procedure …'.
15.   GDPR, article 54(1).
16.   GDPR, article 54(2).

TASKS

[15.07] Supervisory Authorities are not simply devoted to protecting the privacy of subjects. The CJEU expects that they will balance the right to privacy with the free movement of personal data and has indirectly considered how such a balance might be struck on a number of occasions. In *Schrems* the CJEU held that Supervisory Authorities:

> ... must ... ensure a fair balance between, on the one hand, observance of the fundamental right to privacy and, on the other hand, the interests requiring free movement of personal data ...[17]

In *Weltimmo* the Hungarian Supervisory Authority imposed a fine on a Slovakian website which was processing the personal data of Hungarian subjects. The CJEU held that the Hungarian Supervisory Authority would have jurisdiction if it found that the website had an establishment in Hungary; if there was no establishment then concerns about the processing of personal data would have to be raised with the Slovakian Supervisory Authority. The CJEU suggested that the Hungarian and Slovak Supervisory Authority might then co-operate, but also made clear that EU data protection law would not impede the free movement of personal data from Hungary to Slovakia. These supervisory authorities must 'contribute' to the consistent application of the GDPR throughout the EU. To this end the supervisory authorities must cooperate with each other and the EU Commission. They must do this '... in accordance with Chapter VII'.[18] Co-operation between Supervisory Authorities is discussed in further detail below.

[15.08] The tasks of Supervisory Authorities are listed in GDPR, article 57(1). This list is subject to two caveats: it is 'without prejudice to other tasks' set out in the GDPR, and; the tasks listed are to be carried out on the territory of the Supervisory Authority itself. Hence the GDPR does not purport to confer any power on Supervisory Authorities to carry out their tasks on each other's territory. And it does not confer any power on Supervisory Authorities to conduct tasks outside the EU. Hence the GDPR plainly does not intend to confer any power on Supervisory Authorities to act with extra-territorial effect. The tasks of Supervisory Authorities are as follows:

(a) monitor and enforce the application of the GDPR;

(b) promote public awareness and understanding of the risks, rules, safeguards and rights in relation to processing. Activities addressed specifically to children shall receive specific attention;[19]

---

17.   *Schrems* (Case C–362/14) (6 October 2015), para 42.
18.   GDPR, article 51(2).
19.   GDPR, Recital 132 provides that 'Awareness-raising activities by supervisory authorities addressed to the public should include specific measures directed at controllers and processors, including micro, small and medium-sized enterprises, as well as natural persons in particular in the educational context'.

(c) advise, in accordance with Member State law, the national parliament, the government, and other institutions and bodies on legislative and administrative measures relating to the protection of natural persons' rights and freedoms with regard to processing;

(d) promote the awareness of controllers and processors of their obligations under this Regulation;

(e) upon request, provide information to any data subject concerning the exercise of their rights under this Regulation and, if appropriate, cooperate with the supervisory authorities in other Member States to that end;

(f) handle complaints lodged by a data subject, or by a body, organisation or association in accordance with GDPR, article 80, and investigate, to the extent appropriate, the subject matter of the complaint and inform the complainant of the progress and the outcome of the investigation within a reasonable period, in particular if further investigation or coordination with another supervisory authority is necessary;[20]

(g) cooperate with, including sharing information and provide mutual assistance to, other supervisory authorities with a view to ensuring the consistency of application and enforcement of the GDPR;

(h) conduct investigations on the application of this Regulation, including on the basis of information received from another supervisory authority or other public authority;

(i) monitor relevant developments, insofar as they have an impact on the protection of personal data, in particular the development of information and communication technologies and commercial practices;

(j) adopt standard contractual clauses referred to in GDPR, article 28(8) and in point (d) of article 46(2);

(k) establish and maintain a list in relation to the requirement for data protection impact assessment pursuant to GDPR, article 35(4);

(l) give advice on the processing operations referred to in GDPR, article 36(2);

(m) encourage the drawing up of codes of conduct pursuant to article 40(1) and provide an opinion and approve such codes of conduct which provide sufficient safeguards, pursuant to GDPR, article 40(5);

(n) encourage the establishment of data protection certification mechanisms and of data protection seals and marks pursuant to article 42(1), and approve the criteria of certification pursuant to GDPR, article 42(5);

---

20. In respect of this article 57(2) provides that Supervisory Authorities must '... facilitate the submission of complaints ... by measures such as a complaint submission form which can also be completed electronically, without excluding other means of communication'.

(o) where applicable, carry out a periodic review of certifications issued in accordance with GDPR, article 42(7);

(p) draft and publish the criteria for accreditation of a body for monitoring codes of conduct pursuant to Article 41 and of a certification body pursuant to GDPR, article 43;

(q) conduct the accreditation of a body for monitoring codes of conduct pursuant to article 41 and of a certification body pursuant to GDPR, article 43;

(r) authorise contractual clauses and provisions referred to in GDPR, article 46(3);

(s) approve binding corporate rules pursuant to GDPR, article 47;

(t) contribute to the activities of the Board;

(u) keep internal records of infringements of this Regulation and of measures taken in accordance with GDPR, article 58(2); and

(v) fulfil any other tasks related to the protection of personal data.

As the list above makes clear that the tasks of Supervisory Authorities are not just numerous they are also varied ranging from research, public information, supervision and enforcement, approving everything from contractual clauses, codes of conduct, corporate codes of governance and certifications. In addition to these tasks, contributing to the EDPB will also impose a significant burden on individual Supervisory Authorities. As will fulfilling 'any other tasks related to the protection of personal data'. Such tasks may include acting as supervisory authority under Member State's implementations of the Data Protection Directive 2016/680 or the ePrivacy Directive. Finally the Recitals suggest that:

> Member States may specify other tasks related to the protection of personal data under this Regulation.[21]

[15.09] One of the most significant tasks of Supervisory Authorities is the handling of complaints. In *Weltimmo* the CJEU held that:

> … when a supervisory authority receives a complaint … that authority may exercise its investigative powers irrespective of the applicable law and before even knowing which national law is applicable to the processing in question.[22]

This means that a Supervisory Authority may commence investigating a complaint that it receives before it has concluded that it has jurisdiction and, presumably, that the complaint is validly made. This follows from the judgment of the CJEU in *Schrems* in which a complaint about the processing of the applicant's data in the USA was made to the Irish Supervisory Authority. That complaint was rejected as:

> … the allegations raised by Mr Schrems in his complaint could not be profitably put forward since any question of the adequacy of data protection in the United

---

21. GDPR, Recital 129.
22. *Weltimmo* (Judgment) (Case C–230/14) (1 October 2015), para 57.

States had to be determined in accordance with Decision 2000/520 and the Commission had found in that decision that the United States ensured an adequate level of protection.[23]

[15.10] The CJEU held that this decision was incorrect as:

... it would be contrary to the system set up by Directive 95/46 ... for a Commission decision... to have the effect of preventing a national supervisory authority from examining a person's claim concerning the protection of his rights and freedoms in regard to the processing of his personal data which has been or could be transferred from a Member State to the third country covered by that decision.[24]

The CJEU accepted that '... when the national supervisory authorities examine a claim... concerning the compatibility of a Commission decision... with the protection of the privacy and of the fundamental rights and freedoms of individuals, they are not entitled to declare that decision invalid themselves'.[25] Only the CJEU could declare such a Decision invalid, but this did not mean that the Supervisory Authority could not investigate the claim. The CJEU held that what should happen was as follows:

... where a person whose personal data has been or could be transferred to a third country which has been the subject of a Commission decision ... lodges with a national supervisory authority a claim concerning the protection of his rights and freedoms in regard to the processing of that data ... it is incumbent upon the national supervisory authority to examine the claim with all due diligence[26]

[15.11] Article 57(1)(f) provides that it is one of the tasks of Supervisory Authorities to:

... handle complaints lodged by a data subject, or by a body, organisation or association in accordance with Article 80, and investigate, to the extent appropriate, the subject matter of the complaint and inform the complainant of the progress and the outcome of the investigation within a reasonable period, in particular if further investigation or coordination with another supervisory authority is necessary.

[15.12] Article 77 goes on to provide that subjects:

... have the right to lodge a complaint with a supervisory authority, in particular in the Member State of his or her habitual residence, place of work or place of the alleged infringement if the data subject considers that the processing of personal data relating to him or her infringes this Regulation.[27]

---

23. *Schrems* (Case C–362/14) (6 October 2015), para 29.
24. *Schrems* (Case C–362/14) (6 October 2015), para 56.
25. *Schrems* (Case C–362/14) (6 October 2015), para 62.
26. *Schrems* (Case C–362/14) (6 October 2015), para 63.
27. GDPR, article 77(1).

[15.13] A Supervisory Authority with which such a complaint is lodged must:

> ... inform the complainant on the progress and the outcome of the complaint including the possibility of a judicial remedy pursuant to Article 78 ...[28]

[15.14] Article 79 provides that this progress update must be provided within three months. If such an update is not provided, then the subject must have access to an effective judicial remedy.[29] The Recitals provide some further guidance as to how Supervisory Authorities should handle complaints:

> The investigation following a complaint should be carried out, subject to judicial review, to the extent that is appropriate in the specific case. The supervisory authority should inform the data subject of the progress and the outcome of the complaint within a reasonable period. If the case requires further investigation or coordination with another supervisory authority, intermediate information should be given to the data subject. In order to facilitate the submission of complaints, each supervisory authority should take measures such as providing a complaint submission form which can also be completed electronically, without excluding other means of communication.[30]

[15.15] Supervisory Authorities may well receive a great number of complaints, once the GDPR applies and may wish to prioritise some of those complaints in order to manage those volumes. The CJEU has held that the EU Commission can prioritise complaints of breaches of competition law in this way. In *Automec v EU Commission*[31] the CJEU held that:

> ... in the case of an authority entrusted with a public service task, the power to take all the organizational measures necessary for the performance of that task, including setting priorities within the limits prescribed by the law where those priorities have not been determined by the legislature is an inherent feature of administrative activity. This must be the case in particular where an authority has been entrusted with a supervisory and regulatory task as extensive and general as that which has been assigned to the Commission in the field of competition. Consequently, the fact that the Commission applies different degrees of priority to the cases submitted to it in the field of competition is compatible with the obligations imposed on it by Community law.[32]

Supervisory Authorities are entrusted with tasks even more 'extensive and general' than those entrusted to the EU Commission in the field of competition law. However, this does not necessarily mean that Supervisory Authorities will be entitled to prioritise complaints in the same way as the EU Commission can in the field of competition. One of the reasons why the CJEU felt that the EU Commission could prioritise complaints was because '... the Commission is under no obligation to rule on the existence or otherwise of an infringement ...'[33] in the field of competition. In contrast the GDPR

---

28.   GDPR, article 77(2).
29.   GDPR, article 78(2).
30.   GDPR, Recital 141.
31.   *Automec v EU Commission* (Case T–24/90) (18 September 1992).
32.   *Automec v EU Commission* (Case T–24/90) (18 September 1992), para 77.
33.   *Automec v EU Commission* (Case T–24/90) (18 September 1992), para 76.

clearly requires that data subjects be informed of the outcome of their complaint and enables them to complain to Court if a Supervisory Authority '… does not handle a complaint or does not inform the data subject within three months on the progress or outcome of the complaint …'.[34] Whatever discretion Supervisory Authorities may have to prioritise one complaint or type of complaint over another, Supervisory Authorities must progress or conclude those complaints within a three-month period. Therefore, if Supervisory Authorities have any discretion as regards prioritisation, that discretion is limited by this three-month period.

POWERS

[15.16] As the CJEU explained in *Weltimmo* under Directive 95/46:

> … national supervisory authorities have a wide range of powers … Those powers … constitute necessary means to perform their duties … Thus, those authorities possess … investigative powers, such as the power to collect all the information necessary for the performance of their supervisory duties, effective powers of intervention, such as that of imposing a temporary or definitive ban on processing of data, and the power to engage in legal proceedings.[35]

[15.17] GDPR article 58 expands on Directive 95/46, providing that Supervisory Authorities have investigative, corrective, authorisation and advisory powers. It goes on to provide that Supervisory Authorities' exercise of these powers:

> … shall be subject to appropriate safeguards, including effective judicial remedy and due process, set out in Union and Member State law in accordance with the Charter.[36]

This statement is somewhat redundant since appropriate safeguards such as an effective judicial remedy[37] and rights of due process are already required by the Charter. The right to good administration is set out in article 41 of the Charter, para (2) of which provides that this right includes:

- the right of every person to be heard, before any individual measure which would affect him or her adversely is taken;
- the right of every person to have access to his or her file, while respecting the legitimate interests of confidentiality and of professional and business secrecy;
- the obligation of the administration to give reasons for its decisions.

The Recitals go onto suggest:

> The powers of supervisory authorities should be exercised in accordance with appropriate procedural safeguards set out in Union and Member State law,

---

34. GDPR, article 78(2).
35. *Schrems* (Case C–362/14) (6 October 2015), para 43.
36. GDPR, article 58(4).
37. See also article 47 of the Charter.

impartially, fairly and within a reasonable time. In particular each measure should be appropriate, necessary and proportionate in view of ensuring compliance with this Regulation, taking into account the circumstances of each individual case, respect the right of every person to be heard before any individual measure which would affect him or her adversely is taken and avoid superfluous costs and excessive inconveniences for the persons concerned.[38]

[15.18] Supervisory Authorities will have to ensure that subjects, controllers and processors will have at least the above rights respected. In the event of the Supervisory Authority failing to do so then access to effective judicial remedies will have to be ensured in accordance with article 47 of the Charter.[39] The GDPR itself provides:

> Without prejudice to any other administrative or non-judicial remedy, each natural or legal person shall have the right to an effective judicial remedy against a legally binding decision of a supervisory authority concerning them.[40]

[15.19] The GDPR provides that subjects have some specific rights that may be invoked against Supervisory Authorities:

> ... each data subject shall have the right to an effective judicial remedy where the supervisory authority which is competent pursuant to Articles 55 and 56 does not handle a complaint or does not inform the data subject within three months on the progress or outcome of the complaint lodged ...

It goes on to provide that:

> Proceedings against a supervisory authority shall be brought before the courts of the Member State where the supervisory authority is established.

Hence the powers of Supervisory Authorities are not unlimited; subjects, controllers, processors and others such as the not-for-profit body, organisation or associations referenced in GDPR, article 80 may challenge a Supervisory Authority's use of those powers before the Courts. One feature of GDPR, article 58 is that it neither requires nor permits the EU or Member States to further define or articulate those powers through their laws. This means that Supervisory Authorities will have to provide such definitions or articulations through their administrative processes. The GDPR does provide that: 'Each Member State may provide by law that its supervisory authority shall have additional powers to those referred to in paragraphs 1, 2 and 3'. The exercise of such powers may not impair the effective operation of the cooperation and consistency mechanism set out in Ch VII. Member States can add to these powers, but cannot define

---

38. GDPR, Recital 129.
39. 'Everyone whose rights and freedoms guaranteed by the law of the Union are violated has the right to an effective remedy before a tribunal ... Everyone is entitled to a fair and public hearing within a reasonable time by an independent and impartial tribunal previously established by law. Everyone shall have the possibility of being advised, defended and represented. Legal aid shall be made available to those who lack sufficient resources in so far as such aid is necessary to ensure effective access to justice,' Charter, article 47.
40. GDPR, article 78(1).

or adapt them. The only adaptation that article 58 allows Member States to make is the following:

> Each Member State shall provide by law that its supervisory authority shall have the power to bring infringements of this Regulation to the attention of the judicial authorities and where appropriate, to commence or engage otherwise in legal proceedings, in order to enforce the provisions of this Regulation.[41]

INVESTIGATIVE POWERS

[15.20] Article 58(1) provides that each Supervisory Authority shall have the following investigative powers:

(a) to order the controller and the processor, and, where applicable, the controller's or the processor's representative to provide any information it requires for the performance of its tasks;

(b) to carry out investigations in the form of data protection audits;

(c) to carry out a review on certifications issued pursuant to GDPR, article 42(7);

(d) to notify the controller or the processor of an alleged infringement of this Regulation;

(e) to obtain, from the controller and the processor, access to all personal data and to all information necessary for the performance of its tasks; and

(f) to obtain access to any premises of the controller and the processor, including to any data processing.

As regards investigatory powers the Recitals suggest that:

> Investigatory powers as regards access to premises should be exercised in accordance with specific requirements in Member State procedural law, such as the requirement to obtain a prior judicial authorisation. Each legally binding measure of the supervisory authority should be in writing, be clear and unambiguous, indicate the supervisory authority which has issued the measure, the date of issue of the measure, bear the signature of the head, or a member of the supervisory authority authorised by him or her, give the reasons for the measure, and refer to the right of an effective remedy. This should not preclude additional requirements pursuant to Member State procedural law. The adoption of a legally binding decision implies that it may give rise to judicial review in the Member State of the supervisory authority that adopted the decision.[42]

CORRECTIVE POWERS

[15.21] Article 58(2) provides that each Supervisory Authority shall have the following corrective powers:

(a) to issue warnings to a controller or processor that intended processing operations are likely to infringe provisions of this Regulation;

---

41. GDPR, article 58(5).
42. GDPR, Recital 129.

(b) to issue reprimands to a controller or a processor where processing operations have infringed provisions of this Regulation;

(c) to order the controller or the processor to comply with the data subject's requests to exercise his or her rights pursuant to this Regulation;

(d) to order the controller or processor to bring processing operations into compliance with the provisions of this Regulation, where appropriate, in a specified manner and within a specified period;

(e) to order the controller to communicate a personal data breach to the data subject;

(f) to impose a temporary or definitive limitation including a ban on processing;

(g) to order the rectification or erasure of personal data or restriction of processing pursuant to GDPR, articles 16, 17 and 18 and the notification of such actions to recipients to whom the personal data have been disclosed pursuant to GDPR, article 17(2) and article 19;

(h) to withdraw a certification or to order the certification body to withdraw a certification issued pursuant to GDPR, articles 42 and 43, or to order the certification body not to issue certification if the requirements for the certification are not or are no longer met;

(i) to impose an administrative fine pursuant to GDPR, article 83, in addition to, or instead of measures referred to in this paragraph, depending on the circumstances of each individual case;

(j) to order the suspension of data flows to a recipient in a third country or to an international organisation.

AUTHORISATION AND ADVISORY POWERS

[15.22] Article 58(3) provides that each Supervisory Authority shall have the following authorisation and advisory powers:

(a) to advise the controller in accordance with the prior consultation procedure referred to in article 36;

(b) to issue, on its own initiative or on request, opinions to the national parliament, the Member State government or, in accordance with Member State law, to other institutions and bodies as well as to the public on any issue related to the protection of personal data;

(c) to authorise processing referred to in article 36(5), if the law of the Member State requires such prior authorisation;

(d) to issue an opinion and approve draft codes of conduct pursuant to article 40(5);

(e) to accredit certification bodies pursuant to article 43;

(f) to issue certifications and approve criteria of certification in accordance with article 42(5);

(g) to adopt standard data protection clauses referred to in article 28(8) and in point (d) of article 46(2);

(h) to authorise contractual clauses referred to in point (a) of article 46(3);

(i) to authorise administrative arrangements referred to in point (b) of article 46(3);

(j) to approve binding corporate rules pursuant to article 47.

ANNUAL REPORTS

[15.23] Each Supervisory Authority, not just a Member State's lead Supervisory Authority, must prepare an annual report on its activities, which may include '… a list of types of infringement notified and types of measures taken in accordance with Article 58(2)'.[43] So the annual report may list corrective measures taken, but this seems to be at the option of the individual Supervisory Authority. There is no suggestion that the annual report list the uses of other investigative, authorisation or advisory powers. This report must be published. Article 59 goes on to provide that it:

> … shall be transmitted to the national parliament, the government and other authorities as designated by Member State law. They shall be made available to the public, to the Commission and to the Board.

ADMINISTRATIVE FINES

[15.24] The Recitals provide that:

> In order to strengthen the enforcement of the rules of this Regulation, penalties including administrative fines should be imposed for any infringement of this Regulation …[44]

GDPR, article 83 provides that Supervisory Authorities must impose administrative fines that are '… effective, proportionate and dissuasive'.[45] The meaning of this phrase has been considered by the CJEU on a number of occasions in contexts other than EU data protection law. In *Texdata Software*[46] the CJEU considered what were appropriate penalties for breaches of national implementations of the Eleventh Council Directive 89/666/EEC concerning disclosure requirements in respect of branches opened in a Member State by certain types of company governed by the law of another State.[47]

---

43. GDPR, article 59.

44. GDPR, Recital 148.

45. Where administrative fines are imposed on an undertaking, Recital 150 notes that an undertaking should be understood to be an undertaking in accordance with TFEU, Articles 101 and 102 for those purposes. An undertaking for the purposes of TFEU, Articles 101 and 102 is an economic unit (*Mo Och Domsjö AB v Commission* (Case T–352/94), [1998] ECR II–1989, para 87; *General Química v Commission* (Case C–90/09 P), [2011] ECR I–1, paras 34–36). It may comprise several natural or legal persons, which may be referred to as a 'single economic entity' *Hydrotherm Gerätebau v Compact* (Case 170/83), [1984] ECR 2999, para 11.

46. *Texdata Software* (Case C–418/11) (26 September 2013).

47. OJ L 395, 30.12.1989, p 36–39.

Unlike the GDPR, the Eleventh Directive did not 'establish any explicit criterion for the assessment of the proportionality of such penalties'. However, the CJEU considered it appropriate that '... infringements of EU law are penalised under conditions which make the penalty effective, proportionate and dissuasive'.[48] The Court went on to repeat that: '... the severity of penalties must be commensurate with the seriousness of the infringements for which they are imposed, in particular by ensuring a genuinely deterrent effect, while respecting the general principle of proportionality'.[49] What this meant was that measures in national legislation:

> ... must not exceed the limits of what is appropriate and necessary in order to attain the objectives legitimately pursued by the legislation in question: where there is a choice between several appropriate measures, recourse must be had to the least onerous, and the disadvantages caused must not be disproportionate to the aims pursued.[50]

[15.25] The penalties at issue in *Texdata Software* were imposed in respect of failures to comply with disclosure obligations pursuant to Directive 89/666/EEC. The CJEU noted that the minimum penalty imposed was '... the average amount imposed by Member States for breach of the disclosure obligation',[51] which suggests that when imposing such a penalty, a Supervisory Authority may take the level of penalty imposed elsewhere in the EU into account. The CJEU went on to agree with the EU Commission that the severity of penalty had to be weighed against the interests of those disadvantaged by the non-disclosure. This lends support to a view that the severity of penalty imposed on controllers and processors must be weighed against the interests of subjects whose rights have been breached.

[15.26] The Recitals offer some limited guidance as to what may amount to a proportional penalty, providing that:

> In a case of a minor infringement or if the fine likely to be imposed would constitute a disproportionate burden to a natural person, a reprimand may be issued instead of a fine.[52]

They also provide that:

> Where administrative fines are imposed on persons that are not an undertaking, the supervisory authority should take account of the general level of income in the

---

48. *Texdata Software* (Case C–418/11) (26 September 2013), para 50.
49. Citing by analogy, *Asociaţia Accept* (Case C–81/12), *Texdata Software* (Case C–418/11) (26 September 2013), para 51.
50. *Texdata Software* (Case C–418/11) (26 September 2013), para 52. A more concise explanation of what proportionality means in the context of penalties was given by the CJEU in *Urbán* (Case C–210/10), para 53: '... penalties must not ...exceed the limits of what is necessary in order to attain the objectives legitimately pursued by the legislation in question or be disproportionate to those aims'.
51. *Texdata Software* (Case C–418/11) (26 September 2013), para 57.
52. GDPR, Recital 148.

Member State as well as the economic situation of the person in considering the appropriate amount of the fine.[53]

[15.27] The proportionality of a penalty was considered by the CJEU in *Euro-Team*[54] which concerned a Hungarian system of fixed penalties for failing to pay motorway tolls. The CJEU held that '… the Hungarian system of penalties, in light of the severity of the penalties and their regular imposition, is effective and dissuasive'.[55] The fines imposed however failed '… to take account of the nature and gravity of the offence committed' and did not '… take into account the distance travelled without the toll having been paid'.[56] The CJEU therefore held that the Hungarian system of penalties was disproportionate.

Another judgment concerning the imposition of disproportionate penalties under Hungarian law is *Urbán*.[57] The law in question imposed fixed penalties on anyone who breached Council Regulation 3821/85 on recording equipment in road transport,[58] which required that drivers enter on record sheets '… the kilometre count at the end of the last journey recorded on the sheet'.[59] The driver in question had failed to do this and was fined €332.[60] The CJEU held that the Hungarian system of penalties appeared to be disproportionate as:

> … only one out of the 15 discs checked was found not to have been completed properly … In addition, … the failure to complete the recording disc at issue in the main proceedings could not have constituted an abuse inasmuch as the information missing from the record sheet was in fact set out on the bill of lading.[61]

The CJEU went on to note that:

> … the amount of that fine is almost equivalent to the average monthly net income of an employee in Hungary. Consequently, the severity of the penalty appears, in the main proceedings, to be disproportionate to the infringement committed.[62]

A fine must be proportionate, but it must also be dissuasive.[63] The dissuasiveness of a penalty was considered by the CJEU in *LCL*.[64] This concerned a national

---

53. GDPR, Recital 150.
54. *Euro-Team* (Case C–497/15) (22 March 2017).
55. *Euro-Team* (Case C–497/15) (22 March 2017), para 46.
56. *Euro-Team* (Case C–497/15) (22 March 2017), para 47.
57. *Urbán* (Case C–210/10).
58. OJ 1985 L 370, p 8.
59. *Urbán* (Case C–210/10), para 31.
60. *Urbán* (Case C–210/10), para 14.
61. *Urbán* (Case C–210/10), para 56.
62. *Urbán* (Case C–210/10), para 56.
63. In this context it should be noted that one of the objectives of the regulation in question was '…the improvement of working conditions of drivers to whom those regulations apply and the improvement of road safety in general' as well as 'the establishment of common rules on driving times, drivers' breaks and rest periods and their monitoring' *Urbán* (Case C–210/10), para 25.
64. *LCL* (Case C–565/12) (27 March 2014).

implementation of Directive 2008/48/EC on credit agreements for consumers which penalised lenders that failed to check a borrower's credit-worthiness. The penalty in question replaced contractual with statutory interest rates. These would typically be higher and so to the creditor's benefit. Such a penalty, the CJEU suggested, would not be 'genuinely dissuasive'.[65]

[15.28] Administrative fines must be imposed in addition to or instead of, the corrective measures set out in article 58(2)(a) to (h) and (j) depending on the circumstances of each individual case. In other words, fines must be imposed in addition to or instead of warnings, reprimands, orders to comply with data subjects' requests to exercise their rights or bring processing operations into compliance, orders to the controller to communicate a data breach to a data subject, the imposition of a temporary or definitive limitation including a ban on processing, orders to rectify or erase personal data or restrict of processing and notify recipients, withdraw a certification or order the certification body to withdraw a certificate issued or order the suspension of data flows to a recipient in a third country or international organisation.

In deciding whether to impose an administrative fine and deciding on the amount of the administrative fine in each individual case, article 83(2) provides that regard must be had to the following:

> (a) the nature, gravity and duration of the infringement taking into account the nature, scope or purpose of the processing concerned as well as the number of data subjects affected and the level of damage suffered by them;

WP29 has suggested that should a number of different infringements occur together then the supervisory authority will be '... able to apply the administrative fines at a level which is effective, proportionate and dissuasive within the limit of the gravest infringement'. WP29 goes onto suggest that supervisory authorities should have regard to 'whether this is an isolated event or symptomatic of a more systemic breach or lack of adequate routines in place'. Whilst damage to subjects may be taking into account when setting fines, WP29 notes that 'the supervisory authority itself is not competent to award the specific compensation for the damage suffered'. In addition the 'imposition of a fine is not dependent on the ability of the supervisory authority to establish a causal link between the breach and the material loss'. Finally as regards duration, WP29 suggests that this may be illustrative of 'wilful conduct on the data controller's part ... failure to take appropriate preventive measures, or ... inability to put in place the required technical and organisational measures'.[66]

> (b) the intentional or negligent character of the infringement;

WP29 has suggested that '... intentional breaches, demonstrating contempt for the provisions of the law, are more severe than unintentional ones and therefore may be

---

65. *LCL* (Case C–565/12) (27 March 2014), para 51, citing *Commission v United Kingdom* (Case C–382/92), paras 56–58.
66. Article 29 Working Party, *Guidelines on the application and setting of administrative fines for the purposes of the Regulation* 2016/679, 17/EN WP 253, 3 October 2017, pp 10–11.

more likely to warrant the application of an administrative fine'. WP29 suggests that an intentional breach might encompass 'unlawful processing authorised explicitly by the top management hierarchy of the controller, or in spite of advice from the data protection officer or in disregard for existing policies'.[67]

> (c) any action taken by the controller or processor to mitigate the damage suffered by data subjects;

WP29 has noted that the experience of supervisory authorities under Directive 95/46 has shown that '... it can be appropriate to show some degree of flexibility to those data controllers/processors who have admitted to their infringement and taken responsibility to correct or limit the impact of their actions'. Such taking of responsibility might include 'timely action ... to stop the infringement from continuing or expanding to a level or phase which would have had a far more serious impact than it did'.[68]

> (d) the degree of responsibility of the controller or processor taking into account technical and organisational measures implemented by them pursuant to articles 25 and 32;

WP29 has suggested that the question this raises for supervisory authorities is 'to what extent the controller 'did what it could be expected to do' given the nature, the purposes or the size of the processing, seen in light of the obligations imposed on them by the Regulation.[69]

> (e) any relevant previous infringements by the controller or processor;

WP29 has suggested that this is 'meant to assess the track record of the entity committing the infringement' and that supervisory authorities should assess whether '... the controller/processor committed the same infringement earlier ... (or) committed an infringement of the Regulation in the same manner?'. [70]

> (f) the degree of cooperation with the supervisory authority, in order to remedy the infringement and mitigate the possible adverse effects of the infringement;

WP29 has suggested that this might entail asking whether the entity in question has '... responded in a particular manner to the supervisory authority's requests during the investigation phase in that specific case which has significantly limited the impact on individuals' rights as a result?'.[71]

> (g) the categories of personal data affected by the infringement;

---

67. Article 29 Working Party, *Guidelines on the application and setting of administrative fines for the purposes of the Regulation* 2016/679, 17/EN WP 253, 3 October 2017, p 12.

68. Article 29 Working Party, *Guidelines on the application and setting of administrative fines for the purposes of the Regulation* 2016/679, 17/EN WP 253, 3 October 2017, p 13.

69. Article 29 Working Party, *Guidelines on the application and setting of administrative fines for the purposes of the Regulation* 2016/679, 17/EN WP 253, 3 October 2017, p 13.

70. Article 29 Working Party, *Guidelines on the application and setting of administrative fines for the purposes of the Regulation* 2016/679, 17/EN WP 253, 3 October 2017, p 14.

71. Article 29 Working Party, *Guidelines on the application and setting of administrative fines for the purposes of the Regulation* 2016/679, 17/EN WP 253, 3 October 2017, p 14.

WP29 has suggested that this might raise questions such as whether the data in question is special, whether the subjects are directly identified or identifiable, would the dissemination of the data cause immediate damage or distress to subjects or whether the data is encrypted.[72]

    (h) the manner in which the infringement became known to the supervisory authority, in particular whether, and if so to what extent, the controller or processor notified the infringement;

WP29 has suggested that '... a data controller/processor who acted carelessly without notifying, or at least not notifying all of the details of the infringement due to a failure to adequately assess the extent of the infringement may also be considered by the supervisory authority to merit a more serious penalty ie it is unlikely to be classified as a minor infringement'.[73]

    (i) where measures referred to in article 58(2) have previously been ordered against the controller or processor concerned with regard to the same subject-matter, compliance with those measures;

WP29 has suggested that unlike criteria (e) above 'this assessment criteria only seeks to remind supervisory authorities to refer to measures that they themselves have previously issued to the same controller or processors "with regard to the same subject matter"'. [74]

    (j) adherence to approved codes of conduct pursuant to article 40 or approved certification mechanisms pursuant to article 42; and

WP29 has suggested that where a controller or processor has adhered to an approved code of conduct then '... the supervisory authority may be satisfied that the code community in charge of administering the code takes the appropriate action themselves against their member, for example through the monitoring and enforcement schemes of the code of conduct itself. Therefore, the supervisory authority might consider that such measures are effective, proportionate or dissuasive enough in that particular case without the need for imposing additional measures from the supervisory authority itself'.[75]

    (k) any other aggravating or mitigating factor applicable to the circumstances of the case, such as financial benefits gained, or losses avoided, directly or indirectly, from the infringement.[76]

---

72. Article 29 Working Party, *Guidelines on the application and setting of administrative fines for the purposes of the Regulation* 2016/679, 17/EN WP 253, 3 October 2017, pp 14–15.

73. Article 29 Working Party, *Guidelines on the application and setting of administrative fines for the purposes of the Regulation* 2016/679, 17/EN WP 253, 3 October 2017, p 15.

74. Article 29 Working Party, *Guidelines on the application and setting of administrative fines for the purposes of the Regulation* 2016/679, 17/EN WP 253, 3 October 2017, p 15.

75. Article 29 Working Party, *Guidelines on the application and setting of administrative fines for the purposes of the Regulation* 2016/679, 17/EN WP 253, 3 October 2017, p 15.

76. Article 83(2).

WP29 has suggested that 'Information about profit obtained as a result of a breach may be particularly important for the supervisory authorities as economic gain from the infringement cannot be compensated through measures that do not have a pecuniary component. As such, the fact that the controller had profited from the infringement of the Regulation may constitute a strong indication that a fine should be imposed'.[77]

[15.29] In circumstances where a controller or processor 'intentionally or negligently' infringes several provisions of the GDPR for the same or linked processing operations, article 83(3) provides that the total amount of the administrative fine must:

> not exceed the amount specified for the gravest infringement.

Article 83(4) provides for two sets of administrative fines for breaches of certain provisions of the GDPR. Administrative fines of up to €10,000,000 or in the case of an undertaking, up to 2% of the total worldwide annual turnover of the preceding financial year, whichever is higher, must imposed for infringements of the following provisions:

(a) the obligations of the controller and the processor pursuant to article 8 (conditions applicable to a child's consent), article 11 (processing which does not require identification), articles 25 to 39 (data protection by design and default, joint controller's obligations, representatives of controllers or processors not established in the Union, Processors, processing under the authority of the controller or processor, Records of processing activities, cooperation with the supervisory authority, security of personal data, notification of breaches to the supervisory authority, communication of a breach to the data subject, data protection impact assessment and prior consultation, the data protection officer) and article 42 (certification) and article 43 (certification bodies);

(b) the obligations of the certification body pursuant to articles 42 and 43;

(c) the obligations of the monitoring body pursuant to article 41(4).articleis Article requires the monitoring body to take appropriate action in cases of infringement of the code by a controller or processor including suspension or exclusion of the controller or processor from the code. It must also inform the competent supervisory authority of the actions taken and reasons for taking them.

[15.30] Administrative fines up to €20,000,000 or in the case of an undertaking, up to 4% of the total worldwide annual turnover of the preceding financial year, whichever is higher, must be imposed for infringements of the following provisions:

(a) the basic principles for processing, including conditions for consent, pursuant to articles 5 (principles of data processing), 6 (lawfulness of processing), 7 (conditions for consent) and 9 (processing of special categories of personal data);

(b) the data subjects' rights pursuant to articles 12 to 22;

(c) the transfers of personal data to a recipient in a third country or an international organisation pursuant to articles 44 to 49;

---

77. Article 29 Working Party, *Guidelines on the application and setting of administrative fines for the purposes of the Regulation* 2016/679, 17/EN WP 253, 3 October 2017, p 16.

(d) any obligations pursuant to Member State law adopted under Ch IX (processing and freedom of expression, processing and public access to official documentation, processing of the national identification number, processing in the context of employment, safeguards and derogations relation to processing for archiving purposes in the public interest, scientific or historical research purposes or statistical purposes, obligations of secrecy, existing data protection rules of churches and religious associations);

(e) non-compliance with an order or a temporary or definitive limitation on processing or the suspension of data flows by the supervisory authority pursuant to article 58(2) or failure to provide access in violation of article 58(1).articlen-compliance with a corrective order by the supervisory authority in article 58(2) must, in accordance with article 83(2) above, be subject to administrative fines up to €20,000,000, or in the case of an undertaking, up to 4% of the total worldwide annual turnover of the preceding financial year, whichever is higher.articlethout prejudice to the supervisory authorities' corrective powers, each Member State may lay down the rules on whether and to what extent administrative fines may be imposed on public authorities and bodies established in that Member State.articleere administrative fines are imposed on an undertaking, the Recitals note that an undertaking should be understood to be an undertaking in accordance with TFEU, articles 101 and 102 for those purposes.[78] They add that where an administrative fine is imposed on persons other than an undertaking, the supervisory authority should take into account the general level of income in the Member State as well as the economic situation of the person concerned when considering the appropriate amount of the fine. The consistency mechanism, according to the Recitals, may also be used to promote a consistent application of administrative fines and each Member State should determine whether and to what extent public authorities should be subject to them.[79]

[15.31] The Recitals add that Member States should be able to lay down the rules on criminal penalties for infringements of the GDPR and of national rules adopted. Those criminal penalties may allow for the deprivation of the profits obtained through infringements of the GDPR. However, the imposition of such criminal penalties for breaches of national rules and of administrative penalties should not lead to a breach of

---

78. '... according to settled case law, the concept of an undertaking covers any entity engaged in an economic activity, regardless of its legal status and the way in which it is financed ... the term 'undertaking' must be understood as designating an economic unit even if in law that economic unit consists of several persons, natural or legal... As regards the question whether ... a legal person who is not the perpetrator of the infringement may none the less be penalised, it is apparent from the settled case law that the conduct of a subsidiary may be imputed to the parent company in particular when, although having a separate legal personality, that subsidiary does not decide independently upon its own conduct ... but carries out, in all material respects, the instructions given to it by the parent company, having regard in particular to the economic, organisational and legal links which tie those two legal entities,' *General Química* (Case C–90/09 P) (20 January 2011), paras 34–35, 37.
79. Recital 150.

the principles of *ne bis in idem*, as interpreted by the CJEU.[80] This means that a legal action cannot be instituted twice for the same cause of action, a principle more commonly known as 'double jeopardy'.[81] This principle is set out in article 50 of the Charter:

> No one shall be liable to be tried or punished again in criminal proceedings for an offence for which he or she has already been finally acquitted or convicted within the Union in accordance with the law.

This does not mean that a Member State cannot prosecute a controller or processor who has been subject to an administrative fine pursuant to article 83 or other restrictions pursuant to article 58. This follows from the CJEU decision in *Åkerberg Fransson*[82] which concerned a Swede who had made false tax returns, he was subject to a tax surcharge, effectively an administrative sanction as a result. He was then prosecuted. He challenged his prosecution on the basis of *ne bis in idem*; the CJEU held that this principle:

> does not preclude a Member State from imposing successively, for the same acts of non-compliance with declaration obligations in the field of value added tax, a tax penalty and a criminal penalty in so far as the first penalty is not criminal in nature ...[83]

What *ne bis in idem* does mean is that if a prosecution has been concluded in one Member State then proceedings cannot be brought against the same person, for the same offence, in another.[84] A prosecution must be brought to a conclusion for the principle to apply; the mere closure of an investigation may be insufficient.[85]

---

80. GDPR, Recital 149. The significance of the reference to the case law of the CJEU is that it incorporates judgments of the ECJ (as it then was) which predate the incorporation of the Charter into EU law in 2009 (see *Åkerberg Fransson* (Case C–617/10) (26 February 2013).

81. 'The State should not be allowed to make repeated attempts to convict an individual for an alleged offence. Once a trial has been carried out, surrounded by all the appropriate procedural guarantees, and the issue of the individual's possible debt to society has been assessed, the State should not subject him to the ordeal of a new trial (or, as Anglo-American legal systems describe it, to place him in 'double jeopardy'). As Black J of the Supreme Court of the United States concisely put it, 'the underlying idea ... is that the State with all its resources and power should not be allowed to make repeated attempts to convict an individual for an alleged offence ...' *Gasparini* (Case C–467/04), Opinion of Advocate General Sharpston, 15 June 2006, para 72.

82. *Åkerberg Fransson* (Case C–467/04) (26 February 2013).

83. *Åkerberg Fransson* (Case C–467/04) (26 February 2013), para 50.

84. 'The *ne bis in idem* principle ... also applies to procedures whereby further prosecution is barred, such as the procedures at issue in the main actions, by which the Public Prosecutor of a Member State discontinues criminal proceedings brought in that State, without the involvement of a court, once the accused has fulfilled certain obligations and, in particular, has paid a certain sum of money determined by the Public Prosecutor,' *Gözütok and Brügge* (Joined Cases C–187/01 and C–385/01), CJEU, (11 February 2003).

85. '... a decision of the public prosecutor terminating criminal proceedings and finally closing the investigation procedure against a person, albeit with the possibility of its being reopened or annulled, without any penalties having been imposed, (contd .../)

[15.32] The CJEU has repeatedly emphasised that 'in all proceedings in which sanctions, especially fines or penalty payments, may be imposed, observance of the rights of the defence is a fundamental principle of Community law'.[86] Consistent with this approach the CJEU provides that when exercising its powers to impose administrative fines, supervisory authorities must be subject to appropriate procedural safeguards in accordance with Union[87] and Member State law. This includes an effective judicial remedy and due process. Every Member State's legal system provides for administrative fines (the Recitals specify Denmark and Estonia in this regard). The GDPR provides that in such cases article 83 may be applied in such a manner that the fine is initiated by the competent supervisory authority and imposed by competent national courts, while ensuring that those legal remedies are effective and have an equivalent effect to the administrative fines imposed by supervisory authorities. In any event, the fines imposed must be effective, proportionate and dissuasive.[88] The Recitals note that in Denmark the fine is imposed by competent national courts as a criminal penalty and in Estonia the fine is imposed by the supervisory authority in the framework of a misdemeanour procedure provided they have equivalent effect.[89]

OTHER PENALTIES

[15.33] Administrative fines are not the only penalties that may be imposed pursuant to the GDPR, although the GDPR leaves it to Member States to define what these penalties are. Article 84 requires Member States to lay down the rules on other penalties for infringements of the GDPR, in particular for infringements which are not subject to administrative fines and they must take all measures necessary to ensure that they are implemented. Those penalties again must be effective, proportionate and dissuasive.[90]

---

85. (contd) cannot be characterised as a final decision for the purposes of those articles when it is clear from the statement of reasons for that decision that the procedure was closed without a detailed investigation having been carried out ...' *Kossowski* (Case C–486/14) (29 June 2016), para 56.
86. *Groupe Danone v Commission* (Case C–3/06) (8 February 2007), para 68.
87. And the Charter according to Recital 148.
88. Those Member States must notify the Commission of the provisions of their laws which they adopt pursuant to this by 25 May 2018 and, any subsequent amendment law or amendment without delay: article 83(9).
89. 'The legal systems of Denmark and Estonia do not allow for administrative fines as set out in this Regulation. The rules on administrative fines may be applied in such a manner that in Denmark the fine is imposed by competent national courts as a criminal penalty and in Estonia the fine is imposed by the supervisory authority in the framework of a misdemeanour procedure, provided that such an application of the rules in those Member States has an equivalent effect to administrative fines imposed by supervisory authorities. Therefore the competent national courts should take into account the recommendation by the supervisory authority initiating the fine. In any event, the fines imposed should be effective, proportionate and dissuasive,' Recital 151.
90. Each Member State must notify the Commission of such adopting provisions by 25 May 2018 and any subsequent amendments without delay, article 84(2).

Chapter 16

THE INDEPENDENCE OF SUPERVISORY AUTHORITIES

INTRODUCTION

[16.01] The establishment of independent Supervisory Authorities is '... an essential component of the protection of individuals with regard to the processing of personal data'.[1] It is a fundamental obligation of EU law, imposed by both article 8(2) of the Charter and TFEU, article 16(2). The latter provides that the EU's legislature must lay down the rules of data protection and that compliance with these rules:

> ... shall be subject to the control of independent authorities.

The requirement that Supervisory Authorities be independent is carried through to the GDPR, the Recitals to which explain:

> The establishment of supervisory authorities in Member States, empowered to perform their tasks and exercise their powers with complete independence, is an essential component of the protection of natural persons with regard to the processing of their personal data.[2]

[16.02] GDPR, Ch VI provides for such 'independent supervisory authorities'. Article 52(1) sets out the 'independent status' of such authorities:

> Each supervisory authority shall act with complete independence in performing its tasks and exercising its powers in accordance with this Regulation.

The meaning of 'complete independence' was considered by the CJEU in *Commission v Germany*,[3] which held that:

> In relation to a public body, the term 'independence' normally means a status which ensures that the body concerned can act completely freely, without taking any instructions or being put under any pressure.

[16.03] The CJEU then went on to consider what is meant by 'complete independence', holding that:

> ... there is nothing to indicate that the requirement of independence concerns exclusively the relationship between the supervisory authorities and the bodies

---

1. *Transfer of Passenger Name Record data from the European Union to Canada* [2017] EUECJ Avis-1/15_OC (26 July 2017), para 229.
2. GDPR, Recital 117. This adopts the wording of the CJEU in *Commission v Austria* (Case C–614/10) (16 October 2012): 'The establishment in Member States of independent supervisory authorities is thus an essential component of the protection of individuals with regard to the processing of personal data,' para 37.
3. *Commission v Germany* (Case C–518/07) (9 March 2010).

subject to that supervision. On the contrary, the concept of independence is complemented by the adjective 'complete', which implies a decision-making power independent of any direct or indirect external influence on the supervisory authority.[4]

The CJEU then went on to clearly explain why supervisory authorities are independent:

The guarantee of the independence of national supervisory authorities is intended to ensure the effectiveness and reliability of the supervision of compliance with the provisions on protection of individuals with regard to the processing of personal data and must be interpreted in the light of that aim. It was established not to grant a special status to those authorities themselves as well as their agents, but in order to strengthen the protection of individuals and bodies affected by their decisions. It follows that, when carrying out their duties, the supervisory authorities must act objectively and impartially. For that purpose, they must remain free from any external influence ... and not of the influence only of the supervised bodies.[5]

At issue in *Commission v Germany* was a German law, which allowed regional governments '... to influence, directly or indirectly, the decisions of the supervisory authorities or, as the case may be, to cancel and replace those decisions'.[6] The German government claimed that the purpose of this influence was not to enable regional governments to weaken the application of German or EU data protection law and that the German law did not '... aim to oblige those authorities potentially to pursue political objectives inconsistent with the protection of individuals with regard to the processing of personal data ...'.[7] But, the CJEU was concerned that the bodies undertaking this scrutiny were subject to '... the general administration and therefore under the control of the government ...'. In particular, the CJEU noted that German regional governments:

... may have an interest in not complying with the provisions with regard to the protection of personal data where the processing of such data by a non-public body is at issue. That government may itself be an interested party in that processing if it actually or potentially participates therein, for example, in the case of a public-private partnership or in the case of public contracts with the private sector. That government may also have a specific interest if it is necessary or even merely useful for it to have access to databases in order to fulfil certain of its functions, in particular for taxation or law enforcement purposes. Furthermore, that government may also tend to favour economic interests in the application of the provisions on the protection of individuals with regard to the processing of personal data by certain companies which are economically important for the ... region.[8]

---

4.   *Commission v Germany* (Case C–518/07) (9 March 2010), paras 18–19.
5.   *Commission v Germany* (Case C–518/07) (9 March 2010), para 25.
6.   *Commission v Germany* (Case C–518/07) (9 March 2010), para 32.
7.   *Commission v Germany* (Case C–518/07) (9 March 2010), para 33.
8.   *Commission v Germany* (Case C–518/07) (9 March 2010), para 35.

There was no need to prove an actual instance of where such interests had led a German regional government to inappropriately influence the local supervisory authority:

> … the mere risk that the scrutinising authorities could exercise a political influence over the decisions of the supervisory authorities is enough to hinder the latter authorities' independent performance of their tasks.

This led the CJEU to conclude:

> … State scrutiny exercised over the German supervisory authorities responsible for supervising the processing of personal data … is not consistent with the requirement of independence.[9]

[16.04] Complete independence, however, does not mean complete autonomy. Independent though supervisory authorities may be they are still subject to law and law enforcement in the normal way. This is clear from the judgment of the CJEU in *OLAF v ECB*,[10] in which the European Central Bank (ECB) argued that as an independent EU institution it did not fall within the jurisdiction of OLAF, the EU anti-fraud body.[11] The CJEU observed that:

> … recognition that the ECB has … independence does not have the consequence of separating it entirely from the European Community and exempting it from every rule of Community law …[12]

So if allegations of fraud were to be made against the office of a supervisory authority or its staff those allegations would be investigated by the relevant police or anti-fraud unit of the Member State. Of course it is not beyond possibility that such an investigation could infringe the independence of the supervisory authority, but it would be for that supervisory authority to establish that:

> … the fact that it is subject to measures adopted by the Community legislature in the area of fraud prevention and the prevention of any other unlawful activities detrimental to the European Community /[Member State]'s financial interests … is such as to undermine its ability to perform independently [its] specific tasks conferred on it by the EC Treaty.[13]

The GDPR makes clear that supervisory authorities will be subject to appropriate financial and audit controls. GDPR, article 52(6) provides:

> Each Member State shall ensure that each supervisory authority is subject to financial control which does not affect its independence …

---

9. *Commission v Germany* (Case C–518/07) (9 March 2010), para 37.
10. *Commission v BCE* (Case C–11/00) (10 July 2003).
11. 'OLAF investigates fraud against the EU budget, corruption and serious misconduct within the European institutions, and develops anti-fraud policy for the European Commission': https://ec.europa.eu/anti-fraud//home_en.
12. *Commission v BCE* (Case C–11/00) (10 July 2003), para 135.
13. *Commission v BCE* (Case C–11/00) (10 July 2003), para 137.

[16.05] Supervisory authorities will be democratically accountable as well as subject to financial audits. In *Commission v Germany* the CJEU considered whether '... the principle of democracy ... precludes a broad interpretation of that requirement of independence'. At issue was a German law, which allowed German regional authorities to review decisions of their local supervisory authority. The German government argued that this power of review was consistent with the principle of democracy[14] which '... requires that the administration be subject to the instructions of the government which is accountable to its parliament ...'.[15] However the CJEU held that this principle: '... does not preclude the existence of public authorities outside the classic hierarchical administration and more or less independent of the government.'[16] The CJEU did admit that '... the absence of any parliamentary influence over those authorities is inconceivable'. It went on to point out that the requirement of complete independence '... in no way makes such an absence of any parliamentary influence obligatory for the Member'. The CJEU suggested three ways in which a supervisory authority could be made democratically accountable:

1.   '... the management of the supervisory authorities may be appointed by the parliament or the government';

2.   '... the legislator may define the powers of those authorities'; and,

3.   '... the legislator may impose an obligation on the supervisory authorities to report their activities to the parliament'.[17]

This led the CJEU to conclude that:

> ... conferring a status independent of the general administration on the supervisory authorities responsible for the protection of individuals with regard to the processing of personal data outside the public sector does not in itself deprive those authorities of their democratic legitimacy.[18]

Supervisory authorities will also be subject to review by the courts in general and the CJEU in particular. GDPR, article 78(1) provides:

> Without prejudice to any other administrative or non-judicial remedy, each natural or legal person shall have the right to an effective judicial remedy against a legally binding decision of a supervisory authority concerning them.

[16.06] The Recitals expand upon the above, providing that:

> Every data subject should have ... the right to an effective judicial remedy ... if the data subject considers that his or her rights under this Regulation are infringed or where the supervisory authority does not act on a complaint, partially or wholly

---

14.   TEU, article 10.
15.   *Commission v Germany* (Case C–518/07) (9 March 2010), paras 39–40.
16.   *Commission v Germany* (Case C–518/07) (9 March 2010), para 42.
17.   *Commission v Germany* (Case C–518/07) (9 March 2010), paras 44–45.
18.   *Commission v Germany* (Case C–518/07) (9 March 2010), paras 46.

rejects or dismisses a complaint or does not act where such action is necessary to protect the rights of the data subject.[19]

The role of the courts in reviewing decisions of supervisory authorities was considered by the CJEU in *Schrems*. The applicant had made a complaint to the Irish supervisory authority '… by which he in essence asked the latter to exercise its statutory powers by prohibiting Facebook Ireland from transferring his personal data to the United States'.[20] The Irish supervisory authority concluded that this complaint could not be sustained, because the EU Commission deemed the Safe Harbour agreement between it and the US government provided for an adequate standard of data protection. The complainant disagreed with this decision. The CJEU began by recalling its settled case law that:

> … the European Union is a union based on the rule of law in which all acts of its institutions are subject to review of their compatibility with, in particular, the Treaties, general principles of law and fundamental rights …[21]

And so where:

> … the national supervisory authority comes to the conclusion that the arguments put forward in support of such a claim are unfounded and therefore rejects it, the person who lodged the claim must … have access to judicial remedies enabling him to challenge such a decision adversely affecting him before the national courts …[22]

So the independence of supervisory authorities is considerable, though not total. Article 52(2) goes on to provide that:

> The member or members of each supervisory authority shall, in the performance of their tasks and exercise of their powers in accordance with this Regulation, remain free from external influence, whether direct or indirect, and shall neither seek nor take instructions from anybody.

[16.07] In *Commission v Austria*[23] the CJEU held that functional independence was insufficient to fulfil the requirement of complete independence. The fact that members of the Austrian supervisory authority were '… independent and [are not] bound by instructions of any kind in the performance of their duties …' was a necessary but not sufficient condition for their complete independence. The CJEU held that the requirement of complete independence:

> … is intended to preclude not only direct influence, in the form of instructions, but also … any indirect influence which is liable to have an effect on the supervisory authority's decisions.[24]

The Austrian supervisory authority had a managing member who was an official of the Austrian federal government and in charge of managing its day-to-day business. It was

---

19. GDPR, Recital 141.
20. *Schrems* (Case C–362/14) (6 October 2015), para 28.
21. *Schrems* (Case C–362/14) (6 October 2015), para 60.
22. *Schrems* (Case C–362/14) (6 October 2015), para 64.
23. *Commission v Austria* (Case C–614/10) (16 October 2012).
24. *Commission v Austria* (Case C–614/10) (16 October 2012), para 43.

agreed that there was a: '… service-related link between the managing member and that federal authority which allows the activities of the managing member to be supervised by his hierarchical superior'.[25] The CJEU noted that Austrian law granted:

> … the hierarchical superior an extensive power of supervision over the officials in his department. That provision enables the hierarchical superior not only to ensure that his staff carry out their tasks in accordance with the law, efficiently and economically, but also to guide them in carrying out their duties, rectify any faults and omissions and ensure that working hours are adhered to, encourage the promotion of his staff in accordance with their performance and direct them to those tasks which correspond best to their capacities.[26]

Essentially the hierarchical superior had the ability to evaluate the performance of the managing Member. The CJEU accepted that Austrian law was '… designed to prevent the hierarchical superior from issuing instructions to the managing member' but went on to find that this law '… confers on the hierarchical superior a power of supervision that is liable to hinder the [Austria supervisory authority]'s operational independence'. This was because '… the evaluation of the managing member … by his hierarchical superior for the purposes of encouraging his promotion could lead to a form of "prior compliance" on the part of the managing member'.[27] The CJEU went on to conclude:

> … the role assumed by the supervisory authorities as guardians of the right to privacy … requires that their decisions, and therefore the authorities themselves, remain above all suspicion of partiality.[28]

This requirement of non-partiality is reflected in article 52, which requires that EU Member States must '… ensure that each supervisory authority chooses and has its own staff which shall be subject to the exclusive direction of the member or members of the supervisory authority concerned'.[29] GDPR, article 52 also restrains members of a supervisory authority '… from any action incompatible with their duties and shall not, during their term of office, engage in any incompatible occupation, whether gainful or not'.[30] The Recitals explain that this is requirement is imposed:

> In order to ensure the independence of the supervisory authority, the member or members should act with integrity, refrain from any action that is incompatible with their duties and should not, during their term of office, engage in any incompatible occupation, whether gainful or not.[31]

Article 54 requires that Member States stipulate by law which gains and occupations are incompatible with the role of supervisory authority member.[32]

---

25.   *Commission v Austria* (Case C–614/10) (16 October 2012), para 48.
26.   *Commission v Austria* (Case C–614/10) (16 October 2012), para 49.
27.   *Commission v Austria* (Case C–614/10) (16 October 2012), para 51.
28.   *Commission v Austria* (Case C–614/10) (16 October 2012), para 52.
29.   GDPR, article 52(5).
30.   GDPR, article 52(3).
31.   GDPR, Recital 121.
32.   GDPR, article 54(1)(f).

RESOURCES

[16.08] Adequate resources are essential if supervisory authorities are to function effectively. Unlike other supervisory authorities, such as financial or telecommunications supervisors, data protection Supervisory Authorities lack a mechanism to independently raise levies and fees from those that they regulate. Instead supervisory authorities must be directly funded by their Member States. This contrasts to the approach taken in relation to many EU banks, which are supervised pursuant to the Single Supervisory Mechanism (SSM) Regulation which provides: 'The costs of supervision should be borne by the entities subject to it'.[33] GDPR, article 52(4) provides:

> Each Member State shall ensure that each supervisory authority is provided with the human, technical and financial resources, premises and infrastructure necessary for the effective performance of its tasks and exercise of its powers, including those to be carried out in the context of mutual assistance, cooperation and participation in the Board.

Supervisory authorities have significant functions: investigating subject complaints, responding to prior consultation, audits, approval of codes of conduct, participation in EDPB and so forth. It seems likely that discharging these functions will give rise to significant work-loads. Some may wonder whether Member States will, in fact, be willing or able to adequately fund their respective supervisory authorities. Inadequate funding may then threaten supervisory authority independence. As the ECB has repeatedly stated in respect of National Central Banks (NCBs):

> Even if an NCB is fully independent from a functional, institutional and personal point of view … its overall independence would be jeopardised if it could not autonomously avail itself of sufficient financial resources to fulfil its mandate.[34]

Of course supervisory authorities are not NCBs and the supervision of data protection is very different from central banking. But it remains to be seen whether data protection Supervisory Authorities will, in fact, receive adequate funding from their member States. Article 52(4), it should be noted, does not require that supervisory authorities receive independent funding to allocate as they wish. Only that they are provided with a variety of resources: human, technical, financial, premises and infrastructure. Taken together these resources amount to what is 'necessary' for the supervisory authority to effectively perform its tasks. The supervisory authority should have a separate, public annual budget and, as noted above, it should be subject to appropriate financial control. However, the GDPR is silent on how this budget is to be assessed or how a dispute over funding between a supervisory authority and its Member State should be resolved. Should such a dispute arise then the supervisory authority in question might complain to the EU Commission, which might then prosecute the Member State in question before

---

33.   Council Regulation No 1024/2013/EU of 15 October 2013 conferring specific tasks on the European Central Bank concerning policies relating to the prudential supervision of credit institutions, OJ L 287, 29.10.2013, pp 63–89, Recital 77.

34.   ECB, *Convergence Report*, 2016, para 2.2.3, p 25.

the CJEU. Such a complaint is unlikely to make a positive contribution to the relationship between supervisory authority and Member State. Of course supervisory authorities have to be independent and may well become embroiled in disputes with their Member States about supervisory matters. It is therefore unfortunate that the GDPR does not provide more detail about the funding mechanism for supervisory authorities, as it would be preferable if they could avoid also becoming embroiled in disputes about their budget.

Supervisory Authorities may be able to charge for undertaking some, but not all of their tasks, which must be performed:

> ... free of charge for the data subject and, where applicable, for the data protection officer.[35]

[16.09] Article 57 continues to provide that:

> Where requests are manifestly unfounded or excessive, in particular because of their repetitive character, the supervisory authority may charge a reasonable fee based on administrative costs, or refuse to act on the request. The supervisory authority shall bear the burden of demonstrating the manifestly unfounded or excessive character of the request.[36]

So Supervisory Authorities may be able to charge fees to subjects at least in some circumstances. As with the charging of fees by controllers and processors, this may be read as meaning that supervisory authorities may impose reasonable fees on subjects or DPOs who are making manifestly unfounded or excessive requests. The GDPR does not suggest that supervisory authorities cannot charge fees to controllers or processors for undertaking tasks such as responding to prior consultations, conducting accreditation and approving binding corporate rules. This may leave it open to supervisory authorities to charge fees for such functions. The GDPR does not make provision for such fees to be charged, but it does not explicitly exclude them. It is not clear whether the legislatures of Member States will, in fact, charge such fees and whether divergences will emerge between such charging mechanisms.

REMOVAL

[16.10] The GDPR provides that the duties of members of a supervisory authority can only cease in one of three ways:

- firstly '... in the event of the expiry of the term of office, resignation or compulsory retirement, in accordance with the law of the Member State concerned';[37] or

- secondly, where the member is dismissed '... in cases of serious misconduct ...';

---

35.   GDPR, article 57(3).
36.   GDPR, article 57(4).
37.   GDPR, article 53(3).

• finally, where '… the member no longer fulfils the conditions required for the performance of the duties'[38] and so is removed from office.

The removal of a supervisory authority was considered by the CJEU in *Commission v Hungary*.[39] Hungary had amended its data protection law, as a result the existing member of its supervisory authority was removed from office three years before his term was due to expire. The Hungarian law under which the member had been appointed provided that he '… could be called upon to vacate office only upon expiry of his term of office or upon death, resignation, declaration of a conflict of interest, compulsory retirement or compulsory resignation'.[40] It was accepted that the supervisor '… was not compelled to vacate office pursuant to one of those provisions and, in particular, that the Supervisor did not officially resign'.[41] The CJEU therefore found that the sole member of the Hungarian supervisory authority had been compelled '… to vacate office in contravention of the safeguards established by statute in order to protect his term of office'.[42] The fact that this removal 'was because of institutional changes …' was irrelevant to this finding, the CJEU concluded that:

> A mere change in institutional model cannot … objectively justify compelling the person entrusted with the duties of Supervisor to vacate office before expiry of his full term, without providing for transitional measures to ensure that he is allowed to serve his term of office in full.[43]

[16.11] In *Garai*[44] the CJEU considered the position of two members of the Spanish telecommunications supervisor, the CMT, who were dismissed before the expiry of their terms as a result of a merger of Spanish regulatory authorities. The CJEU held that the dismissals '… came about for a reason other than the fact that those appellants no longer fulfilled the conditions required for the performance of their duties, which are laid down in advance in national law'.[45] The CJEU did not suggest that the members could not be dismissed in any circumstance, but held that in this case the members could not be dismissed '… before the expiry of their terms of office in the absence of any rules guaranteeing that such dismissals do not jeopardise the independence and impartiality of such member'.[46] The GDPR only provides for the members' terms to end in the three circumstances outlined above. Members may not be removed in any other circumstances as the GDPR does not allow for this.

---

38. GDPR, article 53(4).
39. *Commission v Hungary* (Case C–288/12) (8 April 2014).
40. *Commission v Hungary* (Case C–288/12) (8 April 2014), para 57.
41. *Commission v Hungary* (Case C–288/12) (8 April 2014), para 58.
42. *Commission v Hungary* (Case C–288/12) (8 April 2014), para 58.
43. *Commission v Hungary* (Case C–288/12) (8 April 2014), para 61.
44. *Ormaetxea Garai and Lorenzo Almendros* (Case C–424/15) (19 October 2016).
45. *Ormaetxea Garai and Lorenzo Almendros* (Case C–424/15) (19 October 2016), para 43.
46. *Ormaetxea Garai and Lorenzo Almendros* (Case C–424/15) (19 October 2016), para 52.

WILL SUPERVISORY AUTHORITIES ACTUALLY HAVE COMPLETE INDEPENDENCE?

[16.12] The most detailed EU analysis of independence is probably that undertaken by the ECB initially in 1998[47] and then repeated on a biannual basis thereafter. Obviously, Central Banks perform quite different functions and have different duties to supervisory authorities. That said, the depth, detail and rigor of the ECB's analysis makes it a useful comparator. The ECB considers that:

> The concept of central bank independence includes various types of independence that must be assessed separately, namely: functional, institutional, personal and financial independence.

Functional independence requires an institution's 'objective to be stated in a clear and legally certain way',[48] which is done by GDPR, article 51(1). Institutional independence means that the decision making bodies of an institution must be prohibited: '… from seeking or taking instructions from EU institutions or bodies, from any government of a Member State or from any other body',[49] which is done by GDPR, article 52(2). Personal independence, which the ECB largely describes as security of tenure,[50] is addressed by article 53(3) and (4). Finally, there is financial independence, which the ECB explains as follows: 'Even if [an institution] is fully independent from a functional, institutional and personal point of view …, its overall independence would be jeopardised if it could not autonomously avail itself of sufficient financial resources to fulfil its mandate'.[51]

In general, the GDPR does a good job of ensuring the independence of supervisory authorities, particularly as regards their functional, institutional and personal independence. Whether that independence is in fact 'complete' may, however, be open to challenge. The basis upon which such a challenge might be brought depends upon the circumstances of any particular case. Two hypothetical circumstances are suggested where a challenge might be brought. An argument might be made that the functional independence of supervisory authorities may be compromised by the power of the EDPB to issue instructions to it; and, the financial independence of supervisory authorities may be compromised by their direct dependence upon Member States for funding. Whether challenges such as this will be brought depends upon circumstance and much depends upon how the GDPR is applied in practice.

---

47. ECB, *Convergence Report 1998,* Frankfurt-am-Main, March 1998, pp 291–195.
48. ECB, *Convergence Report 2016*, Frankfurt-am-Main, June 2016, para 2.2.3, p 20.
49. ECB, *Convergence Report 2016*, Frankfurt-am-Main, June 2016, para 2.2.3, p 21.
50. 'The Statute's provision on security of tenure for members of NCB's decision-making bodies further safeguards central bank independence' ECB, *Convergence Report 2016*, Frankfurt-am-Main, June 2016, para 2.2.3, p 21.
51. 'The Statute's provision on security of tenure for members of NCBs' decision-making bodies further safeguards central bank independence' ECB, *Convergence Report 2016*, Frankfurt-am-Main, June 2016, para 2.2.3, p 25.

Chapter 17

THE JURISDICTION OF SUPERVISORY AUTHORITIES

INTRODUCTION

[17.01] The GDPR provides two distinct supervisory regimes: one for the processing of personal data within the EU; the other for the flow of data out of the EU and processing of personal data outside. Both regimes are significantly different to those which existed under Directive 95/46. These differences are responses to deficiencies in the drafting of Directive 95/46 itself, technological advances and the globalisation of the EU economy. As the Recitals explain:

> Rapid technological developments and globalisation have brought new challenges for the protection of personal data. The scale of the collection and sharing of personal data has increased significantly. Technology allows both private companies and public authorities to make use of personal data on an unprecedented scale in order to pursue their activities. Natural persons increasingly make personal information available publicly and globally. Technology has transformed both the economy and social life, and should further facilitate the free flow of personal data within the Union and the transfer to third countries and international organisations, while ensuring a high level of the protection of personal data.[1]

The internal regime is a relatively straightforward application of the EU's well-understood rules of establishment, albeit with the complication of the European Data Protection Board (EDPB). The external regime is more radical, as the EU asserts a global jurisdiction for the GDPR. These new regimes may well address the deficiencies of Directive 95/45. But as with all of the GDPR, it remains to be seen whether these new regimes will adapt to future developments.

INTERNAL REGIME

[17.02] Article 16(2) TFEU provides that the EU's legislature both '... lay down the rules relating to the protection of individuals with regard to the processing of personal data ...' and '... the rules relating to the free movement of such data ...'. The GDPR makes clear that the purpose of the GDPR is to generally standardise EU data protection rules so that data may flow freely between EU Member States:

> In order to ensure a consistent and high level of protection of natural persons and to remove the obstacles to flows of personal data within the Union, the level of protection of the rights and freedoms of natural persons with regard to the processing of such data should be equivalent in all Member States. Consistent and homogenous application of the rules for the protection of the fundamental rights

---

1. GDPR, Recital 6.

and freedoms of natural persons with regard to the processing of personal data should be ensured throughout the Union.[2]

In order to ensure that personal data can flow freely within the EU the GDPR applies the existing rules of the EU's single market. The GDPR applies two rights provided by the TFEU: the Freedom of Establishment and the Freedom to Supply Services.[3] If a controller is established in a particular Member State it will be subject to the jurisdiction of that State's laws and its supervisory authority in full. Each supervisory authority is responsible for supervising the processing of personal data within its own Member State. Where processing is:

> carried out by public authorities or private bodies[4] ... (pursuant to a legal obligation or public duty)[5] ... the supervisory authority of the Member State concerned shall be competent.[6]

[17.03] Article 55(1) is clear in providing that:

> Each supervisory authority shall be competent for the performance of the tasks assigned to and the exercise of the powers conferred on it in accordance with this Regulation on the territory of its own Member State.[7]

[17.04] Article 56 then goes on to provide that:

> ...the supervisory authority of the main establishment or of the single establishment of the controller or processor shall be competent to act as lead

---

2.   GDPR, Recital 10.

3.   A full analysis of the application of TFEU, articles 49 (Freedom of Establishment) and 56 (Freedom to provide Services) is beyond the scope of this book. The EU Commission published useful guides on the TFEU, article 49 *et seq* (Freedom of Establishment) and TFEU, article 56 *et seq.* (Freedom to Provide Services), which can be found at https://ec.europa.eu/docsroom/documents/22543/attachments/1/translations/en/renditions.pdf and http://ec.europa.eu/DocsRoom/documents/16743/attachments/1/translations/en/renditions/native.

4.   'The rules on the lead supervisory authority and the one-stop-shop mechanism should not apply where the processing is carried out by public authorities or private bodies in the public interest. In such cases the only supervisory authority competent to exercise the powers conferred to it in accordance with this Regulation should be the supervisory authority of the Member State where the public authority or private body is established,' GDPR, Recital 128.

5.   That is on the basis of GDPR, article 6(1)(c) or (e).

6.   The analysis of whether a legal obligation or public duty applies to a processing operation will be determined by the law of the Member State in question, not the GDPR, as TFEU, article 56 is specifically disapplied from this question by GDPR, article 55(2). The Article 29 Working Party suggests that 'Local data processing activity does not fall within the GDPR's cooperation and consistency provisions. Supervisory authorities will respect each other's competence to deal with local data processing activity on a local basis. Processing carried out by public authorities will always be dealt with on a 'local' basis too'. Article 29 WP, *Guidelines for identifying a controller or processor's lead supervisory authority*, revised and adopted on 5 April 2017, 16/EN WP 244 rev 01, para 3.2, p 10.

7.   GDPR, article 55(1).

supervisory authority for the cross-border processing carried out by that controller or processor in accordance with the procedure provided in Article 60.

The question of which supervisory authority is responsible for supervising a particular controller or processor is determined by the location of that controller or processor's establishment. This is consistent with GDPR, article 3 of which provides that it applies to:

... the processing of personal data in the context of the activities of an establishment of a controller or a processor in the Union ...

The question of where a controller is established must be determined in order to decide which supervisory authority has jurisdiction. Where a controller is established in more than one jurisdiction then it is the supervisory authority of the controller's main establishment jurisdiction that will act as lead supervisory authority for the cross-border processing. The identification of the lead authority is significant, the functions of which are summarised by the Recitals as follows:

The lead authority should be competent to adopt binding decisions regarding measures applying the powers conferred on it in accordance with this Regulation. In its capacity as lead authority, the supervisory authority should closely involve and coordinate the supervisory authorities concerned in the decision-making process. Where the decision is to reject the complaint by the data subject in whole or in part, that decision should be adopted by the supervisory authority with which the complaint has been lodged.[8]

[17.05] As the Article 29 Working Party has opined:

... where a multinational company centralises all the decisions relating to the purposes and means of processing activities in one of its establishments in the EU ... only one lead supervisory authority will be identified for the multinational.[9]

Identification of the lead supervisory authority requires answering two questions: firstly, where is a controller or processor established within the EU, and; secondly, if the controller or processor has more than one such establishment, which of these is the main establishment. The first of these questions was considered by the CJEU in *Weltimmo*.[10] The case considered a Slovakian company which ran '... a property dealing website concerning Hungarian properties'[11] which processed the personal data of advertisers. These advertisements were initially free, but a fee became payable after the first month. Some advertisers sought to remove their adverts before these fees were incurred, requesting the deletion of their personal data in the process, however Weltimmo ignored these requests and the charges were imposed. Weltimmo then forwarded the personal data of the advertisers concerned to debt collection agencies. Complaints were made to the Hungarian supervisory authority by the advertisers concerned; that supervisory authority decided it was competent and fined Weltimmo some €32,000. Weltimmo

---

8.   GDPR, Recital 125.
9.   Article 29 *WP, Guidelines for identifying a controller or processor's lead supervisory authority,* revised and adopted on 5 April 2017, 16/EN WP 244 rev 01, para 2.1, p 5.
10.   *Weltimmo* (Case C–230/14) (1 October 2015).
11.   *Weltimmo* (Case C–230/14) (1 October 2015), para 9.

challenged this fine before the Hungarian courts, arguing that it was not within the jurisdiction of the Hungarian courts.

[17.06] The first question considered by the CJEU was whether the supervisory authority of one Member State could '… apply its national law on data protection with regard to a data controller whose company is registered in another Member State and who runs a property dealing website concerning properties situated in the territory of the first of those two States'.[12] The CJEU held that this question divided into parts. Firstly, was Weltimmo established in Hungary, and; secondly was it processing personal data 'in the context of the activities' of that establishment.

The CJEU considered this question in the context of articles 4 and 28 of Directive 95/46. Article 28(1) of that Directive provided that each supervisory authority was '… responsible for monitoring the application, within the territory of its own Member State, of the provisions adopted by the Member States pursuant to that directive.' This is not dissimilar in effect to GDPR, article 55. The CJEU held that:

> The national law applicable to the controller in respect of that processing must therefore be determined not in the light of Article 28 of Directive 95/46, but in the light of Article 4 …

[17.07] Article 4(1)(a) of Directive 95/46 provided that:

> Each Member State shall apply the national provisions it adopts pursuant to this Directive to the processing of personal data where … the processing is carried out in the context of the activities of an establishment of the controller on the territory of the Member State …

Since the GDPR is a regulation, not a Directive, it has no direct equivalent to article 4. However, GDPR, article 3 does state that:

> This Regulation applies to the processing of personal data in the context of the activities of an establishment[13] of a controller or a processor in the Union …[14]

---

12. *Weltimmo* (Case C–230/14) (1 October 2015), para 19.
13. The term 'establishment' has a specific meaning in EU law. The right of establishment provided by the first of these questions, where is a controller or processor established, must be considered in the broader context of EU law. The Right of Establishment is provided by Title IV, Ch 2, TFEU, article 49 of which provides: '…restrictions on the freedom of establishment of nationals of a Member State in the territory of another Member State shall be prohibited.' This right has been considered by the CJEU on many occasions. In (Gebhard (Case C–55/94) [1995] it held that: 'The concept of establishment within the meaning of the Treaty is therefore a very broad one, allowing a Community national to participate, on a stable and continuous basis, in the economic life of a Member State other than his State of origin and to profit therefrom…' (para 25). Whilst EU case law on the TFEU's right of establishment may offer some useful guidance as to what establishment means, there may be significant differences between the concept of establishment used by the TFEU and the GDPR. It is notable that although the CJEU uses similar language when discussing both concepts it did not reference the TFEU case law in either *Google Spain*, *Weltimmo* or *Amazon*.
14. GDPR, article 3(1).

[17.08] The CJEU began its analysis by stating that:

> With regard ... to the concept of 'establishment', it should be noted that ... establishment on the territory of a Member State implies the effective and real exercise of activity through stable arrangements and that the legal form of such an establishment, whether simply a branch or a subsidiary with a legal personality, is not the determining factor.[15]

The CJEU cited Recital 19 of Directive 95/46 (which now appears as GDPR, Recital 22). The Court went on to reiterate its Advocate General's observation that:

> ... this results in a flexible definition of the concept of 'establishment', which departs from a formalistic approach whereby undertakings are established solely in the place where they are registered.[16]

It then went on to hold that: '... the presence of only one representative can, in some circumstances, suffice to constitute a stable arrangement if that representative acts with a sufficient degree of stability through the presence of the necessary equipment for provision of the specific services concerned in the Member State in question'.[17] And the CJEU considered that '... the concept of 'establishment'... extends to any real and effective activity — even a minimal one — exercised through stable arrangements'.[18] As regards to Weltimmo itself, the CJEU noted that its activity consisted of: '... running ... one or several property dealing websites concerning properties situated in Hungary, which are written in Hungarian and whose advertisements are subject to a fee after a period of one month.' The CJEU therefore concluded that Weltimmo pursued '... a real and effective activity in Hungary'.[19] This activity included having '... a representative in Hungary, who is mentioned in the Slovak companies register with an address in Hungary and who has sought to negotiate the settlement of the unpaid debts with the advertisers.' That representative had '... served as a point of contact between that company and the data subjects who lodged complaints and represented the company in the administrative and judicial proceedings'. Weltimmo had a Hungarian bank account and postal address. The CJEU considered that all this information, if verified by the Hungarian courts, was '... capable of establishing ... the existence of an 'establishment ...'.[20] However the CJEU held that it was irrelevant that '... owners of the properties forming the subject-matter of the advertisements have Hungarian nationality ...'.[21]

---

15. *Weltimmo* (Case C–230/14) (1 October 2015), para 28. This language is echoed by GDPR, Recital 22: 'Establishment implies the effective and real exercise of activity through stable arrangements. The legal form of such arrangements, whether through a branch or a subsidiary with a legal personality, is not the determining factor in that respect'.
16. *Weltimmo* (Case C–230/14) (1 October 2015), para 29.
17. *Weltimmo* (Case C–230/14) (1 October 2015), para 30.
18. *Weltimmo* (Case C–230/14) (1 October 2015), para 31.
19. *Weltimmo* (Case C–230/14) (1 October 2015), para 32.
20. *Weltimmo* (Case C–230/14) (1 October 2015), para 33.
21. *Weltimmo* (Case C–230/14) (1 October 2015), para 40.

[17.09] The CJEU went on to consider whether personal data was processed 'in the context of the activities' of that establishment. The CJEU reiterated that such processing did not have to be undertaken 'by' the establishment, but only 'in the context' of its activities.[22] In this case the CJEU held that the processing consisted '… of the publication, on Weltimmo's property dealing websites, of personal data …' and that there was no doubt '… that that processing takes place in the context of the activities … which Weltimmo pursues in Hungary'.[23]

[17.10] If a controller or processor is established across a number of Member States then it will be necessary for a controller to identify which of these Member States is the main establishment of the controller or processor in question. Article 56(1) begins by providing that each supervisory authority is competent

> … to handle a complaint lodged with it or a possible infringement of this Regulation, if the subject matter relates only to an establishment in its Member State or substantially affects data subjects only in its Member State.[24]

This suggests that the jurisdiction of supervisory authorities may have a dual basis, both of which may be interpreted in a manner consistent with the judgment of the CJEU in *Wetltimmo*. The first, that jurisdiction is tied to establishment is clearly consistent with *Weltimmo*. The consistency of the second, that jurisdiction may arise because the actions of a controller established elsewhere substantially affect data subjects only within the Member State of the supervisory authority, is not so clear. As the CJEU made clear in *Weltimmo:*

> … when a supervisory authority receives a complaint … that authority may exercise its investigative powers irrespective of the applicable law and before even knowing which national law is applicable to the processing in question. However, if it reaches the conclusion that the law of another Member State is applicable, it cannot impose penalties outside the territory of its own Member State.[25]

[17.11] The controller's main establishment is defined by the GDPR in the following terms:

> … as regards a controller with establishments in more than one Member State, the place of its central administration in the Union, unless the decisions on the purposes and means of the processing of personal data are taken in another establishment of the controller in the Union and the latter establishment has the

---

22. *Weltimmo* (Case C–230/14) (1 October 2015), para 37, Citing *Google Spain* (Case C–131/12), para 52.
23. *Weltimmo* (Case C–230/14) (1 October 2015), para 38.
24. GDPR, Recital 124 provides that '… the Board should be able to issue guidelines in particular on the criteria to be taken into account in order to ascertain whether the processing in question substantially affects data subjects in more than one Member State …'.
25. *Weltimmo* (Case C–230/14) (1 October 2015), para 57.

power to have such decisions implemented, in which case the establishment having taken such decisions is to be considered to be the main establishment …[26]

Hence the importance of correctly identifying the central administration of a controller or processor. This will be a question of fact. As the EFTA Surveillance Authority submitted to the CJEU in *Ueberseering*.[27]

> Since characterisation as a company's actual centre of administration turns, to a large extent, on the facts, it is always possible that different national legal systems and, within them, different courts may have divergent views on what is an actual centre of administration. Moreover, it is increasingly difficult to identify a company's actual centre of administration in an international, computerised economy, in which the physical presence of decision-makers becomes increasingly unnecessary.[28]

[17.12] TFEU, article 49 links establishment to the location of the '… registered office, central administration or principal place of business …'. The CJEU found that this meant that the TFEU had placed each of these factors on the same footing.[29] The fact that the GDPR only mentions one of these factors, central administration, suggests that the other factors, registered office or principal place of business, are not relevant to the question of where the main establishment is. What is relevant to that question is where '… decisions on the purposes and means of the processing of personal data are taken …'. If such decisions are taken other than where the central administration is located '… and the latter establishment has the power to have such decisions implemented …' then this is where the main establishment of the controller is. This approach should serve to avoid the use of 'brass plate' entities to site a controller in a particular Member State. Such an approach is consistent with the case law of the CJEU.[30]

[17.13] The Article 29 Working Party has suggested that the following factors may be useful for determining a controller's main establishment:

(a) Where are decisions about the purposes and means of the processing given final 'sign off'?

(b) Where are decisions about business activities that involve data processing made?

(c) Where does the power to have decisions implemented effectively lie?

---

26.   GDPR, article 4(16)(a).

27.   *Ueberseering* (Case C–208/00) (5 November 2002).

28.   *Ueberseering* (Case C–208/00) (5 November 2002), para 51.

29.   *Daily Mail* (Case C–81/87), para 21.

30.   '…a fictitious presence, such as that of a "letter box" or "brass plate" company, cannot be described as a place of business… the place of a company's business is the place where the essential decisions concerning its general management are taken and where the functions of its central administration are exercised,' *Planzer Luxembourg* (Case C–73/06) (28 June 2007), paras 62–63.

(d) Where is the Director (or Directors) with overall management responsibility for the cross border processing located?

(e) Where is the controller or processor registered as a company, if in a single territory?[31]

[17.14] The main establishment of a processor is defined as:

> ... the place of its central administration in the Union, or, if the processor has no central administration in the Union, the establishment of the processor in the Union where the main processing activities in the context of the activities of an establishment of the processor take place to the extent that the processor is subject to specific obligations under this Regulation ...[32]

So a processor will be established where its central administration is located. As the Recitals explain:

> The main establishment of a controller in the Union should be determined according to objective criteria and should imply the effective and real exercise of management activities determining the main decisions as to the purposes and means of processing through stable arrangements.[33]

The Recitals go on to make clear that it does not matter where data is, in fact, processed[34] and that:

> Where the processing is carried out by a group of undertakings, the main establishment of the controlling undertaking should be considered to be the main establishment of the group of undertakings, except where the purposes and means of processing are determined by another undertaking.[35]

The Recitals offer some further guidance on the identification of a lead authority:

> Where the processing of personal data takes place in the context of the activities of an establishment of a controller or a processor in the Union and the controller or processor is established in more than one Member State, or where processing taking place in the context of the activities of a single establishment of a controller or processor in the Union substantially affects or is likely to substantially affect data subjects in more than one Member State, the supervisory authority for the main establishment of the controller or processor or for the single establishment of the controller or processor should act as lead authority ... Also where a data subject not residing in that Member State has lodged a complaint, the supervisory

---

31. Article 29 Working Party, *Guidelines for identifying a controller or processor's lead supervisory authority*, 16/EN WP2244 rev 01, 5 April 2017, para 2.1.1, p 7.

32. GDPR, article 4(16)(b).

33. GDPR, Recital 36.

34. 'That criterion should not depend on whether the processing of personal data is carried out at that location. The presence and use of technical means and technologies for processing personal data or processing activities do not, in themselves, constitute a main establishment and are therefore not determining criteria for a main establishment,' GDPR, Recital 36.

35. GDPR, article 4(16)(b).

authority with which such complaint has been lodged should also be a supervisory authority concerned.[36]

The Recitals suggest that the decision as to which supervisory authority should take the lead is not one that any supervisory authority can answer alone.

The decision should be agreed jointly by the lead supervisory authority and the supervisory authorities concerned and should be directed towards the main or single establishment of the controller or processor and be binding on the controller and processor. The controller or processor should take the necessary measures to ensure compliance with this Regulation and the implementation of the decision notified by the lead supervisory authority to the main establishment of the controller or processor as regards the processing activities in the Union.[37]

[17.15] The identification of a lead supervisory authority does not preclude other supervisory authorities from dealing with strictly local issues. The Recitals provide that:

Each supervisory authority not acting as the lead supervisory authority should be competent to handle local cases where the controller or processor is established in more than one Member State, but the subject matter of the specific processing concerns only processing carried out in a single Member State and involves only data subjects in that single Member State, for example, where the subject matter concerns the processing of employees' personal data in the specific employment context of a Member State.

Where a supervisory authority decides to deal with a matter as a local case then:

... the supervisory authority should inform the lead supervisory authority without delay about the matter. After being informed, the lead supervisory authority should decide, whether it will handle the case pursuant to the provision on cooperation between the lead supervisory authority and other supervisory authorities concerned ('one-stop-shop mechanism'), or whether the supervisory authority which informed it should handle the case at local level. When deciding whether it will handle the case, the lead supervisory authority should take into account whether there is an establishment of the controller or processor in the Member State of the supervisory authority which informed it in order to ensure effective enforcement of a decision *vis-à-vis* the controller or processor. Where the lead supervisory authority decides to handle the case, the supervisory authority which informed it should have the possibility to submit a draft for a decision, of which the lead supervisory authority should take utmost account when preparing its draft decision in that one-stop-shop mechanism.[38]

[17.16] The Recitals go on to offer some further guidance as to how such complaints should be handled:

Where another supervisory authority should act as a lead supervisory authority for the processing activities of the controller or processor but the concrete subject

---

36.   GDPR, Recital 124.
37.   GDPR, Recital 126.
38.   GDPR, Recital 127.

matter of a complaint or the possible infringement concerns only processing activities of the controller or processor in the Member State where the complaint has been lodged or the possible infringement detected and the matter does not substantially affect or is not likely to substantially affect data subjects in other Member States, the supervisory authority receiving a complaint or detecting or being informed otherwise of situations that entail possible infringements of this Regulation should seek an amicable settlement with the controller and, if this proves unsuccessful, exercise its full range of powers. This should include: specific processing carried out in the territory of the Member State of the supervisory authority or with regard to data subjects on the territory of that Member State; processing that is carried out in the context of an offer of goods or services specifically aimed at data subjects in the territory of the Member State of the supervisory authority; or processing that has to be assessed taking into account relevant legal obligations under Member State law.[39]

Mutual assistance, joint operations and co-operation between Supervisory Authorities

[17.17] To enable supervisory authorities to work together the GDPR provides co-operation, mutual assistance and dispute resolution mechanisms. Of course, the Article 29 Working Party established by Directive 95/46 demonstrated that supervisory authorities are capable of working together quite productively and successfully.[40] However, effective enforcement and supervision of the GDPR must entail the processing of the personal data of subjects. The GDPR itself requires that such processing have an adequate legal basis and so requires that such co-operation mechanism be explicitly set out. The Recitals to the GDPR provide:

> The supervisory authorities should monitor the application of the provisions pursuant to this Regulation and contribute to its consistent application throughout the Union, in order to protect natural persons in relation to the processing of their personal data and to facilitate the free flow of personal data within the internal market. For that purpose, the supervisory authorities should cooperate with each other and with the Commission, without the need for any agreement between Member States on the provision of mutual assistance or on such cooperation.[41]

---

39. GDPR, Recital 131.
40. And the GDPR does endeavour to ensure the continuance of that atmosphere of co-operation. GDPR, Recital 138 provides that where measures producing mandatory legal effects are not sought then in cases of cross- border relevance '... the cooperation mechanism between the lead supervisory authority and supervisory authorities concerned should be applied and mutual assistance and joint operations might be carried out between the supervisory authorities concerned on a bilateral or multilateral basis without triggering the consistency mechanism'.
41. GDPR, Recital 123.

Mutual assistance

[17.18] GDPR, Article 61 provides that:

> Supervisory authorities shall provide each other with relevant information and mutual assistance in order to implement and apply this Regulation in a consistent manner, and shall put in place measures for effective cooperation with one another. Mutual assistance shall cover, in particular, information requests and supervisory measures, such as requests to carry out prior authorisations and consultations, inspections and investigations.[42]

In particular:

> Each supervisory authority shall take all appropriate measures required to reply to a request of another supervisory authority without undue delay and no later than one month after receiving the request. Such measures may include, in particular, the transmission of relevant information on the conduct of an investigation.[43]

Where such requests are made then they must: '... contain all the necessary information, including the purpose of and reasons for the request. Information exchanged shall be used only for the purpose for which it was requested'.[44] Where such a request is made then:

> The requested supervisory authority shall not refuse to comply with the request unless: ... it is not competent for the subject-matter of the request or for the measures it is requested to execute; or ... compliance with the request would infringe [the GDPR] or Union or Member State law to which the supervisory authority receiving the request is subject.[45]

Where a requested authority refuses to comply with any such request then it shall: '...provide reasons for any refusal to comply ...'. However, the GDPR seems to anticipate that in general supervisory authorities will comply with such requests and:

> ... inform the requesting supervisory authority of the results or, as the case may be, of the progress of the measures taken in order to respond to the request.[46]

---

42. GDPR, article 61(1).
43. GDPR, article 61(2) and Recital 133 reiterate that: 'The supervisory authorities should assist each other in performing their tasks and provide mutual assistance, so as to ensure the consistent application and enforcement of this Regulation in the internal market. A supervisory authority requesting mutual assistance may adopt a provisional measure if it receives no response to a request for mutual assistance within one month of the receipt of that request by the other supervisory authority'.
44. GDPR, article 61(3).
45. GDPR, article 61(4).
46. GDPR, article 61(5).

Requested authorities must facilitate such requests in other ways: providing responses by electronic means, in standardised formats;[47] and, not charging fees, though they may indemnify one another for costs incurred in 'exceptional circumstances'.[48]

Joint operations

[17.19] Supervisory authorities may undertake joint operations with one another. Article 62 provides:

> The supervisory authorities shall, where appropriate, conduct joint operations including joint investigations and joint enforcement measures in which members or staff of the supervisory authorities of other Member States are involved.[49]

The GDPR suggests that supervisory authorities cannot refuse to participate in such joint operations, providing that:

> Where the controller or processor has establishments in several Member States or where a significant number of data subjects in more than one Member State are likely to be substantially affected by processing operations, a supervisory authority of each of those Member States shall have the right to participate in joint operations.

[17.20] The lead authority[50] '... shall invite the supervisory authority of each of those Member States to take part in the joint operations and shall respond without delay to the

---

47. 'Requested supervisory authorities shall, as a rule, supply the information requested by other supervisory authorities by electronic means, using a standardised format,' GDPR, article 61(6). These standardised formats may be specified by the EU Commission: 'The Commission may, by means of implementing acts, specify the format and procedures for mutual assistance referred to in this Article and the arrangements for the exchange of information by electronic means between supervisory authorities, and between supervisory authorities and the Board, in particular the standardised format referred to in para 6 of this Article. Those implementing acts shall be adopted in accordance with the examination procedure referred to in Article 93(2),' GDPR, article 61(9).

48. 'Requested supervisory authorities shall not charge a fee for any action taken by them pursuant to a request for mutual assistance. Supervisory authorities may agree on rules to indemnify each other for specific expenditure arising from the provision of mutual assistance in exceptional circumstances,' GDPR, article 61(7).

49. GDPR, article 62(1) and Recital 134 reiterates that 'Each supervisory authority should, where appropriate, participate in joint operations with other supervisory authorities. The requested supervisory authority should be obliged to respond to the request within a specified time period'.

50. 'The supervisory authority which is competent pursuant to Article 56(1) or (4)...', GDPR, article 62(2).

request of a supervisory authority to participate'.[51] The supervisory authority that extends such an invitation may:

> ... confer powers, including investigative powers on the seconding supervisory authority's members or staff involved in joint operations[52] or ... allow the seconding supervisory authority's members or staff to exercise their investigative powers in accordance with the law of the Member State of the seconding supervisory authority.[53]

The powers of such seconded staff will be limited as they '... may be exercised only under the guidance and in the presence of members or staff of the host supervisory authority'.[54] The host supervisory authority will need to provide this guidance as '... the Member State of the host supervisory authority shall assume responsibility for their actions, including liability, for any damage caused by them during their operations, in accordance with the law of the Member State in whose territory they are operating'.[55] Where seconded staff cause damage then:

> The Member State in whose territory the damage was caused shall make good such damage under the conditions applicable to damage caused by its own staff. The Member State of the seconding supervisory authority whose staff has caused damage to any person in the territory of another Member State shall reimburse that other Member State in full any sums it has paid to the persons entitled on their behalf.[56]

It is only in this situation, where payments to make damage good have actually been made, that one Member State can seek reimbursement from another. GDPR, article 62 provides that 'Without prejudice to the exercise of its rights *vis-à-vis* third parties ... each Member State shall refrain ... from requesting reimbursement from another Member State in relation to damage ...'. The only exception to this is GDPR, article 62(5) which provides for the making good of damage caused by seconded staff. This suggests that the host supervisory authority cannot seek indemnities or other payments from the seconding supervisory authority in advance.

Co-operation

[17.21] In *Weltimmo* the CJEU considered what a supervisory authority should do if it received a complaint about a data controller or processor over which it did not have

---

51. GDPR, article 62(2).
52. This conferral of powers will have to be '... in accordance with Member State law, and with the seconding supervisory authority's authorisation ...,' GDPR, article 62(3).
53. '...in so far as the law of the Member State of the host supervisory authority permits...', GDPR, article 62(3).
54. And will '...be subject to the Member State law of the host supervisory authority,' GDPR, article 62(3).
55. GDPR, article 62(4).
56. GDPR, article 62(5).

jurisdiction. The CJEU held that where a supervisory authority is not the lead authority then it:

> ... must, in fulfilment of the duty of cooperation ... request the supervisory authority of that other Member State to establish an infringement of that law and to impose penalties if that law permits, based, where necessary, on the information which the authority of the first Member State has transmitted to the authority of that other Member State.[57]

And the CJEU went on to find that the supervisory authority to which '... such a complaint has been submitted may, in the context of that cooperation, find it necessary to carry out other investigations, on the instructions of the supervisory authority of the other Member State'.[58] The co-operation mechanism set out by the GDPR is somewhat more complex than that suggested by the CJEU in *Weltimmo,* though it must be expected that the CJEU will expect this mechanism to operate in a manner consistent with that judgment.

[17.22] The GDPR repeatedly reiterates that supervisory authorities must co-operate with one another so as to ensure its consistent application. Article 51 provides that each supervisory authority '... contribute to the consistent application of this Regulation throughout the Union. For that purpose, the supervisory authorities shall cooperate with each other and the Commission ...'.[59] Article 57 provides that each shall:

> ... cooperate with, including sharing information and provide mutual assistance to, other supervisory authorities with a view to ensuring the consistency of application and enforcement of this Regulation ...[60]

[17.23] Article 60(1) then goes on to provide that:

> The lead supervisory authority shall cooperate with the other supervisory authorities concerned in accordance with this Article in an endeavour to reach consensus. The lead supervisory authority and the supervisory authorities concerned shall exchange all relevant information with each other.[61]

[17.24] As the Recitals explain, the lead authority:

> ... should cooperate with the other authorities concerned, because the controller or processor has an establishment on the territory of their Member State, because data subjects residing on their territory are substantially affected, or because a complaint has been lodged with them.[62]

---

57.   *Weltimmo* (Case C–230/14) (1 October 2015), para 57.
58.   *Weltimmo* (Case C–230/14) (1 October 2015), para 58.
59.   GDPR, article 51(2).
60.   GDPR, article 57(1)(g).
61.   Such exchanges of information must take place electronically. GDPR, article 60(12) provides: 'The lead supervisory authority and the other supervisory authorities concerned shall supply the information required under this Article to each other by electronic means, using a standardised format'.
62.   GDPR, Recital 124.

The Recitals make some particular provision for the situation where a complaint is lodged with a supervisory authority other than the lead:

> Where the supervisory authority with which the complaint has been lodged is not the lead supervisory authority, the lead supervisory authority should closely cooperate with the supervisory authority with which the complaint has been lodged in accordance with the provisions on cooperation and consistency laid down in this Regulation. In such cases, the lead supervisory authority should, when taking measures intended to produce legal effects, including the imposition of administrative fines, take utmost account of the view of the supervisory authority with which the complaint has been lodged and which should remain competent to carry out any investigation on the territory of its own Member State in liaison with the competent supervisory authority.[63]

This creates an expectation that the various supervisory authorities will 'endeavour to reach consensus' but that is not the same as obliging the lead authority to abide by that consensus. The lead supervisory authority can impose obligations upon its fellow supervisors:

> The lead supervisory authority may request at any time other supervisory authorities concerned to provide mutual assistance pursuant to Article 61 and may conduct joint operations pursuant to Article 62, in particular for carrying out investigations or for monitoring the implementation of a measure concerning a controller or processor established in another Member State.[64]

And the lead authority must share information and draft decisions with its fellow authorities:

> The lead supervisory authority shall, without delay, communicate the relevant information on the matter to the other supervisory authorities concerned. It shall without delay submit a draft decision to the other supervisory authorities concerned for their opinion and take due account of their views.[65]

[17.25] If none of the supervisory authorities object to the draft decision then they shall be deemed to be in agreement with that draft decision and shall be bound by it.[66] The lead authority shall then:

> … adopt and notify the decision to the main establishment or single establishment of the controller or processor, as the case may be and inform the other supervisory authorities concerned and the Board of the decision in question, including a summary of the relevant facts and grounds. The supervisory authority with which a complaint has been lodged shall inform the complainant on the decision.[67]

---

63. GDPR, Recital 130.
64. GDPR, article 60(2).
65. GDPR, article 60(3).
66. GDPR, article 60(6).
67. GDPR, article 60(7).

A slightly different procedure will be followed where a complaint is being dismissed or rejected. In that case it is '… the supervisory authority with which the complaint was lodged shall adopt the decision and notify it to the complainant and shall inform the controller thereof'.[68] This leads to a quite complex procedure where the lead supervisory authority and the other supervisory authorities concerned agree to dismiss or reject parts of a complaint and to act on other parts of that complaint. Separate decisions will then have to be adopted for each part. On the one hand the:

> … lead supervisory authority shall adopt the decision for the part concerning actions in relation to the controller, shall notify it to the main establishment or single establishment of the controller or processor on the territory of its Member State and shall inform the complainant thereof.

On the other hand:

> … the supervisory authority of the complainant shall adopt the decision for the part concerning dismissal or rejection of that complaint, and shall notify it to that complainant and shall inform the controller or processor thereof.[69]

Splitting the obligation to notify in this way adds an unnecessary layer of complexity to an already complex process which supervisory authorities may struggle to administer. Those authorities will certainly struggle to explain that process to subjects.

[17.26] Once a controller or processor is notified of a decision of the lead authority pursuant to the above procedures it shall:

> … take the necessary measures to ensure compliance with the decision as regards processing activities in the context of all its establishments in the Union. The controller or processor shall notify the measures taken for complying with the decision to the lead supervisory authority, which shall inform the other supervisory authorities concerned.[70]

Authorities that receive draft decisions may express a 'relevant and reasoned objection'[71] to the proposed decision. Where the lead authority decides to follow such an objection it must:

> … submit to the other supervisory authorities concerned a revised draft decision for their opinion. That revised draft decision shall be subject to the procedure referred to in paragraph 4 within a period of two weeks.[72]

---

68. GDPR, article 60(8).
69. GDPR, article 60(9).
70. GDPR, article 60(10).
71. GDPR, Recital 124 provides that the Board may issue guidelines '… on what constitutes a relevant and reasoned objection'.
72. GDPR, article 60(5).

EXTERNAL REGIME

[17.27] GDPR, Recital 22 echoes the language of Recital 19 of Directive 95/46, stating that:

> Establishment implies the effective and real exercise of activity through stable arrangements. The legal form of such arrangements, whether through a branch or a subsidiary with a legal personality, is not the determining factor in that respect.

This language was considered by the CJEU in *Google Spain*[73] which noted that the referring court had determined that: 'Google Search indexes websites throughout the world, including websites located in Spain. The information indexed by its 'web crawlers' or robots, that is to say, computer programs used to locate and sweep up the content of web pages methodically and automatically, is stored temporarily on servers whose State of location is unknown, that being kept secret for reasons of competition'.[74] And that 'Google Spain ... possesses separate legal personality ...'.[75] However, the referring court had failed to determine that '... Google Spain carries out in Spain an activity directly linked to the indexing or storage of information or data contained on third parties' websites'. Therefore, Google Spain did not appear to be the controller of the applicant's personal data. Nevertheless, the referring court had determined that '... the promotion and sale of advertising space, which Google Spain attends to in respect of Spain, constitutes the bulk of the Google group's commercial activity and may be regarded as closely linked to Google Search.[76] Google Spain argued that such activity was insufficient to establish its search engine in Spain, however the CJEU held that:

> ... the processing of personal data for the purposes of the service of a search engine such as Google Search, which is operated by an undertaking that has its seat in a third State but has an establishment in a Member State, is carried out 'in the context of the activities' of that establishment if the latter is intended to

---

73. *Google Spain* (Case C–131/12) (13 May 2014).
74. Google's terms of service stipulate that its services are provided '... by Google Inc. ("Google"), located at 1600 Amphitheatre Parkway, Mountain View, CA 94043, United States.' The terms of service go on to provide that 'The courts in some countries will not apply California law to some types of disputes. If you reside in one of those countries, then where California law is excluded from applying, your country's laws will apply to such disputes related to these terms. Otherwise, you agree that the laws of California, USA, excluding California's choice of law rules, will apply to any disputes arising out of or relating to these terms or the Services. Similarly, if the courts in your country will not permit you to consent to the jurisdiction and venue of the courts in Santa Clara County, California, USA, then your local jurisdiction and venue will apply to such disputes related to these terms. Otherwise, all claims arising out of or relating to these terms or the services will be litigated exclusively in the federal or state courts of Santa Clara County, California, USA, and you and Google consent to personal jurisdiction in those courts,' Google Terms of Service, policy dated 30 April 2017, reviewed on 2 September 2017.
75. *Google Spain* (Case C–131/12) (13 May 2014), para 43.
76. *Google Spain* (Case C–131/12) (13 May 2014), para 46.

promote and sell, in that Member State, advertising space offered by the search engine which serves to make the service offered by that engine profitable.[77]

[17.28] *Google Spain* suggests that a relatively tangential presence in a Member State may be sufficient to establish a controller or processor in the EU. The CJEU noted that Google Spain was legally separate from the subsidiaries of its parent that processed personal data and had no actual role in the processing of personal data. Nevertheless, it held that the existence of Google Spain was sufficient to establish Google Search in Spain. This broad view of establishment may mean that the global jurisdiction that the EU has granted to the GDPR is less significant than at first seems as quite marginal activities may be sufficient to establish a controller within the EU.

[17.29] The EU granted the GDPR a global jurisdiction in order to address significant deficiencies that had been identified by the CJEU in *Lindqvist*[78] on the transfers of personal data outside the EU. GDPR, article 3(2) provides that the GDPR:

> ... applies to the processing of personal data of data subjects who are in the Union by a controller or processor not established in the Union, where the processing activities are related to: ... the offering of goods or services, irrespective of whether a payment of the data subject is required, to such data subjects in the Union; or ... the monitoring of their behaviour as far as their behaviour takes place within the Union.

[17.30] TFEU, article 16 requires that EU data protection rules be subject to the supervision of independent authorities. Hence extending the GDPR's application beyond the borders of the EU means similarly extending the role of Data Protection Authorities.[79] Assertions of extra-territorial jurisdiction have been made before;[80] but

---

77.   *Google Spain* (Case C–131/12) (13 May 2014), para 55.

78.   In *Lindqvist v Sweden* (Case C–101/01) (6 November 2003) the CJEU considered the 'state of development of the internet at the time Directive 95/46 was drawn up' (para 68) and that the transborder data flows provisions of Directive 95/46 failed to 'lay down criteria for deciding whether operations carried out by hosting providers should be deemed to occur in the place of establishment of the service or at its business address or in the place where the computer or computers constituting the service's infrastructure are located' (para 67). The CJEU concluded that it could not be presumed that: 'Community legislature intended the expression transfer [of data] to a third country to cover the loading, by an individual in Mrs Lindqvist's position, of data on to an internet page, even if those data are thereby made accessible to persons in third countries with the technical means to access them'(para 68).

79.   See also the opinion of the CJEU in *Transfer of Passenger Name Record data from the European Union to Canada* (Opinions of the Court) [2017] EUECJ Avis-1/15_OC (26 July 2017) in which the CJEU advised that an agreement providing for the transfer of personal data from the EU to Canada must 'guarantee that the oversight of the rules laid down in the Agreement between Canada and the European Union on the transfer and processing of Passenger Name Record data relating to the protection of air passengers with regard to the processing of Passenger Name Record data concerning them will be carried out by an independent supervisory authority' (para 232).

80.   The enactment of extraterritorial legislation by the EU is extremely rare (Scott, 'The New EU "Extraterritoriality"' (9 July 2014), (contd .../)

they remain relatively uncommon as supervision and enforcement outside the territory of a Member State will be difficult if not impossible.[81] The GDPR seeks to address this difficulty by requiring that those who control or process personal data outside the union designate a representative within the union. GDPR, article 27(1) provides:

> Where Article 3(2) applies, the controller or the processor shall designate in writing a representative in the Union.

This obligation does not apply to every such controller or processor. It will not apply to:

(a) 'processing which is occasional, does not include, on a large scale, processing of special categories of data as referred to in Article 9(1) or processing of personal data relating to criminal convictions and offences referred to in Article 10, and is unlikely to result in a risk to the rights and freedoms of natural persons, taking into account the nature, context, scope and purposes of the processing; or

(b) 'a public authority or body'.

[17.31] Where a representative is designated then that representative cannot be established in just any EU Member State but rather must be:

> ... established in one of the Member States where the data subjects, whose personal data are processed in relation to the offering of goods or services to them, or whose behaviour is monitored, are[82]

When a representative is designated by a controller or processor then they must be:

> ... mandated ... to be addressed in addition to or instead of the controller or the processor by, in particular, supervisory authorities and data subjects, on all issues related to processing, for the purposes of ensuring compliance with this Regulation'.[83]

---

80. (contd) *Common Market Law Review*, Vol 51, 2014, 1343. Available at SSRN: https://ssrn.com/abstract=2464240). But a relevant example of a law which successfully asserted extraterritorial jurisdiction is the US Foreign Account Tax Compliance Act of 2009 (HR 3933), or FATCA, which was enacted as part of the Hiring Incentives to Restore Employment (HIRE) Act, and now comprises Ch 4 of the US Internal Revenue Code. This initially required that financial institutions outside the USA report information about financial accounts held by their institutions by US taxpayers or by foreign entities in which US taxpayers hold a substantial ownership interest.

81. FACTCA imposes a 30% withholding tax on all income and capital payments received by Foreign Financial Institution (FFI) from US sources. This has proven a highly effective enforcement tool as non-US financial institutions have a well-recognised propensity to hold US assets such as Treasuries (a phenomenon described by then French Finance Minister Valéry Giscard d'Estaing as an 'exorbitant privilege,' see Eichengreen, *Exorbitant Privilege: The Rise and Fall of the Dollar and the Future of the International Monetary System* (Oxford University Press, 2011)). The EU, and so the GDPR, lack a similarly effective enforcement mechanism.

82. GDPR, article 27(3).

83. GDPR, article 27(4).

[17.32] The Article 29 Working Party is of the view that such a representative may have to deal with any and all supervisory authorities, not just that of the Member State in which they have been established.[84]

The designation of a representative will not necessarily entail any transfer of liability from the controller or representative who nominates them. GDPR, article 27 concludes with the statement:

> The designation of a representative by the controller or processor shall be without prejudice to legal actions which could be initiated against the controller or the processor themselves.

[17.33] Agreeing to act as the representative for a controller or processor outside the EU may not be without risk, however. Since that controller or representative will be effectively outside the reach of EU Data Protection Authorities, there will be a natural tendency to impose liabilities directly upon the representative. Article 27(5) may ensure that a controller or processor cannot seek to avoid liability on the basis that they have nominated a representative; it does not enable the representative themselves to avoid liability. In addition, the Recitals provide:

> The designated representative should be subject to enforcement proceedings in the event of non-compliance by the controller or processor.[85]

Hence the role of representative is not one to be lightly taken on. It is clear from the GDPR that the role of the representative may go beyond being a simple post-box for the controller or processor who designates them. GDPR, article 30 provides that representatives may be subject to the same record maintenance obligations as the controller or processor who designates them. Representatives are required to co-operate with the supervisory authorities when requested to do so.[86] Such supervisors also have the power '... to order ... the controller's or the processor's representative to provide any information it requires for the performance of its tasks'.[87] The Recitals expand further upon what the role of the representative should be:

> The representative should act on behalf of the controller or the processor and may be addressed by any supervisory authority. The representative should be explicitly designated by a written mandate of the controller or of the processor to act on its behalf with regard to its obligations under this Regulation. The designation of

---

84. 'The GDPR's cooperation and consistency mechanism only applies to controllers with an establishment, or establishments, within the European Union. If the company does not have an establishment in the EU, the mere presence of a representative in a Member State does not trigger the one-stop-shop system. This means that controllers without any establishment in the EU must deal with local supervisory authorities in every Member State they are active in, through their local representative,' Article 29 Working Party, *Guidelines for identifying a controller or processor's lead supervisory authority*, 5 April 2017, para 3.3, p 10.

85. GDPR, Recital 80.

86. GDPR, article 31.

87. GDPR, article 58(1)(a).

such a representative does not affect the responsibility or liability of the controller or of the processor under this Regulation. Such a representative should perform its tasks according to the mandate received from the controller or processor, including cooperating with the competent supervisory authorities with regard to any action taken to ensure compliance with this Regulation.[88]

---

88.   GDPR, Recital 80.

Chapter 18

CONSISTENCY

INTRODUCTION

[18.01] One of the purposes of the GDPR is to '… ensure a consistent and high level of protection of natural persons …'.[1] The Recitals go on to provide that:

> The supervisory authorities should assist each other in performing their tasks and provide mutual assistance, so as to ensure the consistent application and enforcement of this Regulation in the internal market.[2]

And so GDPR, Ch VII, Section 2 provides for 'consistency'. To this end it sets out a consistency mechanism, as article 63 explains:

> In order to contribute to the consistent application of this Regulation throughout the Union, the supervisory authorities shall cooperate with each other and, where relevant, with the Commission, through the consistency mechanism as set out in this Section.

[18.02] The Recitals further explain that:

> In order to ensure the consistent application of this Regulation throughout the Union, a consistency mechanism for cooperation between the supervisory authorities should be established. That mechanism should in particular apply where a supervisory authority intends to adopt a measure intended to produce legal effects as regards processing operations which substantially affect a significant number of data subjects in several Member States. It should also apply where any supervisory authority concerned or the Commission requests that such matter should be handled in the consistency mechanism. That mechanism should be without prejudice to any measures that the Commission may take in the exercise of its powers under the Treaties.[3]

The GDPR provides that its consistency mechanism may be invoked in a variety of situations. Most obviously they may be invoked where differences emerge with regard to co-operation between supervisory authorities. As regards the co-operation mechanism itself, article 60 provides that if the lead authority decides not to follow a relevant and reasoned objection or if it is of the opinion that the objection is neither relevant nor reasoned then it must:

> … submit the matter to the consistency mechanism referred to in Article 63.[4]

---

1.   GDPR, Recital 10.
2.   GDPR, Recital 133.
3.   GDPR, Recital 135.
4.   GDPR, article 60(4).

As regards mutual assistance, GDPR, article 61 provides that where a supervisory authority fails to respond to a request then:

> Where a supervisory authority does not provide the information referred to in paragraph 5 of this Article within one month of receiving the request of another supervisory authority, the requesting supervisory authority may adopt a provisional measure on the territory of its Member State in accordance with Article 55(1). In that case, the urgent need to act under Article 66(1) shall be presumed to be met and require an urgent binding decision from the Board pursuant to Article 66(2).[5]

Finally, as regards joint operations, GDPR, article 62 provides that where a lead supervisory authority fails to invite other supervisory authorities to participate in a joint operation within one month of an intention for such an operation being made then:

> … the other supervisory authorities may adopt a provisional measure on the territory of its Member State in accordance with Article 55. In that case, the urgent need to act under Article 66(1) shall be presumed to be met and require an opinion or an urgent binding decision from the Board pursuant to Article 66(2).[6]

These are not the only situations where the consistency mechanism can be invoked. The consistency mechanism may be applied where lists of processing activities that require a DPIA are adopted by a supervisory authority. It may also be applied when adopting appropriate safeguards for transfers of personal data outside the EU in accordance with article 46(3).[7] The adoption of binding corporate rules must also be in accordance with the consistency mechanism.[8]

EUROPEAN DATA PROTECTION BOARD

[18.03] The European Data Protection Board is referred to by the GDPR as the 'board', though it may be more commonly referred to by its acronym 'EDPB'. The Board is established by article 68 as a body of the Union with legal personality.[9] It is an independent body of the European Union,[10] composed of the head of one supervisory authority of each Member State and the European Data Protection Supervisor, or their respective representatives.[11] Where a Member State has more than one supervisory authority responsible for monitoring the application of the provisions pursuant to the GDPR, a joint representative must be appointed in accordance with that Member State's law.[12] The Commission has the right to participate in the activities and meetings of the

---

5.   GDPR, article 61(8).
6.   GDPR, article 62(7).
7.   GDPR, article 46(4).
8.   GDPR, article 47.
9.   GDPR, article 68(1).
10.   GDPR, article 69(1).
11.   GDPR, article 68(3).
12.   GDPR, article 68(4) 'Where a Member State establishes several supervisory authorities, it should establish by law mechanisms for ensuring the effective participation of those supervisory authorities in the consistency mechanism. (contd .../)

Board but it does so without voting rights and it must designate a representative. It is represented by its Chair[13] who must communicate the activities of the Board to the Commission.[14] Where the Board adopts a binding decision in article 65, the European Data Protection Supervisor has voting rights only on decisions which concern principles and rules applicable to the Union institutions, bodies, offices and agencies which correspond in substance to those of the GDPR.[15] The Board replaces the Working Party on the Protection of Individuals with regard to the Processing of Personal Data established by article 29 of Directive 95/46/EC.[16]

Tasks of the Board

[18.04] The tasks of the Board are set out in article 70 where the Board must either on its own initiative or where relevant, at the request of the Commission undertake a number of tasks. This is to ensure the consistent application of the GDPR. The tasks are as follows:

(a) monitor and ensure the correct application of the GDPR in the cases provided for in articles 64 (Opinions of the Board) and 65 (Dispute Resolution by the Board) without prejudice to the tasks of national supervisory authorities;

(b) advise the Commission on any issue related to the protection of personal data in the Union, including on any proposed amendment of the GDPR;

(c) advise the Commission on the format and procedures for the exchange of information between controllers, processors and supervisory authorities for binding corporate rules;

(d) issue guidelines, recommendations, and best practices on procedures for erasing links, copies or replications of personal data from publicly available communication services;[17]

(e) examine, on its own initiative, on request of one of its members or on request of the Commission, any question covering the application of this Regulation and issue guidelines, recommendations and best practices in order to encourage consistent application of this Regulation;

(f) issue guidelines, recommendations and best practices in accordance with point (e) for further specifying the criteria and conditions for decisions based on profiling;[18]

---

12. (contd) That Member State should in particular designate the supervisory authority which functions as a single contact point for the effective participation of those authorities in the mechanism, to ensure swift and smooth cooperation with other supervisory authorities, the Board and the Commission' GDPR, Recital 119.

13. GDPR, article 68(2).

14. GDPR, article 68(5).

15. GDPR, article 68(6).

16. GDPR, article 92(2).

17. As referred to in GDPR, article 17(2).

18. Pursuant to GDPR, article 22(2).

(g) issue guidelines, recommendations and best practices in accordance with (e) for establishing the personal data breaches and determining undue delay, and for the particular circumstances in which a controller or a processor is required to notify the personal data breach;

(h) issue guidelines, recommendations and best practices in accordance with (e) as to the circumstances in which a personal data breach is likely to result in a high risk to the rights and freedoms of the natural persons;

(i) issue guidelines, recommendations and best practices in accordance with (e) for the purpose of further specifying the criteria and requirements for personal data transfers based on binding corporate rules adhered to by controllers and binding corporate rules adhered to by processors and on further necessary requirements to ensure the protection of personal data of the data subjects concerned;

(j) issue guidelines, recommendations and best practices in accordance with (e) for the purpose of further specifying the criteria and requirements for the transfers of personal data on the basis of article 49(1) (transfers where there is no adequacy decision or appropriate safeguards);

(k) draw up guidelines for supervisory authorities concerning the application of investigative powers, corrective powers, authorisation and advisory powers, and the setting of administrative fines;

(l) review the practical application of the guidelines, recommendations and best practices referred to in (e) and (f);

(m) issue guidelines, recommendations and best practices in accordance with (e) for establishing common procedures for the reporting of infringements of the GDPR by natural persons;[19]

(n) encourage the drawing-up of codes of conduct and the establishment of data protection certification mechanisms and data protection seals and marks;[20]

(o) carry out the accreditation of certification bodies and its periodic review[21] and maintain a public register of accredited bodies[22] and of the accredited controllers or processors established in third countries;[23]

(p) specify the requirements for the accreditation of certification bodies[24] under article 42;

(q) provide the Commission with an opinion on certification requirements;[25]

(r) provide the Commission with an opinion on the icons which may be used to provide data subjects with information;[26]

---

19.   Pursuant to GDPR, article 54(2).
20.   Pursuant to GDPR, articles 40 and 42.
21.   Pursuant to GDPR, article 43.
22.   Pursuant to GDPR, article 43(6).
23.   Pursuant to GDPR, article 42(7).
24.   As referred to in GDPR, article 43(3).
25.   As referred to in GDPR, article 43(8).
26.   Referred to in GDPR, article 12(7).

(s) provide the Commission with an opinion for the assessment of the adequacy of the level of protection in a third country or international organisation, including for the assessment whether a third country, a territory or one or more specified sectors within that third country, or an international organisation no longer ensures an adequate level of protection. In these cases, the Commission must provide the Board with all the necessary documentation, including correspondence with the government of the third country, with regard to that third country, territory or specified sector, or with the international organisation.

(t) issue opinions on draft decisions of supervisory authorities pursuant to the consistency mechanism,[27] on matters submitted pursuant to article 64(2) and to issue binding decisions,[28] including urgent cases referred to in article 66;

(u) promote the cooperation and the effective bilateral and multilateral exchange of information and best practices between the supervisory authorities;

(v) promote common training programmes and facilitate personnel exchanges between the supervisory authorities and, where appropriate, with the supervisory authorities of third countries or with international organisations;

(w) promote the exchange of knowledge and documentation on data protection legislation and practice with data protection supervisory authorities worldwide.

(x) issue opinions on codes of conduct drawn up at Union level[29] and

(y) maintain a publicly accessible electronic register of decisions taken by supervisory authorities and courts on issues handled in the consistency mechanism.

By way of example, the Recitals suggest that the Board could provide guidance on the implementation of appropriate measures and demonstration of compliance by the controller or processor by means of approved codes of conduct, approved certification or guidelines. Guidance could be provided on risks, their origin, nature, likelihood and severity and best practices to mitigate the risk. The Board might issue guidelines on processing operations that are unlikely to result in a high risk to the rights and freedoms of natural persons and indicate what measures may be sufficient in those cases to address such risks.[30] It might also, according to the Recitals, issue guidelines on the criteria to be taken into account in order to ascertain whether processing substantially affects data subjects in more than one Member State and on what constitutes a relevant and reasoned objection.[31]

[18.05] The Board must draw up an annual report regarding the protection of natural persons with regard to processing in the Union and, where relevant, in third countries and international organisations. This report must be made public and transmitted to the

---

27. Referred to in GDPR, article 64(1).
28. Pursuant to GDPR, article 65.
29. Pursuant to GDPR, article 40(9).
30. GDPR, Recital 77.
31. GDPR, Recital 124.

European Parliament, Council and the Commission.[32] It must include a review of the practical application of its guidelines, recommendations and best practices, binding decisions.[33]

The Board must act independently when performing these tasks or exercising its powers[34] and must not either seek or take instructions from anybody.[35] This latter point is stated to be without prejudice to 'requests by the Commission'.[36] Where the Commission seeks advice from the Board on any data protection issue then the Commission may indicate a time limit taking into account the urgency of the matter.[37] All opinions, guidelines, recommendations and best practices must be forwarded to the Commission and committee and they must be made public.[38] Where appropriate the Board must consult interested parties and give them the opportunity to comment within a reasonable period and the results of the consultation procedure must be made public.[39] Article 76 states however, that decisions of the Board are confidential where the Board deems it necessary in its own rules of procedure. Access to documents submitted to members of the Board, experts and representatives of third parties is governed by Regulation (EC) No 1049/2001 regarding public access to European Parliament Council and Commission documents.[40]

Procedure, Chair and Secretariat

[18.06] In terms of procedure, the Board takes decisions by a simple majority of its members, unless otherwise provided for in the GDPR such as where it adopts its own rules of procedure. In that case a two-thirds majority of its members is required. The Board organises its own operational arrangements.[41] It elects its chair and two deputy chairs from amongst its members by simple majority and the Chair's term of office and that of the deputy chairs is five years, renewable once.[42] Article 74 sets out the tasks of the Chair:

(a) to convene the meetings of the Board and prepare its agenda;

(b) to notify the lead supervisory authority and supervisory authorities concerned of dispute resolution decisions adopted by the Board;

---

32. GDPR, article 71(1).
33. GDPR, article 71(2). Those binding decisions referred to in GDPR, article 65.
34. GDPR, article 69(1).
35. GDPR, article 69(2).
36. These are the requests referred to in GDPR, article 70(1)(b).
37. GDPR, article 70(2).
38. GDPR, article 70(3).
39. GDPR, article 70(4).
40. OJ L 145, 31.5.2001, p 43.
41. GDPR, article 72.
42. GDPR, article 73.

(c) to ensure the timely performance of the tasks of the Board, in particular in relation to the consistency mechanism.

The Board lays down the allocation of tasks between the Chair and the deputy chairs in its rules of procedure.[43] The Board is assisted by a secretariat provided by the European Data Protection Supervisor (EDPS) which performs its tasks exclusively under the instructions of the Chair. The staff of the EDPS carrying out the tasks conferred on the Board are subject to separate reporting lines from the staff involved in carrying out tasks conferred on the EDPS. Where it is appropriate, the Board and EDPS must establish and publish a Memorandum of Understanding determining the terms of their cooperation and applicable to the staff of the EDPS involved in carrying out the Board's tasks. The secretariat provides analytical, administrative and logistical support and is responsible in particular for:

(a) the day-to-day business of the Board;

(b) communication between the members of the Board, its Chair and the Commission;

(c) communication with other institutions and the public;

(d) the use of electronic means for internal and external communication;

(e) the translation of relevant information;

(f) the preparation and follow-up of the meetings of the Board;

(g) the preparation, drafting and publication of opinions, decisions on the settlement of disputes between supervisory authorities and other texts adopted by the Board.[44]

The consistency mechanism

[18.07] The consistency mechanism set out in Ch VII, section 2 has three parts: firstly, there is an opinion of the Board; then there is the dispute resolution by the Board; finally, there is exchanges of information, arrangements for which may be specified by the EU Commission. These various mechanisms are discussed below. The Recitals make clear that the consistency mechanism must be followed where it is intended that cross-border measures will produce mandatory legal effects.[45] The mechanism is necessarily complex and therefore may prove time consuming. The GDPR therefore provides for an urgency procedure, which may be invoked in 'exceptional circumstances'. As the Recitals explain, this might arise when the danger exists that the enforcement of a right of a data subject could be considerably impeded. A supervisory authority should be able to adopt 'duly justified provisional measures on its territory'.[46] Such urgency may

---

43. GDPR, article 74(2).

44. GDPR, article 75.

45. 'The application of such mechanism should be a condition for the lawfulness of a measure intended to produce legal effects by a supervisory authority in those cases where its application is mandatory' GDPR, Recital 138.

46. GDPR, Recital 137.

supersede the duty to cooperate. Article 60 sets out details the duty of supervisory authorities to cooperate with one another. It also provides:

> Where, in exceptional circumstances, a supervisory authority concerned has reasons to consider that there is an urgent need to act in order to protect the interests of data subjects, the urgency procedure referred to in Article 66 shall apply[47]

And so, article 66 provides that:

> In exceptional circumstances, where a supervisory authority concerned considers that there is an urgent need to act in order to protect the rights and freedoms of data subjects, it may, by way of derogation from the consistency mechanism referred to in Articles 63, 64 and 65 or the procedure referred to in Article 60, immediately adopt provisional measures intended to produce legal effects on its own territory with a specified period of validity which shall not exceed three months.

Where this arises, the supervisory authority must communicate those measures and the reasons for adopting them to the other supervisory authorities concerned, to the Board and to the Commission. This must be done without delay. Where a supervisory authority has taken such a measure and:

> ... considers that final measures need urgently be adopted, it may request an urgent opinion or an urgent binding decision from the Board, giving reasons for requesting such opinion or decision. [48]

Any supervisory authority may make such a request from the Board where a competent supervisory authority has not taken an appropriate measure in a situation where there is an urgent need to act, in order to protect the rights and freedoms of data subjects. Reasons must be provided for the request including for the urgent need to act.[49] By derogation from articles 64(3) and 65(2), an urgent opinion or an urgent binding decision must be adopted within two weeks by simple majority of the members of the Board.[50]

An opinion of the Board

[18.08] Article 64(1) requires the Board to issue an opinion[51] where a competent supervisory authority intends to adopt any of the following measures and:

---

47. GDPR, article 60(11). GDPR, Recital 137 provides: 'There may be an urgent need to act in order to protect the rights and freedoms of data subjects, in particular when the danger exists that the enforcement of a right of a data subject could be considerably impeded. A supervisory authority should therefore be able to adopt duly justified provisional measures on its territory with a specified period of validity which should not exceed three months.'
48. GDPR, article 66(2).
49. GDPR, article 66(3).
50. GDPR, article 66(4).
51. GDPR, Recital 136 provides: 'In applying the consistency mechanism, the Board should, within a determined period of time, issue an opinion, if a majority of its members so decides or if so requested by any supervisory authority concerned or the Commission'.

the competent supervisory authority must communicate the draft decision to the Board, when it:

(a) aims to adopt a list of the processing operations subject to the requirement for a data protection impact assessment pursuant to Article 35(4);

(b) concerns a matter pursuant to Article 40(7) whether a draft code of conduct or an amendment or extension to a code of conduct complies with this Regulation;

(c) aims to approve the criteria for accreditation of a body pursuant to Article 41(3) or a certification body pursuant to Article 43(3);

(d) aims to determine standard data protection clauses referred to in point (d) of Article 46(2) and in Article 28(8);

(e) aims to authorise contractual clauses referred to in point (a) of Article 46(3); or

(f) aims to approve binding corporate rules within the meaning of Article 47.

In addition to this list, Article 64(2) provides that:

> any supervisory authority, the Chair of the Board or the Commission may request that any matter of general application or producing effects in more than one Member State be examined by the Board with a view to obtaining an opinion in particular where a competent supervisory authority does not comply with the obligations for mutual assistance ... or for joint operations ...[52]

Supervisory authorities and the Commission must communicate to the Board 'any relevant information' including a summary of the facts, the draft decision, the grounds which make the enactment of such a measure necessary and the views of the other supervisory authorities concerned. This must be done without delay by electronic means using a standardised format.[53]

[18.09] The Board must issue its opinion unless it has already issued an opinion on the same matter and that opinion must be adopted within eight weeks by simple majority of the members of the Board. Depending on the complexity of the subject matter, that period may be extended by a further six weeks.[54] The competent supervisory authority must not adopt its draft decision within this period of time. [55] Regarding a draft decision referred to in article 64(1) above circulated to members of the Board, where a member has not objected within a reasonable period of time as indicated by the Chair, they will be deemed to be in agreement with the draft decision.[56] Under article 64(5) the Chair of

---

52. GDPR, article 64(2).
53. GDPR, article 64(4).
54. GDPR, article 64(3).
55. GDPR, article 64(6).
56. GDPR, article 64(3).

the Board must 'without undue, delay' inform the following, by electronic means, of its opinion:

(a) the members of the Board and the Commission of any relevant information which has been communicated to it using a standardised format. Where necessary, the secretariat of the Board must provide translations of relevant information; and

(b) the supervisory authority concerned and the Commission of the opinion and make it public.[57]

In cases referred to under article 64(1) the supervisory authority must take 'utmost account of the opinion of the Board'. Within two weeks after receiving the opinion, it must communicate to the Chair of the Board whether it will maintain or amend its draft decision and, if any, the amended draft decision. This must be done by electronic means using a standardised format.[58] If, however, within that period of time, the supervisory authority does not wish to follow the decision of the Board, the Board can adopt a binding decision in certain cases. Article 64(8) provides that:

> Where the supervisory authority concerned informs the Chair of the Board ... that it does not intend to follow the opinion of the Board, in whole or in part, providing the relevant grounds, Article 65(1) shall apply.

Dispute resolution by the Board

[18.10] Article 65(1) requires the Board to adopt a binding decision in the following cases:[59]

(a) where, in a case referred to in Article 60(4), a supervisory authority concerned has raised a relevant and reasoned objection to a draft decision of the lead authority or the lead authority has rejected such an objection as being not relevant or reasoned. The binding decision will concern all the matters which are the subject of the relevant and reasoned objection, in particular whether there is an infringement of the GDPR;

(b) where there are conflicting views on which of the supervisory authorities concerned is competent for the main establishment;

---

57. GDPR, article 64(5).
58. GDPR, article 64(7).
59. GDPR, Recital 136 provides: 'The Board should also be empowered to adopt legally binding decisions where there are disputes between supervisory authorities. For that purpose, it should issue, in principle by a two-thirds majority of its members, legally binding decisions in clearly specified cases where there are conflicting views among supervisory authorities, in particular in the cooperation mechanism between the lead supervisory authority and supervisory authorities concerned on the merits of the case, in particular whether there is an infringement of this Regulation'.

(c) where a competent supervisory authority does not request the opinion of the Board in the cases referred to in article 64(1), or does not follow the opinion of the Board issued under article 64. In that case, any supervisory authority concerned or the Commission may communicate the matter to the Board.

This is to ensure the 'correct and consistent application' of the GDPR in individual cases. The decision of the Board must be adopted within one month from the referral of the subject-matter by a two-thirds majority of the members of the Board. Given the complexity of the subject matter, the period may be extended by a further month. The Board's decision must be:

> reasoned and addressed to the lead supervisory authority and all the supervisory authorities concerned and binding on them. [60]

During these periods, the supervisory authorities concerned must not adopt a decision on the subject matter submitted to the Board.[61] If the Board is unable to adopt a decision within this time period, it must adopt its decision within two weeks following the expiration of the second month by a simple majority of the members of the Board. Where the members of the Board are split, the decision must be adopted by the vote of its Chair.[62] The Chair of the Board must notify the supervisory authorities concerned of their decision without undue delay and inform the Commission. The decision must be published on the Board's website again without delay after the supervisory authority has notified the Board of its final decision.[63]

[18.11] The lead supervisory authority or, as the case may be, the supervisory authority with which the complaint has been lodged must adopt its final decision without undue delay and at the latest by one month after the Board has notified its decision. It must inform the Board of the date when its final decision is notified respectively to the controller or the processor and to the data subject. The final decision of the supervisory authorities concerned must be adopted under the terms of article 60(7), (8) and (9).[64] The final decision will refer to the decision referred to in article 65(1) and specify that the decision will be published on the Board's website in accordance with article 65(5). The final decision must attach the decision referred to in article 65(1).[65]

If, however, the supervisory authorities in question cannot agree upon which of them has jurisdiction, then the Board provides a dispute resolution procedure. Article 65(1) requires the Board to adopt a binding decision in the following cases:

(a) where, in a case referred to in article 60(4), a supervisory authority concerned has raised a relevant and reasoned objection to a draft decision of the lead authority or the lead authority has rejected such an objection as being not

---

60. GDPR, article 65(2).
61. GDPR, article 65(4).
62. GDPR, article 65(3).
63. GDPR, article 65(5). In accordance with GDPR, article 65(6).
64. See para **17.25**.
65. GDPR, article 65(6).

relevant or reasoned. The binding decision will concern all the matters which are the subject of the relevant and reasoned objection, in particular whether there is an infringement of the GDPR;

(b) where there are conflicting views on which of the supervisory authorities concerned is competent for the main establishment;

(c) where a competent supervisory authority does not request the opinion of the Board in the cases referred to in article 64(1), or does not follow the opinion of the Board issued under article 64. In that case, any supervisory authority concerned or the Commission may communicate the matter to the Board.

This is to ensure the 'correct and consistent application' of the GDPR in individual cases. The decision of the Board must be adopted within one month from the referral of the subject-matter by a two-thirds majority of the members of the Board. Given the complexity of the subject matter, the period may be extended by a further month. The Board's decision must be:

reasoned and addressed to the lead supervisory authority and all the supervisory authorities concerned and binding on them. [66]

During these periods, the supervisory authorities concerned must not adopt a decision on the subject matter submitted to the Board.[67] If the Board is unable to adopt a decision within this time period, it must adopt its decision within two weeks following the expiration of the second month by a simple majority of the members of the Board. Where the members of the Board are split, the decision must be adopted by the vote of its Chair.[68] The Chair of the Board must notify the supervisory authorities concerned of their decision without undue delay and inform the Commission. The decision must be published on the Board's website again without delay after the supervisory authority has notified the Board of its final decision.[69]

The lead supervisory authority or, as the case may be, the supervisory authority with which the complaint has been lodged must adopt its final decision without undue delay and at the latest by one month after the Board has notified its decision. It must inform the Board of the date when its final decision is notified respectively to the controller or the processor and to the data subject. The final decision of the supervisory authorities concerned must be adopted under the terms of article 60(7), (8) and (9). The final decision will refer to the decision referred to in article 65(1) and specify that the decision will be published on the Board's website in accordance with article 65(5). The final decision must attach the decision referred to in article 65(1).[70]

---

66.   GDPR, article 65(2).
67.   GDPR, article 65(4).
68.   GDPR, article 65(3).
69.   GDPR, article 65(5). In accordance with GDPR, article 65(6).
70.   GDPR, article 65(6).

Exchange of information

[18.12] There is a reference in some Articles to 'electronic means' and in particular using a 'standardised format'. Article 67 provides that the:

> Commission may adopt implementing acts of general scope in order to specify the arrangements for the exchange of information by electronic means between supervisory authorities, and between supervisory authorities and the Board, in particular the standardised format referred to in Article 64.

Those implementing acts must be adopted in accordance with the examination procedure set out in article 5 of Regulation No 182/2011 (of the European Parliament and of the Council of 16 February 2011 laying down the rules and general principles concerning mechanisms for control by Member States of the Commission's exercise of implementing powers).

Will the consistency mechanism work?

[18.13] The TFEU recognises data protection as a fundamental right. This greatly complicates the environment in which the GDPR's consistency mechanism will have to operate. The TFEU also requires the independence of supervisory authorities. The Article 29 Working Party is of the Opinion that:

> The GDPR requires lead and concerned supervisory authorities to co-operate, with due respect for each other's views, to ensure a matter is investigated and resolved to each authority's satisfaction – and with an effective remedy for data subjects. Supervisory authorities should endeavour to reach a mutually acceptable course of action. The formal consistency mechanism should only be invoked where co-operation does not reach a mutually acceptable outcome[71]

However, it is for the CJEU to adjudicate whether the actions or legislation of a Member State[72] or EU Institution or body[73] have failed to fulfil their obligations under the EU Treaties or acted illegally. A legally correct decision may not be mutually acceptable to every supervisory authority concerned in a matter. Ultimately it will be for the CJEU to interpret how the GDPR's consistency mechanism should work. And so the Board will have to defer to the CJEU in the same way as the supervisory authorities must do so.

---

71. Article 29 Working Party, Guidelines for identifying a controller or processor's lead supervisory authority, 5 April 2017, para 3.1, p 10.

72. 'If the Court of Justice of the European Union finds that a Member State has failed to fulfil an obligation under the Treaties, the State shall be required to take the necessary measures to comply with the judgment of the Court,' TFEU, article 260.

73. 'The Court of Justice of the European Union shall review the legality of legislative acts, of acts of the Council, of the Commission and of the European Central Bank, other than recommendations and opinions, and of acts of the European Parliament and of the European Council intended to produce legal effects vis-à-vis third parties. It shall also review the legality of acts of bodies, offices or agencies of the Union intended to produce legal effects vis-à-vis third parties,' TFEU, article 263.

Hence the consistency mechanism set out in the GDPR may not be the ultimate decider of whether or not a particular measure is in fact consistent with EU data protection law. This seems to have been accepted by the GDPR itself, which lacks an enforcement mechanism for its binding decisions. Should a supervisory authority disregard a binding decision then the sole enforcement mechanism set out in the GDPR is to bring that supervisory authority back before the Board, so that another binding decision may be made. It seems likely that such a matter would have to be referred to the CJEU, a reality acknowledged by the GDPR which provides that:

> Where proceedings are brought against a decision of a supervisory authority which was preceded by an opinion or a decision of the Board in the consistency mechanism, the supervisory authority shall forward that opinion or decision to the court.[74]

The Recitals expand upon the above, providing that:

> Any natural or legal person has the right to bring an action for annulment of decisions of the Board before the Court of Justice under the conditions provided for in Article 263 TFEU. As addressees of such decisions, the supervisory authorities concerned which wish to challenge them have to bring action within two months of being notified of them, in accordance with Article 263 TFEU. Where decisions of the Board are of direct and individual concern to a controller, processor or complainant, the latter may bring an action for annulment against those decisions within two months of their publication on the website of the Board, in accordance with Article 263 TFEU.[75]

The consistency mechanism provided by the GDPR is more complex than that originally proposed by the Commission. Whether it will work in practice remains to be seen, but it is not without certain disadvantages. Not least that the issuing of opinions and binding decisions may absorb the attention of the Board and the supervisory authorities that participate in it. This may force the Board and supervisory authorities to focus on individual issues to the detriment of more general matters. This may prove unfortunate, as tasks such as issuing 'guidelines, recommendations, and best practices' may prove more advantageous for the EU in the longer term. Much may depend upon how the consistency mechanism works in practice. As the Article 29 Working Party has opined:

> The development of consensus and good will between supervisory authorities is essential to the success of the GDPR's cooperation and consistency process.[76]

---

74.   GDPR, article 78(4).
75.   GDPR, Recital 143.
76.   Article 29 Working Party, *Guidelines for identifying a controller or processor's lead supervisory authority*, 16/EN WP244 rev .01, 5 April 2017, para 3.1, p 10.

PART 7
REMEDIES, LIABILITIES AND PENALTIES

Chapter 19

REMEDIES, LIABILITY AND PENALTIES

REMEDIES

[19.01] The Recitals provide that the GDPR:

> ... respects all fundamental rights and observes the freedoms and principles recognised in the Charter as enshrined in the Treaties, in particular ... the right to an effective remedy ...[1]

This is consistent with article 47 of the Charter:

> Everyone whose rights and freedoms guaranteed by the law of the Union are violated has the right to an effective remedy before a tribunal in compliance with the conditions laid down in this Article.

These remedies are set out in Ch VIII of the GDPR and are as follows:

- right to lodge a complaint with a supervisory authority;

- right to an effective judicial remedy against a supervisory authority;

- right to an effective judicial remedy against a controller or processor;

- right to representation; and

- right to compensation and liability.

These remedies are distinct from the supervision and enforcement mechanisms set out elsewhere in the GDPR as well as the various subject rights that are set out in Ch III of the GDPR. The CJEU explained the relationship between the different remedies in *Schrems:*

> ... legislation not providing for any possibility for an individual to pursue legal remedies in order to have access to personal data relating to him, or to obtain the rectification or erasure of such data, does not respect the essence of the fundamental right to effective judicial protection, as enshrined ... Article 47 of the Charter requires everyone whose rights and freedoms guaranteed by the law of the European Union are violated to have the right to an effective remedy before a tribunal in compliance with the conditions laid down in that article. The very existence of effective judicial review designed to ensure compliance with provisions of EU law is inherent in the existence of the rule of law.[2]

What the CJEU appears to envisage is that a subject would seek a judicial remedy to enforce rights such as access, rectification and erasure. This would suggest that subjects

---

1. GDPR, Recital 4.
2. *Schrems* (Case C–362/14) (6 October 2015), para 95.

must first have asserted such rights before they pursue legal remedies. Such remedies would only be required in the event of a controller failing to respect such rights.

RIGHT TO LODGE A COMPLAINT WITH A SUPERVISORY AUTHORITY

[19.02] The right to lodge a complaint with a supervisory authority was considered by the CJEU in *Schrems*.[3] The applicant had complained about the transfer of his personal data to the USA to the Irish supervisory authority. That authority had rejected that complaint as unfounded as '... the allegations raised by Mr Schrems in his complaint could not be profitably put forward since ... the Commission had found in that decision that the United States ensured an adequate level of protection'[4] The CJEU held that this rejection was incorrect and that '... where a person whose personal data has been or could be transferred to a third country which has been the subject of a Commission decision ... lodges with a national supervisory authority a claim concerning the protection of his rights and freedoms in regard to the processing of that data and contests ... the compatibility of that decision with the protection of the privacy and of the fundamental rights and freedoms of individuals, it is incumbent upon the national supervisory authority to examine the claim with all due diligence'.[5] The right of subjects to bring complaints to the supervisory authorities is therefore clear and the GDPR now provides:

> Without prejudice to any other administrative or judicial remedy, every data subject shall have the right to lodge a complaint with a supervisory authority, in particular in the Member State of his or her habitual residence, place of work or place of the alleged infringement if the data subject considers that the processing of personal data relating to him or her infringes this Regulation.[6]

This makes it clear that the right to complain to a supervisory authority is in addition to other remedies such as an action for damages or other judicial action. This may suggest that the subject does not necessarily have to wait for the conclusion of any complaint that they may have made to a supervisory authority before seeking damages or other intervention of the courts. This may have implications where limitation periods or time limits attach to actions for damages or other remedies under Member State law. If the making of a complaint to a supervisory authority is 'without prejudice' to the seeking of such other remedies, then the subject may have no option but to seek such other remedies in parallel with any complaint that they made to their supervisory authority.

---

3.   *Schrems* (Case C–362/14) (6 October 2015).
4.   *Schrems* (Case C–362/14) (6 October 2015), para 29.
5.   *Schrems* (Case C–362/14) (6 October 2015), para 63.
6.   GDPR, article 77(1).

[19.03] Article 77(2) goes on to provide:

> The supervisory authority with which the complaint has been lodged shall inform
> the complainant on the progress and the outcome of the complaint including the
> possibility of a judicial remedy pursuant to Article 78.

The Recitals provide some further insight as to how supervisory authorities should
respond to a complaint, adding that:

> The investigation following a complaint should be carried out, subject to judicial
> review, to the extent that is appropriate in the specific case. The supervisory
> authority should inform the data subject of the progress and the outcome of the
> complaint within a reasonable period. If the case requires further investigation or
> coordination with another supervisory authority, intermediate information should
> be given to the data subject. In order to facilitate the submission of complaints,
> each supervisory authority should take measures such as providing a complaint
> submission form which can also be completed electronically, without excluding
> other means of communication.[7]

The right of complaint is integrated with the right to an effective judicial remedy which
provides that:

> ... each data subject shall have the right to an effective judicial remedy where the
> (competent) supervisory authority ... does not handle a complaint or does not
> inform the data subject within three months on the progress or outcome of the
> complaint ...[8]

This right is stated to be without prejudice to any other administrative or non-judicial
remedy.

RIGHT TO AN EFFECTIVE JUDICIAL REMEDY AGAINST A SUPERVISORY AUTHORITY

[19.04] In addition to being able to complain to a supervisory authority subjects also
have the right to complain to the courts about the actions or inactions of such an
authority. This right was recognised in *Schrems* in which the CJEU held that where a
subject has complained to a supervisory authority that has come:

> ... to the conclusion that the arguments put forward in support of such a claim are
> unfounded and therefore rejects it, the person who lodged the claim must ... in the
> light of Article 47 of the Charter, have access to judicial remedies enabling him to
> challenge such a decision adversely affecting him before the national courts.

The CJEU went on to outline what should happen where the validity of an EU Act is
being challenged:

> ... those courts must stay proceedings and make a reference to the Court for a
> preliminary ruling on validity where they consider that one or more grounds for

---

7. GDPR, Recital 141.
8. GDPR, article 78(2).

invalidity put forward by the parties or, as the case may be, raised by them of their own motion are well founded.[9]

The CJEU makes clear that this is specific to a situation where the validity of an EU Act is being challenged. But the judgment of the Court is explicitly made '... in the light of Article 47 of the Charter ...' which provides a general right to an effective remedy. The procedure by which national courts may consider such a challenge may vary from case-to-case, but it seems clear that the CJEU expects that national courts will consider such challenges. As the CJEU went on to say:

> ... Article 47 of the Charter requires everyone whose rights and freedoms guaranteed by the law of the European Union are violated to have the right to an effective remedy before a tribunal in compliance with the conditions laid down in that article. The very existence of effective judicial review designed to ensure compliance with provisions of EU law is inherent in the existence of the rule of law ...[10]

The judgment of the CJEU in *Schrems* is now reflected in GDPR, article 78. Of course the right to a judicial remedy against a decision of a supervisory authority cannot be confined to data subjects. Article 78 makes clear that subjects, controllers, processors and indeed anyone else concerned by a legally binding decision of a supervisory authority has the right to complain to court:

> Without prejudice to any other administrative or non-judicial remedy, each natural or legal person shall have the right to an effective judicial remedy against a legally binding decision of a supervisory authority concerning them.[11]

Decisions of supervisory authorities may or may not reflect decisions of the EDPB; the GDPR is silent as to what weight the courts should attach to such decisions. It simply provides that:

> Where proceedings are brought against a decision of a supervisory authority which was preceded by an opinion or a decision of the Board in the consistency mechanism, the supervisory authority shall forward that opinion or decision to the court.[12]

What weight the CJEU considers independent supervisory authorities should attach to decisions, whether binding or non-binding, of the EDPB remains to be seen.

---

9.   *Schrems* (Case C–362/14) (6 October 2015), para 64, Citing *T & L Sugars and Sidul Açúcares v Commission* (Case C–456/13 P), para 48, *Commission and Ors v Kadi* (Cases C–584/10 P, C–593/10 P and C–595/10 P), para 66; *Inuit Tapiriit Kanatami and Ors v Parliament and Council* (Case C–583/11 P), para 91; *Telefónica v Commission* (Case C–274/12 P), para 56, *Melki and Abdeli* (Cases C–188/10 and C–189/10), para 54, and *CIVAD* (Case C–533/10), para 40.

10.   *Schrems* (Case C–362/14) (6 October 2015), para 95.

11.   GDPR, article 78(1).

12.   GDPR, article 78(4).

RIGHT TO AN EFFECTIVE JUDICIAL REMEDY

[19.05] Article 78 provides that:

> ... each data subject shall have the right to an effective judicial remedy where he or she considers that his or her rights under this Regulation have been infringed as a result of the processing of his or her personal data in non-compliance with this Regulation.

This right is explicitly stated to be 'Without prejudice to any available administrative or non-judicial remedy, including the right to lodge a complaint with a supervisory authority pursuant to Article 77 ...'.[13] In theory a subject could invoke their entire suite of remedies at once: invoking their rights under Chapter III, complaining to their competent supervisory authority and seeking a judicial remedy simultaneously. However, it seems more likely that in practice subjects will seek these remedies in sequence. The courts may refer them back to their supervisory authority, which may then direct subjects towards invoking their subject rights.

In *Puskar*[14] the CJEU considered whether national law could provide that '... the exhaustion of available administrative remedies is a prerequisite for bringing such a judicial remedy'.[15] The CJEU recalled that the TEU provided that it was '... for the courts of the Member States to ensure judicial protection of a person's rights under EU law...'[16] and required that Member States '... provide remedies sufficient to ensure effective judicial protection in the fields covered by EU law'.[17] However in this case the right to effective judicial protection was not being called into question, an additional procedural step was merely being imposed in order to exercise it.[18] It appeared to the Court that:

> ... the obligation to exhaust available administrative remedies is intended to relieve the courts of disputes which can be decided directly before the administrative authority concerned and to increase the efficiency of judicial proceedings as regards disputes in which a legal action is brought despite the fact that a complaint has already been lodged.[19]

One of the complaints made in *Puskar* was that '... there was uncertainty as to whether the period for bringing a legal action before the national court begins before a decision has been taken ...'. The CJEU held that if that were the case then '... the obligation to exhaust available administrative remedies, which might prevent access to judicial

---

13.   GDPR, article 79(1).
14.   *Puskar* (Case C–73/16) (27 September 2017).
15.   *Puskar* (Case C–73/16) (27 September 2017), para 56.
16.   Citing TEU, article 4(3).
17.   Citing TEU, article 19(1). *Puskar* (Case C–73/16) (27 September 2017), para 57.
18.   *Puskar* (Case C–73/16) (27 September 2017), para 64.
19.   *Puskar* (Case C–73/16) (27 September 2017), para 67.

protection, would not comply with the right to an effective remedy…'.[20] The CJEU concluded that:

> … Article 47 of the Charter … does not preclude national legislation, which makes the exercise of a judicial remedy by a person stating that his right to protection of personal data… has been infringed, subject to the prior exhaustion of the available administrative remedies.

However the CJEU added that this was:

> … provided that the practical arrangements for the exercise of such remedies do not disproportionately affect the right to an effective remedy before a court referred to in that article. It is important, in particular, that the prior exhaustion of the available administrative remedies does not lead to a substantial delay in bringing a legal action, that it involves the suspension of the limitation period of the rights concerned and that it does not involve excessive costs.[21]

RIGHT TO COMPENSATION

[19.06] The right to compensation may prove to be the most effective enforcement tool provided by the GDPR.[22] On the one hand the prospect of paying damages may create a significant incentive for controllers to be able to demonstrate compliance with the GDPR; on the other hand the prospect of being paid damages may create a significant incentive for subjects to query that compliance. The prospect of damages may provide subjects with a substantive incentive to invoke their rights under GDPR, Ch III. At the same time the prospect of damages may enable supervisory authorities to move on once a controller can demonstrate that it has brought itself into compliance with the GDPR. This is the approach that was taken by the CJEU in *Rotenberg*[23] in which the CJEU did not adopt the 'fruit of the poisonous tree' approach to breaches of EU data protection law. Such an approach would mean the CJEU finding invalid any action resulting from a breach of EU data protection law. Instead the CJEU adopted a more pragmatic approach which might be characterised as 'fix-it, move on, pay damages'.

[19.07] *Rotenberg* arose from Russia's annexation of the Crimea, following which the EU Council introduced sanctions targeted at certain individuals. One such individual was the applicant who was described as: '… a long-time acquaintance of President Putin and his former judo sparring partner'. The initial decision alleged that the applicant controlled a company called Giprotransmost which '… has received a public procurement contract to conduct the feasibility study of the construction of a bridge

---

20. *Puskar* (Case C–73/16) (27 September 2017), para 73.
21. *Puskar* (Case C–73/16) (27 September 2017), para 76.
22. The GDPR is not alone in taking this approach, see similarly Directive 2014/104/EU of the European Parliament and of the Council of 26 November 2014 on certain rules governing actions for damages under national law for infringements of the competition law provisions of the Member States and of the European Union, OJ L 349, 5.12.2014, p 1–19.
23. *Rotenberg v Council* (Case T–720/14) (30 November 2016).

from Russia to the illegally annexed Autonomous Republic of Crimea'.[24] The applicant made submissions to the EU Council, following which resulted in the contested references to Giprotransmost being deleted when EU sanctions were renewed.

The applicant challenged these sanctions before the CJEU on various grounds including '… that the publication by the Council of unsubstantiated, unfounded and incorrect allegations, seriously damaging to his reputation, and which allege that he is involved in cases of corruption and criminal conduct, breaches the principles of protection of personal data …'.[25] Specifically it was alleged that the Council was in breach of Regulation No 45/2001, which sets out the data protection rules that bind EU Institutions. This was rejected by the CJEU which held that: '… if the Council had processed personal data concerning the applicant's shareholding in Giprotransmost in a way that was inconsistent with Regulation No 45/2001 that could not lead to the annulment of … other … acts … were the applicant to succeed in proving that data was processed in that way, he could invoke an infringement of Regulation No 45/2001 in the context of an action for damages'.[26] This suggests that the CJEU is comfortable with an approach of allowing controllers to continue processing personal data once they can demonstrate that they have brought themselves into compliance with the GDPR. Any residual consequences could be dealt with by an award of damages to compensate subjects for the breach of their data protection rights.[27]

[19.08] The GDPR offers no guidance as to what such awards of damages should amount to; nor has the CJEU discussed what the appropriate compensation should be for a breach of a subject's data protection rights. The one exception to this is *Nikolaou*[28] in which the applicant was a former member of the EU's Court of Auditors who had been the subject of an investigation by OLAF, the EU anti-fraud agency. A number of reports had appeared in the media about this investigation, which appeared to have been based on information disclosed by OLAF in breach of its obligation of confidentiality to the applicant.[29] The applicant brought an action against the EU in which he sought €700,000 in respect of the damage to his feelings and €200,000 in respect of the damage to his health, together with costs.[30] These damages and costs were sought in respect of the alleged breach of the applicant's right to privacy as opposed to data protection. However, the CJEU agreed with the applicant that the disclosure of

---

24. *Rotenberg v Council* (Judgment) (Case T–720/14), para 14.
25. *Rotenberg v Council* (Judgment) (Case T–720/14), para 135.
26. *Rotenberg v Council* (Judgment) (Case T–720/14), para 140.
27. It is true that the GDPR does provide supervisory authorities with the corrective power 'to impose a temporary or definitive limitation including a ban on processing'. However, before imposing such a ban the supervisory authority would have to consider all Charter rights including that of conducting a business (article 16), and choosing an occupation and engaging in work earning a livelihood (article 15). It is difficult to see how such a limitation or ban might be imposed if the controller had corrected its breach of data protection law.
28. *Nikolaou* (Case T–259/03), (12 September 2007).
29. *Nikolaou* (Case T–259/03), (12 September 2007), paras 11–27.
30. *Nikolaou* (Case T–259/03), (12 September 2007), para 28.

information about the subject was a processing of his personal data contrary to the obligations imposed on OLAF by Regulation No 45/2001 (which sets out the data protection rules to be followed by EU Institutions).[31] The CJEU then went on to consider the plaintiff's claim for 'moral damages' and damages for the effect that the disclosures had upon his health. As regards the moral damages, the CJEU considered that €3000 was adequate compensation to symbolically repair the moral damage caused to the plaintiff's reputation.[32] So although this award may seem low, the CJEU intended that it be no more than symbolic.[33] Presumably this award would have been more significant if the subject had suffered more substantive damage. As regards damage to the applicant's health, the applicant claimed to have suffered significant psychological damage.[34] However, the CJEU held that the applicant was unable to prove that the plaintiff's disclosure of his personal data was the direct cause of his ill-health.[35]

[19.09] The GDPR provides that compensation may be provided for both material and non-material damage caused by and infringement of its provisions. Non-material damage presumably equates to the moral damage suffered by the applicant in *Nikolaou;* material damage presumably equates to the damage to the applicant's health. Hence the GDPR does seem consistent with the judgment of the CJEU in that case. However, the CJEU judgment in *Nikolaou* dates from 2007; it is clear that the CJEU attaches far more importance to the right to data protection now than it did then.[36] Hence it may well be that the CJEU would no longer consider that the disclosure of the applicant's personal data to the media indicating that he was under investigation by OLAF was a purely 'symbolic' matter. And *Nikolaou* can be read as suggesting that the CJEU may consider quite substantial awards are appropriate for substantial breaches of a subject's data protection rights; €3000 is not insubstantial as an award of symbolic damages after all.

[19.10] GDPR, article 82 provides:

> Any person who has suffered material or non-material damage as a result of an infringement of this Regulation shall have the right to receive compensation from the controller or processor for the damage suffered.[37]

---

31. *Nikolaou* (Case T–259/03), (12 September 2007), paras 208–216.
32. *Nikolaou* (Case T–259/03), (12 September 2007), para 325.
33. *Nikolaou* (Case T–259/03), (12 September 2007), para 333.
34. *Nikolaou* (Case T–259/03), (12 September 2007), para 334.
35. *Nikolaou* (Case T–259/03), (12 September 2007), para 337.
36. Contrast the decision of the CJEU in *Ireland v Parliament and Council* (Case C–301/06) (10 February 2009) with its decision just five years later in *Digital Rights Ireland* (Case C–293/12) (8 April 2014). Both considered the validity of Directive 2006/24. In the former case the CJEU upheld the validity of that directive without discussing privacy in any substantive way; in the latter the CJEU found that Directive to be invalid.
37. GDPR, article 82(1).

Allowing the award of compensation for non-material damage is consistent with the approach of the CJEU which held in *Digital Rights Ireland*:

> To establish the existence of an interference with the fundamental right to privacy, it does not matter whether the information on the private lives concerned is sensitive or whether the persons concerned have been inconvenienced in any way …[38]

However, there is very little guidance from the CJEU as to what the compensation for infringing the GDPR should be. In *Nikolaou*[39] the applicant was the subject of an investigation by OLAF, the EU anti-fraud agency. Information about the investigation leaked to the media. The CJEU held that '… it must be held that the leakage of certain information concerning the OLAF investigation effectively constitutes the processing of personal data concerning the applicant …'. The subject was awarded €3,000 the CJEU holding that: 'That sum is sufficient to remedy the non-pecuniary damage caused to the applicant's reputation as a result of the illegality committed by OLAF and noted in the present judgment, all the relevant circumstances having been taken into account in this respect …'.[40]

Franchet[41] largely concerned the processing of personal data, though a breach of EU data protection law was not directly discussed. The CJEU held that the EU was liable for having processed the applicant's personal data as follows:

> … forwarding of information to the Luxembourg and French judicial authorities without having heard the applicants and its Supervisory Committee and in the leaks relating to the forwarding of the … file to the French judicial authorities …; the errors of the Commission capable of incurring Community liability consist in the publication of the press release … in the speech of its President … and in the initiation of the disciplinary proceedings before the investigations were complete.[42]

In assessing non-material damages the CJEU noted that '… when confidential information is leaked, the publication of that information is the foreseeable and natural consequence of that illegality, so that the causal link remains sufficiently direct'.[43] The

---

38. *Digital Rights Ireland* (Case C–293/12) (8 April 2014), para 33. But contrast with *In CN v Parliament* (French text) (Case T–343/13) (3 December 2015) the applicant was an official of the Council of the European Union who made a petition to the EU Parliament in support of the disabled civil servant. This contained personal data, which the Parliament published on-line following the closure of his case. The CJEU accepted that material damages had been suffered, but refused to award non-material damages as the applicant had not demonstrated the existence of prejudice arising and his claim was limited to the allegation that the dismissive and dilatory attitude of the EU Parliament had hurt him deeply and had caused him great stress, without providing evidence in support of this allegation (para 121).
39. *Nikolaou* (Case T–259/03), (12 September 2007).
40. *Nikolaou* (Case T–259/03), (12 September 2007), para 333.
41. *Franchet* (Case T–48/05) (8 July 2008).
42. *Franchet* (Case T–48/05) (8 July 2008), para 398.
43. *Franchet* (Case T–48/05) (8 July 2008), para 402.

CJEU held that the applicants had '... experienced feelings of injustice and frustration and that they sustained a slur on their honour and their professional reputation on account of the unlawful conduct of OLAF and of the Commission'.[44] The CJEU assessed them as being entitled to damages in the sum of €56,000, though this took into account '... the fact that the applicants' reputation was very seriously affected'.[45]

Article 82 goes on to provide for the allocations of liability and damage between controller and processor. A controller will be liable for:

> ... the damage caused by processing which infringes this Regulation.

Hence it is the controller that is liable in the first instance; processors can be liable but only where they have breached their specific obligations under GDPR or processed personal data other than in accordance with their instructions from the controller. As regards the liability of processors article 82 provides:

> A processor shall be liable for the damage caused by processing only where it has not complied with obligations of this Regulation specifically directed to processors or where it has acted outside or contrary to lawful instructions of the controller.[46]

Article 82 goes on to provide that:

> A controller or processor shall be exempt from liability ... if it proves that it is not in any way responsible for the event giving rise to the damage.[47]

Article 82 creates a substantial incentive for controllers and processors to ensure that their relationship is documented by contract that they have agreed, together with instructions issued by the controller to processor, since it is these documents that may determine their liability. As such, article 82 may provide an effective enforcement mechanism for GDPR, articles 28 and 29. The GDPR goes on to provide for the joint and several liability of controllers and processors, providing that:

> Where more than one controller or processor, or both a controller and a processor, are involved in the same processing and where they are ... responsible for any damage caused by processing, each controller or processor shall be held liable for the entire damage in order to ensure effective compensation of the data subject.[48]

Finally:

> Where a controller or processor has ... paid full compensation for the damage suffered, that controller or processor shall be entitled to claim back from the other controllers or processors involved in the same processing that part of the compensation corresponding to their part of responsibility for the damage ...[49]

---

44.   *Franchet* (Case T–48/05) (8 July 2008), para 411.
45.   *Franchet* (Case T–48/05) (8 July 2008), para 411.
46.   GDPR, article 82(2).
47.   GDPR, article 82(3).
48.   GDPR, article 82(4).
49.   GDPR, article 82(5).

This means that where more than one controller or processor is involved in the processing of a subject's personal data that subject may seek damages from all of them. If an award of damages is made the subject may then seek payment of damages in full from the controller or processor they consider most likely to be in a position to make payment. It will be a matter for that controller and processor to obtain a contribution from their fellow controllers or processors. Hence the contractual or other relationship between controllers and processors will have to provide for the effective and accurate allocation of liabilities. It may also need to provide for the payment of appropriate indemnities.

CLASS ACTIONS

[19.11] One of the distinctive features of modern data processing systems is that they enable the simultaneous processing of very large numbers of data subjects. This is best illustrated by the example of social media networks, which simultaneously process the personal data of many millions of EU data subjects. Given this collective processing of subject data it seems appropriate and proportionate that subjects should have the right to similarly seek collective remedies. The Recitals provide that:

> Where a data subject considers that his or her rights under this Regulation are infringed, he or she should have the right to mandate a not-for-profit body, organisation or association ... to lodge a complaint on his or her behalf with a supervisory authority, exercise the right to a judicial remedy ... or ... exercise the right to receive compensation ...[50]

Article 80 goes on to provide more specifics about such representation. A subject cannot just mandate anybody to exercise his or her rights. Such a mandate may only be granted to:

> ... a not-for-profit body, organisation or association which has been properly constituted in accordance with the law of a Member State, has statutory objectives which are in the public interest, and is active in the field of the protection of data subjects' rights and freedoms with regard to the protection of their personal data
> ...

Such may only be made to a body, organisation or association that is 'not-for-profit'. Of course this does not preclude such bodies, organisations or associations engaging lawyers who may well profit from the exercise of subject mandates. Such a mandate may allow that body, organisation or association to exercise the following rights on behalf of subjects:

- to lodge a complaint with a supervisory authority;
- to seek a judicial remedy against a supervisory authority;
- to seek a judicial remedy against a controller or processor; and
- to seek compensation.

---

50. GDPR, Recital 142.

The GDPR imposes some additional limitations upon the ability of such bodies, organisations or associations to seek compensation on behalf of subjects. One is that they can only seek compensation on behalf of subjects '… where provided for by Member State law'.[51] That other is that they '… may not be allowed to claim compensation on a data subject's behalf independently of the data subject's mandate'.[52] However, Member State law may enable such bodies, organisations or associations to lodge complaints and seek judicial remedies without the consent of subjects if they should consider '… that the rights of a data subject under this Regulation have been infringed as a result of the processing'.[53]

JURISDICTION

[19.12] Somewhat confusingly the GDPR has different rules for jurisdiction for different remedies. Jurisdiction may depend upon who is seeking a remedy, which remedy is being sought and who the remedy is being sought against. These rules on jurisdiction may be different to those that apply to the jurisdiction of supervisory authorities themselves, which are considered in **Chapter 17**.

[19.13] As regards the making of a complaint to a supervisory authority, the Recitals explain that:

> Every data subject should have the right to lodge a complaint with a single supervisory authority, in particular in the Member State of his or her habitual residence …[54]

Article 77 then provides:

> Without prejudice to any other administrative or judicial remedy, every data subject shall have the right to lodge a complaint with a supervisory authority, in particular in the Member State of his or her habitual residence, place of work or place of the alleged infringement if the data subject considers that the processing of personal data relating to him or her infringes this Regulation.[55]

This sets out a number of different bases upon which subjects may identify the supervisory authority which has jurisdiction to consider their complaint. Jurisdiction may be determined by where a subject has his or her habitual residence, place of work or where an infringement of their data protection rights took place. The GDPR does not offer any definition of what it means by these terms. The meaning of 'habitual residence' has been considered by the CJEU on a number of occasions in relation to

---

51.   GDPR, article 80(1).
52.   GDPR, Recital 142.
53.   GDPR, article 80(2).
54.   GDPR, Recital 141.
55.   GDPR, article 77(1).

social security, child custody, staff regulations of the EU Institutions and European Arrest Warrants. In *Swaddling*[56] the CJEU was considering the meaning of residence in the context of social security[57] and held that when identifying a person's habitual residence:

> ... account should be taken in particular of the employed person's family situation; the reasons which have led him to move; the length and continuity of his residence; the fact (where this is the case) that he is in stable employment; and his intention as it appears from all the circumstances.[58]

The CJEU went on to conclude habitual residence in a Member State '... presupposes not only an intention to reside there, but also completion of an appreciable period of residence there'.[59] In *Mercredi*[60] the CJEU was considering the meaning of habitual residence in the context of family law, specifically the habitual residence of a child under Regulation 2201/2003.[61] The CJEU held that 'Among the tests which should be applied by the national court to establish the place where a child is habitually resident, particular mention should be made of the conditions and reasons for the child's stay on the territory of a Member State, and the child's nationality'. The Court went on to note that:

> ... in addition to ... physical presence ... in a Member State, other factors must also make it clear that that presence is not in any way temporary or intermittent ... in order to distinguish habitual residence from mere temporary presence, the former must as a general rule have a certain duration which reflects an adequate degree of permanence.

The CJEU held that:

> Before habitual residence can be transferred to the host State, it is of paramount importance that the person concerned has it in mind to establish there the permanent or habitual centre of his interests, with the intention that it should be of a lasting character.[62]

---

56. *Swaddling* (Case C–90/97) (25 February 1999). See also *Knoch v Bundesanstalt für Arbeit* (Case C–102/91) (8 July 1992).
57. Specifically Regulation 883/2004/EC of the European Parliament and of the Council of 29 April 2004 on the coordination of social security systems, OJ L 166, 30.4.2004, p 1.
58. *Swaddling* (Case C–90/97) (25 February 1999), para 29.
59. *Swaddling* (Case C–90/97) (25 February 1999), para 34.
60. *Mercredi* (Case C–497/10) (22 December 2010) applied by the CJEU in *W v X* (Case C–499/15) (15 February 2017).
61. Specifically Council Regulation 2201/2003/EC of 27 November 2003 concerning jurisdiction and the recognition and enforcement of judgments in matrimonial matters and the matters of parental responsibility, OJ L 338, 23.12.2003, p 1–29.
62. *Mercredi* (Case C–497/10) (22 December 2010), para 48–51.

The CJEU went on to consider in further detail criteria specific to family law that might be used to identify a child's habitual residence.[63] The CJEU went on to conclude that habitual residence was a question for the national court to decide '... taking account of all the circumstances of fact specific to each individual case'.[64]

[19.14] In *Fernandez v EU Commission*[65] the CJEU held that the place of habitual residence of an official of the EU Institutions '... is that in which the official concerned has established, with the intention that it should be of a lasting character, the permanent or habitual centre of his interests. However, for the purposes of determining habitual residence, all the factual circumstances which constitute such residence must be taken into account'.[66] Finally, in *Kozlowski*[67] the CJEU held that for the purposes of the European Arrest Warrant[68] a person was '... resident in the executing Member State when he has established his actual place of residence there ...'.[69]

The above CJEU case law suggests that the identification of a person's habitual residence is a question of fact, to be answered by the national court in question. That court might take a variety of criteria into account when answering that question such as the intentions of the person, the duration of their actual presence there, family circumstances, employment and so forth.

[19.15] Jurisdiction may also be determined by a subject's place of work. In *Weber*[70] the CJEU held that:

> ... the relevant criterion for establishing an employee's habitual place of work ... is, in principle, the place where he spends most of his working time engaged on his employer's business[71]

---

63.   '... the concept of "habitual residence" ... must be interpreted as meaning that such residence corresponds to the place which reflects some degree of integration by the child in a social and family environment ... factors which must be taken into consideration include, first, the duration, regularity, conditions and reasons for the stay in the territory of that Member State and for the mother's move to that State and, second, with particular reference to the child's age, the mother's geographic and family origins and the family and social connections which the mother and child have with that Member State' *Mercredi* (Case C–497/10) (22 December 2010), para 56. See similarly *A (Area of Freedom, Security and Justice)* (Case C–523/07) (2 April 2009), para 44.
64.   *Mercredi* (Case C–497/10) (22 December 2010), para 56.
65.   *Fernandez v EU Commission* (Case C–452/93P) (15 September 1994) See also *Gelabert v EU Commission* (Case T–18/91) (8 April 1992).
66.   *Fernandez v EU Commission* (Case C–452/93P) (15 September 1994), para 22.
67.   *Kozlowski* (Case C–66/08) (17 July 2008).
68.   2002/584/JHA. Council Framework Decision of 13 June 2002 on the European arrest warrant and the surrender procedures between Member States. 2002/584/JHA.
69.   *Kozlowski* (Case C–66/08) (17 July 2008).
70.   *Weber* (Case C–37/00) (27 February 2002).
71.   *Weber* (Case C–37/00) (27 February 2002), para 50.

Subjects may have more than one place of work.[72] Furthermore, the development of information technologies means that people can work anywhere. In *Federacion de Servicios Privados*[73] the CJEU held that:

> ... if a worker who no longer has a fixed place of work is carrying out his duties during his journey to or from a customer, that worker must also be regarded as working during that journey ... given that travelling is an integral part of being a worker without a fixed or habitual place of work, the place of work of such workers cannot be reduced to the physical areas of their work on the premises of their employer's customers.[74]

Finally, the subject may complain to the supervisory authority that has jurisdiction over the 'place of the alleged infringement'. This might be assumed to be the place where the controller is established, but that is not what the GDPR says. Again, much may depend upon the facts of each particular case.

[19.16] Where judicial review of a decision of a supervisory authority is sought then article 78 provides:

> Proceedings against a supervisory authority shall be brought before the courts of the Member State where the supervisory authority is established.[75]

The identification of the jurisdiction in which a supervisory authority is established should be relatively straightforward; it will be the Member under whose laws the supervisory authority was set up. Where a decision of the EDPB is challenged, then that challenge would presumably be brought before the CJEU. Alternatively, a challenge may be brought to a decision of an individual supervisory authority to follow a decision of the EDPB. The GDPR stipulates that in either circumstance '... the supervisory authority shall forward that opinion or decision to the court'.[76]

[19.17] As regards proceedings against a controller or processor article 79(2) provides:

> Proceedings against a controller or a processor shall be brought before the courts of the Member State where the controller or processor has an establishment.

The GDPR then goes on to provide an alternative jurisdiction:

> Alternatively, such proceedings may be brought before the courts of the Member State where the data subject has his or her habitual residence, unless the controller

---

72. See: *Rijksinstituut voor de sociale verzekering des zelfstandigen (RSVZ) v Heinrich Wolf et NV Microtherm Europe and Ors* (Free Movement of Persons) (Case R–155/87) (7 July 1988), para 11; and, *EU Commission v Grand Duchy of Luxembourg* (Case C–351/90) (16 June 1992).
73. *Federacion de Servicios Privados del sindicato Comisiones obreras v Tyco Integrated Security SL* (Case C–266/14) (10 September 2015).
74. *Federacion de Servicios Privados del sindicato Comisiones obreras v Tyco Integrated Security SL* (Case C–266/14) (10 September 2015), para 423.
75. GDPR, article 78(3).
76. GDPR, article 78(4).

or processor is a public authority of a Member State acting in the exercise of its public powers.[77]

Hence subjects have a choice as to which jurisdiction they will seek a remedy against a controller or processor. They may either utilise the jurisdiction in which the controller has an establishment or their own habitual residence.

This will determine the courts from which compensation may be sought in accordance with article 82, which provides:

> Court proceedings for exercising the right to receive compensation shall be brought before the courts competent under the law of the Member State referred to in Article 79(2).[78]

SUSPENSION OF PROCEEDINGS

[19.18] The variety of jurisdictional provisions within the GDPR together with the potential overlap between those provisions makes it seem inevitable that some conflict will arise. The procedure by which the courts may resolve such conflicts is set out in article 81, which provides:

> Where a competent court of a Member State has information on proceedings, concerning the same subject matter as regards processing by the same controller or processor, that are pending in a court in another Member State, it shall contact that court in the other Member State to confirm the existence of such proceedings.[79]

The purpose of contacting the court of the other Member State appears to be to identify the court, which has been first seized of proceedings. Article 81 then goes on to provide:

> Where proceedings concerning the same subject matter as regards processing of the same controller or processor are pending in a court in another Member State, any competent court other than the court first seized may suspend its proceedings.[80]

and:

> Where those proceedings are pending at first instance, any court other than the court first seized may also, on the application of one of the parties, decline jurisdiction if the court first seized has jurisdiction over the actions in question and its law permits the consolidation thereof.

Hence the GDPR allows for courts to suspend proceedings; it does not necessarily require it. How such suspensions will work in practice remains to be seen.

---

77.   GDPR, article 79(2).
78.   GDPR, article 82(6).
79.   GDPR, article 81(1).
80.   GDPR, article 81(2).

PART 8
CRIMINAL JUSTICE

Chapter 20

THE SHARING OF PERSONAL DATA

INTRODUCTION

[20.01] The EU has resolved to establish '… an area of freedom, security and justice …'[1] thus creating a space '… in which the free movement of persons is ensured in conjunction with appropriate measures with respect to external border controls, asylum, immigration and the prevention and combating of crime'.[2] In pursuit of these objectives the EU is granted important functions in relation to police co-operation. The TFEU provides that the EU:

> … shall establish police cooperation involving all the Member States' competent authorities, including police, customs and other specialised law enforcement services in relation to the prevention, detection and investigation of criminal offences.[3]

The TFEU goes on to provide that in pursuit of this objective the EU legislature may establish measures concerning:

> … the collection, storage, processing, analysis and exchange of relevant information.[4]

As the Charter makes clear, these objectives have to be balanced with the right to data protection, providing that:

> Any limitation on the exercise of the rights and freedoms recognised by this Charter must be provided for by law and respect the essence of those rights and freedoms. Subject to the principle of proportionality, limitations may be made only if they are necessary and genuinely meet objectives of general interest recognised by the Union or the need to protect the rights and freedoms of others.[5]

[20.02] The CJEU has examined how this balance is to be set in a number of instances. Opinion 1/15[6] provides a useful analysis of the interaction between TFEU, articles 16

---

1. TEU, Preamble.
2. TEU, article 3(2).
3. TFEU, article 87(1).
4. TFEU, article 87(2)(a). In Opinion 1/15 the CJEU '… observed, first, that relevant information, within the meaning of Article 87(2)(a) TFEU, in relation to the prevention, detection and investigation of criminal offences, may include personal data and, second, that the terms "processing" and "exchange" of such data cover both its transfer to the Member States' competent authorities in this area and its use by those authorities' Opinion 1/15, para 99.
5. Charter, article 52(1).
6. 'Transfer of Passenger Name Record data from the European Union to Canada' [2017] EUECJ Avis-1/OCCUR (26 July 2017).

and 87, together with the Charter. The CJEU began by noting that transfers of personal data from the EU to Canada interfered with both the right to privacy provided by article 7 of the Charter[7] and the right to data protection provided by article 8 of the Charter.[8] However, the CJEU held that:

> ... the rights enshrined in Articles 7 and 8 of the Charter are not absolute rights, but must be considered in relation to their function in society.[9]

[20.03] The CJEU went on to note that '... the envisaged agreement is intended ... to ensure public security ... and the use of that data within the framework of the fight against terrorist offences and serious transnational crime.' The CJEU went on to hold that:

> That objective constitutes, as is apparent from the case law of the Court, an objective of general interest of the European Union that is capable of justifying even serious interferences with the fundamental rights enshrined in Articles 7 and 8 of the Charter. Moreover, the protection of public security also contributes to the protection of the rights and freedoms of others. In this connection, Article 6 of the Charter states that everyone has the right not only to liberty but also to security of the person ...[10]

The CJEU then went on to set out its criteria for how limitations may be placed on the right to data protection.

- Firstly, personal data must be processed 'for specified purposes and on the basis of the consent of the person concerned or some other legitimate basis laid down by law'.[11]

- Secondly, '... any limitation on the exercise of the rights and freedoms recognised by the Charter must be provided for by law,'[12] a requirement which '... implies that the legal basis which permits the interference with those rights must itself define the scope of the limitation on the exercise of the right concerned'.[13]

- Thirdly any such limitation must '... respect the essence of those rights and freedoms.'

- Fourthly '... limitations may be made to those rights and freedoms only if they are necessary and genuinely meet objectives of general interest recognised by the Union or the need to protect the rights and freedoms of others'.

---

7.   Opinion 1/15, para 122, 124.
8.   Opinion 1/15, para 126.
9.   Opinion 1/15, para 136.
10.   Opinion 1/15, para 148–149.
11.   Opinion 1/15, para 137.
12.   Opinion 1/15, para 138.
13.   Opinion 1/15, para 139.

- Fifthly any such limitations will be '… subject to the principle of proportionality …'.[14] The CJEU went on to hold that 'As regards observance of the principle of proportionality, the protection of the fundamental right to respect for private life at EU level requires, in accordance with settled case law of the Court, that derogations from and limitations on the protection of personal data should apply only in so far as is strictly necessary'.[15]

- Finally, in order to satisfy this latter requirement: '… legislation … which entails … interference must lay down clear and precise rules governing the scope and application of the measure in question and imposing minimum safeguards … It must … indicate in what circumstances and under which conditions a measure providing for the processing of such data may be adopted, thereby ensuring that the interference is limited to what is strictly necessary. The need for such safeguards is all the greater where personal data is subject to automated processing. Those considerations apply particularly where the protection of the particular category of personal data that is sensitive data is at stake'.[16]

These criteria go beyond those set out in GDPR, article 6(3). The CJEU is clear that the above must be applied when rights of data protection are being complied with; unlike article 6(3) there is no suggestion that the above are criteria that 'may' be applied. It is also of significance that the above criteria are set out in Opinion 1/15, in which the Grand Chamber of the CJEU was addressing issues raised directly by the EU's parliament, a branch of the EU's legislature. EU measures require the processing of personal data for a variety of police and criminal justice purposes. Some of the more prominent examples are discussed below.[17]

EU measures that provide for data processing for police or criminal justice purposes

[20.04] The EU is determined 'to lay the foundations of an ever-closer union among the peoples of Europe' and resolved 'to ensure … economic and social progress … by

---

14. Opinion 1/15, para 138.
15. Opinion 1/15, para 140.
16. Opinion 1/15, para 141.
17. The legal base that might apply to such measures was considered by the CJEU in Opinion 1/15. The Court began by noting that both articles '… provide for the use of the ordinary legislative procedure …' and so '… the use of both of those provisions does not entail, in principle, different adoption procedures' (para 106). Opinion 1/15 concerned an agreement providing for the transfer of personal data from the EU to Canada. The EU Council submitted that there were subtle differences between the voting rules for TFEU, articles 16(2) and 87(2)(a). These differences stemmed from the non-participation of Denmark in votes on measures proposed pursuant to TFEU, Pt 3, Title V (paras 105-118). This argument was rejected by the CJEU which held that the Council Decision must be '… based jointly on Article 16(2) and Article 87(2)(a) TFEU' (para 118). Requiring that such Council Decisions have a joint legal base means that they cannot just address information sharing, as required by article 87(2)(a), but also data protection, as required by TFEU, article 16(2).

common action to eliminate the barriers which divide Europe'.[18] Unfortunately criminal networks can also be built upon such foundations. As the Europol Regulation explains:

> Large-scale criminal and terrorist networks pose a significant threat to the internal security of the Union and to the safety and livelihood of its citizens. Available threat assessments show that criminal groups are becoming increasingly poly-criminal and cross-border in their activities. National law enforcement authorities therefore need to cooperate more closely with their counterparts in other Member States.[19]

[20.05] The dangers that such cross-border networks pose to the EU were illustrated by the Paris attacks of November 2015. The perpetrators[20] and their weapons[21] were able to move freely across the internal borders of the EU.[22] Following those attacks the EU committed to improved information sharing measures.[23] Measures enacted since then include:

- Europol Regulation; and the
- PNR Directive.

These build upon existing measures such as:

- data retention;
- ECRIS;
- Eurojust;
- European Investigation Orders;
- Anti-money laundering Directive;
- European Information Exchange Model; and
- the Schengen Information System.

These measures are discussed briefly below, however this is not intended to be a comprehensive discussion of all EU measures that provide for the processing of personal

---

18.   TFEU, Preamble.
19.   Europol Regulation, Recital 4.
20.   Traynor, 'EU ministers order tighter border checks in response to Paris attacks', (2015) *The Guardian*, 20 November.
21.   'For EU officials, the Paris and Copenhagen attacks this year have confirmed a suspicion that illegal weapons are flowing freely through Europe's 26-country Schengen zone ...' Bajekal and Walt, 'How Europe's Terrorists get their Guns', (2015) *Time Magazine*, 7 December.
22.   Hewitt, 'Paris attacks: The crisis of Europe's borders', (2015) bbc.com, 18 November.
23.   See generally the EU Council's page on Response to foreign terrorist fighters and recent terrorist attacks in Europe: http://www.consilium.europa.eu/en/policies/fight-against-terrorism/foreign-fighters/. See in particular the Final Report of the High-level expert group on information systems and interoperability, May 2017: http://ec.europa.eu/transparency/regexpert/index.cfm?do=groupDetail.groupDetailDoc&id=32600&no=1.

data.[24] Instead this seeks to give an overview of how the EU is harmonising the processing of personal data for police and criminal justice purposes in the EU. These various measures are interesting, because they demonstrate the extent to which the EU is now mandating the processing of personal data. Each of these measures contains some specific mechanism to provide for the protection of personal data. These measures must be considered in the context of the Law Enforcement Directive, which is discussed in detail in the chapter that follows.

Data retention

[20.06] In *Digital Rights Ireland*[25] the CJEU held the EU's Data Retention Directive 2006/24[26] to be invalid. That Directive required that providers of electronic communications services

> ... retain ... data necessary to trace and identify the source of a communication and its destination, to identify the date, time, duration and type of a communication, to identify users' communication equipment, and to identify the location of mobile communication equipment, data which consist, inter alia, of the name and address of the subscriber or registered user, the calling telephone number, the number called and an IP address for Internet services. Those data make it possible, in particular, to know the identity of the person with whom a subscriber or registered user has communicated and by what means, and to identify the time of the communication as well as the place from which that communication took place. They also make it possible to know the frequency of the communications of the subscriber or registered user with certain persons during a given period.[27]

The CJEU began its judgment by noting that the retention of data for the purpose of allowing the competent national authorities to have possible access to those data in the fight against terrorism and serious crime '... genuinely satisfies an objective of general interest'.[28] The CJEU went on to find that the retention of this data provided the police with '... additional opportunities to shed light on serious crime and ... they are therefore

---

24. Other systems that are not discussed include the Customs Information System (CIS) and the Vate Information Exchange System (VIES). See respectively Council Regulation 515/97/EC of 13 March 1997 on mutual assistance between the administrative authorities of the Member States and cooperation between the latter and the Commission to ensure the correct application of the law on customs or agricultural matters, OJ L 82 22 March 1997 and http://ec.europa.eu/taxation_customs/vies/.
25. *Digital Rights Ireland* (Case C–293/12) (8 April 2014).
26. Directive 2006/24/EC of the European Parliament and of the Council of 15 March 2006 on the retention of data generated or processed in connection with the provision of publicly available electronic communications services or of public communications networks and amending Directive 2002/58/EC (OJ 2006 L 105, p 54).
27. *Digital Rights Ireland* (Case C–293/12) (8 April 2014), para 26.
28. *Digital Rights Ireland* (Case C–293/12) (8 April 2014), para 44.

a valuable tool for criminal investigations' and so '... the retention of such data may be considered to be appropriate for attaining the objective pursued ...'.[29]

[20.07] The CJEU then considered whether it was possible to 'verify the proportionality of the interference found to exist.' The CJEU began by explaining that '... the principle of proportionality requires that acts of the EU institutions be appropriate for attaining the legitimate objectives pursued by the legislation at issue and do not exceed the limits of what is appropriate and necessary in order to achieve those objectives ...'.[30] However, the CJEU went on to note that '... where interferences with fundamental rights are at issue, the extent of the EU legislature's discretion may prove to be limited, depending on a number of factors, including, in particular, the area concerned, the nature of the right at issue guaranteed by the Charter, the nature and seriousness of the interference and the object pursued by the interference'.[31] As regards the retention of telecommunications data in the case before it the CJEU held that:

> ... in view of the important role played by the protection of personal data in the light of the fundamental right to respect for private life and the extent and seriousness of the interference with that right caused by Directive 2006/24, the EU legislature's discretion is reduced, with the result that review of that discretion should be strict.[32]

The CJEU accepted that the fight against serious crime, organised crime and terrorism was 'of the utmost importance'. And noted that the effectiveness of this fight might '... depend to a great extent on the use of modern investigation techniques'. However, the CJEU refused to accept that even a fundamental objective of general interest such as this could of itself justify the Directive 2006/24 as '... being considered to be necessary for the purpose of that fight'.[33] The CJEU reiterated its settled case law[34] that '... derogations and limitations in relation to the protection of personal data must apply only in so far as is strictly necessary'.[35] And so EU legislation which interferes with the right to data protection:

> ... must lay down clear and precise rules governing the scope and application of the measure in question and imposing minimum safeguards so that the persons whose data have been retained have sufficient guarantees to effectively protect their personal data against the risk of abuse and against any unlawful access and use of that data.[36]

---

29. *Digital Rights Ireland* (Case C–293/12) (8 April 2014), para 49. In making this assessment the CJEU did not consider the effectiveness of data retention as relevant to the question of whether it was appropriate (para 50).
30. *Digital Rights Ireland* (Case C–293/12) (8 April 2014), para 46.
31. *Digital Rights Ireland* (Case C–293/12) (8 April 2014), para 47.
32. *Digital Rights Ireland* (Case C–293/12) (8 April 2014), para 48.
33. *Digital Rights Ireland* (Case C–293/12) (8 April 2014), para 51.
34. Citing *Institut professionnel des agents immobiliers (IPI)* (Case C–473/12) (7 November 2013).
35. *Digital Rights Ireland* (Case C–293/12) (8 April 2014), para 52.
36. *Digital Rights Ireland* (Case C–293/12) (8 April 2014), para 54.

[20.08] The CJEU noted that the need for such safeguards was '... all the greater where ... personal data are subjected to automatic processing and where there is a significant risk of unlawful access to those data'.[37] The CJEU then turned to consider whether Directive 2006/24 went beyond what was strictly necessary. It began by observing that Directive 2006/24:

> ... requires the retention of all traffic data concerning fixed telephony, mobile telephony, Internet access, Internet e-mail and Internet telephony. It therefore applies to all means of electronic communication, the use of which is very widespread and of growing importance in people's everyday lives. Furthermore ... the directive covers all subscribers and registered users. It therefore entails an interference with the fundamental rights of practically the entire European population.[38]

The CJEU identified three particular difficulties that it had with Directive 2006/24. The first was the comprehensive nature of the retention that it required as it:

> ... affects all persons using electronic communications services, but without the persons whose data are retained being, even indirectly, in a situation which is liable to give rise to criminal prosecutions. It ... applies even to persons for whom there is no evidence capable of suggesting that their conduct might have a link, even an indirect or remote one, with serious crime. Furthermore, it does not provide for any exception, with the result that it applies even to persons whose communications are subject ... to the obligation of professional secrecy.[39]

The second difficulty was that although Directive 2006/24 did seek to contribute to the fight against serious crime it did not:

> ... require any relationship between the data whose retention is provided for and a threat to public security and, in particular, it is not restricted to a retention in relation (i) to data pertaining to a particular time period and/or a particular geographical zone and/or to a circle of particular persons likely to be involved, in one way or another, in a serious crime, or (ii) to persons who could, for other reasons, contribute, by the retention of their data, to the prevention, detection or prosecution of serious offences.[40]

This '... general absence of limits ...' led to the third difficulty that the CJEU had with Directive 2006/24, which was that it failed to:

> ... lay down any objective criterion by which to determine the limits of the access of the competent national authorities to the data and their subsequent use for the purposes of prevention, detection or criminal prosecutions concerning offences that, in view of the extent and seriousness of the interference with the fundamental rights enshrined in Articles 7 and 8 of the Charter, may be considered to be sufficiently serious to justify such an interference.[41]

---

37. *Digital Rights Ireland* (Case C–293/12) (8 April 2014), para 55.
38. *Digital Rights Ireland* (Case C–293/12) (8 April 2014), para 56.
39. *Digital Rights Ireland* (Case C–293/12) (8 April 2014), para 58.
40. *Digital Rights Ireland* (Case C–293/12) (8 April 2014), para 59.
41. *Digital Rights Ireland* (Case C–293/12) (8 April 2014), para 60.

This was a particular difficulty for the CJEU, which went on to note that Directive 2006/ 24: '... does not contain substantive and procedural conditions relating to the access of the competent national authorities to the data and to their subsequent use'.[42] The CJEU went on to explain what such conditions might amount to, noting that Directive 2006/14 did not:

> ... lay down any objective criterion by which the number of persons authorised to access and subsequently use the data retained is limited to what is strictly necessary ... access ... is not made dependent on a prior review carried out by a court or by an independent administrative body whose decision seeks to limit access to the data and their use to what is strictly necessary ... and which intervenes following a reasoned request of those authorities submitted within the framework of procedures of prevention, detection or criminal prosecutions.[43]

[20.09] The fourth difficulty that the CJEU had with Directive 2006/24 was that it failed to provide '... sufficient safeguards ... to ensure effective protection of the data retained against the risk of abuse and against any unlawful access and use of that data. And in particular Directive 2006/24 did not:

> ... lay down rules which are specific and adapted to (i) the vast quantity of data whose retention is required by that directive, (ii) the sensitive nature of that data and (iii) the risk of unlawful access to that data, rules which would serve, in particular, to govern the protection and security of the data in question in a clear and strict manner in order to ensure their full integrity and confidentiality.[44]

In particular the CJEU noted that Directive 2006/24 failed to '... ensure the irreversible destruction of the data at the end of the data retention period'.[45] The final difficulty which the CJEU had with Directive 2006/24 was that it did not '... require the data in question to be retained within the European Union, with the result that it cannot be held that the control ... by an independent authority of compliance with the requirements of protection and security ... is fully ensured'. Having outlined the various difficulties that it had with Directive 2006/24 the CJEU concluded that it was invalid.

[20.10] Following *Digital Rights Ireland* some Member States were of the opinion that the invalidity of Directive 2006/24/EU did not affect the validity of their domestic data retention laws. However, in *Tele2 Sverige*[46] the CJEU held that such national measures

---

42.   *Digital Rights Ireland* (Case C–293/12) (8 April 2014), para 61.
43.   *Digital Rights Ireland* (Case C–293/12) (8 April 2014), para 62. The CJEU had particular difficulty with the generalised nature of the retention periods imposed by Directive 2006/24 which required that: '... data be retained for a period of at least six months, without any distinction being made between the categories of data ... on the basis of their possible usefulness for the purposes of the objective pursued or according to the persons concerned ... that period is set at between a minimum of 6 months and a maximum of 24 months, but it is not stated that the determination of the period of retention must be based on objective criteria in order to ensure that it is limited to what is strictly necessary,' paras 63–64.
44.   *Digital Rights Ireland* (Case C–293/12) (8 April 2014), para 66.
45.   *Digital Rights Ireland* (Case C–293/12) (8 April 2014), para 67.
46.   *Tele2 Sverige* (Case C–203/15) (21 December 2016).

fell within the scope of EU law in general and the Charter in particular.[47] EU law did not prevent Member States adopting such national measures, but imposed certain requirements. As regards the retention of data, the CJEU held that the objective of fighting serious crime '… cannot in itself justify that national legislation providing for the general and indiscriminate retention of all traffic and location data should be considered to be necessary for the purposes of that fight'.[48]

Firstly, the national legislation in question which allowed access to retained telecommunications data would have to be '… proportionate to the seriousness of the interference in fundamental rights that that access entails, it follows that, in the area of prevention, investigation, detection and prosecution of criminal offences, only the objective of fighting serious crime is capable of justifying such access to the retained data' and would have to ensure '… that such access does not exceed the limits of what is strictly necessary'.[49] This meant that national legislation would have to '… lay down clear and precise rules indicating in what circumstances and under which conditions …'.[50] access would be granted to retained data. Such rules would have to set out the '… substantive and procedural conditions …' pursuant to which access would be granted. This meant that national legislation would have to set out objective criteria which defined the circumstances and conditions under which access was to be granted to retained data. And so, as a general rule access might only be granted '… in relation to the objective of fighting crime, only to the data of individuals suspected of planning, committing or having committed a serious crime or of being implicated in one way or another in such a crime'. However, the CJEU did suggest that there might be other situations such as '… where … vital national security, defence or public security interests are threatened by terrorist activities' in which '… access … might also be granted where there is objective evidence from which it can be deduced that that data might, in a specific case, make an effective contribution to combating such activities.'[51] In order to ensure that such conditions were respected the CJEU anticipated that applications to access retained data would be:

> … subject to a prior review carried out either by a court or by an independent administrative body, and that the decision of that court or body should be made following a reasoned request by those authorities submitted, inter alia, within the framework of procedures for the prevention, detection or prosecution of crime.[52]

Police and other authorities granted access to such retained data would have to '… notify the persons affected, under the applicable national procedures, as soon as that notification is no longer liable to jeopardise the investigations being undertaken by those authorities'. The purpose of such notification was '… to enable the persons affected to exercise… their right to a legal remedy … where their rights have been infringed'.[53]

---

47. *Tele2 Sverige* (Case C–203/15) (21 December 2016), paras 62–81.
48. *Tele2 Sverige* (Case C–203/15) (21 December 2016), para 103.
49. *Tele2 Sverige* (Case C–203/15) (21 December 2016), paras 115–116.
50. *Tele2 Sverige* (Case C–203/15) (21 December 2016), para 117.
51. *Tele2 Sverige* (Case C–203/15) (21 December 2016), para 119.
52. *Tele2 Sverige* (Case C–203/15) (21 December 2016), para 120.
53. *Tele2 Sverige* (Case C–203/15) (21 December 2016), para 121.

[20.11] However, the CJEU is not opposed to the retention of data in every instance, only its generalised retention. In *Tele2 Sverige* the CJEU explained that the Charter:

> ... does not prevent a Member State from adopting legislation permitting, as a preventive measure, the targeted retention of traffic and location data, for the purpose of fighting serious crime, provided that the retention of data is limited, with respect to the categories of data to be retained, the means of communication affected, the persons concerned and the retention period adopted, to what is strictly necessary.[54]

In terms of targeting such measures the CJEU observed '... the national legislation must be based on objective evidence which makes it possible to identify a public whose data is likely to reveal a link, at least an indirect one, with serious criminal offences, and to contribute in one way or another to fighting serious crime or to preventing a serious risk to public security. Such limits may be set by using a geographical criterion ...'.[55] And the CJEU approved a quite generalised form of data retention in *Breyer*,[56] which concerned German government websites that stored:

> ... information on all access operations in logfiles. The information retained in the logfiles after those sites have been accessed include the name of the web page or file to which access was sought, the terms entered in the search fields, the time of access, the quantity of data transferred, an indication of whether access was successful, and the IP address of the computer from which access was sought.

This was done for the purpose of '... preventing attacks and making it possible to prosecute "pirates"...'.[57] The CJEU accepted that the objective of ensuring the '... the general operability of those services may justify the use of those data after a consultation period of those websites'.[58]

---

54. *Tele2 Sverige* (Case C–203/15) (21 December 2016), para 108.
55. *Tele2 Sverige* (Case C–203/15) (21 December 2016), para 111.
56. *Breyer* (Case C–582/14) (19 October 2016).
57. *Breyer* (Case C–582/14) (19 October 2016), para 14.
58. *Breyer* (Case C–582/14) (19 October 2016), para s, 65. See also *McFadden* (Case C–484/14) (15 September 2016) in which the CJEU accepted that providers of internet access, specifically public wi-fi, might have to identify users. Identification would, of course, be pointless if data relating to that identification were not retained by the internet service providers. Some might therefore speculate that the EU Commission would bring forward a new data retention proposal. Such speculation was explicitly rejected by an EU Commission statement: 'We have been very clear that the Commission is not coming forward with any new initiatives on Data Retention. In the absence of EU rules, Member States are free to maintain their current data retention systems or set up new ones, providing of course they comply with basic principles under EU law, such as those contained in the ePrivacy Directive' EU Commission, Statement on national data retention laws, 16 September 2015. In January 2017 the EU Commission explained that its Proposal for a new ePrivacy Regulation would not '... harmonise rules on data retention...' but would rather maintain '...the existing possibility to limit these rights for reasons related to national security or criminal law enforcement,' EU Commission, Fact Sheet, Digital Single Market – Stronger privacy rules for electronic communications, 10 January 2017. (contd .../)

The Europol Regulation

[20.12] Europol is established pursuant to TFEU, article 88. Its mission is:

> … to support and strengthen action by the Member States' police authorities and other law enforcement services and their mutual cooperation in preventing and combating serious crime affecting two or more Member States, terrorism and forms of crime which affect a common interest covered by a Union policy.[59]

Article 88 goes on to provide that it is for the EU legislature to determine the '… structure, operation, field of action and tasks …' of Europol. These tasks may include:

> … the collection, storage, processing, analysis and exchange of information, in particular that forwarded by the authorities of the Member States or third countries or bodies.[60]

[20.13] The Europol Regulation[61] establishes a European Union Agency for Law Enforcement Cooperation or Europol '… with a view to supporting cooperation among law enforcement authorities in the Union'.[62] This is an agency with a variety of tasks, including to: '… collect, store, process, analyse and exchange information, including criminal intelligence';[63] '… notify the Member States … without delay of any information and connections between criminal offences concerning them';[64] and '… support Member States' cross-border information exchange activities …'.[65] Chapter IV of the Europol Regulation sets out detailed provisions on the processing of information. It provides that personal data may be processed only for the purposes of:

> (a) 'cross-checking aimed at identifying connections or other relevant links between information related to:
>
> > (i) 'persons who are suspected of having committed or taken part in a criminal offence in respect of which Europol is competent, or who have been convicted of such an offence;

---

58.   (contd) As of 29 September 2017 the EU Commission position was that following the judgment of the CJEU in *Digital Rights Ireland* it had '… started to monitor developments at national level, in particular as regards the assessment by Member States of their data retention legislation'.
59.   TFEU, article 88(1).
60.   TFEU, article 88(2)(a).
61.   Regulation 794/2016/EU of the European Parliament and of the Council of 11 May 2016 on the European Union Agency for Law Enforcement Cooperation (Europol) and replacing and repealing Council Decisions 2009/371/JHA, 2009/934/JHA, 2009/935/JHA, 2009/936/JHA and 2009/968/JHA, OJ L 135, 24.5.2016, p 53–114.
62.   Regulation 794/2016/EU, article 1(1).
63.   Regulation 794/2016/EU, article 4(1)(a).
64.   Regulation 794/2016/EU, article 4(1)(b).
65.   Regulation 794/2016/EU article 4(1)(h).

    (ii) 'persons regarding whom there are factual indications or reasonable grounds to believe that they will commit criminal offences in respect of which Europol is competent;

(b) 'analyses of a strategic or thematic nature;

(c) 'operational analyses;

(d) 'facilitating the exchange of information between Member States, Europol, other Union bodies, third countries and international organisations'.[66]

[20.14] Chapter IV goes on to impose restrictions on who can access such information. Chapter V sets out how Europol may exchange information with partner organisations, including those outside the EU. Chapter VI provides for data protection safeguards. It sets out codes against which the reliability and accuracy of information must be assessed[67] and goes on to provide general data protection principles,[68] protections for sensitive data,[69] data protection by design[70] and time limits on the storage of data.[71] Provision is made for the security of data[72] and the notification of subjects in the event of a breach.[73] Provision is also made for the division of responsibility between the police authorities of Member States and Europol;[74] provision is similarly made for the division of supervisory authorities between national data protection supervisory[75] authorities and the EDPS.[76] A DPO is to be appointed.[77] Subjects are granted the right to access the following information:

(a) confirmation as to whether or not data related to him or her are being processed;

(b) information on at least the purposes of the processing operation, the categories of data concerned, and the recipients or categories of recipients to whom the data are disclosed;

(c) communication in an intelligible form of the data undergoing processing and of any available information as to their sources;

(d) an indication of the legal basis for processing the data;

(e) the envisaged period for which the personal data will be stored;

---

66. Regulation 794/2016/EU, article 18(2).
67. Regulation 794/2016/EU, article 29.
68. Regulation 794/2016/EU, article 28.
69. Regulation 794/2016/EU, article 30.
70. Regulation 794/2016/EU, article 33.
71. Regulation 794/2016/EU, article 31.
72. Regulation 794/2016/EU, article 32.
73. Regulation 794/2016/EU, article 35.
74. Regulation 794/2016/EU, article 38.
75. Regulation 794/2016/EU, article 42.
76. Regulation 794/2016/EU, articles 43 and 44.
77. Regulation 794/2016/EU, article 41.

(f)   the existence of the right to request from Europol rectification, erasure or restriction of processing of personal data concerning the data subject.[78]

However, such a request may be refused or the response restricted if such a refusal or restriction is necessary to:

(a)   enable Europol to fulfil its tasks properly;

(b)   protect security and public order or prevent crime;

(c)   guarantee that any national investigation will not be jeopardised; or

(d)   protect the rights and freedoms of third parties;[79]

Subjects have rights of rectification, erasure and restriction.[80]

PNR Directive

[20.15] Passenger Name Records or PNR are essentially detailed passenger manifests of commercial aeroplanes. PNR is defined as:

> a record of each passenger's travel requirements which contains information necessary to enable reservations to be processed and controlled by the booking and participating air carriers for each journey booked by or on behalf of any person, whether it is contained in reservation systems, departure control systems used to check passengers onto flights, or equivalent systems providing the same functionalities.[81]

The PNR Directive[82] now provides for the transfer of Passenger Name Record (PNR) data[83] from air carriers to the Passenger Information Unit or PIU which has been nominated by the Member States. These PIU are that Member State's '… authority

---

78.   Regulation 794/2016/EU, article 36(1).
79.   Regulation 794/2016/EU, article 36(6).
80.   Regulation 794/2016/EU, article 37.
81.   Directive 2016/681/EU, article 3(5).
82.   Directive 2016/681/EU of the European Parliament and of the Council of 27 April 2016 on the use of passenger name record (PNR) data for the prevention, detection, investigation and prosecution of terrorist offences and serious crime, OJ L 119, 4.5.2016, p 132–149.
83.   Annex 1 lists the passenger name record data as far as collected by air carriers: PNR record locator, date of reservation/issue of ticket 'providing' date(s) of intended travel, name(s), address and contact information (telephone number, e-mail address), all forms of payment information, including billing address, complete travel itinerary for specific PNR, frequent flyer information, travel agency/travel agent, travel status of passenger, including confirmations, check-in status, no-show or go-show information, split/divided PNR information, general remarks (including all available information on unaccompanied minors under 18 years, such as name and gender of the minor, age, language(s) spoken, name and contact details of guardian on departure and relationship to the minor, name and contact details of guardian on arrival and relationship to the minor, departure and arrival agent), ticketing field information, including ticket number, date of ticket issuance and one-way tickets, automated ticket fare quote fields, seat number and other seat information, code share information, all baggage information, number and other names of travellers on the PN and any advance passenger information (API) data collected (including the type, number, (contd .../)

competent for the prevention, detection, investigation or prosecution of terrorist offences and of serious crime …'.[84] These PIU may process PNR only for the following purposes:

    (a) carrying out an assessment of passengers prior to their scheduled arrival in or departure from the Member State to identify persons who require further examination by the competent authorities …and, where relevant, by Europol in accordance … in view of the fact that such persons may be involved in a terrorist offence or serious crime;[85]

    (b) responding, on a case-by-case basis, to a duly reasoned request based on sufficient grounds from the competent authorities to provide and process PNR data in specific cases for the purposes of preventing, detecting, investigating and prosecuting terrorist offences or serious crime, and to provide the competent authorities or, where appropriate, Europol with the results of such processing; and

    (c) analysing PNR data for the purpose of updating or creating new criteria to be used in … assessments … in order to identify any persons who may be involved in a terrorist offence or serious crime.[86]

PNR data must be retained for five years, but must be depersonalised after six months. Disclosure of full PNR will then only be permitted where it is reasonably believed that it is necessary for the purposes set out in article 6(2)(b) (ie responding to a request) and where it is approved by a judicial authority or another national authority competent under national law to verify whether the conditions for disclosure are met.[87] The PNR Directive contains specific provisions on data protection[88] and requires that each PIU appoint a DPO.[89] Member States must transpose the Directive by 25 May 2018[90] and the

---

83.   (contd) country of issuance and expiry date of any identity document, nationality, family name, given name, gender, date of birth, airline, flight number, departure date, arrival date, departure port, arrival port, departure time and arrival time) and all historical changes to the PNR). If the data transferred includes data that is not listed in Annex 1, the PIU must delete the data immediately and permanently upon receipt (article 6(1)).

84.   Directive 2016/681/EU, article 4(1).

85.   The PIU may do this by comparing 'a) compare PNR data against databases relevant for the purposes of preventing, detecting, investigating and prosecuting terrorist offences and serious crime, including databases on persons or objects sought or under alert, in accordance with Union, international and national rules applicable to such databases; or (b) process PNR data against pre-determined criteria.' The latter form of assessment must '… be carried out in a non-discriminatory manner. Those pre-determined criteria must be targeted, proportionate and specific. Member States shall ensure that those criteria are set and regularly reviewed by the PIU in cooperation with the competent authorities …The criteria shall in no circumstances be based on a person's race or ethnic origin, political opinions, religion or philosophical beliefs, trade union membership, health, sexual life or sexual orientation,' Directive 2016/681/EU, article 6(3) and (4).

86.   Directive 2016/681/EU, article 6(2).

87.   Directive 2016/681/EU, article 12.

88.   Directive 2016/681/EU, article 4(1).

89.   Directive 2016/681/EU, article 6(2).

90.   Directive 2016/681/EU, article 18.

EU Commission must then undertake a review within two years.[91] The PNR Directive requires transfers of data in respect of extra-EU flights but limits the circumstances under which such data can be transferred outside the EU.[92] It allows Member States some flexibility in respect of intra-EU flights.[93]

ECRIS

[20.16] ECRIS is the European Criminal Records Information System[94] which was established by Council Framework Decision 2009/315/JHA.[95] This Decision provides that Member States must nominate a central authority,[96] which must:

> … as soon as possible, inform the central authorities of the other Member States of any convictions handed down within its territory against the nationals of such other Member States, as entered in the criminal record.[97]

The central authority of a person's nationality must store all information relating to that person's convictions.[98] ECRIS allows for Member States' central authorities to provide information about a person's criminal convictions on request to the central authorities of other Member States for the purposes of criminal proceedings and otherwise. Such requests must be made in accordance with national laws.[99] Council Framework Decision 2009/315/JHA imposes conditions on the use of personal data and was to have been implemented by 27 April 2012.[100]

Eurojust

[20.17] Eurojust was established by Council Decision 2002/187[101] and describes itself as the EU's judicial cooperation unit.[102] The objectives of Eurojust are to stimulate and

---

91.   Directive 2016/681/EU, article 19.
92.   Directive 2016/681/EU, article 11. The EU has existing agreements with a number of third countries (USA and Australia) that allow for the transfer of PNR data. However, the CJEU failed to sanction a new agreement for the transfer of PNR data to Canada in Transfer of Passenger Name Record data from the European Union to Canada [2017] Avis-1/15 (26 July 2017).
93.   Directive 2016/681/EU, article 2.
94.   See generally http://ec.europa.eu/justice/criminal/european-e-justice/ecris/index_en.htm.
95.   Council Framework Decision 2009/315/JHA of 26 February 2009 on the organisation and content of the exchange of information extracted from the criminal record between Member States, OJ L 93, 7.4.2009, p 23–32.
96.   Council Framework Decision 2009/315/JHA, article 3.
97.   Council Framework Decision 2009/315/JHA, article 4(2).
98.   Council Framework Decision 2009/315/JHA, article 5(1).
99.   Council Framework Decision 2009/315/JHA, article 6(1).
100. Council Framework Decision 2009/315/JHA, article 13.
101. Council Decision 2002/187/JHA of 28 February 2002 setting up Eurojust with a view to reinforcing the fight against serious crime, OJ L 63 of 6 March 2002, amended by Decision 2003/659/JHA (OJ L 245 of 29 September 2003 and Decision 2009/426/JHA OJ L 138 of 4 June 2009.
102. http://www.eurojust.europa.eu/Pages/home.aspx.

improve coordination, improve cooperation and otherwise support the national competent authorities that are its members.[103] The tasks of Eurojust may be discharged through its members or by acting as a college. Tasks discharged through members of Eurojust include undertaking investigations, providing information and assisting one another.[104] Tasks that Eurojust may discharge include undertaking investigations and ensuring that its members inform one another of investigations and prosecutions.[105] Council Decision 2002/187 goes on to provide that: '... competent authorities of the Member States shall exchange with Eurojust any information necessary for the performance of its tasks ...'.[106] whilst 'Eurojust shall provide competent national authorities with information and feedback on the results of the processing of information ...'.[107] As regards the processing of personal data it provides:

> Insofar as it is necessary to achieve its objectives, Eurojust may, within the framework of its competence and in order to carry out its tasks, process personal data, by automated means or in structured manual files.[108]

Council Decision 2002/187 requires that Eurojust adhere to the Strasbourg Convention, a requirement that will be overridden by the Data Protection Police Directive. It goes on to set out restrictions on the processing of personal data[109] and to provide for the establishment of a Case Management System, index and temporary work files.[110] Limitations are placed upon the periods for which data may be retained[111] and restrictions are imposed on access to personal data[112] as well as obligations in relation to data security[113] and confidentiality.[114] Cooperation with third states and international organisations such as Interpol is provided for.[115] Before information is exchanged with states or organisations outside the EU '..., the national member of the Member State which submitted the information shall give his consent to the transfer of that information'.[116] Subjects are granted a right of access,[117] together with the right to seek the correction and deletion of their personal data.[118] The appointment of a DPO is provided for,[119] together with a Joint Supervisory Body to monitor the processing of

---

103. Council Decision 2002/187/JHA, article 5.
104. Council Decision 2002/187/JHA, article 6.
105. Council Decision 2002/187/JHA, article 7.
106. Council Decision 2002/187/JHA, article 13(1).
107. Council Decision 2002/187/JHA, article 13a(1).
108. Council Decision 2002/187/JHA, article 14.
109. Council Decision 2002/187/JHA, article 15.
110. Council Decision 2002/187/JHA, article 16.
111. Council Decision 2002/187/JHA, article 21.
112. Council Decision 2002/187/JHA, article 18.
113. Council Decision 2002/187/JHA, article 22.
114. Council Decision 2002/187/JHA, article 25.
115. Council Decision 2002/187/JHA, article 26a.
116. Council Decision 2002/187/JHA, article 27.
117. Council Decision 2002/187/JHA, article 19.
118. Council Decision 2002/187/JHA, article 20.
119. Council Decision 2002/187/JHA, article 17.

personal data pursuant to Council Decision 2002/187. Finally: 'Eurojust shall be liable … for any damage caused to an individual which results from unauthorised or incorrect processing of data carried out by it'.[120]

European Investigation Orders[121]

[20.18] European Investigation Orders or EIOs are designed to supplant existing measures, such as the European Evidence Warrant (EEW). As the Recitals to Directive 2014/41 of 3 April 2014 regarding the European Investigation Order in criminal matters[122] explain:

> An EIO is to be issued for the purpose of having one or several specific investigative measure(s) carried out in the State executing the EIO ('the executing State') with a view to gathering evidence. This includes the obtaining of evidence that is already in the possession of the executing authority ....[123] The EIO establishes a single regime for obtaining evidence. Additional rules are however necessary for certain types of investigative measures which should be indicated in the EIO, such as the temporary transfer of persons held in custody, hearing by video or telephone conference, obtaining of information related to bank accounts or banking transactions, controlled deliveries or covert investigations.[124]

Directive 2014/41 also provides for the interception of telecommunications[125] and there are protections for confidentiality[126] and personal data.[127] Directive 2014/41 was to have been implemented by 22 May 2017.

European Information Exchange Model

[20.19] The European Information Exchange Model or EIXM was described in a communication from the EU Commission.[128] The EIXM consists of two main elements:

---

120. Council Decision 2002/187/JHA, article 24(1).
121. Directive 2014/41/EU of the European Parliament and of the Council of 3 April 2014 regarding the European Investigation Order in criminal matters, OJ L 130, 1.5.2014, p 1–36. See also the CoE's European Convention on Mutual Assistance in Criminal Matters, Strasbourg, 20 April 1959.
122. Directive 2014/41/EU of 3 April 2014 regarding the European Investigation Order in criminal matters, OJ L 130, 1.5.2014, p 1–36.
123. Directive 2014/41, Recital 7.
124. Directive 2014/41, Recital 24.
125. Directive 2014/41, article 30.
126. Directive 2014/41, article 19.
127. Directive 2014/41, article 20.
128. Communication from the Commission to the European Parliament and the Council on strengthening law enforcement cooperation in the EU: the European Information Exchange Model (EIXM) doc. 17680/12 JAI 913 DAPIX 163 ENFOPOL 418 JURINFO 64.

the Prüm Decision;[129] and the Swedish Initiative.[130] The Prüm Decision enables the sharing of personal data for major events:

> For the prevention of criminal offences and in maintaining public order and security for major events with a cross-border dimension, in particular for sporting events or European Council meetings, Member States shall, both upon request and of their own accord, supply one another with personal data if any final convictions or other circumstances give reason to believe that the data subjects will commit criminal offences at the events or pose a threat to public order and security ...[131]

The Prüm Decision also provides for the supply of information '... in order to prevent terrorist offences'.[132] More generally it enables the sharing of DNA, fingerprint and number plate data.[133] The Swedish Initiative sets out rules for exchanges of criminal information and intelligence between Member States.[134] Both the *Prüm* decision[135] and the Swedish Initiative[136] provide some data protection safeguards.

Anti-money laundering Directive

[20.20] The Anti-Money Laundering Directive[137] or AMLD is now in its fourth iteration,[138] the first such Directive dates back to 1991.[139] The AMLD begins with a Recital of why it is necessary:

> Flows of illicit money can damage the integrity, stability and reputation of the financial sector, and threaten the internal market of the Union as well as international development. Money laundering, terrorism financing and organised crime remain significant problems ... targeted and proportionate prevention of the

---

129. Council Decision 2008/615/JHA of 23 June 2008 on the stepping up of cross-border cooperation, particularly in combating terrorism and cross-border crime, OJ L 210, 6.8.2008, p 1–11.
130. Council Framework Decision 2006/960/JHA of 18 December 2006 on simplifying the exchange of information and intelligence between law enforcement authorities of the Member States of the European Union, OJ L 386, 29.12.2006, pp 89–100.
131. Council Decision 2008/615/JHA, article 14(1).
132. Council Decision 2008/615/JHA, article 16(1).
133. Council Decision 2008/615/JHA, Ch 2.
134. Council Framework Decision 2006/960/JHA, article 3.
135. Council Decision 2008/615/JHA, Ch 6.
136. Council Framework Decision 2006/960/JHA, article 8.
137. Council Framework Decision 2006/960/JHA, article 3.
138. Directive 2015/849/EU of the European Parliament and of the Council of 20 May 2015 on the prevention of the use of the financial system for the purposes of money laundering or terrorist financing, amending Regulation 648/2012/EU of the European Parliament and of the Council, and repealing Directive 2005/60/EC of the European Parliament and of the Council and Commission Directive 2006/70/EC, OJ L 141, 5.6.2015, pp 73–117.
139. Council Directive 91/308/EEC of 10 June 1991 on prevention of the use of the financial system for the purpose of money laundering (OJ L 166, 28.6.1991, p 77).

use of the financial system for the purposes of money laundering and terrorist financing is indispenable.[140]

A very broad variety of entities are now subject to AMLD ranging from credit and financial institutions, to auditors and accountants, lawyers, estate agents, bookies and casinos.[141] Such entities must undertake customer due diligence in specified circumstances such as establishing a business relationship, undertaking occasional transactions or 'when there is a suspicion of money laundering or terrorist financing, regardless of any derogation, exemption or threshold'.[142] Customer due diligence comprises:

(a) identifying the customer and verifying the customer's identity on the basis of documents, data or information obtained from a reliable and independent source;

(b) identifying the beneficial owner and taking reasonable measures to verify that person's identity so that the obliged entity is satisfied that it knows who the beneficial owner is, including, as regards legal persons, trusts, companies, foundations and similar legal arrangements, taking reasonable measures to understand the ownership and control structure of the customer;

(c) assessing and, as appropriate, obtaining information on the purpose and intended nature of the business relationship;

(d) conducting ongoing monitoring of the business relationship including scrutiny of transactions undertaken throughout the course of that relationship to ensure that the transactions being conducted are consistent with the obliged entity's knowledge of the customer, the business and risk profile, including where necessary the source of funds and ensuring that the documents, data or information held are kept up-to-date.[143]

Member States must establish a Financial Intelligence Unit or FIU. They must then oblige entities that are subject to the AMLD, together with their directors and employees, to inform:

> ... the FIU, including by filing a report, on their own initiative, where the obliged entity knows, suspects or has reasonable grounds to suspect that funds, regardless of the amount involved, are the proceeds of criminal activity or are related to terrorist financing ...[144]

AMLD goes on to provide for co-operation between national bodies[145] and between FIUs and the supervisory authorities for the financial services sector[146] and the EU

---

140. AMLD, Recital 1.
141. AMLD, article 2(1).
142. AMLD, article 11.
143. AMLD, article 13(1).
144. AMLD, article 33(1)(a).
145. AMLD, article 49.
146. AMLD, article 50.

Commission.[147] FIUs must cooperate with each other '... to the greatest extent possible, regardless of their organisational status'.[148] And:

> Member States shall ensure that FIUs exchange, spontaneously or upon request, any information that may be relevant for the processing or analysis of information by the FIU related to money laundering or terrorist financing and the natural or legal person involved ...[149]

Such information must be shared using protected channels of communication.[150] Some restrictions are imposed upon the extent to which such shared information may be used, the AMLD providing that:

> Member States shall ensure that the information exchanged (with each other) is used only for the purpose for which it was sought or provided and that any dissemination of that information by the receiving FIU to any other authority, agency or department, or any use of this information for purposes beyond those originally approved, is made subject to the prior consent by the FIU providing the information.[151]

The Schengen Information System

[20.21] The Schengen *acquis*[152] is a set of rules and legislation which enable the abolition of border controls within the Schengen area of the EU. The Schengen *acquis* is now recognised by TFEU, Protocol 19. The Schengen Information System (SIS) assists border control and law enforcement cooperation and is set out in three measures:

(a) Regulation 1987/2006 on the establishment, operation and use of the second generation Schengen Information System (SIS II);[153]

(b) Council Decision 2007/533/JHA of 12 June 2007 on the establishment, operation and use of the second generation Schengen Information System;[154] and

---

147. AMLD, article 51.
148. AMLD, article 52.
149. AMLD, article 53.
150. AMLD, article 56(1).
151. AMLD, article 55(1).
152. The Schengen *acquis* – Convention implementing the Schengen Agreement of 14 June 1985 between the governments of the States of the Benelux Economic Union, the Federal Republic of Germany and the French Republic on the gradual abolition of checks at their common borders, OJ L 239, 22/09/2000, pp 19–62.
153. Regulation 1987/2006/EC on the establishment, operation and use of the second generation Schengen Information System (SIS II) OJ L 381, 28.12.2006, pp 4–23.
154. Council Decision 2007/533/JHA of 12 June 2007 on the establishment, operation and use of the second generation Schengen Information System (SIS II), OJ L 205, 7.8.2007, pp 63–84.

(b) Regulation 1986/2006 regarding access to the Second Generation Schengen Information System (SIS II) by the services in the Member States responsible for issuing vehicle registration certificates.[155]

These regulations underpin a system which enables the sharing of information relating to persons from third countries, alerts about missing persons together with alerts on vehicles, registration certificates and number plates.

---

155. Regulation 1986/2006 regarding access to the Second Generation Schengen Information System (SIS II) by the services in the Member States responsible for issuing vehicle registration certificates, OJ L 381, 28.12.2006, pp 1–3.

Chapter 21

THE LAW ENFORCEMENT DIRECTIVE

INTRODUCTION

[21.01] Directive 2016/680/EU on the protection of natural persons with regard to the processing of personal data by competent authorities for the purposes of the prevention, investigation, detection or prosecution of criminal offences or the execution of criminal penalties, and on the free movement of such data[1] (LED) is due to be implemented by 6 May 2018. LED has its legal basis in article 8(1) of the Charter and TFEU, article 16(1),[2] a legal base it shares with the GDPR. Article 16(2), TFEU requires that the EU legislature: '… lay down the rules relating to the protection of individuals with regard to TFEU, article 16(2) to the processing of personal data … and the rules relating to the free movement of such data'. Consistent with this requirement LED requires that Member States:

(a) protect the fundamental rights and freedoms of natural persons and in particular their right to the protection of personal data; and

(b) 'ensure that the exchange of personal data by competent authorities within the Union, where such exchange is required by Union or Member State law, is neither restricted nor prohibited for reasons connected with the protection of natural persons with regard to the processing of personal data.[3]

---

1.   Directive 2016/680/EU on the protection of natural persons with regard to the processing of personal data by competent authorities for the purposes of the prevention, investigation, detection or prosecution of criminal offences or the execution of criminal penalties, and on the free movement of such data, OJ L 119, 4.5.2016, p. 89–131. For a discussion of the original Commission proposal see the Article 29 Working Party, Opinion 03/2015 on the draft directive on the protection of individuals with regard to the processing of personal data by competent authorities for the purposes of prevention, investigation, detection or prosecution of criminal offences or the execution of criminal penalties, and the free movement of such data, 3211/15/EN WP 233, 1 December 2015 and also EDPS, A further step towards comprehensive EU data protection, Opinion 6/2015, 28 October 2015.

2.   LED, Recital.

3.   LED, article 1(2). LED, article 1(1) reiterates that it 'lays down the rules relating to the protection of natural persons with regard to the processing of personal data by competent authorities for the purposes of the prevention, investigation, detection or prosecution of criminal offences or the execution of criminal penalties, including the safeguarding against and the prevention of threats to public security'. Article 1(3) states that it does '… not preclude Member States from providing higher safeguards than those established in this Directive for the protection of the rights and freedoms of the data subject with regard to the processing of personal data by competent authorities'.

[21.02] LED recites that it is '… intended to contribute to the accomplishment of an area of freedom, security and justice',[4] an area which the EU resolved to accomplish in the TEU.[5] LED recites that it is necessary because:

> Rapid technological developments and globalisation have brought new challenges for the protection of personal data. The scale of the collection and sharing of personal data has increased significantly. Technology allows personal data to be processed on an unprecedented scale in order to pursue activities such as the prevention, investigation, detection or prosecution of criminal offences or the execution of criminal penalties.[6]

LED goes on to recite that its purpose is to facilitate the '… free flow of personal data between competent authorities for the purposes of the prevention, investigation, detection or prosecution of criminal offences or the execution of criminal penalties, including the safeguarding against and the prevention of threats to public security within the Union and the transfer of such personal data to third countries and international organisations …'. Such flows should be facilitated '… while ensuring a high level of protection of personal data'. This requires '… building of a strong and more coherent framework for the protection of personal data in the Union, backed by strong enforcement'.[7]

Scope

[21.03] LED applies to the processing of personal data by what article 1(1) terms 'competent authorities'.[8] Such authorities are defined by LED as including public authorities such as judicial authorities, the police or other law enforcement authorities and are defined in the Directive as:

(a) any public authority competent for the prevention, investigation, detection or prosecution of criminal offences[9] or the execution of criminal penalties, including the safeguarding against and the prevention of threats to public security; or

(b) any other body or entity entrusted by Member State law to exercise public authority and public powers for the purposes of the prevention, investigation, detection or prosecution of criminal offences or the execution of criminal penalties, including the safeguarding against and the prevention of threats to public security.[10]

Therefore, competent authorities include not only the police but also other bodies or entities entrusted by Member State law to exercise public authority and public powers

---

4.   LED, Recital 2.
5.   TEU, Preamble.
6.   LED, Recital 3.
7.   LED, Recital 4.
8.   LED, article 2(1).
9.   LED, Recital 13 provides that the term 'criminal offence' should be an autonomous concept of Union law as interpreted by the Court of Justice of the European Union.
10.   LED, article 3(7).

for the purposes of this Directive. The Recitals explain that where such a body or entity processes personal data other than for purposes of the LED, the GDPR will apply. The GDPR therefore will apply in cases where a body or entity collects personal data for other purposes and further processes those personal data in order to comply with a legal obligation to which it is subject. For example, a financial institution might retain personal data for the purposes of investigation detection or prosecution of criminal offences and give it to the competent national authorities in accordance with member state laws. A body or entity which processes personal data on behalf of such authorities does so in accordance with the LED and should be bound by a contract or other legal act and by the provisions applicable to processors pursuant to this Directive, while the application of the GDPR remains unaffected for the processing of personal data by the processor outside the scope of this Directive.[11]

[21.04] The Recitals provide some examples of activities to which the LED applies including police activities carried out without prior knowledge if an incident is a criminal offence or not, or taking coercive measures at demonstrations, major sporting events and riots. They also include maintaining law and order where necessary to safeguard against and prevent threats to public security and to fundamental interests of the society protected by law which may lead to a criminal offence. The Recitals provide that Member States may entrust competent authorities with other tasks which are not necessarily carried out for the purposes of the prevention, investigation, detection or prosecution of criminal offences, including the safeguarding against and the prevention of threats to public security, so that the processing of personal data for those other purposes, in so far as it is within the scope of Union law, falls within the scope of the GDPR.[12]

As in the case of the GDPR, the LED applies to:

> the processing of personal data wholly or partly by automated means, and to the processing other than by automated means of personal data which form part of a filing system or are intended to form part of a filing system.[13]

[21.05] The Recitals explain that files or sets of files, as well as their cover pages, which are not structured according to specific criteria, would not fall within the scope of the LED.[14] LED has no application to the processing of personal data:

(a) in the course of an activity which falls outside the scope of Union law;

(b) by the Union institutions, bodies, offices and agencies.[15]

---

11. LED, Recital 11.
12. LED, Recital 12. LED, Recital 16 acknowledges that the Directive is without prejudice to the principle of public access to official documents.
13. LED, article 2(2).
14. LED, Recital 18.
15. LED, article 2(3). Regulation 45/2001/EC applies to processing by Union institution (see Proposal for a Regulation COM (2017) 8 final). Other Union legal acts to such processing of personal data should be adapted to the GDPR principles.

Few activities now remain outside scope of EU law. In terms of personal data processing the most significant of those that remain outside is probably Member State competencies in the area of national security. The EU is '... to implement a common foreign and security policy including the progressive framing of a common defence policy, which might lead to a common defence ...'.[16] However, the:

> ... essential State functions, including ensuring the territorial integrity of the State, maintaining law and order and safeguarding national security. In particular, national security remains the sole responsibility of each Member State.[17]

[21.06] TEU, Title V, Ch 2 goes on to provide for the EU's Common Foreign and security policy.

> The common security and defence policy shall be an integral part of the common foreign and security policy ... The common security and defence policy shall include the progressive framing of a common Union defence policy. This will lead to a common defence ...[18]

TEU, article 39 then provides:

> ... the Council shall adopt a decision laying down the rules relating to the protection of individuals with regard to the processing of personal data by the Member States when carrying out activities which fall within the scope of this Chapter, and the rules relating to the free movement of such data. Compliance with these rules shall be subject to the control of independent authorities.

Such a decision has yet to be adopted by the EU Council.

[21.07] LED repeals Council Framework Decision 2008/977/JHA with effect from 6 May 2018[19] which applied in the area of judicial cooperation in criminal matters and police cooperation. That Decision however, was limited to the processing of personal data transmitted or made available between Member States[20] as opposed to internal data, for example. LED bridges the gap by protecting personal data processed by competent authorities. According to the Recitals, activities concerning national security, activities of agencies or units dealing with national security issues and the processing of personal data by the Member States when carrying out activities which fall within the scope of the Treaty on European Union (TEU), Title V, Ch 2 should not be considered to be activities falling within the scope of this Directive.[21]

All Member States are affiliated to the International Criminal Police Organisation (Interpol) which receives, stores and circulates personal data to assist competent authorities in preventing and combating international crime. This Directive applies

---

16.   TEU, Preamble.
17.   TEU, article 4(2).
18.   TEU, article 42(1) and (2).
19.   LED, article 59.
20.   LED, Recital 6.
21.   LED, Recital 14.

where personal data are transferred from the Union to Interpol and to countries which have delegated members to Interpol.[22]

Lawfulness of processing

[21.08] Unlike the GDPR, which sets out a variety of bases upon which the processing of personal data may be lawful, the LED provides that the processing of personal data by competent authorities will only be lawful if and to the extent that processing is necessary for the performance of a task carried out on the basis of EU or Member State law.[23] Member State law regulating processing within the scope of the LED must specify at least the objectives of processing, the personal data to be processed and the purposes of the processing.[24]

The Recitals add that in the performance of its tasks, competent authorities may require or order natural persons to comply with requests. In these cases, the consent of the data subject should not provide a legal ground for processing personal data by competent authorities because the data subject has 'no genuine and free choice' so their decision could not be considered to be a freely given indication of his wishes. The Recitals note that this does not preclude Member States from providing by law that data subjects may agree to processing such as DNA tests or the monitoring of his location with electronic tags.[25]

Data protection principles

[21.09] Chapter II of the Directive sets out the principles relating to the processing of personal data. The principles should apply to any information concerning an identified or identifiable natural person and do not apply to anonymous information.[26] Article 4 requires Member States to provide for personal data to be:

(a) 'processed lawfully and fairly'. The Recitals explain that this principle does not prevent law-enforcement authorities from carrying out activities such as covert investigations or video surveillance because they are done for the purposes of the prevention, investigation, detection or prosecution of criminal offences or the execution of criminal penalties, including the safeguarding against and the prevention of threats to public security. This is so long as such activities are laid down by law and constitute a necessary and proportionate measure in a democratic society with due regard for the legitimate interests of the natural person concerned. The Recitals explain that the principle of fair processing is a distinct notion from the right to a fair trial (as defined in article 47 of the Charter

---

22. LED, Recital 25. This Directive is without prejudice to the rules in Council Common Position 2005/69/JHA and Council Decision 2007/533/JHA.
23. LED, article 8(1).
24. LED, article 8(2).
25. LED, Recital 35.
26. LED, Recital 21.

and in article 6 of the European Convention for the Protection of Human Rights and Fundamental Freedoms (ECHR);[27]

(b) collected for specified, explicit and legitimate purposes and not processed in a manner that is incompatible with those purposes. The Recitals add that this purpose should be determined at the time of collection;[28]

(c) adequate, relevant and not excessive in relation to the purposes for which they are processed. The term 'excessive' is used here rather than 'limited' in the GDPR;

(d) accurate and, where necessary, kept up to date; every reasonable step must be taken to ensure that personal data that are inaccurate, having regard to the purposes for which they are processed, are erased or rectified without delay. When assessing this principle account should be taken of the nature and purpose of the processing concerned. The Recitals offer the example of evidence taken in judicial proceedings where statements are made containing personal data which are based on the subjective perception of a person and which are not always verifiable. As a result, the requirement of accuracy should not relate to the accuracy of a statement but merely to the fact that a specific statement has been made;[29]

(e) kept in a form which permits identification of data subjects for no longer than is necessary for the purposes for which they are processed;

(f) processed in a manner that ensures appropriate security of the personal data, including protection against unauthorised or unlawful processing and against accidental loss, destruction or damage, using appropriate technical or organisational measures.[30] The Recitals add that in order to maintain security, processing must ensure both security and confidentiality by preventing unauthorised access to or use of personal data and the equipment used for the processing. The measures taken to ensure this may take into account available state of the article and technology, the costs of implementation in relation to the risks and the nature of the personal data to be protected.[31] As in the case of the GDPR, an appropriate standard of security for personal data is that which results in its integrity and confidentiality.

[21.10] Article 5 further provides that Member States must provide for appropriate time limits to be established for the erasure of personal data or for a periodic review of the need for the storage of personal data. Procedural measures must ensure that those time

---

27.   LED, Recital 26.
28.   LED, Recital 26.
29.   LED, Recital 30.
30.   LED, article 4(1).
31.   LED, Recital 28.

limits are observed. The Article 29 WP has issued an *Opinion on some key issues of the Law Enforcement Directive*[32] which recommends that:

> National laws on data processing within the scope of the Directive always should foresee maximum storage periods as well as periodic reviews… The review proceeding should be documented and the decision to extend the data storage period should be duly justified.[33]

Processing by the same or another controller (competent authority) for any of the purposes set out in article 1(1) other than that for which the personal data are collected is permitted in so far as:

(a) the controller is authorised to process such personal data for such a purpose in accordance with Union or Member State law; and

(b) processing is necessary and proportionate to that other purpose in accordance with Union or Member State law.[34]

The Recitals give the example of processing personal data collected in the context of the prevention, investigation, detection or prosecution of specific criminal offences beyond that context in order to develop an understanding of criminal activities and to make links between different criminal offences detected.[35] Processing by the same or another controller may include archiving in the public interest, scientific, statistical or historical use, for the purposes of the prevention, investigation, detection or prosecution of criminal offences or the execution of criminal penalties including the safeguarding against and the prevention of threats to public security subject to appropriate safeguards for the rights and freedoms of data subjects.[36] The controller is responsible for ensuring compliance with the principles and must be able to demonstrate this compliance.[37]

Distinction between different categories of data subject

[21.11] In the area of police and criminal justice there are many categories of data subject: suspects, convicted persons, victims, witnesses, persons possessing relevant information or contacts, associates of suspects and convicted criminals. Article 6 provides that Member States must provide for the controller, where applicable and as far as possible, to make a clear distinction between personal data of different categories of data subjects, such as:

> (a) persons with regard to whom there are serious grounds for believing that they have committed or are about to commit a criminal offence;

---

32. Article 29 WP, *Opinion on some key issues of the Law Enforcement Directive*, 17/EN WP 258, 29 November 2017.
33. Article 29 WP, *Opinion on some key issues of the Law Enforcement Directive*, 17/EN WP 258, 29 November 2017, p 6.
34. LED, article 4(2).
35. LED, Recital 27.
36. LED, article 4(3).
37. LED, article 4(4).

    (b) persons convicted of a criminal offence;

    (c) victims of a criminal offence or persons with regard to whom certain facts give rise to reasons for believing that he or she could be the victim of a criminal offence; and

    (d) other parties to a criminal offence, such as persons who might be called on to testify in investigations in connection with criminal offences or subsequent criminal proceedings, persons who can provide information on criminal offences, or contacts or associates of one of the persons referred to in points (a) and (b).

This should not prevent the application of the right of presumption of innocence as guaranteed by the Charter and ECHR as interpreted by the ECtHR and CJEU in case law.[38]

Distinction between personal data and verification of quality of personal data

[21.12] Article 7 provides that personal data based on facts must be distinguished, as far as possible, from personal data based on personal assessments.[39] Competent authorities must take all reasonable steps to ensure that personal data which are inaccurate, incomplete or no longer up to date are not transmitted or made available. Each authority must, in so far as is practicable, verify the quality of personal data before they are transmitted or made available. As far as possible, in all transmissions of personal data, necessary information enabling the receiving competent authority to assess the degree of accuracy, completeness and reliability of personal data, and the extent to which they are up to date must be added.[40]

If incorrect personal data have been transmitted or personal data have been unlawfully transmitted, the recipient must be notified without delay and the personal data rectified or erased or processing restricted in accordance with article 16.[41] Article 3(10) defines 'recipient' as meaning a natural or legal person, public authority, agency or another body, to which the personal data are disclosed, whether a third party or not. The Recitals explain that public authorities to which personal data are disclosed in accordance with a legal obligation for the exercise of their duties are not considered recipients. The Recitals provide the example of tax and customs authorities, financial investigation units, independent administrative authorities or financial market authorities responsible for the regulation and supervision of securities markets and who receive personal data which are necessary to carry out a particular inquiry in the general interest, in accordance with Union or Member State law.[42]

---

38.   LED, Recital 31.
39.   LED, article 7(1).
40.   LED, article 7(2).
41.   LED, article 7(3).
42.   LED, Recital 22.

Specific processing conditions

[21.13] Personal data collected by competent authorities for article 1(1) purposes must not be processed for purposes other than those set out in article 1(1) unless authorised by Union or Member State law. Where personal data are processed for such other purposes, the GDPR will apply unless the processing is carried out in an activity which falls outside the scope of Union law.[43] Where competent authorities are entrusted by Member State law with the performance of tasks not compatible with article 1(1), the GPR will apply to processing for such purposes including for archiving purposes in the public interest, scientific or historical research purposes or statistical purposes, unless the processing is carried out in an activity which falls outside the scope of Union law.[44] Where Union or Member State law applicable to the transmitting competent authority provides specific conditions for processing, Member State law must provide for the transmitting competent authority to inform the recipient of such personal data of those conditions and the requirement to comply with them.[45] Conditions do not apply to recipients in other Member States or to agencies, offices and bodies established pursuant to TFEU, Chs 4 (Judicial Co-Operation in Criminal Matters) and 5 (Police Co-Operation) of Title V (Area of Freedom, Security and Justice) other than those applicable to similar transmissions of data within the Member State of the transmitting competent authority.[46]

Processing of special categories of personal data

[21.14] Personal data which is particularly sensitive in relation to fundamental rights and freedoms are given greater protection. Article 10 provides that the:

> processing of personal data revealing racial or ethnic origin, political opinions, religious or philosophical beliefs, or trade union membership, and the processing of genetic data,[47] biometric data for the purpose of uniquely identifying a natural person, data concerning health or data concerning a natural person's sex life or sexual orientation shall be allowed only where strictly necessary, subject to appropriate safeguards for the rights and freedoms of the data subject, and only:
>
> (a) where authorised by Union or Member State law;
>
> (b) to protect the vital interests of the data subject or of another natural person; or
>
> (c) where such processing relates to data which are manifestly made public by the data subject.[48]

---

43. LED, article 9(1).
44. LED, article 9(2).
45. LED, article 9(3).
46. LED, article 9(4).
47. The definitions of genetic and health data mirror those set out in the GDPR but add that considering the complexity and sensitivity of genetic information, there is a great risk of misuse and re-use for various purposes by the controller. Any discrimination based on genetic features should in principle be prohibited. LED, Recital 23.
48. LED, article 10.

The processing of such sensitive or special categories of data requires the use of appropriate safeguards for the rights and freedoms of the data subject and the Recitals suggest that such safeguards could include collecting this data only in connection with other data on the person concerned, securing the data collected adequately, stricter rules on the access of staff to special categories of data and prohibiting the transmission of that data. Where the data subject has agreed, processing should be allowed, however 'the consent of the data subject should not provide in itself a legal ground for processing such sensitive personal data by competent authorities'.[49] The Article 29 WP has recommended that: 'The processing of special categories of data, if not foreseen by Union law, always requires a specific legal basis in national law'.[50]

Automated individual decision-making

[21.15] A data subject should have the right not to be subject to a decision evaluating personal aspects relating to him which is based solely on automated processing and which 'significantly affects him'.[51] So Member States must ensure that:

> a decision based solely on automated processing, including profiling, which produces an adverse legal effect concerning the data subject or significantly affects him or her, to be prohibited unless authorised by Union or Member State law to which the controller is subject and which provides appropriate safeguards for the rights and freedoms of the data subject, at least the right to obtain human intervention on the part of the controller.[52]

The Recitals provide that this human intervention might include allowing him to express his point of view, obtain an explanation of the decision reached after such assessment or to challenge the decision.[53] The decision referred to in this Article must not be based on the special categories of personal data in article 10 unless suitable measures to safeguard the data subject's rights and freedoms and legitimate interests are in place.[54] Profiling that results in discrimination against natural persons on the basis of special categories of personal data referred to in article 10 are prohibited, in accordance with Union law.[55] The prohibition provided by LED, article 11 may be compared to the right '... not to be subject to a decision based solely on automated processing, including profiling ...' provided by GDPR, article 22. There are similarities between the two; both restrict the automated processing of special categories of personal data, for example. One difference is that GDPR does grant subjects broader rights over the processing of their

---

49.   LED, Recital 37.
50.   Article 29 WP, *Opinion on some key issues of the Law Enforcement Directive*, 17/EN WP 258, 29 November 2017, p 10.
51.   LED, Recital 38.
52.   LED, article 11(1).
53.   LED, Recital 38.
54.   LED, article 11(2).
55.   LED, article 11(3).

personal data, notably a right to object.[56] This reflects the broader bases upon which the processing of personal data is permitted by the GDPR. In contrast, the LED only permits the automated processing of personal data on a single legal basis: Union or Member State law.

Rights of the data subject

[21.16] LED, Ch III sets out the rights of data subjects. These may be compared to those provided by GDPR, Ch III; the LED does provide subjects with rights that are, in many ways, similar to those provided by the GDPR. The LED grants subjects fewer rights than the GDPR, it provides no right to object,[57] for example. Rights granted by the LED are as follows:

(a)   information;

(b)   access;

(c)   rectification, erasure and restriction.

Each is discussed below. These rights may be considered as a whole, not necessarily individually. As the Article 29 WP has noted '… it is important to see the interrelation of data subjects rights …'[58] as the Criminal Justice Directive '… provides for a new architecture of the rights of data subjects …'.[59] Article 12 sets out the rules governing the communication and modalities for exercising these rights. Member States must ensure that the controller takes:

> reasonable steps to provide any information referred to in Article 13 [information] and make any communication with regard to Articles 11 [automated decisions], 14 [access, rectification, erasure and restriction] to 18 and 31 [notification of personal data breaches] relating to processing to the data subject in a concise, intelligible and easily accessible form, using clear and plain language.

The Recitals add that the information should be easily accessible such as on the controller's website and should be adapted to the needs of vulnerable persons such as children.[60] The information must be provided by any appropriate means, generally in the same format as the request, including by electronic means.[61] Controllers must facilitate the exercise of the rights of the data subject under articles 11 and 14 to 18[62] and inform the data subject in writing about the follow up to his request without undue delay.[63] This

---

56.   LED, article 21.

57.   LED, article 21.

58.   Article 29 WP, *Opinion on some key issues of the Law Enforcement Directive*, 17/EN WP 258, 29 November 2017, p 16.

59.   Article 29 WP, *Opinion on some key issues of the Law Enforcement Directive*, 17/EN WP 258, 29 November 2017, p 24.

60.   LED, Recital 39.

61.   LED, article 12(1).

62.   LED, article 12(2).

63.   LED, article 12(3).

information must be provided free of charge.[64] If a data subject abuses his rights a charge may be imposed. Article 12(4) provides that where requests from a data subject are manifestly unfounded or excessive, in particular because of their repetitive character, the controller may either:

(a) charge a reasonable fee to cover the administrative costs involved in providing the information or communication or taking the action requested; or

(b) refuse to act on the request.

In either case, the burden will be on the controller to show the manifestly unfounded or excessive character of the request.[65] Where the controller has reasonable doubts concerning the identity of a person making a request in article 14 or 16, additional information may be requested by the controller in order to confirm the identity of the data subject.[66] The Recitals add that the additional information provided should only be processed for that specific purpose and should not be stored for longer than needed for that purpose.[67]

[21.17] Controllers are obliged to make, at least, the following information available to the data subject:

(a) the identity and the contact details of the controller;

(b) the contact details of the data protection officer, where applicable;

(c) the purposes of the processing for which the personal data are intended;

(d) the right to lodge a complaint with a supervisory authority and the contact details of the supervisory authority;

(e) the existence of the right to request from the controller access to and rectification or erasure of personal data and restriction of processing of the personal data concerning the data subject.[68]

The Recitals suggest that this information could be provided on the competent authority's website.[69] In addition to this information in specific cases the data subjects must be informed of the legal basis for the processing and how long it will be stored. Member States must provide by law for the controller to give to the data subject, in specific cases, the following further information to enable the exercise of his rights:

(a) the legal basis for the processing;

(b) the period for which the personal data will be stored, or, where that is not possible, the criteria used to determine that period;

---

64.   LED, article 12(4).
65.   LED, article 12(4).
66.   LED, article 12(5).
67.   LED, Recital 41.
68.   LED, article 13(1).
69.   LED, Recital 42.

(c) where applicable, the categories of recipients of the personal data, including in third countries or international organisations;[70]

(d) where necessary, further information, in particular where the personal data are collected without the knowledge of the data subject.[71]

Member States however may adopt legislative measures delaying, restricting or omitting the provision of this further piece of information to the data subject

to the extent that, and for as long as, such a measure constitutes a necessary and proportionate measure in a democratic society with due regard for the fundamental rights and the legitimate interests of the natural person concerned, in order to:

(a) avoid obstructing official or legal inquiries, investigations or procedures;

(b) avoid prejudicing the prevention, detection, investigation or prosecution of criminal offences or the execution of criminal penalties;

(c) protect public security;

(d) protect national security;

(e) protect the rights and freedoms of others.[72]

Member States may adopt legislative measures in order to determine categories of processing which may wholly or partly fall under any of these points.[73]

[21.18] Subject to some limitations on the right of access set out in article 15, data subjects have the right to obtain confirmation from the controller as to whether or not data concerning them are being processed and if that is the case, access to the personal data and to information setting out the following:

(a) the purposes of and legal basis for the processing;

(b) the categories of personal data concerned;

(c) the recipients or categories of recipients to whom the personal data have been disclosed, in particular recipients in third countries or international organisations;

(d) where possible, the envisaged period for which the personal data will be stored, or, if not possible, the criteria used to determine that period;

(e) the existence of the right to request from the controller rectification or erasure of personal data or restriction of processing of personal data concerning the data subject;

---

70. An 'international organisation,' an organisation and its subordinate bodies governed by public international law, or any other body which is set up by, or on the basis of, an agreement between two or more countries' – LED, article 3(6).

71. LED, article 13(2).

72. LED, article 13(3).

73. LED, article 13(4).

(f) the right to lodge a complaint with the supervisory authority and the contact details of the supervisory authority;

(g) communication of the personal data undergoing processing and of any available information as to their origin.[74]

The Recitals explain that a natural person should be able to exercise this right easily and at reasonable intervals in order to be aware of and verify the lawfulness of the processing. Where the communication includes information as to the origin of the information, the Recitals note that the information provided should not reveal the identity of natural persons in particular confidential sources. The Recitals explain that for this right to be compiled with the data subject can receive a full summary of the data in an intelligible form and it could be provided in the form of a copy of the personal data undergoing processing.[75]

[21.19] The Directive anticipates that there may be circumstances justifying limiting this right of access and so in article 15(1) Member States may adopt legislative measures:

restricting, wholly or partly, the data subject's right of access to the extent that, and for as long as such a partial or complete restriction constitutes a necessary and proportionate measure in a democratic society with due regard for the fundamental rights and legitimate interests of the natural person concerned, in order to:

(a) avoid obstructing official or legal inquiries, investigations or procedures;

(b) avoid prejudicing the prevention, detection, investigation or prosecution of criminal offences or the execution of criminal penalties;

(c) protect public security;

(d) protect national security;

(e) protect the rights and freedoms of others.[76]

According to the Recitals, the controller should assess by way of a concrete and individual examination of each case, whether the right of access should be partially or completely restricted.[77] Member States may adopt legislative measures in order to determine the categories of processing which may wholly or partly fall under points (a) to (e).[78] In these cases, the controller must inform the data subject, without undue delay, in writing of any refusal or restriction of access and of the reasons for the refusal or the restriction. The Recitals anticipate that the reasons for the decision may be factual or legal.[79] If the provision of this information would undermine a purpose under

---

74. LED, article 14.
75. LED, Recital 43.
76. LED, article 15(1).
77. LED, Recital 44.
78. LED, article 15(2).
79. LED, Recital 45.

article 15(1) that information may be omitted. Controllers must inform the data subject that they may lodge a complaint with a supervisory authority or seek a judicial remedy[80] and are required to document the factual or legal reasons upon which the decision is based. That information must be made available to the supervisory authorities.[81] The Recitals add that any restriction of the rights of the data subject must comply with the Charter and ECHR, and in particular respect the essence of those rights and freedoms.[82]

[21.20] Article 16 provides that data subjects must have the right to rectify inaccurate personal data relating to him without undue delay. The Recitals add that this right would not affect the content of witness testimony.[83] Depending on the purposes of the processing, data subjects have the right to have incomplete personal data completed, including by means of providing a supplementary statement.[84] The controller must erase personal data without undue delay and provide for the right of the data subject to obtain from the controller the erasure of personal data concerning him without undue delay where processing infringes the provisions adopted pursuant to article 4, 8 or 10, or where personal data must be erased in order to comply with a legal obligation to which the controller is subject.[85]

Article 16(3) provides that in some cases, instead of erasure, the controller must restrict processing. Processing must be restricted where:

(a) the accuracy of the personal data is contested by the data subject and their accuracy or inaccuracy cannot be ascertained (the controller must inform the data subject before lifting the restriction); or

(b) the personal data must be maintained for the purposes of evidence.

By way of example, the Recitals provide that the data should be restricted if there are reasonable grounds to believe that erasure could affect the legitimate interests of the data subject. In that case, restricted data should only be processed for the purpose which prevented their erasure. The Recitals provide examples of methods to restrict the processing such as moving the selected data to another processing system for archiving purposes for example or making the data unavailable. In the case of automated filing systems, the restriction should be ensured by technical means and it should be clearly indicated on the system that the data is restricted.[86]

[21.21] Article 16(4) requires the controller to inform the data subject in writing of any refusal of rectification or erasure of personal data or restriction of processing and of the reasons for the refusal. National legislative measures may be adopted restricting:

wholly or partly, the obligation to provide such information where a restriction constitutes a necessary and proportionate measure in a democratic society with

---

80. LED, article 15(3).
81. LED, article 15(4).
82. LED, Recital 46.
83. LED, Recital 47.
84. LED, article 16(1).
85. LED, article 16(2).
86. LED, Recital 47.

due regard for the fundamental rights and legitimate interests of the natural person concerned in order to:

(a) avoid obstructing official or legal inquiries, investigations or procedures;

(b) avoid prejudicing the prevention, detection, investigation or prosecution of criminal offences or the execution of criminal penalties;

(c) protect public security;

(d) protect national security;

(e) protect the rights and freedoms of others.

Data subjects must be informed by the controller that a complaint may be made to a supervisory authority or a judicial remedy may be sought.[87] The controller must communicate the rectification of inaccurate personal data to the competent authority from which the inaccurate personal data originate.[88] Where data has been rectified, erased or restricted the controller must notify the recipients and the recipients must rectify or erase the personal data or restrict processing of personal data under their responsibility.[89] The Recitals add that controllers should abstain from further dissemination of such data.[90]

Exercise and verification of rights by the supervisory authority

[21.22] Some aspects of the subject's rights of information,[91] access,[92] rectification or restriction[93] may also be exercised through the competent supervisory authority.[94] The controller must inform the data subject of this possibility.[95] Where a data subject exercises this right, the supervisory authority must inform the data subject at least that all necessary verifications or a review by the supervisory authority have taken place. The data subject must also be informed by the authority of their right to seek a judicial remedy.[96]

Rights of the data subject in criminal investigations and proceedings

[21.23] Article 18 provides that where the personal data are contained in a judicial decision, record or case file in the course of a criminal investigation and proceedings, Member States may provide for the exercise of the data subject's rights to information,

---

87.   LED, article 16(4).
88.   LED, article 16(5).
89.   LED, article 16(6).
90.   LED, Recital 47.
91.   LED, article 13(3).
92.   LED, article 15(3).
93.   LED, article 16(4).
94.   LED, article 17(1).
95.   LED, article 17(2).
96.   LED, article 17(3).

access, rectification, erasure and restriction to be carried out in accordance with Member State law.

Obligations of the Controller – data protection by design and default

[21.24] Chapter IV is divided into three sections: the first section sets out the obligations of the controller and processor, the second provides for security obligations and the third section details the role and function of the data protection officer.

Article 19 requires controllers to implement appropriate technical and organisational measures and be able to demonstrate that processing is performed in accordance with the LED. The controller is 'the competent authority which alone or jointly with others, determines the purposes and means of the processing of personal data; where the purposes and means of such processing are determined by Union or Member State law, the controller or the specific criteria for its nomination may be provided for by union or Member State law'.[97] The technical and organisational measures should take into account the nature, scope, context and purposes of processing together with risks and these measures must be reviewed and updated where necessary. Where proportionate to the processing activities undertaken, this would include the implementation of appropriate data protection policies.[98] The Recitals add that specific safeguards in respect of the treatment of personal data of vulnerable natural persons such as children should also be taken into account.[99] Possible risks are identified in the Recitals such as physical, material or non-material damage; in particular it could give rise to discrimination, identity theft or fraud, financial loss, damage to the reputation, loss of confidentiality of data protected by professional secrecy, authorised reversal of pseudonymisation or any other significant economic or social disadvantage.[100]

[21.25] At the time of determining the means for processing and the time of the processing itself, organisational and technical measures such as pseudonymisation[101] and data minimisation must be implemented in an effective manner with necessary safeguards integrated into the processing, in order to comply with the Directive and protect the rights of data subjects.[102] Account can be taken of the state of the article, the costs and the nature, scope, context and purposes of processing together with risks for the rights and freedoms of data subjects[103] but, according to the Recitals, the 'implementation of such measures should not depend solely on economic

---

97.   LED, article 3(8).
98.   LED, article 19(2).
99.   LED, Recital 50.
100. LED, Recital 51.
101. 'As early as possible,' LED, Recital 53. This Recital goes on to provide that the use of pseudonymisation for the purposes of this Directive can serve as a tool that could facilitate the free flow of personal data within the area of freedom, security and justice.
102. LED, article 20(1).
103. LED, article 20(1).

considerations'.[104] Controllers must implement measures ensuring that by default only personal data which are necessary for each specific purpose of the processing are processed. This obligation applies to the amount of personal data collected, the extent of their processing, the period of their storage and their accessibility. In particular, such measures must ensure that by default personal data are not made accessible without the individual's intervention to an indefinite number of natural persons.[105]

Where two or more controllers jointly determine the purposes and means of processing, the Directive requires that Member States ensure they are considered as joint controllers and that their respective responsibilities for compliance are set out in a transparent manner. They should arrange between them their responsibilities regarding the data subject's rights and duty to provide information unless their respective responsibilities are determined by Union or Member State law to which the controller is subject. The arrangement between joint controllers should designate which of them acts as a single contact point for data subjects exercising their rights[106] but the Directive permits Member States to provide in adopting legislation that the data subjects may exercise their rights against each of the controllers regardless of any terms of the arrangement between joint controllers.[107]

Processor

[21.26] A processor is defined as the natural or legal person, public body, agency or other body which processes personal data on behalf of the controller.[108] Article 22 sets out the obligations of the processor: The Directive requires Member States to ensure that where processing is carried out by a processor, the controller must only use processors providing sufficient guarantees to implement appropriate technical and organisational measures to ensure compliance with the Directive and the protection of data subject rights.[109] The Recitals add that the processor should take into account the principle of data protection by design and by default.[110] The processor must not engage another processor without the prior specific or general written authorisation by the controller. In the case of general written authorisation, the processor must inform the controller of any intended changes concerning the addition or replacement of other processors so as to give the controller an opportunity to object to such changes.[111] It is the controller who determines the purposes and means of processing but if a processor determines it, then that processor will be considered to be a controller in respect of that processing.[112]

---

104. LED, Recital 53.
105. LED, article 20(2).
106. LED, article 21(1).
107. LED, article 21(2).
108. LED, article 3(9).
109. LED, article 22(1).
110. LED, Recital 55.
111. LED, article 22(2).
112. LED, article 22(5).

[21.27] Member States must ensure that processing by a processor is governed by a contract or other legal act that is binding on the processor with regard to the controller and the agreement must set out 'the subject-matter and duration of the processing, the nature and purpose of the processing, the type of personal data and categories of data subjects and the obligations and rights of the controller'. Article 22(3) provides that in particular, the contract or other legal act must be in writing, including in an electronic form[113] and must specify that the processor:

    (a) acts only on instructions from the controller;

    (b) ensures that persons authorised to process the personal data have committed themselves to confidentiality or are under an appropriate statutory obligation of confidentiality;

    (c) assists the controller by any appropriate means to ensure compliance with the provisions on the data subject's rights;

    (d) at the choice of the controller, deletes or returns all the personal data to the controller after the end of the provision of data processing services, and deletes existing copies unless Union or Member State law requires storage of the personal data;

    (e) makes available to the controller all information necessary to demonstrate compliance with this Article;

    (f) complies with the conditions referred to in paragraphs 2 and 3 for engaging another processor.

The processor and any person acting under the authority of the controller or of the processor, who has access to personal data, must not process those data except on instructions from the controller, unless required to do so by Union or Member State law.[114]

Record keeping

[21.28] Both controllers and processors are obliged to maintain records on all categories of processing activities under their responsibility. Article 24 provides that Member States must ensure that controllers maintain a record of all categories of processing activities under their responsibility and that the controller and the processor must make those records available to the supervisory authority on request.[115] The records must be in writing, including in electronic form[116] and contain all of the following information:

    (a) the name and contact details of the controller and, where applicable, the joint controller and the data protection officer;

    (b) the purposes of the processing;

    (c) the categories of recipients to whom the personal data have been or will be disclosed including recipients in third countries or international organisations;

---

113. LED, article 22(4).
114. LED, article 23.
115. LED, article 24(4).
116. LED, article 24(3).

(d) a description of the categories of data subject and of the categories of personal data;

(e) where applicable, the use of profiling;

(f) where applicable, the categories of transfers of personal data to a third country or an international organisation;

(g) an indication of the legal basis for the processing operation, including transfers, for which the personal data are intended;

(h) where possible, the envisaged time limits for erasure of the different categories of personal data;

(i) where possible, a general description of the technical and organisational security measures referred to in Article 29(1).

Processors must maintain a record of all categories of processing activities carried out on behalf of a controller, containing:

(a) the name and contact details of the processor or processors, of each controller on behalf of which the processor is acting and, where applicable, the data protection officer;

(b) the categories of processing carried out on behalf of each controller;

(c) where applicable, transfers of personal data to a third country or an international organisation where explicitly instructed to do so by the controller, including the identification of that third country or international organisation;

(d) where possible, a general description of the technical and organisational security measures referred to in Article 29(1).[117]

In the case non-automated processing systems the controller or processor should have effective methods of demonstrating the lawfulness of the processing, enabling self-monitoring and of ensuring data integrity and data security such as logs or other forms of records.[118] Logs must be kept for at least the following processing operations in automated processing systems: 'collection, alteration, consultation, disclosure including transfers, combination and erasure'. The use of logs of consultation and disclosure must make it possible to establish 'the justification, date and time of such operations and, as far as possible, the identification of the person who consulted or disclosed personal data, and the identity of the recipients of such personal data'.[119] The logs can only be used to verify the lawfulness of processing, self-monitoring, ensuring the integrity and security of the personal data, and for criminal proceedings.[120] The Recitals add that 'self-monitoring also includes internal disciplinary proceedings of competent authorities'.[121] The logs must be made available to the supervisory authority on request.[122] Indeed it is a requirement of the Directive that controllers and the processors cooperate, on request,

---

117. LED, article 24(2).
118. LED, Recital 56.
119. LED, article 25(1).
120. LED, article 25(2).
121. LED, Recital 57.
122. LED, article 25(3).

with the supervisory authority in the performance of its tasks.[123] The Article 29 WP has explained that: 'Logging has a two-fold goal once it can be used as a deterrent action of non-authorised use, which can only be effectively if a log analysis rule is implemented, and a punitive action when a breach is discovered'.[124] The Article 29 WP went on to recommend that:

> … the use of logs in criminal proceedings can only be considered adequate when the lawfulness of a data processing operation – for instance, data consultation or disclosure – is being challenged, when there is a security breach in dispute or if data integrity is at stake. The use of logs for any other kind of criminal proceedings would be excessive and could undermine the real goals of the logging activity.[125]

Data Protection Impact Assessment

[21.29] Before processing, controllers are required to carry out an assessment of the impact of the envisaged processing operation on the protection of personal data. This is required where a type of processing is likely to result in a high risk to the rights and freedoms of natural persons. Account may be taken of the use of new technologies, the nature, scope, context and purposes of the processing in determining whether it would be likely to result in a high risk.[126] This assessment must contain 'at least a general description of the envisaged processing operations, an assessment of the risks to the rights and freedoms of data subjects, the measures envisaged to address those risks, safeguards, security measures and mechanisms to ensure the protection of personal data and to demonstrate compliance with this Directive, taking into account the rights and legitimate interests of the data subjects and other persons concerned'.[127] The Recitals add that these assessments should cover relevant systems and processes of processing operations but should not cover individual cases.[128] The Article 29 WP has recommended that national legislators '… place an obligation on controllers to carry out a DPIA in connection with automated decisions'.[129]

Prior consultation of the supervisory authority

[21.30] In certain cases, controllers and processors must consult the supervisory authority prior to processing. The authority must be consulted before processing which

---

123. LED, article 26.
124. Article 29 WP, *Opinion on some key issues of the Law Enforcement Directive*, 17/EN WP 258, 29 November 2017, p 26.
125. Article 29 WP, *Opinion on some key issues of the Law Enforcement Directive*, 17/EN WP 258, 29 November 2017, p 29.
126. LED, article 27(1).
127. LED, article 27(2).
128. LED, Recitals 58.
129. Article 29 WP, *Opinion on some key issues of the Law Enforcement Directive*, 17/EN WP 258, 29 November 2017, p 15.

will form part of a new filing system in two situations (a) if a data protection impact assessment indicates that processing would result in a high risk without measures taken by the controller to mitigate the risk or (b) the type of processing, in particular where using new technologies, mechanisms or procedures, involves a high risk to the rights and freedoms of data subjects.[130] The supervisory authority may establish a list of processing operations requiring prior consultation in these situations. [131] Where the supervisory authority is consulted and is of the opinion that the intended processing would infringe the Directive, in particular where the controller has insufficiently identified or mitigated the risk, the Directive requires that the supervisory authority provide written advice to the controller and where applicable to the processor and may use any of its powers as set out in article 47. This written advice must be provided within a period of up to six weeks of receipt of the request for consultation. Depending on the complexity of the intended processing the period may be extended by a month. The supervisory authority must inform the controller and, where applicable, the processor of an extension within one month of the receipt of the request for consultation, together with the reasons for the delay.[132]

The authority must be consulted during the preparation of a proposal for a legislative measure which concerns processing. The legislative measure may be one to be adopted by a national parliament or a regulatory measure pursuant to such a measure.[133]

The controller must provide the data protection impact assessment to the supervisory authority and any other information upon request in order to allow the supervisory authority to evaluate whether the processing is in compliance with the Directive and in particular assess the risks for the protection of personal data of the data subject and of the related safeguards.[134]

Security of personal data

[21.31] In order to maintain security, including confidentiality and prevent a breach of this Directive, the controller or processor should evaluate risks inherent in the processing and implement measures to mitigate those risks such as encryption.[135] Article 29 requires that Member States ensure that controllers and processors implement 'appropriate technical and organisational measures to ensure a level of security appropriate to the risk, in particular as regards the processing of special categories of personal data'. The state of the article, costs of implementation and the nature, scope, context and purposes of the processing as well as the risk of varying likelihood and severity for the rights and freedoms of natural persons, can all be taken into account.[136]

---

130. LED, article 28(1).
131. LED, article 28(3).
132. LED, article 28(5).
133. LED, article 28(2).
134. LED, article 28(4).
135. LED, Recital 60.
136. LED, article 29(1).

In automated processing the controller or processor, following an evaluation of the risks, must implement measures designed to:

(a) deny unauthorised persons access to processing equipment used for processing ('equipment access control');

(b) prevent the unauthorised reading, copying, modification or removal of data media ('data media control');

(c) prevent the unauthorised input of personal data and the unauthorised inspection, modification or deletion of stored personal data ('storage control');

(d) prevent the use of automated processing systems by unauthorised persons using data communication equipment ('user control');

(e) ensure that persons authorised to use an automated processing system have access only to the personal data covered by their access authorisation ('data access control');

(f) ensure that it is possible to verify and establish the bodies to which personal data have been or may be transmitted or made available using data communication equipment ('communication control');

(g) ensure that it is subsequently possible to verify and establish which personal data have been input into automated processing systems and when and by whom the personal data were input ('input control');

(h) prevent the unauthorised reading, copying, modification or deletion of personal data during transfers of personal data or during transportation of data media ('transport control');

(i) ensure that installed systems may, in the case of interruption, be restored ('recovery');

(j) ensure that the functions of the system perform, that the appearance of faults in the functions is reported ('reliability') and that stored personal data cannot be corrupted by means of a malfunctioning of the system ('integrity'). [137]

Notification of personal data breach to the supervisory authority

[21.32] The Recitals acknowledge that a personal data breach could result in physical, material or non-material damage such as a loss of control over their personal data or identity theft or fraud, financial loss, an unauthorised reversal of psuedonymisation, damage to reputation or loss of confidentiality of personal data protected by professional secrecy.[138] Therefore article 30 requires that controllers notify the supervisory authority of a personal data breach without undue delay and, where feasible, not later than 72 hours after having become aware of it unless the breach is unlikely to result in a risk to the rights and freedoms of natural persons. The Recitals add that controllers should be able to demonstrate, in accordance with the accountability principle, that the breach is unlikely to result in such a risk. Where the notification is not made within 72 hours, the reasons for such delay must accompany the notification.[139]

---

137. LED, article 29(2).

138. LED, Recital 61.

139. LED, article 30(1).

Processors must notify the controller of a breach without undue delay.[140] The notification must at least contain the following:

(a) a description of the nature of the personal data breach including, where possible, the categories and approximate number of data subjects and personal data records concerned;

(b) the name and contact details of the data protection officer or other contact point where more information can be obtained;

(c) a description of the likely consequences of the personal data breach;

(d) a description of the measures taken or proposed to be taken by the controller to address the breach. Where appropriate this might include measures to mitigate its possible adverse effects.[141]

The process anticipates that it might not be possible to provide this information at the same time and the Directive provides that the information 'may be provided in phases without undue further delay'.[142] Where the personal data breach involves personal data that have been transmitted by or to the controller of another Member State, this information must be communicated to the controller of that Member State without undue delay.[143]

Controllers are required to document the facts surrounding any personal data breaches, its effects and the remedial action taken. This will enable the supervisory authority to verify compliance.[144]

Communication of a personal data breach to the data subject

[21.33] Article 31 provides that where the personal data breach is likely to result in a high risk to the rights and freedoms of natural persons, the controller must communicate the personal data breach to the data subject without undue delay.[145] The Recitals explain that this is to allow them to 'take the necessary precautions'.[146] The nature of the breach must be communicated to them in 'clear and plain language' and contain at least the information and measures set out in article 30(3)(b),(c) and (d).[147] In other words, data subjects must receive the similar information to that required to be provided to the supervisory authority. The Recitals add that this communication might include recommendations for the natural person to mitigate potential adverse effects and it should be done in close cooperation with the supervisory authority, and respecting

---

140. LED, article 30(2).
141. LED, article 30(3).
142. LED, article 30(4).
143. LED, article 30(6).
144. LED, article 30(5).
145. LED, article 31(1).
146. LED, Recital 62.
147. LED, article 31(2).

guidance provided by it or other relevant authorities. The Recitals explain that the need to mitigate an immediate risk of damage would call for a prompt communication to data subjects, whereas the need to implement appropriate measures against continuing or similar data breaches may justify more time for the communication.[148] Therefore the Directive provides that no communication needs to be made to the data subject if any of the following conditions are met:

(a) the controller has implemented appropriate technological and organisational protection measures, and those measures were applied to the personal data affected by the personal data breach, in particular those that render the personal data unintelligible to any person who is not authorised to access it, such as encryption;

(b) the controller has taken subsequent measures which ensure that the high risk to the rights and freedoms of data subjects ... is no longer likely to materialise;

(c) it would involve a disproportionate effort. In such a case, there shall instead be a public communication or a similar measure whereby the data subjects are informed in an equally effective manner.[149]

If a communication has not been made to the data subject, the supervisory authority may require that one be made if the authority considers that there is a likelihood of the data breach resulting in a high risk. Alternatively it may decide that there is no need to make a communication as the requirements in (a)–(c) above are met.[150] The communication to the data subject may be delayed, restricted or omitted in accordance with article 13(3) where legislative measures are adopted in order to avoid: obstructing official or legal inquiries, investigation or procedures, prejudicing the prevention, detection, investigation or prosecution of criminal offences or the execution of criminal penalties, in order to protect public or national security or to protect the rights and freedoms of others.[151]

Data Protection Officer

[21.34] In order to ensure compliance with this Directive the controller should designate a person who 'would assist it in monitoring internal compliance,'[152] so article 32 provides that controllers 'must designate a data protection officer'. The Directive provides that Member States may exempt the courts and other independent judicial authorities when acting in their judicial capacity from that obligation. The Data Protection Officer must be designated on the basis of their 'professional qualities and, in particular ... expert knowledge of data protection law and practice and their ability to fulfil the tasks' set out in article 34 below.[153] The Recitals add that the data protection

---

148. LED, Recital 62.
149. LED, article 31(3).
150. LED, article 31(4).
151. LED, article 31(5).
152. LED, Recital 63.
153. LED, article 32(2).

officer might be an existing member of staff who has received special training in data protection law and practice in order to acquire that expertise. The necessary level of expert knowledge should be determined according to the data processing being carried out and could be carried out on a part-time or full-time basis.[154] A single data protection officer may be designated for several competent authorities, taking account of their organisational structure and size.[155] The Recitals provide the example of a situation of shared resources in central units and add that the person could be appointed to different positions within the structure of the relevant controllers.[156] The controller must publish the contact details of the data protection officer and communicate them to the supervisory authority.[157] The controller must ensure that the data protection officer is 'involved, properly and in a timely manner, in all issues which relate to the protection of personal data'[158] and must be supported in performing his tasks by providing the resources necessary to carry out those tasks and access to personal data and processing operations. The controller must also provide the supports necessary to maintain their expert knowledge.[159] Article 34 provides that controllers must entrust the data protection officer at least with the following tasks:

(a) to inform and advise the controller and the employees who carry out processing of their obligations pursuant to this Directive and to other Union or Member State data protection provisions;

(b) to monitor compliance with this Directive, with other Union or Member State data protection provisions and with the policies of the controller in relation to the protection of personal data, including the assignment of responsibilities, awareness-raising and training of staff involved in processing operations, and the related audits;

(c) to provide advice where requested as regards the data protection impact assessment and monitor its performance pursuant to Article 27;

(d) to cooperate with the supervisory authority;

(e) to act as the contact point for the supervisory authority on issues relating to processing, including the prior consultation referred to in Article 28, and to consult, where appropriate, with regard to any other matter.

The tasks are similar to the tasks of the DPO set out in the GDPR. The role of the data protection officer and tasks entrusted, the Recitals add, should be performed in 'an independent manner in accordance with member state law'.[160]

---

154. LED, Recital 63.
155. LED, article 32(3).
156. LED, Recital 63.
157. LED, article 32(4).
158. LED, article 33(1).
159. LED, article 33(2).
160. LED, Recital 63.

Transfers of personal data

[21.35] Chapter V sets out the general rules governing the transfers of personal data to third countries or international organisations. Transfers by competent authorities of personal data undergoing processing or are intended for processing after transfer to a third country or to an international organisation including for onward transfers to another third country or international organisation may be made provided domestic legislation transposing this Directive is complied with together with the conditions set out in this Chapter. These are as follows:

(a) the transfer is necessary for the purposes of the prevention, investigation, detection or prosecution of criminal offences or the execution of criminal penalties, including the safeguarding against and the prevention of threats to public security;

(b) the personal data are transferred to a controller in a third country or international organisation that is an authority competent for these purposes;

(c) where personal data are transmitted or made available from another Member State, that Member State has given its prior authorisation to the transfer in accordance with its national law;

(d) the Commission has adopted an adequacy decision (pursuant to article 36) or appropriate safeguards have been provided or exist pursuant to article 37, or, in the absence of an adequacy decision pursuant to article 36 and of appropriate safeguards in accordance with article 37, derogations for specific situations apply pursuant to article 38; and

(e) in the case of an onward transfer to another third country or international organisation, the competent authority that carried out the original transfer or another competent authority of the same Member State authorises the onward transfer, after taking into due account all relevant factors, including the seriousness of the criminal offence, the purpose for which the personal data was originally transferred and the level of personal data protection in the third country or an international organisation to which personal data are onward transferred.[161] The Recitals add that the competent authority that carried out the original transfer should also be able to subject the onward transfer to specific conditions which could be described in handling codes for example.[162]

In the case of (c) above, transfers may be made without the prior authorisation where the transfer of the personal data is necessary for the prevention of an immediate and serious threat to the public security of a Member State or its essential interests or a third country and prior authorisation cannot be obtained in good time. The authority responsible for giving prior authorisation must be informed without delay.[163] The Directive provides

---

161. LED, article 35(1).
162. LED, Recital 65.
163. LED, article 35(2).

that all provisions in Ch V must be applied in order to ensure that the level of protection of natural persons ensured by this Directive is not undermined.[164]

[21.36] Transfers to a third country or international organisation may take place where 'the Commission has decided that the third country, a territory or one or more specified sectors within that third country, or the international organisation in question ensures an adequate level of protection. Such a transfer shall not require any specific authorisation'.[165] The Recitals explain that this should provide legal certainty and uniformity throughout the Union.[166] In assessing the adequacy of the level of protection the Commission must take into account the following:

(a) the rule of law, respect for human rights and fundamental freedoms, relevant legislation, both general and sectoral, including concerning public security, defence, national security and criminal law and the access of public authorities to personal data, as well as the implementation of such legislation, data protection rules, professional rules and security measures, including rules for the onward transfer of personal data to another third country or international organisation, which are complied with in that country or international organisation, case law, as well as effective and enforceable data subject rights and effective administrative and judicial redress for the data subjects whose personal data are transferred;

(b) the existence and effective functioning of one or more independent supervisory authorities in the third country or to which an international organisation is subject, with responsibility for ensuring and enforcing compliance with data protection rules, including adequate enforcement powers, for assisting and advising data subjects in exercising their rights and for cooperation with the supervisory authorities of the Member States; and

(c) the international commitments the third country or international organisation concerned has entered into, or other obligations arising from legally binding conventions or instruments as well as from its participation in multilateral or regional systems, in particular in relation to the protection of personal data.[167]

The Recitals note that account could be taken of a third country's accession to the Council of Europe Convention of the 28 January 1981 for the Protection of individuals with regard to the automatic processing of personal data and its Additional Protocol. They also add that the Commission should consult with the European Data Protection Board when assessing the level of protection and take into account any relevant Commission adequacy decisions adopted in accordance with article 45 of the GDPR.[168] Where the Commission is satisfied of the adequacy of the level of protection, the Commission may do so by way of an implementing act. This act must provide a mechanism for periodic review, at least every four years, which takes into account all

---

164. LED, article 35(3).
165. LED, article 36(1).
166. LED, Recital 65.
167. LED, article 36(2).
168. LED, Recital 68.

relevant developments in the third country or international organisation. The act must specify its territorial and sectoral application and, where applicable, identify the supervisory authority or authorities referred to in article 36(2)(b) above. It must be adopted in accordance with the examination procedure set out in article 58(2).[169] The Commission must monitor developments in these third countries and international organisations on an ongoing basis.[170]

[21.37] If, following a review, the Commission finds that there is not an adequate level of protection, the Commission can, to the extent necessary, repeal, amend or suspend the decision without retroactive effect. Again, the implementing act must be adopted in accordance with the examination procedure. On the grounds of urgency, the Commission must adopt applicable implementing acts immediately[171] and the Commission must enter into consultations with the third country or international organisation in an effort to remedy the situation.[172] Such a decision must be made without prejudice to the transfers of personal data to the third country, the territory or one or more specified sectors within that third country or the international organisations in accordance with articles 37 and 38 (derogations in certain situations).[173] The Commission is obliged to publish in the *Official Journal of the European Union* and on its website a list of the third countries, territories and specified sectors within a third country and international organisations for which it has decided that an adequate level of protection is or is no longer ensured.[174]

Article 37 provides that where no decision has been issued pursuant to article 36(3), transfers to a third country or an international organisation may take place where (a) appropriate safeguards are provided for in a legally binding instrument or (b) the controller 'has assessed all the circumstances surrounding the transfer of personal data and concludes that appropriate safeguards exist with regard to the protection of personal data'.[175] In the case of (b), the transfer must be documented and the documentation must be made available to the supervisory authority on request. The documentation should set out the date and time of transfer, information about the receiving competent authority, the justification for the transfer and the personal data transferred.[176] The Recitals provide the example of a bilateral agreement which has been concluded by the Member States, implemented in their legal order and which could be enforced by their data subjects, thus ensuring compliance with the data protection requirements. The Recitals add that the controller should be able to take into account cooperation agreements between Europol or Eurojust and third countries which allow for the exchange of personal data when carrying out the assessment of all the circumstances surrounding the

---

169. LED, article 36(3).
170. LED, article 36(4).
171. LED, article 36(5).
172. LED, article 36(6).
173. LED, article 36(7).
174. LED, article 36(8).
175. LED, article 37(2).
176. LED, article 37(3).

transfer of data. The controller should be able to take into account confidentiality obligations and the principle of specificity which ensures that the data will not be processed for purposes other than the transfer. The Recitals go on to provide that the controller should take into account the fact that the personal data will not be used to request, hand down or execute a death penalty or any form of cruel and inhuman treatment.[177]

[21.38] Article 38 sets out the derogations for specific situations. Where there is no adequacy decision (pursuant to article 36), or appropriate safeguards (pursuant to article 37) transfers to a third country or international organisation may take place only on the condition that the transfer is necessary:

(a) in order to protect the vital interests of the data subject or another person;

(b) to safeguard legitimate interests of the data subject, where the law of the Member State transferring the personal data so provides;

(c) for the prevention of an immediate and serious threat to public security of a Member State or a third country;

(d) in individual cases for the purposes set out in Article 1(1); or

(e) in an individual case for the establishment, exercise or defence of legal claims relating to the purposes set out in Article 1(1).[178]

Personal data must not be transferred if the 'transferring competent authority determines that fundamental rights and freedoms of the data subject concerned override the public interest in the transfer set out in points (d) and (e)' above.[179] Again, any such transfer must be documented and made available to the supervisory authority on request setting out details such as the date and time of transfer, information about the receiving competent authority, the justification for the transfer and the personal data transferred'.[180] The Recitals note that these derogations should be interpreted restrictively and should 'not allow frequent, massive and structural transfers of personal data or large scale transfers of data' and limited to data strictly necessary.[181]

[21.39] Member States may provide for competent authorities (ie public authorities competent for the prevention, investigation, detection or prosecution of criminal offences or the execution of criminal penalties, including the safeguarding against and the prevention of threats to public security)[182] in 'individual and specific cases', to transfer personal data directed to recipients established in third countries only if the

---

177. LED, Recital 71.
178. LED, article 38(1).
179. LED, article 38(2).
180. LED, article 38(3).
181. LED, Recital 72.
182. LED, article 3(7)(a).

other provisions of this Directive are complied with and all of the following conditions are fulfilled:

(a) the transfer is strictly necessary for the performance of a task of the transferring competent authority as provided for by Union or Member State law for the purposes set out in Article 1(1);

(b) the transferring competent authority determines that no fundamental rights and freedoms of the data subject concerned override the public interest necessitating the transfer in the case at hand;

(c) the transferring competent authority considers that the transfer to an authority that is competent for the purposes referred to in Article 1(1) in the third country is ineffective or inappropriate, in particular because the transfer cannot be achieved in good time;

(d) the authority that is competent for the purposes referred to in Article 1(1) in the third country is informed without undue delay, unless this is ineffective or inappropriate;

(e) the transferring competent authority informs the recipient of the specified purpose or purposes for which the personal data are only to be processed by the latter provided that such processing is necessary.[183]

This is by way of derogation from article 35(1)(b) and without prejudice to any international agreement, Union or Member State law.[184] The Recitals explain that this transfer might arise where there is an urgent need to transfer personal data to save the life of a person who is in danger of becoming a victim of a crime or in the interest of preventing an imminent perpetration of a crime, including terrorism.[185] Where such a transfer is made the transferring competent authority must inform the supervisory authority[186] and again the transfer must be documented.[187]

International cooperation

[21.40] Article 40 replicates article 50 of the GDPR providing that where personal data moves across borders it makes it difficult to exercise data protection rights, supervisory authorities may find that they are unable to pursue complaints or conduct investigations relating to activities outside their borders and there may be inconsistent legal regimes. There is therefore a need to promote closer cooperation between data protection supervisory authorities to help them exchange information with their foreign counterparts.[188] Therefore, article 40 provides that in relation to third countries and

---

183. LED, article 39(1).
184. LED, article 35(1). An international agreement means any bilateral or multilateral international agreement in force between Member States and third countries in the field of judicial cooperation in criminal matters and police cooperation – LED, article 39(2).
185. LED, Recital 73.
186. LED, article 39(3).
187. LED, article 39(4).
188. LED, Recital 74.

international organisations, the Commission and Member States will take appropriate steps to:

(a) develop international cooperation mechanisms to facilitate the effective enforcement of legislation for the protection of personal data;

(b) provide international mutual assistance in the enforcement of legislation for the protection of personal data, including through notification, complaint referral, investigative assistance and information exchange, subject to appropriate safeguards for the protection of personal data and other fundamental rights and freedoms;

(c) engage relevant stakeholders in discussion and activities aimed at furthering international cooperation in the enforcement of legislation for the protection of personal data;

(d) promote the exchange and documentation of personal data protection legislation and practice, including on jurisdictional conflicts with third countries.

Independent supervisory authorities

[21.41] Each Member State is obliged in article 41 to provide 'for one or more independent public authorities to be responsible for monitoring' the application of the LED. This is to protect the fundamental rights and freedoms of natural persons in relation to processing and to facilitate the free flow of personal data within the Union. The Recitals explain that permitting a Member State to have more than one supervisory authority could reflect the constitutional, organisational and administrative structure in that state.[189] Each authority will contribute to the consistent application of the Directive in the Union and cooperate with each other and the Commission in accordance with Chapter VII.[190] The LED permits the supervisory authority established under the GDPR to be the appropriate authority under this Directive and to assume responsibility for the relevant tasks.[191] Where there is more than one supervisory authority established in a Member State, that Member State must designate the supervisory authority which represents those authorities in the Board referred to in article 51.[192] For the most part the provisions concerning the supervisory authorities mirror provisions in the GDPR and are dealt with elsewhere in this book. The requirement of independence both in terms of the authority and its members is set out in article 42. This Article mirrors that provided in GDPR, article 52.[193] The general conditions for the members of the supervisory authority are set out in article 43 and replicate the provisions of GDPR, article 53. The rules on the establishment of the supervisory authority in article 44 replicate the

---

189. LED, Recital 77.
190. LED, article 41(2).
191. LED, article 41(3).
192. LED, article 41(4).
193. See **Chapter 16**.

provisions of GDPR, article 54 save the first appointment after 6 May 2016 which is the date the LED must be transposed into domestic law.[194]

[21.42] Each supervisory authority must be competent in the performance of its tasks and in the exercise of its powers on the territory of its own Member State.[195] Member States must ensure that each supervisory authority is not to be competent to supervise the processing operations of courts when acting in their judicial capacity. Member States may provide for their supervisory authority not to be competent to supervise processing operations of other independent judicial authorities when acting in their judicial capacity[196] such as in a public prosecutor's office.[197] This exemption, the Recitals explain, is to safeguard the independence of judges in the performance of their judicial tasks and it should only apply to judicial activities in court cases and not to other activities where judges might be involved in accordance with Member State law.[198]

The tasks of the supervisory authority are set out in article 46 and provide, on its territory, for each supervisory authority to:

(a) monitor and enforce the application of the provisions adopted pursuant to this Directive and its implementing measures;

(b) promote public awareness and understanding of the risks, rules, safeguards and rights in relation to processing;

(c) advise, in accordance with Member State law, the national parliament, the government and other institutions and bodies on legislative and administrative measures relating to the protection of natural persons' rights and freedoms with regard to processing;

(d) promote the awareness of controllers and processors of their obligations under this Directive;

(e) upon request, provide information to any data subject concerning the exercise of their rights under this Directive and, if appropriate, cooperate with the supervisory authorities in other Member States to that end;

(f) deal with complaints lodged by a data subject, or by a body, organisation or association in accordance with Article 55, and investigate, to the extent appropriate, the subject-matter of the complaint and inform the complainant of the progress and the outcome of the investigation within a reasonable period, in particular if further investigation or coordination with another supervisory authority is necessary;[199]

---

194. LED, article 63.
195. LED, article 45(1).
196. LED, article 45(2).
197. LED, Recital 80.
198. LED, Recital 80.
199. LED, Recital 81 adds that the investigation should be carried out, subject to the judicial review, to the extent that is appropriate in the case. The supervisory authority should inform the data subject of the progress and outcome of the complaint and if it requires further investigation or coordination with another supervisory authority, intermediate information should be provided to the data subject.

(g) check the lawfulness of processing pursuant to Article 17, and inform the data subject within a reasonable period of the outcome of the check pursuant to paragraph 3 of that Article or of the reasons why the check has not been carried out;

(h) cooperate with, including by sharing information, and provide mutual assistance to other supervisory authorities, with a view to ensuring the consistency of application and enforcement of this Directive;

(i) conduct investigations on the application of this Directive, including on the basis of information received from another supervisory authority or other public authority;[200]

(j) monitor relevant developments insofar as they have an impact on the protection of personal data, in particular the development of information and communication technologies;

(k) provide advice on the processing operations referred to in Article 28; and

(l) contribute to the activities of the Board.

Each supervisory authority must facilitate the submission of complaints in (f) such as providing a complaint submission form which can be completed electronically, without excluding other means of communication.[201] And competent authorities must put in place effective mechanisms to encourage confidential reporting of infringements of the LED.[202] The performance of the tasks above must be free of charge for the data subject and for the data protection officer.[203] If a request is manifestly unfounded or excessive, because it is repetitive a reasonable fee may be charged by the supervisory authority based on its administrative costs, or it may refuse to act on the request. The burden will be placed on the supervisory authority to demonstrate that the request is manifestly unfounded or excessive.[204]

[21.43] Each supervisory authority must be given effective investigative powers by law including at least the power to obtain access to all personal data from the controller and the processor and to all information necessary for the performance of its tasks.[205] The supervisory authority must have effective corrective powers such as, for example:

(a) to issue warnings to a controller or processor that intended processing operations are likely to infringe the provisions adopted pursuant to the LED;

(b) to order the controller or processor to bring processing operations into compliance with the provisions adopted pursuant to the LED, where appropriate, in a specified manner and within a specified period, in particular by ordering the

---

200. LED, Recital 82 adds that investigative powers such as accessing premises should be exercised in accordance with specific requirements in Member State law such as a prior judicial authorisation.
201. LED, article 46(2).
202. LED, article 48.
203. LED, article 46(3).
204. LED, article 46(4).
205. LED, article 47(1).

rectification or erasure of personal data or restriction of processing pursuant to article 16;

(c) to impose a temporary or definitive limitation, including a ban, on processing.[206]

Each supervisory authority must be given effective advisory powers enabling it to advise the controllers in accordance with the prior consultation procedure in article 28 and to issue, on its own initiative or on request, opinions to its national parliament and its government or, in accordance with its national law, to other institutions and bodies as well as to the public on any issue related to the protection of personal data.[207] In exercising these powers, appropriate safeguards must be provided including an effective judicial remedy and due process, as set out in Union and Member State law in accordance with the Charter.[208] The Recitals add that measures taken by the supervisory authorities should be appropriate, necessary and proportionate taking into account the circumstances of each individual case, respect for the right of every person to be heard before any individual measure that would adversely affect the person concerned is taken and avoiding superfluous costs and excessive inconvenience to the person concerned.[209]

[21.44] The supervisory authority must be given the power to bring infringements of provisions adopted pursuant to this Directive to the attention of judicial authorities. Where appropriate this would include the power to commence or otherwise engage in legal proceedings.[210] An annual report must be drawn up on its activities including a list of the types of infringement notified and penalties imposed. The reports must be transmitted to the national parliament, government and other authorities as designed by Member State law and made available to the public, Commission and the Board. [211]

Mutual assistance

[21.45] Supervisory authorities are obligated to provide each other with relevant information and mutual assistance so as to ensure that the Directive is implemented and applied consistently and must put in place measures for effective cooperation with one another. Mutual assistance covers information requests and supervisory measures such as requests to carry out consultations, inspections and investigations.[212] Replies to the requests of another supervisory authority must be made without undue delay and no later than one month after receiving the request. Such measures may include the transmission of relevant information on the conduct of an investigation.[213] Requests for assistance must contain all the necessary information, including the purpose of and

---

206. LED, article 47(2).
207. LED, article 47(3).
208. LED, article 47(4).
209. LED, Recital 82.
210. LED, article 47(5).
211. LED, article 49.
212. LED, article 50(1).
213. LED, article 50(2).

reasons for the request and information exchanged can only be used for the purpose for which it was requested.[214] A requested supervisory authority cannot refuse to comply with the request unless:

(a) it is not competent for the subject-matter of the request or for the measures it is requested to execute; or

(b) compliance with the request would infringe this Directive or Union or Member State law to which the supervisory authority receiving the request is subject.[215]

The requested supervisory authority must inform the requesting supervisory authority of the results or progress of the measures taken in order to respond to the request and reasons must be provided for any refusal to comply with such a request.[216] Replies, as a rule, should be made by electronic means using a standardised format.[217] No fee may be imposed for any action taken by them pursuant to a request for mutual assistance and supervisory authorities may agree to indemnify each other for specific expenditure arising from the provision of mutual assistance in exceptional circumstances.[218] The Commission may specify the format and procedures for mutual assistance and arrangements for the exchange of information by electronic means between supervisory authorities and between authorities and the Board. The Commission may do so by means of implementing an act adopted in accordance with the examination procedure referred to in article 58(2).[219]

Tasks of the Board

[21.46] The tasks of the Board (as established by the GDPR) are set out in article 51 in respect of processing within the scope of the LED as follows:

(a) advise the Commission on any issue related to the protection of personal data in the Union, including on any proposed amendment of the LED;

(b) examine, on its own initiative, on request of one of its members or on request of the Commission, any question covering the application of the LED and issue guidelines, recommendations and best practices so as to encourage consistent application of this Directive;

(c) draw up guidelines for supervisory authorities concerning the application of measures referred to in article 47(1) and (3);

(d) issue guidelines, recommendations and best practices in accordance with point (b) of this subparagraph for establishing personal data breaches and determining the undue delay referred to in article 30(1) and (2) and for the particular

---

214. LED, article 50(3).
215. LED, article 50(4).
216. LED, article 50(5).
217. LED, article 50(6).
218. LED, article 50(7).
219. LED, article 50(8).

circumstances in which a controller or a processor is required to notify the personal data breach;

(e) issue guidelines, recommendations and best practices in accordance with point (b) of this subparagraph as to the circumstances in which a personal data breach is likely to result in a high risk to the rights and freedoms of natural persons as referred to in article 31(1);

(f) review the practical application of the guidelines, recommendations and best practices referred to in points (b) and (c);

(g) provide the Commission with an opinion for the assessment of the adequacy of the level of protection in a third country, a territory or one or more specified sectors within a third country, or an international organisation, including for the assessment whether that third country, territory, specified sector, or international organisation no longer ensures an adequate level of protection. In this case, the Commission must provide the Board with all the necessary documentation including correspondences;

(h) promote the cooperation and the effective bilateral and multilateral exchange of information and best practices between the supervisory authorities;

(i) promote common training programmes and facilitate personnel exchanges between the supervisory authorities and, where appropriate, with the supervisory authorities of third countries or with international organisations;

(j) promote the exchange of knowledge and documentation on data protection law and practice with data protection supervisory authorities worldwide.

If the Commission requests advice from the Board, a time limit may be set which takes into account the urgency of the matter.[220] The Board must forward its opinions, guidelines, recommendations and best practices to the Commission and to the committee (referred to in article 58(1)) and make them public.[221] The Commission must inform the Board of the action it has taken following opinions, guidelines, recommendations and best practices issued by the Board.[222]

Remedies

[21.47] The LED sets out the remedies that are available to data subjects alone in some instances, in others to the broader categories of 'any person' or 'natural or legal persons':

> 1. Each data subject has the right to lodge a complaint with a single supervisory authority, if the data subject considers that the processing of personal data relating to him infringes provisions adopted pursuant to the LED. [223] This is without prejudice to any other administrative of judicial remedies. The

---

220. LED, article 51(2).
221. LED, article 51(3).
222. LED, article 51(4).
223. LED, article 52(1).

supervisory authority with which the complaint has been lodged to must transmit it to the competent supervisory authority, without undue delay if the complaint is not lodged with the supervisory authority that is competent pursuant to article 45(1). In this case, the data subject must be informed about the transmission[224] and the supervisory authority with which the complaint has been lodged to must provide further assistance on request of the data subject.[225] The competent supervisory authority must inform the data subject of the progress and the outcome of the complaint, including of the possibility of a judicial remedy pursuant to article 53.[226] The Recitals add that in order to facilitate the submission of complaints, each supervisory authority should takes measures such as providing a complaint submission form which can also be completed electronically without excluding other means of communication.[227]

2. A natural or legal person has the right to an effective judicial remedy against a legally binding decision of a supervisory authority concerning them. This remedy is not confined to data subjects alone, its extension to natural or legal persons means that it may be invoked by controllers and processors also. This is without prejudice to any other administrative or non-judicial remedy.[228] The Recitals add that this right is against a decision that produces legal effects concerning that person. This decision might concern in particular the exercise of investigative, corrective and authorisation powers by the supervisory authority or the dismissal or rejection of complaints. This right does not include other measures of supervisory authorities which are not legally binding such as opinions issued or advice provided by the supervisory authority. [229]

3. Each data subject has the right to an effective judicial remedy where the supervisory authority which is competent pursuant to article 45(1) does not handle a complaint or does not inform the data subject within three months of the progress or outcome of the complaint lodged pursuant to article 52.[230] Proceedings against a supervisory authority must be brought before the courts of the Member State where the supervisory authority is established in this case and under point 2.[231]

4. The data subject has the right to an effective judicial remedy where he considers that his rights have been infringed as a result of the processing of his personal data in non-compliance with the LED. This is without prejudice to any

---

224. LED, article 52(2).
225. LED, article 52(3).
226. LED, article 52(4).
227. LED, Recital 85.
228. LED, article 53(1).
229. LED, Recital 86.
230. LED, article 53(2). This is without prejudice to any other administrative or non-judicial remedy.
231. LED, article 53(3).

available administrative or non-judicial remedy, including the right to lodge a complaint with a supervisory authority pursuant to article 52. [232]

5. The data subject has the right to mandate a not-for-profit body, organisation or association which has been properly constituted with statutory objectives which are in the public interest and is active in the field of protection of data subject's right to and freedoms to lodge the complaint on his behalf and to exercise the rights set out in Articles on his behalf. [233]

6. 'Any person' who has suffered material or non-material damage as a result of an unlawful processing operation or of any act infringing national provisions adopted pursuant to the LED to have the right to receive compensation for the damage suffered from the controller or any other authority competent under Member State law. [234] The Recitals explain that the concept of damage should be broadly interpreted in the light of the case law of the CJEU in a manner which fully reflects the objectives of the LED. They further provide that data subjects should receive full and effective compensation for the damage that they have suffered.[235] The use of the phrase 'any person' suggests that compensation may be sought by persons other than data subjects, though it remains to be seen how Member States will implement this provision and what it may mean in practice.

Each Member State must set out the rules on penalties applicable to infringements and take all measures necessary to ensure that they are implemented. The penalties must be effective, proportionate and dissuasive.[236] And the Recitals add that such penalties may be imposed upon any natural or legal person whether governed by private or public law and Member States should take all measures to implement the penalties.[237]

[21.48] The specific provisions for the protection of personal data in Union legal acts that entered into force on or before 6 May 2016 in the field of judicial cooperation in criminal matters and police cooperation, which regulate processing between Member States and the access of designated authorities of Member States to information systems established pursuant to the Treaties within the scope of this Directive, remain unaffected.[238] International agreements involving the transfer of personal data to third countries or international organisations which were concluded by Member States prior to 6 May 2016 and which comply with Union law remain in force until amended, replaced or revoked.[239]

---

232. LED, article 54.
233. LED, article 55, in accordance with Member State procedural law. Recital 87 notes that the right of representation of data subjects should be without prejudice to Member State procedural law which may require mandatory representation of data subjects by a lawyer, as defined in Council Directive 77/249/EEC.
234. LED, article 56.
235. LED, Recital 88.
236. LED, article 57.
237. LED, Recital 89.
238. LED, article 60.
239. LED, article 61.

Commission reports

[21.49] By 6 May 2022, and every four years thereafter, the Commission is obliged to submit a report on the evaluation and review of the LED to the European Parliament and to the Council and they must be made public.[240] The Commission must examine, in particular, the application and functioning of Ch V on the transfer of personal data to third countries or international organisations with particular regard to decisions adopted pursuant to articles 36(3) and 39.[241] In order to undertake this report, it may request information from Member States and supervisory authorities[242] and in carrying out the evaluations and reviews the Commission must take into account the positions and findings of the European Parliament, of the Council and of other relevant bodies or sources.[243] If necessary, taking account of developments in information technology and state of progress in the information society, the Commission must submit appropriate proposals with a view to amending the LED.[244] By 6 May 2019, the Commission must review other legal acts adopted by the Union which regulate processing by the competent authorities for the purposes set out in article 1(1) including those referred to in article 60, in order to assess the need to align them with this Directive and to make, where appropriate, the necessary proposals to amend those acts to ensure a consistent approach to the protection of personal data within the scope of this Directive.[245]

[21.50] Article 63 requires Member States to adopt and publish, by 6 May 2018, the laws, regulations and administrative provisions necessary to comply with the LED. The text must be notified to the Commission and the provisions are applicable from 6 May 2018. There are two derogations provided in article 63. Firstly Member States:

> may provide, exceptionally, where it involves disproportionate effort, for automated processing systems set up before 6 May 2016 to be brought into conformity with article 25(1) by 6 May 2023.[246]

And secondly a Member State:

> may, in exceptional circumstances, bring an automated processing system as referred to in paragraph 2 of this Article into conformity with Article 25(1) within a specified period after the period referred to in paragraph 2 of this Article, if it would otherwise cause serious difficulties for the operation of that particular automated processing system.

The Member State concerned must notify the Commission of the grounds for those serious difficulties and the grounds for the specified period within which it must bring

---

240. LED, article 62(1).
241. LED, article 62(2).
242. LED, article 62(3).
243. LED, article 62(4).
244. LED, article 62(5).
245. LED, article 62(6).
246. LED, article 63(2).

that particular automated processing system into conformity with article 25(1). The specified period cannot be later than 6 May 2026.[247]

Member States must communicate to the Commission the text of the main provisions of national law which they adopt in the field covered by this Directive.[248] The Commission is assisted by the committee established by GDPR, article 93. That committee is a committee within the meaning of Regulation 182/2011/EU.[249]

247. LED, article 63(3).
248. LED, article 63(4).
249. LED, article 58(1).

PART 9
PROCESSING BY COMMUNITY
INSTITUTIONS

Chapter 22

PROCESSING BY COMMUNITY INSTITUTIONS

INTRODUCTION

[22.01] TFEU, article 16(2) requires that the EU's legislature:

> ... lay down the rules relating to the protection of individuals with regard to the processing of personal data by Union institutions, bodies, offices and agencies ...

At present the rules on the processing of personal data by EU institutions, bodies, offices and agencies are set out in EU Regulation 45/2001. GDPR, article 98 suggests that the EU Commission may wish to consider that Regulation's amendment:

> The Commission shall, if appropriate, submit legislative proposals with a view to amending other Union legal acts on the protection of personal data, in order to ensure uniform and consistent protection of natural persons with regard to processing. This shall in particular concern the rules relating to the protection of natural persons with regard to processing by Union institutions, bodies, offices and agencies and on the free movement of such data.

On foot of these provisions the EU Commission proposed a new Regulation on the processing of personal data by the Union institutions, bodies, offices and agencies in January 2017.[1] However the GDPR provides that Regulation 45/2001 will be adapted in accordance with the GDPR until this Proposal is enacted:

> For the processing of personal data by the Union institutions, bodies, offices and agencies, Regulation (EC) No 45/2001 applies. Regulation (EC) No 45/2001 and other Union legal acts applicable to such processing of personal data shall be adapted to the principles and rules of [Regulation 45/2001] in accordance with Article 98.[2]

The GDPR explains that this adaptation is required:

> In order to provide a strong and coherent data protection framework in the Union, the necessary adaptations of Regulation (EC) No 45/2001 should follow after the adoption of this Regulation, in order to allow application at the same time as this Regulation.[3]

Hence the continuing relevance of Regulation 45/2001 is open to question. It would appear that the GDPR will apply to EU institutions, bodies, offices and agencies in the

---

1.   Proposal for a Regulation of the European Parliament and of the Council on the protection of individuals with regard to the processing of personal data by the Union institutions, bodies, offices and agencies and on the free movement of such data, and repealing Regulation 45/2001/EC and Decision No 1247/2002/EC, COM (2017) 8: Brussels, 10 January 2017.
2.   GDPR, article 2(3).
3.   GDPR, Recital 17.

same manner as it will apply to the government institutions, bodies, offices and agencies of a Member State. However, there are some provisions of Regulation 45/2001 that will remain relevant as the GDPR lacks direct equivalents, these provisions include: the establishment of the European Data Protection Supervisor (EDPS); specific rules on transfers from one EU institution to another; and more detailed obligations to secure the data.

EU REGULATION 45/2001

[22.02] EU Regulation 45/2001 governs the protection of personal data processing by the Community Institutions and bodies and the free movement of such data. Article 1 sets out its objective as ensuring that Community Institutions or bodies

> ... protect the fundamental rights and freedoms of natural persons, and in particular their right to privacy with respect to the processing of personal data and shall neither restrict nor prohibit the free flow of personal data between themselves or to recipients subject to the national law of the Member States implementing Directive 95/46/EC.

The European Data Protection Supervisor (EDPS) is established as an independent supervisory authority tasked with monitoring its application to all processing operations carried out by a Community institution or body.[4] This Regulation applies to the processing by all Community institutions and bodies '... insofar as such processing is carried out in the exercise of activities all or part of which fall within the scope of Community law'.[5] It applies to processing of personal data whether by automated means or not.

General rules on the lawfulness of processing personal data

[22.03] The persons to be protected under Regulation 45/2001 are those whose personal data are processed by Community institutions or bodies '... in any context whatsoever, for example because they are employed by those institutions or bodies'.[6] Data controllers[7] must ensure that personal data is:

    (a)   processed fairly and lawfully;

    (b)   collected for specified, explicit and legitimate purposes and not further processed in a manner incompatible with those purposes;

---

4.   Regulation 45/2001/EC, article 1.

5.   Regulation 45/2001/EC, article 3(1).

6.   Regulation 45/2001/EC, Recital 7.

7.   A data controller is defined in article 2(d) as meaning the Community institution or body, the Directorate-General, the unit or any other organisational entity which alone or jointly with others determines the purposes and means of the processing of personal data; where the purposes and means of processing are determined by a specific Community act, the controller or the specific criteria for its nomination may be designated by such Community act.

(c) adequate, relevant and not excessive in relation to the purposes for which they are collected and/ further processed;

(d) accurate and where necessary, kept up to date;

(e) kept in a form which permits identification of data subjects for no longer than is necessary for the purposes for which the data were collected or for which they are further processed. The community institution or body must ensure that data which are to be stored for longer periods for historical, statistical or scientific use are kept either in anonymous form only or, if that is not possible, only with the identity of the data subjects encrypted.[8]

Personal data may only be processed if

(a) processing is necessary for the performance of a task carried out in the public interest on the basis of the Treaties establishing the European Communities or other legal instruments adopted on the basis thereof or in the legitimate exercise of official authority vested in the Community institution or body or in a third party to whom the data are disclosed, or

(b) processing is necessary for compliance with a legal obligation to which the controller is subject, or

(c) processing is necessary for the performance of a contract to which the data subject is party or in order to take steps at the request of the data subject prior to entering into a contract, or

(d) the data subject has unambiguously given his or her consent, or

(e) processing is necessary in order to protect the vital interests of the data subject.[9]

Article 6 adds that without prejudice to the above personal data can only be processed for purposes other than those for which they have been collected 'if the change of purpose is expressly permitted by the internal rules of the Community institution or body'. Personal data 'collected exclusively for ensuring the security or the control of the processing systems or operations shall not be used for other purpose, with the exception of the prevention, investigation, detection and prosecution of serious criminal offences'.[10]

Transfer of personal data

[22.04] Personal data can be transferred within or to other Community institutions or bodies 'if the data are necessary for the legitimate performance of tasks covered by the competence of the recipient'. If data are transferred following a request from the recipient, both the controller and the recipient are responsible for the legitimacy of the transfer. The controller must be able to verify the competence of the recipient and to

---

8.   Regulation 45/2001/EC, article 4.

9.   Regulation 45/2001/EC, article 5.

10.   Regulation 45/2001/EC, article 6(2).

make a provisional evaluation of the necessity for the transfer of the data. If there are any doubts in relation to this necessity, the controller must seek further information from the recipient and the recipient must ensure that the necessity for the transfer of the data can be subsequently verified. The recipient is only permitted to process the personal data for the purposes for which they were transmitted.[11]

Regulation 45/2001, article 9 provides for transfers to recipients that are outside the scope of Directive 95/46 and so the GDPR. This will encompass transfers to recipients outside the EU; within the EU it might encompass transfers to recipients that are subject to the LED. The latter form of transfer has proven controversial in the past. In *Franchet*[12] the CJEU held that the EU was liable for having processed the applicant's personal data as follows:

> ... forwarding of information to the Luxembourg and French judicial authorities without having heard the applicants and its Supervisory Committee and in the leaks relating to the forwarding of the ... file to the French judicial authorities ...; the errors of the Commission capable of incurring Community liability consist in the publication of the press release ... in the speech of its President ... and in the initiation of the disciplinary proceedings before the investigations were complete.[13]

The CJEU assessed them as being entitled to damages in the sum of €56,000, though this took into account '... the fact that the applicants' reputation was very seriously affected'.[14] Regulation 45/2001 provides that such data may be '... transferred solely to allow tasks covered by the competence of the controller to be carried out'. It also provides for transfers to recipients outside the EU. From May 2018 such transfers will then be subject to GDPR, Ch V.[15] Regulation 45/2001 allows for the data transfers where there is an adequate level of protection ensured in the country of the recipient or within the recipient international organisation and transferred solely to allow tasks covered by the competence of the controller to be carried out. The adequacy is assessed in the light of all the circumstances surrounding a data transfer operation.[16] The EDPS may authorise a transfer to a third country or international organisation which does not ensure an adequate level of protection where the controller adduces adequate safeguards with respect to the protection of the privacy and fundamental rights and freedoms of individuals and as regards the exercise of the corresponding rights. Those safeguards may result from appropriate contractual clauses.[17]

---

11.   Regulation 45/2001/EC, article 7.
12.   *Franchet* (Case T–48/05) (8 July 2008).
13.   *Franchet* (Case T–48/05) (8 July 2008), para 398.
14.   *Franchet* (Case T–48/05) (8 July 2008), para 411.
15.   The text of Regulation 45/2001/EC, article 8 refers to Directive 95/46.
16.   Regulation 45/2001/EC, article 9.
17.   Regulation 45/2001/EC, article 9(7).

The processing of special categories of data

[22.05] Regulation 45/2001 prohibits the processing of personal data revealing racial or ethnic origin, political opinions, religious or philosophical beliefs, trade-union membership, and of data concerning health or sex life. This list will have to be expanded to include genetic or biometric data to accord with GDPR, article 9, which may in turn supplant article 10(6) which provides that the EDPS may determine the conditions under which a personal number or other identifier of general application may be processed by a Community institution or body.[18] The exceptions set out in Regulation 45/2001, article 10(2) will have to be read in accordance with GDPR, article 9(2).

Information to be given to the data subject

[22.06] Where data is collected from a data subject, they must be given the following information unless they already have it: The identity of the controller, purposes of processing, recipients, whether replies to questions are obligatory or voluntary and the consequences of failing to reply, the existence of the right of access, rectification and any further information such as the legal basis of the processing, time limits for storing the data and the right to have recourse at any time to the EDPS. This is to ensure fair processing.[19] Where it is not obtained directly from the data subject, that information must be provided at the time of undertaking the recording of the personal data or if a disclosure to a third party is envisaged, no later than the time when the data are first disclosed. The origin of the data must also be provided in this case.[20]

Rights of the data subject

[22.07] The data subject has a number of rights: The right of access,[21] the right of rectification,[22] the right to block inaccurate data, data no longer needed by the controller or where the processing is unlawful,[23] the right of erasure if processing their personal data is unlawful,[24] the right to obtain from the controller the notification to third parties of any rectification, erasure or blocking of processing,[25] the right to object to processing[26] and the right not to be subject to automated decisions.[27]

---

18. Regulation 45/2001/EC, article 10.
19. Regulation 45/2001/EC, article 11.
20. Regulation 45/2001/EC, article 12.
21. Regulation 45/2001/EC, article 13.
22. Regulation 45/2001/EC, article 14.
23. Regulation 45/2001/EC, article 15.
24. Regulation 45/2001/EC, article 16.
25. Regulation 45/2001/EC, article 17.
26. Regulation 45/2001/EC, article 18.
27. Regulation 45/2001/EC, article 19.

Exemptions and restrictions

[22.08] The Community institutions and bodies may restrict the application of provisions relating to the principles relating to data quality, the information to be given to data subjects, data subject rights set out in articles 13 to 17 and the provisions relating to traffic and billing data in article 37(1) where such restriction constitutes 'a necessary measure to safeguard:

    (a) the prevention, investigation, detection and prosecution of criminal offences;

    (b) an important economic or financial interest of a Member State or of the European Communities, including monetary, budgetary and taxation matters;

    (c) the protection of the data subject or of the rights and freedoms of others;

    (d) the national security, public security or defence of the Member States;

    (e) a monitoring, inspection or regulatory task connected, even occasionally, with the exercise of official authority in the cases referred to in (a) and (b).[28]

If a restriction is imposed, the data subject must be informed of the principal reasons on which the application of the restriction is based and his right to have recourse to the EDPS (EDPS).[29] Where the restriction involves the denial of access to the data subject, the EDPS must when investigating a complaint only inform him or her of whether the data have been processed correctly and if not, whether any corrections have been made.[30] The provision of information in these cases may be deferred for 'as long as such information would deprive the restriction of its effect'.[31]

Data subject rights set out in articles 13 to 16 do not apply when data are processed solely for purposes of scientific research or are kept in personal form for a period which does not exceed the period necessary for the sole purpose of compiling statistics. This is provided that there is clearly no risk of breaching the privacy of the data subject and that the controller provides adequate legal safeguards.[32]

Confidentiality and security of processing

[22.09] A person employed with a Community institution or body and any Community institution or body itself acting as processor, with access to personal data, must '... not process them except on instructions from the controller, unless required to do so by national or Community law'.[33] Appropriate technical and organisational measures to ensure the security must be used taking into account the state of the article and costs. These measures are there to prevent any unauthorised disclosure or access, accidental or unlawful destruction or accidental loss, or alteration, and to prevent all other unlawful forms of processing.

---

28. Regulation 45/2001/EC, article 20(1).
29. Regulation 45/2001/EC, article 20(3).
30. Regulation 45/2001/EC, article 20(4).
31. Regulation 45/2001/EC, article 20(5).
32. Regulation 45/2001/EC, article 20(2).
33. Regulation 45/2001/EC, article 21.

When processing is by automated means, the security measures must be taken '... as appropriate in view of the risks in particular with the aim of:

(a) preventing any unauthorised person from gaining access to computer systems processing personal data;

(b) preventing any unauthorised reading, copying, alteration or removal of storage media;

(c) preventing any unauthorised memory inputs as well as any unauthorised disclosure, alteration or erasure of stored personal data;

(d) preventing unauthorised persons from using data-processing systems by means of data transmission facilities;

(e) ensuring that authorised users of a data-processing system can access no personal data other than those to which their access right refers;

(f) recording which personal data have been communicated, at what times and to whom;

(g) ensuring that it will subsequently be possible to check which personal data have been processed, at what times and by whom;

(h) ensuring that personal data being processed on behalf of third parties can be processed only in the manner prescribed by the contracting institution or body;

(i) ensuring that, during communication of personal data and during transport of storage media, the data cannot be read, copied or erased without authorisation;

(j) designing the organisational structure within an institution or body in such a way that it will meet the special requirements of data protection.[34]

The controller is obliged to choose a processor providing sufficient guarantees in respect of the technical and organisational security measures described above. Processing carried out by a processor must be governed by a contract or legal act binding on the processor to the controller and stipulating in particular that the processor will only act on instructions from the controller and comply with security and confidentiality obligations.[35] The contract or legal act must be in writing or in another equivalent form.[36]

The Data Protection Officer

[22.10] Article 24 requires each Community institution and Community body to appoint a Data Protection Officer (DPO) and sets out their tasks as follows:

(a) ensuring that controllers and data subjects are informed of their rights and obligations;

---

34. Regulation 45/2001/EC, article 22.

35. Unless, by virtue of Directive 95/46/EC, article 16 or article 17(3), the processor is already subject to obligations with regard to confidentiality and security laid down in the national law of one of the Member States.

36. Regulation 45/2001/EC, article 23.

(b)   responding to requests from the EDPS and cooperating with the EDPS;

(c)   ensuring in an independent manner the internal application of the provisions of this Regulation;

(d)   keeping a register of the processing operations carried out by the controller, containing the relevant information;

(e)   notifying the EDPS of the processing operations likely to present specific risks.

The DPO must ensure that 'the rights and freedoms of the data subjects are unlikely to be adversely affected by the processing operations'. The DPO should be selected on the basis of their personal and professional qualities and in particular, their expert knowledge of data protection and there should be no conflict of interest between their duty as DPO and other official duties in particular in relation to the application of the provisions of this Regulation. Their appointment should be for a term of between two and five years and they may be reappointed up to a maximum total term of ten years. The institution or body must register the appointment with the EDPS. The DPO may be dismissed from their post only with the consent of the EDPS where they no longer fulfil the conditions required for the performance of their duties. Staff and resources necessary to carry out their tasks must be provided. In terms of carrying out their duties, the DPO '... may not receive any instructions'.

Further implementing rules concerning the Data Protection Officer must be adopted by each Community institution or body in accordance with provisions set out in the Annex. The implementing rules must in particular concern the tasks, duties and powers of the Data Protection. The Annex provides that the DPO may make recommendations for the practical improvement of data protection to the Community institution or body and advise it and the controller concerned on matters concerning the application of data protection provisions. Furthermore, he or she may investigate matters and occurrences directly relating to their tasks and which come to their notice, and report back to the person who commissioned the investigation or to the controller. The DPO may be consulted by the Community institution or body which appointed them, by the controller concerned, by the Staff Committee concerned and by any individual, without going through the official channels, on any matter concerning the interpretation or application of this Regulation. No one must suffer prejudice by virtue of bringing breaches of Regulation 45/2001 to the attention of the DPO. Every controller concerned must assist the DPO in performing their duties and to give information in reply to questions. In performing their duties, the DPO must have access at all times to the data forming the subject matter of processing operations and to all offices, data-processing installations and data carriers. To the extent required, the DPO must be relieved of other activities. The DPO and staff must not disclose information which they obtain in the course of their duties.

Notification to the Data Protection Officer

[22.11] The controller must give prior notice to the DPO of processing operations intended to serve a single purpose or several related purposes. The information to be given must include:

(a) the name and address of the controller and an indication of the organisational parts of an institution or body entrusted with the processing of personal data for a particular purpose;

(b) the purpose or purposes of the processing;

(c) a description of the category or categories of data subjects and of the data or categories of data relating to them;

(d) the legal basis of the processing operation;

(e) the recipients or categories of recipient to whom the data might be disclosed;

(f) a general indication of the time limits for blocking and erasure of the different categories of data;

(g) proposed transfers of data to third countries or international organisations;

(h) a general description allowing a preliminary assessment to be made of the appropriateness of the security measures undertaken.

Changes must be notified promptly to the DPO.[37] The DPO must also keep a register of processing operations and should contain the information listed in (a) to (g) above. The register may be inspected by any person directly or indirectly through the EDPS.[38]

Prior checking by the EDPS and obligation to cooperate

[22.12] Processing operations are likely to present specific risks to the rights and freedoms of data subjects by virtue of their nature, their scope or their purposes are subject to prior checking by the EDPS.[39] The following processing operations are likely to present these risks:

(a) processing of data relating to health and to suspected offences, criminal convictions or security measures;

(b) processing operations intended to evaluate personal aspects relating to the data subject, including his or her ability, efficiency and conduct;

(c) processing operations allowing linkages not provided for pursuant to national or Community legislation between data processed for different purposes;

(d) processing operations for the purpose of excluding individuals from a right, benefit or contract.[40]

---

37. Regulation 45/2001/EC, article 25.
38. Regulation 45/2001/EC, article 26.
39. Regulation 45/2001/EC, article 27(1).
40. Regulation 45/2001/EC, article 27(2).

Prior checks are carried out by the EDPS following receipt of a notification from the DPO[41] and it will deliver an opinion within two months. This period may be suspended until the EDPS has obtained further information where requested. If the matter is complex, the period may also be extended for a further two months, by decision of the EDPS and this must be notified to the controller prior to the expiry of the initial two-month period. If the opinion has not been delivered by the end of the two-month period, or any extension, it will be deemed to be favourable.

Where the EDPS decides that the notified processing involves a breach of the Regulation, appropriate proposals may be made to avoid such breach. Where the controller does not modify the processing operation accordingly, the EDPS may exercise their power under article 47(1). [42] The EDPS must keep a register of all notified processing operations containing the information referred to in article 25 and it is open to public inspection.[43]

The Community institutions and bodies must inform the EDPS when drawing up administrative measures relating to the processing of personal data involving a Community institution or body alone or jointly with others. When it adopts a legislative proposal relating to the protection of individuals' rights and freedoms with regard to the processing of personal data, the Commission must consult the EDPS.[44] Community institutions and bodies must inform the EDPS of the measures taken further to the EDPS's decisions or authorisations.[45]

Where requested, controllers must assist the EDPS in the performance of their duties, in particular by providing any information requested and by granting access.[46] In response to the EDPS's exercise of power, the controller must inform it of its views within a reasonable period to be specified by the Supervisor. The reply must also include a description of the measures taken, if any, in response to the remarks of the EDPS.[47]

Remedies

[22.13] Chapter III sets out the remedies where a dispute arises. Article 32 provides that the CJEU has jurisdiction to hear all disputes which relate to the provisions of the Regulation, including claims for damages. Every data subject can lodge a complaint with the EDPS if they consider that their data protection rights have been infringed as a result of the processing of their personal data by a Community institution or body.[48] In

---

41.   Regulation 45/2001/EC, article 27(3).
42.   Regulation 45/2001/EC, article 27(4).
43.   Regulation 45/2001/EC, article 27(5).
44.   Regulation 45/2001/EC, article 28.
45.   As set out in Regulation 45/2001/EC, article 46(h). Regulation 45/2001/EC, article 29.
46.   Regulation 45/2001/EC, article 30.
47.   Regulation 45/2001/EC, article 31.
48.   Regulation 45/2001/EC, article 32 refers to subject rights pursuant to what was then TEC, article 286, which then specifically provided for the establishment of the ECPS and that EC (contd .../)

the absence of a response by the EDPS within six months, the complaint will be deemed to have been rejected. Actions against decisions of the EDPS must be brought before the CJEU. Any person who has suffered damage because of an unlawful processing operation or any action incompatible with Regulation 45/2001 has the right to have the damage made good.[49] Any person employed with a Community institution or body may lodge a complaint with the EDPS regarding an alleged breach of Regulation 45/2001 without acting through official channels and no-one must suffer prejudice on account of making such a complaint.[50]

Protection of personal data and privacy in the context of internal telecommunications networks

[22.14] Article 34 contains specific provisions in relation to the processing of personal data in connection with the use of telecommunications networks or terminal equipment operated under the control of a Community institution or body. The Community institutions and bodies must

> take appropriate technical and organisational measures to safeguard the secure use of the telecommunications networks and terminal equipment, if necessary in conjunction with the providers of publicly available telecommunications services or the providers of public telecommunications networks. Having regard to the state of the article and the cost of their implementation, these measures shall ensure a level of security appropriate to the risk presented.

In the event of any particular risk of a breach of the security of the network and terminal equipment, the Community institution or body concerned must inform users of the existence of that risk and of any possible remedies and alternative means of communication.[51] A 'user' is defined as meaning '... any natural person using a telecommunications network or terminal equipment operated under the control of a Community institution or body'. Community institutions and bodies must also ensure the 'confidentiality of communications by means of telecommunications networks and terminal equipment, in accordance with the general principles of Community law'.[52]

Traffic data relating to users which are processed and stored to establish calls and other connections over the telecommunications network must be erased or made anonymous upon termination of the call or other connection. If necessary, traffic data as indicated in a list agreed by the EDPS may be processed for the purpose of telecommunications budget and traffic management, including the verification of authorised use of the telecommunications systems. These data must be erased or made

---

48. (contd) 'acts on the protection of individuals with regard to the processing of personal data and the free movement of such data apply to the Community institutions and bodies'. Article 286 has now been supplanted by article 8 of the Charter and TFEU, article 16.
49. Regulation 45/2001/EC, article 32.
50. Regulation 45/2001/EC, article 33.
51. Regulation 45/2001/EC, article 35.
52. Regulation 45/2001/EC, article 36.

anonymous as soon as possible and no later than six months after collection, unless they need to be kept for a longer period to establish, exercise or defend a right in a legal claim pending before a court. The processing of traffic and billing data can only be carried out by persons handling billing, traffic or budget management and users of the telecommunication networks have the right to receive non-itemised bills or other records of calls made.[53]

Personal data contained in printed or electronic directories of users and access to such directories must be limited to what is strictly necessary for the specific purposes of the directory and Community institutions and bodies must take necessary measures to prevent that personal data being used for direct marketing purposes.[54] Where call-line identification is offered, the calling user must have the possibility via a simple means, free of charge, to eliminate the presentation of the call-line identification. A called user must have the possibility via a simple means, free of charge, to prevent the presentation of the call-line identification of incoming calls. Where connected-line identification is offered, the called user must have the possibility via a simple means and free of charge, to eliminate the presentation of the connected-line identification to the calling user. Where presentation of calling or connected-line identification is offered, users must be informed.[55] There must also be transparent procedures governing the way in which Community institutions and bodies can override the elimination of call line identification: in cases of where there are malicious or nuisance calls or emergencies.[56]

EUROPEAN DATA PROTECTION SUPERVISOR (EDPS)

[22.15] The EDPS is established by article 41 of Regulation 45/2001, which provides that the EDPS is responsible for ensuring that the fundamental rights and freedoms of natural persons, and in particular their right to privacy, are respected by the Community institutions and bodies. Of course as with the supervisory authorities of Member States, the basis of the powers of the EDPS lies in article 8(3) of the Charter and TFEU, article 16(2) which requires that EU data protection law be subject to the control of independent authorities. Regulation 45/2001 requires that the EDPS act '... in complete independence in the performance of his or her duties' and must neither seek nor take instructions from anybody in the performance of their duties. The EDPS must refrain from any action incompatible with their duties and must not, during their term of office, engage in any other occupation, whether gainful or not. The EDPS is obliged to 'behave with integrity and discretion as regards the acceptance of appointments and benefits after their term of office'.[57] The EDPS and staff are subject to 'a duty of professional secrecy with regard to any confidential information which has come to their knowledge

---

53. Regulation 45/2001/EC, article 37.
54. Regulation 45/2001/EC, article 38.
55. Regulation 45/2001/EC, article 39.
56. Regulation 45/2001/EC, article 40.
57. Regulation 45/2001/EC, article 44.

in the course of the performance of their official duties'. This applies both during and after their term of office.[58]

[22.16] The EDPS is responsible:

> for monitoring and ensuring the application of the provisions of this Regulation and any other Community act relating to the protection of the fundamental rights and freedoms of natural persons with regard to the processing of personal data by a Community institution or body, and for advising Community institutions and bodies and data subjects on all matters concerning the processing of personal data. To these ends he or she shall fulfil the duties provided for in Article 46 and exercise the powers granted in Article 47.

The European Parliament and the Council appoint the EDPS for a term of five years by common accord and on the basis of a list drawn up by the Commission following a public call for candidates. The EDPS is chosen from persons whose independence is beyond doubt and who are acknowledged as having the experience and skills required to perform the duties of EDPS, for example because they belong or have belonged to supervisory authorities in Member States. The EDPS is eligible for reappointment and their duties end when they resign or on compulsory retirement. The EDPS may be dismissed or deprived of their right to a pension or other benefits in its stead by the Court of Justice at the request of the European Parliament, the Council or the Commission, if they no longer fulfil the conditions required for the performance of their duties or if they are guilty of serious misconduct. In the case of a normal replacement or voluntary resignation, the EDPS remains in office until they have been replaced. Articles 12 to 15 and 18 of the Protocol on the Privileges and Immunities of the European Communities also apply to the EDPS. These provisions also apply to the Assistant Supervisor who must also be appointed following the same procedure and for the same term. This Assistant Supervisor acts as a replacement when the Supervisor is absent or prevented from attending to them.[59]

The European Parliament, the Council and the Commission must by common accord determine the regulations and general conditions governing the performance of the EDPS's duties and in particular the salary, allowances and any other benefits in lieu of remuneration.[60] The budget authority ensures that the EDPS is provided with the human and financial resources necessary for the performance of their tasks. The EDPS is assisted by a Secretariat and the officials and the other staff members of the Secretariat are appointed by the EDPS; their superior is the EDPS and they are subject exclusively to the Supervisor's direction. Their numbers are decided each year as part of the budgetary procedure.

---

58. Regulation 45/2001/EC, article 45.
59. Regulation 45/2001/EC, article 42.
60. Decision No 1247/2002/EC.

[22.17] Article 46 sets out the duties of the EDPS. He or she must:

(a) hear and investigate complaints, and inform the data subject of the outcome within a reasonable period;

(b) conduct inquiries either on his or her own initiative or on the basis of a complaint, and inform the data subjects of the outcome within a reasonable period;

(c) monitor and ensure the application of the provisions of this Regulation and any other Community act relating to the protection of natural persons with regard to the processing of personal data by a Community institution or body with the exception of the Court of Justice of the European Communities acting in its judicial capacity;

(d) advise all Community institutions and bodies, either on his or her own initiative or in response to a consultation, on all matters concerning the processing of personal data, in particular before they draw up internal rules relating to the protection of fundamental rights and freedoms with regard to the processing of personal data;

(e) monitor relevant developments, insofar as they have an impact on the protection of personal data, in particular the development of information and communication technologies;

(f) (i) cooperate with the national supervisory authorities referred to in Article 28 of Directive 95/46/EC in the countries to which that Directive applies to the extent necessary for the performance of their respective duties, in particular by exchanging all useful information, requesting such authority or body to exercise its powers or responding to a request from such authority or body; (ii) also cooperate with the supervisory data protection bodies established under Title VI of the Treaty on European Union particularly with a view to improving consistency in applying the rules and procedures with which they are respectively responsible for ensuring compliance;

(g) participate in the activities of the Working Party on the Protection of Individuals with regard to the Processing of Personal Data set up by Article 29 of Directive 95/46/EC;

(h) determine, give reasons for and make public the exemptions, safeguards, authorisations and conditions mentioned in Article 10(2)(b), (4), (5) and (6), in Article 12(2), in Article 19 and in Article 37(2);

(i) keep a register of processing operations notified to him or her by virtue of Article 27(2) and registered in accordance with Article 27(5), and provide means of access to the registers kept by the Data Protection Officers under Article 26;

(j) carry out a prior check of processing notified to him or her;

(k) establish his or her Rules of Procedure.

[22.18] The EDPS may:

(a) give advice to data subjects in the exercise of their rights;

(b) refer the matter to the controller in the event of an alleged breach of the provisions governing the processing of personal data, and, where appropriate, make proposals for remedying that breach and for improving the protection of the data subjects;

(c) order that requests to exercise certain rights in relation to data be complied with where such requests have been refused in breach of Articles 13 to 19;[61]

(d) warn or admonish the controller;

(e) order the rectification, blocking, erasure or destruction of all data when they have been processed in breach of the provisions governing the processing of personal data and the notification of such actions to third parties to whom the data have been disclosed;

(f) impose a temporary or definitive ban on processing;

(g) refer the matter to the Community institution or body concerned and, if necessary, to the European Parliament, the Council and the Commission;

(h) refer the matter to the Court of Justice of the European Communities under the conditions provided for in the Treaty;

(i) intervene in actions brought before the Court of Justice of the European Communities.[62]

[22.19] The EDPS has the power:

(a) to obtain from a controller or Community institution or body access to all personal data and to all information necessary for his or her enquiries;

(b) to obtain access to any premises in which a controller or Community institution or body carries on its activities when there are reasonable grounds for presuming that an activity covered by this Regulation is being carried out there.[63]

The EDPS is obliged to submit an annual report on their activities to the European Parliament, the Council and the Commission and at the same time make it public. The Supervisor must forward the activities report to the other Community institutions and bodies.[64]

The EDPS and the GDPR

[22.20] The EDPS is a member of the European Data Protection Board (EDPB),[65] however he has '… voting rights only on decisions which concern principles and rules applicable to the Union institutions, bodies, offices and agencies which correspond in

---

61. Data subject rights of access, rectification, block, erasure, notification to third parties, object, automated processing.
62. Regulation 45/2001/EC, article 47(1).
63. Regulation 45/2001/EC, article 47(2).
64. Regulation 45/2001/EC, article 48.
65. GDPR, article 68(3).

substance to those of (the GDPR)'.[66] The GDPR requires that the EDPS provide the secretariat for the EDPB.[67] That secretariat will provide the EDPB with its '... analytical, administrative and logistical support ...'[68] and will be responsible for the following tasks 'in particular':

(a) the day-to-day business of the Board;
(b) communication between the members of the Board, its Chair and the Commission;
(c) communication with other institutions and the public;
(d) the use of electronic means for internal and external communication;
(e) the translation of relevant information;
(f) the preparation and follow-up of the meetings of the Board;
(g) the preparation, drafting and publication of opinions, decisions on the settlement of disputes between supervisory authorities and other texts adopted by the Board.

That secretariat must perform these tasks 'exclusively under the instructions of the Chair of the EDPB';[69] Staff of the ECPS who support the EDPB must be '... subject to separate reporting lines from the staff involved in carrying out tasks conferred on the European Data Protection Supervisor'.[70] If appropriate the EDPS and EDPB may enter into a memorandum of understanding with the EDPB, which they are obliged to publish. This memorandum will determine the terms of cooperation between the EDPS and EDPB and be applicable to the staff assigned to the secretariat of the EDPB.

FINAL PROVISIONS

[22.21] An official or other servant of the European Communities will be liable to disciplinary action where they fail to comply with obligations under Regulation 45/2001.[71]

---

66. GDPR, article 68(5).
67. GDPR, article 75(1).
68. GDPR, article 75(5).
69. GDPR, article 75(2).
70. GDPR, article 75(3).
71. Regulation 45/2001/EC, article 49.

PART 10
ePRIVACY DIRECTIVE

Chapter 23

ePRIVACY

INTRODUCTION

[23.01] The regulatory framework for electronic communications networks and services is an EU Single Market success story.[1] This framework consists of four directives and two regulations:

- Directive 2002/20/EC, the Authorisation Directive;[2]
- Directive 2002/19/EC, the Access Directive;[3]
- Directive 2002/22/EC, the Universal Service Directive;[4]
- Directive 2002/58/EC, the ePrivacy Directive;[5]
- Regulation 1211/2009 which established a Body of European Regulators for Electronic Communications (BEREC);[6] and
- Regulation 531/2012 on roaming on public mobile communications networks.[7]

[23.02] Directive 2002/58 is part of this framework and aims to protect personal data, privacy and the confidentiality of communications in electronic communications networks. It also guarantees the free movement of personal data on such electronic communications networks within the EU. Hence it has a significant impact upon the EU Commission's Digital Single Market strategy.[8] A review undertaken by the EU

---

1. 'Over the last decade EU electronic communications policy has been successful in delivering more competition, lower prices and more choice for businesses and consumers,' EU Commission, Connectivity for a Competitive Digital Single Market – Towards a European Gigabit Society, COM(2016) 587 final, Brussels, 14 September 2016, p 2.
2. Directive 2002/20/EC of 7 March 2002 on the authorisation of electronic communications networks and services, OJ L 108, 24.4.2002, pp 21–32.
3. Directive 2002/19/EC of 7 March 2002 on access to, and interconnection of, electronic communications networks and associated facilities, OJ L 108, 24.4.2002, pp 7–20.
4. Directive 2002/22/EC of 7 March 2002 on universal service and users' rights relating to electronic communications networks and services, OJ L 108, 24.4.2002, pp 51–77.
5. Directive 2002/58/EC of 12 July 2002 concerning the processing of personal data and the protection of privacy in the electronic communications sector, OJ L 201, 31.7.2002, pp 37–47.
6. Regulation 1211/2009 of 25 November 2009 establishing the Body of European Regulators for Electronic Communications (BEREC), OJ L 337, 18.12.2009, pp 1–10.
7. Regulation 531/2012 13 June 2012 on roaming on public mobile communications networks within the Union, OJ L 172, 30.6.2012, p 10–35.
8. EU Commission, *Communication from the Commission to the European Parliament, the Council, the European Economic and Social Committee and the Committee of the Regions, A Digital Single Market Strategy for Europe*, COM(2015) 192 final.

Commission on Directive 2002/58's regulatory fitness and performance concluded that '... the objectives and principles of the current framework remain sound ...', however, important technological and economic developments have taken place:

> Consumers and businesses increasingly rely on new internet-based services enabling inter-personal communications such as Voice over IP, instant messaging and web-based e-mail services, instead of traditional communications services.

These communications services, which the EU Commission describes as 'Over-The-Top' or OTT services, fall outside the scope of Directive 2002/58. Arguably they might then fall within the scope of the GDPR, however the EU Commission is concerned that:

> ... the Directive has not kept pace with technological developments, resulting in a void of protection of communications conveyed through new services.[9]

Some might take the view that such OTT might be regulated by the GDPR, however what the EU Commission proposes would be a '*lex specialis* to the GDPR' which would:

> ... particularise and complement it as regards electronic communications data that qualify as personal data.[10]

In any event, the Recitals to the GDPR now suggest that:

> In order to clarify the relationship between this Regulation and Directive 2002/58/EC, that Directive should be amended accordingly. Once this Regulation is adopted, Directive 2002/58/EC should be reviewed in particular in order to ensure consistency with this Regulation.[11]

[23.03] In January 2017 the EU Commission proposed a regulation concerning the respect for private life and the protection of personal data in electronic communications and repealing Directive 2002/58/EC.[12] It identified the following as being the 'cornerstones' of its proposal:

- all electronic communications must be confidential;
- confidentiality of users' online behaviour and devices has to be guaranteed;
- processing of communications content and metadata is conditioned to consent; and
- spam and direct marketing communications require prior consent.

---

9.   EU Commission, Proposal for a Regulation concerning the respect for private life and the protection of personal data in electronic communications and repealing Directive 2002/58/EC, 2017/0003 (COD), COM(2017) 10 final, Brussels, 10 January 2017, p 1, para 1.1.

10. EU Commission, Proposal for a Regulation concerning the respect for private life and the protection of personal data in electronic communications and repealing Directive 2002/58/EC, 2017/0003 (COD), COM(2017) 10 final, Brussels, 10 January 2017, p 1, para 1.2.

11. GDPR, Recital 173.

12. EU Commission, Proposal for a Regulation concerning the respect for private life and the protection of personal data in electronic communications and repealing Directive 2002/58/EC, 2017/0003 (COD), COM(2017) 10 final, Brussels, 10 January 2017.

As with the GDPR there are many similarities between what the EU Commission has proposed and the existing law. Article 5 of the EU Commission proposal begins by providing that 'Electronic communications data shall be confidential' whilst article 5 of Directive 2002/58 begins 'Member States shall ensure the confidentiality of communications ...'.[13] Both Directive 2002/58[14] and the EU Commission proposal impose controls upon the processing of traffic data and the proliferation of spam and direct marketing communications.[15] The more significant changes proposed concern standardisation, scope and supervision. As regards standardisation, the EU Commission is proposing a regulation, which has direct effect, as opposed to a Directive, which has to be implemented by Member States. As regards scope, the EU Commission is proposing that the new ePrivacy Regulation would apply to OTT services such as voice-over IP.[16] And as regards supervision, the EU Commission proposes that ePrivacy will be supervised by the authorities responsible for monitoring the application of the GDPR[17] and that subjects will be able to avail of the same remedies as the GDPR provides.[18]

DIRECTIVE 2002/58

[23.04] For now, Directive 2002/58[19] remains in place. Back in 2002 the need for this Directive was explained by its recitals:

> New advanced digital technologies are currently being introduced in public communications networks in the Community, which give rise to specific requirements concerning the protection of personal data and privacy of the user. The development of the information society is characterised by the introduction of

---

13.   ePrivacy Directive, article 5(1).

14.   ePrivacy Directive, article 6; article 6, Proposal for a Regulation concerning the respect for private life and the protection of personal data in electronic communications and repealing Directive 2002/58/EC.

15.   ePrivacy Directive, article 13; article 16, Proposal for a Regulation concerning the respect for private life and the protection of personal data in electronic communications and repealing Directive 2002/58/EC.

16.   Article 4(3)(b), Proposal for a Regulation concerning the respect for private life and the protection of personal data in electronic communications and repealing Directive 2002/58/EC.

17.   Chapter IV, Proposal for a Regulation concerning the respect for private life and the protection of personal data in electronic communications and repealing Directive 2002/58/EC.

18.   Chapter V, Proposal for a Regulation concerning the respect for private life and the protection of personal data in electronic communications and repealing Directive 2002/58/EC.

19.   Directive 2002/58/EC concerns the processing of personal data and the protection of privacy in the electronic communications sector (Directive on privacy and electronic communications) OJ L 201, 31.7.2002, p.37 and has been amended by Directive 2009/136/EC and corrected by Corrigendum OJ L 241 (2009/136/EC). It had also been amended by Directive 2006/24 but the CJEU found that Directive invalid in *Digital Rights Ireland*.

new electronic communications services. Access to digital mobile networks has become available and affordable for a large public. These digital networks have large capacities and possibilities for processing personal data. The successful cross-border development of these services is partly dependent on the confidence of users that their privacy will not be at risk.[20] The Internet is overturning traditional market structures by providing a common, global infrastructure for the delivery of a wide range of electronic communications services. Publicly available electronic communications services over the Internet open new possibilities for users but also new risks for their personal data and privacy.[21]

To this end, article 1 provides for the harmonisation of national provisions required to ensure 'an equivalent level of protection of fundamental rights and freedoms, and in particular the right to privacy and confidentiality, with respect to the processing of personal data in the electronic communication sector and to ensure the free movement of such data and of electronic communication equipment and services in the Community'.

The provisions of Directive 2002/58 particularised and complemented Directive 95/46; from May 2018 they will have to be read in the context of the GDPR. The relationship between Directive 2002/58 and the GDPR is explained by GDPR, article 95, which provides:

> This Regulation shall not impose additional obligations on natural or legal persons in relation to processing in connection with the provision of publicly available electronic communications services in public communication networks in the Union in relation to matters for which they are subject to specific obligations with the same objective set out in Directive 2002/58 …

[23.05] The GDPR Recitals expand somewhat on the above, providing that it:

> … should apply to all matters concerning the protection of fundamental rights and freedoms *vis-à-vis* the processing of personal data which are not subject to specific obligations with the same objective set out in Directive 2002/58/EC … including the obligations on the controller and the rights of natural persons.[22]

One significant difference between the GDPR and Directive 2002/58 is that the latter provides for the 'protection of the legitimate interests of subscribers who are legal persons'. The Directive does not apply to activities falling outside the scope of Treaty establishing the EC and activities concerning public security, defence, State security (including the economic well-being of the State when the activities relate to State security matters) and the activities of the State in areas of criminal law. Directive 2002/58 applies to the processing of personal data:

> in connection with the provision of publicly available electronic communications services in public communications networks in the Community, including public communications networks supporting data collection and identification devices.[23]

---

20. Directive 2002/58/EC, Recital 5.
21. Directive 2002/58/EC, Recital 6.
22. GDPR, Recital 173.
23. Directive 2002/58/EC, article 3.

Security of processing and notification of personal data breaches

[23.06] Article 4 imposes security obligations upon providers of a publicly available electronic communications service, which must take:

> appropriate technical and organisational measures to safeguard security of its services, if necessary in conjunction with the provider of the public communications network with respect to network security. Having regard to the state of the article and the cost of their implementation, these measures shall ensure a level of security appropriate to the risk presented.

[23.07] Without prejudice to Directive 95/46 (or the GDPR from May 2018) these measures must at least:

- ensure that personal data can be accessed only by authorised personnel for legally authorised purposes,

- protect personal data stored or transmitted against accidental or unlawful destruction, accidental loss or alteration, and unauthorised or unlawful storage, processing, access or disclosure, and,

- ensure the implementation of a security policy with respect to the processing of personal data.[24]

Relevant national authorities can audit these security measures and issue recommendations on best practices.[25] In case of a particular risk of a breach of the security of the network, the provider of a publicly available electronic communications service:

> must inform the subscribers concerning such risk and, where the risk lies outside the scope of the measures to be taken by the service provider, of any possible remedies, including an indication of the likely costs involved.[26]

[23.08] There are obligations on the provider of a public available electronic communications service to notify of personal data breaches. A personal data breach is a 'breach of security leading to the accidental or unlawful destruction, loss, alteration, unauthorised disclosure of, or access to, personal data transmitted, stored or otherwise processed in connection with the provision of a publicly available electronic communications service in the Community'.[27] If there has been such a breach, the provider must notify the competent national authority without undue delay. Where the breach is likely to adversely affect the personal data or privacy of a subscriber or individual, then that subscriber or individual must also be notified by the provider without undue delay. There is no obligation to notify the subscriber or individual if the provider 'has demonstrated to the satisfaction of the competent authority that it has

---

24. Directive 2002/58/EC, article 4(1a).
25. Directive 2002/58/EC, article 4(1a).
26. Directive 2002/58/EC, article 4(2).
27. Directive 2002/58/EC, article 2(i).

implemented appropriate technological protection measures, and that those measures were applied to the data concerned by the security breach'. Such technological protection measures must have rendered the data unintelligible to any unauthorised person. The competent national authority may require a provider to notify the individual or subscriber having considered the likely adverse effects of the breach.

[23.09] In terms of notifying the subscriber or individual, the notification should, at least, describe the nature of the personal data breach, contact points where more information can be obtained, and recommendations to mitigate the possible adverse effects of the personal data breach. This description together with a description of the consequences of, and the measures proposed or taken by the provider to address the personal data breach must be notified to the competent national authority.[28]

The competent national authorities may adopt guidelines on such notifications of personal data breaches and audit whether providers have complied with their notification obligations. Such authorities can impose appropriate sanctions where there has been a failure to do so.

Providers are also required to maintain an inventory of personal data breaches comprising:

> the facts surrounding the breach, its effects and the remedial action taken which shall be sufficient to enable the competent national authorities to verify compliance .... The inventory shall only include the information necessary for this purpose.[29]

In order to ensure consistency, the Commission may, following consultation with the European Network and Information Security Agency (ENISA), the Working Party on the Protection of Individuals with regard to the Processing of Personal Data and the European Data Protection Supervisor, adopt technical implementing measures concerning the circumstances, format and procedures applicable to the information and notification requirements referred to above.[30]

Confidentiality of the communications

[23.10] The confidentiality of communications and the related traffic data by means of a public communications network and publicly available electronic communications services, must be ensured through national legislation. Communication in this regard means any information:

> exchanged or conveyed between a finite number of parties by means of a publicly available electronic communications service. This does not include any information conveyed as part of a broadcasting service to the public over an

---

28.   Directive 2002/58/EC, article 4(3).
29.   Directive 2002/58/EC, article 4(4).
30.   Directive 2002/58/EC, article 4(5).

electronic communications network except to the extent that the information can be related to the identifiable subscriber or user[31] receiving the information.[32]

Such legislation must:

> prohibit listening, tapping, storage or other kinds of interception or surveillance of communications and the related traffic data by persons other than users, without the consent of the users concerned, except when legally authorised to do so in accordance with Article 15(1).[33]

This does not however prevent technical storage which is necessary for the conveyance of a communication. Neither does it affect:

> any legally authorised recording of communications and the related traffic data when carried out in the course of lawful business practice for the purpose of providing evidence of a commercial transaction or of any other business communication.[34]

The recitals add that in this case the recorded communication should be erased as soon as possible and in any case at the latest by the end of the period during which the transaction can be lawfully challenged.[35]

Cookies

[23.11] Directive 2002/58 does not define cookies, but the EU Commission has explained that:

> A cookie is a small piece of data that a website asks your browser to store on your computer or mobile device. The cookie allows the website to 'remember' your actions or preferences over time.

The Commission goes on to explain that websites mainly use cookies to: identify users; remember users' custom preferences; and help users complete tasks without having to re-enter information when browsing from one page to another or when visiting the site later. It notes that cookies can also be used for online behavioural target advertising and to show adverts relevant to something that the user searched for in the past.

---

31. A user is defined in Directive 2002/58/EC, article 2(a) as 'any natural person using a publicly available electronic communications service for private or business purposes, without necessarily having subscribed to this service'.
32. Directive 2002/58/EC, article 2(d). The example of video-on-demand services is provided by Recital 16. The Recitals further define communications as including 'any naming, numbering or addressing information provided by the sender ... to carry out the communication.' Directive 2002/58/EC, Recital 15.
33. Article 5. Recital 3 adds that the confidentiality of communications is guaranteed in accordance with international instruments such as the European Convention for the Protection of Human Rights and Fundamental Freedoms (ECHR) and the constitutions of Member States.
34. Directive 2002/58/EC, article 5(2).
35. Directive 2002/58/EC, Recital 23.

Cookies may be classified by the time for which they will identify subjects. There are 'session cookies' which are erased when the user closes the browser; there are also persistent cookies which remain on the user's computer for a pre-defined period of time. Alternatively, cookies may be classified by reference to the domain to which they belong. 'First-party cookies' are set by the web server of the visited page and share the same domain; third-party cookies are stored by a different domain to the visited page's domain.[36] Cookies are commonplace. In 2014 a survey was undertaken by EU Data Protection Supervisory Authorities in 8 Member States across 478 websites. This survey found '… an average of 10.3 first-party cookies and 24.4 third-party cookies per site';[37] and, '… an average of 4.8 session cookies and 29.8 persistent third-party cookies per site'.[38]

[23.12] Subjects may be identified or identifiable from the cookies that have been left on their computers. As such cookies may be personal data and processing will then be subject to EU data protection law. The Recitals to Directive 2002/58 explain that the terminal equipment of users are part of the private sphere of the users:

> spyware, web bugs, hidden identifiers and other similar devices can enter the user's terminal without their knowledge in order to gain access to information, to store hidden information or to trace the activities of the user and may seriously intrude upon the privacy of these users. The use of such devices should be allowed only for legitimate purposes, with the knowledge of the users concerned.[39]

Such devices or 'cookies' can however be legitimate in for example analysing the effectiveness of website design and advertising and in verifying the identity of users of on-line transactions. Where they are for legitimate purposes their use should be permitted:

> on condition that users are provided with clear and precise information … about the purposes of cookies or similar devices so as to ensure that users are made aware of information being placed on the terminal equipment they are using. Users should have the opportunity to refuse to have the cookie or similar device stored on their terminal equipment.[40]

Directive 2002/58 then requires that Member States ensure that the storing of information, or the gaining of access to information already stored, in the terminal equipment of a subscriber or user is only allowed where the subscriber or user concerned has given their consent, having been provided with clear and comprehensive information about the purposes of the processing. This again does not prevent any technical storage or access for the sole purpose of carrying out the transmission of a communication over an electronic communications network, or as strictly necessary in order for the provider of an information society service explicitly requested by the subscriber or user to

---

36.   http://ec.europa.eu/ipg/basics/legal/cookies/index_en.htm.
37.   A29 WP, *Cookie Sweep Combined Analysis – Report,* 14/EN WP 229, 3 February 2015, p 6.
38.   A29 WP, *Cookie Sweep Combined Analysis – Report,* 14/EN WP 229, 3 February 2015, p 7.
39.   Directive 2002/58/EC, Recital 24.
40.   Directive 2002/58/EC, Recital 25.

provide the service.[41] The term consent corresponds to the data subject's consent in Directive 95/46/EC.[42]

These controls on the use of cookies have been the subject of Opinions and Guidelines from the WP, article 29, which concluded that cookies notifications should contain the following elements: specific information, prior consent, indication of wishes expressed by user's active behaviour and an ability to choose freely.[43] From May 2018 those notifications will have to conform to the information requirements of articles 13 and 14 as well as the consent requirements of GDPR, article 7.

Traffic data

[23.13] Traffic data relating to subscribers and users processed and stored by the provider must be erased or made anonymous when it is no longer needed for the purpose of the transmission of a communication. However, it may be necessary for the purposes of billing and interconnection payments and such processing is permissible only up to the end of the period during which the bill may lawfully be challenged or payment pursued. Traffic data refers to any data 'processed for the purpose of the conveyance of a communication on an electronic communications network or for the billing'.[44] The Recitals expand upon this definition by adding that traffic data 'may, inter alia, consist of data referring to the routing, duration, time or volume of a communication, to the protocol used, to the location of the terminal equipment of the sender or recipient, to the network on which the communication originates or terminates, to the beginning, end or duration of a connection. They may also consist of the format in which the communication is conveyed by the network'.[45]

[23.14] The provider may process traffic data for marketing electronic communications services or for the provision of value added services to the extent and duration necessary for such services where the subscriber or user has given their prior consent. A 'value added service' is defined in article 2(g) as 'any service which requires the processing of traffic data or location data other than traffic data beyond what is necessary for the transmission of a communication or the billing thereof'. The Recitals give the examples of advice on least expensive tariff packages, route guidance, traffic information, weather forecasts and tourist information.[46]

---

41. Directive 2002/58/EC, article 5(3).
42. Directive 2002/58/EC, article 2(f).
43. A29 WP, *Working Document 02/2013 providing guidance on obtaining consent for cookies*, 1676/13/EN WP 208 2 October 2013, p 3. See also, Article 29 WP, *Opinion 04/2012 on Cookie Consent Exemption,* 00879/12/EN, WP 194, 7 June 2012.
44. Directive 2002/58/EC, article 2(b). Consent may be obtained by ticking a box on an internet website according to Recital 17.
45. Directive 2002/58/EC, Recital 15.
46. Directive 2002/58/EC, Recital 18.

[23.15] The subscriber or user must have the possibility of withdrawing that consent for the processing of traffic data at any time. The service provider must inform the subscriber or user of the types of traffic data which are processed, the duration of processing and, prior to obtaining consent, the purposes of processing.

The processing of traffic data must:

> be restricted to persons acting under the authority of providers of the public communications networks and publicly available electronic communications services handling billing or traffic management, customer enquiries, fraud detection, marketing electronic communications services or providing a value added service, and must be restricted to what is necessary for the purposes of such activities.

Competent bodies may be informed of traffic data in conformity with applicable legislation with a view to settling disputes, in particular interconnection or billing disputes.[47] In *Probst v mr.nexnet*[48] the applicant disputed his bill from his electronic communications provider. The matter found its way to the CJEU which was asked:

> ... essentially whether, and in what circumstances, Article 6(2) and (5) of Directive 2002/58 allows a service provider to pass traffic data to the assignee of its claims for payment and allows the latter to process those data.[49]

[23.16] The CJEU concluded that article 6(2) meant that:

> ... a service provider is authorised to pass traffic data to the assignee of its claims for payment for the purpose of their recovery and that the latter is authorised to process those data on condition, first, that it acts 'under the authority' of the service provider as regards the processing of those data and, second, that it processes only traffic data which are necessary for the purpose of the recovery of those claim.[50]

The CJEU then considered the meaning of the phrase 'under the authority' and concluded that '... a person acts under the authority of another where the former acts on instructions and under the control of the latter'.[51] The CJEU considered that this term had to be strictly construed[52] and in accordance with Directive 95/46. This led the CJEU to conclude that

> ... the assignee of a claim for payment relating to the payment of telecommunications charges acts 'under the authority' of the service provider ... where, for the processing of traffic data that such an activity involves, the assignee acts only on instructions and under the control of the service provider ...

---

47.   Directive 2002/58/EC, article 6.
48.   *Probst v mr.nexnet* (Case C–119/12) (22 November 2012).
49.   *Probst v mr.nexnet* (Case C–119/12) (22 November 2012), para 16.
50.   *Probst v mr.nexnet* (Case C–119/12) (22 November 2012), para 19.
51.   *Probst v mr.nexnet* (Case C–119/12) (22 November 2012), para 21.
52.   *Probst v mr.nexnet* (Case C–119/12) (22 November 2012), para 23.

This was subject to the contract between the controller and processor containing '... provisions of such a kind as to ensure the lawful processing of traffic data by the latter and must allow the service provider to ensure at all times that those provisions are being complied with by the assignee'.[53]

Itemised billing

[23.17] Subscribers have the right to receive non-itemised bills. National provisions should reconcile the rights of subscribers receiving itemised bills with the right to privacy of calling users and called subscribers, by ensuring, for example, that sufficient alternative privacy enhancing methods of communications or payments are available to such users and subscribers.[54]

Presentation and restriction of calling and connected line identification

[23.18] Where call-line identification is offered, the service provider must offer the calling user the possibility of preventing the presentation of the calling line identification on a per-call basis. This must be offered free of charge and by a simple means. The calling subscriber must have this possibility on a per-line basis. This also applies in the case of calls to third countries originating in the Community. The called subscriber must be given the possibility, using a simple means and free of charge for reasonable use of this function, of preventing the presentation of the calling line identification of incoming calls. The called subscriber must be given the possibility, using a simple means, of rejecting incoming calls where the presentation of the calling line identification has been prevented by the calling user or subscriber. The called subscriber must also be given the possibility, using a simple means and free of charge, of preventing the presentation of the connected line identification to the calling user. These provisions also apply to incoming calls originating in third countries. Where presentation of calling and/or connected line identification is offered, the providers must inform the public thereof and of these possibilities.[55]

Location data other than traffic data

[23.19] Where location data other than traffic data, relating to users or subscribers of public communications networks or publicly available electronic communications services, can be processed:

> such data may only be processed when they are made anonymous, or with the consent of the users or subscribers to the extent and for the duration necessary for the provision of a value added service.

---

53. *Probst v mr.nexnet* (Case C–119/12) (22 November 2012), para 31.
54. Directive 2002/58/EC, article 7.
55. Directive 2002/58/EC, article 8.

Location data means any data processed in an electronic communications network or by an electronic communications service, indicating:

> the geographic position of the terminal equipment of a user of a publicly available electronic communications service.[56]

The Recitals add that location data may refer to the:

> latitude, longitude and altitude of the user's terminal equipment, to the direction of travel, to the level of accuracy of the location information, to the identification of the network cell in which the terminal equipment is located at a certain point in time and to the time the location information was recorded.[57]

The service provider must inform the users or subscribers of: (1) the type of location data other than traffic data which will be processed; (2) the purposes; (3) duration of the processing; and (4) whether the data will be transmitted to a third party for the purpose of providing the value added service. This information must be provided before the giving of consent and users or subscribers must be given the possibility to withdraw their consent for the processing of location data other than traffic data at any time. Where consent has been obtained the user or subscriber must continue to have the possibility of temporarily refusing the processing of such data for each connection to the network or for each transmission of a communication. This must be facilitated using a simple means and free of charge. Processing of this data must be restricted to persons acting under the authority of the provider of the public communications network or publicly available communications service or of the third party providing the value added service, and must be restricted to what is necessary for the purposes of providing the value added service.[58]

There must be transparent procedures governing the way in which a provider can override the elimination of the presentation of calling line identification, on a temporary basis, upon the application of a subscriber requesting the tracing of malicious or nuisance calls. Similarly, there must be transparent procedures where a provider can override the elimination of calling line identification and the temporary denial or absence of consent of a subscriber or user for the processing of location data, on a per-line basis for organisations dealing with emergency calls and including law enforcement agencies, ambulance services and fire brigades, for the purpose of responding to such calls.[59]

Automatic call forwarding

[23.20] Subscribers must be given the possibility of stopping automatic call forwarding by a third party to the subscriber's terminal. This must be via a simple means and free of charge.[60]

---

56.   Directive 2002/58/EC, article 2(c).
57.   Directive 2002/58/EC, Recital 14.
58.   Directive 2002/58/EC, article 9.
59.   Directive 2002/58/EC, article 10.
60.   Directive 2002/58/EC, article 11.

Directories of subscribers

[23.21] Subscribers must be informed about the purposes of a printed or electronic directory of subscribers available to the public or available from a directory enquiry service. They should be informed free of change and before inclusion. They should also be informed of any 'further usage possibilities based on search functions embedded in electronic versions of the directory'. Subscribers must be given the opportunity to determine whether their personal data are included and if so, to verify, correct or withdraw such data free of charge. This applies to subscribers who are natural persons. Member States must also ensure that the legitimate interests of subscribers other than natural persons with regard to their entry in public directories are sufficiently protected.

Member States may require that for any purpose of a public directory other than the search of contact details of persons on the basis of their name and, where necessary, a minimum of other identifiers, additional consent be asked of the subscribers.[61]

Unsolicited communications

[23.22] The use of automated calling and automatic calling machines, faxes or electronic mail for the purposes of direct marketing is only allowed where subscribers or users (a natural person) have given their prior consent. The term 'electronic mail' is widely defined as:

> any text, voice, sound or image message sent over a public communications network which can be stored in the network or in the recipient's terminal equipment until it is collected by the recipient.[62]

If a natural or legal person obtains from its customers their electronic contact details for electronic mail, in the context of the sale of a product or a service, in accordance with Directive 95/46/EC, that natural or legal person may use these electronic contact details

> for direct marketing of its own similar products or services provided that customers clearly and distinctly are given the opportunity to object, free of charge and in an easy manner, to such use of electronic contact details at the time of their collection and on the occasion of each message in case the customer has not initially refused such use.[63]

[23.23] The Recitals note that unsolicited commercial communications may be easy and cheap to send but they impose a burden and/or cost on the recipient, therefore consent is required.[64] Unsolicited communications for the purposes of direct marketing are not allowed either:

> without the consent of the subscribers or users concerned or in respect of subscribers or users who do not wish to receive these communications, the choice

---

61. Directive 2002/58/EC, article 12.
62. Directive 2002/58/EC, article 2(h).
63. Directive 2002/58/EC, article 13(2).
64. Directive 2002/58/EC, Recital 40.

between these options to be determined by national legislation, taking into account that both options must be free of charge for the subscriber or user.[65]

Sending an electronic mail for the purposes of direct marketing which disguises or conceals the identity of the sender (contravening article 6 of Directive 2000/31/EC), which do not have a valid address to which the recipient may send a request that such communications cease or which encourage recipients to visit websites that contravene that article are prohibited.[66]

Articles 13(1) and (3) apply to subscribers who are natural persons but Member States should also ensure that the legitimate interests of other subscribers with regard to unsolicited communications are sufficiently protected.[67]

Natural or legal persons who are adversely affected by infringements of national provisions adopted pursuant to this article may bring legal proceedings in respect of such infringements. Member States may also lay down 'specific rules on penalties applicable to providers of electronic communications services which by their negligence contribute to infringements of national provisions adopted pursuant to this Article'.[68]

Technical features and standardisation

[23.24] Member States must ensure that there are no mandatory requirements for specific technical features on terminal or other electronic communication equipment which could impede the placing of equipment on the market and the free circulation of such equipment in and between Member States. Where provisions of the Directive require specific technical features in electronic communications networks, Member States are required to inform the Commission. Where required, measures may be adopted to ensure that terminal equipment is constructed in a way that is compatible with the right of users to protect and control the use of their personal data.[69]

Application of certain provisions of Directive 95/46/EC

[23.25] Member States can adopt legislation which restricts the scope of the rights and obligations provided for in article 5 (confidentiality of the communications), article 6 (traffic data), article 8(1), (2), (3) and (4) (presentation and restriction of calling and connected line identification), and article 9 (location data other than traffic data) of this Directive when it is a:

> necessary, appropriate and proportionate measure within a democratic society to safeguard national security (i.e. State security), defence, public security, and the

---

65.   Directive 2002/58/EC, article 13(3).

66.   Directive 2002/58/EC, article 13(4).

67.   Directive 2002/58/EC, article 13(5).

68.   Directive 2002/58/EC, article 13(6).

69.   This is in accordance with Directive 1999/5/EC and Council Decision 87/95/EEC of 22 December 1986 on standardisation in the field of information technology and communications. Directive 2002/58/EC, article 14.

prevention, investigation, detection and prosecution of criminal offences or of unauthorised use of the electronic communication system, as referred to in Article 13(1) of Directive 95/46/EC.

To this end, Member States may, *inter alia*, adopt legislative measures providing for the:

retention of data for a limited period justified on the grounds [above] ... All the measures ... shall be in accordance with the general principles of Community law, including those referred to in Article 6(1) and (2) of the Treaty on European Union.[70]

[23.26] *Bonnier Audio*[71] which concerned a law enabling the owners of intellectual property rights to apply to the Swedish courts '... for an order for the disclosure of data for the purpose of communicating the name and address of the person ...'[72] who had breached their rights by sharing their intellectual property on-line. The CJEU concluded that Directive 2002/58 did not preclude:

... national legislation ... insofar as that legislation enables the national court seized of an application for an order for disclosure of personal data, made by a person who is entitled to act, to weigh the conflicting interests involved, on the basis of the facts of each case and taking due account of the requirements of the principle of proportionality.[73]

However in *Tele2 Sverige*[74] the CJEU concluded that this provision must be interpreted firstly as '... precluding national legislation which, for the purpose of fighting crime, provides for general and indiscriminate retention of all traffic and location data of all subscribers and registered users relating to all means of electronic communication' and secondly as '... precluding national legislation governing the protection and security of traffic and location data and, in particular, access of the competent national authorities to the retained data, where the objective pursued by that access, in the context of fighting crime, is not restricted solely to fighting serious crime, where access is not subject to prior review by a court or an independent administrative authority, and where there is no requirement that the data concerned should be retained within the European Union'.[75]

Providers are required to establish internal procedures for responding to requests for access to users' personal data based on national provisions and provide the competent national authority, on demand, 'with information about those procedures, the number of requests received, the legal justification invoked and their response'.[76]

---

70. Directive 2002/58/EC, article 15(1).
71. *Bonnier Audio* (Case C–461/10) (19 April 2012).
72. *Bonnier Audio* (Case C–461/10) (19 April 2012), para 28.
73. *Bonnier Audio* (Case C–461/10) (19 April 2012), para 62.
74. *Tele2 Sverige* (Case C–203/15) (21 December 2016).
75. *Tele2 Sverige* (Case C–203/15) (21 December 2016), para 134.
76. Directive 2002/58/EC, article 15.

SCHEDULE

DPIA TEMPLATE

Step 1A: Description "a systematic description of the envisaged processing operations"

What is the processing operation?

Is this personal data?

Is this personal data being processed?

Are there any exemptions that apply to the processing?

- Is it domestic? (see CJEU in Rynes)

- Is it for national security or defence? (see CJEU in Tele2 Sverige)

Step 1B: Is this a processing operation likely to result in a high risk to the rights and freedoms of natural persons?

In particular:

- Does this processing involve a systematic and extensive evaluation of personal aspects relating to natural persons which is based on automated processing?

- Is it processing on a large scale of special categories or of criminal convictions and offences? Or

- Is it a systematic monitoring of a publicly accessible area on a large scale?

Have you checked DPC lists?

- Is it definitively in?

- Is it definitively out?

Step 2: Analysis: "a systematic description of the...purposes of the processing..."

What is the lawful basis of the processing?

- Law: legal obligation/public duty

- Agreement: consent/contract

- Legitimate/vital/public interest

How will processing complying with the principles?

- lawfulness, fairness and transparency

- purpose limitation

- data minimisation

- accuracy

- storage limitation

- integrity and confidentiality

- accountability

Are there any other rules that may be engaged?

- Special categories of data?

- Transborder data flows?

- Profiling?

Step 3: Consultation

When will you consult with DPO?

Will you consult with the public?

- What about?

- When?

Step 4A: Necessity & proportionality

Purpose of Processing	Is processing necessary for that purpose?	Is processing proportionate to that purpose?

Step 4B: Risk rating

Processing operation	Risk	Risk rating before	measure	Risk rating after

Step 4C: Conclusion

Do measures to:

"…ensure the protection of personal data and to demonstrate compliance with [GDPR] taking into account the rights and legitimate interests of data subjects and other persons concerned"?

Step 5: Prior consultation

Would processing "…result in a high risk in the absence of measures taken by the controller to mitigate the risk…"?

Step 6: Repetition?

What will the trigger be for a repetition?

- Time based?
- Event based?

INDEX

Charter of Fundamental Rights of the European Union (contd)
  right to data protection, 1.02
  right to privacy, 1.06
  right to rectification, 9.17
  sharing of personal data as to justice and home affairs, 20.01
  supervisory authorities
    independence, 16.01
    powers, 15.17

Children
  consent to processing, 7.09–7.10
  modalities, 10.02

Churches
  application of GDPR, 3.25
  special categories of data, 8.09

Class actions
  remedies, 19.11

Codes of conduct
  controllers and processors
    generally, 14.01–14.03
    monitoring, 14.04
  transfers of personal data, 5.23

Communication of data breach to data subject
  sharing of personal data, 21.33

Community institutions
  processing
    confidentiality, 22.09
    co-operation, 22.12
    Data Protection Officer, 22.10
    data subjects' rights, 22.07
    EDPS, 22.15–22.20
    EU Regulation 45/2001, 22.02–22.14
    exemptions, 22.08
    final provisions, 22.21
    information to be given to data subject, 22.06
    internal communications netwrosk, 22.14
    introduction, 22.01
    lawfulness, 22.03–22.12

    notification to DPO, 22.11
    prior checking by EDPS, 22.12
    remedies, 22.13–22.14
    restrictions, 22.08
    security, 22.09
    special categories of data, 22.05
    transfer of personal data, 22.04

Compensation
  remedies, 19.06–19.10

Competencies of EU and member states
  co-ordinated, 3.06
  exclusive, 3.03
  shared, 3.05
  supported, co-ordinated and supplemented, 3.07

Competent authorities
  crime prevention purposes, 3.10

Competition banning agreements
  right to data protection, 1.13

Competition law
  interaction with right to data protection, 1.13

Compensation
  remedies, 19.06–19.10

Complaint to supervisory authority
  generally, 19.02–19.03
  habitual residence of subject, 19.13–19.14
  jurisdiction, 19.13–19.16
  place of alleged infringement, 19.15
  place of work of subject, 19.15

Compliance with lawful obligation
  lawfulness, 7.12–7.19

Concise
  modalities, 10.02

Confidentiality
  ePrivacy, 23.10
  processing by Community institutions, 22.09
  security measures, 13.26

Connected line identification
  ePrivacy, 23.18